clinical evidence

For a catalog of publications available from ACP-ASIM, contact:

Customer Service Center
American College of Physicians–American Society of Internal Medicine
190 N. Independence Mall West
Philadelphia, PA 19106-1572
215-351-2600
800-523-1546, ext. 2600

Visit our Web site at www.acponline.org

1

JANUARY 2000

clinical evidence

A compendium of the best available evidence for effective health care

BMJ Publishing Group

ACP ASIM

Manager, Book Publishing: David Myers
Administrator, Book Publishing: Diane McCabe
Production Supervisor: Allan S. Kleinberg
Production Editor: Scott Thomas Hurd

Printed in the United States of America
Composition by Fulcrum Data Services, Inc.
Printing/binding by R.R. Donnelley
Design by Peter Wilder, The Designers Collective Limited, UK

ISBN 0943126-86-X
ISSN 1526-9531

Subscriptions
Clinical Evidence is published twice a year by the American College of Physicians–American Society of Internal Medicine and the BMJ Publishing Group. The 2000 subscription rates are: $99.00 for individuals, $89.00 for ACP–ASIM members, $192.00 for institutions, and $59.00 for students.

For all US subscriptions, please contact ACP-ASIM, 190 N. Independence Mall West, Philadelphia, PA 19106-1572. Phone: 215-351-2600 or 800-523-1546, ext. 2600 Fax: 215-351-2799

For all UK and overseas subscriptions, please contact BMJ Publishing Group, PO Box 299, London, WC1H 9TD, United Kingdom. Phone: 44-171-383-6270 Fax: 44-171-383-6402
E-mail: subscriptions@bmjgroup.com.

Feedback
We want *Clinical Evidence* to be as useful, accurate, and up to date as possible. Please give us your views, comments, and suggestions via e-mail at CEfeedback@bmjgroup.com. Also, visit our Web site at www.evidence.org for more information about *Clinical Evidence*.

Permissions
Please contact Joshua Roberts at jroberts@mail.acponline.org or by fax at 215-351-2644 when requesting permission to reprint all or part of any contribution in *Clinical Evidence*.

Material in this publication was reviewed by ACP-ASIM for general medical accuracy and applicability in the United States; however, the information provided herein does not necessarily reflect the specific recommendations or opinions of ACP-ASIM. The authors, editors, and publishers are not responsible for errors of omission or for any consequences from the application of the information in this publication and make no warranty, express or implied, with respect to the contents of the publication. The naming of any organization, product, or alternative therapy in this publication is not an ACP-ASIM endorsement, and the omission of any such name does not indicate ACP-ASIM disapproval.

The authors and publisher have exerted every effort to ensure that drug selection and dosage set forth in this issue are in accord with current recommendations and practice at the time of publication. In view of ongoing research, occasional changes in government regulations, and the constant flow of information relating to drug therapy and drug reactions, the reader is urged to check the package insert for each drug for any change in indications and dosage and for added warnings and precautions. This care is particularly important when the recommended agent is a new or infrequently used drug.

What is *Clinical Evidence*?

Updated twice a year, *Clinical Evidence* is a compendium of evidence on the effects of common clinical interventions produced jointly by the American College of Physicians—American Society of Internal Medicine and the BMJ Publishing Group. It provides a concise account of the current state of knowledge and uncertainty about the prevention and treatment of a wide range of clinical conditions based on thorough searches of the literature. It is neither a textbook of medicine nor a book of guidelines. It summarizes the best available evidence, and where there is no good evidence, it says so.

With each successive issue, *Clinical Evidence* will both update and expand its coverage. The initial focus will be on the effects of preventive and therapeutic interventions as demonstrated by randomized trials and systematic reviews of such trials.

Acknowledgements

Clinical Evidence is very much an international effort, the result of much hard work by many people. The production of the North American edition of *Clinical Evidence* would not have been possible without the concerted efforts of many colleagues at the Johns Hopkins University School of Medicine and the Publishing Division of the American College of Physicians–American Society of Internal Medicine.

In addition, we thank the following people and organizations for their advice and support: the Cochrane Collaboration, and especially Iain Chalmers, Phil Alderson, and Carol Lefebvre; the NHS Centre for Reviews and Dissemination, and especially Trevor Sheldon, Jos Kleijnen, and Julie Glanville; the NHS Executive, and especially Andre Burnett, Tom Mann, Gina Radford, and Graham Winyard; the British National Formulary, and especially Dinesh Mehta and Anne Prasad; the Health Information Research Unit at McMaster University, and especially Anne McKibbon; the clinicians and epidemiologists who have acted as peer reviewers; and Martin Shipley and Doug Altman for statistical advice. Finally, we are grateful to the clinicians and patients who have spared time to take part in the focus groups, which have been crucial to the development of *Clinical Evidence*.

Foreword to the North American Edition

We at the American College of Physicians–American Society of Internal Medicine are proud to bring you the first American edition of *Clinical Evidence*. In doing so, we continue our effort to bring the best scientific evidence to clinical practice in the hope of improving the quality of health care. *Clinical Evidence* joins a growing line of the College's publications—both print and electronic—devoted to this purpose, including *ACP Journal Club*, *Evidence-Based Medicine*, and *Best Evidence*. Thanks are owed to our colleagues in the Cochrane Collaboration, at McMaster University, and at the BMJ Publishing Group, with whom we have joined to produce and disseminate these publications.

This first American version of *Clinical Evidence* appears six months after the introduction of the initial issue in the United Kingdom. Although the contents are nearly identical, we have substituted U.S. background statistics, identified pharmacologic agents that are not available, and in some cases added data from important new trials. We are in the process of integrating our editorial process more fully with that of our colleagues at the BMJ Publishing Group to allow eventual simultaneous publication of the same clinical material in forms amenable to our respective readers on both sides of the Atlantic.

In the introduction to this volume, Fiona Godlee—my counterpart in the United Kingdom—has outlined the genesis of *Clinical Evidence*, its underlying philosophy, and how it is put together. As a compendium of the best available evidence for effective health care, it offers syntheses of data from the highest-quality randomized trials, systematic reviews, and meta-analyses on therapeutic interventions for a wide array of diseases. *Clinical Evidence* combines the work of the Cochrane Collaboration and other evidence-based–medicine publications and organizes it around clinical questions. In presenting the data in hard quantitative terms, *Clinical Evidence* attempts to inform clinicians about what works and what does not. Its authors conscientiously have avoided including information from studies farther down the hierarchy of evidence, and they stop short of offering guidelines or recommendations. It is left to the clinician to decide how the evidence applies to individual patients and how best to use it to help make therapeutic decisions. We hope that the organization of *Clinical Evidence* will make it an easily accessible reference to which users will turn time and again.

Although the primary purpose of *Clinical Evidence* is to serve as a constant companion at the bedside and in the examination room, it can be used in several other important ways. As more data are generated and synthesized and as the number of topics covered continues to grow, *Clinical Evidence* will supply health care providers with an invaluable means of continuing education. As an educational resource for medical students and postgraduate trainees, *Clinical Evidence* provides not only the best current information for taking care of patients but also a means for applying critical quantitative thinking to clinical problems. For clinicians and researchers alike, the developing body of information in *Clinical Evidence* reveals as much about what we do *not* know as what we do; in so doing, it identifies potentially important areas of investigation. Finally, in an era of increasing competition for available resources, information in evidence-based–medicine publications like *Clinical Evidence* will be invaluable in molding health care policy by government and the private sector.

What lies ahead for *Clinical Evidence*? Because clinical research is moving constantly forward, we intend to bring out a new issue every six months, covering new topics and additional issues within topics and eventually extending our purview to diagnosis, screening, and prevention. An electronic version is planned for the near future, both to improve user convenience and to manage the growing volume of material. Because the amount of high-quality clinical data continues to grow almost exponentially, a large electronic archive is essential and can be used to produce different customized print versions for use by different specialty groups and other specific users. Over time, we expect ongoing change in format and presentation inspired by the constructive comments from our readers. Most important, we trust that *Clinical Evidence* will increase awareness of evidence-based medicine in the Americas—a part of the world where the heterogeneity of health care systems and widely differing practice patterns make dissemination and adoption of newer trends in medicine an ongoing challenge. We hope that *Clinical Evidence* will serve as an important next step in this process of bringing better care to our patients.

David R. Goldmann, MD, FACP
Editor

Contents

About *Clinical Evidence*

The inspiration for *Clinical Evidence* came in a phone call in 1995. Tom Mann and his colleagues at the NHS Executive asked the BMJ Publishing Group to explore the possibility of developing an evidence "formulary" along the lines of the *British National Forumulary*. They recognized that clinicians were under increasing pressure to keep up to date and to base their practice more firmly on evidence but that few had the necessary time or skills to do this. Their idea was to provide concise and regularly updated summaries of the best available evidence on clinical interventions. However, they did not think that the NHS could develop such a formulary itself. "It would be marvelous," said Tom Mann, "if somebody would just do it." A small team at the BMJ set to work to produce a pilot version of what was then called the *Clinical Effectiveness Directory*.

Between that pilot and this first issue, a great deal has changed. The BMJ Publishing Group and the American College of Physicians–American Society of Internal Medicine convened an international advisory board, held focus groups of clinicians, talked to patient-support groups, and adopted countless good ideas from early drafts by our contributors. Throughout, we have kept in mind an equation set out by Shaughnessy and coworkers.[1] This states that the usefulness of any source of information is equal to its relevance, multiplied by its validity, divided by the work required to extract the information. In order to be as useful as possible, we aimed for high relevance, high validity, and low work in terms of the reader's time and effort. We also kept in mind principles of transparency and explicitness. Readers needed to understand where our information came from and how it was assembled.

A UNIQUE RESOURCE

Clinical Evidence joins a growing number of sources of evidence-based information for clinicians, but it has several features that make it unique:

- Its contents are driven by questions rather than by the availability of research evidence. Rather than start with the evidence and summarize what is there, we have tried to identify important clinical questions and then searched for and summarized the best available evidence to answer them.
- It identifies but does not try to fill important gaps in the evidence. We feel that it will be helpful for clinicians to know when their uncertainty stems from gaps in the evidence rather than gaps in their own knowledge.
- It is updated twice a year, which means that you can rely on it to keep you up to date in the areas that are covered.
- It specifically aims *not* to make recommendations. This is because we feel that simply summarizing the evidence will make it more widely applicable. The experience of the clinical practice guideline movement has shown that it is nearly impossible to make recommendations that are appropriate for every situation. Differences in baseline risks and preferences of individual patients and in the local availability of interventions will always mean that the evidence must be interpreted individually rather than applied across the board. *Clinical Evidence* provides the raw material for developing locally applicable clinical practice guidelines and for clinicians and patients to make up their own minds on the best course of action. We supply the evidence; you make the decisions.

COMPLEMENTARY BUT DIFFERENT

We are often asked how *Clinical Evidence* differs from two other high-quality sources of evidence-based information: the Cochrane Library and the evidence-based journals *ACP Journal Club*, *Evidence-Based Medicine*, *Evidence-Based Mental Health*, and *Evidence-Based Nursing*.

Clinical Evidence is complementary to but different from the work of the Cochrane Collaboration, which produces and publishes high-quality systematic reviews of controlled trials.[2] *Clinical Evidence* might be seen as the friendly front end of the Cochrane Library, because it takes this and other high-quality information and pulls it together in one place in a concise format. Many of our advisors and contributors are active members of the Cochrane Collaboration.

Clinical Evidence is also complementary to but different from the evidence-based journals, which select and summarize the best and most clinically relevant articles as they appear in the world's medical literature. Together these journals form a growing archive of high-quality abstracts of individual articles, many of which are now pooled on the *Best Evidence* CD-ROM. *Clinical Evidence* takes a different approach. It begins not with the journals but with clinical questions. It is able to answer some, but for others it simply reports that no good evidence was found.

A WORK IN PROGRESS

Clinical Evidence is an evolving project. We knew before we started that we were undertaking an enormous task, but the more we worked the more we realized its enormity. We recognize that there is some mismatch between what we eventually want to achieve, and what we have succeeded in achieving with this first issue. Although we have made every effort to ensure that the searches were thorough and that the appraisals of studies were objective, inevitably we will have missed some important studies. In order not to make unjustified claims about the accuracy of the information, we use phrases such as "we found no systematic review" rather than "there is no systematic review." In addition, approximately one third of contributors to the first issue helped us out in the early stages by performing their own searches and appraisals in line with our guidance notes. To be as explicit as possible about the methods used for each contribution, we have asked contributors to provide a brief methods section describing the searches that were performed and how individual studies were selected.

UPDATING AND EXPANDING *CLINICAL EVIDENCE*

Our expectation is that *Clinical Evidence* will evolve rapidly in its early years, just as the *British National Formulary* did when it first appeared. Indeed, *Clinical Evidence* may well become a family of products, appearing in different formats and languages for different audiences. In particular, it will evolve in response to the needs of clinicians. We have tried hard to anticipate those needs (not least by involving clinicians at every stage), but it is only when people begin to use *Clinical Evidence* in daily practice that we can know how best to develop it. That is why your feedback is so important to us and why we are arranging for various ways to evaluate the product.

Clinical Evidence will be updated twice a year and expanded to include summaries of the evidence on additional diseases, syndromes, and clinical questions. We also intend to include evidence on screening and possibly diagnosis in future issues. An electronic version of *Clinical Evidence* is in development.

REFERENCES

1. **Shaughnessy AF, Slawson DC, Bennett JH.** Becoming an information master: a guidebook to the medical information jungle. *J Fam Pract* 1994;39:489–499.
2. **The Cochrane Collaboration Web site.** Accessed 28 Oct 1999 at http://hiru.mcmaster.ca/cochrane/default.htm.

A Guide to the Text

SUMMARY PAGE

The summary page for each topic presents the questions addressed, some key messages, and a list of the interventions covered, which have been categorized according to whether they have been found effective or not. We have borrowed the categories of effectiveness from one of the Cochrane Collaboration's first and most popular products, *A Guide to Effective Care in Pregnancy and Childbirth*.[1] These categories are:

Beneficial: Interventions whose effectiveness has been demonstrated by clear evidence from controlled trials
Likely to be beneficial: Interventions for which effectiveness is less well established than for those listed under "beneficial"
Trade-off between benefits and harms: Interventions for which clinicians and patients should weigh the beneficial and harmful effects according to individual circumstances and priorities
Unknown effectiveness: Interventions for which there are currently insufficient data or data of inadequate quality
Unlikely to be beneficial: Interventions for which lack of effectiveness is less well established than for those listed under "likely to be ineffective or harmful"
Likely to be ineffective or harmful: Interventions whose ineffectiveness or harmfulness has been demonstrated by clear evidence

Putting interventions into these categories is not always straightforward. For one thing, much of the evidence that is most relevant to clinical decisions relates to comparisons between different interventions rather than to comparison with placebo or no intervention. Where necessary, we have indicated the comparisons in brackets. Another problem is that interventions may have been tested or found to be effective in only one group of people. Again, we have indicated this where possible.

NEGATIVE FINDINGS

An aspect surprisingly difficult to get right has been the reporting of negative findings. As we have had to keep reminding ourselves, absence of evidence of benefit is not the same as absence of benefit. Or, to put this another way, saying that there is no good evidence that a treatment works is not the same as saying that the treatment doesn't work. We hope that the text makes this distinction clear throughout.

EFFECTS, NOT EFFECTIVENESS

A key aim of *Clinical Evidence* is to emphasize the important trade-offs between the benefits and harms, advantages and disadvantages, of different treatment options. We therefore discuss the effects of interventions, both positive and negative, rather than the effectiveness, and for each question or intervention option we present data on benefits and harms under separate headings. "Harms" include adverse effects of treatment and inconvenience to the patient. We have asked contributors to keep these negative effects in mind at all times. Where possible, from good data, we aim to give some indication of the frequency of adverse effects and to highlight which adverse effects have not been adequately studied.

DRUG INFORMATION

We make no attempt to provide information on drug dosages, formulations, indications, contraindications, or adverse effects. For this information we refer readers to drug formularies and textbooks. Drug dosages are included when a question explores the relative effectiveness or safety of different doses.

INFORMATION ON COST

We have decided not to include information on the cost or cost effectiveness of interventions, for at least the first few issues of *Clinical Evidence*. This is not because we believe costs to be unimportant, but because the question of what constitutes good evidence on costs is much disputed and because costs vary greatly both within and among countries. However, because we believe that it will become increasingly untenable for clinicians to act without paying attention to the financial resources of their patients, future issues of *Clinical Evidence* may provide relevant information on costs.

NUMERICAL DATA

Whenever possible, data are presented in the same form as in the original studies. However, sometimes we have changed the units or type of information used to allow comparison with results from other studies. Mainly, this involved converting odds ratios into relative risks. For many situations (when the absolute risk of an outcome is low and the 95% confidence interval is not too wide), the relative risk and odds ratio are comparable. Where this is not the case, relative risks and their confidence intervals have been calculated from baseline event rates and odds ratios cited in studies, or, where appropriate, from pooled results.[2,3]

COMPETING INTERESTS

In line with the policies of the *BMJ* and the *Annals of Internal Medicine*,[4,5] our aim is not to try to eliminate conflicts of interest but to make them explicit, so that readers can judge for themselves what influence, if any, these may have had on the contributors' interpretation of the evidence. We therefore asked all contributors to let us know about any potential conflicts, or, as we now call them, competing interests; we append any that are declared to the end of the contribution. Where the contributor gives no competing interests, we record "none declared."

HOW TO USE THE INFORMATION IN *CLINICAL EVIDENCE*

The type of information contained in *Clinical Evidence* is necessary but not sufficient for the provision of effective, high-quality health care. It is intended as an aid to clinical decision making to be used in conjunction with other important sources of information. These other sources include estimates of patients' baseline risk of a condition or outcome based on history, physical examination, and clinical and laboratory investigations; patient preferences; economic arguments; availability of treatments; and local expertise.

Some guidance on how to apply research evidence in practice is available on p. xix.

REFERENCES

1. **Enkin M, Keirse M, Renfrew M, et al.** *A Guide to Effective Care in Pregnancy and Childbirth*. Oxford: Oxford University Press; 1998.
2. **Zhang J, Yu KF.** What is the relative risk? A method of correcting the odds ratio in cohort studies of common outcomes. *JAMA* 1998;280:1690–1691.
3. **Demets DL.** Methods for combining randomized clinical trials: strengths and limitations. *Stat Med* 1987;6:341–348.
4. **Smith R.** Beyond conflict of interest. *BMJ* 1998;317:291–292.
5. ***Annals of Internal Medicine* Information for Authors.** Accessed 18 Nov 1999 at http://www.acponline.org/journals/resource/infor4aut.htm

How *Clinical Evidence* Is Put Together

The summaries in *Clinical Evidence* result from a rigorous process aimed at ensuring that the information they contain is both reliable and relevant to clinical practice.

SELECTING TOPICS

Clinical Evidence aims to cover common or important clinical conditions seen in primary and hospital care. To decide which conditions to cover in the initial issues, we reviewed national data on consultation rates, morbidity, and mortality and took advice from generalist clinicians and patient groups.

SELECTING THE QUESTIONS

The questions in *Clinical Evidence* concern the benefits and harms of preventive and therapeutic interventions, with emphasis on outcomes that matter to patients. Questions were selected for their relevance to clinical practice by section editors and contributors in collaboration with primary care clinicians and patient groups. Each issue of *Clinical Evidence* will include new questions as well as updates of existing questions. Readers can suggest new clinical questions using the feedback cards found at the back of the book and on the *Clinical Evidence* Web site (www.evidence.org) or by writing directly to *Clinical Evidence*.

SEARCHING AND APPRAISING THE LITERATURE

For each question, the literature is searched using the Cochrane Library, Medline, EMBASE, and, occasionally, other electronic databases, looking first for good systematic reviews and then for primary studies with designs that are most appropriate for answering the question. For most questions on interventions, this means finding randomized controlled trials, but some questions (e.g., those examining etiology, prognosis, or rare outcomes) may require observational studies.

Of the studies that are identified in the search, we selected and summarized only a small proportion. The selection was done by critically appraising the abstracts of the studies identified in the search, a task performed independently by a clinician and an information scientist using validated criteria similar to those of Sackett and coworkers[1] and Jadad and coworkers.[2,3] Where the search identifies more than one or two good reviews or trials, we select those we judge to be the most robust or relevant, using the full text of the article. Where we identify few or no good reviews or trials, we include other studied but highlight their limitations. Contributors, who are chosen for their expertise in the field and their skill in epidemiology, are asked to review our selection of studies and to justify any additions or exclusions they wish to make.

Our search strategy and critical appraisal criteria are available on our Web site (www.evidence.org).

SUMMARIZING THE EVIDENCE, PEER REVIEW, AND EDITING

The contributors summarize the evidence relating to each question. Each topic is then peer reviewed by the section editors, by at least two external expert clinicians, by members of our advisory board, and by an international editorial committee of generalist clinicians who have expertise in epidemiology. The revised text is then edited by editors with clinical and epidemiological training, and data are checked against the original study reports.

FEEDBACK

Despite the extensive peer review and quality checks described above, we expect that the text will contain some errors and inconsistencies. Please let us know of any you find by using the response card at the back of the book or the form found on the Web site or by sending an e-mail to CEfeedback@bmjgroup.com.

We also hope to hear from you with your views on what we are doing, how we could do it better, and what we should include in future issues of *Clinical Evidence*.

REFERENCES

1. **Sackett DL, Haynes RB, Guyatt GH, Tugwell P.** *Clinical Epidemiology: A Basic Science for Clinical Medicine*, 2nd ed. Boston: Little, Brown; 1991.
2. **Jadad AR.** Assessing the quality of RCTs: why, what, and by whom? In: Jadad AR. *Randomised Controlled Trials*. London: BMJ Books, 1998:45–60.
3. **Jadad AR, Moore RA, Carroll D, Jenkinson C, et al.** Assessing the quality of reports of randomized clinical trials: Is blinding necessary? *Control Clin Trial* 1996;17:1–12.

Glossary

Absolute risk increase (ARI) The absolute difference in rates of adverse events between the experimental and control groups in a trial or between an exposed and an unexposed group in an observational study. This figure does not give any idea of the proportional increase between the two groups; for this, relative risk increase (*see* definition below) is needed.

Absolute risk reduction (ARR) The absolute difference in rates or risk of events between the experimental and control groups in a trial or between an exposed and an unexposed group in an observational study. This figure does not give any idea of the proportional reduction between the two groups; for this, relative risk reduction (*see* definition below) is needed.

Bias Systematic deviation of observed study results from the true results, because of the way(s) in which the study is conducted.

Case-control study A study design that examines to what extent (usually adverse) events are related to earlier exposure. This type of study design is most useful for trying to ascertain the cause of rare events, such as rare cancers.

Clinically significant A finding that is clinically important, as opposed to being statistically significant (*see* definition below), which may or may not be due to chance.

Cohort study A study design that examines to what extent a treatment or exposure is likely to cause specified events. Prospective cohort studies (which track participants forward in time) can be more reliable than retrospective cohort studies (which look back in time to ascertain whether or not participants were exposed to the agent in question) because the temporal relationship between exposure and outcome is certain.

Confidence interval (CI) A range of values calculated from the sample observations that are believed, with a particular probability, to contain the true parameter value.

Controls The participants in the comparison group of a randomized controlled trial (*see* definition below). They are allocated either placebo, no treatment, or the standard treatment.

Cross-sectional study A study design that involves surveying a population about an exposure, or condition, or both at one moment in time. It can be used for assessing the prevalence of a condition in the population.

Effect size The magnitude of the effect of treatment (or exposure) as measured by differences or ratios of means for continuous or interval scales; risk differences, relative risks (*see* definition below), and odds ratios (*see* definition below) for proportions; rate differences or rate ratios for person-time data; or hazard ratios (*see* definition below) for survival data. In social science, effect size usually refers to the difference in means divided by the standard deviation in the control (unexposed) group.

Hazard ratio (HR) A phrase used in the context of survival over time broadly equivalent to the relative rate of death. If the ratio is 0.5, then the relative rate of dying in one group is half the rate of dying in the other group.

Heterogeneity Dissimilarity. In the context of meta-analysis, heterogeneity may be either statistical (meaning that studies used different statistical methods) or clinical (meaning that studies evaluated different types of patients, treatments, or outcomes). Either type of heterogeneity may render pooling of data in meta-analysis inappropriate.

Homogeneity Similarity (*see* Heterogeneity).

Incidence The number of new cases of a condition occurring in a population over a specified period of time.

Meta-analysis A statistical technique that summarizes the results of several studies in a single estimate.

Morbidity Illness, but not death.

Mortality Death.

Negative predictive value (NPV) The chance of not having a disease given a negative test result.

Number needed to harm (NNH) One measure of treatment harm. The number of people needed to be treated with a specific intervention for a given period of time to cause one additional adverse outcome. NNH can be calculated as 1/ARI (*see* Absolute risk increase).

Number needed to treat (NNT) One measure of treatment effectiveness. The number of people needed to be treated with a specific intervention for a given period of time to prevent one additional adverse outcome or achieve one additional beneficial outcome. NNT can be calculated as 1/ARR (*see* Absolute risk reduction).

Odds ratio (OR) One measure of treatment effectiveness. It is the ratio of the odds of an event happening rather than not happening. If the OR is equal to one, then the effects of the treatment are no different from those of the control treatment. If the OR is greater (or less) than one, then the effects of the treatment are more (or less) then those of the control treatment. Note that the effects being measured may be adverse (e.g., death or disability) or desirable (e.g., survival).

Odds reduction The complement of odds ratio (1 – OR) analogous to relative risk reduction.

***p* value** The probability, under the assumption of no effect or no difference (the null hypothesis), of obtaining a result equal to or more extreme than what was actually observed. A p value $<$ 0.05 is usually said to be statistically significant.

Placebo A biologically inert treatment given to control-group participants in trials.

Positive predictive value (PPV) The chance of having a disease given a positive test result.

Prevalence The proportion of people with a finding or disease in a given population at a given time.

Publication bias The notion that studies with positive results are more likely to be published than studies with negative results, thus making it appear from surveys of the published literature that treatments have more positive results than is truly the case.

Randomized controlled trial (RCT) A trial in which participants are assigned randomly to groups: one or more experimental groups receiving the intervention that is being tested and one comparison (control) group receiving an alternative treatment or placebo. The different treatment groups allow assessment of the relative effects of intervention.

Relative risk (RR) The number of times more likely (if RR $>$ 1) or less likely (if RR $<$ 1) something is to happen in one group compared with another. It is similar in concept to an odds ratio (*see* definition above).

Relative risk increase (RRI) The proportional increase in rates of adverse events between experimental and control participants in a trial or between the exposed and unexposed participants in an observational study.

Relative risk reduction (RRR) The proportional reduction in rates of adverse events between experimental and control participants in a trial or between the exposed and unexposed participants in an observational study.

Sensitivity The chance of having a positive test result given that you have a disease (not to be confused with positive predictive value (*see* definition above), which is the opposite.

Specificity The change of having a negative test result given that you have a disease (not to be confused with negative predictive value (*see* definition above), which is the opposite.

Statistical power A study has adequate statistical power if it is big enough to detect reliably a difference (for instance, between two treatments) if one actually exists.

Statistically significant means that the findings of a study are unlikely to be due to chance (*see* Clinically significant).

Systematic review A review in which all trials on a topic have been systematically identified, appraised, and summarized according to predetermined criteria. It can, but need not, involve meta-analysis (*see* definition above) as a statistical method of adding together and numerically summarizing the results of the trials that meet minimum quality criteria.

Validity The soundness or rigor of a study. A study is valid if the way it is designed and carried out means that the results are unbiased and give a true estimate of the measured effect.

Weighted mean difference (WMD) The difference between groups, expressed as means, when continuous variables (e.g., height, weight, symptom scores) are used, rather than dichotomous outcomes (e.g., death, myocardial infarction).

Abbreviations

AR	Absolute risk	**NS**	Not significant
ARI	Absolute risk increase	**OR**	Odds ratio
ARR	Absolute risk reduction	***p***	*p* value
CCT	Controlled clinical trial	**RCT**	Randomized controlled trial
CI	Confidence interval	**RR**	Relative risk
HR	Hazard ratio	**RRI**	Relative risk increase
NNH	Number needed to harm	**RRR**	Relative risk reduction
NNT	Number needed to treat	**WMD**	Weighted mean difference

How To Calculate Risk

AR	=	# events (good or bad) in treated or control group / # people in group	**ARR**	=	ARC – ART
			RR	=	ART/ARC = 1 – RRRf
			RRR	=	(ARC – ART)/ARC = 1 – RR
ARC	=	AR of events in control group	**NNT**	=	1/AR
ART	=	AR of events in treated group			

To express decimals as percentages, multiply by 100.

If the RR (or OR) = 1, or the CI includes 1, there is no significant difference between treatment and control groups.

If the RR > 1 and the CI does not include 1, events are significantly more likely in the treatment than the control group.

If the RR < 1 and the CI does not include 1, events are significantly less likely in the treatment than the control group.

RR of 0.8 means a RRR of 0.2. In turn, this means a 20% reduction in the relative risk of an adverse outcome in the treatment group compared with the control group.

RRR is usually constant across a range of absolute risks, but the ARR is higher and the NNT lower in people with higher absolute risks.

EXAMPLE

If a person's AR of stroke is 25% without treatment but falls to 20% with treatment, the ARR is 25% – 20% or 5% or 0.05; the RRR is (25% – 20%)/20% or 0.2; and the NNT is 1/0.05 or 20. In a person with an AR of stroke of only 2.5% without treatment, the same treatment will still produce a 20% RRR, but this will reduce his or her AR of stroke to 2%, giving a much smaller ARR of 2.5% – 2.0% or 0.5% or 0.005 and a NNT of 200.

Primary prevention of cardiovascular diseases

Clinical Evidence writers on primary prevention of cardiovascular diseases

QUESTIONS

INTERVENTIONS

Key Messages

Exercise

- We found observational evidence that moderate to high physical activity reduces coronary artery disease and stroke.
- Observational studies found that sudden death after strenuous exercise is very rare, more common in the sedentary, and does not outweigh the benefits.

Diet

- Fruit and vegetable consumption is associated with reduced ischemic vascular disease in observational studies.
- Randomized controlled trials (RCTs) found that β-carotene supplements are not effective at reducing heart disease and may be harmful.
- We found insufficient evidence to support the use of antioxidant supplements in healthy individuals.

Smoking

- There is a strong association in observational data between smoking and overall mortality and ischemic vascular disease.
- Several large cohort studies found that the increased risks associated with smoking fall after cessation of smoking.

Hypertension

- Lifestyle interventions have been shown to have beneficial effects on blood pressure but have not been shown to reduce mortality or morbidity.
- Drugs reduce blood pressure more than lifestyle interventions.
- A systematic review found that the main determinant of treatment benefit is the pretreatment absolute cardiovascular disease risk.
- The evidence of beneficial effects of blood pressure reduction on mortality and morbidity is strongest for diuretics and then β-blockers.
- We found no direct evidence of the beneficial effects of lowering blood pressure beyond 140/80 mm Hg.

Cholesterol

- Systematic reviews found that cholesterol reduction in asymptomatic people lowers the rate of cardiovascular events but does not reduce the overall death rate.
- Systematic reviews and RCTs have found that combined use of cholesterol-lowering diet and lipid-lowering drugs reduces cholesterol more than lifestyle interventions alone.

Antithrombotic drugs

- We found insufficient randomized evidence to identify which asymptomatic individuals would benefit overall and which would be harmed by regular treatment with aspirin.
- One RCT found that the benefits and harms of oral anticoagulation among individuals without symptoms of cardiovascular disease also are balanced very finely, and the net effects are uncertain.

DEFINITION Primary prevention in this context is the long-term management of people at increased risk but with no evidence of cardiovascular disease. Clinically overt ischemic vascular disease includes acute myocardial infarction (AMI), angina, stroke, and peripheral vascular disease. Many adults have no symptoms or obvious signs of vascular disease, even though they have atheroma and are at increased risk of ischemic vascular events due to one or more risk factors (*see* below).

INCIDENCE/ PREVALENCE In the US, approximately 42% of all deaths are from vascular disease. AMI and its sequelae remain the most common single cause of death.

ETIOLOGY Identified major risk factors for ischemic vascular disease include increasing age, male sex, raised serum cholesterol (from low-density lipoprotein cholesterol), reduced high-density lipoprotein cholesterol, hypertension, smoking, diabetes, family history of cardiovascular disease, obesity, and sedentary lifestyle. For many of these risk factors, observational studies show a continuous gradient of increasing risk of cardiovascular disease with increasing levels of the risk factor, with no obvious threshold level. In a population, most ischemic vascular events occur in people with intermediate levels of absolute risk, because there are many more such people than there are people at high risk.[1]

PROGNOSIS Most people in industrialized countries eventually develop overt cardiovascular disease. Twenty-five percent of people die suddenly of coronary artery disease,[1a] and two thirds of AMIs occur before reaching hospital.[2] The benefits of intervention in an unselected population with no evidence of cardiovascular disease (primary prevention) may be small because their baseline risk is small. However, absolute risk of ischemic vascular events varies dramatically, even among people with similar levels of blood pressure or cholesterol. Estimates of absolute risk can be based on simple risk equations or tables.[3,4]

AIMS To reduce mortality and morbidity from cardiovascular disease, with minimum adverse effects.

OUTCOMES Incidence of fatal and nonfatal cardiovascular events (includes coronary and cerebrovascular disease, and heart failure). Changes in levels of individual risk factors, such as blood pressure, are surrogate outcomes.

METHODS We searched the Cochrane Library, MEDLINE, and EMBASE in July 1998.

EXERCISE

David Whiteman, Michael Murphy

QUESTION **Does physical activity reduce the risk of vascular events in asymptomatic people?**

We found strong observational evidence that moderate to high levels of physical activity reduce the risk of nonfatal and fatal coronary artery disease (CAD) and stroke. People who are physically active (those who undertake moderate levels of activity daily or almost daily) typically experience 30–50% reductions in relative risk of CAD compared with people who are sedentary, after adjusting for other risk factors. The absolute risk of sudden death after strenuous activity is small (though greatest in people who are habitually sedentary) and does not outweigh the observed benefits.

Benefits: **Effects of physical activity on CAD:** We found no RCTs. Three systematic reviews published between 1989 and 1992 evaluated observational studies and found increased risk of CAD in sedentary compared with active people.[5–7] Since 1990, 12 large well-conducted prospective nonrandomized studies with follow up periods ranging from five to 26 years have specifically addressed the association between physical activity and risk of nonfatal or fatal CAD.[8–19] All adjusted extensively for confounding factors and reported reductions in the RR of death from CAD of 20% to 50% for people engaged in moderate to high levels of physical activity. Risk declined with increasing levels of activity (for examples of activity levels, *see* Table 1). In absolute terms, people leading sedentary lives (those who never or rarely engaged in any physical activity) suffered approximately 70 CAD deaths per 10,000 person-years compared with 40 per 10,000 person-years among the most active participants (those who expend >3500 kcal/wk). This means a benefit from high levels of physical activity of approximately 30 lives saved per 10,000 person-years at risk. **Effects of physical fitness on CAD:** We found no RCTs. A systematic review published in 1992 identified seven large, well-designed prospective, nonrandomized studies of the effects of physical fitness on CAD.[20] All used reproducible measures of physical fitness. Five studies adjusted for other CAD risk factors. These found increased RRs of death from CAD in people with low levels of physical fitness (lowest quartile) compared with those with high levels (highest quartile); the RRs ranged from 1.2 to 4.0. Most studies reported only baseline measures of physical fitness, thus not accounting for changes in fitness. A recent large follow-up study found lower risk among people who increased their fitness level (RR for CAD death compared with those whose level of fitness did not change 0.48, 95% CI 0.31–0.74).[21] **Effects of physical activity on stroke:** We found no RCTs and no systematic review of observational studies. Since 1990, 10 observational studies have been published, based on more than 3000 strokes among North American, Japanese, and European populations.[22–33] Most of these studies identified a beneficial effect of exercise on the order of a halving in risk for those who were moderately active or more so compared with those who were inactive. (The only exception was the Japanese cohort,[33] which reported a significant threefold increased risk of stroke in men who took part in "heavy" as opposed to "moderate" physical activity.) The benefits were greater in older people and men, but most studies were conducted in white men in late middle age. The results usually persisted after adjustment for other known risk factors for stroke (blood pressure, blood lipids, body mass index, and smoking) and after excluding people with pre-existing diseases that might limit physical activity and increase stroke risk. Some studies, but not all, reported increased risk reduction with increasing levels of activity.

Harms: No direct evidence of harm was reported in the studies described above. Two studies[34,35] conducted in the US and Germany, each involving more than 1000 cases of nonfatal myocardial infarction, observed that 4% to 7% of these events occurred within 1 hour of strenuous physical activity.[36] Strenuous activity was estimated to have raised the RR of AMI between two- and sixfold in the hour after activity, with risks returning to baseline after that. However, the AR remained low, variously estimated at six deaths per 100,000 middle-aged men per year,[37] or 0.3 to 2.7 events per 10,000 person-hours of exercise.[38] Both studies found that the risks associated with strenuous activity were much higher in people who were habitually sedentary (RR 107, 95% CI 67–171)[34] compared with those who engaged in heavy physical exertion on five or more occasions per week (RR 2.4, 95% CI 1.5–3.7).[34] Overuse injuries of the musculoskeletal system are likely to be the most common adverse event, but few population data are available to quantify the magnitude of risk.

Comment: The findings from these observational studies should be interpreted with caution. The studies varied in their precise definitions of levels of activity and fitness. The level of activity or fitness experienced by each participant was not assigned experimentally by an investigator (as in a RCT) but was the result of self-selection. Active (or fit) participants are likely to differ from inactive (or unfit) participants in other ways that also influence their risk of cardiovascular disease. Confounding of this type can be controlled partially by adjustment for other known risk factors (e.g., age, smoking status, and body mass index), but it is likely that some residual confounding will remain, which could overestimate the effect of exercise. The AR of sudden death during or immediately after physical activity is small and does not outweigh the observed benefits. Because risks of sudden death are highest among habitually sedentary persons, gradual commencement of exercise seems prudent.

QUESTION **What intensity and frequency of physical activity improves fitness?**

Small RCTs have found that at least moderate-intensity exercise (equivalent to brisk walking) is necessary to improve fitness. There is no evidence of a difference between short bouts of exercise several times a day compared with longer daily bouts.

Benefits: **Intensity:** We found no systematic review. Numerous small RCTs of varying quality have been conducted in various subpopulations. In general, these found that over a period of 6 to 12 months, low-intensity activity programs produced no measurable changes in maximum oxygen consumption (VO_2max), whereas moderate intensity activity programs (equivalent to brisk walking) typically produced improvements of 20% in sedentary subjects. (Table 1 gives the intensity of effort required for a range of physical activities.) **Frequency:** No systematic review. An RCT in 36 men compared 8 weeks of a single daily bout of 30-minutes' exercise versus three daily bouts of 10 minutes each.[39] It found no significant difference in fitness benefit between groups.

Harms: None reported.

Comment: These trials should be interpreted with caution because small sample sizes increase the chances that groups were not comparable at baseline.

DIETARY INTERVENTIONS

Andy Ness

QUESTION **Does eating more fruits and vegetables reduce the risk of heart attack or stroke in asymptomatic people?**

Cohort studies have found that eating more fruits and vegetables reduces the risk of heart attack and stroke, although the evidence is less consistent for stroke. The size and nature of any real protective effect is uncertain.

Benefits: We found no RCTs. Two systematic reviews examined the evidence from observational studies for ischemic heart disease[40,41] and one for stroke.[40] **Ischemic heart disease:** Adding recently published studies[42–44] to those reported in the first review,[40] a protective association was observed for ischemic heart disease in eight of 19 cohort studies. In the second review, the authors calculated a summary measure of the protective association of 15% comparing those in the 90th percentile and those in the 10th percentile for consumption of fruits and vegetables.[42] The validity of this estimate is questionable. The most informative published cohort study gives a better idea of the magnitude of the protective association.[45] There was an RRR for coronary death of 0.34 (95% CI 0.04–0.54) for men consuming 117 g/d or more of vegetables compared with those consuming <61 g/d. There was no significant benefit from increased fruit consumption alone (RRR for coronary death 0.23, 95% CI 0.12 relative risk increase to 0.46 relative risk reduction) for men consuming ≥159 g/d of fruit compared with those consuming <75 g/d). **Stroke:** Adding recently published studies[42,46–48] to those reported in the first review,[40] a protective association was observed in eight of 12 cohorts for stroke. The single most informative study used a food frequency questionnaire and long follow-up.[49] It reported a RRR for stroke of 0.26 (95% CI not available, $p = 0.03$) in the fifth of the population eating the most vegetables compared to the fifth eating the least.

Harms: None have been identified.

Comment: Lack of trial evidence and deficiencies in the data available from observational studies mean that the size and nature[50,51] of any real protective effect is uncertain. The observed associations could be a result of confounding, because people who eat more fruit and vegetables often come from higher socioeconomic groups and adopt other healthy lifestyles.[52]

QUESTION Do antioxidants reduce the risk of heart attack and stroke in asymptomatic people?

We found no evidence that β-carotene supplements are effective, and RCTs suggest that these may be harmful. Other antioxidant supplements may be beneficial, but there is insufficient trial evidence to support their use.

Benefits: **β-Carotene:** Most prospective cohort studies of β-carotene have reported a modest protective association with increased intake.[53–55] However, several large trials of β-carotene supplementation failed to show a benefit,[55,56] but found that supplements may be harmful, with an RRI for cardiovascular deaths of 0.12 (95% CI 0.04 to 0.22).[55] Various explanations for these results have been put forward. These include the use of the wrong isomer, the wrong dose, or a detrimental effect on other carotenoid levels.[57,58] **Vitamin C:** A systematic review identified 12 cohort studies, three of which reported a significant protective association for CAD.[59] Adding a recently published study[47] to the review,[59] a protective association between vitamin C and stroke was observed in two of eight cohort studies. No large trials of vitamin C supplementation alone have been reported. Two large trials have been carried out in Linxian, China.[60–63] One trial was carried out in 29,584 participants drawn from the general population. Using a factorial design, subjects were randomized to one of four arms: arm A–retinol (10,000 IU) and zinc (22.5 mg); arm B–riboflavin (5.2 mg) and niacin (40 mg); arm C–vitamin C (120 mg) and molybdenum (30 µg); arm D–β-carotene (15 mg), selenium (50 µg), and vitamin E (30 mg). After 6 years there was an RRR in death from all causes of 0.09 (95% CI 0.01–0.16) in arm D; deaths from stroke also were reduced. There was no reduction in stroke or all-cause mortality in the other arms.[61] The other trial was carried out in 3318 people with esophageal dysplasia. Subjects were randomized to receive a multivitamin supplement that contained 14 vitamins and 12 minerals including vitamin C (180 mg), vitamin E (60 IU [1 IU = 0.67 mg]), β-carotene (15 mg), and selenium (50 µg). The RRR for death from all causes was 0.07 (95% CI 0.16 relative risk increase to 0.25 relative risk reduction). The RRR for stroke was 0.33 (95% CI 0.07 relative risk increase to 0.63 relative risk reduction) after 6 years.[60,62] **Vitamin E:** All six large cohort studies that examined the association between vitamin E intake and ischemic heart disease have reported a protective association,[45,64–67] although in one this was not significant.[68] In three studies, the protective association was with dietary vitamin E.[45,65,68] In the others, it was vitamin E supplement uses.[64,66,67] Cohort studies have reported no association between rates of ischemic heart disease and vitamin E status,[54] but blood concentrations of vitamin E are a poor marker of intake,[69] and deterioration of vitamin E may have occurred with storage of blood samples.[54] A trial of 50 mg of vitamin E in 29,133 Finnish smokers showed a slight increase in the RR of death of 0.02 (95% CI 0.09 relative increase to 0.05 relative reduction) after 5 to 8 years.[70] (*See* also the results of the Linxian trials[60–63] described in the section on vitamin C.) **Antioxidant minerals:** There is little epidemiologic evidence to confirm or refute a cardioprotective role of copper, zinc, or manganese.[71] Cohort studies reported an increased risk of ischemic heart disease in people with low blood selenium concentrations.[72] Most of these were carried out in Finland, a country with low intakes.[72] (*See* also the results of the Linxian trials[60–63] described in the section on vitamin C.) **Flavonoids:** Two[73,74] of four cohort studies[73–76] have reported a reduced risk of ischemic heart disease with increased flavonoid intake. One observational study reported a reduced risk of stroke with increased flavonoid intake.[46]

Comment: More trials of antioxidant supplementation are under way.[77]

SMOKING CESSATION

Julian J Nicholas, Thomas Kottke

QUESTION **By how much does smoking cessation, or avoidance of starting smoking, reduce risk?**

Observational studies have found that cigarette smoking is strongly related to overall mortality. We found evidence from both observational and randomized studies that cigarette smoking increases the risk of CAD and stroke. The evidence is strongest for stroke.

Benefits: Several large cohort studies examining the links between smoking and disease have been extensively reviewed by the US Surgeon General[78] and the Royal College of Physicians.[79] The reviews concluded that cigarette smoking was causally related to disease and that smoking cessation substantially reduced the risk of cancer, respiratory disease, CAD, and stroke. **Death from all causes:** The longest prospective study reported death rates within a cohort of 34,439 male British doctors whose smoking habits were assessed periodically over 40 years (1951–1991). Smokers were approximately three times more likely to die in middle age (45–64 years) and twice as likely to die in older age (65–84 years) compared with lifelong nonsmokers (CIs were not identifiable from this study).[80] The prospective Nurses' Health Study followed 117,001 middle-aged female nurses for 12 years. It found that the total mortality in current smokers was nearly twice that in lifelong nonsmokers (RR of death 1.87, 95% CI 1.65–2.13).[81] **CAD:** One review, published in 1990, identified 10 cohort studies, involving 20 million person-years of observation.[78] All studies found a higher incidence of CAD among smokers (RR of death from CAD compared with nonsmokers 1.7, CI could not be identified from the study).[78] People smoking more than 20 cigarettes per day were more likely to have a coronary event (RR 2.5, CI not stated in the study).[79] The RR of a first nonfatal AMI in middle-aged smokers compared with never smokers was 2.9 in men (95% CI 2.4–3.4)[82] and 3.6 in women (95% CI 3.0–4.4).[83] A RCT of smoking cessation in 1445 men aged 40 to 59 years[84] reported an average fall in cigarette consumption of 53% in the intervention group compared with the controls and a corresponding fall in the RR of death from CAD (RRR of CAD death compared with the control group 0.18, 95% CI –0.18 to 0.43). The wide CI means that there could have been anything from a 43% decrease to an 18% increase in CAD death identified in the intervention group. **Stroke:** A systematic review published in 1989 of 32 studies (17 cohort studies with concurrent or historical controls, 14 case control studies, and one hypertension intervention trial). It found a RR of stroke in cigarette smokers compared with nonsmokers of 1.5 (95% CI 1.4–1.6).[85] The RR was raised significantly for cerebral infarction (RR 1.92, 95% CI 1.71–2.16) and subarachnoid hemorrhage (RR 2.93, 95% CI 2.48–3.46) but not for intracerebral hemorrhage excluding subarachnoid hemorrhage (RR 0.74, 95% CI 0.56–0.98). The RR of stroke was highest in those aged under 55 years (2.9, 95% CI 2.40–3.59) and lowest in those aged over 74 years (RR 1.11, 95% CI 0.96–1.28).

Harms: We found no evidence that stopping smoking increases mortality in any subgroup of smokers but may lead to depression in some people.[85a]

Comment: We found no evidence of publication or other overt bias that may explain the observed association between smoking and death from all causes, CAD, and stroke. There was a dose-response curve between the number of cigarettes smoked and the RR, which is consistent with a causal relationship. The ARR from stopping smoking will be highest for those with the highest AR of vascular events.

QUESTION How quickly do risks diminish when smokers stop smoking?

Observational studies have found that the relative risk of mortality and of cardiovascular morbidity falls after cessation of smoking. The risk can take many years to approximate that of nonsmokers, particularly in those with a history of heavy smoking.

Benefits: **Death from all causes:** In people who stopped smoking, death rates fell gradually to lie between those of lifelong smokers and never smokers. Estimates for the time required for former smokers to bring their risk of death in line with never smokers varied among studies, but it may be longer than 15 years.[86] Nevertheless, actuarial projections from the British doctors' study predicted improved life expectancy even among those who stopped smoking in later life (≥65 years).[80] **CAD:** Observational studies found that, in both men and women ex-smokers, the risk of coronary events rapidly declined to a level comparable to that of never smokers after 2 to 3 years and was independent of the number of cigarettes smoked before quitting.[78] **Stroke:** The US Surgeon General's review of observational studies found that the risk of stroke decreased in ex-smokers compared with smokers (RR 1.2, 95% CI not available) but remained increased for 5 to 10 years after cessation compared with those who had never smoked (RR 1.5).[78] The more recent British regional heart study in 7735 middle aged men found that, 5 years after smoking cessation, the risk of stroke in light smokers (<20 cigarettes per day) was identical to that of lifelong nonsmokers, but the risk in heavy smokers (≥20 cigarettes per day) was still raised (RR 2.2, 95% CI 1.1–4.3).[87] The Nurses' Health Study of 117,001 middle-aged female nurses also reported a fall in risk after stopping smoking. The RR in former smokers 2 to 4 years after stopping smoking was 1.17 (95% CI, 0.49–2.23), but the fall was observed equally in people who had been light and heavy smokers.[81]

Harms: We found no evidence that stopping smoking increases mortality in any subgroup of smokers.

Comment: For a review of the evidence on methods of changing smoking behavior, *see* p. 29.

TREATING ESSENTIAL HYPERTENSION

Cindy Mulrow, Rod Jackson

QUESTION **What are the effects of lifestyle modification in people with essential hypertension?**

OPTION **AEROBIC EXERCISE**

A systematic review of RCTs has found that aerobic exercise reduces blood pressure (*see* Table 2).

Benefits: No RCTs have examined the effects of exercise on morbidity, mortality, or quality of life. A systematic review published in 1996 identified 29 RCTs of at least 4-weeks' duration in 1533 hypertensive or normotensive sedentary adults aged 18 to 79 years.[88] Aerobic exercise interventions were walking/jogging, cycling, or both, often lasting 45 to 60 minutes per session for 3 days per week. Mean exercise intensity was approximately 60% to 70% of VO_2max. The changes in blood pressure seen in the trials were heterogeneous depending on the baseline blood pressure and duration of the intervention. Compared with nonexercising control groups, aerobic exercise reduced systolic blood pressure by 4.7 mm Hg (95% CI 4.4–5.0 mm Hg) and diastolic blood pressure by 3.1 mm Hg (95% CI 3.0–3.3 mm Hg). Greater reductions were seen in people with higher initial blood pressures. Trials using interventions longer than 6-months' duration in hypertensive adults aged 45 years or over found smaller mean reductions in blood pressure, but with wide CIs (systolic reduction 0.8 mm Hg, 95% CI 5.9 mm Hg reduction to 4.2 mm Hg increase).[89]

Harms: Musculoskeletal injuries may occur, but their frequency was not documented.

Comment: Some adults may find such programs difficult to maintain. In common with other studies of lifestyle modifications, we found that these short-term clinical trials were too small to assess the effect of the interventions on cardiovascular mortality or morbidity.

OPTION LOW-FAT, HIGH-FRUIT-AND-VEGETABLE DIET

One RCT found that a low-fat, high-fruit-and-vegetable diet modestly reduced blood pressure.

Benefits: We found no RCTs examining the effects of low-fat, high-fruit-and-vegetable diet on morbidity or mortality. (For evidence from cohort studies, *see* p. 5.) A RCT of 459 adults with systolic blood pressures of less than 160 mm Hg and diastolic blood pressures of 80 to 90 mm Hg compared effects of three diets on blood pressure.[90] Diets were 1) a control diet low in magnesium and potassium; 2) a fruit-and-vegetable diet high in potassium, magnesium, and fiber; and 3) a combination of the fruit-and-vegetable diet with a low-fat diet high in calcium and protein. After 8 weeks, when compared with the control diet, the fruit-and-vegetable diet reduced systolic blood pressure by 2.8 mm Hg (97.5% CI 0.9 to 4.7 mm Hg) and diastolic blood pressure by 1.1 mm Hg (97.5% CI 2.4 mm Hg decrease to 0.3 mm Hg increase, $p = 0.07$), and the combination diet reduced systolic blood pressure by 5.5 mm Hg (97.5% CI 3.7–7.4 mm Hg) and diastolic blood pressure by 3.0 mm Hg (97.5% CI 1.6–4.3 mm Hg). The blood pressure reductions in the subgroup of hypertensive patients (≥140 mm Hg systolic and/or ≥90 mm Hg diastolic) were more dramatic (11.4/15.5 mm Hg).

Harms: We found no direct evidence that a low-fat, high-fruit-and-vegetable diet is harmful. Depending on prior diet and accessibility to particular foods, adaptation of this diet may have some added costs.

Comment: This trial was short and participants were supplied with food during the intervention period.[90] Other trials show that long-term maintenance of particular diets is difficult for many people, although low-fat diets may have multiple benefits.

OPTION REDUCED ALCOHOL CONSUMPTION

The scant evidence about the effect of reducing alcohol consumption on lowering blood pressure in people with mild hypertension is inconclusive.

Benefits: We found no RCTs examining the effects of reducing alcohol consumption on morbidity or mortality. (No systematic review.) Over 60 population studies have reported associations between alcohol consumption and blood pressure levels; the relation is generally linear, although several studies reported a threshold effect at approximately two to three standard drinks per day.[91] Any adverse effect of up to two drinks per day on blood pressure levels is either very small or nonexistent. A RCT of 44 treated hypertensive men (initial blood pressures 142/85 mm Hg) who were moderate to heavy drinkers showed that reducing alcohol consumption from 452 to 64 mL of ethanol per week lowered systolic blood pressure by 5 mm Hg (95% CI 2.1–7.9 mm Hg) and diastolic blood pressure by 3 mm Hg (95% CI 1.1–4.9 mm Hg).[92] Another RCT of 641 men with mild hypertension showed that a treatment program designed to reduce alcohol intake by 50% or to two or fewer drinks daily resulted in only a 1.2 mm Hg greater reduction in systolic blood pressure ($p = 0.17$) and a 0.7 mm Hg greater reduction in diastolic blood pressure ($p = 0.18$) than the control group.[92a]

Harms: We found no direct evidence that reducing alcohol intake to as few as two drinks a day is harmful.

Comment: Given the likely cardioprotective effect of regular light drinking in middle-aged and older people, current drinkers should be advised to limit consumption to approximately two drinks per day.

OPTION SALT RESTRICTION

A systematic review of RCTs has found that salt restriction may lead to modest reductions in blood pressure, with more benefit in people older than 45 years than in younger people (*see* Table 2).

Benefits: No RCTs have examined the effects of salt restriction on morbidity or mortality. We found a systematic review published in 1998 that identified 58 trials involving 2161 people with hypertension aged 23 to 73 years (mean age 49 years).[93] We also found a subsequent RCT lasting 30 months in 875 hypertensive men and women aged 60 to 80 years (mean age 66 years).[94] Interventions were low-salt diets with or without weight reduction. Control subjects took their usual diet. Changes in salt intake in trials in the systematic review were heterogeneous: a mean reduction in sodium intake of 118 mmol (6.7 g) per day for 28 days led to reductions of 3.9 mm Hg (95% CI 3.0–4.8 mm Hg) in systolic blood pressure and 1.9 mm Hg (95% CI 1.3–2.5 mm Hg) in diastolic blood pressure.[93] The subsequent trial in elderly people found that a mean decrease in salt intake of approximately 40 mmol (2.35 g) per day reduced systolic blood pressure by 2.6 mm Hg (95% CI 0.4–4.8 mm Hg) and diastolic blood pressure by 1.1 mm Hg (95% CI 0.3 mm Hg rise in diastolic to 2.5 mm Hg fall). An earlier systematic review published in 1996 identified 28 RCTs in 1131 hypertensive people. It found that lesser reductions of 60 mmol/d led to smaller reductions in systolic/diastolic blood pressure of 2.2/0.5 mm Hg, and found greater effects in trials where mean age was greater than 45 years (6.3/2.2 mm Hg).[95]

Harms: We found no direct evidence that low-salt diets may increase morbidity or mortality. Epidemiologic data conflict, with one observational study suggesting that very low salt intakes may be associated with increased incidence of myocardial infarction in middle-aged men.[96]

Comment: Small trials tended to report larger reductions in systolic and diastolic blood pressure than larger trials. This is consistent with publication bias or less rigorous methodology in small trials.[95]

OPTION **SMOKING CESSATION**

Epidemiologic data clearly identify that smoking is a significant risk factor for cardiovascular disease (*see* p. 7). There is no direct evidence that stopping smoking decreases mortality, morbidity, or blood pressure in people with hypertension (*see* Table 2).

OPTION **WEIGHT LOSS**

Modest weight reductions of 3% to 9% of body weight are achievable in motivated middle-aged and older adults and may lead to modest reductions in blood pressure in obese people with hypertension. Many adults find it difficult to maintain weight loss (*see* Table 2).

Benefits: No RCTs have examined the effects of weight loss on morbidity and mortality. A systematic review published in 1998 identified 18 RCTs. These involved a total of 2611 middle-aged people (mean age 50 years, mean weight 85 kg, mean blood pressures 152/98 mm Hg, 55% men).[97] Caloric intakes ranged from 450 to 1500 kcal/d; most diets led to weight reductions of 3% to 9% of body weight. Combined data from the six trials that did not vary antihypertensive regimens during the intervention period showed mean blood pressure reductions of 3 mm Hg systolic (95% CI 0.7–6.8 mm Hg) and 2.9 mm Hg diastolic (95% CI 0.1–5.7 mm Hg). Trials that allowed adjustment of antihypertensive regimens found that lower doses and fewer antihypertensive drugs were needed in the weight reduction groups compared with control groups.

Harms: We found no direct evidence that intentional gradual weight loss of less than 10% of body weight is harmful in obese hypertensive adults.

Comment: None.

QUESTION **What are the effects of dietary supplements in asymptomatic people with essential hypertension?**

OPTION **POTASSIUM SUPPLEMENTATION**

A systematic review of RCTs has found that potassium supplementation of about 60 mmol (2000 mg, which is roughly the amount contained in five bananas) per day is feasible for most adults and modestly reduces blood pressure (*see* Table 3).

Benefits: No RCTs have examined the effects of potassium supplementation on morbidity or mortality. A systematic review published in 1997 of 21 RCTs, involving 1560 hypertensive adults aged 19 to 79 years, found that potassium supplementation can lower blood pressure.[98] Interventions most often consisted of potassium chloride supplementation ranging from 60 to 100 mmol/d. Control subjects took placebo tablets or their usual diet. The mean decrease in blood pressure in the intervention groups compared with controls was 4.4 mm Hg systolic (95% CI 2.2–6.6 mm Hg) and 2.5 mm Hg diastolic (95% CI 0.1–4.9 mm Hg). There was a suggestion of greater drops in blood pressure in people with higher urinary sodium excretion and in black compared with white people.

Harms: We found no direct evidence of harm in people without kidney failure and in people not taking drugs that increase serum potassium. Gastrointestinal adverse effects (e.g., belching, flatulence, diarrhea, or abdominal discomfort) occur in 2% to 10% of people.

Comment: We found no direct evidence that potassium-supplementation diets affect morbidity or mortality, but reductions in blood pressure and lipids may have important cardioprotective effects.

OPTION FISH OIL SUPPLEMENTATION

One systematic review of RCTs has found that fish oil supplementation in large doses of ≥3 g/d modestly lowers blood pressure (see Table 3).

Benefits: No RCTs have examined the effects of fish oil supplementation on morbidity or mortality. A systematic review published in 1993 found seven RCTs involving 339 people with hypertension.[99] Participants were mainly middle-aged white men (mean age 50 years). The trials were mostly of short duration (mean follow-up 8 weeks). Interventions were usually capsules that contained ≥3 g of fish oil. Control participants took usual diets with or without oil mixtures that did not contain omega-3 polyunsaturated fatty acids. The mean decrease in blood pressure in the treatment group relative to the control group was 4.5 mm Hg systolic (95% CI 1.2–7.8 mm Hg) and 2.5 mm Hg diastolic (95% CI 0.6–4.4 mm Hg).

Harms: Belching, bad breath, fishy taste, and/or abdominal pain occur in approximately one third of people taking high doses of fish oil capsules.

Comment: The trials were short and used high doses of fish oil. Such high intake may be difficult to maintain. There was an apparent dose-dependent effect of fish oil on blood pressure. Fish oil supplementation may have additional benefits, such as improving dyslipidemia.

OPTION CALCIUM SUPPLEMENTATION

We found limited evidence suggesting that calcium supplementation may reduce systolic blood pressure by very small amounts (see Table 3).

Benefits: No RCTs have examined the effects of calcium supplementation on morbidity or mortality. A systematic review published in 1996 found 12 placebo-controlled RCTs with a median duration of 8 weeks involving 383 middle-aged hypertensive adults.[100] Baseline consumption of calcium ranged from 1000 to 3000 mg/d; calcium supplementation ranged from 800 to 1500 mg/d. Mean systolic blood pressure reduction was 2.1 mm Hg (95% CI 0.6–3.6 mm Hg); no significant diastolic reductions were found.

Harms: Adverse gastrointestinal effects, such as abdominal pain, were generally mild and varied among particular preparations.

Comment: The pooled estimate shows significant small decreases in systolic blood pressure with calcium supplementation; however, the effect was too small to support the use of calcium as a means to control blood pressure.

OPTION MAGNESIUM SUPPLEMENTATION

We found no good evidence on the effect of magnesium supplementation on blood pressure in people with hypertension and normal magnesium concentrations (*see* Table 3).

Benefits: No RCTs have examined the effects of magnesium supplementation on morbidity or mortality. A few small, short-term RCTs had inconsistent results in terms of blood pressure reduction.

Harms: Inadequate data.

Comment: None.

QUESTION Which pharmacologic interventions reduce the risk of cardiovascular events in people with essential hypertension?

OPTION DRUG TREATMENT

One systematic review of RCTs has found that drug treatment can decrease the risk of fatal and nonfatal stroke, cardiac events, and total mortality in specific patient populations. The biggest benefit is seen in those with the highest baseline cardiovascular disease risk.

Benefits: We found one systematic review published in 1996, which identified 17 RCTs of at least 1-year's duration with morbidity and mortality outcomes in 37,000 people.[101] Systolic/diastolic blood pressure reductions achieved in the trials varied but averaged around 12–16/5–10 mm Hg. There was evidence of benefit in total death rate, cardiovascular death rate, stroke, major coronary events, and congestive cardiac failure, but the absolute results depended on age and the severity of the hypertension (*see* below). The biggest benefit was seen in those with the highest baseline risk. The trials most often compared placebo with diuretics (usually thiazides with the addition of amiloride or triamterene) and β-blockers (usually atenolol or metoprolol) in a stepped care approach. We found only one published, large, well-designed, placebo-controlled RCT of a long-acting dihydropyridine calcium-channel blocker in people with hypertension.[102] A total of 4695 people (aged at least 60 years with isolated systolic hypertension but no severe cardiovascular or other disease) were randomized to treatment for approximately 2 years with either placebo or nisoldipine. The baseline risk of fatal or nonfatal cardiovascular events was 3.4% per year. The RR of cardiovascular events with active treatment was reduced by 0.31 (95% CI 0.14–0.45). The NNT to avoid one additional cardiovascular event per year was 94. **Target diastolic blood pressure:** A trial involving 18,790 people with a mean age of 62 years and diastolic blood pressures between 100 to 115 mm Hg evaluated target diastolic blood pressures of 90, 85, and 80 mm Hg.[103] However, mean achieved diastolic blood pressures were 85, 83, and 81 mm Hg respectively, which limited power to detect group differences. There were no significant differences in major cardiovascular events between the three groups.

Harms: **Mortality and major morbidity:** A systematic review of RCTs of diuretic and β-blocker–based pharmacotherapy found no increase in noncardiovascular mortality in treated people.[101] Comparable data on noncardiovascular morbidity is not available, although trials and case control studies found no consistent increase in cancer incidence with antihypertensive treatment. **Quality of life and tolerability:** Recent studies of low-dose drugs found good tolerance. For example, over 4 years of double-blind treatment with placebo or one of five antihypertensive agents, 59% of people on placebo and 72% assigned to pharmacotherapy remained on their initially assigned treatment.[88] A systematic review and several recent trials show quality of life is not affected adversely and may be improved in those who remain on treatment.[104,105]

Comment: Trials have included people healthier than in the general population, with lower rates of cardiovascular risk factors, cardiovascular disease, and comorbidity. People with higher cardiovascular risk can expect greater short-term absolute risk reduction than seen in the trials, whereas people with major competing risks, such as terminal cancer or end stage Alzheimer's disease, can expect smaller risk reduction. In the systematic review,[101] five of the trials were in middle-aged adults with mild to moderate hypertension. Seven of the trials were in people older than 60 years of age. On average, every 1000 patient years of treatment in older adults prevented five strokes (95% CI 2–8; NNT 197 treated for 1 year to prevent one event), three coronary events (95% CI 1–4; NNT 362), and four cardiovascular deaths (95% CI 1–8, NNT 225). Drug treatment in middle-aged adults prevented one stroke (95% CI 0–2; NNT 833) for every 1000 patient-years of treatment and did not affect significantly coronary events or mortality.

QUESTION What is the drug treatment of choice for essential hypertension?

Two systematic reviews have found that initial treatment with diuretics or β-blockers has proven mortality and morbidity benefits with minimal adverse effects. No other intervention has consistent evidence of reduced mortality and morbidity.

Benefits: A systematic review published in 1997 of RCTs that included over 48,000 people compared effects of high- and low-dose diuretics and β-blockers.[106] A second systematic review published in 1998 was limited to 10 trials involving 16,164 elderly people.[107] These reviews did not summarize direct comparisons of diuretics with β-blockers, but compared results of trials that used diuretics as first line agents with results of trials that used β-blockers as first-line agents. The reviews found no significant difference between diuretics and β-blockers, although only diuretics showed a significant reduction in CAD events. Other agents have not been compared.

Harms: **Quality of life and tolerability:** In the three long-term, double-blind comparisons of low-dose diuretics, β-blockers, angiotensin-converting–enzyme (ACE) inhibitors and calcium-channel blockers, tolerability and overall quality-of-life indicators tended to be more favorable for diuretics and β-blockers than for newer drugs.[108,109,110] Symptomatic adverse effects vary by drug class and by agents within classes. **Metabolic changes:** Many studies have reported adverse effects of diuretics and β-blockers on blood lipids (both drug groups), blood glucose, potassium, and uric acid (diuretics). Most of these studies were either of short duration or used high doses. Low-dose diuretics and β-blockers do not produce long-term metabolic effects likely to be of clinical importance.[111–113] For example, secondary analysis of results from a large trial of diuretics in the treatment of elderly people with isolated systolic hypertension showed similar cardiovascular RRRs in diabetic and nondiabetic people.[114] **Major harm controversies:** Case control and cohort studies suggest that short- and intermediate-acting dihydropyridine calcium-channel blockers, such as nifedipine and isradipine, may increase cardiovascular morbidity and mortality.[115] Results of RCTs are not conclusive.

Comment: None.

CHOLESTEROL LOWERING

Jeffrey L Probstfield

QUESTION **What are the effects of cholesterol lowering in asymptomatic people?**

We found little direct evidence that cholesterol reduction lowers overall mortality in people with no existing cardiovascular symptoms (primary prevention). Benefit is related to an individual's baseline risk and to the degree of cholesterol lowering rather than to the individual's absolute cholesterol concentration.

Benefits: There are numerous systematic reviews of the effects of cholesterol lowering on cardiovascular event rates, CAD mortality, and total mortality. Most conclude that cholesterol reduction lowers cardiovascular events but that there is little evidence that cholesterol reduction lowers overall mortality when used in people with no existing cardiovascular symptoms (primary prevention).[116,117] We found one systematic review published in 1998 which analyzed 43 RCTs with at least 2-years' follow-up, including five RCTs comparing the effects of pharmacotherapy versus placebo in 27,387 people with no prior myocardial infarction (primary prevention; although these trials included people with angina).[118] This review found no difference between primary and secondary prevention trials in the link between degree of cholesterol reduction and the RRR for total CAD mortality; a fall in total cholesterol of 10% (~ 0.6 mM/L) was associated with a RRR for CAD mortality of 0.15 and for total mortality of 0.11. A recent large RCT[119] evaluated primary prevention of coronary events in 6605 men and women with average total cholesterol, low high-density lipoprotein cholesterol, and no history of CAD. It found that treatment with a statin and a cholesterol-lowering diet for 5.2 years reduced the risk of acute major coronary events (fatal or nonfatal myocardial infarction, unstable angina, or sudden cardiac death) when compared with placebo and diet (AR 5.5% over 5.2 years with placebo, 3.5% with the statin; RRR 0.37, 95% CI 0.21–0.50; ARR 0.02 over 5.2 years, NNT for 5.2 years to avoid one additional acute major coronary event = 49, 95% CI 36–88). Similar results were found for reduction in rates of myocardial infarction (ARs 2.9% for placebo over 5.2 years, 1.7% for statin; RRR 0.40, 95% CI 0.17–0.57; NNT to avoid one additional AMI = 87, 95% CI 61–204). Coronary revascularization procedures also were decreased (RRR 0.33, 95% CI 0.14–0.47; NNT to avoid one additional procedure = 65, 95% CI 45–149). However, the study was not large enough to detect any change in the number of fatal CAD events (ARs 0.45% over 5.2 years for placebo, 0.33% for statin; RRR 0.27, 95% CI 0.59 increased risk to 0.66 reduced risk) or total mortality (AR 2.3% over 5.2 years for placebo, 2.4% for statin; RRI 0.04, 95% CI 0.41 increased risk to 0.24 decreased risk). In the large statin trials,[119–123] the ARR for CAD events, CAD mortality, and total mortality varied with the baseline risk in the placebo group of each trial (Figure 1). One systematic review published in 1997 analyzed 17 RCTs examining the effect in primary prevention of low-fat dietary behavior interventions of at least 3-months' duration versus no intervention.[124] It found a small but sustained fall in total cholesterol of only 0.2 mM/L. Another systematic review published in 1998 of 19 RCTs found similar results.[125] More intense diets produced a greater reduction in cholesterol, but diets were limited probably because of failure to implement fully the dietary recommendations.

Harms: We found no systematic review of studies on the harms of cholesterol-lowering interventions. Specific harms of statins are discussed on p. 89.

Comment: Figure 1 shows that the baseline risk of the populations selected in each statin trial varied considerably.[119–123] The observed lack of benefit in total mortality may merely reflect the small magnitude of any benefit to be expected in these trials and the design of many trials primarily to detect changes in event rates rather than mortality rates. Even if the relative reduction of overall mortality seen in the secondary prevention trials can be extrapolated to primary prevention in the general population, the NNTs to prevent one death per year of treatment will be large (~1000 treated for 1 year to avoid one additional death per year).

ANTITHROMBOTIC TREATMENT

Cathie Sudlow, Colin Baigent

QUESTION **What is the role of antiplatelet treatment in asymptomatic people?**

The role of antiplatelet treatment in individuals without symptoms of cardiovascular disease is uncertain. We found insufficient evidence from RCTs to identify which individuals would benefit overall and which would be harmed by regular treatment with aspirin.

Benefits: The most recent antiplatelet trialists' (APT) systematic overview published in 1994 included nearly 30,000 individuals with no clinically apparent arterial disease. Most participants were invloved in two large trials of aspirin versus control among male doctors in the UK (aspirin 500 mg/d) and the US (aspirin 325 mg every other day).[126–128] Since then, two further RCTs of aspirin versus control among asymptomatic individuals with identifiable risk factors for vascular events have been published.[129,130] The thrombosis prevention trial (TPT) was a 2 × 2 factorial RCT of aspirin (75 mg/d) versus placebo and of low-intensity oral anticoagulation with warfarin (target International Normalized Ratio, INR, 1.5) versus placebo, among approximately 5000 men aged 45 to 69 years. Participants were recruited from the general population, were in the top 20% to 25% of a CAD risk score distribution, and were followed for approximately 6 years.[129] The hypertension optimal treatment (HOT) trial also used a factorial design, with comparisons of aspirin 75 mg/d versus placebo and of three different intensities of blood pressure reduction, among approximately 19,000 hypertensive individuals (the majority of whom had no history of vascular disease).[130] Data on vascular events (nonfatal myocardial infarction, nonfatal stroke, or vascular death) from the primary prevention trials are summarized in Table 4. Overall, antiplatelet treatment produced a 13% (95% CI 5%–20%) proportional reduction in the odds of a vascular event, corresponding to the avoidance of only approximately one vascular event per 1000 individuals treated per year. There was a clear reduction in myocardial infarction: among the three trials in the APT overview the odds of a nonfatal myocardial infarction were reduced by 29% (95% CI 14%–41%); in TPT the rate of all (fatal or nonfatal) ischemic heart disease was reduced by 20% (95% CI 1%–35%); and in HOT the rate of all myocardial infarction was reduced by 36% (95% CI 15%–51%). However, although antiplatelet treatment seemed to reduce the risk of ischemic stroke, it also seemed to increase the risk of hemorrhagic stroke. In the 1994, APT overview the odds of a nonfatal stroke were increased by 21% (95% CI 0%–38%); in TPT there was a nonsignificant 3% (95% CI –45% to 35%) reduction in the rate of all stroke; and in HOT there was a nonsignificant 2% (95% CI –24% to 22%) reduction in the rate of all stroke. Considering all the randomized evidence, there was no clear evidence of a reduction in vascular death or in all-cause mortality.

Harms: Serious, potentially life-threatening bleeding is the most important adverse effect of antiplatelet treatment. Intracranial bleeds are uncommon, but they can be fatal and usually cause substantial disability in survivors. Major extracranial bleeds occur mainly in the gastrointestinal tract and may require hospital admission or blood transfusion but do not generally result in permanent disability and are rarely fatal. Table 5 shows the approximate excess annual rates for intracranial and major extracranial bleeds.

Comment: Individuals in primary prevention trials were at much lower risk of vascular events (average 1% per year in the control group) than the high-risk patients with clinical manifestations of cardiovascular disease that also were included in the APT overview (average 9% per year in the control group).[126] The absolute benefit of aspirin was therefore very small and, because it was of similar magnitude to the bleeding risks, the net effects were statistically uncertain. The size and direction of the effects of aspirin in particular individuals may well depend on specific factors, such as age, blood pressure, smoking status, or history of diabetes mellitus. At present there is insufficient information to identify which individuals would benefit overall and which would be harmed by regular treatment with aspirin, although some professional organizations recommend its use in people with risk factors for cardiovascular disease. Further information will become available soon from the Women's Health Study, a RCT comparing aspirin 100 mg/d versus placebo among 40,000 apparently healthy postmenopausal women,[131] and subsequently from a detailed overview of individual participant data from all available trials.

QUESTION **What is the role of anticoagulant treatment with warfarin in asymptomatic people?**

The available randomized evidence shows that, as for aspirin, the benefits and risks of low-intensity oral anticoagulation with warfarin among individuals without evidence of cardiovascular disease are finely balanced, and the net effects are uncertain.

Benefits: The TPT is currently the only trial to have addressed the possible role of anticoagulation (with a low target INR of 1.5) among individuals without evidence of cardiovascular disease.[129] The proportional effects of warfarin were similar among patients allocated aspirin or placebo; overall, warfarin produced a nonsignificant 14% (95% CI –2% to 28%) reduction in the odds of a vascular event, corresponding to a small absolute reduction of approximately two per 1000 individuals per year (253/2762 [9.2%] warfarin vs. 288/2737 [10.5%] placebo over ~6.5 years). The rate of all ischemic heart disease was reduced by 21% (95% CI 4%–35%), the rate of all stroke was nonsignificantly increased by 15% (–22% to 68%), and there was no effect on other causes of vascular death.

Harms: Allocation to warfarin was associated with a nonsignificant excess of approximately 0.4 intracranial bleeds per 1000 individuals per year (14/2762 [0.5%] warfarin vs. 7/2737 [0.3%] placebo), and a nonsignificant excess of extracranial bleeds of approximately 0.5 per 1000 individuals per year (21/2545 [0.8%] warfarin vs. 12/2540 [0.5%] placebo).

Comment: As is the case for aspirin, the benefits and risks of low-intensity oral anticoagulation among individuals without evidence of cardiovascular disease are finely balanced. The number of individuals randomized to date is only approximately one tenth of the number included in primary prevention trials of aspirin (*see* above); thus, the reliable identification of those who may benefit from such treatment will require further large-scale randomized evidence.

REFERENCES

1. Heller RF, Chinn S, Pedoe HD, Rose G. How well can we predict coronary heart disease? Findings of the United Kingdom heart disease prevention project. *BMJ* 1984;288:1409–1411
1a. Cleeman JI, Lenfant C. The National Cholesterol Education Program. *JAMA* 1998;280:2099–2104.
2. Tunstall-Pedoe H, Morrison C. Woodward M, Fitzpatrick B, Watt G. Sex differences in myocardial infarction and coronary deaths in the Scottish MONICA population of Glasgow 1985 to 1991: presentation, diagnosis, treatment, and 28-day case fatality of 3991 events in men and 1551 events in women. *Circulation* 1996;93:1981–1992.
3. Anderson KV, Odell PM, Wilson PW, Kannel WB. Cardiovascular disease risk profiles. *Am Heart J* 1991;121:293–298.
4. National Health Committee. Guidelines for the management of mildly raised blood pressure in New Zealand. Wellington Ministry of Health, 1993. (http://www.nzgg.org.nz/library/gl_complete/bloodpressure)
5. Powell KE, Thompson PD, Caspersen CJ, Kendrick JS. Physical activity and the incidence of coronary heart disease. *Ann Rev Public Health* 1987;8:253–287.
6. Berlin JA, Colditz GA. A meta-analysis of physical activity in the prevention of coronary heart

disease . *Am J Epidemiol* 1990;132:612–628. Search date not stated; primary sources review articles and MEDLINE.
7. Eaton CB. Relation of physical activity and cardiovascular fitness to coronary heart disease, part I: a meta-analysis of the independent relation of physical activity and coronary heart disease. *J Am Board Fam Pract* 1992;5:31–42. Search date not stated; primary source MEDLINE.
8. Fraser GE, Strahan TM, Sabate J, Beeson WL, Kissinger D. Effects of traditional coronary risk factors on rates of incident coronary events in a low-risk population: the Adventist health study. *Circulation* 1992;86:406–413.
9. Lindsted KD, Tonstad S, Kuzma JW. Self-report of physical activity and patterns of mortality in Seventh-Day Adventist men. *J Clin Epidemiol* 1991;44:355–364.
10. Folsom AR, Arnett DK, Hutchinson RG, Liao F, Clegg LX, Cooper LS. Physical activity and incidence of coronary heart disease in middle-aged women and men. *Med Sci Sports Exerc* 1997; 29:901–909.
11. Jensen G, Nyboe J, Appleyard M, Schnohr P. Risk factors for acute myocardial infarction in Copenhagen, II: Smoking, alcohol intake, physical activity, obesity, oral contraception, diabetes, lipids, and blood pressure. *Eur Heart J* 1991;12:298–308.
12. Simonsick EM, Lafferty ME, Phillips CL, et al. Risk due to inactivity in physically capable older adults. *Am J Public Health* 1993;83:1443–1450.
13. Haapanen N, Miilunpalo S, Vuori I, Oja P, Pasanen M. Association of leisure time physical activity with the risk of coronary heart disease, hypertension and diabetes in middle-aged men and women. *Int J Epidemiol* 1997;26:739–747.
14. Sherman SE, D'Agostino RB, Cobb JL, Kannel WB. Does exercise reduce mortality rates in the elderly? Experience from the Framingham heart study. *Am Heart J* 1994;128:965–972.
15. Rodriguez BL, Curb JD, Burchfiel CM, et al. Physical activity and 23-year incidence of coronary heart disease morbidity and mortality among middle-aged men: the Honolulu heart program. *Circulation* 1994;89:2540–2544.
16. Eaton CB, Medalie JH, Flocke SA, Zyzanski SJ, Yaari S, Goldbourt U. Self-reported physical activity predicts long-term coronary heart disease and all-cause mortalities: 21-year follow-up of the Israeli ischemic heart disease study. *Arch Fam Med* 1995;4:323–329.
17. Stender M, Hense HW, Doring A, Keil U. Physical activity at work and cardiovascular disease risk: results from the MONICA Augsburg study. *Int J Epidemiol* 1993;22:644–650.
18. Leon AS, Myers MJ, Connett J. Leisure time physical activity and the 16-year risks of mortality from coronary heart disease and all-causes in the multiple risk factor intervention trial (MRFIT). *Int J Sports Med* 1997;18(suppl 3):S208–215.
19. Rosolova H, Simon J, Sefrna F. Impact of cardiovascular risk factors on morbidity and mortality in Czech middle-aged men: Pilsen longitudinal study. *Cardiology* 1994;85:61–68.
20. Eaton CB. Relation of physical activity and cardiovascular fitness to coronary heart disease, part II: cardiovascular fitness and the safety and efficacy of physical activity prescription. *J Am Board Fam Pract* 1992;5:157–165.
21. Blair SN, Kohl HW 3rd, Barlow CE, Paffenbarger RS Jr, Gibbons LW, Macera CA. Changes in physical fitness and all-cause mortality: a prospective study of healthy and unhealthy men. *JAMA* 1995;273:1093–1098.
22. Sacco RL, Gan R, Boden-Albala B, et al. Leisure-time physical activity and ischemic stroke risk: the Northern Manhattan stroke study. *Stroke* 1998;29:380–387.
23. Shinton R. Lifelong exposures and the potential for stroke prevention: the contribution of cigarette smoking, exercise, and body fat. *J Epidemiol Community Health* 1997;51:138–143.
24. Gillum RF, Mussolino ME, Ingram DD. Physical activity and stroke incidence in women and men. The NHANES I epidemiologic follow-up study. *Am J Epidemiol* 1996;143:860-869.
25. Kiely DK, Wolf PA, Cupples LA, Beiser AS, Kannel WB. Physical activity and stroke risk: the Framingham study [published erratum appears in *Am J Epidemiol* 1995 Jan 15;141:178]. *Am J Epidemiol* 1994;140:608–620.
26. Abbott RD, Rodriguez BL, Burchfiel CM, Curb JD. Physical activity in older middle-aged men and reduced risk of stroke: the Honolulu heart program. *Am J Epidemiol* 1994;139:881–893.
27. Haheim LL, Holme I, Hjermann I, Leren P. Risk factors of stroke incidence and mortality: a 12-year follow-up of the Oslo Study. *Stroke* 1993; 24:1484–1489.
28. Wannamethee G, Shaper AG. Physical activity and stroke in British middle aged men. *BMJ* 1992;304:597–601.
29. Menotti A, Keys A, Blackburn H, et al. Twenty-year stroke mortality and prediction in twelve cohorts of the seven countries study. *Int J Epidemiol* 1990;19:309–315.
30. Lindenstrom E, Boysen G, Nyboe J. Risk factors for stroke in Copenhagen, Denmark. II Lifestyle factors. *Neuroepidemiology* 1993;12:43–50.
31. Lindenstrom E, Boysen G, Nyboe J. Lifestyle factors and risk of cerebrovascular disease in women: the Copenhagen City heart study. *Stroke* 1993;24:1468–1472.
32. Folsom AR, Prineas RJ, Kaye SA, Munger RG. Incidence of hypertension and stroke in relation to body fat distribution and other risk factors in older women. *Stroke* 1990;21:701–706.
33. Nakayama T, Date C, Yokoyama T, Yoshiike N, Yamaguchi M, Tanaka H. A 15.5-year follow-up study of stroke in a Japanese provincial city: the Shibata study. *Stroke* 1997;28:45–52.
34. Mittleman MA, Maclure M, Tofler GH, Sherwood JB, Goldberg RJ, Muller JE. Triggering of acute myocardial infarction by heavy physical exertion. Protection against triggering by regular exertion: determinants of myocardial infarction onset study investigators. *N Engl J Med* 1993;329: 1677–1683.
35. Willich SN, Lewis M, Lowel H, Arntz HR, Schubert F, Schroder R. Physical exertion as a trigger of acute myocardial infarction: triggers and mechanisms of myocardial infarction study group. *N Engl J Med* 1993;329:1684–1690.
36. Pate RR, Pratt M, Blair SN, et al. Physical activity and public health. A recommendation from the Centers for Disease Control and Prevention and the American College of Sports Medicine. *JAMA* 1995;273:402–407.
37. Thompson PD. The cardiovascular complications of vigorous physical activity. *Arch Intern Med* 1996;156:2297–2302.
38. Oberman A. Exercise and the primary prevention of cardiovascular disease. *Am J Cardiol* 1985;55:10D–20D.
39. DeBusk RF, Stenestrand U, Sheehan M, Haskell WL. Training effects of long versus short bouts of exercise in healthy subjects. *Am J Cardiol* 1990;65:1010–1013.
40. Ness AR, Powles JW. Fruit and vegetables and cardiovascular disease: a review. *Int J Epidemiol* 1997;26:1–13.

41. Law MR, Morris JK. By how much does fruit and vegetable consumption reduce the risk of ischaemic heart disease? *Eur J Clin Nutr* 1998; 52:549–556.
42. Key TJ, Thorogood M, Appleby PN, Burr ML. Dietary habits and mortality in 11,000 vegetarians and health conscious people: results of a 17 year follow up. *BMJ* 1996;313:775–779.
43. Pietinen P, Rimm EB, Korhonen P, et al. Intake of dietary fibre and risk of coronary heart disease in a cohort of Finnish men. *Circulation* 1996;94:2720–2727.
44. Mann JI, Appleby PN, Key TJ, Thorogood M. Dietary determinants of ischaemic heart disease in health conscious individuals. *Heart* 1997;78:450–455.
45. Knekt P, Reunanen A, Jarvinen R, Seppanen R, Heliovaara M, Aromaa A. Antioxidant vitamin intake and coronary mortality in a longitudinal population study. *Am J Epidemiol* 1994;139:1180–1189.
46. Keli SO, Hertog MG, Feskens EJ, Kromhout D. Dietary flavonoids, antioxidant vitamins, and incidence of stroke. *Arch Intern Med* 1996;156: 637–642.
47. Daviglus ML, Orencia AJ, Dyer AR, et al. Dietary vitamin C, beta-carotene and 30-year risk of stroke: results from the Western Electric study. *Neuroepidemiology* 1997;16:69–77.
48. Ascherio A, Rimm EB, Hernan MA, et al. Prospective study of potassium intake and risk of stroke among US men. *Can J Cardiol* 1997;13:44B.
49. Manson JE, Willett WC, Stampfer MJ, Colditz GA, Speizer FE, Hennekens CH. Vegetable and fruit consumption and incidence of stroke in women. *Circulation* 1994;89:932.
50. Ness AR, Powles JW. Does eating fruit and vegetables protect against heart attack and stroke? *Chemistry and Industry* 1996;792–794.
51. Ness AR, Powles JW. Dietary habits and mortality in vegetarians and health conscious people: several uncertainties still exist. *BMJ* 1997;314:148–149.
52. Serdula MK, Byers T, Mokdad AH, Simoes E, Mendleim JM, Coates RJ. The association between fruit and vegetable intake and chronic disease risk factors. *Epidemiology* 1996;7: 161–165.
53. Jha P, Flather M, Lonn E, Farkouh M, Yusuf S. The antioxidant vitamins and cardiovascular disease: a critical review of epidemiologic and clinical trial data. *Ann Intern Med* 1995;123: 860–872.
54. Roxrode KM, Manson JE. Antioxidants and coronary heart disease: observational studies. *J Cardiovasc Risk* 1996;3:363–367.
55. Egger M, Schneider M, Davey Smith G. Spurious precision? Meta-analysis of observational studies. *BMJ* 1998;316:140–144.
56. Gaziano JM. Randomized trials of dietary antioxidants in cardiovascular disease prevention and treatment. *J Cardiovasc Risk* 1996;3:368–371.
57. Pietrzik K. Antioxidant vitamins, cancer, and cardiovascular disease. *N Engl J Med* 1996;335: 1065–1068.
58. Pietrzik K. Antioxidant vitamins, cancer, and cardiovascular disease. *N Engl J Med* 1996;335: 1065–1068.
59. Ness AR, Powles JW, Khaw KT. Vitamin C and cardiovascular disease - a systematic review. *J Cardiovasc Risk* 1997;3:513–521.
60. Li J, Taylor PR, Li B, et al. Nutrition intervention trials in Linxian, China: multiple vitamin/mineral supplementation, cancer incidence, and disease-specific mortality among adults with esophageal dysplasia. *J Natl Cancer Inst* 1993;85:1492–1498.
61. Blot WJ, Li J, Taylor PR, et al. Nutrition intervention trials in Linxian, China: supplementation with specific vitamin/mineral combinations, cancer incidence, and disease-specific mortality in the general population. *J Natl Cancer Inst* 1993;85:1483–1492.
62. Mark SD, Wang W, Fraumeni JF, et al. Lowered risks of hypertension and cerebrovascular disease after vitamin/mineral supplementation. *Am J Epidemiol* 1996;143:658–664.
63. Mark SD, Wang W, Fraumeni JF, et al. Do nutritional supplements lower the risk of stroke or hypertension? *Epidemiology* 1998;9:9–15.
64. Rimm EB, Stampfer MJ, Ascherio A, Giovannucci E, Colditz GA, Willett WC. Vitamin E consumption and the risk of coronary heart disease in men. *N Engl J Med* 1993;328:1450–1456.
65. Kushi LH, Folsom AR, Prineas RJ, Mink PJ, Wu Y, Bostick RM. Dietary antioxidant vitamins and deaths from coronary heart disease in postmenopausal women. *N Engl J Med* 1996;334: 1156–1162.
66. Stampfer MJ, Hennekens CH, Manson JE, Colditz GA, Rosner B, Willett WC. Vitamin E consumption and the risk of coronary heart disease in women. *N Engl J Med* 1993;328:1444–1449.
67. Losonczy KG, Harris TB, Havlik RJ. Vitamin E and vitamin C supplement use and risk of all-cause and coronary mortality in older persons: the established populations for epidemiologic studies of the elderly. *Am J Clin Nutr* 1996;64:190–196.
68. Sahyoun NR, Jacques PF, Russell RM. Carotenoids, vitamins C and E, and mortality in an elderly population. *Am J Epidemiol* 1996;144:501–511.
69. Bates CJ, Thurnham DI, Bingham SA, Margetts BM, Nelson M. Biochemical markers of nutrient intake. In: Margetts BM, Nelson M, eds. *Design concepts in nutritional epidemiology*. Oxford: Oxford Medical Publications, 1991.
70. The Alpha-Tocopherol Beta Carotene Cancer Pevention Study Group. The effect of vitamin E and beta carotene on the incidence of lung cancer and other cancers in male smokers. *N Engl J Med* 1994;330:1029–1035.
71. Houtman JP. Trace elements and cardiovascular disease. *J Cardiovasc Risk* 1996;3:18–25.
72. Nève J. Selenium as a risk factor for cardiovascular diseases. *J Cardiovasc Risk* 1996;3:42–47.
73. Hertog MGL, Feskens EJM, Hollman PCH, Katan MB, Kromhout D. Dietary antioxidant flavonoids and risk of coronary heart disease: the Zutphen elderly study. Lancet 1993;342:1007–1011.
74. Knekt P, Jarvinen R, Reunanen A, Maatela J. Flavonoid intake and coronary mortality in Finland: a cohort study. *BMJ* 1996;312: 478–481.
75. Rimm EB, Katan MB, Ascherio A, Stampfer MJ, Willett WC. Relation between intake of flavonoids and risk for coronary heart disease in male health professionals. *Ann Intern Med* 1996;125:384–389.
76. Kromhout D. Diet-heart issues in a pharmacological era. *Lancet* 1996;348(suppl):s20–22.
77. Hennekens CH, Gaziano JM, Manson JE, Buring JE. Antioxidant vitamin cardiovascular disease hypothesis is still promising, but still unproven: the need for randomised trials. *Am J Clin Nutr* 1995;62(suppl):1377S–1380S.
78. Smoking 1 US Department of Health and Human Services. *The health benefits of smoking cessation : a report of the Surgeon General*. Rockville, Maryland: US Department of Health and Human Services, Public Health Service, Centers for Disease Control: 1990. DHHS Publication (CDC) 90-8416.
79. Royal College of Physicians. *Smoking and health now*. London: Pitman Medical and Scientific Publishing, 1971.

80. Doll R, Peto R, Wheatley K, Gray R, Sutherland I. Mortality in relation to smoking: 40 years' observations on male British doctors. *BMJ* 1994;309:901–911.
81. Kawachi I, Colditz GA, Stampfer MJ, et al. Smoking cessation in relation to total mortality rates in women: a prospective cohort study. *Ann Intern Med* 1993;119:992–1000.
82. Rosenberg L, Kaufman DW, Helmrich SP, Shapiro S. The risk of myocardial infarction after quitting smoking in men under 55 years of age. *N Engl J Med* 1985;313:1511–1514.
83. Rosenberg L, Palmer JR, Shapiro S. Decline in the risk of myocardial infarction among women who stop smoking. *N Engl J Med* 1990;322: 213–217.
84. Rose G, Hamilton PJ, Colwell L, Shipley MJ. A randomised controlled trial of anti-smoking advice: 10-year results. *J Epidemiol Community Health* 1982;36:102–108.
85. Shinton R, Beevers G. Meta-analysis of relation between cigarette smoking and stroke. *BMJ* 1989;298:789–794.
85a. Covey LS, Glassman AH, Stetner F. Major depression following smoking cessation. *Am J Psychiatry* 1997;154:263–265.
86. Rogot E, Murray JL. Smoking and causes of death among US veterans: 16 years of observation. *Public Health Rep* 1980;95:213–222.
87. Wannamethee SG, Shaper AG, Ebrahim S. History of parental death from stroke or heart trouble and the risk of stroke in middle-aged men. *Stroke* 1996;27:1492–1498.
88. Halbert JA, Silagy CA, Finucane P, Withers RT, Hamdorf PA, Andrews GR. The effectiveness of exercise training in lowering blood pressure: a meta-analysis of randomised controlled trials of 4 weeks or longer. *J Hum Hypertens* 1997;11:641–649. (Search date 1996; primary sources MEDLINE, EMBASE, Science Citation Index.)
89. Ebrahim S, Davey Smith G. Lowering blood pressure: a systematic review of sustained non-pharmacological interventions. *J Public Health Med* 1998;20:441–448. (Search date 1995, primary source MEDLINE.)
90. Appel LJ, Moore TJ, Obarzanek E, et al. A clinical trial of the effects of dietary patterns on blood pressure. *N Engl J Med* 1997;336:1117–1124.
91. Beilin LJ, Puddey IB, Burke V. Alcohol and hypertension: kill or cure? *J Hum Hypertens* 1996; 10(suppl 2):S1–5.
92. Puddey IB, Beilin LJ, Vandongen R. Regular alcohol use raises blood pressure in treated hypertensive subjects. *Lancet* 1987;i:647–651.
92a. Cushman WC, Cutler JA, Hanna E, et al. Prevention and Treatment of Hypertension Study (PATHS): effects of an alcohol treatment program on blood pressure. *Arch Intern Med* 1998;158:1197–1207.
93. Graudal NA, Galloe AM, Garred P. Effects of sodium restriction on blood pressure, renin, aldosterone, catecholamines, cholesterols, and triglyceride. *JAMA* 1998;279:1383–1391. (Search date 1997; primary source MEDLINE.)
94. Whelton PK, Appel LJ, Espeland MA, et al. Sodium reduction and weight loss in the treatment of hypertension in older persons: a randomized controlled trial of non pharmacologic interventions in the elderly (TONE). *JAMA* 1998; 279:839–846.
95. Midgley JP, Matthew AG, Greenwood CM, Logan AG. Effect of reduced dietary sodium on blood pressure. *JAMA* 1996;275:1590–1597. (Search date 1994; primary sources MEDLINE, Current Contents.)
96. Alderman MH, Madhavan S, Cohen H, Sealey JE, Laragh JH. Low urinary sodium associated with greater risk of myocardial infarction among treated hypertensive men. *Hypertension* 1995;25:1144–1152.
97. Brand MB, Mulrow CD, Chiquette E, et al. Weight-reducing diets for control of hypertension in adults. (Cochrane Review). In: The Cochrane Library, Issue 3, 1998. Oxford: Update Software. (Search date 1997; primary source Cochrane Library, MEDLINE.)
98. Whelton PK, He J, Cutler JA, et al. Effects of oral potassium on blood pressure: meta-analysis of randomized controlled clinical trials. *JAMA* 1997;277:1624–1632. (Search date 1995; primary source MEDLINE.)
99. Morris MC, Sacks F, Rosner B. Does fish oil lower blood pressure? A meta-analysis of controlled clinical trials. *Circulation* 1993;88:523–533. (Search date not given; primary source Index Medicus.)
100. Bucher HC, Cook RJ, Guyatt GH, et al. Effects of dietary calcium supplementation on blood pressure. *JAMA* 1996;275:1016–1022. (Search date 1994; primary sources MEDLINE, EMBASE.)
101. Gueyffier F, Froment A, Gouton M. New meta-analysis of treatment trials of hypertension: improving the estimate of therapeutic benefit. *J Human Hypertens* 1996;10:1–8. (Search date 1997; primary source MEDLINE).
102. Staessen JA, Fagard R, Thijs L, et al. Randomised double-blind comparison of placebo and active treatment for older patients with isolated systolic hypertension. *Lancet* 1997;350:757–764.
103. Hansson L, Zanchetti AZ, Carruthers SG, et al. Effects of intensive blood pressure lowering and low-dose aspirin in patients with hypertension: principal results of the hypertension optimal treatment (HOT) trial. *Lancet* 1998;351: 1755–1762.
104. Beto JA, Bansal VK. Quality of life in treatment of hypertension: a meta-analysis of clinical trials. *Am J Hypertens* 1992;5:125–133. (Search date 1990; primary sources MEDLINE, ERIC.)
105. Croog SH, Levine S, Testa MA. The effects of antihypertensive therapy on quality of life. *N Engl J Med* 1986;314:1657–1664.
106. Psaty BM, Smith NL, Siscovick DS, et al. Health outcomes associated with antihypertensive therapies used as first line agents: a systematic review and meta-analysis. *JAMA* 1997;277: 739–745. (Search date 1995; primary source MEDLINE.)
107. Messerli FH, Grossman E, Goldbourt U. Are beta blockers efficacious as first-line therapy for hypertension in the elderly? A systematic review. *JAMA* 1998;279:1903–1907. (Search date 1998; primary source MEDLINE.)
108. Neaton JD, Grimm RH, Prineas RJ, et al. Treatment of mild hypertension study: final results. *JAMA* 1993;270:713–724.
109. Materson BJ, Reda DJ, Cushman WC, et al. Single drug therapy for hypertension in men. *N Engl J Med* 1993;328:914–921.
110. Philipp T, Anlauf M, Distler A, Holzgreve H, Michaelis J, Wellek S. Randomised, double blind, multicentre comparison of hydrochlorothiazide, atenolol, nitrendipine, and enalapril in antihypertensive treatment: results of the HANE study. *BMJ* 1997;315:154–159.
111. Weir MR, Flack JM, Applegate WB. Tolerability, safety, and quality of life and hypertensive therapy: the case for low-dose diuretics. *Am J Med* 1996;101(suppl 3A):83S–92S.
112. Grimm RH, Flack JM, Grandits GA, et al. Long-term effects on plasma lipids of diet and drugs to treat hypertension. *JAMA* 1996;275:1549–1556.

113. Berglund G, Andersson OK, Widgren BR. Low-dose antihypertensive treatment with a thiazide diuretic is not diabetogenic: a ten-year controlled trial with bendroflumethiazide. *Acta Med Scand*, 1986;220(5):419–424.
114. Curb JD, Pressel SL, Cutler JA, et al. Effect of diuretic-based antihypertensive treatment on cardiovascular disease risk in older diabetic patients with isolated systolic hypertension. *JAMA* 1996;276:1886–1892.
115. Cutler JA. Calcium channel blockers for hypertension – uncertainty continues. *N Engl J Med* 1998;338:679–681.
116. Katerndahl DA, Lawler WR. Variability in meta-analytic results concerning the value of cholesterol reduction in coronary heart disease: a meta-meta-analysis. *Am J Epidemiol* 1999;149:429–441. (Search date 1995; primary sources MEDLINE and meta-analysis bibliographies.)
117. Froom J, Froom P, Benjamin M, Benjamin BJ. Measurement and management of hyperlipidaemia for the primary prevention of coronary heart disease. *J Am Board Fam Pract* 1998;11: 12–22.
118. Gould AL, Rossouw JE, Santanello NC, Heyse JF, Furberg CD. Cholesterol reduction yields clinical benefit: impact of statin trials. *Circulation* 1998;97:946–952.
119. Downs JR, Clearfield M, Weis S, et al. Primary prevention of acute coronary events with lovastatin in men and women with average cholesterol levels: results of the AFCAPS/TexCAPS. *JAMA* 1998;279:1615–1622.
120. Scandinavian Simvastatin Survival Study Group. Randomized trial of cholesterol lowering in 4444 patients with coronary heart disease: the Scandinavian simvastatin survival study (4S). *Lancet* 1995;344:1383–1389.
121. Long-term Intervention with Pravastatin in Ischemic Disease (LIPID) Study Group Program. Prevention of cardiovascular events and death with pravastatin in patients with coronary heart disease and a broad range of initial cholesterol levels. *N Engl J Med* 1998;339:1349–1357.
122. Sacks FM, Pfeffer MA, Moye LA, et al for the Cholesterol and Recurrent Events Trial Investigators. The effect of pravastatin on coronary events after myocardial infarction in patients with average cholesterol levels. *N Engl J Med* 1996;335:1001–1009.
123. Shepherd J, Cobbe SM, Ford I, et al for the West of Scotland Coronary Prevention Study Group. Prevention of coronary heart disease with pravastatin in men with hypercholesterolemia. *N Engl J Med* 1995;333:1301–1307.
124. Brunner E, White I, Thorogood M, et al. Can dietary interventions change diet and cardiovascular risk factors? A meta-analysis of randomized controlled trials. *Am J Public Health* 1997;87:1415–1422. Search date: July 1993, primary sources not specified in detail.
125. Tang JL, Armitage JM, Lancaster T, Silagy CA, Fowler GH, Neil HAW. Systematic review of dietary intervention trials to lower blood total cholesterol in free living subjects. *BMJ* 1998; 316:1213–1220. (Search date 1996; primary sources MEDLINE, Human Nutrition, EMBASE and Allied and Alternative Health,1966–1995, hand search of *Am J Clin Nutr* and reference list checks.)
126. Antiplatelet Trialists' Collaboration. Collaborative overview of randomised trials of antiplatelet therapy – I: prevention of death, myocardial infarction, and stroke by prolonged antiplatelet therapy in various categories of patients. *BMJ* 1994;308:81–106.
127. Peto R, Gray R, Collins R, et al. Randomized trial of prophylactic daily aspirin in British male doctors. *BMJ* 1988;296:313–316.
128. Steering Committee of the Physicians' Health Study Research Group. Final report on the aspirin component of the ongoing physicians' health study. *N Engl J Med* 1989;321:129–135.
129. The Medical Research Council's General Practice Research Framework. Thrombosis prevention trial: randomised trial of low-intensity anticoagulation with warfarin and low-dose aspirin in the primary prevention of ischaemic heart disease in men at increased risk. *Lancet* 1998;351:233–241.
130. Hansson L, Zanchetti A, Carruthers SG, et al for the HOT Study Group. Effects of intensive blood-pressure lowering and low-dose aspirin in patients with hypertension: principal results of the hypertension optimal treatment (HOT) randomised trial. *Lancet* 1998;351:1755–1762.
131. Buring JE, Hennekens CH, for the Women's Health Study Research Group. Women's health study: summary of the study design. *Journal of Myocardial Ischemia* 1992;4:27–29.

The affiliations of the authors who contributed to this chapter are:

David Whiteman
Nuffield Medical Research Fellow
Univeristy of Oxford
Oxford
UK

Andy Ness
Senior Lecturer in Epidemiology
University of Bristol
Bristol
UK

Michael Murphy
Director, ICRF General Practice
Research Group
University of Oxford
Oxford
UK

Julian J Nicholas
Resident Physician
Mayo Clinic
Rochester
US

Thomas Kottke
Consultant
Mayo Clinic
Rochester
Minnesota
US

Jeffrey L. Probstfield
Professor of Medicine
University of Washington
Seattle
US

Cindy Mulrow
Professor of Medicine
University of Texas Health Science Center
San Antonio
US

Rod Jackson
Associate Professor of Epidemiology
University of Auckland
Auckland
New Zealand

Cathie Sudlow
Wellcome Research Fellow in Clinical Epidemiology
University of Oxford
Oxford
UK

Colin Baigent
MRC Scientist
University of Oxford
Oxford
UK

Competing interests: None declared.

TABLE 1 **Examples of common physical activities by intensity of effort required in multiples of the resting rate of oxygen consumption during physical activity. Based on table from Pate et al.[36] (*See* text p. 5.)**

Activity type	Light activity (< 3.0 METs)	Moderate activity (3.0–6.0 METs)	Vigorous activity (> 6.0 METs)
Walking	Slowly (1–2 mph)	Briskly (3–4 mph)	Briskly uphill or with a load
Swimming	Treading slowly	Moderate effort	Fast treading or swimming
Cycling	–	For pleasure or transport (≤ 10 mph)	Fast or racing (> 10 mph)
Golf	Power cart	Pulling cart or carrying clubs	–
Boating	Power boat	Canoeing leisurely	Canoeing rapidly (> 4 mph)
Home care	Carpet sweeping	General cleaning	Moving furniture
Mowing lawn	Riding mower	Power mower	Hand mower
Home repair	Carpentry	Painting	–

mph, miles per hour; METs, work metabolic rate/resting metabolic rate; 1 MET represents the rate of oxygen consumption of a seated adult at rest.

TABLE 2 **Effectiveness of lifestyle interventions for lowering blood pressure in people with essential hypertension: results of RCTs. (See text p. 9.)**

Intervention	Mean decrease in syst/diast BP (mm Hg)	No. of RCTs (people)	Participants	Duration	Mean change in targeted factor
Exercise	5/3	29 (1533)	80% men aged 28–72	>4 weeks	50 min aerobic 3× per week
Low-fat, high-fruit–vegetable diet	5.5/3	1 (459)*	50% men mean age 44	8 weeks	
Weight loss	3/3	18 (2611)	55% male mean age 50	2–52 weeks	3%–9% of body weight
Reduced alcohol consumption	5/3	1 (44)	100% male mean age 53	6 weeks	From 452–464 mL ethanol per week
Salt restriction	4/2 2/0.5	58 (2161) 28 (1131)	Mean age 49 Mean age 47	1–52 weeks 4 weeks	118 mmol/day 60 mmol/day

syst/diast BP, systolic/diastolic blood pressure.

*Note that the mean decreases in BP in a subgroup of patients (n = 133) with hypertension (systolic pressure ≥ 140 mm Hg, diastolic pressure ≥ 90 mm Hg, or both) were more dramatic (systolic pressure 11.4 mm Hg, diastolic pressure 5.5 mm Hg).

TABLE 3 **Effectiveness of dietary supplementation for lowering blood pressure in people with essential hypertension: results of RCTs. (See text p. 12.)**

Intervention	Decrease in syst/diast BP (mm Hg)	No. of RCTs (people)	Participants	Duration	Change in targeted factor
Potassium supplementation	4/2.5	21 (1560)	Age 19–79	1–24 weeks mean 8 weeks	60–100 mmol/day
Fish oil supplementation	4.5/2.5	7 (339)	Mean age 50	Mean 8 weeks	≥3 g
Calcium supplementation	2/0	12 (383)	Not clear	8 weeks median	800–1500 mg/day

TABLE 4 **Effects of antiplatelet treatment (mainly aspirin) on vascular events* (nonfatal myocardial infarction, nonfatal stroke, or vascular death) in RCTs among individuals without evidence of cardiovascular disease. (*See* text p. 17.)**

Trials	Antiplatelet (events/patients)	Controls (events/patients)	OR (CI[†])	Approx average duration of treatment (years)	Approx control group risk (per year)	Approx vascular events avoided per 1000 patients treated per year (95% CI)
APT 1994[129] (3 trials)	652/14,608 (4.5%)	708/14,604 (4.8%)	0.90 (0.77–1.05)	5.2[‡]	0.9%	0.7
TPT[131¶]	211/2545 (8.3%)	250/2540 (9.8%)	0.83 (0.64–1.07)	6.4	1.5%	2.4
HOT[132]	315/9399 (3.4%)	368/9391 (3.9%)	0.85 (0.70–1.04)	3.8	1.0%	1.5
All trials	1178/26,552 (4.4%)	1326/26,535 (5.0%)	0.87 (0.80–0.95)	5.0[‡]	1.0%	1.1 (0.4–1.8)

*Published data from TPT and HOT; data provided by trialists for trials in the APT overview. [†]99% CI for 1994 APT overview, TPT and HOT; 95% CI for "all trials." [‡]Weighted by study size. [¶]The proportional effects of aspirin were similar in the absence or presence of warfarin, so the data presented are not stratified by warfarin allocation. Heterogeneity of ORs between five trials: χ^2 (4 df) = 4.5; NS.

TABLE 5 **Effects of aspirin on intracranial bleeds and major extracranial bleeds in RCTs among individuals without evidence of cardiovascular disease. (*See text p. 18.*)**

	Antiplatelet (events/ patients)	Controls (events/ patients)	Approx average duration of treatment (years)	Approx excess bleeds per 1000 patients treated per year (95% CI)
Intracranial bleeds				
APT 1994 (2 trials)[128]	44/14,466 (0.3%)	24/14,454 (0.2%)	5.2	
TPT[131]	12/2545 (0.5%)	6/2540 (0.2%)	6.4	
HOT[132]	14/9399 (0.1%)	15/9391 (0.2%)	3.8	
All trials	70/26,410 (0.3%)	45/26,385 (0.2%)	5.0	0.2 (0.02–0.4)
Major extracranial bleeds				
APT 1994 (2 trials)[128]	69/14,466 (0.5%)	49/14,454 (0.3%)	5.2	
TPT[131]	20/2545 (0.8%)	13/2540 (0.5%)	6.4	
HOT[132]	122/9399 (1.3%)	63/9391 (0.7%)	3.8	
All trials	211/26,410 (0.8%)	125/26,385 (0.5%)	5.0	0.7 (0.4–0.9)

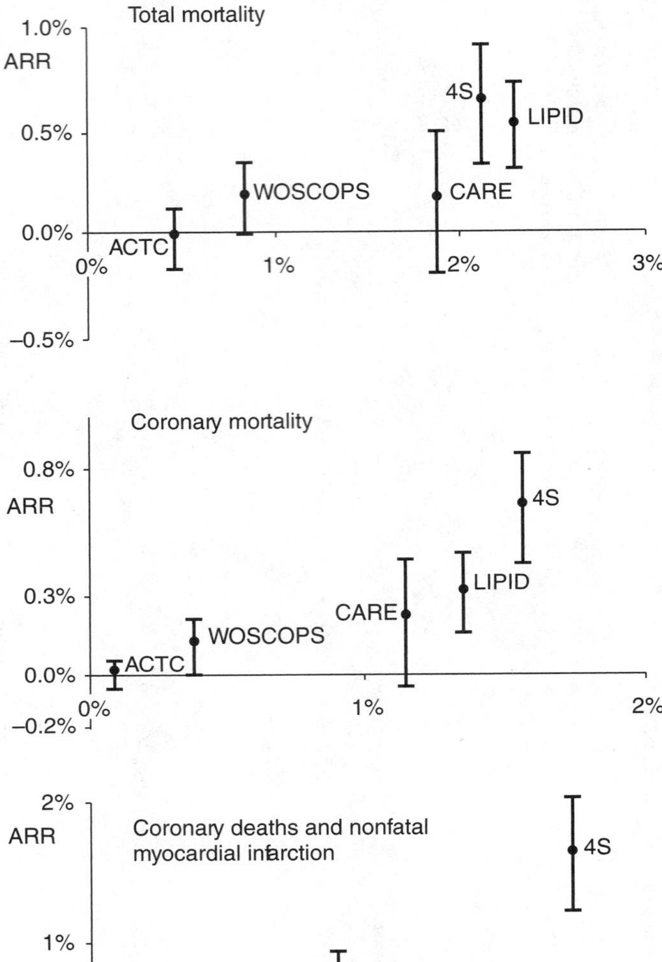

FIGURE 1 **Effects of cholesterol lowering: relation between the ARR (for annual rates of total mortality, coronary artery disease mortality and coronary deaths and nonfatal myocardial infarction in patients treated with statins) and the baseline risk of those events in the placebo group for each of the five large statin trials (ACTC = AFCAPS/TexCAPS[119], 4S[120], LIPID[121], CARE[122], WOSCOPS[123]).** ***(See text p. 16.)***

Modifying lifestyle behaviors

Margaret Thorogood, PhD

QUESTIONS

INTERVENTIONS

*In terms of producing behavioral change

Key Messages

- Systematic reviews have found that simple once-only advice from a physician results in 2% of smokers quitting smoking and not relapsing for 1 year. More intense interventions may increase the percentage quitting smoking by a further 3%. Psychologists achieve a similar quit rate (3%) to that of physicians, but there are insufficient data for nurses.
- One systematic review has found that nicotine replacement treatment is an effective component of cessation strategies in smokers who smoke at least 10 cigarettes daily. We found no clear evidence that any method of delivery of nicotine is more effective than the others.
- Systematic reviews have found that smoking interventions are more effective in pregnant women than in healthy nonpregnant women. Smoking interventions have greater impact in men at higher risk of death from heart disease.
- One systematic review has found that training of health professionals increases the effectiveness of smoking interventions.
- We found weak evidence that sedentary people increase physical activity after counseling. One randomized controlled trial (RCT) has found that exercise advice increases physical activity in women over 80 years of age and reduces their risk of falling.

- Systematic reviews have found that advice on cholesterol-lowering diet (i.e., advice to lower fat intake or increase the ratio of polyunsaturated to saturated fatty acid) leads to a small reduction in blood cholesterol concentrations in the long term (≥6 months).
- Systematic reviews have found that advice on eating a diet that will reduce blood pressure (i.e., advice to reduce sodium intake, increase potassium intake, or both) leads to a very small reduction in blood pressure in the long term. We found no good evidence to support the effectiveness of such advice in a primary care setting.
- Systematic reviews have found that a combination of advice on diet and exercise supported by behavior therapy is probably more effective than either diet or exercise advice alone in the treatment of obesity and may lead to sustained weight loss.

DEFINITION Cigarette smoking, diet, and level of physical activity are important in the etiology of many chronic diseases, and individual change in behavior has potential to decrease the burden of chronic disease, particularly cardiovascular disease.

INCIDENCE/ PREVALENCE In the developed world, the decline in smoking has slowed and the prevalence of regular smoking is increasing in young people. A sedentary lifestyle is becoming increasingly common, and the prevalence of obesity is increasing rapidly.

AIMS To encourage individuals to reduce or abandon unhealthy behaviours and to take up healthy behaviors; and to support the maintenance of these changes in the long term.

OUTCOMES Ideally the outcomes considered would be clinical, relate to the underlying conditions (longevity, quality of life, rate of stroke or myocardial infarction). However, most studies report proxy outcomes, such as the proportion of people changing behavior in a specified period (e.g., stopping smoking).

METHODS Searches of MEDLINE and EMBASE were performed in July 1998. Recent appropriate systematic reviews were identified as well as more recent RCTs.

QUESTION What interventions reduce cigarette smoking?

OPTION COUNSELING

Systematic reviews of RCTs have found that simple once-only advice from a physician during a routine consultation results in 2% of smokers quitting smoking and not relapsing for 1 year. Additional encouragement or support may increase (by an additional 3%) the effectiveness of the advice. Individual advice from a psychologist achieves a similar quit rate (3%). There are insufficient data on advice given by a nurse to estimate the effect.

Benefits: We found two systematic reviews.[1,2] One, published in 1995, identified 17 trials in 14,438 smokers in which physicians provided simple advice, typically of less than 5-minutes' duration. It found that 1.9% of smokers (95% CI 0.1–2.8) stopped smoking as a direct result of the advice and did not relapse for at least 1 year.[1] Rates of cessation in the control groups ranged from 1.1% to 14.1% and in the intervention group from 1.5% to 14.5%. The results were similar when the analysis was confined to the six trials in which cessation was confirmed by biochemical markers. Ten trials tested the effect of additional support, such as additional visits and encouragement or demonstrations of exhaled carbon monoxide in the patient's breath. There was a high degree of heterogeneity (with rates of cessation ranging from –0.5% to 29%), but the overall estimate of effectiveness was 5% (95% CI 1%–8%) of smokers quitting for 1 year. Five trials of individual sessions with a psychologist gave a summary statistic of 2.8% (95% CI 1.3%–4.2%) of smokers quitting at 1 year. Only two trials of nurse advice were identified and these were too small to estimate the effect.[1] The other systematic review published in 1997 identified 23 trials of smoking advice in general practice.[2] In 20 of the trials, a general practitioner was involved in giving advice, although nurses or counselors also were involved in four of these trials. In three trials the advice was given solely by a nurse or health visitor. Smoking cessation was measured for between 6 months and 2 years. There was significant heterogeneity because of the inclusion of two trials (both involving only general practitioners) with notably larger effects. When these two trials were excluded the summary statistic for the odds of smoking cessation was 1.32 (95% CI 1.18–1.48). Intensive advice was marginally more effective than brief advice. The OR for quitting after brief advice was 1.27 (1.11–1.45), whereas the similar OR after intensive advice was 1.46 (1.18–1.80). Fifty smokers would need to be given brief advice (or 25 smokers given intensive advice) for one additional person to quit for at least 6 months.[2]

Harms: We found no evidence of harm.

Comment: The effects of advice may be considered disappointingly small, but the cost is small, and a year-on-year reduction of 2% in the number of smokers would represent a significant public health gain (see pp. 7, 93).

OPTION NICOTINE REPLACEMENT

One systematic review has found that nicotine replacement is an effective component of cessation strategies in smokers who smoke at least 10 cigarettes per day. Fifteen such smokers would have to be treated with nicotine patches to produce one extra nonsmoker at 12 months. This is reduced to nine smokers if the nicotine patches are provided together with a high-intensity support program. There is no clear evidence that any one method of delivery of nicotine is more effective.

Benefits: One systematic review published in 1998 identified 47 trials of nicotine gum, 22 trials of nicotine transdermal patches, three of nicotine intranasal spray, and two of inhaled nicotine.[3] When the abstinence rates for all trials were pooled according to the longest duration of follow-up available, 18% of smokers allocated to nicotine replacement successfully quit, compared with 11% in the control group. The odds of abstinence were increased 76% (95% CI 63%–90%) by the use of nicotine replacement. There was no significant difference in the OR for abstinence with the different forms of nicotine replacement, which ranged from 1.65 for nicotine gum to 2.45 for nicotine nasal spray. There was weak evidence to support repeat use of nicotine replacement in relapsed smokers. The NNT to produce one extra nonsmoker at 12 months was 15 with the nicotine patch or 22 with the gum. These numbers fell to 9 and 11 if the nicotine replacement was provided together with a high-intensity support program.[3]

Harms: Nicotine gum has been associated with hiccups, gastrointestinal disturbances, jaw pain, and orodental problems. Nicotine transdermal patches have been associated with skin sensitivity and irritation. Nicotine inhaler and nasal spray have been associated with local irritation at the site of administration.

Comment: Nicotine replacement does not represent an easy cure from nicotine addiction but does improve the cessation rate. Even so, the majority of smokers attempting cessation will fail at any one attempt, and multiple attempts may be needed.

QUESTION **Are smoking cessation interventions more effective if targeted at high-risk individuals?**

OPTION **IN PREGNANT WOMEN**

One systematic review of RCTs has found that the effect of smoking interventions in pregnant women is greater than that found in trials in healthy nonpregnant women.

Benefits: We found no trials in which the same intervention was used in both pregnant and nonpregnant women. One systematic review published in 1995 identified 10 trials of antismoking interventions in 4815 pregnant women.[1] It included one trial of physician advice, one trial of advice by a health educator, one trial of group sessions, and seven trials of behavior therapy based on self-help manuals. The overall absolute increase in the percentage of smokers who stopped smoking as a result of the intervention was 7.6% (95% CI 4.3%–10.8%). The absolute percentage with advice giving was 3.3% (95% CI 0.3%–6.2%) and with self-help manuals 9.0% (95% CI 4.8%–13.1%). Cessation rates ranged from 1.9% to 16.7% in the control groups and from 7.1% to 36.1 % in the intervention groups.[1] Another systematic review identified 11 trials in which smoking status was verified by biochemical measures between the sixth and ninth month of pregnancy.[4] One trial found an outlying result of a sevenfold increase in smoking cessation. The summary OR for smoking cessation in the 10 homogenous trials was 1.50 (95% CI 1.22–1.86), indicating a 50% increase in cessation over control group cessation rates, which ranged from 1.4% to 17.2%.

Harms: None documented.

Comment: The effect in pregnant women was greater than that found in trials in healthy nonpregnant women.

OPTION **IN MEN AT HIGH RISK OF CARDIOVASCULAR DISEASE**

A systematic review of RCTs has found that the effect of smoking interventions in men at higher than average risk of death from heart disease is considerably greater than that found in trials of lower-risk men.

Benefits: We found no trials where the same intervention was used in high- and low-risk men. One systematic review published in 1995 identified four trials of 13,208 healthy men with relatively high levels of heart disease risk factors. It found the absolute increase in the percentage of men quitting smoking in the antismoking advice group compared with the control group was 21% (95% CI 10.2%–30.9%).[1] Approximately five men at high risk of heart disease would need antismoking advice for one additional person to quit smoking. One relatively early trial (reported in 1974), in 223 men surviving a myocardial infarction and given intensive advice by members of the therapeutic team while still in the coronary care unit, found a self-reported cessation rate at 1 year or more of 63% in the intervention group compared with 28% in the control group, a relative difference of 36% (95% CI 23%–48%).[5] Three men who smoke after a myocardial infarction would need to receive intensive advice for one additional person to quit smoking at 1 year.

Harms: None were documented.

Comment: There was heterogeneity in the four trials; this is explained partly by a less intense intervention in one trial and the recording of a change from cigarettes to other forms of tobacco as success in another trial. The 1974 trial was weakened by use of reported smoking cessation and nonrandom allocation to the intervention.[5]

QUESTION **Does training of professionals increase the effectiveness of smoking cessation interventions?**

One systematic review has found that smoking interventions are more effective if the health professionals delivering the interventions have received training. One extra ex-smoker can be expected for approximately 50 patients advised by a trained, compared with an untrained, physician.

Benefits: We found one systematic review, which identified eight trials of training medical practitioners, and one trial of training dental practitioners to give antismoking advice.[6] All the trials took place in the USA. The training was provided on a group basis, and variously included lectures, videotapes, role plays, and discussion. The importance of setting quit dates and offering follow-up was emphasized in most of the training programs. The OR for quitting was 1.48 (95% CI 1.20–1.83) in smokers offered advice by health professionals who had received training compared with smokers who attended untrained practitioners. Three trials used prompts and reminders to practitioners to deploy smoking cessation techniques and found an OR of quitting of 2.4 (95% CI 1.4–3.9).

QUESTION **Which interventions increase physical activity in sedentary people?**

OPTION **COUNSELING**

We found weak evidence from systematic reviews that sedentary people can be encouraged to increase their physical activity. Interventions that encourage moderate rather than vigorous exercise and do not require attendance at a special facility are more likely to be successful.

Benefits: We found two systematic reviews and a subsequent RCT. One review, published in 1996, identified 11 RCTs of single-factor physical activity promotion in 1699 people, all of them based in the USA.[7] Seven trials evaluated advice to undertake exercise from the home (mainly walking, but including jogging and swimming), and six evaluated advice to undertake facility-based exercise (including jogging and walking on sports tracks, endurance exercise, games, swimming, and exercise to music classes). An increase in activity in the intervention groups was seen in trials in which home-based moderate exercise was encouraged and regular, brief follow-up of participants was provided. In most of the trials, the participants were self-selected volunteers, so the effects of the interventions may have been exaggerated. Only one of the trials was designed specifically to test the effect of physicians' advice to increase physical activity, and this showed no difference between intervention and control groups in uptake of physical activity. The other systematic review, published in 1997, identified four RCTs of exercise promotion based in primary care that reported measures of exercise as an outcome variable. Three of these trials found a significant increase in physical activity in the intervention group, although one of these had a limited follow-up time of 2 months, so the change may not have been sustained.[8] In the subsequent RCT, 714 sedentary people were randomized to be either invited by their general practitioner to meet a fitness adviser (who advised on exercise, including use of local exercise facilities) or to receive advice about local exercise facilities through the mail. There was a small but significant relative reduction of 11% (95% CI 5%–17%) in the number of people classed as sedentary in the intervention group compared with the control group.[9]

Harms: Neither of the reviews, nor the trial, reported any incidences of harm from taking up exercise.

Comment: The evidence for the effectiveness of physical activity interventions is weak. Little relevant, good-quality research has been undertaken. Several trials are in progress, including one in the UK (the move-it trial) in which people in primary care have been randomized to two different methods of encouraging an increase in walking or to a no-intervention control arm. An ongoing multisite trial in the USA has randomized 874 patients to one of three experimental counseling interventions. Both trials are due to report in 1999.[10]

QUESTION **Does targeting interventions about exercise to high-risk people increase effectiveness?**

OPTION **IN WOMEN AGED OVER 80 YEARS**

One RCT found exercise advice increased physical activity and decreased the risk of falling in women aged over 80 years.

Benefits: We found no systematic review. In a trial in New Zealand, 233 women aged over 80 years were randomized to four visits from a physiotherapist (who advised a course of 30 minutes of home-based exercises three times per week that was appropriate for the individual) or to a similar number of social visits without exercise.[11] After 1 year, the group allocated to the physiotherapist visits was significantly more active than the control group, and 42% were still completing the recommended exercise program at least three times a week. The mean annual rate of falls in the intervention group was 0.87 compared with 1.34 in the control group, a difference of 0.47 falls per year (95% CI 0.04–0.90 falls per year).

Harms: No additional harms in the intervention group were reported.

Comment: The ability to generalize the results of this trial is difficult to estimate until the results have been confirmed in other trials.

QUESTION **Which interventions successfully change peoples' diet?**

OPTION **COUNSELING**

Systematic reviews have found that advice on eating a cholesterol-lowering diet (i.e., advice to reduce fat intake or increase the ratio of saturated to polyunsaturated fatty acid in the diet) leads to a small reduction in blood cholesterol concentrations in the long term (≥6 months). We found no good evidence to support the effectiveness of such advice in a primary care setting.

Benefits: We found three systematic reviews. One review, published in 1997, identified five trials of cholesterol-lowering dietary advice (principally advice from nutritionists or specially trained counselors) with follow-up for between 9 to 18 months. It found a reduction in blood cholesterol concentration in the intervention group of 0.22 mmol/L (95% CI 0.05–0.39) compared with the control group.[12] However, there was significant heterogeneity ($p < 0.02$), with two outlying studies; one showing no effect and one showing a larger effect. This review excluded trials of patients at high risk of heart disease. Another systematic review, published in 1998, identified 13 trials of more than 6-months' duration and included patients at high risk of heart disease.[13] It found a mean reduction of 4.5% (95% CI 3.9%–5.1%) in blood cholesterol concentration. The average baseline blood cholesterol concentration was 6.3 mmol/L, which translates to an approximate reduction of 0.3 mmol/L. The third systematic review, published in 1997, of dietary interventions in a primary care setting identified six trials measuring differences in lipid concentrations. In three of these trials, no significant differences were found, and in an additional two, the significant differences were confined to women in one and men in the other.[14]

Harms: We found no data on potential harm.

Comment: Compliance with dietary advice will inevitably be imperfect, so the finding of a 2- to 3-mmol/L reduction in blood cholesterol in the two systematic reviews accords surprisingly well with the findings of a meta-analysis of the plasma lipid response to changes in dietary fat and cholesterol.[15] The analysis included data from 244 published studies and concluded that compliance with current dietary recommendations (30% energy from fat, <10% saturated fat, and <300 mg/d cholesterol) would reduce blood cholesterol by approximately 5% compared with the average US dietary intake.

QUESTION **Does dietary advice lead to a sustained fall in blood pressure?**

Systematic reviews have found that advice on eating a diet that will reduce blood pressure (i.e., advice to reduce sodium intake, increase potassium intake, or both) leads to a very small reduction in blood pressure in the long term. We found no good evidence to support the effectiveness of such advice in a primary care setting.

Benefits: We found two systematic reviews. One, published in 1997, identified five trials of blood pressure–lowering dietary advice (principally advice from nutritionists or specially trained counselors) with follow-up for between 9 and 18 months. It found a reduction in blood pressure in the intervention group compared with the control group of 1.2 mm Hg in diastolic blood pressure (95% CI a fall of 2.6 mm Hg to a rise of 0.2 mm Hg), and a reduction of 1.9 mm Hg systolic blood pressure (95% CI 0.8–3.0).[12] A systematic review of dietary intervention in a primary care setting identified five trials that collected data on blood pressure, but none found a significant effect.[14]

QUESTION **Which interventions to change lifestyle result in sustained weight loss?**

OPTION **COUNSELING**

A combination of advice on diet and exercise supported by behavior therapy is probably more effective than either diet or exercise advice alone, and may lead to sustained weight loss.

Benefits: We found two systematic reviews. One, published in 1997, identified 99 studies, including a small number of studies that tested either dietary interventions with or without a behavior intervention component, or physical activity interventions with or without a behavior intervention component. The combination of diet and exercise in conjunction with behavioral therapy was more beneficial for weight loss than diet alone. However, this finding was based on the results of one study, in which a mean weight loss of 3.8 kg at 1 year was observed in a group receiving diet guidelines and behavior intervention compared with a significantly different mean loss of 7.9 kg in a group receiving the same intervention plus a program of walking.[16] The other systematic review, published in 1997, identified 493 studies using diet, exercise, or diet plus exercise, including studies that were not RCTs. It concluded that, at 1-year follow-up, diet plus exercise "tended to be the superior program" (*see* Comment).[17]

Harms: The two reviews cited do not provide data on harm resulting from diet or exercise interventions for weight loss.

Comment: In the first systematic review the authors' comment that health care professionals may have a negative attitude toward obesity and may benefit from training in methods for improving the delivery of weight loss/maintenance programs.[16] The second review included nonrandomized studies that might overestimate the effect of interventions. The findings of the second review should be treated with caution.

REFERENCES

1. Law M, Tang JL. An analysis of the effectiveness of interventions intended to help people stop smoking. *Arch Intern Med* 1995;155:1933–1941. (Search date not specified but before 1995; primary sources MEDLINE and *Index Medicus*; dates not given, but selected trials range from 1967–1993.)
2. Ashenden R, Silagy C, Weller D. A systematic review of the effectiveness of promoting lifestyle change in general practice. *Family Pract* 1997;14:160–176. (Search date May 1995; primary sources MEDLINE, Psychlit, Sociofile, Cinahl, EMBASE and Drug, all searched from the year of their inception up to May 1995.)
3. Silagy C, Mant D, Fowler G, Lancaster T. Nicotine replacement therapy for smoking cessation. In: The Cochrane Library, Issue 2, 1998. Oxford: Update Software. (Search date 1998; primary sources specialised register of the Cochrane Tobacco Addiction Group, 1966–1998, MEDLINE May 1998, Psychlit September 1997, Science Citation Index April 1998.)
4. Dolan-Mullen P, Ramirez G, Groff JY. A meta-analysis of randomized trials of prenatal smoking cessation interventions. *Am J Obstet Gynecol* 1994;171:1328–1334 (Search date 1993; primary sources Healthline 1981 to August 1993, dissertation abstracts 1982 to December 1992, MEDLINE and CancerLit 1987 to October 1993, Psychlit 1974 to June 1993, hand search of bibliographies of review articles and studies published 1993.)
5. Burt A, Thornley P, Illingworth D, White P, Shaw TRD, Turner R. Stopping smoking after myocardial infarction. *Lancet* 1974;i:304–306.
6. Lancaster T, Silagy C, Fowler G, Spiers I. Training health professionals in smoking cessation. In: The Cochrane Library, Issue 2, 1998. Oxford: Update Software. (Search date February 1998; primary sources specialised register of the Cochrane Tobacco Addiction Group 1966–1998.)
7. Hillsdon M, Thorogood M. A systematic review of physical activity promotion strategies. *Br J Sports Med* 1996;30:84–89. (Search date 1996; primary sources MEDLINE, Excerpta Medica, Sport, SCISearch 1966–1996, handsearch of reference lists.)
8. Ashenden R, Silagy C, Weller D. A systematic review of the effectiveness of promoting lifestyle change in general practice. *Fam Pract* 1997;14:160–176.
9. Stevens W, Hillsdon M, Thorogood M, McArdle D. The cost effectiveness of a primary care based physical activity intervention in 45–74 year old men and women: a randomised controlled trial. *Br J Sports Med* 1998;32:236–241.
10. King A, Sallis JF, Dunn AL, et al. Overview of the activity counselling trial (ACT) intervention for promoting physical activity in primary health care settings. *Med Sci Sports Exerc* 1998;30:1086–1096.
11. Campbell AJ, Robertson MC, Gardner MM, Norton RN, Tilyard MW, Buchner DM. Randomised controlled trial of a general practice programme of home based exercise to prevent falls in elderly women. *BMJ* 1997;315:1065–1069.
12. Brunner E, White I, Thorogood M, Bristow A, Curle D, Marmot M. Can dietary interventions change diet and cardiovascular risk factors? A meta-analysis of randomised controlled trials. *Am J Public Health* 1997;87:1415–1422. (Search date July 1993; primary sources computer and manual searches of databases and journals. No further details given.)
13. Tang JL, Armitage JM, Lancaster T, Silagy CA, Fowler GH, Neil HAW. Systematic review of dietary intervention trials to lower blood total cholesterol in free living subjects. *BMJ* 1998;316:1213–1220. (Search date 1996; primary sources MEDLINE, Human Nutrition, EMBASE and Allied and Alternative Health, 1966–1995, hand search of *Am J Clin Nutr* and reference list checks.)
14. Ashenden R, Silagy C, Weller D. A systematic review of the effectiveness of promoting lifestyle change in general practice. *Fam Pract* 1997;14:160–176. (Search date May 1995; primary sources MEDLINE, Psychlit, Sociofile, Cinahl, EMBASE and Drug, all searched from the year of their inception up to May 1995.)
15. Howell WH, McNamara DJ, Tosca MA, Smith BT, Gaines JA. Plasma lipid and lipoprotein responses to dietary fat and cholesterol: a meta-analysis. *Am J Clin Nutr* 1997;65:1747–1764. (Search date 1994 primary source MEDLINE 1966 to february 1994. Hand search of selected review publications and bibliographies.)
16. Glenny A-M, O'Meara S, Melville A, Sheldon T, Wilson C. The treatment and prevention of obesity: a systematic review of the literature. *Int J Obesity Related Metab Disord* 1997;21:715–737. (Search date 1995; primary sources MEDLINE, EMBASE, DHSS data, Current Research in UK, Science citation index, Social Science citation index, Conference Proceedings index, SIGLE, Dissertation abstracts, Sport, Drug Info., AMED (Allied and alternative medicine), ASSI (abstracts and indexes), CAB, NTIS (National technical information dB), Directory of Published Proceedings (Interdok), Purchasing Innovations Database, Health promotion database S.S.R.U., DARE (CRD – data base of systematic reviews), NEED (CRD – data base of health economic reviews). All databases searched from starting date to the end of 1995.)
17. Miller WC, Koceja DM, Hamilton EJ. A meta-analysis of the past 25 years of weight loss research using diet, exercise, or diet plus exercise intervention. *Int J Obesity Relat Metab Disord* 1997;21:941–947. (Search date 1994; primary source MEDLINE 1969 to 1994.)

Margaret Thorogood, PhD
Reader in Public Health and Preventative Medicine
School of Hygiene and Tropical Medicine
London
UK

Competing interests: None declared.

Preventing cardiovascular disease in diabetes

Ronald J Sigal, MD, MPH, FRCPC

QUESTIONS

INTERVENTIONS

Key Messages

- Diabetes mellitus increases the risk of cardiovascular disease (CVD). CVD risk factors in people with diabetes include conventional risk factors (age, prior CVD, cigarette smoking, hypertension, dyslipidemia, sedentary lifestyle, family history of premature CVD), and more diabetes specific risk factors (elevated urine protein excretion, poor glycemic control).
- A systematic review has found that aggressive control of hypertension in diabetic patients, with target blood pressures of 130/80–85 or lower reduces cardiovascular morbidity and mortality.
- Randomized controlled trials (RCTs) have found that statins reduce CVD morbidity and mortality in patients with diabetes after myocardial infarction (MI), in people with and without elevated low-density lipoprotein cholesterol (LDL-C). There is evidence from RCTs that statins and fibrates are effective in primary prevention of CVD events in people with diabetes and dyslipidemia.
- RCTs and an overview of RCTs have found that aspirin is effective in primary and secondary prevention of CVD in people with diabetes.
- RCTs have found that aggressive control of blood glucose with insulin and oral agents or both does not increase the risk of CVD and may decrease this risk.

DEFINITIONS **Diabetes mellitus:** *See* p. 130. **Cardiovascular disease (CVD):** Atherosclerotic disease of the heart and/or the coronary, cerebral, or peripheral vessels leading to clinical events (e.g., acute myocardial infarction, congestive heart failure, sudden cardiac death, stroke, gangrene, and/or need for revascularization procedures).

INCIDENCE/ PREVALENCE Diabetes mellitus is a major risk factor for CVD. In the USA, 60% to 75% of people with diabetes die of cardiovascular causes.[1] The annual incidence of CVD is increased two- to threefold in diabetic men and three- to fourfold in diabetic women after adjustment for age and other cardiac risk factors.[2] Approximately 45% of white people with diabetes have evidence of coronary artery disease, compared with approximately 25% of people without diabetes in the same populations.[2] In a population-based cohort study of 1059 diabetic and 1373 nondiabetic Finnish adults aged 45 to 64 years, the 7-year risk of MI was as high in adults with diabetes without previous cardiac disease as it was in people without diabetes with prior coronary artery disease.[3]

ETIOLOGY **Conventional risk factors for CVD** contribute to increasing the relative risk of CVD in people with diabetes to approximately the same extent as in those without diabetes and are reviewed elsewhere in this volume (see p. 2). Female sex is not protective against CVD in diabetes; the risk of CVD is the same in diabetic women as in diabetic men. **Relatively diabetes-specific CVD risk factors** include longer duration of diabetes during adulthood (the years of exposure to diabetes before age 20 add little to the risk of CVD);[4] elevated blood glucose concentrations (reflected in fasting blood glucose or glycated hemoglobin); and microalbuminuria (albuminuria 30–299 mg/d). Diabetic people with microalbuminuria have approximately two to three times the coronary morbidity and mortality risks of their normoalbuminuric counterparts with similar durations of diabetes,[5,6] and with persistent clinical proteinuria (~ 300 μg/24 h) this relative risk is approximately nine times greater than their normoalbuminuric counterparts.[4,7,8]

PROGNOSIS Diabetes mellitus increases the risk of mortality or serious morbidity after a coronary event approximately 1.5- to 3-fold.[2,3,9,10] This excess risk is only partly accounted for by the greater prevalence of other cardiac risk factors in people with diabetes.

AIMS To reduce mortality and morbidity from CVD with minimum adverse effects.

OUTCOMES Incidence of fatal or nonfatal acute MI, congestive heart failure (CHF), sudden cardiac death, coronary revascularization, stroke, gangrene; angiographic evidence of coronary, cerebral vascular, or peripheral arterial stenosis.

METHODS Searches of MEDLINE and EMBASE were performed in July 1998. We searched for systematic reviews of RCTs with at least 10 confirmed clinical CVD events among people with diabetes. Studies reporting only intermediate end points (e.g., regression of plaque on angiography, lipid changes) were not considered. When a systematic review was available, only randomized trials published after the date of search for the systematic review were included.

QUESTION **What are the effects of screening for high cardiovascular risk?**

We found no good evidence.

Benefits: We found no systematic reviews and no large RCTs of screening people with diabetes for cardiovascular risk.

Harms: Inadequate data.

Comment: Screening for conventional risk factors as well as regular determination of HbA1c (up to quarterly), lipid profile, and urinary albumin excretion will identify people at high risk.[11,12] Screening for CVD with exercise stress testing in previously sedentary adults with diabetes who are planning to undertake vigorous exercise programs has been recommended on the basis of consensus of expert opinion,[11,13] but such testing has not been shown to prevent cardiac events.

QUESTION **Which interventions improve cardiovascular outcomes in people with diabetes?**

OPTION **SMOKING CESSATION**

Observational studies have found that cigarette smoking is associated with increased cardiovascular death in people with diabetes. In nondiabetic people, smoking cessation has been shown to be associated with reduced risk.

Benefits: We found no systematic review. Cohort studies have found that cigarette smoking increased the incidence of cardiovascular death in diabetic people up to fourfold, depending on the amount smoked.[14]

Harms: None known.

Comment: There is little published literature on smoking cessation specifically in people with diabetes. However, these patients are likely to benefit from smoking cessation at least as much as nondiabetic patients. (*See* p. 7.)

OPTION **ANTIHYPERTENSIVE TREATMENT**

A systematic review of RCTs has found that angiotensin-converting–enzyme (ACE) inhibitors, diuretics, and β-blockers are effective for primary prevention of cardiovascular events in people with diabetes. It is not clear whether one class is better than another. Two large trials found that long-acting dihydropyridine calcium-channel blockers caused excess cardiovascular morbidity compared with ACE inhibitors. Setting lower target blood pressures reduces CVD events. β-blockers and ACE inhibitors reduce the risk of major cardiovascular events in people with diabetes and a previous acute MI. No class of medication had significant adverse effects on metabolism or quality of life at the doses used in the trials reviewed below.

Benefits: A systematic review on antihypertensive treatment in diabetes was last updated in August 1997.[15] It analyzed individual patient data for 5823 people with diabetes within 14 RCTs in which people without diabetes also were enrolled. **Primary prevention:** *See* Table 1. The systematic review identified two primary prevention studies, including 1355 people with diabetes who received either active treatment (stepped care beginning with a diuretic) or less active treatment (either placebo[16] or referral to usual care in the community[17]). CVD morbidity and mortality were reduced significantly with active treatment (OR for morbidity and mortality 0.64, 95% CI 0.50–0.82, and for overall mortality 0.85, 95% CI 0.62–1.17). The absolute risk of major CVD events found in these studies was high: 27% of controls and 19% of those receiving active treatment during a 5-year period. Thirteen middle-aged and older adults with diabetes would have to be treated for 5 years to prevent one major CVD event. **Secondary prevention:** *See* Table 2. The systematic review also included seven trials of secondary prevention (with follow up of at least 1 year), including 2564 people with diabetes.[15] The review found that both ACE inhibitors and β-blockers reduced the risk of subsequent cardiac events in people with diabetes with previous MI, with or without hypertension.[15] The OR for all-cause mortality (from six trials with 2402 people) was 0.82 (95% CI 0.69–0.99) and for cardiovascular morbidity and mortality (two trials with 654 people) 0.82 (95% CI 0.60–1.13). Five other trials of secondary prevention for 1904 people with diabetes had follow-up of less than 1 year. The OR for all-cause mortality was 0.64 (95% CI 0.50–0.83) and for CVD morbidity and mortality (from three trials with 1612 people) 0.68 (95% CI 0.43–1.05). **Target blood pressure:** We found several recent trials with large numbers of participants with diabetes (*See* Tables 1 and 2). In the UK Prospective Diabetes Study (UKPDS) Hypertension in Diabetes study[18,19] and Hypertension Optimal Treatment (HOT) study[20], tighter control of blood pressure reduced the risks of major cardiovascular events. In the HOT study, people with diabetes who were randomized to target diastolic blood pressure $\leq$80 mm Hg had half the risk of major CVD events compared with their counterparts randomized to target blood pressure $\leq$90 mm Hg. In the UKPDS, hypertensive patients with type 2 diabetes randomized to "tight" blood pressure control (<150/<85 mm Hg) with atenolol ($n = 358$) or captopril ($n = 400$) had reduced incidence of "any diabetes-related end point," deaths related to diabetes (primarily CVD deaths), stroke, and microvascular disease.

Harms: In the UKPDS, patients taking atenolol gained 1.8 kg more weight (3.4 ± 8.0 versus 1.6 ± 9.1 kg, $p = 0.02$) compared with those allocated to captopril.[19] Over the first 4 years of the trial, patients allocated to atenolol had higher mean HbA1c (7.5% ± 1.4% vs. 7.0 ± 1.4%, $p = 0.0044$), but there was no difference between groups over the subsequent 4 years. There was no difference between atenolol and captopril in rates of hypoglycemia or lipid concentrations, nor were differences found between atenolol and captopril in tolerability, blood pressure lowering, or prevention of disease events. Two trials[21,22] compared a long-acting dihydropyridine calcium antagonist with an ACE inhibitor in people with type 2 diabetes. In both trials, the two classes of drug were equally effective in lowering blood pressure, but people randomized to the calcium-channel blocker had two-to fivefold greater risk of a major CVD event compared with those randomized to the ACE inhibitor. However, in the HOT study,[20] all study groups received the long-acting calcium antagonist felodipine, and the cardiovascular morbidity and mortality were relatively low.

Comment: None.

OPTION LIPID-LOWERING AGENTS

Subgroup analysis of data from people with diabetes enroled into large trials of HMGCo-A reductases have found that these are effective in primary and secondary prevention of AMI. Fibrates are effective in primary prevention of AMI; so far, there is little evidence regarding their role in secondary prevention.

Benefits: **Primary prevention:** We found no systematic reviews. Three large RCTs have compared lipid-lowering agents versus placebo (*See* Table 1). In the AFCAPS/TexCAPS study,[23] men aged 45 to 73 years and postmenopausal women aged 55 to 73 years were randomized to diet plus lovastatin 20 to 40 mg/d or diet plus placebo and followed for a mean of 5.2 years. Lipid concentrations for inclusion were total cholesterol 179 to 263 mg/dL, LDL-C 130 to 191 mg/dL, HDL-C ≤44.7 mg/dL (men) or ≤47.1 mg/dL (women), and triglycerides ≤400 mg/dL. In the Helsinki Heart Study,[24] 4081 Finnish men aged 40 to 55 years were randomized to gemfibrozil 600 mg twice daily or placebo and followed for 5 years. Required baseline lipid concentrations were (total minus HDL-C) ~201 mg/dL; patients were not excluded on the basis of triglyceride level. In the SENDCAP study,[25] 164 men and women with type 2 diabetes aged 35 to 65 years were randomized to bezafibrate or placebo for 3 years. Required baseline lipids included one or more of the following: total cholesterol 209 to 309 mg/dL, serum triglyceride 159 to 708 mg/dL, HDL-C ≤42.5 mg/dL or total–to–HDL-C ratio ≈5.9. **Secondary prevention:** *See* Table 2. In the Scandinavian Simvastatin Survival Study,[26] 4444 men and women aged 35 to 70 years with previous MI or angina pectoris, total cholesterol concentrations of 212 to 309 mg/dL and triglycerides ≤221 mg/dL were randomized to simvastatin or placebo and followed for a median of 5.4 years. Simvastatin dosage was initially 20 mg/d, with blinded dosage titration up to 40 mg/d, according to cholesterol response during the first 6 to 18 weeks. The RRs of main end points in simvastatin treated diabetic patients were as follows: total mortality 0.57 (95% CI 0.30–1.08), major CHD events 0.45 (95% CI 0.27–0.74) and any atherosclerotic event 0.63 (95% CI 0.43–0.92).[19] In the Cholesterol and Recurrent Events (CARE) trial,[27] 4159 men and women aged 21 to 75 (mean 59) years, 3 to 20 months post MI and with total cholesterol <239 mg/dL, triglycerides <347 mg/dL and LDL-C 116 to 174 mg/dL were randomized to pravastatin 40 mg/d or placebo and followed for a median of 5 years. Among the participants with diabetes, the absolute risk of major coronary events (death from coronary disease, nonfatal MI, coronary artery bypass grafting [CABG], or percutaneous transluminal coronary angioplasty [PTCA] was 37% (112/304) in those randomized to placebo and 29% (81/282) in those randomized to pravastatin (RR 0.75, 95% CI 0.57–1.0). In the Long-term Intervention with Pravastatin in Ischaemic Disease (LIPID) trial, 9014 men and women aged 31 to

75 (median 62) years with acute MI or unstable angina (as hospital discharge diagnosis) 3 to 36 months before enrolment, plasma total cholesterol 154 to 270 mg/dL and plasma triglycerides < 442 mg/dL were randomized to receive pravastatin 40 mg/d or placebo for a mean of 6.1 years.[28] Among the 782 participants with diabetes, the absolute risk of CVD death or nonfatal acute MI was 22.8% (88/386) in those randomized to placebo and 19.2% (76/396) in those randomized to pravastatin (RR 0.84, 95% CI 0.59–1.10).

Harms: None reported.

Comment: Most published clinical trials (as of August 1998) with sufficient statistical power to detect effects on cardiovascular events have enrolled comparatively small numbers of diabetic patients or excluded them altogether. The available evidence is therefore based almost entirely on subgroup analyses of larger trials. Several large ongoing trials are evaluating the effects of fibrates in people with diabetes.

OPTION BLOOD GLUCOSE CONTROL

In most cohort studies, higher average concentrations of blood glucose in people with diabetes are associated with a higher incidence of CVD. Clinical trials provide modest support for glucose lowering with insulin, sulfonylureas, or metformin in primary prevention of CVD[29,30] and strong support for intensive insulin treatment after a acute MI.[31,32]

Benefits: **Primary prevention:** We found no systematic review. In patients with diabetes, higher average levels of blood glucose are associated with higher incidence of CVD. In two large RCTs, intensive treatment aimed at lowering blood glucose clearly decreased the risks of microvascular diabetic complications in both type 1 and type 2 diabetes. However, the reduction of cardiovascular risk with intensified glucose control in both the Diabetes Control and Complications Trial (DCCT)[33,34] and UKPDS[29] was nonsignificant. In the DCCT, 1441 patients with type 1 diabetes aged 13 to 39 years and free of CVD, hypertension, hypercholesterolemia, and obesity at baseline were randomly assigned to conventional or intensive diabetes treatment and followed for a mean of 6.5 years. Major macrovascular events were almost twice as frequent in the conventionally treated group (40 events) as in the intensive treatment group (23 events), although the differences were not significant (ARR 2.2%; RRR 0.41, 95% CI −0.10–+0.68).[24] In the UKPDS, 3867 patients aged 25 to 65 years (median 54 years) with type 2 diabetes that was inadequately controlled on diet alone were randomized to conventional treatment (diet only, $n = 1138$, drugs added only if needed to keep fasting glucose < 15.0 mM/L) or intensive treatment with a sulphonylurea ($n = 1573$), insulin ($n = 1156$). Patients in UKPDS > 120% of ideal body weight were randomized to conventional treatment ($n = 411$), metformin ($n = 342$), sulphonylureas ($n = 542$), or insulin ($n = 409$). Intensive treatment beginning with a sulphonylurea or insulin resulted in improved glycemic control (HbA1c 7.9% with conventional treatment compared with 7% with intensive treatment), and a 12% RRR for any diabetes related end point compared with conventional treatment (RR 0.88, 95% CI 0.8–0.99; NNT 39 for 5 years to prevent one addition-

al diabetes-related end point). The absolute risk of acute MI was 14.7 per 1000 patient-years (intensive) compared with 17.4 per 1000 patient-years (conventional) (RR 0.84, 95% CI 0.71–1.0). Risks of stroke and amputation did not differ significantly among groups.[29]
Secondary prevention: In the DIGAMI study[31,32] 620 people (mean age 68 years, 63% men, 84% type 2) with random blood glucose ~ 11 mmol/L were randomized within 24 hours of an acute MI to either standard treatment or intensive insulin treatment. The intensive insulin group received an insulin glucose infusion for 24 hours followed by subcutaneous insulin four times daily for at least 3 months. The standard treatment group received insulin only when it was clinically indicated. HbA1c and mortality fell significantly with intensive insulin treatment (HbA1c 1.1% vs. 0.4% with standard treatment at 3 months and 0.9% vs. 0.4% at 12 months: mortality 19% vs. 26% at 1 year and 33% vs. 44% at a mean of 3.4 years; RR = 0.72, 95% CI 0.55–0.92). Nine diabetic patients would have to be treated for 3.4 years to prevent one additional premature death. The absolute reduction in the risk of mortality was particularly striking in patients who were not previously taking insulin and had no more than one of the following risk factors before the immediate prerandomization acute MI: age > 70 years, history of previous acute MI, history of congestive heart failure, current treatment with digitalis. In this low-risk subgroup, the ARR was 15% (NNT 7 for 3.4 years).

Harms: Sulphonylureas and insulin, but not metformin, increased the risks of weight gain and hypoglycemia. On an intention to treat basis, the proportions of patients per year with severe hypoglycemic episodes were 0.7%, 1.2%, 1%, 2%, and 0.6% for conventional, chlorpropamide, glibenclamide, insulin, and metformin groups, respectively. These frequencies of hypoglycemia are vastly lower than those observed with intensive treatment in patients with type 1 diabetes in the DCCT.[34,35] There was no evidence that any specific treatment (insulin, sulphonylurea, or metformin) increased overall risk of CVD.[29,30]

Comment: The role of intensive glucose-lowering treatment in primary prevention of cardiovascular events remains unclear. However, such treatment clearly reduces the risk of microvascular disease and does not increase the risk of CVD. The potential of the UKPDS to demonstrate an effect of tighter glycemic control was limited by the small achieved difference in median HbA1c between intensive and conventional treatment. In contrast, the DCCT achieved a larger 1.9% difference in median HbA1c was between groups, but the young age of the participants and consequent low incidence of cardiovascular events limited the power of the study to detect an effect of treatment on incidence of CVD.[34,35] The mortality reduction in patients receiving insulin infusion soon after acute MI followed by intensive insulin treatment compared with those receiving conventional treatment is extremely impressive. The study design does not allow us to distinguish whether the early insulin infusion or the later intensive subcutaneous insulin treatment was most important in this improved survival. UKPDS found no evidence that oral hypoglycemics increase cardiovascular mortality,[29,30] but the possibility that oral hypoglycemics may be harmful in the post–acute MI setting cannot be ruled out.

OPTION ASPIRIN

A systematic review of secondary prevention and very large clinical trials of primary and mixed primary and secondary prevention support a cardioprotective role for aspirin.

Benefits: **Primary prevention:** In the only large primary prevention trial that compared aspirin versus placebo and that reported data on people with diabetes, 22,701 US male physicians aged 40 to 85 years were randomly assigned to aspirin 325 mg every other day or placebo and followed for an average of 5 years.[36] Among the 533 participants with diabetes, acute MI occurred in 4% (11/275) of those randomized to aspirin and 10.1% (26/258) of those randomized to placebo. The relative risk of acute MI was 0.39 (95% CI 0.20–0.79). To prevent one MI, 16 (95% CI 12–47) men with diabetes would have to be treated with aspirin for 5 years. In the HOT study, numbers for aspirin treatment versus placebo were not reported, but the authors stated that the effect of aspirin was "about the same ... as in the whole HOT population," which had a relative risk reduction for acute MI of 15%.[21] **Primary and early secondary prevention:** The Early Treatment Diabetic Retinopathy Study (ETDRS)[36] was the largest randomized trial of aspirin prophylaxis in people with diabetes. 3711 diabetic men and women (30% with type 1, 48% with previous CVD) were assigned randomly to aspirin 650 mg/d or placebo and followed for a mean of 5 years. There was a statistically nonsignificant reduction in overall mortality in the aspirin-treated patients (RR 0.91, 95% CI 0.75–1.11). Acute MI occurred in 289 (16%) people in the aspirin group and 336 (18%) in the placebo group (ARR 2%, 95% CI 0.1%–4.9%). Fifty patients would need to be treated for 5 years with aspirin 650 mg/d to prevent one additional acute MI. **Secondary prevention:** The Antiplatelet Trialists' Collaboration (ATC)[37] analyzed 145 clinical trials of antiplatelet treatment (primarily aspirin) published before March 1990. Results for those with diabetes are included in Table 2.

Harms: In ETDRS,[38] fatal or nonfatal stroke occurred in 5% on aspirin and 4.2% on placebo (NS). There was no significant increase with aspirin in the risks of vitreous, retinal, gastrointestinal, or cerebral hemorrhage. In the ATC analysis, doses of aspirin ranged from 75 mg to 1500 mg/d. Most trials used 75 to 325 mg/d of aspirin; doses higher than 325 mg/d increased the risk of hemorrhagic adverse effects without improving preventive efficacy. No difference in efficacy or adverse effects was found in the dose range 75 to 325 mg.[37]

Comment: We found insufficient evidence to define precisely who with diabetes should be treated with aspirin. The risk of CVD is very low before 30 years of age, and most white diabetic adults aged over age 30 are at increased risk for CVD. In the absence of contraindications, the American and Canadian diabetes associations have suggested that aspirin 75 to 325 mg should be prescribed to all diabetic adults over age 30 who are at "high risk" of CVD. Contraindications to aspirin treatment include aspirin allergy, bleeding tendency, anticoagulant treatment, recent gastrointestinal bleeding, and clinically active liver disease.[11,37]

OPTION REDUCTION OF PROTEINURIA

Elevated urinary protein excretion is a risk factor for CVD. The cardiovascular benefit, if any, of reducing proteinuria by interventions such as ACE inhibitors remains unknown.

REFERENCES

1. Geiss LS, Herman WH, Smith PJ. Mortality in non-insulin-dependent diabetes. In: Harris MI, ed. *Diabetes in America*. 2nd ed. Bethesda, MD: National Institutes of Health, 1995:233–255.
2. Wingard DL, Barrett-Connor E. Heart disease and diabetes. In: Harris MI, ed. *Diabetes in America*. 2nd ed. Bethesda, MD: National Institutes of Health, 1995:429–448.
3. Haffner SM, Lehto S, Ronnemaa T, et al. Mortality from coronary heart disease in subjects with type 2 diabetes and in nondiabetic subjects with and without prior myocardial infarction. *N Engl J Med* 1998;339:229–234.
4. Krolewski AS, Warram JH, Freire MB. Epidemiology of late diabetic complications. A basis for the development and evaluation of preventive programs. *Endocrinol Metab Clin North Am* 1996;25(2):217–242.
5. Messent JW, Elliott TG, Hill RD, et al. Prognostic significance of microalbuminuria in insulin-dependent diabetes mellitus: a twenty-three year follow-up study. *Kidney Int* 1992;41(4):836–839.
6. Dinneen SF, Gerstein HC. The association of microalbuminuria and mortality in non-insulin-dependent diabetes mellitus - a systematic overview of the literature. Arch Int Med 1997;157(13):1413–1418. (Search date: 1995; primary sources MEDLINE 1966-94, Scisearch, hand-searching of bibliographies).
7. Borch Johnsen K, Andersen PK, Deckert T. The effect of proteinuria on relative mortality in type 1 (insulin-dependent) diabetes mellitus. *Diabetologia* 1985;28(8):590–596.
8. Warram JH, Laffel LM, Ganda OP, et al. Coronary artery disease is the major determinant of excess mortality in patients with insulin-dependent diabetes mellitus and persistent proteinuria. *J Am Soc Nephrol* 1992;3(4 Suppl):S104–110.
9. Behar S, Boyko V, Reicher-Reiss H, et al. Ten-year survival after acute myocardial infarction: comparison of patients with and without diabetes. SPRINT Study Group. Secondary Prevention Reinfarction Israeli Nifedipine Trial. *Am Heart J* 1997;133:290–296.
10. Mak KH, Moliterno DJ, Granger CB, et al. Influence of diabetes mellitus on clinical outcome in the thrombolytic era of acute myocardial infarction. GUSTO-I Investigators. Global Utilization of Streptokinase and Tissue Plasminogen Activator for Occluded Coronary Arteries. *J Am Coll Cardiol* 1997;30:171–179.
11. Meltzer S, Leiter L, Daneman D, et al. 1998 Clinical practice guidelines for the management of diabetes in Canada. *CMAJ* 1998;159(Suppl. 8):S1–S29.
12. American Diabetes Association. Clinical practice recommendations 1998. *Diabetes Care* 1998; 21(Suppl. 1):S1–S97.
13. American Diabetes Association. Diabetes mellitus and exercise. *Diabetes Care* 1997;20(12): 1908–1912.
14. Stamler J, Vaccaro O, Neaton JD, et al. Diabetes, other risk factors, and 12-year cardiovascular mortality for men screened in the Multiple Risk Factor Intervention Trial. *Diabetes Care* 1993;16:434.
15. Fuller J, Stevens LK, Chaturvedi N, et al. Antihypertensive therapy in diabetes mellitus. The Cochrane Library 1998, Issue 2, 1998. Last update August 1997. Primary sources MEDLINE, EMBASE, and heand searches of specialty journals in cardiovascular disease, stroke, renal disease, and hypertension.
16. Curb JD, Pressel SL, Cutler JA, et al. Effect of diuretic-based antihypertensive treatment on cardiovascular disease risk in older diabetic patients with isolated systolic hypertension. Systolic Hypertension in the Elderly Program Cooperative Research Group. *JAMA* 1996;276(23):1886–1892.
17. Davis BR, Langford HG, Blaufox MD, et al. The association of postural changes in systolic blood pressure and mortality in persons with hypertension: the Hypertension Detection and Follow-up Program experience. *Circulation* 1987;75(2): 340–346.
18. UK Prospective Diabetes Study Group. Tight blood pressure control and risk of macrovascular and microvascular complications in type 2 diabetes: UKPDS 38. *BMJ* 1998;317:703–713.
19. UK Prospective Diabetes Study Group. Efficacy of atenolol and captopril in reducing risk of macrovascular and microvascular complications in type 2 diabetes: UKPDS 39. *BMJ* 1998;317: 713–720.
20. Hansson L, Zanchetti A, Carruthers SG, et al. Effects of intensive blood-pressure lowering and low-dose aspirin in patients with hypertension: principal results of the Hypertension Optimal Treatment (HOT) randomised trial. *Lancet* 1998; 351:1755–1762.
21. Estacio RO, Jeffers BW, Hiatt WR, et al. The effect of nisoldipine as compared with enalapril on cardiovascular events in patients with non-insulin-dependent diabetes and hypertension. *N Engl J Med* 1998;338:645–652.
22. Tatti P, Pahor M, Byington RP, et al. Outcome results of the Fosinopril versus Amlodipine Cardiovascular Events randomised Trial (FACET) in patients with hypertension and NIDDM. *Diabetes Care* 1998;21:597–603.
23. Downs JR, Clearfield M, Weis S, et al. Primary prevention of acute coronary events with lovastatin in men and women with average cholesterol levels: results of AFCAPS/TexCAPS. Air Force/Texas Coronary Atherosclerosis Prevention Study. *JAMA* 1998;279(20):1615–1622.
24. Koskinen P, Manttari M, Manninen V, et al. Coronary heart disease incidence in NIDDM patients in the Helsinki Heart Study. *Diabetes Care* 1992;15(7):820–825.
25. Elkeles RS, Diamond JR, Poulter C, et al. Cardiovascular outcomes in type 2 diabetes. A double-blind placebo- controlled study of bezafibrate: the St. Mary's, Ealing, Northwick Park Diabetes Cardiovascular Disease Prevention (SENDCAP) Study. *Diabetes Care* 1998;21(4): 641–648.
26. Pyorala K, Pedersen TR, Kjekshus J, et al. Cholesterol lowering with simvastatin improves prognosis of diabetic patients with coronary heart disease. A subgroup analysis of the

Scandinavian Simvastatin Survival Study (4S). *Diabetes Care* 1997;20(4):614–620.
27. Sacks FM, Pfeffer MA, Moye LA, et al. The effect of pravastatin on coronary events after myocardial infarction in patients with average cholesterol levels. Cholesterol and Recurrent Events Trial investigators. *N Engl J Med* 1996;335(14):1001–1009.
28. The Long-term Intervention with Pravastatin in Ischaemic Disease (LIPID) Study Program. Prevention of Cardiovascular Events and Death with Pravastatin in Patients with Coronary Heart Disease and a Broad Range of Initial Cholesterol Levels. *N Engl J Med* 1998;339:1349–1357.
29. UK Prospective Diabetes Study Group. Intensive blood-glucose control with sulphonylureas or insulin compared with conventional treatment and risk of complications in patients with type 2 diabetes (UKPDS 33). *Lancet* 1998;352(9131):837–853.
30. UK Prospective Diabetes Study Group. Effect of intensive blood-glucose control with metformin on complications in overweight patients with type 2 diabetes (UKPDS 34). *Lancet* 1998;352(9131):854–865.
31. Malmberg K, Ryden L, Efendic S, et al. Randomised trial of insulin-glucose infusion followed by subcutaneous insulin treatment in diabetic patients with acute myocardial infarction (DIGAMI study): effects on mortality at 1 year. *J Am Coll Cardiol* 1995;26(1):57–65.
32. Malmberg K. Prospective randomised study of intensive insulin treatment on long term survival after acute myocardial infarction in patients with diabetes mellitus. DIGAMI (Diabetes Mellitus, Insulin Glucose Infusion in Acute Myocardial Infarction) Study Group. *BMJ* 1997;314: 1512–1515.
33. DCCT Research Group. The effect of intensive treatment of diabetes on the development and progression of long-term complications in insulin-dependent diabetes mellitus. *N Engl J Med* 1993;329(14):977–986.
34. DCCT Research Group. Effect of intensive diabetes management on macrovascular events and risk factors in the Diabetes Control and Complications Trial. *Am J Cardiol* 1995;75(14):894–903.
35. Steering Committee of the Physicians' Health Study Research Group. Final report on the aspirin component of the ongoing Physicians' Health Study. *N Engl J Med* 1989;321(3):129–135.
36. ETDRS Investigators. Aspirin effects on mortality and morbidity in patients with diabetes mellitus. *JAMA* 1992;268:1292–1300.
37. American Diabetes Association. Aspirin therapy in diabetes. *Diabetes Care* 1997;20:1772–1773.
38. Collaborative overview of randomised trials of antiplatelet therapy–I: Prevention of death, myocardial infarction, and stroke by prolonged antiplatelet therapy in various categories of patients. Antiplatelet Trialists' Collaboration. *BMJ* 1994;308(6921):81–106.

Ronald J Sigal, MD, MPH, FRCPC
Assistant Professor of Medicine
University of Ottawa
Canada

Competing interests: The author has received lecture fees and expenses from Eli Lilly, Nova-Nordisk, and Bristol Myers Squibb.

TABLE 1 Primary prevention of cardiovascular events in people with diabetes: evidence from systematic reviews (SR) and RCTs. The data refer only to people with diabetes

Study	Intervention	Outcome	No of cases (%)		NNT[b]
			Intervention	Control	(95% CI)
Antihypertensive medication[a]					
Diabetes and Hypertension (SR)[15]	ACE inhibitors, diuretics, or β-blockers (5 years)	CVD mortality and morbidity	121/647 (18.7%)	188/708 (26.6%)	13 (8–29)
UKPDS Hypertension Study (RCT)[18,19]	"Tight" target BP (<150/<85) with captopril or atenolol *v* "less tight" target BP (<180/<105) (8.4 years)	AMI (fatal or nonfatal)	107/758 (14.1%)	83/390 (21.3%)	–
		Stroke	38/758 (5.0%)	34/390 (8.7%)	27 (14–199)
		Peripheral vascular events	8/758 (1.1%)	8/390 (2.1%)	–
HOT[20]	Felodipine and ACE-inhibitor, or β-blocker, with 3 distinct target BPs (3.8 years)	AMI (fatal or nonfatal), stroke (fatal or nonfatal) or other cardiovascular death	22/499 (4.4%) (Target diastolic BP 80 mm Hg)	45/501 (9.0%) (Target diastolic BP 90 mm Hg)	22[d] (13–67)
FACET[22]	Fosinopril vs. amlodipine (2.9 years)	AMI, stroke, or admission to hospital for angina	14/189 (7.4%) (Fosinopril)	27/191 (14.1%) (Amlodipine)	15[e] (8–187)
ABCD[21]	Enalapril vs. nisoldipine (5 years)	AMI (fatal or nonfatal)	5/235 (2.1%) (Enalapril)	25/235 (10.6%) (Nisoldipine)	12[f] (8–24)
Lipid lowering medication					
AFCAPS/TexCAPS[23]	Lovastatin (5 years)	AMI, unstable angina or sudden cardiac death	4/84 (4.8%)	6/71 (8.5%)	–
SENDCAP[g,25]	Bezafibrate (3 years)	AMI or new ischemic changes on ECG	5/64 (7.8%)	16/64 (25.0%)	6 (3–21)
Helsinki Heart Study[24]	Gemfibrozil (5 years)	AMI or cardiac death	2/59 (3.4%)	8/76 (10.5%)	–

TABLE 1 Continued

Blood glucose control					
DCCT[33,34]	Intensive insulin treatment in type 1 diabetes (6.5 years)	Major macrovascular events[c]	23/711 (3.2%)	40/730 (5.5%)	45 (23–700)
UKPDS[29]	Intensive (insulin and/or sulphonylurea) vs. conventional treatment (5 years)	AMI (fatal or nonfatal)	387/2729 (14.2%)	186/1138 (16.3%)	–
UKPDS[30]	Intensive (metformin) vs. conventional treatment (5 years)	AMI (fatal or nonfatal)	39/342 (11.4%)	73/411 (17.8%)	16 (10–40)
Aspirin					
Physicians' Health Study[35]	Aspirin (5 years)	AMI (fatal or nonfatal)	11/275 (4.0%)	26/258 (10.1%)	17 (10–58)
ETDRS[h,36]	Aspirin (5 years)	AMI (fatal or nonfatal)	289/1856 (15.6%)	336/1855 (18.1%)	39 (20–739)

[a]For antihypertensive medications, only RCTs published after the 1997 systematic review are included. [b]NNT are shown only where the study found a significant absolute risk reduction. [c]Combined AMI (fatal or nonfatal), sudden cardiac death, revascularization procedure, angina with coronary artery disease confirmed by angiography or by noninvasive testing, stroke, lower limb amputation, peripheral arterial events requiring revascularization, claudication with angiographic evidence of peripheral vascular disease. [d]To prevent one major cardiovascular event, 22 diabetic people aged 50–80 years need treatment for 3.8 years to target diastolic BP of 80 mm Hg rather than 90 mm Hg. The group with target diastolic BP of ≤85 mm Hg had results between those for the two groups presented here. [e]To prevent one event, 15 middle-aged and older (mean age 63) hypertensive diabetic people need treating for 2.9 years with fosinopril rather than amlodipine. [f]To prevent one fatal or nonfatal MI, 12 middle-aged and older (mean age 57) hypertensive people with diabetes need treatment for 5 years with enalapril rather than nisoldipine. [g]SENDCAP study results reported for the first 3 years of follow up. [h]ETDRS was a mixed primary and secondary prevention study; half of participants had CVD at baseline.

TABLE 2 Secondary prevention of CVD events in people with diabetes: evidence from systematic reviews (SR) and RCTs (data only for people with diabetes)

Study	Intervention	Outcome	No of cases (%)		NNT
			Intervention	Control	(95% CI)
Antihypertensive medication					
Long-term secondary prevention (SR)[15]	ACE inhibitors and β-blockers (~ 1 year)	CVD mortality and morbidity	130/316 (41.1%)	157/338 (46.4%)	–
Short-term secondary prevention (SR)[15]	Various antihypertensive medications (<1 year)	CVD mortality and morbidity	8/245 (3.3%)	21/288 (7.3%)	25 (13–346)
Lipid lowering					
4S[26]	Simvastatin (5.4 years)	CHD death or nonfatal MI	24/105 (22.9%)	44/97 (43.8%)	5 (3–18)
CARE[27]	Pravastatin (5 years)	Coronary disease death, nonfatal MI, or revascularization	81/282 (28.7%)	112/304 (36.8%)	12 (6–182)
LIPID[28]	Pravastatin (6.1 years)	CHD death or nonfatal MI	76/396 (19.2%)	88/386 (22.8%)	–
Blood glucose control					
DIGAMI[32]	Insulin infusion followed by intensive insulin treatment vs. usual care (3.4 years)	Overall mortality	102/306 (33.3%)	138/314 (43.9%)	9 (5–33)
Aspirin					
Antiplatelet trialists (SR)[38]	Aspirin vs. placebo (median 2 years)		415/2248 (18.5%)	502/2254 (22.3%)	26 (16–69)

Unstable angina

Madhu K Natarajan, MD, FRCPC, FACC

QUESTIONS

INTERVENTIONS

Key Messages

- A systematic review of randomized controlled trials (RCTs) has found that aspirin reduces the risk of death or myocardial infarction (MI) in people with unstable angina.
- One RCT found ticlopidine to be effective in unstable angina, but its use is limited by the risk of neutropenia.
- We found limited evidence for the effectiveness of GP IIb/IIIa inhibitors beyond that provided by heparin.
- A meta-analysis shows that adding unfractionated heparin or LMWH to aspirin most likely reduces rates of death and MI in people with unstable angina.
- Large RCTs have found that any short-term advantage of hirudin plus aspirin over unfractionated heparin plus aspirin is not maintained after cessation of treatment.
- A systematic review has found no evidence that calcium-channel blockers prevent death or MI in people with unstable angina.
- The value of nitrates or β-blockers in reducing death or MI in unstable angina has not yet been evaluated adequately.
- We found little evidence about the superiority of early medical treatment over early invasive treatment in unstable angina.

DEFINITION Unstable angina is distinguished from stable angina, acute MI, and noncardiac pain by the pattern (characteristic pain present at rest or on lower levels of activity) or severity (recently increasing intensity, frequency, or duration) of symptoms and the absence of persistent ST elevation on a resting electrocardiogram (ECG). It includes a variety of different clinical patterns: rest angina within 1 week of onset; angina increasing in severity to moderate or severe pain; variant angina, non–Q-wave MI; and post-MI angina after the first 24 hours.

INCIDENCE/ PREVALENCE In industrialized countries, the annual incidence of unstable angina is approximately six per 10,000 people in the general population.

ETIOLOGY Risk factors are the same as for other manifestations of ischemic heart disease: older age, previous atheromatous cardiovascular disease, diabetes mellitus, smoking cigarettes, hypertension, hypercholesterolemia, male sex, and a family history of ischemic heart disease. Unstable angina also can occur in association with other disorders of the circulation, including heart valve disease, arrhythmia, and cardiomyopathy.

PROGNOSIS Despite optimal treatment, the incidence of serious adverse outcomes (e.g., death, acute MI, or refractory angina requiring emergency revascularization) is 5% to 7% within the first 7 days and approximately 15% at 30 days. Between 5% to 14% of people with unstable angina die in the year after diagnosis, with approximately half of these deaths occurring within 4 weeks of diagnosis. No single factor identifies people at higher risk of an adverse event. Risk factors include: severity of presentation (e.g., duration of pain, rapidity of progression, evidence of heart failure); medical history (e.g., previous unstable angina, acute MI, left ventricular dysfunction); other clinical parameters (e.g., age, diabetes); ECG changes (for example, severity of ST segment depression, deep T-wave inversion, transient ST elevation); biochemical parameters (e.g., troponin concentration); and change in clinical status (e.g., recurrent chest pain, silent ischemia, hemodynamic instability).

AIMS To relieve pain and ischemia; to prevent death and MI; to identify high-risk patients requiring revascularization; to facilitate early hospital discharge in low- and medium-risk patients; to modify risk factors; and to prevent death, MI, and recurrent ischemia after discharge from hospital.

OUTCOMES Rate of death or MI (often measured at 2, 7, and 30 days and at 6 months after randomization). Some RCTs include rates of refractory ischemia or readmission for unstable angina.

METHODS We searched MEDLINE and EMBASE in July 1998 to identify relevant systematic reviews. Individual high-quality trials published after the last acceptable systematic review also were selected.

QUESTION What are the effects of treatment?

ANTIPLATELET TREATMENT

OPTION **ASPIRIN**

A systematic review of RCTs has found that aspirin alone reduces the risk of death and MI in people with unstable angina. The evidence suggests no added benefit and possible added harm from doses of aspirin over 325 mg daily.

Benefits: A systematic review published in 1994 compared antiplatelet treatment versus placebo in 100,000 patients in 145 RCTs.[1] Seven of these trials included a total of 4000 patients with unstable angina. The 6-month event rate (vascular death, MI, or stroke) was 14% on placebo and 9% on antiplatelet treatment (mostly medium-dose aspirin 75–325 mg/d) (RRR 0.35, 95% CI 0.21–0.49). This means that 20 people would need to be treated with aspirin rather than placebo to prevent one additional vascular event in 6 months (NNT 20, 95% CI 15–34). Individual trials within the systematic review showed consistent benefit from daily aspirin in terms of reduced deaths and MIs.

Harms: On doses of aspirin ranging from 75 to 1200 mg/d, no significant adverse events, especially gastrointestinal intolerance or bleeding, were reported.[1] However, the sum of the evidence suggests no added benefit and greater incidence of gastrointestinal effects for aspirin dosages higher than 325 mg/d. Some people are allergic to aspirin.

Comment: The systematic review covered a wide range of patients with different morbidities and levels of risk. Its results should be able to be generalized to routine practice.[1] People with unstable angina who are allergic or who are nonresponders to aspirin will need alternative antiplatelet treatment.

OPTION **TICLOPIDINE**

One RCT found that ticlopidine was more effective than conventional treatment (without aspirin) in people with unstable angina. Therefore, it may serve as an alternative in patients who are intolerant or allergic to aspirin.

Benefits: We found no systematic review of ticlopidine in unstable angina. An RCT published in 1990 compared ticlopidine versus conventional treatment without aspirin in 652 people with unstable angina (72% male) treated within 48 hours of admission and followed up for 6 months.[2] At 6 months, there were significantly fewer vascular deaths or nonfatal MIs on ticlopidine (RRR compared with control 0.46, 95% CI 0.12–0.81), meaning that 16 people would need to be treated with ticlopidine rather than conventional treatment to avoid one additional event in 6 months (NNT 16, 95% CI 9–62). We found no trial of ticlopidine versus aspirin in the treatment of unstable angina.

Harms: Reversible neutropenia has been reported in 1% to 2% of patients. Other adverse effects that may result in discontinuation of treatment are diarrhea and skin rash.

Comment: Ticlopidine is an alternative for people with unstable angina who are allergic or intolerant to aspirin. The OASIS 4 (CURE study) is comparing clopidogrel plus aspirin versus aspirin alone in this group of patients (Yusuf S, personal communication).

OPTION GP IIb/IIIa PLATELET-RECEPTOR INHIBITORS

RCTs have found that adding parenteral GP IIb/IIIa inhibitors to standard treatment with unfractionated heparin and aspirin reduces deaths and MIs. There is no clear evidence that GP IIb/IIIa inhibitors are superior to heparin in patients taking aspirin.

Benefits: We found no systematic review, but three RCTs have examined the effect of adding GP IIb/IIIa inhibitors to standard treatment,[3–5] and one RCT has compared a GP IIb/IIIa inhibitor versus heparin.[6] The primary end points varied, but all trials included data on rates of death and MI at 30 days. These are summarized in Table 1. **Added to heparin:** We found one RCT comparing tirofiban, heparin, or both as an infusion for a mean of 72 hours in 1915 patients with unstable angina or non–Q-wave MI.[3] The study was stopped prematurely because of an excess of deaths at 7 days in those who received tirofiban alone. **Added to heparin plus aspirin:** We found two RCTs comparing GP IIb/IIIa inhibitors plus heparin and aspirin versus heparin and aspirin alone in 13,000 patients with unstable angina.[4,5] The larger trial (9461 evaluable patients) found significantly fewer deaths and nonfatal MIs when eptifibatide was added to standard treatment.[4] The smaller trial (2282 patients) found no significant difference in rates of death or nonfatal MI at 30 days between heparin alone (AR 11.7%), low-dose lamifiban (AR 10.6%) or high-dose lamifiban (AR 12.0%).[5] However, at 6 months there were significantly fewer deaths or MIs in patients on low-dose lamifiban (AR 13.7%) than high-dose lamifiban (AR 16.4%) or placebo (AR 17.9%). **Versus heparin:** One RCT compared intravenous tirofiban versus heparin for 48 hours in 3232 patients who were already receiving aspirin.[6] The primary composite end point of death, MI, or refractory ischemia at 48 hours was significantly lower on tirofiban (AR 3.8% vs. 5.6%, RRR 33%, 95% CI 8%–52%), but at 30 days there was no significant difference in the end point of death or MI (Table 1).

Harms: There was no difference in the rate of major bleeding between tirofiban and heparin (AR 0.4% in both groups).[6] When high-dose lamifiban was added to heparin there were more intermediate or major bleeds than with heparin alone (AR 12.1% vs. 5.5%, $p = 0.002$).[5] Reversible thrombocytopenia occurred more frequently with tirofiban than with heparin (AR 1.1 % vs. 0.4%, $p = 0.04$).[6]

Comment: The smaller trial of adding a GP IIb/IIIa inhibitor to standard treatment[5] suggests that a "dose ceiling" may exist beyond which escalation of dose results in higher bleeding complications with no increase in efficacy. Several ongoing trials of oral agents are evaluating long-term outcomes of continued treatment with GP IIb/IIIa inhibitors. Lamifiban is currently in phase III trials in the US.

ANTITHROMBIN TREATMENT

OPTION UNFRACTIONATED HEPARIN

A systematic review of six small RCTs has found that adding unfractionated heparin to aspirin in people with unstable angina is likely to be beneficial in reducing mortality and myocardial infarction.

Benefits: **Added to aspirin:** A systematic review published in 1996 identified six RCTs in 1353 people with unstable angina who were treated with either heparin and aspirin or aspirin alone.[7] Duration of treatment was 2 to 7 days. It found that the AR of death or MI during treatment with heparin plus aspirin (55/698, 8%) was less than that for aspirin alone (AR 68/655, 10%); however, the differences could have arisen by chance (RR 0.67, 95% CI 0.44–1.02). There was also no significant difference between the two groups, in the subset of four RCTs with data available, in the rate of death or MI from the discontinuation of randomized treatment to 12 weeks after randomization (ARs 12% on heparin and aspirin, 14% on aspirin alone; RR 0.82, 95% CI 0.56–1.20). **Versus LMWH:** *See* below.

Harms: Major bleeding occurred in 0.4% of those on aspirin and 1.5% of those on aspirin plus heparin (RR 1.89, 95% CI 0.66–5.38; $p=0.68$).

Comment: Investigators were blinded in only two of the six RCTs. The review was limited to trials that included data on acute MI or death during the treatment period, raising the possibility of publication bias, which would be difficult to detect with only six studies. Biases also may have arisen within individual trials by exclusion of substantial numbers of randomised participants. The review did not explore the clinical significance of the ARR for death or MI of approximately 3% and the ARI of major bleeding of approximately 1%. Much larger trials are required.

OPTION LOW-MOLECULAR-WEIGHT HEPARINS (LMWH)

RCTs have found that aspirin plus LMWH is more effective than aspirin alone in the first 30 days after an episode of unstable angina. Four large RCTs in patients with unstable angina or non–Q-wave MI who were taking aspirin found no clear difference in rates of death or MI between LMWH and unfractionated heparin, although significant effects were seen in individual trials. LMWH is easier to use and requires no monitoring.

Benefits: We found no systematic review. **Adding LMWH to aspirin:** Two RCTs compared LMWH versus placebo in people with unstable angina taking aspirin. Both found a significant short-term reduction in death or MI with aspirin plus LMWH. One RCT compared subcutaneous LMWH (nadroparin) versus intravenous unfractionated heparin or placebo in 219 patients within 6 hours of rest pain.[8] All patients received aspirin. LMWH was significantly more effective than either unfractionated heparin or placebo in reducing the combined end point of in hospital death, MI, recurrent angina, or urgent revascularization (OR for LMWH vs. placebo 2.26, 95% CI 1.0–5.8, $p=0.03$; OR for LMWH vs. unfractionated heparin 3.07, 95% CI 1.36–7.0). There were no deaths. The other RCT compared LMWH (dalteparin) versus placebo in 1506 patients with unstable angina or non–Q-wave MI.[9] All patients received aspirin. At 6 days, LMWH significantly reduced death or MI (ARs dalteparin 1.8%, placebo 4.8%; RR 0.37, 95% CI 0.20–0.68) and the composite end point of death, MI, or revascularization (ARs dalteparin 2.2%, placebo 5.7%; RR 0.38, 95% CI 0.22–0.66). At 40 days, there was no significant difference for the end point of death or MI (ARs dalteparin 8.0%, placebo 10.7%; RR 0.75, 95% CI 0.54–1.03) but a significant benefit when revascularization was added to the composite end point (ARs dalteparin 18.0%, placebo 23.7%; RR 0.76, 95% CI 0.62–0.92). **Versus unfractionated heparin:** We found four RCTs comparing LMWH versus unfractionated heparin in over 10,000 patients with unstable angina or non–Q-wave MI.[10–13] All patients received aspirin. Two trials compared 5 to 8 days of intravenous unfractionated heparin versus 6 to 14 days of subcutaneous LMWH.[10,12] The other two compared LMWH versus unfractionated heparin for 3 to 6 days, followed by LMWH versus placebo injections for up to day 45.[11,13] Two trials[11,12] found no significant difference in rates of death, MI, or angina at 6, 14, and 45 days (AR at days 6–45 12.3% in both groups; RR for LMWH compared with unfractionated 1.01, 95% CI 0.74–1.38[11]; ARs at 14 days LMWH 20%, unfractionated 18.1%, 95% CI not available, p = ns).[12] The other two[10,13] found a significantly lower rate of death, MI, or angina in patients on LMWH (ARs at 14 days LMWH 16.6%, unfractionated 19.8%; RR for LMWH compared with unfractionated heparin 0.80, 95% CI 0.67–0.96[10]; ARs at 42 days LMWH 17.3%, unfractionated 19.6%, 95% CI not available, $p = 0.049$).[13] However, most of the benefit from LMWH in the fourth trial was seen in the first few days.[13] By contrast, when the rate of death alone was analyzed in the second trial, this was found to be significantly higher with LMWH in the first 6 days of treatment (ARs LMWH 1.5% [11 deaths], unfractionated 0.4% [three deaths]; RR compared to unfractionated 3.37, 95% CI 1.01–11.24).[11]

Harms: In one RCT there was no significant difference in the frequency of major bleeds between LMWH and unfractionated heparin (ARs 6.5% and 7%) but bleeding overall was more common (ARs 18.4% and 14.2%, $p = 0.001$).[10] In another trial, major bleeds were more frequent in patients on LMWH (ARs 2.9% vs. 1.5%, 95% CI not available, $p = 0.02$).[13]

Comment: Several features make LMWH potentially more attractive than unfractionated heparin for routine use, including the fact that no monitoring of activated partial thromboplastin time (aPTT) is required and that LMWH can be administered by patients after discharge. The trials used different doses and regimens for both LMWH and unfractionated heparin, which makes comparison without formal meta-analysis difficult. Note that nadroparin is not yet available in the US.

OPTION HIRUDIN

RCTs have found that, in people with unstable angina taking aspirin, rates of death and MI are significantly lower during infusion of hirudin than during infusion of unfractionated heparin. However, this advantage does not persist once the infusion stops. Longer durations of hirudin infusion (> 72 hours) are

being evaluated currently. Compared with heparin, hirudin causes more major bleeds requiring transfusion but no more life-threatening bleeds or hemorrhagic strokes.

Benefits: We found no systematic review. **Versus unfractionated heparin:** Three recent large RCTs have compared r-hirudin versus unfractionated heparin given for either 2 or 3 days in over 19,000 people with unstable angina who also received aspirin.[14–16] **During infusion:** All three trials found that, during the infusion, there was a significant reduction in rates of death or new MI on hirudin (ARs hirudin 2.3%, heparin 3.1%; RRs hirudin vs. unfractionated heparin 0.73, 95% CI 0.59–0.91[14] and RR 0.76, 95% CI 0.59–0.98[16]). **After infusion:** All three trials found that, once the infusion stopped, the clear benefit from hirudin disappeared (AR for death or new MI at 30 days with hirudin 8.3%, heparin 9.1%; RR 0.90, 95% CI 0.78–1.06[14]; RR for death, new MI or severe angina at 7 days 0.57, 95% CI 0.32–1.02[15]; RR for death or new MI at 7 days 0.83, 95% CI 0.68–1.02[16]).

Harms: In the largest RCT, hirudin was associated with a significant increase in the need for transfusion (ARs 10.2% vs. 8.4%, $p=0.01$), and a trend for increased extracranial hemorrhage (ARs 10.2% vs. 8.6%, $p=0.06$) and intracranial hemorrhage (ARs 0.2% vs. 0.02%, $p=0.06$) compared with unfractionated heparin.[14] In the second largest RCT, hirudin was associated with an excess of major bleeding (ARs 1.2% vs. 0.7%; RR 1.71, 95% CI 1.13–2.58) but no increase in life-threatening bleeds or strokes at day 7.[16] The smallest RCT reported no hemorrhagic strokes and no difference in the rate of major bleeds (~ 1% in all groups).[15] Hirudin was associated with a higher rate of minor bleeding (ARs low-dose hirudin [LDHir] 16.2%, medium-dose hirudin [MDHir] 21.3%, heparin 10.5%; RR LDHir versus heparin 1.54, 95% CI 1.03–2.31; RR MDHir versus heparin 2.03, 95% CI 1.39–2.96).[15]

Comment: The margin of benefit of hirudin over heparin decreases after stopping the infusion. Whether longer duration of treatment has greater benefits is the target of future trials (Yusuf S, personal communication). Two of the trials gave doses of hirudin in proportion to the body weight but with fixed doses of heparin.[14,15]

ANTI-ISCHEMIC TREATMENT

OPTION NITRATES, β-BLOCKERS, CALCIUM-CHANNEL BLOCKERS

The effects of nitrates, β-blockers, and calcium-channel blockers on rates of death or MI have not yet been evaluated adequately in people with unstable angina. Short-acting dihydropyridine calcium-channel blockers may increase mortality.

Benefits: **Nitrates:** We found no systematic reviews or RCTs of nitrates versus placebo in unstable angina. **β-Blockers:** We found no systematic review of β-blockers versus placebo in unstable angina. The HINT study randomized 338 patients with rest angina not receiving β-blocker treatment to nifedipine, metoprolol, both, or neither in a double-blind, placebo-controlled fashion.[17] The main outcome was recurrent angina or MI within 48 hours. Metoprolol was significantly more effective than nifedipine. Another trial randomly assigned 81 patients with unstable angina on "optimal doses" of nitrates and nifedipine to placebo or at least 160 mg/d of propranolol.[18] The incidence of cardiac death, MI, and requirement for coronary artery bypass grafting (CABG) or percutaneous coronary interventions at 30 days did not differ between the two groups (propranolol 16/42 vs. placebo 18/39, $p=$ns). The propranolol group had a lower cumulative probability of experiencing recurrent rest angina over the first 4 days of the trial. The mean number of clinical episodes of angina, duration of angina, nitroglycerine requirement, and ischemic ST changes by continuous ECG monitoring was also lower. **Calcium-channel blockers:** We found one systematic review published in 1989. This reported that calcium-channel blockers reduced symptoms and ischemia but had no effect on rates of MI or death.[19]

Harms: Hypotension is a potential adverse effect of nitrates. However, both older and more recent large RCTs in people with other ischemic conditions showed that nitrates were safe and well tolerated when used judiciously in clinically appropriate doses. Potential adverse effects of β-blockers include bradycardia, exacerbation of reactive airways disease, and hypoglycemia in diabetics. Observational studies have reported increased mortality with short-acting dihydropyridines (e.g., nifedipine) in people with coronary heart disease.[20,21]

Comment: We found no good evidence that anti-ischemic drugs (nitrates, β-blockers, calcium-channel blockers) prevent death or MI. By consensus, until further data are available, intravenous nitrates remain a first-line treatment together with heparin and aspirin in unstable angina.

INVASIVE TREATMENT

OPTION EARLY ROUTINE CARDIAC CATHETERIZATION AND REVASCULARIZATION

RCTs have found that early invasive treatment reduces symptoms and promotes early discharge compared with early conservative treatment in patients with unstable angina. However, early invasive treatment does not seem to reduce rates of death and MI. It is not yet clear whether certain patients (e.g., those who are refractory to medical treatment) are more likely than others to benefit from early invasive treatment.

Benefits: We found no systematic review. Two RCTs have compared early routine angiography/revascularization versus medical treatment alone. The larger trial, TIMI IIIB study, used a factorial design to compare tissue plasminogen activator versus placebo and to compare early invasive treatment (cardiac catheterization at 18–48 hours) versus early conservative treatment in 1473 patients with unstable angina presenting within 24 hours of ischemic chest discomfort.[22,23] All patients received aspirin and unfractionated heparin. Within 6 weeks, 64% of patients randomized to conservative treatment underwent cardiac catheterization, 26% underwent percutaneous transluminal coronary angioplasty (PTCA), and 24% underwent CABG. At 6 weeks, there was no significant difference in the composite end point (death, MI, or a symptom limited exercise stress test) (invasive 18.1% vs. conservative 16.2%, $p=0.78$). However, invasive treatment significantly reduced rehospitalizations (7.8% vs. 14.1%, $p<0.001$), rehospitalization days (365 vs. 930, $p<0.001$), and need for antianginal medications ($p<0.02$). At 1 year, there was no significant difference in rates of death or MI (invasive 10.8% vs. conservative 12.2%, $p=0.42$), but the lower numbers of repeat hospital admissions and hospital days with invasive treatment persisted. The VANQWISH trial compared invasive versus conservative treatment in 920 patients.[24] Over 23-months' follow-up (range 12–44 months) there was no significant difference in the combined primary end point of death or MI (RR 0.87, 95% CI 0.68–1.10).

Harms: The larger RCT reported no differences in complication rates (death, MI, emergency CABG, abrupt vessel closure, hemorrhage, or serious hypotension) between invasive and conservative treatment (14% vs. 13%, $p=0.38$).[22,23] In the smaller RCT, patients who underwent early invasive treatment were significantly more at risk of death or MI at hospital discharge (36 vs. 15 patients, $p=0.004$), 30 days after randomization (48 vs. 26 patients, $p=0.012$), and 1 year (111 vs. 85 patients, $p=0.05$).[24]

Comment: It is not yet clear whether there are subgroups of patients that benefit particularly from either invasive or conservative treatment. Further studies are needed to compare the current consensus strategy (bed rest and aggressive medical treatment, with cardiac catheterization in those who are refractory to medical treatment) versus routine early cardiac catheterization and appropriate revascularization.

REFERENCES

1. Antiplatelet Trialists' Collaboration. Collaborative overview of randomised trials of antiplatelet therapy - I: prevention of death, myocardial infarction, and stroke by prolonged antiplatelet therapy in various categories of patients. *BMJ* 1994;308: 81–106. (Trials available in March 1990 were included; primary sources MEDLINE, Current Contents.)
2. Balsano F, Rizzon P, Violi F, et al and the Studio della Ticlopidina nell'Angina Instabile Group. Antiplatelet treatment with ticlopidine in unstable angina: a controlled multicentre clinical trial. *Circulation* 1990;82:17–26.
3. PRISM-PLUS Study Investigators. Inhibition of the platelet glycoprotein IIb/IIIa receptor with tirofiban in unstable angina and non-Q-wave myocardial infarction. *N Engl J Med* 1998;338:1488–1497.
4. Pursuit Trial Investigators. Inhibition of platelet glycoprotein IIb/IIIa with eptifibatide in patients with acute coronary syndromes. *N Engl J Med* 1998;339:436–443.
5. PARAGON Investigators. International, randomized, controlled trial of lamifiban (a platelet glycoprotein IIb/IIIa inhibitor), heparin, or both in unstable angina. *Circulation* 1998;97: 2386–2395.
6. PRISM Study Investigators. A comparison of aspirin plus tirofiban with aspirin plus heparin for unstable angina. *N Engl J Med* 1998;338: 1498–1505.
7. Oler A, Whooley MA, Oler J, Grady D. Adding heparin to aspirin reduces the incidence of myocardial infarction and death in patients with unstable angina: a meta-analysis. *JAMA* 1996; 276:811–815. (Search date 1995; primary sources MEDLINE 1966 to September 1995, hand search of reference lists, consultation with experts.)
8. Gurfinkel EP, Manos EJ, Mejaíl RI, et al. Low molecular weight heparin versus regular heparin or aspirin in the treatment of unstable angina and silent ischemia. *J Am Coll Cardiol* 1995;26: 313–318.
9. FRISC Study Group. Low-molecular-weight heparin during instability in coronary artery disease. *Lancet* 1996;347:561–568.
10. Cohen M, Demers C, Gurfinkel EP, et al. A comparison of low molecular-weight heparin with unfractionated heparin for unstable coronary artery disease. *N Engl J Med* 1997;337: 447–452.
11. Klein W, Buchwald A, Hillis SE, et al for the FRIC Investigators. Comparison of low-molecular-weight heparin with unfractionated heparin acutely and with placebo for 6 weeks in the management of unstable coronary artery disease: fragmin in unstable coronary artery disease study. *Circulation* 1997;96:61–68.
12. Leizorovicz A. The FRAXIS study. Presented at XXth Congress of the European Society of Cardiology, Vienna, Austria, 1998.
13. Antman EM. The TIMI IIB study. Presented at XXth congress of the European Society of Cardiology, Vienna, Austria, 1998.
14. GUSTO IIb Investigators. A comparison of recom-

binant hirudin with heparin for the treatment of acute coronary syndromes. *N Engl J Med* 1996; 335:775–782.
15. OASIS Investigators. Comparison of the effects of two doses of recombinant hirudin compared with heparin in patients with acute myocardial ischemia without ST elevation: a pilot study. *Circulation* 1997;96:769–777.
16. Yusuf S. OASIS 2 study. Presented at the XXth Congress of the European Society of Cardiology, August, 1998.
17. HINT Research Group. Early treatment of unstable angina in the coronary care unit: a randomized, double blind, placebo controlled comparison of recurrent ischaemia in patients treated with nifedipine or metoprolol or both. *Br Heart J* 1986;56:400–413.
18. Gottlieb SO, Weisfeldt ML, Ouyang P, et al. Effect of the addition of propranolol to therapy with nifedipine for unstable angina pectoris: a randomized, double-blind, placebo-controlled trial. *Circulation* 1986;73:331–337.
19. Held PH, Yusuf S, Furberg CD. Calcium channel blockers in acute myocardial infarction and unstable angina: an overview. *BMJ* 1989;299: 1187–1192. (Search date not stated; primary sources not specified in detail.)
20. Furberg CD, Psaty BM, Meyer JV. Nifedipine: dose-related increase in mortality in patients with coronary heart disease. *Circulation* 1995;92:1326–1331. (Search date and primary sources not specified).
21. WHO-ISH Study. Ad hoc subcommittee of the liaison committee of the World Health Organisation and the International Society of Hypertension: effects of calcium antagonists on the risks of coronary heart disease, cancer and bleeding. *J Hypertens* 1997:15:105–115.
22. The TIMI IIIB Investigators. Effects of tissue plasminogen activator and a comparison of early invasive and conservative strategies in unstable angina and non-Q-wave myocardial infarction. results of the TIMI IIIB trial. *Circulation* 1994;89: 1545–1556.
23. Anderson V, Cannon CP, Stone PH, et al for the TIMI IIIB Investigators. One-year results of the thrombolysis in myocardial infarction (TIMI) IIIB clinical trial: a randomized comparison of tissue-type plasminogen activator versus placebo and early invasive versus early conservative strategies in unstable angina and non-Q wave myocardial infarction. *J Am Coll Cardiol* 1995;26: 1643–1650.
24. Boden WE, O'Rourke RA, Crawford MH, et al for the VANQWISH Trial Investigators. Outcomes in patients with acute non-Q-wave myocardial infarction randomly assigned to an invasive as compared with a conservative management strategy. *N Engl J Med* 1998;338:1785–1792.

Madhu K Natarajan, MD, FRCPC, FACC
Division of Cardiology
McMaster University
Hamilton, Ontario
Canada

Competing interests: None declared.

TABLE 1 **Effects of GP IIb/IIIa inhibitors in unstable angina and non–Q-wave myocardial infarction: results of main RCTs.** **(*See* text p. 54.)**

Trial	Total patients	Comparison	RRR for death or MI at 30 days*	NNT to avoid one additional death or MI at 30 days
PRISM-PLUS[3]	1570	Tirofiban and heparin vs. heparin alone	0.30 (95% CI 0.04–0.49)	31
PURSUIT[4]	10,948	Eptifibatide and heparin vs. heparin alone	0.11 (95% CI 0.013–0.20)	67
PARAGON[5]	2282	Lamifiban and heparin vs. heparin alone	0.04 (95% CI –0.32 to 0.30	–
PRISM[6]	3232	Aspirin and tirofiban vs. aspirin and heparin	0.20 (95% CI –0.05 to 0.39)	–

* = 1-OR

Acute myocardial infarction

Shamir R Mehta, MD, FRCPC, and Salim Yusuf, DPhil, FRCPC

QUESTIONS

INTERVENTIONS

To be covered in future issues of *Clinical Evidence*
Management of complicated AMI
Cardiogenic shock
Cardiac arrest
Arrhythmias
Myocardial rupture

Key Messages

- Good evidence from systematic reviews of randomized controlled trials (RCTs) supports the following interventions in people presenting with symptoms of AMI:
  - aspirin (at least 160 mg chewed and swallowed immediately and continued daily for at least a few years and perhaps for life)
  - thrombolytic treatment (streptokinase ± intravenous/subcutaneous heparin or tissue plasminogen activator [tPA] + intravenous heparin) in people with ST elevation on the presenting electrocardiogram (ECG)
  - a β-blocker (started intravenously within hours of infarction and continued orally for several years) in people without contraindications
  - an ACE inhibitor (started within 24 hours of infarction and continued daily) for approximately 1 month in people at low risk of death and for several months in people with heart failure at any time during hospital admission or with a left ventricular ejection fraction less than 40%
  - nitrates (shown to be safe for symptomatic relief in this setting, but to have at most a modest effect on mortality).
- Systematic reviews of RCTs have found no evidence of mortality benefit from calcium-channel blockers during or after AMI; there is potential for increased mortality in people with heart failure.
- A systematic review of RCTs has found that, in high-risk people who present early (< 4 hours after onset of symptoms) and have ST elevation, primary PTCA is more effective than thrombolytic treatment, provided that it can be performed quickly (< 90 minutes after hospital arrival) by an experienced operator and staff in a high-volume center.

DEFINITION AMI is the sudden occlusion of a coronary artery leading to myocardial death.

INCIDENCE/ PREVALENCE AMI is one of the most common causes of mortality in both developed developed and developing nations. In 1990, ischemic heart disease was the leading cause of death worldwide, accounting for approximately 6.3 million deaths. The age standardized incidence varies among and within countries.[1] Each year, approximately 900,000 people in the USA experience an AMI, and approximately 225,000 of them die. Approximately half of these patients die within 1 hour of symptoms and before reaching a hospital emergency room.[2] Event rates increase with age for both sexes and are higher in men than women at all ages. The incidence of death from AMI has fallen in many Western countries over the past 20 years.

ETIOLOGY The immediate mechanism of AMI is rupture of an atheromatous plaque, causing thrombosis and occlusion of coronary arteries and myocardial death. Factors that may convert a stable plaque into an unstable plaque (the "active plaque") have yet to be elucidated fully; however, shear stresses, inflammation, and autoimmunity have been proposed. The changing rates of coronary heart disease in different populations are explained only partly by changes in the standard risk factors for ischemic heart disease (particularly fall in blood pressure and smoking).

PROGNOSIS AMI may lead to a host of mechanical and electrical complications, including death, ventricular dysfunction, congestive heart failure, cardiogenic shock, fatal and nonfatal arrhythmia, valvular dysfunction, or myocardial rupture.

AIMS To relieve pain, to restore blood supply to heart muscle, to reduce incidence of complications (e.g., congestive heart failure, myocardial rupture, valvular dysfunction, fatal and nonfatal arrhythmia), to prevent recurrent ischemia and infarction, and to decrease mortality.

OUTCOMES Efficacy outcomes: rates of major cardiovascular events, including death, recurrent AMI, refractory ischemia, and stroke. Safety outcomes: rates of major bleeding and intracranial hemorrhage.

METHODS We searched MEDLINE, EMBASE, and Cochrane electronic databases in July 1998 to identify relevant systematic reviews. Individual high-quality trials published after the last acceptable systematic review also were selected.

QUESTION Which treatments improve outcomes in AMI?

OPTION ASPIRIN AND OTHER ANTIPLATELET TREATMENTS

A systematic review of RCTs has found that, in people with AMI, aspirin reduces mortality (one life saved per 40 people treated during the acute phase), reinfarction (one fewer nonfatal reinfarction per 100 people treated), and stroke (one fewer nonfatal stroke per 300 people treated). The evidence suggests an optimal dose of aspirin of 160 to 325 mg acutely, followed by long-term treatment with at least 75 mg/d indefinitely.

Benefits: **Aspirin versus placebo:** A systematic review published in 1994 identified nine trials in 18,773 people treated with antiplatelet agents or placebo soon after the onset of AMI and for a period of at least 1 month afterward.[3] The absolute and relative benefits found in the systematic review are shown in Figure 1. The largest of the trials was ISIS-2, which involved 17,187 people with suspected AMI randomized to receive either placebo or aspirin (162.6 mg) chewed and swallowed on the day of AMI and continued daily for 1 month.[4] In subsequent long-term follow-up of the ISIS-2 trial, the mortality benefit was maintained for up to 4 years.[5] In the systematic review, the most widely tested aspirin regimens were 75 to 325 mg/d.[3] Doses throughout this range seemed similarly effective, with no evidence that "higher" doses (500–1500 mg/d) were more effective (odds reduction compared with placebo 21%, 95% CI 14%–27%) than "medium" doses (160–325 mg/d) (odds reduction 28%, 95% CI 0.22–0.33) or "lower" doses (75–160 mg/d) (odds reduction 26%, 95% CI 5%–42%). There was insufficient evidence for efficacy of doses below 75 mg/d. One study supports the administration of a loading dose of 160 to 325 mg/d to achieve a prompt antiplatelet effect.[6]

Harms: In ISIS-2, there was no significant increase in rates of cerebral hemorrhage or bleeds requiring transfusion (0.4% on aspirin and placebo).[4] There was a small absolute excess of "minor" bleeding (ARI 0.6%, 95% CI not available, $p < 0.01$), which might be expected with any clinically effective antiplatelet/antithrombotic treatment.

Comment: Although there was no evidence of a difference in effectiveness of the different doses of aspirin, it seems prudent to administer a dose of at least 160 to 325 mg in the acute setting followed by at least 75 mg/d. Future issues of *Clinical Evidence* will explore the benefits and harms of other antiplatelet agents, including ticlopidine, clopidogrel, and the glycoprotein IIb/IIIa inhibitors.

OPTION THROMBOLYTIC TREATMENT

Systematic reviews of RCTs have found that prompt administration of thrombolytic treatment (within 6 hours and perhaps up to 12 hours and longer after the onset of symptoms) reduces mortality in people of all age groups with AMI and ST elevation or bundle branch block on their presenting ECG. Fifty-six people would need treatment in the acute phase to prevent one death. Strokes, intracranial hemorrhage, and major bleeds are more common in people given thrombolysis; one additional stroke for every 250 people treated and one additional major bleed for every 143 people treated. Intracranial hemorrhage is more common in people of advanced age and low body weight, those with hypertension on admission, and those given tPA rather than another thrombolytic agent.

Benefits: **Thrombolytic treatment versus placebo:** A systematic review published in 1994 identified nine RCTs, each including at least 1000 people with suspected AMI who received either thrombolytic treatment or placebo ($n = 58,600$).[7] Baseline ECGs showed ST-segment elevation in 68% of people, and ST-segment depression, T-wave abnormalities, or no abnormality in the rest. The AR of mortality was 9.6% on thrombolytic treatment and 11.5% on placebo (ARR 1.9%, RRR 0.18, 95% CI 13%–23%). The number needing treatment in the acute phase to prevent one additional death was 56 (95% CI 43–77). The greatest benefit was observed in the large group of people presenting with ST elevation (RRR 0.21 , 95% CI not available) or bundle branch block (RRR 0.25). **Timing of treatment:** The earlier thrombolytic treatment was given, the greater the absolute benefit (Figure 2). For each hour of delay, the ARR for death decreased by 0.16% (ARR for death if given within 6 hours of symptoms 3%; ARR for death if given 7–12 hours after the onset of symptoms 2%).[8] Too few people in the systematic review received treatment more than 12 hours after the onset of symptoms to determine whether the benefits of thrombolytic treatment would outweigh the risks. Extrapolation of the data in Figure 2 suggests that, at least for people with ST elevation, there may be some net benefit of treatment between 12 and 18 hours after symptom onset (ARR for death 1%). **Type of infarct:** Reduced rates of death were seen in people with all types of infarct, but the benefit was several times greater in those with anterior infarction (3.7%) compared with those with inferior infarction (0.8%) or infarctions in other zones (2.7%). **Different thrombolytic agents:** A systematic review[8] published in 1997 identified three large RCTs comparing streptokinase versus tPA: GISSI-2,[9] ISIS-3,[10] and GUSTO-1.[11] The data are summarized in Table 1. In the GISSI-2 trial, people with ST elevation and symptoms of AMI for less than 6 hours were randomized in an open-label fashion to intravenous tPA 100 mg over 3 hours or streptokinase 1.5 MU over 1 hour and were further randomized to subcutaneous heparin 12,500 U twice daily beginning 12 hours later or no heparin.[9] Heparin added little benefit (AR of death in hospital 8.5% vs. 8.9% on no heparin, RRR 0.05, 95% CI –0.04 to 0.14). In ISIS-3, people with suspected AMI presenting within 24 hours of symptoms were randomized to receive either streptokinase 1.5 MU over 1 hour, tPA 0.6 MU/kg every 4 hours, or anisoylated plasminogen streptokinase activator complex (APSAC) (30 U/3 min), and then further randomized to subcutaneous heparin 12,500 U starting at 7 hours and continued for 7 days or no heparin.[10] All received aspirin on admission. At 35 days, mortality was similar among the three regimens (streptokinase 10.6%, APSAC 10.5%, tPA 10.3%), and the addition of heparin made no significant difference (AR of death 10.3% vs. 10.6% on no heparin). In the GUSTO-1 trial, people with ST segment elevation presenting within 6 hours of symptom onset were randomized in an open-label fashion to one of four regimens: 1) streptokinase 1.5 MU over 1 hour plus subcutaneous heparin 12,500 U twice daily starting 4 hours after thrombolytic treatment; 2) streptokinase 1.5 MU over 1 hour plus intravenous heparin 5000 U bolus followed by 1000 U/h; 3) accelerated tPA 15 mg bolus then 0.75 mg/kg over 30 minutes followed by 0.50 mg/kg over 60 minutes, plus intravenous heparin 5000 U bolus then 1000 U/h; and 4) tPA 1.0 mg/kg over 60 minutes, 10% given as a bolus, plus streptokinase 1.0 MU over 60 minutes.[11] When the results of the three trials were combined using weighting proportional to their sample sizes, the combined outcome of any stroke or death (unrelated to stroke to avoid "double counting") was 9.4% for streptokinase only regimens and 9.2% for tPA-based regimens (including the combined tPA and streptokinase arm in GUSTO-1). RRR for tPA versus streptokinase was 2.1% and was not significant ($p = 0.4$), and ARR was 0.2% (95% CI, a reduction in risk of 0.5% to an increase of 0.2%).[8]

Harms: **Stroke/intracerebral hemorrhage:** The risk of stroke was increased by thrombolytic treatment given in the acute phase (ARI compared to placebo 0.4%, 95% CI 0.2%–0.5%, NNH 250).[7] In GUSTO-1, the overall incidence of intracerebral hemorrhage was 0.7% and of stroke 1.4%, of which 31% were severely disabling and 50% were intracerebral hemorrhages. The risk of hemorrhagic stroke was higher with tPA (AR 0.72%) than with streptokinase and subcutaneous heparin (AR 0.49%) or with streptokinase and intravenous heparin (AR 0.54%, $p=0.03$ for tPA compared with combined streptokinase arms).[11] **Predictive factors for stroke/intracranial hemorrhage:** Multivariate analysis of data from a large database of people who experienced intracerebral hemorrhage after thrombolytic treatment[12] identified four independent predictors of increased risk of intracerebral hemorrhage: age > 65 years (OR 2.2, 95% CI 1.4–3.5), weight < 70 kg (OR 2.1, 95% CI 1.3–3.2), hypertension on admission (OR 2.0, 95% CI 1.2–3.2), and use of tPA rather than another thrombolytic agent (OR 1.6, 95% CI 1.0–2.5). AR of intracranial hemorrhage was 0.26% on streptokinase in the absence of risk factors, and 0.96%, 1.32%, and 2.17% in people with one, two, or three risk factors. The GUSTO-1 researchers analyzed 592 strokes in 41,021 people and found seven factors to be predictors of intracerebral hemorrhage: advanced age, lower weight, history of cerebrovascular disease, history of hypertension, higher systolic or diastolic pressure on presentation, and use of tPA rather than streptokinase.[13,14] **Major bleeding:** The risk of major bleeding was increased by thrombolytic treatment given in the acute phase (ARI compared with placebo 0.7%, 95% CI 0.6%–0.9%, NNH 143).[7] Bleeding was most common in people undergoing procedures (coronary artery bypass grafting or PTCA). Spontaneous bleeds were observed most often in the gastrointestinal tract.[11]

Comment: The evidence suggests that it is far more important to administer prompt thrombolytic treatment than to debate which thrombolytic agent should be used. In this regard, a strategy of rapid use of any thrombolytic in a broad population is likely to lead to the greatest impact on reducing mortality. When the results of GISSI-2, ISIS-3, and GUSTO-1 are taken together, tPA-based regimens do not seem to confer a significant advantage in the combined outcome of any stroke and death (unrelated to stroke) over streptokinase. The legitimacy of combining the results of the three trials can be questioned, as the selection criteria and protocols differed in important aspects (*see* Collins et al[8] for arguments to justify combining the results of these trials despite their apparent differences). A rational approach may be to individualize treatment by weighing the risks of bleeding with overall benefit and cost effectiveness, instead of adopting a single-agent strategy.

OPTION β-BLOCKERS

Systematic reviews of RCTs have found that oral β-blockers given within hours of infarction reduce both mortality and reinfarction in people with AMI. Adding β-blockers to thrombolytic treatment confers additional benefit.

Benefits: **β-Blockers given within hours of infarction:** Systematic reviews published in 1985 and 1987 identified 27 RCTs of early use of β-blockers. They found that, within 1 week of treatment, β-blockers significantly reduced the risk of death compared with placebo (RRR 13%, 95% CI 2%–25%, $p<0.02$).[15,16] The greatest benefit was observed in the first 2 days of treatment (RRR for death approximately 25%), highlighting the importance of initiating treatment early. Incidence of other major vascular events was also reduced: the combined outcome of death, nonfatal cardiac arrest, or nonfatal reinfarction had RRR of 16% (1110 events vs. 1298 events, 95% CI not available, $p<0.001$). The largest of these trials, ISIS-1, compared atenolol (5–10 mg immediately intravenously followed by 100 mg/d orally for 7 days) versus standard treatment (no β-blocker) in 16,027 people with AMI.[17] After 7 days, the AR of vascular mortality was 3.89% on atenolol vs. 4.57% in the controls (RRR 15%, 95% CI 19%–27%; ARR 0.7%). Thus, the NNT to prevent one death by 7 days is 143. There was more benefit in people with ECG evidence of AMI at entry (probable anterior infarction, inferior infarction, both, or bundle branch block). In this group, the AR of death was 5.33% on atenolol and 6.49% in the controls (ARR 1.16%, NNT 86, 95% CI not available). People over 65 years of age and those with large infarcts had the most benefit. **In people receiving thrombolytic treatment:** The TIMI-IIB study compared early versus delayed metoprolol in 1434 people with AMI receiving tPA.[18] Early treatment began on day 1 (intravenous then oral) and delayed treatment on day 6 (oral). At 6 days, patients receiving early treatment had significantly lower rates of reinfarction (AR 2.7% early vs. 5.1% delayed, 95% CI not available, $p=0.02$) and recurrent chest pain (AR 18.8% vs. 24.1%, $p<0.02$). There were no early (6 days) or late (1 year) differences observed in mortality or left ventricular ejection fraction between the two groups. **Long-term use of β-blockers:** *See* p. 73.

Harms: Patients with asthma or severe congestive cardiac failure were excluded from most trials. Many of the early trials tended to enrol people at low risk of death soon after AMI. In those given immediate rather than delayed β-blockers in TIMI-IIB, there was a nonsignificant increased frequency of heart failure during the initial admission to hospital (15.3% vs. 12.2%, $p=0.10$).[18] First-degree heart block and bundle branch block increased the frequency of adverse events.

Comment: β-Blockers may reduce rates of cardiac rupture and ventricular fibrillation. This may explain why patients over 65 years of age and those with large infarcts had the most benefit, because they also have higher rates of these complications. The trials mostly were conducted in the prethrombolytic era. The TIMI-IIB trial established that β-blockers significantly decrease reinfarction rates even when added to thrombolytic treatment. The absence of deaths or changes in left ventricular ejection fraction in this trial is probably because the trial was too small to detect a reduction in deaths over and above that observed with tPA.

OPTION ACE INHIBITORS

A systematic review of four large RCTs has found that ACE inhibitors used within 24 hours of onset of symptoms reduce mortality in people with AMI. The question of whether ACE inhibitors should be offered to everyone

presenting with AMI or only to people with signs of heart failure remains unresolved.

Benefits: **In all people after an AMI:** A systematic review published in 1998 identified four large RCTs (each including >1000 patients) comparing ACE inhibitors versus placebo given to all people (irrespective of clinical heart failure or left ventricular dysfunction) within 36 hours of the onset of symptoms of AMI. Data from 98,496 people were pooled.[19] The AR of death from any cause by 30 days was 7.1% in the ACE inhibitor group and 7.6% in the control group (RRR 7%, 95% CI 2%–11%, NNT 200 to save one life by 30 days). Most of this benefit was in the first 7 days after AMI. The absolute benefit was particularly large in some high-risk groups: those in Killip class 2–3 (RRR 9.1%, NNT 71, 99% CI 36–10 000); those with heart rates >100 beats/min at entry (RRR 14.5%, NNT 44 , 99% CI 25–185); and those with an anterior AMI (RRR 12.8%, NNT 94, 99% CI 56–303). ACE inhibitors also reduced the incidence of nonfatal cardiac failure (AR 14.6% vs. 15.2%, 95% CI not available, $p=0.01$). **In selected people after an AMI:** A selective strategy was tested in three trials (SAVE,[20] AIRE,[21] and TRACE[22]). Treatment was restricted to people with clinical heart failure, objective evidence of left ventricular dysfunction, or both ($n=\sim 6000$) and was started a few days after AMI. These trials found consistently that long-term treatment with ACE inhibitors in this selected population was associated with a significant reduction in mortality and reinfarction. In the SAVE trial, for example, there was a 21% (95% CI 5%–35%, $p=0.014$) RRR for cardiovascular death, a 37% (95% CI 20%–50%, $p<0.001$) RRR for the development of severe heart failure, a 22% (95% CI 4%–37%, $p=0.019$) RRR for congestive heart failure requiring hospitalization, and a 25% (95% CI 5%–40%, $p=0.015$) RRR for recurrent AMI.[20]

Harms: The systematic review[19] found an excess of persistent hypotension (AR 17.6% vs. 9.3%, 95% CI for difference not available, $p<0.01$) and renal dysfunction (AR 1.3% vs. 0.6%, $p<0.01$) in patients given ACE inhibitors. The relative and absolute risks of these adverse effects were distributed uniformly across both the high and lower cardiovascular risk groups.

Comment: The largest benefits of ACE inhibitors in the setting of AMI are seen when treatment is started within 24 hours. The evidence does not answer the questions of which people with an AMI should be offered ACE inhibitors and for how long after AMI it remains beneficial to start treatment with an ACE inhibitor.

OPTION NITRATES

RCTs performed before and during the thrombolytic era have found that intravenous nitrates are safe in the acute management of symptoms in people with AMI but may reduce mortality only slightly.

Benefits: **Without thrombolysis:** A systematic review published in 1988 identified 10 RCTs comparing intravenous nitroglycerine or nitroprusside versus placebo in 2000 people with AMI.[23] The trials were all conducted in the prethrombolytic era. Nitrates reduced the RR of death by 35% (95% CI 16%–55%). The observed benefit of nitrates appeared to be mostly during the acute hospitalization period, with very modest or little long-term survival benefit. **With aspirin/thrombolysis:** During the thrombolytic era, two large RCTs, ISIS-4[24] and GISSI-3,[25] compared nitrates given acutely versus placebo in 58,050 and 17,817 people with AMI (90% received aspirin and approximately 70% received thrombolytic treatment). In ISIS-4, people received oral controlled-release mononitrate 30 to 60 mg/d.[24] In GISSI-3 people received intravenous nitroglycerine for 24 hours then transdermal nitroglycerine 10 mg/d.[25] Neither trial found a significant improvement in survival, either in the total sample or in subgroups of people at different risk of death. Nitrates were a useful adjunctive treatment to help control symptoms in people with AMI.

Harms: The systemic review and the large trials found no significant harm associated with routine use of nitrates in people with AMI.[23–25]

Comment: In ISIS-4 and GISSI-3, a large proportion of people took nonstudy nitrates, there was a high rate of concurrent use of other hypotensive agents, people were relatively low risk, and nitrates were not titrated to blood pressure and heart rate.[24,25] All or some of these reasons may explain the lack of benefit observed.

OPTION CALCIUM-CHANNEL BLOCKERS

RCTs have found that calcium-channel blockers given to people within the first few days of an AMI do not reduce deaths, and may increase deaths in people with reduced left ventricular function.

Benefits: **Dihydropyridine agents:** No systematic review. Two large RCTs have compared short-acting nifedipine versus placebo in people treated within the first few days of AMI.[26,27] Neither found evidence of benefit and both found trends toward increased mortality on nifedipine. The SPRINT-II trial was terminated prematurely because of lack of efficacy. It found a 33% increase in mortality on nifedipine that did not reach significance.[27] There are insufficient data on sustained release nifedipine, amlodipine, or felodipine in this setting. **Verapamil:** The DAVIT-I trial compared placebo versus verapamil started intravenously on admission for AMI then continued orally for six months in 1436 people.[28] At 6 months, there was no significant difference in mortality (AR 12.8% verapamil vs. 13.9% placebo), and at 12 months no significant difference in reinfarction (AR 7% vs. 8.3%) or mortality (AR 15.2% vs. 16.4%) between the two groups.

Harms: Two systematic reviews of trials of any kind of calcium-channel blockers in people with AMI found a nonsignificant increase of mortality of approximately 4%[29] and 6%.[30] The MDPIT study randomized 2466 people with AMI to receive either diltiazem (60 mg orally four times daily started 3–15 days after AMI) or placebo.[31] Overall there was no effect on total mortality or reinfarction between the two groups, but subgroup analysis found a 41% increase in death or reinfarction in patients with congestive heart failure (RRI 1.41, 95% CI 1.01–1.96).

Comment: Currently there is no evidence to support the routine use of calcium-channel blockers in the acute management of AMI. Long-acting calcium-channel blockers may be useful after non–Q-wave AMI in people without congestive heart failure in whom β-blockers cannot be used.

OPTION PRIMARY PTCA VERSUS THROMBOLYSIS

A systematic review of RCTs has found that, in the short term, primary PTCA is at least as effective as (and possibly superior to) thrombolysis in the treatment of AMI in terms of reduced rates of death, reinfarction, and haemorrhagic stroke. However, the trials were conducted mainly in high volume, specialist centers. The effectiveness of PTCA in less specialist hands compared to thrombolysis remains to be defined.

Benefits: A systematic review published in 1997 identified 10 trials of primary PTCA versus thrombolysis in people with AMI ($n = 2606$).[32] None of the trials had sufficient power to detect mortality reductions individually. **Death and reinfarction:** The review found reduced mortality with PTCA. At 30 days, the AR of death was 4.4% with primary PTCA compared with 6.5% with thrombolysis (OR 0.66, 95% CI 0.46–0.94, ARR 2.1%, NNT 48).[32] The effect was similar independent of the thrombolytic regimen used. There was also a significant reduction in the combined end point of death and reinfarction with PTCA (OR 0.58, 95% CI 0.44–0.76). The largest single trial, GUSTO-IIb, compared primary PTCA versus accelerated tPA in 1138 people with AMI (with ST elevation on the ECG) who presented within 12 hours of symptom onset.[33] At 30 days, there was no significant difference in mortality between the two groups (AR 5.7% vs. 7.0%), but primary PTCA significantly reduced the primary end point of death, nonfatal AMI, or nonfatal disabling stroke (AR 9.6% vs. 13.7% on tPA, OR 0.67, 95% CI 0.47–0.97). This effect was substantially attenuated by 6 months.

Harms: **Stroke:** The review found that PTCA was associated with a significant reduction in total stroke (AR 0.7% vs. 2.0%) and hemorrhagic stroke (AR 0.1% vs. 1.1%).[32] In GUSTO-IIb, the collective rate of hemorrhagic stroke in people given thrombolysis was 1.1%, substantially higher than that observed in trials comparing thrombolysis with placebo. This may have been because the trials summarized above were in older people and used tPA. However, the lower rates of hemorrhagic stroke with PTCA were consistent across almost all of the trials, and this may be the major advantage of PTCA over thrombolysis.

Comment: Although collectively the trials show an overall (short-term) reduction in deaths with PTCA compared with thrombolysis, there are several pitfalls common to the individual trials, most of which inflate the benefit of PTCA.[34] Trials comparing PTCA with thrombolysis cannot be blinded easily, and ascertainment of end points that require some judgment (e.g., reinfarction or stroke) may have been influenced by the investigators' knowledge of the treatment allocation (only one trial had a blinded adjudication events committee). Also, people allocated to PTCA were discharged 1 to 2 days earlier than those allocated to thrombolysis, which favored PTCA by reducing the time for detection of in hospital events. In addition, the trials before GUSTO-IIb should be viewed only as hypothesis generating in that the composite outcome (death, reinfarction, and stroke) was not defined prospectively and attention was placed only on these end points after there seemed to be some benefit on *post hoc* analysis. The results are based also on short-term outcomes only and do not provide information on the collective long-term benefit. For example, in GUSTO-IIb, the composite end point was significant at 30 days, but with a wide degree of uncertainty, and this was attenuated substantially to a nonsignificant difference by 6 months. The lower mortality and reinfarction rates reported with PTCA are promising but not conclusive, and the real benefits may well be smaller. Only in a minority of centers that perform a high volume of direct PTCA and in the hands of experienced interventionalists may primary PTCA be clearly superior to thrombolytic treatment. Elsewhere, primary PTCA may have its greatest benefit in people with contraindications to thrombolysis, in people in cardiogenic shock, or in people in whom the mortality reduction with thrombolysis is modest and the risk of intracranial hemorrhage is increased (e.g., in elderly people).[30] The value of direct PTCA over thrombolysis in people presenting to hospital more than 12 hours after onset of chest pain remains to be tested.

REFERENCES

1. Murray C, Lopez A. Mortality by cause for eight regions of the world: global burden of disease study. *Lancet* 1997;349:1269–1276.
2. National Heart, Lung, and Blood Institute. *Morbidity and mortality: chartbook on cardiovascular, lung, and blood diseases*. Bethesda, Maryland: US Department of Health and Human Services, Public Health Service, National Institutes of Health; May 1992.
3. Antiplatelet Trialists' Collaboration. Collaborative overview of randomised trials of antiplatelet therapy I: prevention of death, myocardial infarction, and stroke by prolonged antiplatelet therapy in various categories of patients. *BMJ* 1994;308: 81–106. (Search date, trials available at March 1990; primary sources MEDLINE, Current Contents.)
4. Second International Study of Infarct Survival (ISIS-2) Collaborative Group. Randomized trial of intravenous streptokinase, oral aspirin, both or neither among 17,187 cases of suspected acute myocardial infarction. *Lancet* 1988;ii:349–360.
5. Baigent C, Collins R. ISIS-2: four year mortality of 17 187 patients after fibrinolytic and antiplatelet therapy in suspected acute myocardial infarction study [abstract]. *Circulation* 1993; Suppl I:I-291.
6. Patrignani P, Filabozzi P, Patrono C. Selective cumulative inhibition of platelet thromboxane production by low-dose aspirin in healthy subjects. *J Clin Invest* 1982;69:1366–1372.
7. Fibrinolytic Therapy Trialists' (FTT) Collaborative Group. Indications for fibrinolytic therapy in suspected acute myocardial infarction: collaborative overview of early mortality and major morbidity results of all randomized trials of more than 1000 patients. *Lancet* 1994;343:311–322. (Search date and primary sources not stated.)
8. Collins R, Peto R, Baigent C, Sleight P. Aspirin, heparin and fibrinolytic therapy in suspected acute myocardial infarction. *N Engl J Med* 1997;336:847–860. (Search date and primary sources not stated.)
9. Gruppo Italiano per lo studio della Sopravvivenza nell'infarto miocardico (GISSI). GISSI-2: a factorial randomised trial of alteplase versus streptokinase and heparin versus no heparin among 12,490 patients with acute myocardial infarction. *Lancet* 1990;336:65–71.
10. Third International Study of Infarct Survival (ISIS-3) Collaborative Group. ISIS-3: a randomised comparison of streptokinase vs tissue plasminogen activator vs anistreplase and of aspirin plus heparin vs aspirin alone among 41,299 cases of suspected acute myocardial infarction. *Lancet* 1992;339:753–770.
11. The GUSTO Investigators. An international randomized trial comparing four thrombolytic strategies for acute myocardial infarction. *N Engl J Med* 1993;329:673–682.
12. Simoons ML, Maggioni AP, Knatterud G, et al. Individual risk assessment for intracranial hemorrhage during thrombolytic therapy. *Lancet* 1993;342:1523–1528.
13. Gore JM, Granger CB, Simoons ML, et al. Stroke after thrombolysis: mortality and functional outcomes in the GUSTO-1 trial. *Circulation* 1995;92: 2811–2818.
14. Berkowitz SD, Granger CB, Pieper KS, et al. Incidence and predictors of bleeding after contemporary thrombolytic therapy for myocardial infarction. *Circulation* 1997;95:2508–2516.
15. Yusuf S, Peto R, Lewis S, et al. Beta-blockade during and after myocardial infarction: an overview of the randomized trials. *Prog Cardiovasc Dis* 1985;27:335–371. (Search date not stated; primary sources: computer-aided search of the literature; manual search of reference lists and inquiries to colleagues about relevant papers)
16. Sleight P for the ISIS Study Group. Beta blockade early in acute myocardial infarction. *Am J Cardiol* 1987;60:6A–12A.
17. First International Study of Infarct Survival (ISIS-1). Randomised trial of intravenous atenolol among 16,027 cases of suspected acute myocardial infarction. *Lancet* 1986;ii:57–66.
18. Roberts R, Rogers WJ, Mueller HS, et al. Immediate versus deferred beta-blockade following thrombolytic therapy in patients with acute myocardial infarction: results of the thrombolysis in myocardial infarction (TIMI) II-B study. *Circulation* 1991;83:422–437.
19. ACE-inhibitor MI Collaborative Group. Indications for ACE inhibitors in the early treatment of acute myocardial infarction: systemic overview of indi-

vidual data from 100,000 patients in randomized trials. *Circulation* 1998;97:2202–2212.
20. Pfeffer MA, Braunwald E, Moye LA, et al. Effect of captopril on mortality and morbidity in patients with left ventricular dysfunction after myocardial infarction. *N Engl J Med* 1992; 327:669-677.
21. The Acute Infarction Ramipril Efficacy (AIRE) Study Investigators. Effect of ramipril on mortality and morbidity of survivors of acute myocardial infarction with clinical evidence of heart failure. *Lancet* 1998;1993:821-828.
22. The Trandolapril Cardiac Evaluation (TRACE) Study Group. A clinical trial of the angiotensin-converting-enzyme inhibitor trandolapril in patients with left ventricular dysfunction after myocardial infarction. *N Engl J Med* 1995;333:1670-6.
23. Yusuf S, Collins R, MacMahon S, Peto R. Effect of intravenous nitrates on mortality in acute myocardial infarction: an overview of the randomised trials. *Lancet* 1988;1:1088—1092. (Search date: not stated; primary sources literature, colleagues, investigators and pharmaceutical companies.)
24. Fourth International Study of Infarct Survival (ISIS-4) Collaborative Group. ISIS-4: a randomised factorial trial assessing early oral captopril, oral mononitrate, and intravenous magnesium sulphate in 58,050 patients with suspected acute myocardial infarction. *Lancet* 1995;345:669–685.
25. Gruppo Italiano per lo studio della Sopravvivenza nell'infarto miocardico (GISSI). GISSI-3: effects of lisinopril and transdermal glyceryl trinitrate singly and together on 6-week mortality and ventricular function after acute myocardial infarction. *Lancet* 1994;343:1115–1122.
26. Wilcox RG, Hampton JR, Banks DC, et al. Early nifedipine in acute myocardial infarction: the TRENT study. *BMJ* 1986;293:1204–1208.
27. Goldbourt U, Behar S, Reicher-Reiss H, et al. Trial of early administration of nifedipine in suspected acute myocardial infarction: the secondary prevention reinfarction Israel nifedipine trial 2 study. *Arch Intern Med* 1993;153:345–353.
28. The Danish Study Group on Verapamil in Myocardial Infarction. Verapamil in acute myocardial infarction. *Eur Heart J* 1984;5:516–528.
29. Yusuf S, Furberg CD. Effects of calcium channel blockers on survival after myocardial infarction. *Cardiovasc Drugs Ther* 1987;1:343–344.
30. Teo KK, Yusuf S, Furberg CD. Effects of prophylactic antiarrhythmic drug therapy in acute myocardial infarction: an overview of results from randomized controlled trials. *JAMA* 1993;270: 1589–1595. (Search date not stated; primary sources MEDLINE and correspondence with investigators and pharmaceutical companies.)
31. The Multicenter Diltiazem Post Infarction Trial Research Group. The effect of diltiazem on mortality and reinfarction after myocardial infarction. *N Engl J Med* 1988;319:385–392.
32. Weaver WD, Simes RJ, Betriu A, et al. Comparison of primary coronary angioplasty and intravenous thrombolytic therapy for acute myocardial infarction: a quantitative review. *JAMA* 1997;278:2093–2098. (Search date March 1996; primary sources MEDLINE and scientific session abstracts of stated journals.)
33. The GUSTO IIb Angioplasty Substudy Investigators. A clinical trial comparing primary coronary angioplasty with tissue plasminogen activator for acute myocardial infarction. *N Engl J Med* 1997;336:1621–1628.
34. Yusuf S, Pogue J. Primary angioplasty compared with thrombolytic therapy for acute myocardial infarction [editorial]. *JAMA* 1997;278:2110–2111.
35. Van de Werf F, Topol EJ, Lee KL, et al. Variations in patient management and outcomes for acute myocardial infarction in the United States and other countries: results from the GUSTO trial. *JAMA* 1995;273:1586–1591.

Shamir R Mehta, MD, FRCPC
Interventional Cardiologist
Clinical Scholar
Department of Medicine
Division of Cardiology
McMaster University
Hamilton
Ontario
Canada

Salim Yusuf, DPhil, FRCPC
Professor of Medicine
Director, Division of Cardiology
McMaster University
Hamilton
Ontario
Canada

Competing interests: SRM, none declared. SY has received honoraria for speaking and consulting. SY has also received research grants from over 10 companies.

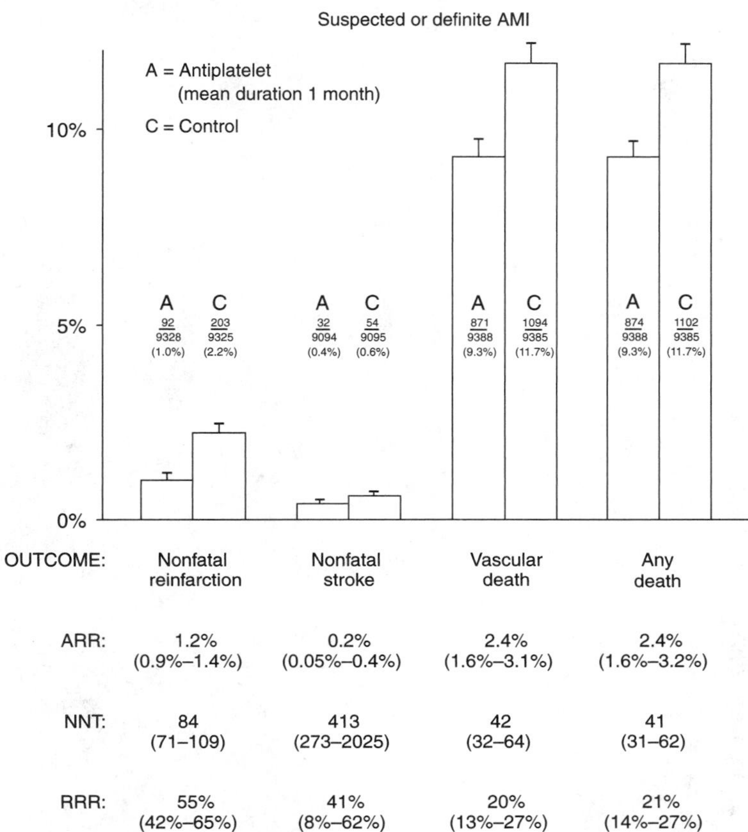

FIGURE 1 **Absolute effects of antiplatelet treatment on various outcomes in patients with a prior suspected or definite AMI.[3] The columns show the absolute risks over 1 month for each category; the error bars are the upper 95% CI. In the "any death" column, nonvascular deaths are represented by lower horizontal lines. The table displays for each outcome the absolute risk reduction (ARR), the number of patients needing treatment for 1 month to avoid one additional event (NNT), and the relative risk reduction (RRR), with their 95% CIs. (*See* text p. 64.) Published with permission.[3]**

TABLE 1 **Direct randomized comparisons of the standard streptokinase regimen with various tPA-based fibrinolytic regimens in patients with suspected AMI in the GISSI-2, ISIS-3, and GUSTO-1 trials.[9–11]** (*See* text p. 65.)

Trial and treatment	No. of patients randomized	Any stroke	Any death	Death not related to stroke[†]	Stroke or death
GISSI-2[‡]					
Streptokinase	10,396	98 (0.9)	958 (9.2)	916 (8.8)	1014 (9.8)
tPA	10,372	136 (1.3)	993 (9.6)	931 (9.0)	1067 (10.3)
Effect/1000 patients treated with tPA instead of streptokinase		3.7±1.5 more	3.6±4.0 more	1.7±4.0 more	5.3±4.2 more
ISIS-3[§]					
Streptokinase	13,780	141 (1.0	1455 (10.6)	1389 (10.1)	1530 (11.1)
tPA	13,746	188 (1.4)	1418 (10.3)	1325 (9.6)	1513 (11.0)
Effect/1000 patients treated with tPA instead of streptokinase		3.5±1.3 more	2.4±3.7 fewer	4.4±3.6 fewer	1.0±3.8 fewer
GUSTO-1[¶]					
Streptokinase (subcutaneous heparin)	9841	117 (1.2)	712 (7.3)	666 (6.8)	783 (8.0)
Streptokinase (intravenous heparin)	10,410	144 (1.4)	763 (7.4)	709 (6.8)	853 (8.2)
tPA alone	10,396	161 (1.6)	653 (6.3)	585 (5.6)	746 (7.2)
tPA plus streptokinase	10,374	170 (1.6)	723 (7.0)	647 (6.2)	817 (7.9)
Effect/1000 patients treated with tPA-based regimens instead of streptinokinase		3.0±1.2 more	6.6±2.5 fewer	8.6±2.4 fewer	5.5±2.6 fewer
*X*2/2 heterogeneity of effects between 3 trials		0.7	5.6	7.0	5.4
p value		0.3	0.06	0.03	0.07
Weighted average of all 3 trials*					
Effect/1000 patient treated with tPA-based regimens instead of streptokinase		3.3±0.8 more	2.9±1.9 fewer	4.9±1.8 fewer	1.6±1.9 fewer
p value		<0.001	>0.1	0.01	0.4

Values are number (%). This table should not be used to make direct nonrandomized comparisons between the absolute event rates in different trials, because the patient populations may have differed substantially in age and other characteristics. Deaths recorded throughtout the first 35 days are included for GISSI-2 and ISIS-3 and throughout the first 30 days for GUSTO-1. Numbers randomized and numbers with follow-up are from the ISIS-3 report[10] and GUSTO-1[11] (supplemented with revised GUSTO-1 data from the National Auxiliary Publications Service), and numbers with events and the percentages (based on patients with follow-up) are from the ISIS-3 report[10] and Van de Werf et al[35] plus-minus values are ± SD. In all three trials, streptokinase was given in an intravenous infusions of 1.5 million units over a period of 1 hour.

† Death not related to stroke was defined as death without recorded stroke. ‡In the GISSI-2 trial, the tPA regimen involved an initial bolus of 10 mg, followed by 50 mg in the first hour and 20 mg in each of the second and third hours. §In the ISIS-3 trial, the tPA regimen involved 40,000 clot-lysis units per kilogram of body weight as an initial bolus, followed by 360,000 units per kilogram in the first hour and 67,000 units per kilogram in each of the next 3 hours. ¶In the GUSTO-1 trial, the t-PA alone regimen involved an initial bolus of 15 mg, followed by 0.75 mg per kilogram (up to 50 mg) in the first 30 minutes and 0.5 mg per kilogram (up to 35 mg) in the next hour in the GUSTO-1 trial the other tPA-based regimen involved 0.1 mg of tPA per kilogram (up to 9 mg) as an initial bolus and 0.9 mg per kilogram (up to 81 mg) in the remainder of the first hour, plus 1 million units of streptokinase in the first hour. *The weights are proportional to the sample sizes of the trials, so this average gives most weight to the GUSTO-1 trial and least to the GISSI-2 trials.[9] Reproduced from Collins R, Peto R, Baigent BM, Sleight DM. Aspirin, heparin and fibrinolytic therapy in suspected AMI. *N Engl J Med* 1997;336:847–60, with permission of the publisher.

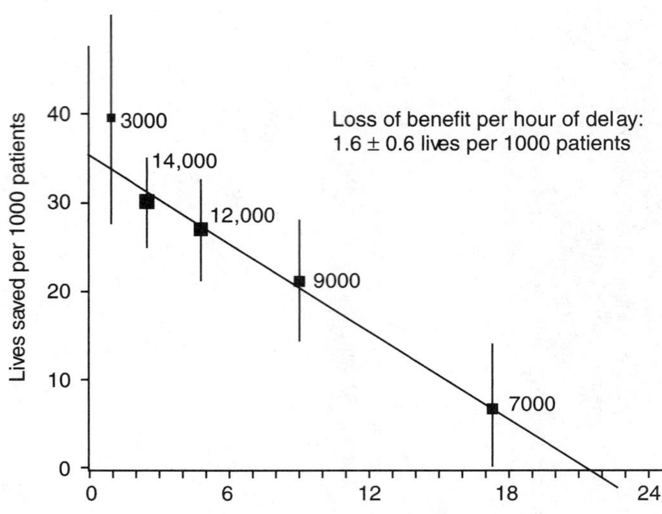

FIGURE 2 **Absolute number of lives saved at 1 month per 1000 patients receiving thrombolytic treatment plotted against the time from the onset of symptoms to randomization among 45,000 patients with ST-segment elevation or bundle branch block.[7] Numbers along the curve are the number of patients treated at different times. (*See* text p. 64.) Published with permission.[8]**

Secondary prevention of ischemic cardiac events

Clinical Evidence writers on secondary prevention of ischemic cardiac events

QUESTIONS

INTERVENTIONS

Key Messages

Antithrombotic treatment

- A collaborative overview found that antiplatelet treatment produces substantial reductions in the risk of serious vascular events.
- The overview found that aspirin (75 mg/d) is as effective as higher doses. We found no clear evidence that any other antiplatelet regimen is definitely superior to medium-dose aspirin (i.e., 75 to 325 mg/d) in the prevention of vascular events. Clopidogrel is a safe and effective alternative to aspirin. A systematic review found that anticoagulants produce a similar reduction in the risk of serious vascular events to that produced by aspirin. However, the greater risk of hemorrhage and the need for regular monitoring of oral anticoagulants make medium-dose aspirin the most appropriate first-line

antithrombotic treatment. We found no clear evidence that the addition of oral anticoagulants to aspirin produces additional benefit.

Other drug treatments

- Systematic reviews have found that:
  - β-Blockers reduce the risk of all cause mortality, coronary mortality, recurrent nonfatal myocardial infarction (MI), and sudden death in people after MI.
  - In people who have had a MI and have left ventricular dysfunction, ACE inhibitors reduce rates of death, hospitalization for congestive heart failure, and recurrent nonfatal MI. The effects of ACE inhibitors in people who have had a MI but do not have left ventricular dysfunction have not yet been evaluated adequately.
  - The use of class I antiarrhythmic agents after MI increases the risk of cardiovascular mortality and sudden death.
  - Amiodarone reduces the risk of sudden death and marginally reduces overall mortality in people at high risk of death after MI. We found limited evidence on the effects of D-sotalol, namely that it may be harmful rather than beneficial in this setting.
  - Calcium-channel blockers do not reduce mortality in people after MI or with chronic coronary heart disease. Diltiazem and verapamil may reduce rates of reinfarction and refractory angina in people after MI who do not have heart failure.
- Data from the only large well-designed randomized controlled trial (RCT) published to date provide no evidence that hormone replacement therapy (HRT) reduces major cardiovascular events in postmenopausal women with established coronary artery disease, despite strong evidence from RCTs that HRT improves some cardiovascular risk factors.

Cholesterol reduction

- A systematic review found that cholesterol lowering with statins substantially reduces the risk of cardiovascular mortality and morbidity with no increase in noncardiovascular mortality.

Blood pressure reduction

- We found no direct evidence of the effects of blood pressure lowering in people with established coronary artery disease. Observational studies and extrapolation from trials of blood pressure reduction in people with no history of ischemic cardiac events support the lowering of blood pressure in those at high risk of ischemic coronary events. The evidence for benefit is strongest for β-blockers.

Nondrug treatments

- The role of vitamin E, β-carotene, and vitamin C remains unclear.
- Evidence from RCTs shows that advising coronary patients to eat more fish (particularly fatty fish) or more fruit and vegetables, bread, pasta, potatoes, olive oil, and rapeseed margarine (i.e., a more Mediterranean diet) may result in a substantial survival benefit. We found no strong evidence from RCTs for a beneficial effect of low-fat or high-fiber diets on major nonfatal coronary artery disease events or coronary artery disease mortality.
- Systematic reviews have found that cardiac rehabilitation improves coronary risk factors and reduces the risk of major cardiac events in patients after MI. The role of exercise alone in reducing the risk of adverse cardiovascular outcomes is not clear.
- We found no RCTs of the effects of smoking cessation on cardiovascular events in people with coronary artery disease. Epidemiologic studies indicate that people with coronary artery disease who stop smoking rapidly reduce their risk of recurrent coronary events or death. The use of nicotine patches seems safe in people with coronary artery disease.

- One systematic review of mainly poor quality RCTs suggests that psychological and stress management may decrease rates of myocardial infarction or cardiac death in people with coronary artery disease.

Surgical treatments

- Randomized controlled trials (RCTs) performed up to the mid-1980s found that, in comparison to medical treatment, coronary artery bypass grafting carries a greater risk of death in the first year but reduces the risk of death from coronary artery disease at 5 and 10 years. Greatest benefit occurs in people with more severe disease (multivessel disease, left ventricular dysfunction, or MI). We found no evidence of increased protection against subsequent MI. A more recent RCT, using modern techniques and with optimal background medical treatment, found even greater superiority of revascularization.
- RCTs found that, in comparison to percutaneous transluminal coronary angioplasty, intracoronary stents afford superior acute and long-term clinical and angiographic results.

DEFINITION Secondary prevention in this context is the long-term management of people with a prior acute MI, and of people at high risk of ischemic cardiac events for other reasons, such as a history of angina or coronary surgical procedures.

INCIDENCE/ PREVALENCE Coronary artery disease is the leading cause of death in developed countries and is becoming a major cause of mortality and morbidity in developing countries. There are pronounced international, regional, and temporal differences in death rates. In the USA, the prevalence of overt coronary artery disease approaches 4%.[1]

ETIOLOGY Most ischemic cardiac events are associated with atherosclerotic plaques that can cause acute obstruction of coronary vessels. Atherosclerosis is more likely in elderly people, in those with established coronary artery disease, and in those with risk factors (e.g., smoking, hypertension, high cholesterol, diabetes mellitus).

PROGNOSIS Approximately half of those who suffer an acute MI die before they reach hospital. Of those hospitalized, 7% to 15% die in hospital and another 7% to 15% die during the following year. Observational studies suggest a decline in 1-year mortality in the last decade of life.[2] People who survive the acute stage of MI fall into three prognostic groups based on their baseline risk (see Table 1): high (20% of all survivors), moderate (55%), and low (25%) risk. Long-term prognosis depends on the degree of left ventricular dysfunction, the presence of residual ischemia, and the extent of any electrical instability. Further risk stratification procedures include evaluation of left ventricular function (by echocardiography or nuclear ventriculography) and of myocardial ischemia (by noninvasive stress testing).[5–9] Those with low left ventricular ejection fraction, ischemia, or poor functional status may be evaluated further by cardiac catheterization and may benefit from revascularization.[10]

AIMS To improve long-term survival and quality of life, to prevent (recurrent) MI, unstable angina, left ventricular dysfunction, heart failure, and sudden cardiac death, and to restore and maintain normal activities.

OUTCOMES Mortality (total, cardiovascular, coronary, sudden death, noncardiovascular), morbidity (MI, severe angina, and stroke), or quality of life.

METHODS Searches of the Cochrane Library, MEDLINE, and EMBASE databases were performed in July 1998. Recent appropriate systematic reviews were identified as well as more recent RCTs.

QUESTION What are the effects of antithrombotic treatment?

Cathie Sudlow, Colin Baigent

OPTION ANTIPLATELET TREATMENT

Prolonged antiplatelet treatment produces substantial reductions in the risk of serious vascular events among patients at high risk of ischemic cardiac events. For prolonged use, aspirin 75 mg/d is as effective as higher doses. Although the risks of gastrointestinal bleeding with aspirin doses in the range 75 to 325 mg/d appear similar, it seems reasonable to choose the lowest conveniently available dose in this range. We found no clear evidence that any other antiplatelet regimen is superior to medium-dose aspirin (i.e., 75–325 mg/d) in the prevention of vascular events, although clopidogrel is a safe and effective (but more expensive) alternative to aspirin.

Benefits: **Antiplatelet treatment versus placebo:** The most recent antiplatelet trialists' (APT) collaborative overview, published in 1994, found that a month or more of antiplatelet treatment produced a highly significant reduction of approximately one quarter in the odds of a vascular event (nonfatal MI, nonfatal stroke, or vascular death) among approximately 70,000 patients at high risk of occlusive arterial disease.[11] Although most of these patients were at high risk of ischemic cardiac events, patients with established coronary artery disease were at particularly high risk. These included those with a history of MI, those with stable angina, and those who had undergone coronary revascularization procedures. Among the 20,000 patients with a prior MI, antiplatelet treatment prevented 18 nonfatal recurrent MIs, six nonfatal strokes, and 13 vascular deaths per 1000 patients treated for approximately 2 years. There was also a clear reduction in all-cause mortality (Figure 1). **Different daily doses of aspirin:** Approximately two thirds of the RCTs in the 1994 APT overview involved an aspirin regimen, and medium-dose aspirin (75–325 mg/d) was the most widely tested regimen. Indirect comparisons showed that daily doses of less than 160 mg (mostly 75–150 mg), 160 to 325 mg, and 500 to 1500 mg prevented similar proportions of vascular events among high-risk patients, whereas direct comparisons also showed that daily aspirin doses of 75 to 325 mg or 500 to 1500 mg were similarly effective.[11] In the main APT analyses, limited numbers of patients at high risk of ischemic cardiac events had been studied in trials using daily doses of less than 160 mg, but clear evidence for the effectiveness of aspirin 75 mg/d among patients at high risk of ischemic cardiac events has subsequently become available from the Swedish angina pectoris aspirin trial (SAPAT), which randomized approximately 2000 patients with stable angina to aspirin 75 mg/d or placebo.[12] Aspirin produced a proportional reduction of 34% (95% CI 24%–49%) in the risk of the primary outcome of "MI and sudden death." **Alternative antiplatelet regimens to aspirin:** In the

APT 1994 overview, there was no evidence that any antiplatelet regimen was more effective than medium-dose aspirin alone in the prevention of vascular events.[11] More recently, the clopidogrel versus aspirin in patients at risk of ischemic events (CAPRIE) study compared the effects of clopidogrel (a thienopyridine agent similar to ticlopidine) versus aspirin (325 mg/d) among approximately 20,000 high-risk patients with a recent MI, a recent ischemic stroke, or peripheral arterial disease.[13] Clopidogrel produced an 8.7% (95% CI 0.3%–16.5%) proportional reduction in the risk of a vascular event (defined in this trial as a nonfatal MI, nonfatal ischemic stroke, or nonhemorrhagic vascular death) that was conventionally significant ($p=0.04$). A similar proportional reduction in vascular events was observed among approximately 3500 high-risk patients included in previous trials comparing ticlopidine versus aspirin.[11] Hence, if the trials of thienopyridines (clopidogrel and ticlopidine) are considered together, they suggest that such agents are at least as effective as medium-dose aspirin and may offer greater protection against vascular events. However, the size of any absolute benefits that may arise from replacing aspirin with clopidogrel among particular types of high-risk patients remains statistically uncertain; overall, approximately five vascular events were avoided per 1000 patients treated per year, but the 95% CI ranged from the prevention of 10 such vascular events to minimal absolute benefit.

Harms: Serious, potentially life-threatening bleeding is the most important adverse effect of antiplatelet treatment. Intracranial hemorrhages are uncommon, but they are often fatal and usually cause significant disability in survivors and thus constitute the main hazard that could offset treatment benefit. The APT 1994 overview showed that any excess risk of intracranial bleeding with antiplatelet treatment was small, at most one or two per 1000 patients per year in trials of long-term treatment.[11] Unlike serious vascular events, extracranial bleeds rarely result in permanent disability or death. Antiplatelet treatment produced a small but significant excess of nonfatal major extracranial bleeds of three per 1000, but there was no clear excess of fatal extracranial bleeds.[11] Among patients at high risk of ischemic cardiac events, therefore, the large absolute reductions in serious vascular events produced by antiplatelet treatment far outweigh any absolute hazards. In a direct randomized comparison, aspirin 1200 mg/d was associated with more gastrointestinal bleeding than 325 mg/d,[14] but there is no definite evidence for a variation in gastrointestinal bleeding risk in the range 75 to 325 mg/d. Clopidogrel was found to be safe in CAPRIE, with a much lower incidence of neutropenia than had been observed previously in trials of ticlopidine.[13]

OPTION ORAL ANTICOAGULANTS IN THE ABSENCE OF ANTIPLATELET TREATMENT

In the absence of antiplatelet treatment, oral anticoagulants produce a similar proportional reduction in the risk of serious vascular events to that produced by aspirin. However, the more substantial risks of bleeding and need for regular monitoring of oral anticoagulants make medium-dose aspirin the most appropriate first-line antithrombotic treatment for people at high risk of ischemic cardiac events.

Benefits: A systematic overview of RCTs of the effects of oral anticoagulation (with most regimens maintaining INR > 3) versus control in the absence of antiplatelet treatment among approximately 10,000 patients with a prior MI found that anticoagulation produced a 39% reduction in the odds of stroke or death ($2p < 0.0001$).[15] This corresponded to an absolute reduction of approximately 15 major vascular events per 1000 patients treated per year.

Harms: There was an excess of four to five major extracranial bleeds per 1000 patients treated per year.[15] Data on the effects on intracranial bleeding were not available for all trials included in this overview, but in the two largest trials (together including approximately 5000 patients) there was an excess of approximately three intracranial bleeds per 1000 patients per year.[16,17]

Comment: Medium-dose aspirin (75–325 mg/d) produces similar proportional reduction in the risk of serious vascular events to those produced by oral anticoagulation. However, aspirin does not require regular monitoring, and any associated bleeding risks are relatively small (*see* Antiplatelet Treatment above). Medium-dose aspirin is therefore the most appropriate first-line antithrombotic treatment for people at high risk of ischemic cardiac events.

OPTION ORAL ANTICOAGULANTS IN ADDITION TO ANTIPLATELET TREATMENT

We found no clear evidence that the addition of low-intensity oral anticoagulation (target INR < 1.5) to aspirin produces additional benefit. The effects of adding a more intensive anticoagulant regimen are unknown but are being assessed in ongoing RCTs.

Benefits: Two recent trials have assessed whether the addition of an appropriate oral anticoagulant regimen to medium-dose aspirin may produce a further worthwhile reduction in vascular events.[18,19] In the coumadin aspirin reinfarction study (CARS), approximately 7000 patients with a prior MI were randomized to aspirin 160 mg/d versus aspirin 80 mg with 3 mg fixed-dose warfarin daily. (Randomization to a third group receiving 80 mg aspirin with 1 mg fixed dose warfarin daily was terminated early.) Because daily aspirin doses of 80 mg and 160 mg would be expected to have similar effects on serious vascular events (*see* Antiplatelet Treatment above), the primary comparison can be regarded as an assessment of the addition of low-intensity warfarin (median INR 1.2) to medium-dose aspirin. During a median follow-up of approximately 14 months, there were no detectable differences between the two main treatment groups in the risks of any of the primary events (nonfatal MI, nonfatal ischemic stroke, cardiovascular death), either separately or in combination.[18] In the post–coronary artery bypass grafting (CABG) trial approximately 1300 patients who had previously undergone CABG were randomized to warfarin (up to 4 mg/d, INR ~1.4) versus placebo (and, in a 2 × 2 factorial design, to receive either aggressive or moderate lipid-lowering treatment). All patients were encouraged to take aspirin. After a mean follow-up of approximately 4 years, there were no significant differences between the warfarin and placebo groups in the primary outcome of progression of significant graft atherosclerosis or in the combined clinical outcome of MI, stroke, vascular death, or a further revascularization procedure.[19]

Harms: In CARS, there was a nonsignificant excess of seven major extracranial bleeds per 1000 patients treated for approximately year with 3 mg warfarin and 80 mg aspirin compared with 160 mg aspirin alone, but with no apparent excess of intracranial bleeds.[18] No excess of major extracranial bleeds occurred with warfarin in the post CABG trial, and intracranial hemorrhages were not reported separately.[19]

Comment: The addition of low-intensity oral anticoagulant treatment (i.e., INR <1.5) to aspirin among patients at high risk of ischemic cardiac events does not seem to produce further clinical benefit. But, because such regimens do not produce a clear excess of major bleeding, adding a more intensive oral anticoagulant regimen (e.g., INR 2.0–2.5) to aspirin may be beneficial without producing unacceptable bleeding risks. This question is currently being assessed in several ongoing RCTs.

QUESTION What are the effects of other drug treatments?

Eva Lonn

OPTION β-BLOCKERS

We found strong evidence from systematic reviews of RCTs that β-blockers reduce the risk of all-cause mortality, coronary mortality, recurrent nonfatal MI, and sudden death in people after MI. Most benefit is seen in those at highest risk of death after an MI (> 50 years old; previous MI, angina pectoris, hypertension, or treatment with digitalis; transient mechanical or electrical failure; higher heart rate at study entry). Approximately one quarter of patients suffer adverse effects.

Benefits: **Survival and reinfarction:** A systematic review published in 1993 identified 26 RCTs in over 24,000 people in whom β-blockers were started orally within days or weeks of an acute MI (late intervention trials) and continued for between 6 weeks to 3 years. Most trials followed participants for 1 year. The review found improved survival in people given β-blockers (RRR 0.23, 95% CI 0.14–0.30).[20] A previous systematic review published in 1985 identified 24 RCTs of long-term use of β-blockers after MI. It found reductions in total mortality (~ 20%), sudden death (~ 30%), and nonfatal reinfarction (~ 25%). The number of people who would need to be treated for 1 year with a β-blocker rather than placebo was 48 to prevent one additional death, 56 to prevent one additional recurrent MI, and 63 to prevent one additional sudden death.[21] **Anginal symptoms:** We found no good RCTs evaluating the antianginal effects of β-blockers in people after MI. One trial found atenolol more effective than placebo in people with chronic stable effort angina or silent ischemia.[22] **Different types of β-blockers:** The earlier review found no differences between β-blockers with and without cardioselectivity or membrane-stabilizing properties, but it raised concerns about the lack of efficacy of β-blockers with intrinsic sympathomimetic activity in long-term management after MI.[21] These concerns were addressed by the Acebutolol Prevention of Secondary Infarction (APSI) trial in 607 people at high risk after MI, which found that acebutolol, a β-blocker with moderate partial agonist activity, decreased 1 year mortality (AR of death: 11% with placebo, 6% with acebutolol; RRR 0.48, 95% CI 0.09–0.71).[23] **Effects in different subgroups:** A systematic review published in 1988 evaluated 1-year mortality in clinically relevant subgroups.[24] It identified nine RCTs comparing placebo versus β-blockers started more than 24 hours after onset of symptoms of acute MI and continued for 9 to 24 months. Pooled analysis of individual patient data ($n = 13\,679$) found that the beneficial effects of β-blockers on mortality seemed comparable in men and women. The highest absolute benefit from β-blockers was seen in subgroups with the highest baseline risks (i.e., those with the highest mortality on placebo): those over 50 years of age; those with a history of previous MI, angina pectoris, hypertension, or treatment with digitalis; those with transient signs or symptoms of mechanical or electrical failure in the early phases of MI; and those with a higher heart rate at study entry. Low-risk subgroups had smaller absolute benefit, which was inconsistent across trials.

Harms: Adverse effects include shortness of breath, bronchospasm, bradycardia, hypotension, heart block, cold hands and feet, diarrhea, fatigue, reduced sexual activity, depression, nightmares, faintness, insomnia, blacking out, and hallucinations. Rates vary in different studies. One RCT reported an ARI for any adverse effect on propranolol compared with placebo of 0.24 (95% CI not available). Serious adverse effects were uncommon and only a small proportion of patients withdrew as a result.[25]

Comment: Continued benefit has been reported from the use of β-blockers up to 6 years after MI (ARR for mortality 0.059, 95% CI not available, $p = 0.003$; RRR 0.18). However, the study was not blinded after 33 months.

OPTION ANGIOTENSIN-CONVERTING–ENZYME (ACE) INHIBITORS

In people who have had an MI and have left ventricular dysfunction, there is strong evidence from a systematic review of RCTs that ACE inhibitors reduce rates of death, hospitalization for congestive heart failure, and recurrent nonfatal MI. The effects of ACE inhibitors in people who have had an MI but do not have left ventricular dysfunction has not yet been evaluated adequately.

Benefits: **In people with low left ventricular ejection fraction:** A systematic review[26] published in 1997 identified three RCTs comparing placebo versus ACE inhibitors (captopril, ramipril, or trandolapril) started 3 to 16 days after acute MI and continued for 15 to 42 months. It analyzed individual patient data from 5966 people with a recent MI and with clinical manifestations of congestive heart failure or moderate left ventricular dysfunction (left ventricular ejection fraction ≤35%–40%). ACE inhibitors significantly reduced rates of death (RRR 0.26, 95% CI 0.17–0.34, NNT 17 people needed treating for approximately 2 years to prevent one death), hospitalization for congestive heart failure (RRR 0.27, 95% CI 0.15–0.37, NNT 28), and recurrent nonfatal MI (RRR 0.20, 95% CI 0.06–0.31, NNT 43). **In people without impaired ventricular fraction or evidence of congestive heart failure:** We found no systematic review or RCTs.

Harms: The major adverse effects reported in these trials were cough (ARI versus placebo of 5%–10%), dizziness, hypotension (5%–10%), renal failure (<3%), hyperkalemia (<3%), angina, syncope, diarrhea (2%) and, for captopril, alteration in taste (2% of captopril users).[26]

Comment: The use of ACE inhibitors in people with a recent MI without symptoms or signs of CHF and with no or only mild impairment in left ventricular function is currently under investigation in the heart outcomes prevention evaluation (HOPE) study in 9541 people, in the prevention of events with ACE inhibitors (PEACE) study in 8000 people, and in the EUROPA study in 10,500 people.[27]

OPTION CLASS I ANTIARRHYTHMIC AGENTS (QUINIDINE, PROCAINAMIDE, DISOPYRIMIDE, ENCAINIDE, FLECAINIDE, MORIZICINE)

A systematic review of RCTs has found that the use of class I antiarrhythmic agents after MI increases the risk of cardiovascular mortality and sudden death.

Benefits: None (*see* Harms).

Harms: A systematic review published in 1993 identified 51 RCTs comparing placebo versus class I antiarrhythmic drugs, given both acutely and later in the management of MI, in 23,229 people.[20] The review found that the antiarrhythmic agents increased mortality (AR of death 5.6% vs. 5.0% on placebo, OR 1.14, 95% CI 1.01–1.28). In individual RCTs, the clearest evidence for harm emerged from the Cardiac Arrhythmia Suppression Trials (CAST I and CAST II). CAST I compared encainide or flecainide versus placebo in 1498 people with MI and with asymptomatic or mildly symptomatic ventricular arrhythmia. After 10 months of follow-up, there was an increase in the RR of death or cardiac arrest in actively treated patients (RR 2.38, 95% CI 1.59–3.57), equivalent to one additional death or cardiac arrest for every 17 patients treated for approximately 10 months with encainide or flecainide rather than placebo.[28]

Comment: The evidence implies that these drugs should not be used in people after MI or with significant coronary artery disease.

OPTION CLASS III ANTIARRHYTHMIC AGENTS (AMIODARONE, D-SOTALOL)

Two systematic reviews of RCTs have found that amiodarone reduces the risk of sudden death and marginally reduces overall mortality in people at high risk of death after MI. Limited evidence on the effects of D-sotalol suggests that it may be harmful rather than beneficial in this setting.

Benefits: A systematic review published in 1997 analyzed individual patient data from 13 RCTs of amiodarone in high-risk patients. A total of 6553 patients were involved, 78% with a recent MI from eight trials and 22% with congestive heart failure from five trials.[29] Most trials were placebo controlled with a mean follow-up of approximately 1.5 years. People were selected with a recent MI and a high risk of death from cardiac arrhythmia (based on low left ventricular ejection fraction, frequent ventricular premature depolarizations or nonsustained ventricular tachycardia, but no history of sustained symptomatic ventricular tachycardia or ventricular fibrillation). Patients with congestive heart failure were symptomatic but compensated and did not have a recent MI, although in most cases the heart failure was ischemic in origin. All trials used a loading dose of amiodarone (400 mg/d for 28 days or 800 mg/d for 14 days) followed by a maintenance dose (200–400 mg/d). Amiodarone significantly reduced total mortality (ARs 10.9 % per year on amiodarone, 12.3% per year with placebo; RRR 0.13, 95% CI 0.01–0.22, NNT 71 people treated per year to avoid one additional death) and rates of sudden cardiac death (RRR 0.29, 95% CI 0.15–0.41, NNT 59). Amiodarone had similar effects in the post-MI and congestive heart failure studies. Comparable findings emerged from another systematic review published in 1997. This reviewed amiodarone trials in 5864 people with MI, congestive heart failure, left ventricular dysfunction, or cardiac arrest.[30]

Harms: Adverse events leading to discontinuation of amiodarone, and expressed per 100 person-years, were hypothyroidism (7.0 vs. 1.1 on placebo, OR 7.3), hyperthyroidism (1.4 vs. 0.5, OR 2.5), peripheral neuropathy (0.5 vs. 0.2, OR 2.8), lung infiltrates (1.6 vs. 0.5, OR 3.1), bradycardia (2.4 vs. 0.8, OR 2.6), and liver dysfunction (1.0 vs. 0.4, OR 2.7).[29]

Comment: The reviews' conclusions are probably specific to amiodarone.[29,30] One RCT found increased mortality with the class III antiarrhythmic agent D-sotalol compared with placebo in 3121 patients with MI and left ventricular dysfunction (ARs for death 5% vs. 3.1%; RR 1.65, 95% CI 1.15–2.36). The trial was terminated prematurely after less than 1 year of follow-up.[31] The two largest RCTs of amiodarone after MI found a favorable interaction between β-blockers and amiodarone with additional reduction in cardiac mortality.[32,33]

OPTION CALCIUM-CHANNEL BLOCKERS

A systematic review of RCTs found no benefit from calcium-channel blockers in people after MI or with chronic coronary artery disease. Diltiazem and verapamil may reduce rates of reinfarction and refractory angina in people after MI who do not have heart failure.

Benefits: A systematic review published in 1993 identified 24 RCTs of calcium-channel blockers (including dihydropyridines, diltiazem, and verapamil) administered early or late during the course of acute MI or unstable angina and continued in the intermediate or long term.[20] Two of the trials used angiographic coronary regression as an outcome in people with stable coronary artery disease treated with calcium-channel blockers. The review found overall no significant difference in the AR of death compared with placebo (AR 9.7% vs. 9.3%, ARI on calcium-channel blockers compared with placebo 0.004, 95% CI –0.004 to 0.012, OR 1.04, 95% CI 0.95–1.14). **Diltiazem and verapamil:** The review found no significant effect compared with placebo (OR 0.95, 95% CI 0.82–1.09).[20] Three trials comparing diltiazem or verapamil versus placebo reported benefit on active treatment (decreased rates of recurrent infarction and refractory angina) but only for those people without signs or symptoms of heart failure. For those with clinical manifestations of heart failure, the trends were toward harm.[34–36] **Dihydropyridines:** The review found no significant effect compared with placebo (OR 1.16, 95% CI 0.99–1.35). Several individual RCTs of dihydropyridines found increased mortality, particularly when these agents were started early in the course of acute MI and in the absence of β-blockers.

Harms: Adverse effects reported on verapamil and diltiazem include atrioventricular block, atrial bradycardia, new-onset heart failure, hypotension, dizziness, edema, rash, constipation, and pruritus.

Comment: Newer-generation dihydropyridines, such as amlodipine and felodipine, have not been well studied in people after MI but have been found to be safe in people with heart failure, including heart failure of ischemic origin.

OPTION HORMONE REPLACEMENT THERAPY

We found no clear evidence from RCTs that hormone replacement therapy reduces major cardiovascular events in postmenopausal women with established coronary artery disease, despite strong evidence from RCTs that hormone replacement therapy improves some cardiovascular risk factors.

Benefits: **Combined estrogen and progestins:** No systematic review. One large RCT has evaluated the effects of estrogens plus progestins on clinical outcomes in 2763 postmenopausal women with coronary artery disease.[37] This found no benefit. It compared placebo versus conjugated equine estrogen 0.625 mg/d plus medroxyprogesterone acetate 2.5 mg/d for an average of 4.1 years. There were no differences in rates of nonfatal MI or deaths caused by coronary artery disease; 172 women on hormone replacement therapy and 176 women on placebo suffered an MI or death because of coronary artery disease (RRR compared with placebo 0.01, 95% CI –0.22 to 0.20). It also found no difference in the other secondary cardiovascular outcomes (coronary revascularization, unstable angina, congestive heart failure, resuscitated cardiac arrest, stroke or transient ischemic attack, and peripheral arterial disease) or in all-cause mortality. **Estrogen alone:** We found no good RCTs of estrogen alone (without progestins) in the secondary prevention of coronary artery disease in postmenopausal women. One RCT found that high-dose estrogen (5 mg conjugated equine estogens per day) was associated with increased risk of MI and thromboembolic events in men with pre-existing coronary artery disease.[38]

Harms: Pooled estimates from observational studies show an increased risk of endometrial cancer (RR > 8) and of breast cancer (RR 1.25–1.46) when estrogen is used for over 8 years. In most observational studies, the addition of progestins prevented endometrial cancer but not breast cancer. The risk of venous thromboembolism, including pulmonary embolism and deep vein thrombosis, was three to four times higher on hormone replacement therapy; however, because the incidence of venous thromboembolism is low in postmenopausal women, the absolute increase in risk was only approximately one to two additional cases of venous thromboembolism in 5000 users per year.[39] In the RCT described above,[37] more women in the hormone replacement therapy than in the placebo group experienced venous thromboembolism (34 vs. 12, OR 2.89, 95% CI 1.50–5.58) and gallbladder disease (84 vs. 62, OR 1.38, 95% CI 0.84–1.38).

Comment: Many observational studies have found reduced rates of clinical events caused by coronary artery disease in postmenopausal women using hormone replacement therapy, especially in women with coronary artery disease. Hormone users experienced 35% to 80% fewer recurrent events than nonusers.[40,41] Meanwhile, several RCTs have found that hormone replacement therapy improves cardiovascular risk factors.[42] It is not known whether studies longer than 4 years would show a benefit.

QUESTION What are the effects of cholesterol reduction?

Jeffrey L Probstfield

OPTION CHOLESTEROL-LOWERING DRUGS

A systematic review and large subsequent RCTs have found that cholesterol reduction in people at high risk of ischemic coronary events substantially reduces the risk of cardiovascular mortality, morbidity, and interventions, with no increase in noncardiovascular mortality and little increase in noncardiovascular morbidity. Benefit is related to an individual's baseline risk and to the degree of cholesterol lowering but does not seem to be influenced by the individual's absolute cholesterol concentration. Because they are generally at higher baseline risk, elderly people are likely to benefit more than younger people, but direct evidence of the effects of cholesterol-lowering drugs in older people (>75 years of age) is awaited. The available evidence does not yet indicate the most effective or cost-effective means of using cholesterol-lowering drugs along with other means of reducing cholesterol or interventions to modify other cardiovascular risk factors.

Benefits: **In people aged up to 75 years:** We found one systematic review published in 1998[43] and two large subsequent RCTs.[44,45] The review identified 43 RCTs with at least 2-years' follow-up. Participants were 96,227 people receiving pharmacotherapy, diet, surgery, or multifactorial interventions.[43] Fourteen trials compared pharmacotherapy versus placebo in 23,655 people with a history of ischemic cardiac events. The review found that, with the exception of hormone treatments, a fall of total cholesterol of 10% (~ 0.6 mM/L) was associated with an RRR for coronary artery disease of 0.15 and for total mortality of 0.11. The effect of statins was fully explained by the observed lowering of cholesterol. The RRR for coronary death and nonfatal MI in the five large statin trials was consistent across the trials, but the number of people needing treatment for 1 year to prevent one coronary death or nonfatal MI varied between the trials according to the AR of the placebo group (Table 2). Differences between the baseline cholesterol concentration of people recruited to each trial seemed to play no role in determining the results of the trials, at least in the ranges studied to date. The two subsequent

RCTs were in people with a history of ischemic cardiac events[44] or a saphenous vein CABG.[45] The first included 9014 people aged 31 to 75 years with a history of MI or unstable angina. Over 6 years compared with placebo, statins produced reductions in coronary artery disease death or nonfatal MI (ARs 15.9% placebo vs. 12.3% statin, ARR 0.036, RRR 0.24, 95% CI 0.15–0.32), total mortality (ARs 14.1% placebo vs. 11% statin; ARR 0.031; RRR 0.22, 95% CI 0.13–0.31), MI (ARs 10.3% placebo vs. 7.4% statin, ARR 0.029, RRR 0.29, 95% CI 0.18–0.38), stroke (ARs 4.5% placebo vs. 3.7% statin, RRR 0.19, 95% CI 0–0.34, $p = 0.048$), and coronary revascularization (ARs 15.7% placebo vs. 13.0% statin, ARR 0.027, RRR 0.20, 95% CI 0.10–0.28). The effect of cholesterol lowering on the RR of coronary artery disease death or nonfatal MI seemed broadly similar in all predefined subgroups (both sexes, at all ages studied, and at different levels of risk factors), although there was inadequate power to detect moderate differences in RRR between the subgroups.[44] **In people aged over 75 years:** No systematic review or RCTs (*see* Comment).

Harms: We found no systematic review of studies on harms. One double-blind RCT specifically investigated the long-term adverse effects of lovastatin against placebo in 8245 people over 48 weeks.[46] All eight long-term RCTs included in the systematic review described above[30] recorded adverse events with up to 6 years of treatment.[47–54] The type, frequency, and severity of reported adverse effects was similar for all the statins investigated in these trials. Increases in liver transaminase concentrations occurred in approximately 0.5% of all patients and were more common after several months of treatment and at higher doses (0.1% in placebo and with 20 mg/d lovastatin, 0.9% with 40 mg/d, and 1.5% for 80 mg/d; $p < 0.001$ for trend). Mild muscle enzyme increases occurred in 5% to 10% of individuals. Rare (< 0.1%) and reversible increases of more than 10-fold in creatine phosphokinase concentrations have been described. Total noncardiovascular events, total and tissue specific cancers, and accident and violent deaths have been reported consistently in statin trials. In the recent trial of secondary prevention, the AR for non-CVD death was 4.4% with placebo vs. 3.7% with pravastatin; RRR 0.17, 95% CI 0.02 relative risk increase to 0.32 relative risk decrease.[54] One trial found a nonsignificant increase in breast cancer with pravastatin,[49] but this was not confirmed by another.[54] We found no evidence of additional harm associated with cholesterol lowering in elderly people. We found no evidence from existing studies to suggest that harm occurs when lowering cholesterol immediately after an acute MI.

Comment: The evidence indicates that, in a wide range of clinical contexts, RRR depends on the size of the fall in cholesterol and is not otherwise dependent on the method by which cholesterol is lowered. The absolute benefit over several years of lowering cholesterol therefore will be greatest in people with the highest AR of an ischemic cardiac event. Even if the RRR attenuates at older age, the AR for ischemic cardiac events is much higher in elderly people than in younger individuals. However, long-term benefit for cholesterol lowering has not yet been shown directly in those over 75 years of age. Additional information may be provided by the heart protection study (20,000 participants, completion 2000, simvastatin, up to age 75 years),[55] the women's health initiative (48,000 participants, completion 2007, diet, up to age 79 years),[56] and the antihypertensive and lipid-lowering treatment to prevent heart disease trial (10,000 participants, completion 2002, pravastatin, no upper age limit).[57] It is not known whether cholesterol reduction will provide benefit for those with initial cholesterol concentrations lower than those selected in the published trials. We found no evidence to indicate whether starting statin treatment immediately after acute infarction provides additional benefits. Because the main aim of treatment is to reduce AR (rather than to reduce the cholesterol to any particular concentration), treatments aimed at lowering cholesterol need evaluating for effectiveness and cost effectiveness in comparison with other possible risk-factor interventions in each individual.

QUESTION What are the effects of blood pressure reduction?

Eva Lonn

We found no direct evidence of the effects of blood pressure lowering in people with established coronary artery disease. Observational studies and extrapolation of primary prevention trials of blood pressure reduction support the lowering of blood pressure in those at high risk of ischemic coronary events. The evidence for benefit is strongest for β-blockers, although not specifically in people with raised blood pressure. The target blood pressure in these people is not clear.

Benefits: We found no systematic review and no RCTs designed specifically to examine blood pressure reduction in those with established coronary artery disease. Prospective epidemiologic studies have established that blood pressure continues to be a risk factor for cardiovascular events in people who have already experienced a MI. The prospective follow-up of 5362 men who reported prior MI during screening for the Multiple Risk Factor Intervention Trial (MRFIT) found no detectable association between systolic blood pressure and coronary artery disease mortality, and increased coronary artery disease mortality for those with lowest diastolic blood pressure in the first 2 years of follow-up.[58] After 15 years, there were highly significant linear associations between both systolic and diastolic blood pressure and increased risk of coronary artery disease mortality (stronger relation for systolic blood pressure), with apparent benefit for men with blood pressure maintained at levels lower than the arbitrarily defined "normal" levels. The evidence of benefit from lowering of blood pressure in those with coronary artery disease requires extrapolation from primary prevention trials. Trials of antihypertensive treatment in elderly people[59–61] are likely to have included people with preclinical coronary artery disease. Mortality benefit has been established for β-blockers after MI and for ACE inhibitors after MI, especially in those with heart failure (see sections above). A reduction in secondary end points has been observed for verapamil and diltiazem after MI in those without heart failure.

Harms: Some observational studies have found increased mortality among those with low diastolic blood pressure.[62] Trials in elderly people of both blood pressure lowering for hypertension or while treating heart failure[63] found no evidence of a J-shaped relation between blood pressure and death.

Comment: Without specific studies comparing different antihypertensive treatments, the available evidence is strongest for a beneficial effect of β-blockers when treating survivors of an MI who have raised blood pressure. We found no specific evidence about the target level of blood pressure.

QUESTION What are the effects of nondrug treatments?

Andy Ness, Eva Lonn

OPTION DIETARY INTERVENTIONS

RCTs found that advising coronary patients to eat more fish (particularly oily fish), more fruit and vegetables, bread, pasta, potatoes, olive oil, and rapeseed margarine (i.e., a more Mediterranean diet) may result in a substantial survival benefit. We found no strong evidence from RCTs for a beneficial effect of low-fat or high-fiber diets on major nonfatal coronary heart disease events or coronary heart disease mortality.

Benefits: **Low-fat diets:** A systematic review published in 1998 found no evidence of reduced mortality from coronary artery disease in people after MI who were allocated a low-fat diet (RR 0.94, 95% CI 0.84–1.06).[64] The Diet and Reinfarction Trial (DART) randomized 2033 middle-aged men with a recent MI to three dietary arms: fat advice (to eat less fat); fiber advice (to eat more cereal fiber); and fish advice (to eat at least two portions of fatty fish a week).[65] Advise to reduce fat was complicated and, although fat intake reduced only slightly in the fat advice group, fruit and vegetable intake increased by approximately 40 g/d.[66] There was, however, no clear reduction in mortality (unadjusted RR at 2 years for death from any cause 0.97, 95% CI 0.75–1.27). **High-fiber diets:** In DART, people advised to eat more fiber doubled their intake, but survival was, if anything, slightly worse (unadjusted RR at 2 years for death from any cause 1.23, 95% CI 0.95–1.60). **High-fish diets:** In DART, those advised to eat more fish ate three times as much fish, although approximately 14% could not tolerate the fish and were given fish oil capsules. Those given fish advice were significantly less likely to die within 2 years (RRR 0.29, 95% CI 0.07–0.46, NNT 30). **Mediterranean diet:** An RCT randomized 605 middle-aged people with a recent MI to receive advice to eat a Mediterranean diet (more bread, more vegetables, more fruit, more fish, and less meat), and to replace butter and cream with rapeseed margarine. Controls took usual dietary advice.[67] There were several dietary differences between the groups. Fruit intake, for example, was approximately 50 g/d higher in the intervention group. After 27 months, the trial was stopped prematurely because of better outcomes in the intervention group. There were 20 deaths in the control group and eight in the intervention group (adjusted RRR of death 0.70, 95% CI 0.18–0.89, NNT 25 over 2 years).

Harms: No major adverse effects have been established.

Comment: Two further Mediterranean diet trials are planned in Edinburgh and Oslo (Renaud S, personal communication). Diets low in saturated fat and cholesterol can lead to 10% to 15% reductions in cholesterol concentrations in highly controlled settings, such as in metabolic wards.[68] In free living individuals the effects are more modest: 3% to 5% reductions in cholesterol concentrations in general population studies and 9% reductions in people after MI.[64,69–71] Several RCTs of intensive dietary intervention in conjunction with multifactorial risk reduction treatment found decreased progression of anatomic extent of coronary artery disease on angiography.[72] A trial of advice to eat more fruit and vegetables in men with angina is under way (Burr M, personal communication). **Effect on cardiovascular risk factors:** Other studies have investigated the effects of dietary interventions on cardiovascular risk factors rather than the effect on cardiovascular morbidity and mortality. A systematic review published in 1996 suggested that garlic may reduce cholesterol by approximately 10%.[73] Some trials in this review had methodologic flaws. More recent reports published in 1998 found no effects of garlic powder or garlic oil on cholesterol concentrations.[74,75] A systematic review reported modest reductions in cholesterol levels of 2% to 5% from oats and psyllium-enriched cereals (high-fiber diets).[76] A systematic review of soy protein also reported modest reductions in cholesterol concentrations.[77]

OPTION ANTIOXIDANT VITAMINS (VITAMIN E, β-CAROTENE, VITAMIN C)

The role of vitamin E, β-carotene, and vitamin C in the long-term management of people at high risk for ischemic cardiac events remains unclear.

Benefits: No systematic review of RCTs. Two large RCTs have looked at vitamin E in coronary patients.[78,79] The Cambridge heart antioxidant study recruited 2002 patients with angiographically proved ischemic heart disease.[78] The dose of vitamin E was high (400 IU or 800 IU) and the duration of follow-up short (a median of 510 days). There was a substantial reduction in the RR of nonfatal coronary events (RRR 0.77, 95% CI 0.53–0.89) but a nonsignificant increase in the RR of coronary death (RRI 0.18, –0.004 to 1.27) and all-cause mortality. The Finnish Alpha-Tocopherol Beta-Carotene (ATBC) cancer prevention study compared β-carotene versus vitamin E supplements or placebo, and included 1862 male Finnish smokers with a history of MI. The dose of vitamin E (50 mg/d) was smaller than that used in the Cambridge study. In the subgroup analysis of data from the 1862 men with prior MI, there was a decrease in the RR of nonfatal MI (RRR 0.38, 95% CI 0.04–0.59) but a nonsignificant increase in RR of coronary death (RRI 0.33, 95% CI –0.14 to 1.05) in the vitamin E group.[79] The interpretation of these two secondary prevention trials has differed.[80–82] There were significantly more deaths from coronary artery disease on β-carotene than placebo.

Harms: The trials of vitamin E both reported nonsignificant increases in the risk of coronary death (*see* above).[78,79] Four large RCTs of β-carotene supplementation in primary prevention found no cardiovascular benefits, and two of the trials raised concerns about increased mortality (RRI for cardiovascular death 0.12, 95% CI 0.04–0.22) and cancer rates.[83]

Comment: The balance of benefits and harms in the vitamin E studies is difficult to interpret because of the statistically insignificant but potentially clinically important increase in the risk of coronary death. A systematic review of epidemiologic studies published in 1997 found consistent associations between increased dietary or supplemental intake of vitamin E, or both, and lower cardiovascular risk and less consistent associations for β-carotene and vitamin C.[83] Most observational studies of antioxidants have excluded people with preexisting disease.[84,85] Ongoing clinical trials are further evaluating the use of vitamin E in the primary and secondary prevention of cardiovascular diseases.

OPTION CARDIAC REHABILITATION INCLUDING EXERCISE

Systematic reviews of RCTs have found that cardiac rehabilitation improves coronary risk factors and reduces the risk of major cardiac events in patients after MI. The role of exercise alone in reducing the risk of adverse cardiovascular outcomes is not clear.

Benefits: **Cardiac rehabilitation:** Three systematic reviews identified RCTs of cardiac rehabilitation including exercise in people after MI. Rehabilitation included medical evaluation, prescribed exercise, cardiac risk-factor modification, education, and counseling. The reviews found 20% to 25% reductions in cardiovascular deaths in the treatment groups.[86–88] One review identified 22 RCTs in 4554 people with a recent MI. After a mean follow-up of 3 years, there were significant reductions in total mortality (RRR 0.20), cardiovascular mortality (RRR 0.22), and fatal reinfarction (RRR 0.25), but no significant difference in rates of nonfatal reinfarction.[87] **Exercise alone:** A more recent qualitative systematic review published in 1995 found that rehabilitation with exercise alone had little effect on rates of nonfatal MI or overall mortality but a small beneficial effect on angina.[89]

Harms: No study documented an increased risk of reinfarction or other adverse cardiovascular outcomes for exercise rehabilitation compared to control. Rates of adverse cardiovascular outcomes (syncope, arrhythmia, MI, or sudden death) were low (2–3/100,000 patient-hours) in supervized rehabilitation programs, and rates of fatal cardiac events during or immediately after exercise training were reported in two older surveys as ranging from 1/116,400 to 1/784,000 patient-hours.[89]

Comment: The three reviews included RCTs performed before the widespread use of thrombolytic agents and β-blockers after MI. Most participants were men under 70 years of age. Other interventions aimed at risk-factor modification were often provided in the intervention groups (including nutritional education, counseling in behavioral modification and, in some trials, lipid-lowering medications). We found no strong evidence that exercise training and cardiac rehabilitation programs increase the proportion of people returning to work after MI.

OPTION SMOKING CESSATION

We found no RCTs of the effects of smoking cessation on cardiovascular events in people with coronary artery disease. Moderate evidence from epidemiologic studies indicates that people with coronary artery disease who stop smoking rapidly reduce their risk of recurrent coronary events or death.

The use of nicotine patches seems safe in people with coronary artery disease.

Benefits: We found no RCTs evaluating the effects of smoking cessation on coronary mortality and morbidity. Many observational studies found that people with coronary artery disease who stop smoking, rapidly reduce their risk of cardiac death and MI (RRR ~ 0.50 for recurrent coronary events or premature death compared with continuing smokers).[90] (*See also* p. 7.) Approximately half of the benefits occur in the first year of stopping smoking, followed by a more gradual decrease in risk, reaching the risk of never smokers after several years of abstinence.[90] Among people with peripheral arterial disease and stroke, smoking cessation has been shown in observational studies to be associated with improved exercise tolerance, decreased risk of amputation, improved survival, and reduced risk of recurrent stroke.

Harms: Two recent RCTs of nicotine replacement treatment in patients with stable coronary artery disease showed no significant increases in cardiovascular events in people using transdermal nicotine patches.[91,92]

Comment: One RCT compared the impact of firm and detailed advice to stop smoking in 125 survivors of acute MI versus conventional advice in 85 people.[93] Allocation to the intervention or control group was determined by day of admission. At follow-up, over 1 year after admission, 62% of the intervention group and 28% of the control group were nonsmokers. Mortality and morbidity were not reported.

OPTION PSYCHOLOGICAL AND STRESS MANAGEMENT INTERVENTIONS

A systematic review of mainly poor-quality RCTs has found that psychological and stress management may decrease rates of MI or cardiac death in people with coronary artery disease.

Benefits: A systematic review published in 1996 of 23 RCTs involved 3180 people with coronary artery disease; 2024 received one of a diverse range of psychosocial treatments and 1156 were controls who received usual treatment.[94] Mortality data were only available in 12 studies. Psychosocial interventions were associated with a 41% reduction in mortality (OR 1.70, 95% CI 1.09–2.64) and a 46% reduction in nonfatal events in the first 2 years of follow up after MI (OR 1.84, 95% CI 1.12–2.99).[94]

Harms: No specific harms were reported.

Comment: These results should be interpreted with caution because of the methodologic limitations of the individual RCTs and the use of a diverse range of interventions (relaxation, stress management, counseling). The RCTs were generally small, with short follow-up, and used nonuniform outcome measures. Measures to ensure concealment of randomization from those making measurements were not assessed. The authors of the review acknowledged the strong possibility of publication bias but made no attempt to quantify it. The results were inconsistent across trials.[95] Several observational studies have found that depression and social isolation (lack of social and emotional support) are independent predictors of mortality and nonfatal coronary artery disease events in people after MI.[96]

QUESTION **What are the effects of surgical treatments?**

Charanjit Rihal

OPTION **CORONARY ARTERY BYPASS GRAFTING (CABG) VERSUS MEDICAL TREATMENT**

RCTs performed up to the mid 1980s found that, in comparison to medical treatment, CABG carried a greater risk of death in the first year but reduced the risk of death from coronary artery disease at 5 and 10 years. Greatest benefit occurred in people with more severe disease (multivessel disease, left ventricular dysfunction, or MI). There was no evidence of increased protection against subsequent MI. Data from a more recent RCT, using modern techniques and with optimal background medical treatment, suggest even greater superiority of revascularization.

Benefits: A systematic review published in 1994 analyzed individual data from 2649 patients with coronary artery disease in seven RCTs comparing CABG versus medical treatment. Patients were enrolled from 1972 to 1984: 97% were male, 82% 41 to 60 years old, 80% with ejection fraction more than 50%, 60% with prior MI, and 83% with two- or three-vessel disease.[97] Patients assigned to CABG also received medical treatment, and 40% of patients assigned to initial medical treatment underwent CABG in the following 10 years. A subsequent RCT compared medical treatment versus revascularization (CABG or percutaneous transluminal coronary angioplasty [PTCA]) in 558 patients with asymptomatic but definite ischemia (positive exercise test or ambulatory electrocardiogram).[98] **Mortality and MI:** The systematic review found a reduced risk of death with CABG at 5 years (RRR compared with medical treatment alone 0.39, 95% CI 0.23–0.52), 7 years (RRR 0.32, 95% CI 0.17–0.44), and 10 years (RRR 0.17, 95% CI 0.02–0.30).[97] In the subsequent RCT, mortality at 2 years was significantly lower after routine revascularization (AR of death 1.1% vs. 6.6% and 4.4% in the two medical groups, $p<0.02$).[98] No overall impact of CABG on subsequent infarction was found either in individual trials or in the systematic review, possibly because those assigned to surgery had increased rates of infarction in the perioperative period (*see* below). In the subsequent RCT, rates of death or MI were 4.7% with revascularization vs. 8.8% and 12.1% on medical treatment ($p<0.04$).[98] **Other nonfatal end points:** Most trials did not prospectively collect data on rehospitalization, recurrent angina, or quality of life. **Effects in different people:** The systematic review found that the relative benefits were similar in patients with different baseline risk (OR for death 0.61 if left ventricular function normal and 0.59 if abnormal). The absolute benefit of CABG was greatest in people with an abnormal ejection fraction, because the baseline risk of death was twice as high in this group (ejection fraction > 50%, ARR of death over 5 years 0.05; ejection fraction < 50%, ARR 0.10). Both absolute and relative mortality benefits were higher in people with a greater number of diseased coronary arteries, especially those with three vessel disease (OR of death 0.58, $p<0.001$), and those with left main coronary artery disease (OR 0.32, $p=0.004$) or any involvement of the left anterior descending coronary artery (OR 0.58), even if only one or two vessels were involved.[97]

Harms: **Perioperative complications:** In the systematic review, of the 1240 patients who underwent CABG, 40 (3.2%) died and 7.1% had documented nonfatal MI within 30 days of the procedure. At 1 year, the life table estimated incidence of death or MI was 11.6% with CABG and 8% with medical treatment (RRI 0.45, 95% CI 0.18–1.03).[97] Because the diagnosis of MI after CABG is difficult, its true incidence may be higher. In the recent RCT, after 2 years of follow-up, rates of death or MI were significantly lower in people assigned to routine revascularization (AR for death 1.1% vs. 6.6% and 4.4% for the two medical groups, $p<0.02$; AR for death or MI 4.7% vs. 12.1% and 8.8% in the two medical groups, $p<0.04$).[98]

Comment: The results of the systematic review may not be able to be generalized to current practice. Participants were 65 years or younger, but over half of CABG procedures are now performed on patients over 65. Almost all participants were men. High-risk patients, such as those with severe angina and left main coronary artery stenosis, were underrepresented. Internal thoracic artery grafts were used in less than 5% of participants. Lipid-lowering agents (particularly HMG-CoA reductase inhibitors) and aspirin were used infrequently (aspirin used in 3% of participants at enrollment). Only approximately half of the patients were taking β-blockers. Moreover, the systematic review probably underestimates the real benefits of CABG in comparison with medical treatment alone, because medical and surgical treatment for coronary artery disease were not mutually exclusive; by 5 years, 25% of medical patients (and by 10 years 41%) had undergone CABG surgery. Underestimation would be greatest among high-risk patients. Patients with previous CABG have not been studied in RCTs, although they now represent a growing proportion of patients undergoing CABG.

OPTION PERCUTANEOUS TRANSLUMINAL CORONARY ANGIOPLASTY (PTCA) VERSUS MEDICAL TREATMENT

RCTs have found that, in comparison to medical treatment, coronary PTCA is more effective in alleviating angina pectoris, myocardial ischemia, and improving exercise tolerance. However, it is associated with increased risk of MI during and soon after the procedure, emergency CABG, and repeat procedures for restenosis.

Benefits: No systematic review. We found two good RCTs in 212 and 1018 people with stable coronary artery disease.[99,100] **Mortality, MI, and unstable angina:** After an average of 5 years' follow-up, the smaller trial found no significant difference in rates of death (AR 9.5% for PTCA vs. 10.3% for medical groups, $p=$NS) or nonfatal MI (7.6% vs. 6.5%, $p=$NS).[101] However, more patients initially assigned to medical treatment required PTCA or CABG during follow-up (35.5% vs. 13.3%, $p<0.0001$) or presented with unstable angina (25.2% vs. 6.7%, $p=0.001$).[6] The larger trial found a significant increase in rates of death or MI with PTCA (AR by 3 years with PTCA 6.3%

vs. 3.3% on medical treatment; ARI 0.03, 95% CI 0.004–0.057). The higher rate of death or MI with PTCA was attributable to one death and seven procedure related MIs.[100] **Angina pectoris:** In the smaller trial, although PTCA was technically successful in only 80% of patients, it led to a higher proportion of patients free of angina at 6 months (64% vs. 46%, $p<0.01$), fewer monthly anginal episodes in those who were still symptomatic, lower use of medication, and greater improvement in duration of treadmill exercise, even though the use of concomitant antianginal medications was discontinued before the test (improvement 2.1 vs. 0.5 minutes, $p<0.0001$).[99] In the larger trial, angina pectoris and treadmill exercise time improved significantly in both groups at 3 months, but more so in those given PTCA; ARR of moderate to severe angina (grade 2 or worse) compared with the medical group was 16.5%. The NNT was six people needing PTCA rather than medical treatment alone to prevent one additional person suffering from moderate to severe angina in the 3 months after randomization. At 3 years, the ARR for angina had fallen to 7.6% because patients with severe symptoms in both groups underwent PTCA for symptom control.[100] **Effects in different people:** Antianginal benefit from PTCA was limited to people with moderate to severe (grade 2 or worse) angina (20% lower incidence of angina and 1-minute longer treadmill exercise times compared with medical treatment); people with mild symptoms at enrollment derived no significant improvement in symptoms.[100]

Harms: Procedural death and MI, as well as repeat procedures for restenosis, are the main hazards of PTCA. In the smaller trial, two (1.9%) emergency CABG operations and five (4.8%) MIs occurred at the time of the procedure. By 6 months, the PTCA group had higher rates of CABG surgery (7% vs. 0%) and nonprotocol PTCA (15.2% vs. 10.3%).[99] In the larger trial, the higher rate of death or MI with PTA was attributable to one death and seven procedure-related MIs.[100]

Comment: PTCA has become one of the most commonly performed invasive procedures. We found good evidence that it treats the symptoms of angina pectoris, but it has not been shown to reduce the overall incidence of death or MI in people with stable angina. This is likely to be because of the risk of complications during and soon after the procedure and the fact that most PTCAs are performed for single vessel disease. Technical improvements that lower the procedural risk would improve the risk-to-benefit ratio for PTCA.

OPTION PTCA VERSUS CABG FOR MULTIVESSEL DISEASE

One systematic review of RCTs has found no evidence of a difference in efficacy between PTCA and CABG in low- to medium-risk patients, in terms of rates of death and MI and quality of life. However, these trials were too small to exclude a 20% to 30% difference in mortality. PTCA is associated with a greater need for repeat procedures.

Benefits: A systematic review published in 1995 identified eight RCTs in 3371 patients with multivessel disease.[102] A subsequent RCT included 1829 patients.[103] **Angina pectoris:** In all trials at 1 year, the prevalence of moderate to severe angina pectoris (grade 2 or worse) was significantly higher after PTCA than after CABG (RR 1.6, 95% CI 1.3–1.9). After 3 years this difference had decreased as rates of repeat revascularization increased in the patients allocated to PTCA (RR 1.2, 95% CI –0.99 to 1.5). **Mortality:** When data from all nine trials were pooled, there was no significant difference in all cause mortality between groups (AR 7.3% vs. 6.8%, OR 1.09, 95% CI 0.88–1.35).[104] In the largest of these studies (BARI) among people with treated diabetes, a significant mortality difference was found in favor of CABG (AR of death by 5 years with CABG 19.4% vs. 34.5% with PTCA, 95% CI for difference not available, $p = 0.003$).[103] **Death or MI:** In all trials, the combined end point of death or MI was not significantly different between groups (AR 13.8% vs. 13.4%, OR 1.05, 95% CI 0.89–1.23).[104] **Repeat procedures:** In all trials, the need for repeat procedures was significantly higher in patients with PTCA (AR 44% vs. 6.0% in patients allocated to CABG, OR 7.9, 95% CI 6.9–9.0).[103] **Quality of life:** Subanalyses of the trial data have found no difference between groups in quality of life or return to employment over 3 to 5 years of follow-up.[105]

Harms: *See* above. CABG is more invasive than PTCA, but PTCA is associated with a greater need for repeat procedures.

Comment: Although no major differences in death or MI were observed in the nine RCTs, these trials enrolled relatively low-risk patients. It is therefore premature to conclude PTCA and CABG are equivalent for all patients with multivessel disease. Fewer than 20% of patients had left ventricular dysfunction, almost 70% had one- or two-vessel disease, and observed mortality was only 2.6% for the first year and 1.1% per year thereafter. Patients enrolled in the largest trial more closely approximated to moderate-risk patients, but this was caused primarily by the higher proportion of patients with diabetes mellitus.[103] Even in that trial, nearly 60% of patients had two-vessel coronary artery disease. Finally, even though nine trials have been performed, the total enrolment of 5200 patients falls short of what would be needed to show mortality differences of 20% to 30% among low- and moderate-risk patients. Large mortality differences between the two procedures (40% to 50%) are unlikely.

OPTION PTCA VERSUS INTRACORONARY STENTS

RCTs have found that, in comparison to coronary PTCA, intracoronary stents afford superior acute and long-term clinical and angiographic results.

Benefits: No systematic review. **For disease of native coronary arteries:** We found three RCTs comparing elective stenting versus PTCA.[106–108] At 12 months, intracoronary stents significantly reduced the risk of recurrent angina (13% vs. 30%, $p = 0.04$)[107] but not of death, MI, or need for CABG. At 6 months, all three trials found a lower prevalence of angiographic restenosis (31% vs. 42%, $p = 0.046$[106]; 22% vs. 32%, $p = 0.02$[107]; and 17% vs. 40%, $p = 0.02$[108]), and a lower need for repeat PTA (13.5% vs. 23.3%, RR 0.58, 95% CI 0.40–0.85).[108] **For saphenous vein graft lesions in patients with prior CABG:** We found one RCT comparing elective stents versus standard balloon angioplasty in 220 patients.[109] Acute angiographic results were better with stents than balloon angioplasty. At 6 months, there was no difference in rates of restenosis (37% vs. 46%, $p=0.24$), but the overall incidence of death, MI, CABG, or repeat PTCA was lower in the stent group (27% vs. 42%, $p=0.03$). **For treatment of chronic total occlusions:** Chronic occlusions of the coronary arteries are particularly prone to restenosis and reocclusion following PTCA. We found two RCTs comparing PTCA alone versus PTCA followed by insertion of stents. One trial involved 119 people with chronic total occlusion and found 57% of the stent group were free from angina at 6-month follow-up versus 24% of the PTCA-only group (95% CI not available, $p<0.001$). Angiographic restenosis (> 50% stenosis on follow-up angiography) occurred in 74% of PTCA and 32% of stent patients ($p<0.001$). Repeat procedures were needed less often among stent patients (22% vs. 42%, $p=0.025$).[110] In the second trial involving 110 people, those treated with stents experienced less ischemia (14% vs. 46%, $P=0.002$), had less restenosis (32% vs. 68%, $p<0.001$), and underwent fewer repeat procedures (5.3% vs. 22%, $p=0.038$) by 9 months.[111]

Harms: Initially, aggressive combination antithrombotic and anticoagulant regimens were used because of a high incidence of stent thrombosis and MI. These regimens led to a high incidence of arterial access-site bleeding.[107] More recently, improved stent deployment techniques and use of aspirin and ticlopidine have reduced both stent thrombosis and arterial access-site bleeding.[109,112] Currently, the risk of stent thrombosis is less than 1%.[108,112,113] Hemorrhage (particularly femoral artery bleeding) was more frequent after stenting than PTA alone[110] but occurred in less than 3% following stenting when antiplatelet drugs were used without long-term anticoagulants.

Comment: It remains to be determined if stenting influences the relative benefits and harms of percutaneous procedures versus CABG.

REFERENCES

1. Greaves EJ, Gillum BS. *1994 Summary: national hospital discharge survey*. Advance data from Vital and Health Statistics, no. 278. Hyattsville, Maryland: National Center for Health Statistics, 1996.
2. Rouleau JL, Talajic M, Sussex B, et al. Myocardial infarction patients in the 1990s – their risk factors, stratification and survival in Canada: the Canadian assessment of myocardial infarction (CAMI) study. *J Am Coll Cardiol* 1996;27:1119–1127.
3. Shaw LJ, Peterson ED, Kesler K, Hasselblad V, Califf RM. A meta-analysis of predischarge risk stratification after acute myocardial infarction with stress electrocardiographic, myocardial perfusion, and ventricular function imaging. *Am J Cardiol* 1996;78:1327–1337. (Search date 1995; primary sources MEDLINE 1980–1995, and hand search of bibliographies of review articles published 1985–1995.)
4. Kudenchuk PJ, Maynard C, Martin JS, et al. Comparison, presentation, treatment, and outcome of acute myocardial infarction in men versus women. *Am J Cardiol* 1996;78:9–14.
5. The Task Force on the Management of Acute Myocardial Infarction of the European Society of Cardiology. Acute myocardial infarction: pre-hospital and in-hospital management. *Eur Heart J* 1996;17:43–63.
6. Peterson ED, Shaw LJ, Califf RM. Clinical guideline: part II. Risk stratification after myocardial infarction. *Ann Intern Med* 1997;126:561–582.
7. The Multicenter Postinfarction Research Group. Risk stratification and survival after myocardial infarction. *N Engl J Med* 1983;309;331–336.
8. American College of Cardiology /American Heart Association Task Force on Practice Guidelines (Committee on Exercise Testing). ACC/AHA guidelines for exercise testing. *J Am Coll Cardiol* 1997;30:260–311.
9. Fallen E, Cairns J, Dafoe W, et al. Management of the postmyocardial infarction patient: a consensus report – revision of the 1991 CCS guidelines. *Can J Cardiol* 1995;11:477–486.
10. Madsen JK, Grande P, Saunamaki, et al. Danish multicenter randomized study of invasive versus conservative treatment in patients with inducible ischemia after thrombolysis in acute myocardial infarction (DANAMI). *Circulation* 1997;96: 748–755.
11. Antiplatelet Trialists' Collaboration. Collaborative overview of randomised trials of antiplatelet therapy – I: prevention of death, myocardial infarction, and stroke by prolonged antiplatelet therapy in various categories of patients. *BMJ* 1994;308:81–106.
12. Juul-Möller S, Edvardsson N, Jahnmatz B, Rosen A, Sorenson S, Omblus R, for the Swedish Angina

Pectoris Aspirin Trial (SAPAT) Group. Double-blind trial of aspirin in primary prevention of myocardial infarction in patients with stable chronic angina pectoris. *Lancet* 1992;340:1421–1425.
13. CAPRIE Steering Committee. A randomised, blinded, trial of clopidogrel versus aspirin in patients at risk of ischaemic events. *Lancet* 1996;348:1329–1339.
14. Farrell B, Godwin J, Richards S, Warlow C. The United Kingdom transient ischaemic attack (UK-TIA) aspirin trial: final results. *J Neurol Neurosurg Psychiatry* 1991;54:1044–1054.
15. Yusuf S, Michaelis W, Hua A, et al. Effects of oral anticoagulants on mortality, reinfarction and stroke after myocardial infarction [abstr]. *Circulation* 1995;92(suppl):I-343.
16. Anticoagulants in the Secondary Prevention of Events in Coronary Thrombosis (ASPECT) Research Group. Effect of long-term oral anticoagulant treatment on mortality and cardiovascular morbidity after myocardial infarction. *Lancet* 1994;343:499–503.
17. Smith P, Arnesen H, Holme I. The effect of warfarin on mortality and reinfarction after myocardial infarction. *N Engl J Med* 1990;323:147–152.
18. Coumadin Aspirin Reinfarction Study (CARS) Investigators. Randomised double-blind trial of fixed low-dose warfarin with aspirin after myocardial infarction. *Lancet* 1997;350:389–396.
19. Post Coronary Artery Bypass Graft Trial Investigators. The effect of aggressive lowering of low-density lipoprotein cholesterol levels and low-dose anticoagulation on obstructive changes in saphenous-vein coronary-artery bypass grafts. *N Engl J Med* 1997;336:153–162.
20. Teo KK, Yusuf S, Furberg CD. Effects of prophylactic antiarrhythmic drug therapy in acute myocardial infarction. *JAMA* 1993;270:1589–1595. (Search date 1993; primary sources MEDLINE 1960–1993, hand search of reference lists, details of unpublished trials sought from pharmaceutical industry/other investigators.)
21. Yusuf S, Peto R, Lewis J, Collins R, Sleight P. Beta blockade during and after myocardial infarction: An overview of the randomized trials. *Prog Cardiovasc Dis* 1985;27:335–371. (No details of search date or primary sources given.)
22. Pepine CJ, Cohn PF, Deedwania PC, et al for the ASIST Study Group. Effects of treatment on outcome in mildly symptomatic patients with ischemia during daily life: the atenolol silent ischemia study (ASIST). *Circulation* 1994;90: 762–768.
23. Boissel J-P, Leizerovicz A, Picolet H, et al, for the APSI Investigators. Secondary prevention after high-risk acute myocardial infarction with low-dose acebutolol. *Am J Cardiol* 1990;66:251–260.
24. The Beta-Blocker Pooling Project Research Group. The beta-blocker pooling project (BBPP): subgroup findings from randomized trials in post infarction patients. *Eur Heart J* 1988;9:8–16. (Search date, placebo controlled trials published by December 1983; details of primary sources not given.)
25. Beta-blocker Heart Attack Trial Research Group. A randomized trial of propranolol in patients with acute myocardial infarction: I. Mortality results. *JAMA* 1982;247:1707–1714.
26. Flather M, Kober L, Pfeffer MA, et al. Meta-analysis of individual patient data from trials of long-term ACE-inhibitor treatment after acute myocardial infarction (SAVE, AIRE, and TRACE studies). *Circulation* 1997;96(suppl 1):I-706. (No details of search date or primary sources given.)
27. Yusuf S, Lonn E. Anti-ischaemic effects of ACE inhibitors: review of current clinical evidence and ongoing clinical trials. *Eur Heart J* 1998;19(suppl J):J36–44.
28. Echt DS, Liebson PR, Mitchell LB, et al. Mortality and morbidity in patients receiving encainide, flecainide, or placebo. *N Engl J Med* 1991;324: 781–788.
29. Amiodarone Trials Meta-Analysis Investigators. Effect of prophylactic amiodarone on mortality after acute myocardial infarction and in congestive heart failure: meta-analysis of individual data from 6500 patients in randomised trials. *Lancet* 1997;350:1417–1424. (No details of search date or primary sources given.)
30. Sim I, McDonald KM, Lavori PW, Norbutas CM, Hlatky MA. Quantitative overview of randomized trials of amiodarone to prevent sudden cardiac death. *Circulation* 1997;96:2823–2829. (Search date 1997; primary sources MEDLINE and Biosis 1985–March 1997.)
31. Waldo AL, Camm AJ, de Ruyter H, et al for the SWORD Investigators. Effect of d-sotalol on mortality in patients with left ventricular dysfunction after recent and remote myocardial infarction. *Lancet* 1996;348:7–12.
32. Cairns JA, Connolly SJ, Roberts R, Gent M, for the Canadian Amiodarone Myocardial Infarction Arrhythmia Trial Investigators. Randomized trial of outcome after myocardial infarction in patients with frequent or repetitive ventricular premature depolarisations: CAMIAT. *Lancet* 1997;349:675–682.
33. Julian DG, Camm AJ, Janse MJ, et al for the European Myocardial Infarct Amiodarone Trial Investigators. Randomised trial of effect of amiodarone on mortality in patients with left-ventricular dysfunction after recent myocardial infarction: EMIAT. *Lancet* 1997;349:667–674.
34. Gibson R, Boden WE, Theroux P et al. Diltiazem and reinfarction in patients with non-Q-wave myocardial infarction. *N Engl J Med* 1986;315: 423–429.
35. The Multicenter Diltiazem Postinfarction Trial Research Group. The effect of diltiazem on mortality and reinfarction after myocardial infarction. *N Engl J Med* 1988;319:385–392.
36. The Danish Study Group on Verapamil in Myocardial Infarction. Effect of verapamil on mortality and major events after acute myocardial infarction: the Danish verapamil infarction trial II (DAVIT II). *Am J Cardiol* 1990;66:779–785.
37. Hulley S, Grady D, Bush T, et al. Randomized trial of estrogen plus progestin for secondary prevention of coronary heart disease in postmenopausal women. *JAMA* 1998;280:605–613.
38. Coronary Drug Research Project Research Group. The coronary drug project: initial findings leading to modifications of its research protocol. *JAMA* 1970;214:1303–1313.
39. Daly E, Vessey MP, Hawkins MM, Carson JL, Gough P, Marsh S. Risk of venous thromboembolism in users of hormone replacement therapy. *Lancet* 1996;348:977–980.
40. Newton KM, LaCroix AZ, McKnight B, et al. Estrogen replacement therapy and prognosis after first myocardial infarction. *Am J Epidemiol* 1997;145:269–277.
41. Sullivan JM, El-Zeky F, Vander Zwaag R, et al. Effect on survival of estrogen replacement therapy after coronary artery bypass grafting. *Am J Cardiol* 1997;79:847–850.
42. The Writing Group for the PEPI Trial. Effects of estrogen or estrogen/progestin regimens on heart disease risk factors in postmenopausal women. *JAMA* 1995; 273:199–208.
43. Gould AL, Rossouw JE, Santanello NC, Heyse JF, Furberg CD. Cholesterol reduction yields clinical benefit: impact of statin trials. *Circulation* 1998;

97:946–952.
44. Long-term Intervention with Pravastatin in Ischemic Disease (LIPID) Study Program. Prevention of cardiovascular events and death with pravastatin in patients with coronary heart disease and a broad range of initial cholesterol levels. *N Engl J Med* 1998;339:1349–1357.
45. Post Coronary Artery Bypass Graft Trial Investigators. The effect of aggressive lowering of low-density lipoprotein cholesterol levels and low-dose anticoagulation on obstructive changes in saphenous-vein coronary-artery bypass grafts. *N Engl J Med* 1997;336:153–162.
46. Bradford RH, Shear CL, Chremos AN, et al. Expanded clinical evaluation of lovastatin (EXCEL) study results, I: efficacy in modifying plasma lipoproteins and adverse event profile in 8245 patients with moderate hypercholesterolemia. *Arch Intern Med* 1991;151:43–49.
47. Scandinavian Simvastatin Survival Study Group. Randomized trial of cholesterol lowering in 4444 patients with coronary heart disease: the Scandinavian simvastatin survival study (4S). *Lancet* 1995;344:1383–1389.
48. Shepherd J, Cobbe SM, Ford I, et al for the West of Scotland Coronary Prevention Study Group. Prevention of coronary heart disease with pravastatin in men with hypercholesterolemia. *N Engl J Med* 1995;333:1301–1307.
49. Sacks FM, Pfeffer MA, Moye LA, et al for the Cholesterol and Recurrent Events Trial Investigators. The effect of pravastatin on coronary events after myocardial infarction in patients with average cholesterol levels. *N Engl J Med* 1996;335:1001–1009.
50. Brown G, Albers JJ, Fisher LD, et al. Regression of coronary artery disease as a result of intensive lipid-lowering therapy in men with high levels of apolipoprotein B. *N Engl J Med* 1990;323: 1289–1298.
51. Furberg CD, Adams HP, Applegate WB, et al for the Asymptomatic Carotid Artery Progression Study (ACAPS) Research Group. Effect of lovastatin on early carotid atherosclerosis and cardiovascular events. *Circulation* 1994;90:1679–1687.
52. Post Coronary Artery Bypass Graft Trial Investigators. The effect of aggressive lowering of low-density lipoprotein cholesterol levels and low-dose anticoagulation on obstructive changes in saphenous-vein coronary-artery bypass grafts. *N Engl J Med* 1997;336:153–162.
53. Downs JR, Clearfield M, Weis S, et al for the AFCAPS/TexCAPS Research Group. Primary prevention of acute coronary events with lovastatin in men and women with average cholesterol levels. *JAMA* 1998;279:1615–1622.
54. Long-term Intervention with Pravastatin in Ischemic Disease (LIPID) Study Program. Prevention of cardiovascular events and death with pravastatin in patients with coronary heart disease and a broad range of initial cholesterol levels. *N Engl J Med* 1998;339:1349–1357.
55. The Cholesterol Treatment Trialists' (CTT) Collaboration. Protocol for a prospective collaborative overview of all current and planned randomized trials of cholesterol treatment regimens. *Am J Cardiol* 1995;75:1130–1134.
56. The Women's Health Initiative Study Group. Design of the women's health initiative clinical trial and observational study. *Cont Clin Trials* 1998;19:61–109.
57. Davis BR, Cutler JA Gordon DJ, et al for the ALLHAT Research Group. Rationale and design for the antihypertensive and lipid lowering treatment to prevent heart attack trial (ALLHAT). *Am J Hypertens* 1996;9:342–360.
58. Flack JM, Neaton J, Grimm R, et al. Blood pressure and mortality among men with prior myocardial infarction. *Circulation* 1995:92;2437–2445.
59. Dahlof B, Lindholm LH, Hansson L et al. Morbidity and mortality in the Swedish trial in old patients with hypertension (STOP-hypertension). *Lancet* 1991;338:1281–1285.
60. Medical Research Council Working Party. MRC trial of treatment of hypertension in older adults: principal results. *BMJ* 1992;304:405–412.
61. Systolic Hypertension in Elderly Patients (SHEP) Cooperative Research Group. Prevention of stroke by antihypertensive drug treatment in older persons with isolated systolic hypertension. *JAMA* 1991;265:3255-3264.
62. D'Agostino RB, Belanger AJ, Kannel WB, et al. Relationship of low diastolic blood pressure to coronary heart disease death in presence of myocardial infarction: the Framingham study. *BMJ* 1991;303:385–389.
63. Pfeffer MA, Braunwald E, Moye LA, et al on behalf of the SAVE investigators. Effect of captopril on mortality and morbidity in patients with left ventricular dysfunction after myocardial infarction: results of the survival and ventricular enlargement trial. *N Engl J Med* 1992;327:669–677.
64. NHS Centre for Reviews and Dissemination, York University. Cholesterol and coronary heart disease: screening and treatment. *Effective Health Care* 1998;4: Number 1.
65. Burr ML, Fehily AM, Gilbert JF, et al. Effects of changes in fat, fish, and fibre intakes on death and myocardial reinfarction: diet and reinfarction trial (DART). *Lancet* 1989;ii:757–761.
66. Fehily AM, Vaughan-Williams E, Shiels K, et al. The effect of dietary advice on nutrient intakes: evidence from the diet and reinfarction trial (DART). *Journal of Human Nutrition and Dietetics* 1989;2:225–235.
67. de Lorgeril M, Renaud S, Mamelle N, et al. Mediterranean alpha-linolenic acid-rich diet in secondary prevention of coronary heart disease. *Lancet* 1994;343:1454–1459.
68. Clarke R, Frost C, Collins R, et al. Dietary lipids and blood cholesterol: quantitative meta-analysis of metabolic ward studies. *BMJ* 1997;314: 112–117. (Search date 1995; primary sources MEDLINE 1960–1995, hand search of reference lists and nutrition journals.)
69. Tang JL, Armitage JM, Lancaster T, et al. Systematic review of dietary intervention trials to lower blood total cholesterol in free-living subjects. *BMJ* 1998;316:1213–1220. (Search date 1997, primary sources MEDLINE, Human Nutrition, EMBASE, and Allied and Alternative Medicine 1966–1997, hand searching the *Am J Clin Nutr* and references of review articles.)
70. Brunner E, White I, Thorogood M, et al. Can dietary interventions change diet and cardiovascular risk factors? A meta-analysis of randomized controlled trials. *Am J Public Health* 1997;87:1415–1422. (Search date 1993; primary sources MEDLINE 1966–July 1993 and manual search of selected journals.)
71. Ebrahim S, Davey SG. *Health promotion in older people for the prevention of coronary heart disease and stroke*. London: Health Education Authority, 1996.
72. Waters D. Lessons from coronary atherosclerosis "regression" trials. *Cardiology Clinics* 1996;14:31–50.
73. Neil H, Silagy C, Lancaster T, et al. Garlic powder in the treatment of moderate hyperlipidemia: a controlled trial and meta-analysis. *J R Coll Physicians Lond* 1996;30:329–334.
74. Isaacshon JL, Moser M, Stein EA, et al. Garlic powder and plasma lipids and lipoproteins. *Arch Intern Med* 1998;158:1189–1194.
75. Berthold HK, Sudhop T, von Bergmann K. Effect of a garlic oil preparation on serum lipoproteins and

cholesterol metabolism. *JAMA* 1998;279:1900–1902.
76. Ripsin CM, Keenan JM, Jacobs DR Jr, et al. Oat products and lipid lowering: a meta-analysis. *JAMA* 1992;267:3317–3325. (Search date 1991; primary sources MEDLINE 1966–1991, unpublished trials solicited form all known investigators of lipid-oats association.)
77. Anderson J, Johnstone B, Cook-Newell M. Meta-analysis of the effects of soy protein intake on serum lipids. *N Engl J Med* 1995;333:276–282. (No details of search date or primary sources given.)
78. Stephens NG, Parsons A, Schofield PM, et al. Randomised controlled trial of vitamin E in patients with coronary disease: Cambridge heart antioxidant study (CHAOS). *Lancet* 1996;347: 781–786.
79. Rapola JM, Virtamo J, Ripatti S, et al. Randomised trial of α-tocopherol and β-carotene supplements on incidence of major coronary events in men with previous myocardial infarction. *Lancet* 1997;349:1715–1720.
80. Stephens NG. Anti-oxidant therapy for ischaemic heart disease: where do we stand? *Lancet* 1997;349:1710–1711.
81. Shahar E. Antioxidants and ischaemic heart disease. *Lancet* 1997;350:667–668.
82. Rapola JM, Virtamo J, Huttunen JK. Antioxidants and ischaemic heart disease – author's reply. *Lancet* 1997;350:668.
83. Lonn EM, Yusuf S. Is there a role for antioxidant vitamins in the prevention of cardiovascular diseases? An update on epidemiological and clinical trials data. *Can J Cardiol* 1997;13:957–965. (Search date 1996; primary sources MEDLINE 1965–96, plus one reference added from 1997.)
84. Jha P, Flather M, Lonn E, Farkouh M, Yusuf S. The antioxidant vitamins and cardiovascular disease: a critical review of epidemiologic and clinical trial data. *Ann Intern Med* 1995;123:860–872.
85. Ness AR, Powles JW, Khaw KT. Vitamin C and cardiovascular disease—a systematic review. *J Cardiovasc Risk* 1996;3:513–521.
86. Oldridge NB, Guyatt GH, Fischer MS, Rimm AA. Cardiac rehabilitation after myocardial infarction: combined experience of randomized clinical trials. *JAMA* 1988;260:945-950.
87. O'Connor GT, Buring JE, Yusuf S et al. An overview of randomized trials of rehabilitation with exercise after myocardial infarction. *Circulation* 1989;80:234–244. (No details of search date or primary sources given.)
88. Berlin JA, Colditz GA. A meta-analysis of physical activity in the prevention of coronary heart disease. *Am J Epidemiol* 1990;132:612–628. (No details of search date or primary sources given.)
89. Wenger NK, Froelicher NS, Smith LK, et al. *Cardiac rehabilitation and secondary prevention*. Rockville, Maryland: Agency for Health Care Policy and Research and National Heart, Lung and Blood Institute, 1995.
90. US Department of Health and Human Services. *The health benefits of smoking cessation: a report of the surgeon general*. Bethesda, Maryland: US DHSS,1990.
91. Working Group for the Study of Transdermal Nicotine in Patients with Coronary Artery Disease. Nicotine replacement therapy for patients with coronary artery disease. *Arch Intern Med* 1994;154:989–995.
92. Joseph AM, Norman SM, Ferry LH, et al. The safety of transdermal nicotine as an aid to smoking cessation in patients with cardiac disease. *N Engl J Med* 1996;335:1792–1798.
93. Burt A, Thornley P, Illingworth D, White P, Shaw TRD, Turner R. Stopping smoking after myocardial infarction. *Lancet* 1974;I:304–306.
94. Linden W, Stossel C, Maurice J. Psychosocial interventions for patients with coronary artery disease: a meta-analysis. *Arch Intern Med* 1996; 156:745–752. (No details of search date or primary sources given.)
95. US Department of Health and Human Services. *Cardiac rehabilitation*. AHCPR Publication No 96-0672, 1995;121–128.
96. Hemingway H, Marmot M. Psychosocial factors in the primary and secondary prevention of coronary heart disease: a systematic review. In Yusuf S, Cairns JA, Camm AJ, Fallen EL, Gersh BJ, eds. *Evidence based cardiology*. London: BMJ Books, 1998. (Search date 1996; primary sources MEDLINE 1966–1996, manual searching of bibliographies of retrieved articles and review articles.)
97. Yusuf S, Zucker D, Peduzzi P, *et al.* Effect of coronary artery bypass graft surgery on survival: overview of 10-year results from randomized trials by the coronary artery bypass graft surgery trialists collaboration. *Lancet* 1994; 344: 563–570.
98. Davies RF, Goldberg AD, Forman S, *et al.* Asymptomatic cardiac ischemia pilot (ACIP) study two-year follow-up: outcomes of patients randomized to initial strategies of medical therapy versus revascularization. *Circulation* 1997;95:2037–2043.
99. Parisi AF, Folland ED, Hartigan P. A comparison of angioplasty with medical therapy in the treatment of single-vessel coronary artery disease. *N Engl J Med* 1992;326:10–16.
100.RITA-2 Trial Participants. Coronary angioplasty versus medical therapy for angina: the second randomized intervention treatment of angina (RITA-2) trial. *Lancet* 1997;350:461–468.
101.Morris KG, Folland ED, Hartigan PM, Parisi AF. Unstable angina in late follow-up of the ACME trial. *Circulation* 1995;92(suppl I): I-725.
102.Pocock SJ, Henderson RA, Rickards AF, *et al.* Meta-analysis of randomized trials comparing coronary angioplasty with bypass surgery. *Lancet* 1995;346:1184–1189. (No details of search date or primary sources given.)
103.Bypass Angioplasty Revascularization Investigation (BARI) Investigators. Comparison of coronary bypass surgery with angioplasty in patients with multivessel disease: *N Engl J Med* 1996;335: 217–225.
104.Rihal CS, Gersh BJ, Yusuf S. Chronic coronary artery disease: coronary artery bypass surgery vs percutaneous transluminal coronary angioplasty vs medical therapy. In: Yusuf S, Cairns JA, Camm JA, Fallen EL, Gersh BJ, eds. *Evidence based cardiology*. London: BMJ Books, 1998.
105.Hlatky MA, Rogers WJ, Johnstone I, et al. Medical care costs and quality of life after randomization to coronary angioplasty or coronary bypass surgery. *N Engl J Med* 1997;336:92–99.
106.Fischman DL, Leon MB, Bain DS, et al. A randomized comparison of coronary-stent placement and balloon angioplasty in the treatment of coronary artery disease. *N Engl J Med* 1994;331:496–501.
107.Serruys PW, de Jaegere P, Kiemeneij F, et al. A comparison of balloon-expandable-stent implantation with balloon angioplasty in patients with coronary artery disease. *N Engl J Med* 1994;33:489–495.
108.Versaci F, Gaspardone A, Tomai F, Crea F, Chiariello L, Gioffre PA. A comparison of coronary-artery stenting with angioplasty for isolated stenosis of the proximal left anterior descending coronary artery. *N Engl J Med* 1997;336: 817–822.
109.Savage MP, Douglas JS, Fischman DL, et al. Stent placement compared with balloon angioplasty for obstructed coronary bypass grafts. *N*

Engl J Med 1997;337:740–747.
110.Sirnes P, Golf S, Myreng Y, et al. Stenting in chronic coronary occlusion (SICCO): a randomized controlled trial of adding stent implantation after successful angioplasty. *J Am Coll Cardiol* 1996;28:1444–1451.
111.Rubartelli P, Niccoli L, Verna E, et al. Stent implantation versus balloon angioplasty in chronic coronary occlusions: results from the GISSOC trial. *J Am Coll Cardiol* 1998;32:90–96.
112.Schomig A, Neumann FJ, Kastrati A, et al. A randomized comparison of antiplatelet and anticoagulant therapy after the placement of coronary artery stents. *N Engl J Med* 1996;334:1084–1089.
113.Leon MB, Baim DS, Gordon P, et al. Clinical and angiographic results from the stent anticoagulation regimen study (STARS). *Circulation* 1996; 94:I-685.

Cathie Sudlow
Wellcome Research Fellow in Clinical Epidemiology
University of Oxford
Oxford
UK

Colin Baigent
MRC Scientist
University of Oxford
Oxford
UK

Eva Lonn
Assistant Professor of Medicine
Hamilton General Hospital
Hamilton
Canada

Jeffrey L Probstfield
Professor of Medicine
University of Washington
Seattle
USA

Andy Ness
Senior Lecturer in Epidemiology
University of Bristol
Bristol
UK

Charanjit Rihal
Consultant Cardiologist
Mayo Clinic and Mayo Foundation
Rochester
USA

Competing interests: CS, CB, AN, CR none declared. JLP has been reimbursed and received honoraria from the Merck Company. EL has received honoraria for delivering lectures from different companies including Hoechst Marion Roussel, the Merck Company, Parke-Davies; and research grants part awarded by Hoechst Marion Roussel and part by the Medical Research Council of Canada.

TABLE 1 Prognostic groups for people who survive the acute stage of MI. (*See text p. 79.*)

Baseline risk	1-year mortality	Clinical markers[3–5]
High	10%–50%	Older age; history of previous MI; reduced exercise tolerance (New York Heart Association functional classes II–IV) before admission; clinical signs of heart failure in the first 2 days (Killip classes IIb, III, and IV) or persistent heart failure on days 3–5 after infarction; early increased heart rate; persistent or early appearance of angina at rest or with minimal exertion; and multiple or complex ventricular arrhythmias during monitoring in hospital.
Moderate	10%	–
Low	2%–5%	Younger age (< 55 years), no previous MI, an event-free course during the first 5 days after MI.[3]

TABLE 2 **Baseline risk, NNT and RRR for the five large statin trials.[30] (*See* text p. 88.)**

Trial	AR (placebo group)	NNT (people needing treatment to prevent one event per year)	RRR (95% CI)
4S[47]	5.2%	63	0.34 (0.25–0.41)
CARE[49]	2.6%	167	0.24 (0.09–0.36)
LIPID[44]	2.6%	172	0.24 (0.15–0.32)
WOSCOPS[48]	1.5%	217	0.31 (0.17–0.43)
AFCAPS/TexCAPS[53]	2.9%	87	0.40 (0.17–0.57)

The outcomes chosen in each trial are those nearest to definite myocardial infarction and coronary artery disease death. The NNTs rise as the baseline risk (indicated by the event rate in the placebo group) falls. RRR seems unaffected by changes in baseline risk.

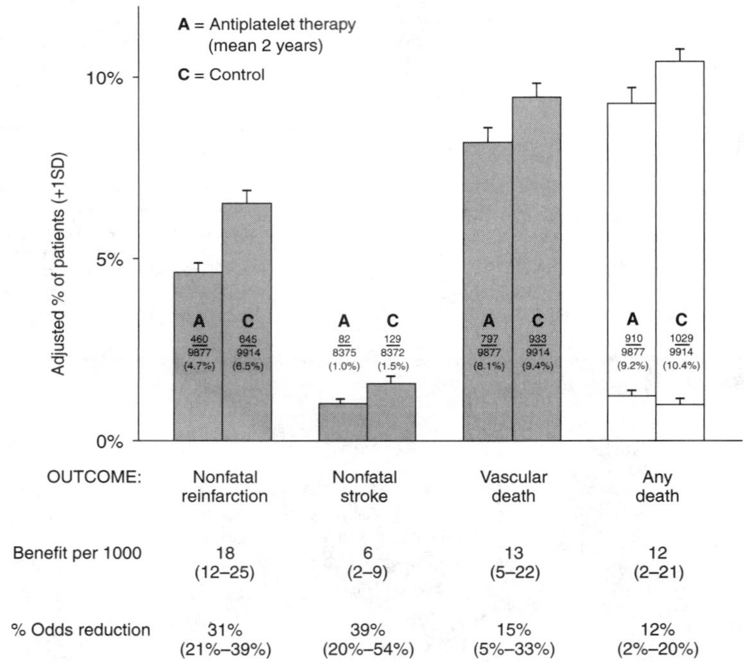

FIGURE 1 **The absolute effects of antiplatelet treatment on various outcomes in patients with prior MI: results of a systematic review.[11] The columns show the absolute risks over 2 years for each outcome. The error bars represent standard deviations. In "any death" column, nonvascular deaths are represented by lower horizontal lines. (*See* text p. 80.)**

Acute ischemic stroke

Gord Gubitz, MD, FRCPC, and Peter Sandercock, MD

QUESTIONS

INTERVENTIONS

To be covered in future issues of *Clinical Evidence*
Corticosteroids
Neuroprotective agents
Fibrinogen-depleting agents
Glycerol
Hemodilution techniques

Key Messages

- Systematic reviews of randomized controlled trials (RCTs) have found that:
  - Stroke rehabilitation units reduce death and severe disability.
  - Thrombolysis reduces the risk of dependency but increases the risk of death (both from intracranial hemorrhage and from any cause).
  - Early use of aspirin after a known ischemic stroke reduces the chance of death and dependency and improves the chance of complete recovery.
  - Immediate systemic anticoagulation does not improve outcome after ischemic stroke.
- Blood pressure reduction soon after acute ischemic stroke has not been tested in large-scale RCTs and may be harmful.
- Systematic reviews of RCTs have found no evidence of benefit from surgical evacuation of cerebral or cerebellar hematomas.

DEFINITION Stroke is characterized by rapidly developing clinical symptoms and signs of focal and, at times, global loss of cerebral function lasting more than 24 hours or leading to death, with no apparent cause other than that of vascular origin.[1]

INCIDENCE/PREVALENCE Stroke is the third most common cause of death in most developed countries.[2] It is a worldwide problem: approximately 4.5 million people worldwide die from stroke each year. Stroke can occur at any age, but half of all strokes occur in people aged over 70 years.[3]

ETIOLOGY Approximately 80% of all acute strokes are caused by cerebral infarction, usually resulting from thrombotic or embolic occlusion of a cerebral artery[4]; the remainder are caused by either intracerebral or subarachnoid hemorrhage.

PROGNOSIS Approximately 10% of all people with acute ischemic strokes will die within 30 days of stroke onset.[5] Of those who survive the acute event, approximately 50% will experience some level of disability after 6 months.[6]

AIMS To achieve rapid restoration and maintenance of blood supply to the ischemic area in the brain and to minimize brain damage and hence, impairment, disability, and secondary complications.

OUTCOMES Risk of death or dependency (generally assessed as the proportion of patients dead or requiring physical assistance for transfers, mobility, dressing, feeding, or toileting[7] 3–6 months after stroke onset); quality of life.

METHODS The systematic reviews and RCTs were selected after searching the Cochrane Library (Issue 3, 1998). Information on RCTs not yet published on the Cochrane Library was obtained by searching the Cochrane Stroke Review Group (Cochrane Library, Issue 2, 1999).

QUESTION What are the effects of specialized care?

One systematic review of RCTs has found that 1) stroke patients managed in specialist stroke rehabilitation units are more likely to be alive and living at home 1 year after the stroke than those managed in general medical wards, and 2) that stroke unit care reduces the time spent in hospital.

Benefits: We found one systematic review published in 1999.[7] This identified 20 RCTs in 3864 people with stroke comparing specialized stroke rehabilitation units with conventional care. In most of these trials, the specialized stroke rehabilitation unit consisted of a designated area or ward, although some trials used a mobile "stroke team." Participants in these trials usually were transferred to stroke care within the first week or two following stroke onset. Those cared for in a stroke rehabilitation unit were more likely to benefit; RRR for death or dependency after a median follow-up time of 1 year was 10% (95% CI 5%–15%). The NNT to prevent one additional death or dependence by one year was 16 (95% CI 11–32). (*See* Figure 1 for comparison with other interventions.) Care in a stroke rehabilitation unit significantly reduced the time spent in hospital; stay in hospital was a mean of 1.9 days shorter in patients admitted to a stroke unit than in those given conventional care (95% CI 1–2.8 days shorter).

Harms: No detrimental effects attributable to stroke units were reported.

Comment: Of all of the interventions available for the treatment of stroke, admission to a stroke unit (or system of organized stroke care) is the most effective (Figure 1). Although the proportional reduction in death or dependency seems similar with stroke unit care and with thrombolysis, stroke units lead to the greatest benefit to the population. Stroke unit care is applicable to most stroke patients, whereas thrombolysis is applicable only to a very small proportion. In a region with 1000 strokes per year, of which 700 are admitted to hospital, perhaps 70 (10%) might be eligible for and treated with thrombolysis, and five people would avoid death or dependency. On the other hand, perhaps 500 would be admitted to a stroke unit, and 30 people would avoid death or dependency. The trials do not provide data on which aspects of the multidisciplinary approach lead to improved outcome. Most of the trials excluded mildest and severest strokes, and the lengths of stay were calculated in different ways, limiting the ability to infer general conclusions.

QUESTION What are the effects of medical treatment?

OPTION THROMBOLYSIS

The balance between benefits and harms from thrombolysis in acute ischemic stroke is not clear. One systematic review found that thrombolysis given soon after acute ischemic stroke reduced overall risk of death and dependency in the long term, but this benefit was achieved at the cost of an increased short-term risk of fatal intracranial hemorrhage. It remains unclear which patients are most likely to benefit.

Benefits: We found one systematic review published in 1997.[8] This identified 12 RCTs with a total of 3435 patients comparing intravenous thrombolytic treatment versus placebo given soon after the onset of stroke. All trials included a computed tomographic (CT) or magnetic resonance imaging (MRI) scan before randomization to exclude intracranial hemorrhage or other nonstroke disorders. The review included information on three different thrombolytic agents: streptokinase, urokinase, and recombinant tissue plasminogen activator (rt-PA), but direct comparison of different thrombolytic drugs was not possible. Thrombolysis reduced the RR of being dead or dependent at the end of the studies by 9% (95% CI 4%–16%). The NNT to prevent one additional death or disability at 6 months was 15 (95% CI 9–35). (*See* Figure 1 for comparison with other interventions.) Two important trials of intravenous rt-PA recently have been completed: one has been published in full[9] and the other has been published as an abstract[10]; their results seem consistent with the overall results of the systematic review, but the results of both will need to be incorporated in an update of the review.

Harms: **Fatal and nonfatal intracranial hemorrhage:** In the systematic review,[8] the RRI of fatal intracranial hemorrhage in patients treated with thrombolysis was 533% (95% CI 321%–2778%). The NNH to cause one additional fatal intracranial hemorrhage was 19 (95% CI 15–25). **Death:** In the systematic review,[8] thrombolytic treatment was associated with an increase in the RR of death at the end of the trials of 20% (95% CI 11%–46%). The NNH was 20 patients (95% CI 12–49). However, as noted above, this excess of deaths was offset by a decrease in the number of patients alive with disability 6 months after stroke onset; the net effect is a reduction in the number of patients "dead or dependent."

Comment: There was significant heterogeneity between the 12 trials for total deaths at the end of the trials (Figure 2).[8] Explanations may include variations between trials in the type of thrombolytic agent used; its dose; the concomitant use of antithrombotic agents (aspirin or heparin) within the first 24 hours of thrombolysis; severity of the strokes; and time from onset of the stroke to randomization (which was <6 hours in nine of the trials, but up to 5 days in two trials, and up to 2 weeks in the last trial). The balance of risk and benefit may be more favorable if the thrombolytic is given within 3 hours of onset.[9] The duration of follow-up in each trial varied from 2 weeks to 6 months. There is inadequate evidence to justify thrombolysis in patients who have not had a CT or MRI scan to exclude intracerebral hemorrhage.

OPTION ANTIPLATELET TREATMENT

One systematic review of RCTs has found that antiplatelet treatment with aspirin started within 48 hours of acute ischemic stroke reduces the risk of death and dependence, as does the continued long-term use of aspirin (*see* p. 118). Most patients included in the systematic review had had a CT scan to exclude hemorrhage before treatment was started: in such patients aspirin was beneficial. There is less evidence about the effect of aspirin in patients not scanned first.

Benefits: **Early use of aspirin (6 months):** We found one systematic review published in 1997.[12] This evaluated five small RCTs comparing antiplatelet treatment started within 14 days of the stroke versus placebo in 501 patients with definite or presumed ischemic stroke; too few events were recorded to make any firm conclusion. Aspirin alone was compared with placebo in only one of the five RCTs in the review as well as in two subsequent large RCTs involving more than 40,000 patients.[11,13] Patients in these trials were randomized and started on treatment within 48 hours of the onset of the stroke; most had an ischemic stroke confirmed by CT scan before randomization, but conscious patients could be randomized before CT if the stroke was very likely to be ischemic on clinical grounds. Treatment duration varied from 10 to 28 days. The results of the three trials of aspirin alone have been combined.[11] Aspirin (150–300 mg/d) started within the first 48 hours of acute ischemic stroke reduced the RR of death or dependency at the end of follow-up (an average of 4 weeks in one study[11] and 6 months in the other two) by 2.7% (95% CI 0.6%–4.8%). The NNT to avoid an additional death or dependency by the end of follow-up was 78 (95% CI 43–370), and for one extra patient to make a complete recovery from their stroke the NNT was 100. (*See* Figure 1 for comparison with other interventions.) **Long-term treatment (3 years):** *See* p. 118.

Harms: Although aspirin caused an excess within the treatment period of approximately two intracranial and two extracranial hemorrhages per 1000 patients treated, these small risks were more than offset by the reductions in death and disability from other causes.[11–14]

Comment: There is no clear evidence that any one dose of aspirin is more effective than any other. As the symptoms of aspirin toxicity (dyspepsia and constipation) are dose related,[15] the smallest effective dose should be used. On the basis of trial data,[11,13] this currently means a dose of 150 to 300 mg/d for the acute phase of ischemic stroke. Although patients truly intolerant to aspirin could be treated with ticlopidine, clopidogrel, or dipyridamole, these drugs are more expensive than aspirin. Patients unable to swallow safely after a stroke can be given aspirin as a suppository.

OPTION SYSTEMIC ANTICOAGULANTS

One systematic review of RCTs has found that immediate treatment with systemic anticoagulants (including unfractionated heparin, low-molecular-weight heparin, heparinoids, or specific thrombin inhibitors) offers no short- or long-term improvement in acute ischemic stroke. The risk of deep venous thrombosis and pulmonary embolus is reduced, but this benefit is offset by a dose-dependent risk of intracranial and extracranial hemorrhage.

Benefits: **Death or dependency:** We found one systematic review published in 1997 as part of the International Stroke Trial (IST) report.[13] This identified three RCTs which involved 19,759 patients; 97.6% of these came from the IST trial itself, which randomized patients with any severity of stroke to treatment with either subcutaneous heparin or placebo, usually after exclusion of hemorrhagic stroke by CT scan. There was no difference in the proportion of patients dead or dependent in the treatment and placebo groups at the end of follow-up at 3 to 6 months after the stroke: RRR 0.53% (95% CI –1.8% to 2.7%); ARR 0.33% (95% CI –1% to 1.68%). (See Figure 1 for comparison with other interventions.) Also, in the IST there was no clear short- or long-term benefit of heparin in the prespecified subgroups, including patients with acute ischemic stroke of presumed cardioembolic origin. A recent RCT of the heparinoid, danaparoid, in 1281 patients[16] also provided no evidence of clear benefit in terms of death or dependency at the end of the follow up period. **Deep venous thrombosis:** A systematic review[17] published in 1998 found 15 small heterogeneous RCTs, with a total of 1599 patients randomized to early treatment of ischemic stroke with one of several different types of systemic anticoagulant. The RRR of deep vein thrombosis in nine of those was 68% (95% CI 58%–75%). The NNT to avoid one additional deep venous thrombosis was 3 (95% CI 2–4).

Harms: The IST[13] found a RRI for symptomatic intracranial hemorrhages within 14 days of starting treatment of 193% (95% CI 132%–253%). The NNH for one additional symptomatic intracranial hemorrhage was 123 (95% CI 95–179). This effect was dose dependent; the RRI of medium-dose heparin compared with low-dose heparin at 14 days of treatment was 143% (95% CI 82%–204%). The NNH to cause one extra symptomatic intracranial hemorrhage by using medium-dose heparin instead of low-dose heparin was 97 (95% CI 68–169). The

IST also reported a dose-dependent RRI of major extracranial hemorrhages by 14 days of treatment with heparin: RRI 249% (95% CI 181%–317%). The NNH to cause one additional symptomatic extracranial hemorrhage was 106 (95% CI 83–145). Increased risk of intracranial and extracranial hemorrhage also was noted with low-molecular-weight heparin[17] and heparinoid.[16]

Comment: The IST included strokes of all severities, increasing the ability of the study to be generalized. The nine studies in the systematic review[18] studied deep vein thrombosis rates only during a brief treatment period, which was as short as 14 days in four trials. Alternative treatments to prevent deep vein thrombosis and pulmonary embolism after acute ischemic stroke include aspirin and compression stockings. The evidence relating to these will be reviewed in a future issue of *Clinical Evidence*.

OPTION BLOOD PRESSURE REDUCTION

One systematic review of RCTs provides no evidence that blood pressure reduction in patients with acute ischemic stoke has benefits but suggests treatment is harmful.

Benefits: We found one systematic review[19] published in 1998, which identified three RCTs comparing blood pressure–lowering treatment versus placebo in 113 patients with acute stroke. Several different antihypertensive agents were used. The trials collected insufficient clinical data to allow an analysis of the relation between changes in blood pressure and clinical outcome.

Harms: Individual RCTs have suggested that patients treated with antihypertensive agents may have a worse clinical outcome and increased mortality.[20,21] A systematic review published in 1994 evaluated nine placebo-controlled RCTs of the calcium-channel antagonist nimodipine in 3719 patients treated with acute stroke; no net benefit was found.[22] A more comprehensive review published in 1998 of 24 trials of calcium antagonists involving 6894 patients found a non-significant increase in the RR of death of 8% (95% CI 1% reduction to 18% increase).[23] Although treatment with calcium antagonists in these trials was intended for neuroprotection, blood pressure was lower in the treatment group in several trials.

Comment: Population-based data suggest a direct and continuous association between blood pressure and the risk of recurrent stroke.[24] However, acute blood pressure lowering in acute stroke may lead to increased cerebral ischemia. Immediate treatment of raised blood pressure may be indicated in certain patients, including those with intracerebral hemorrhage, severe hypertension, hypertensive encephalopathy, aortic dissection, cardiac failure, or cardiac ischemia.[25]

QUESTION What are the effects of surgical treatments?

OPTION EVACUATION OF INTRACEREBRAL HEMATOMAS

The balance between benefits and harms is not clearly established. Patients with infratentorial (cerebellar) hematomas whose consciousness level is declining probably benefit from evacuation, but there is no supporting evidence from RCTs.

Benefits: **For supratentorial hematomas:** We found two systematic reviews[26,27] published in 1997, which assessed the same four RCTs comparing surgery (craniotomy or endoscopy) versus best medical treatment in 350 patients with primary supratentorial intracerebral hemorrhage. Neither review found any short- or long-term benefit for the surgically treated patients: RRI for death or disability 5.2% (95% CI –8% to 18.4%). The NNT ranged from eight to cause one additional death or disability to 18 to prevent one additional adverse outcome. **For infratentorial hematomas:** We found no evidence from RCTs to suggest that either surgical evacuation or ventricular shunting is beneficial, although these techniques are regarded as the "standard of care" for such patients.[28]

Harms: The systematic reviews[26,27] found that the relative risk of death or dependency was increased by open craniotomy (RR 18%, 95% CI 3%–33%). The NNH for one additional death or dependence was seven people having a craniotomy (95% CI 4–54).

Comment: The balance between benefits and harms is not established clearly, but practice is based on the consensus opinion that patients with infratentorial (cerebellar) hematomas whose conscious level is declining probably benefit from evacuation.

REFERENCES

1. Hatano S. Experience from a multicentre stroke register: a preliminary report. *Bull World Health Organ* 1976;54:541–553.
2. Bonita R. Epidemiology of stroke. *Lancet* 1992;339:342–344.
3. Bamford J, Sandercock P, Dennis M, Warlow C, Jones L, McPherson K. A prospective study of acute cerebrovascular disease in the community: the Oxfordshire community stroke project, 1981–1986. 1. Methodology, demography and incident cases of first ever stroke. *J Neurol Neurosurg Psychiatry* 1988;51:1373–1380.
4. Bamford J, Dennis M, Sandercock P, Burn J, Warlow C. A prospective study of acute cerebrovascular disease in the community: the Oxfordshire community stroke project, 1981–1986. *J Neurol Neurosurg Psychiatry* 1990;53:16–22.
5. Bamford J, Dennis M, Sandercock P, Burn J, Warlow C. The frequency, causes and timing of death within 30 days of a first stroke: the Oxfordshire community stroke project. *J Neurol Neurosurg Psychiatry* 1990;53:824–829.
6. Wade DT, Hewer RL. Functional abilities after stroke: measurement, natural history and prognosis. *J Neurol Neurosurg Psychiatry* 1988;50:177–182.
7. Stroke Unit Trialists' Collaboration. Collaborative systematic review of the randomised trials of organised inpatient (stroke unit) care after stroke. *BMJ* 1997;314:1151–1159. (Search date 1995, primary sources, a wide range including Index Medicus and MEDLINE.)
8. Wardlaw JM, Warlow CP, Counsell C. Systematic review of evidence on thrombolytic therapy for acute ischaemic stroke. *Lancet* 1997;350: 607–414. (Search date 1996; primary sources, a wide range including MEDLINE and EMBASE and Cochrane stroke group specialist trials register.)
9. Hacke W, Kaste M, Fieschi C, et al, for the Second European-Australasian Acute Stroke Study Investigators. Randomised double-blind placebo-controlled trial of thrombolytic therapy with intravenous alteplase in acute ischaemic stroke (ECASS II). *Lancet* 1998:352:1245–1251.
10. Clarke W, Albers G, ATLANTIS investigators. The ATLANTIS rt-PA study acute stroke trial: final results [abstr]. *Stroke* 1999;30:234.
11. CAST (Chinese Acute Stroke Trial) Collaborative Group. CAST: randomised placebo controlled trial of early aspirin use in 20,000 patients with acute ischaemic stroke. *Lancet* 1997;349:1641–1649.
12. Counsell C, Sandercock P. Antiplatelet therapy for acute ischaemic stroke (Cochrane Review). In: The Cochrane Library, Issue 1, 1999. Oxford: Update Software.

13. International Stroke Trial Collaborative Group. The international stroke trial (IST): a randomised trial of aspirin, subcutaneous heparin, both or neither among 19,435 patients with acute ischaemic stroke. *Lancet* 1997;349:1569–1581.
14. Antiplatelet Trialist's Collaboration. Collaborative overview of randomised trials of antiplatelet therapy I: Prevention of death, myocardial infarction and stroke by prolonged antiplatelet therapy in various categories of patients. *BMJ* 1994;308: 81–106. (Search date 1990, primary sources, a wide range including MEDLINE and Current Contents.)
15. Slattery J, Warlow CP, Shorrock CJ, Langman MJS. Risks of gastrointestinal bleeding during secondary prevention of vascular events with aspirin – analysis of gastrointestinal bleeding during the UK-TIA trial. *Gut* 1995;37:509–511.
16. Publications Committee for the Trial of ORG 10172 in Acute Stroke Treatment (TOAST) Investigators. Low molecular weight heparinoid ORG 10172 (danaparoid), and outcome after acute ischaemic stroke. *JAMA* 1998;279:1265–1272.
17. Hommel M, for the FISS-bis Investigators Group. Fraxiparine in ischaemic stroke study (FISS-bis) [abstr]. *Cerebrovasc Dis* 1998;8(suppl 4):19.
18. Counsell C, Sandercock PA. The efficacy and safety of anticoagulant therapy in patients with acute presumed ischaemic stroke. (Cochrane Review). In: The Cochrane Library, Issue 2, 1998. Oxford: Update Software. Updated quarterly.
19. Blood pressure in Acute Stroke Collaboration (BASC). Blood pressure management in acute stroke. Part I: assessment of trials designed to alter blood pressure. (Cochrane Review). In: The Cochrane Library, Issue 2, 1998. Oxford: Update Software. Updated quarterly.
20. Wahlgren NG, MacMahon DG, DeKeyser J, Ingredavik B, Ryman, T. Intravenous nimedipine west European stroke trial (INWEST) of nimedipine in the treatment of acute ischaemic stroke. *Cerebrovasc Dis* 1994;4:204–210.
21. Barer DH, Cruickshank JM, Ebrahim SB, Mitchell JRA. Low dose beta blockade in acute stroke (BEST trial): an evaluation. *BMJ* 1988;296:737–741.
22. Mohr JP, Orgogozo JM, Harrison MJG, et al. Meta-analysis of oral nimodipine trials in acute ischaemic stroke. *Cerebrovasc Dis* 1994;4:197–203.
23. Horn J, Orgogozo JM, Limburg M. Review on calcium antagonists in ischaemic stroke; mortality data [abstr]. *Cerebrovasc Dis* 1998;8(suppl 4):27.
24. Rodgers A, MacMahon S, Gamble G, et al. Blood pressure and risk of stroke in patients with cerebrovascular disease. *BMJ* 1996;313:147.
25. O'Connell JE, Gray CS. Treating hypertension after stroke. *BMJ* 1994;308:1523–1524.
26. Prasad K, Browman G, Srivastava A, Menon G. Surgery in primary supratentorial intracerebral hematoma: a meta-analysis of randomised trials. *Acta Neurol Scand* 1997;95:103–110. (Search date 1995, primary sources, a wide range including MEDLINE and Current Contents.)
27. Hankey GJ, Hon C. Surgery for primary intracerebral haemorrhage: is it safe and effective? A systematic review of case series and randomized trials. *Stroke* 1997;28:2126–2132. (Search date 1966; primary source MEDLINE.)
28. Treatment of primary intracerebral haemorrhage. In: Warlow CP, Dennis MS, van Gijn J, et al, eds. *Stroke: a practical guide to management*. Oxford: Blackwell Science,1996:435.

Gord Gubitz, MD, FRCPC
Clinical Research Fellow

Peter Sandercock, MD
Reader in Neurology

University of Edinburgh
Edinburgh
UK

Competing interests: GG, none declared. PS has received honoraria for lectures, funds for research, funds for members of his staff and fees for single consultancies from Glaxo Wellcome, Boehringer Ingelheim, Sanofi/BMS.

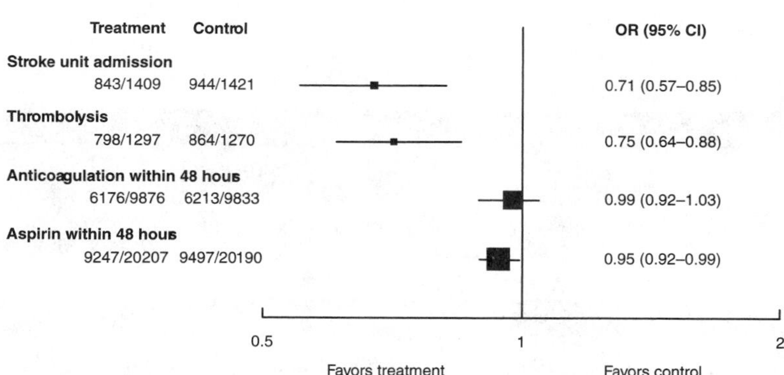

FIGURE 1 The proportional effects of different interventions on "death or dependency" at the end of scheduled follow-up: results of systematic reviews.[7,8,11,13] The data refer only to benefits and not to harms.

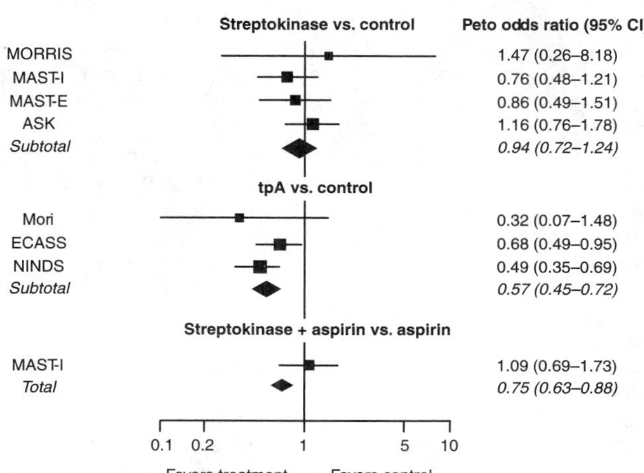

FIGURE 2 Effect of thrombolysis on death and dependency at end of trial follow-up: results of a systematic review of RCTs. Published with permission.[8] (*See* text p. 107.)

Stroke prevention

Clinical Evidence writers on secondary stroke prevention

QUESTIONS

INTERVENTIONS

Key Messages

In people with a prior stroke or TIA, the available randomized evidence shows that:

- There is insufficient evidence to support routine blood pressure reduction.
- A statin may prevent stroke in people who also have a history of coronary artery disease. In those with no history of coronary artery disease, the evidence is inconclusive.
- Routine use of prolonged antiplatelet treatment is beneficial unless there is a clear contraindication.
- Aspirin 75 mg/d is as effective as higher doses. There is no evidence that any other antiplatelet regimen is definitely superior to medium-dose aspirin (75–325 mg/d) in the prevention of vascular events. Clopidogrel or the combination of aspirin and dipyridamole are safe and effective (but more costly) alternatives to medium-dose aspirin.
- There is no evidence of benefit from anticoagulation in people in sinus rhythm, but there is an increased risk of serious bleeding.

- Carotid endarterectomy reduces the risk of major stroke in people with severe carotid stenosis provided the risks of imaging and surgery are small.
- The role of percutaneous transluminal angioplasty has not been adequately evaluated.

In people with atrial fibrillation and a prior stroke or TIA, the available randomized evidence shows that:

- Anticoagulants reduce the risk of stroke, provided there is a low risk of bleeding and careful monitoring.
- Aspirin reduces the risk of stroke, but less effectively than anticoagulants. These findings support the use of aspirin among those people with atrial fibrillation and contraindications to anticoagulants.

In people with atrial fibrillation but with no other major risk factors for stroke, the available randomized evidence shows that:

- Anticoagulants reduce the risk of stroke, provided there is a low risk of bleeding and careful monitoring.
- Aspirin reduces the risk of stroke in people with contraindications to anticoagulants.

DEFINITION Primary prevention in this context is the management of people with risk factors for the initial occurrence of stroke or TIA. Secondary prevention in this context is the long-term management of people with a prior stroke or TIA. Stroke: *See* p. 106. TIA: Similar to a mild ischemic stroke except that symptoms last for less than 24 hours.[1]

INCIDENCE/ PREVALENCE *See* p. 106.

ETIOLOGY *See* p. 106. Risk factors for stroke include prior stroke or TIA, increasing age, hypertension, diabetes, cigarette smoking, and emboli associated with atrial fibrillation, artificial heart valves, or myocardial infarction. The relation with cholesterol is less clear; an overview of prospective studies among apparently healthy middle-aged individuals found no overall association between total cholesterol and stroke risk.[2] However, the lack of any overall relation may have concealed a positive relation with ischemic stroke and a negative association with hemorrhagic stroke, as was observed in an overview of prospective studies conducted in eastern Asian populations.[3]

PROGNOSIS Patients with a history of stroke or TIA are at particularly high risk of subsequent stroke (~ 10% in the first year and ~ 5% per year thereafter), but they are also at increased risk of other serious vascular events, including myocardial infarction.[4] The most frequent subsequent event is another stroke or TIA rather than any other vascular event (compare Figure 1, p. 127 with Figure 1, p. 104).

AIMS To prevent death or disabling stroke as well as other serious nonfatal outcomes, especially myocardial infarction.

OUTCOMES Rates of TIA or stroke, recurrent TIA or stroke, or death.

METHODS Searches of electronic databases were performed in July 1998. Recent appropriate systematic reviews were identified as well as more recent RCTs.

QUESTION **What are the effects of interventions in people with previous stroke or TIA?**

OPTION **BLOOD PRESSURE REDUCTION**

Cathie Sudlow, Colin Baigent

We found insufficient randomized evidence to recommend routine blood pressure reduction among patients with a prior stroke or TIA, but this issue currently is being addressed in a large RCT.

Benefits: An overview of RCTs of antihypertensive treatment (generally comprising a diuretic, a β-blocker, or both) pooled data among approximately 48,000 people with hypertension, most of whom had no history of vascular disease. It found a reduction of approximately 5 to 6 mm Hg in diastolic blood pressure over 2 to 3 years reduced the odds of stroke by 38% (95% CI 31%–45%).[6] The proportional effects of treatment on stroke were similar among patients with differing degrees of hypertension, among middle-aged and elderly patients, and among patients with or without a prior stroke or TIA.[7] However, only two of the trials (including approximately 500 patients) specifically aimed to assess the effects of blood pressure reduction among hypertensive patients with a prior stroke or TIA.[7] A subsequent overview of individual patient data from many of the same trials also found no significant difference between the effects of antihypertensive treatment on patients with or without a history of a cerebrovascular event.[8] Similar, but statistically uncertain, results were obtained in an overview of four RCTs of antihypertensive treatment versus placebo in approximately 3000 patients with a history of a cerebrovascular event (with or without hypertension): an average diastolic blood pressure reduction of 3 mm Hg produced a nonsignificant reduction of 19% (95% CI –1% to 39%) in the odds of stroke within approximately 3 years.[7] In a preliminary report from a further trial in China in which 5665 patients with a prior stroke or TIA were randomized to receive either the diuretic indapamide or placebo, a reduction of approximately 2 mm Hg in diastolic blood pressure over 2 years produced a reduction in stroke incidence of 29% (95% CI 12%–42%).[9] It is appropriate to await final results before including this trial in any formal assessment of the randomized evidence.

Harms: Among patients with a history of stroke, reports of an apparently J-shaped relationship between blood pressure and subsequent stroke have led to concerns that blood pressure reduction actually may increase the risk of recurrent stroke, perhaps because of reduced cerebral perfusion.[9] This possibility may be of particular concern for patients with hemodynamically significant stenosis of the extracranial carotid or vertebral arteries. However, preliminary analyses of data from over 15,000 patients with a history of cerebrovascular or coronary events included in trials in the antithrombotic trialists' collaboration showed a positive log-linear relation between usual diastolic blood pressure and the subsequent risk of stroke; for every 5 mm Hg decrease in usual diastolic blood pressure there was approximately 15% proportional reduction in stroke risk, with no evidence of any threshold below which a lower diastolic blood pressure was not associated with a lower stroke risk.[10,11] The RCTs found no evidence that reducing diastolic blood pressure was hazardous, at least down to approximately 80 mm Hg.[5]

Comment: In the light of persisting uncertainty about the net effects of blood pressure reduction among patients with a previous cerebrovascular event, a large RCT (the perindopril protection against recurrent stroke study [PROGRESS]) is currently assessing the balance of benefits and risks of treatment with an angiotensin-converting–enzyme (ACE) regimen among 6000 patients with a history of stroke or TIA.[7]

OPTION CHOLESTEROL REDUCTION

Cathie Sudlow, Colin Baigent

We found insufficient randomized evidence about the effects of cholesterol reduction among patients with a prior stroke or TIA to recommend routine treatment for such patients. The existing randomized evidence does, however, support cholesterol reduction with a statin in such patients who also have a definite history of coronary heart disease.

Benefits: Tens of thousands of individuals have been randomized in trials that primarily assessed the effects of reducing cholesterol on coronary artery disease risk, both among those with a history of coronary artery disease and among apparently healthy individuals. These trials did not aim specifically to include patients with a prior stroke or TIA, but many reported the effects of reducing cholesterol concentrations on stroke as an outcome.[12,13] Overviews of these have shown that, whereas a mean reduction in total cholesterol of around 11% with a fibrate, resin, or dietary regimen produced no clear effect on stroke, a mean reduction of approximately 22% in total cholesterol with a statin produced approximately a 30% reduction in the risk of stroke (as well as approximately a 30% reduction in the risk of coronary artery disease) (Table 1).[12,13] Only two small early RCTs have assessed directly the effects of reducing cholesterol among patients with a prior stroke or TIA, but the drug used (clofibrate in both cases) produced only a small fall in the mean cholesterol, and the results were inconclusive.[14,15]

Harms: There was a nonsignificant 17% increase in the odds of fatal stroke in the statin trials, albeit with a wide 95% CI ranging from approximately a twofold increase to a 30% reduction (Table 1).[12] Because a hemorrhagic stroke is more likely to be fatal than an ischemic stroke, this finding raises the concern that reducing cholesterol concentrations may produce a small excess risk of hemorrhagic stroke. However, very few trials reported reliable information on pathologic types of stroke,[13] and the issue awaits further clarification from ongoing studies.

Comment: The effect of reducing cholesterol concentrations among patients with a previous stroke or TIA but no history of coronary artery disease remains uncertain. To date, only two large-scale statin trials (CARE[16] and 4S[17]) have reported separately the results for hemorrhagic stroke; because only 10 such strokes were recorded in these two studies (six in people allocated statin compared with four in those allocated placebo) no reliable conclusions can be drawn. The randomized evidence supports cholesterol reduction with a statin among those patients who also have a definite history of coronary artery disease. A prospective overview of individual patient data from all RCTs of cholesterol reduction eventually will provide a reliable summary of the overall effects of reducing cholesterol concentrations among various groups of patients with a previous stroke or TIA.[18]

OPTION ANTIPLATELET TREATMENT

Cathie Sudlow, Colin Baigent

The available randomized evidence shows that prolonged antiplatelet treatment is beneficial for patients with a prior (presumed ischemic) stroke or TIA, unless there is a clear contraindication. There is no clear evidence that any other antiplatelet regimen is superior to medium-dose aspirin (75–325 mg/d) in the prevention of vascular events. Aspirin 75 mg daily is as effective as higher doses in the long-term prevention of vascular events, but it remains unclear whether doses lower than 75 mg/d are sufficient. Clopidogrel or the combination of aspirin and dipyridamole are safe and effective (but more costly) alternatives to medium-dose aspirin.

Benefits: **Antiplatelet treatment versus control:** The most recent antiplatelet trialists' (APT) collaborative overview published in 1994 showed that a month or more of antiplatelet treatment produced a highly significant reduction of approximately one quarter in the odds of a vascular event (nonfatal myocardial infarction, nonfatal stroke, or vascular death) among approximately 70,000 patients at high risk of occlusive arterial disease.[5] These included approximately 10,000 patients with a previous (presumed ischemic) stroke or TIA, among whom approximately 20 nonfatal strokes, nine nonfatal myocardial infarctions, and 11 vascular deaths were prevented per 1000 patients treated with antiplatelet treatment for approximately 3 years. There was also a clear reduction in all-cause mortality (Figure 1). **Different daily doses of aspirin:** Approximately two thirds of the RCTs in the 1994 APT overview involved an aspirin regimen, and medium-dose aspirin (75–325 mg/d) was the most widely tested. Indirect comparisons showed that daily doses of more than 160 mg (mostly 75–150 mg), 160 to 325 mg, and 500 to 1500 mg prevented similar proportions of vascular events among high-risk patients, whereas direct comparisons also showed that daily doses of 75 to 325 mg or 500 to 1500 mg were similarly effective.[5] The inclusion of data from two more recent large trials among high-risk patients (one of them including almost 1400 patients with a previous ischemic stroke or TIA[19]) assessing a daily dose of exactly 75 mg versus control,[19,20] showed that this aspirin dose produced a definite reduction in vascular events (odds reduction 29%, 95% CI 17%–39%).[5] However, the effects of doses lower than 75 mg/d have been studied less extensively in RCTs. In the second European stroke prevention study (ESPS-2), which included approximately 6000 patients with a previous stroke or TIA, aspirin 50 mg/d produced a reduction of only 13% (95% CI 1%–25%) in the primary outcome of "stroke or death" compared with placebo.[21] The only directly randomized comparison of medium- versus low-dose aspirin found that the effects of daily doses of 30 mg and 283 mg were similar among approximately 3000 patients with a recent TIA or minor ischemic stroke but could not exclude the possibility of moderate (and clinically important) differences between these two doses.[22] **Alternative antiplatelet regimens to aspirin:** In the APT 1994 overview, neither direct nor indirect comparisons between different antiplatelet regimens provided clear evidence that any regimen was more effective than medium-dose aspirin alone in the prevention of vascular events.[18] Two recent large trials have provided further information about two new antiplatelet regimens: the combination of low-dose aspirin (50 mg/d) and dipyridamole,[21] and clopidogrel.[23] In the 1994 APT overview, the addition of dipyridamole to aspirin did not seem to produce any worthwhile reduction in vascular events compared with aspirin alone, but the possibility of a small additional benefit was not excluded.[5] More recently, ESPS-2 showed that although the addition of dipyridamole to aspirin 50 mg/d produced a significant 23% reduction in the risk of stroke, the 13% reduction in the risk of "stroke or death" was more modest and statistically uncertain.[21] More detailed analyses of all the trials that have assessed the effects of adding dipyridamole to aspirin currently are being prepared by the antithrombotic trialists' (ATT) collaboration.[24] The clopidogrel versus aspirin in patients at risk of ischemic events (CAPRIE) trial compared clopidogrel (75 mg/d) versus aspirin (325 mg/d) among approximately 20,000 high-risk patients with a recent ischemic stroke, a recent myocardial infarction, or peripheral arterial disease. Clopidogrel produced a significant reduction in the risk of a vascular event (defined in this trial as a nonfatal myocardial infarction, nonfatal stroke, or nonhemorrhagic vascular death; RRR 8.7%, 95% CI 0.3%–16.5%; $p=0.04$).[23] A similar proportional reduction in vascular events was observed among approximately 3500 high-risk patients included in previous trials comparing ticlopidine versus aspirin.[18] Hence, if the trials of thienopyridines (clopidogrel and ticlopidine) are considered together, they suggest that such agents are at least as effective as medium-dose aspirin and may offer greater protection against vascular events. Clopidogrel also was found to be safe in CAPRIE, with a much lower incidence of neutropenia than had been observed previously in trials of ticlopidine. However, the size of any absolute benefits that may arise from replacing aspirin with clopidogrel among particular types of high-risk patients remains statistically uncertain: overall, approximately five vascular events were avoided per 1000 patients treated per year (95% CI 0–10).[23]

Harms: Serious, potentially life-threatening bleeding is the most important adverse effect of antiplatelet treatment. **Intracranial hemorrhages:** These are uncommon, but they are often fatal and usually cause significant disability in survivors and thus constitute the main hazard that could offset treatment benefit. The APT 1994 overview showed that any excess risk of intracranial bleeding with antiplatelet treatment was small, at most one or two per 1000 patients per year in trials of long-term treatment.[5] **Extracranial hemorrhages:** Unlike serious vascular events, extracranial bleeds rarely result in permanent disability or death. Antiplatelet treatment produced a small but significant excess of three per 1000 nonfatal major extracranial bleeds, but there was no clear excess of fatal extracranial bleeds.[5] In a direct randomized comparison, aspirin 1200 mg/d was associated with more gastrointestinal bleeding than 325 mg/d[25] but there is no definite evidence for any clinically relevant variation in gastrointestinal bleeding risk in the range 75 to 325 mg/d. However, it seems reasonable to choose the lowest conveniently available dosage in this range.

Comment: Among patients with a previous stroke or TIA, therefore, the large absolute reductions in serious vascular events produced by antiplatelet treatment far outweigh any absolute hazards. Additional Cochrane systematic reviews on the subject of antiplatelet therapy are currently in preparation.

OPTION LONG-TERM ORAL ANTICOAGULATION FOR PEOPLE IN NORMAL SINUS RHYTHM

Gord Gubitz, Peter Sandercock

One systematic review of RCTs provides no evidence that long-term oral anticoagulation reduces the risk of stroke recurrence after presumed ischemic stroke in patients in normal sinus rhythm. The risk of fatal intracranial and extracranial hemorrhage is increased.

Benefits: We found one systematic review published in 1998, which evaluated nine small trials (mean duration 1.8 years) comparing oral anticoagulants (warfarin, dicoumarol, phenindione) versus placebo.[26] The review included 1214 patients in normal sinus rhythm with previous nonembolic presumed ischemic stroke or TIA. There was no clear benefit of anticoagulation on mortality, death or dependency, or recurrent stroke; for death or dependency the AR by the end of the trials was 67% in the anticoagulation group and 71% in the control group (RRR 0.05, 95% CI –0.09 to 0.20; ARR 4%, 95% CI –6% to 14%), which included the possibility that anticoagulants might lead to an additional 14% of treated patients being alive and independent or, equally, an additional 6% being dead or dependent.

Harms: By the end of the trials, the systematic review found a significantly increased risk of fatal intracranial hemorrhage (RRI 1.76, 95% CI 0.36–3.16; NNH 49 people treated with anticoagulants over 1.8 years to produce one additional nonfatal extracranial hemorrhage, 95% CI 27–240) and of fatal and nonfatal extracranial hemorrhage (RRI 3.73, 95% CI 1.47–7.91, NNH for one additional extracranial hemorrhage 20, 95% CI 14–33).[26] **Warfarin versus aspirin:** One RCT compared aspirin versus oral anticoagulant (target International Normalized Ratio [INR] 3.0–4.5) in 1316 patients for approximately 14 months after TIA or nondisabling stroke.[27] The trial was stopped early because of an excess of intracranial hemorrhages in the warfarin-treated group (RRI 1.3, 95% CI 0.6–2.5).

Comment: The trials in the systematic review[26] all had major methodologic problems, including poor monitoring of anticoagulation. All were completed before the introduction of routine computed tomography (CT) scanning, which means that patients with primary hemorrhagic strokes could have been included. The systematic review could therefore not provide a reliable and precise overall estimate of the balance of risk and benefit with respect to death or dependency. Most patients in the trial comparing warfarin and aspirin did have a CT scan, but an adverse outcome still was seen with anticoagulants.

OPTION CAROTID ENDARTERECTOMY FOR PEOPLE WITH RECENT CAROTID TERRITORY ISCHEMIA

Gord Gubitz, Peter Sandercock

RCTs have found that carotid endarterectomy reduces the risk of major stroke and death in people with a recent carotid territory TIA or nondisabling

ischemic stroke who have severe symptomatic stenosis of the ipsilateral carotid artery (> 70%). We found no clear evidence on the balance of benefits and harms in people with lesser degrees of symptomatic stenosis. Weak evidence from one RCT suggests possible benefit in people with asymptomatic but severe stenosis, but new large-scale trials are awaited.

Benefits: **In people with symptomatic stenosis:** We found no systematic review. Two large RCTs have compared carotid surgery versus control treatment in which surgery was avoided if at all possible in 5909 people with some degree of ipsilateral carotid stenosis.[28,29] The trials included 1235 people with severe stenosis (>70% or >80%[28]). Participants were randomized within 4[29] and 6[28] months of the onset of vascular symptoms. Both trials found significant reductions in the risk of major stroke or death, but with benefit limited to people with severe stenosis. In one trial, RRR at 2 years was 0.56 (95% CI 0.27–0.84, NNT to avoid one additional major stroke or death by two years = 10, 95% CI 7–20)[29]; in the other trial, RRR at 3 years was 0.44 (95% CI 0.18–0.70, NNT to avoid one additional major stroke or death by 3 years = 9, 95% CI 5–21).[28] After 3 years, the beneficial effect of carotid surgery disappeared because the risk of ipsilateral stroke in the control group decreased.[28] **In people with asymptomatic stenosis:** We found one systematic review, published in 1998, of five trials of carotid endarterectomy for asymptomatic carotid stenosis (e.g., no carotid territory TIA or minor stroke within past few months), which included 2440 patients.[30] Carotid surgery reduced the risk of odds of ipsilateral stoke or death by 38% (95% CI 16% to 56%), ARR 2%, NNT 50 to prevent one ipsilateral stroke or death over 3 years. Although the risk of perioperative stroke or death from carotid surgery for people with asymptomatic stenosis (2.3%) appears to be lower than in people with symptomatic stenosis, the risk of stroke without surgery is low and, for most people, the balance of risk and benefit from surgery is unclear.[30]

Harms: Carotid surgery in symptomatic people is associated with a small but definite risk of stroke and death. In the two RCTs described above, the ARs of major stroke or death at 30 days in treatment and control groups were 7% vs. 0.2%[28] and 2.1% vs. 0.9%.[29] Postoperative complications included wound hematoma, lower cranial nerve injury, hypertension, hypotension, and recurrent stenosis.

Comment: **People with symptomatic stenosis:** The two RCTs used different techniques to measure the degree of carotid stenosis, but conversion charts are available. The trials, as well as observational studies,[31] show that the risk of recurrent stroke is highest around the time of the symptomatic event. Therefore, surgery probably should be performed as soon as possible, and targeted at patients with the highest risk of further stroke (e.g., those with frequent TIAs, ulcerated rather than smooth stenosis, and cerebral rather than ocular symptoms). It also would seem reasonable that surgery should be conducted only in centers with high patient volumes and acceptable rates of angiographic and operative risk, but we found no evidence from RCTs to back up this statement. **People with asymptomatic stenosis:** A large-scale trial (ACST) is ongoing and aims to confirm or refute the findings of the systematic review[31] described above.

OPTION **CAROTID PERCUTANEOUS TRANSLUMINAL ANGIOPLASTY**

Gord Gubitz, Peter Sandercock

Carotid percutaneous transluminal angioplasty (PTA) has not been evaluated adequately in people with a recent carotid territory TIA or nondisabling ischemic stroke who have severe stenosis of the ipsilateral carotid artery.

Benefits: We found no systematic review. **Carotid PTA:** One RCT[32] compared "best medical treatment plus carotid PTA" versus "best medical treatment plus carotid endarterectomy" in 504 people with a recent carotid territory TIA or nondisabling ischemic stroke with stenosis of the ipsilateral carotid artery. Too few patients were randomized between angioplasty and best medical care to provide reliable estimates of efficacy. Preliminary data have been presented but not yet published, suggesting that the rates of stroke or death at 30 days are similar. The final data on short- and long-term outcome are awaited. **Vertebral artery PTA:** The RCT[32] randomized only 16 patients between vertebral PTA and best medical treatment. This did not provide enough data for reliable estimates of efficacy.

Harms: We found insufficient randomized data on which to comment. An audited analysis of the safety data of the RCT[32] has not yet been published.

Comment: We found insufficient evidence at present to advise practice. PTA should continue to be evaluated in RCTs.

QUESTION **What are the effects of interventions in people with atrial fibrillation?**

Gord Gubitz, Peter Sandercock, Gregory YH Lip

OPTION **ANTICOAGULATION AND ANTIPLATELET TREATMENT FOR PEOPLE IN ATRIAL FIBRILLATION**

One systematic review of RCTs has found that people at high risk of stroke who are in atrial fibrillation and have no contraindication to anticoagulants will benefit from anticoagulation. Aspirin is less effective than warfarin, but is a reasonable alternative if warfarin is contraindicated. The best time to start anticoagulation after an ischemic stroke is unclear.

Benefits: **Warfarin versus placebo in people with atrial fibrillation and a previous stroke or TIA:** We found one systematic review[33] published in 1998 of the effects of anticoagulation in two RCTs, including 1053 people with chronic nonrheumatic atrial fibrillation. Ninety-eight percent of the people came from one trial,[34] which started treatment within 3 months of a minor stroke or TIA: 669 were randomized to open-label anticoagulant or double-blinded aspirin or placebo; 338 had contraindications to anticoagulants and were randomized to aspirin or placebo. Anticoagulation (target INR 2.5–4.0) compared with placebo for 2.3 years reduced recurrent stroke (ARs 12% per year for placebo, 4% for warfarin, RRR 0.64, 95% CI 0.42–0.78; NNT 7, 95% CI 5–14). **Warfarin versus placebo in people with atrial fib-**

rillation but no previous stroke or TIA: We found one systematic review, published by the atrial fibrillation investigators in 1994. This evaluated the five initial primary prevention trials involving 2461 people over a mean of 1.5 years found that anticoagulation compared with placebo reduced the rate of stroke (ARs 4.5% per year for placebo, 1.4% for warfarin, RRR 0.68, 95% CI 0.50–0.79, NNT for 1 year to prevent one additional stroke = 32).[35] **Warfarin versus aspirin:** Aspirin was less effective than warfarin in people with a prior stroke or TIA (RRR for stroke with warfarin compared with aspirin 0.65, 95% CI 0.4–0.8, equivalent to NNT per year to avoid one additional stroke = 17).[34] **Aspirin versus placebo:** We found one systematic review, published in 1997, involving 2574 people in three RCTs (including one RCT of people with prior stroke or TIA). This found a reduction of the stroke rate by aspirin compared with placebo in people with atrial fibrillation (RRR 0.21, 95% CI 0–0.38, $p = 0.05$).[36] **Adjusted-dose warfarin versus low-dose warfarin and aspirin:** The SPAF-III trial compared the use of low- and fixed-dose warfarin (target INR 1.2–1.5) plus aspirin (325 mg/d) with standard dose-adjusted warfarin treatment (INR 2–3) in 1044 patients with atrial fibrillation who were at high risk for stroke and thromboembolism (i.e., women aged > 75 years, systolic blood pressure > 160 mm Hg, poor left ventricular function, or prior thromboembolic event).[37] Compared with adjusted-dose warfarin treatment, low/fixed-dose warfarin plus aspirin was associated with significantly higher rates of: ischemic stroke or systemic embolism (7.9% vs. 1.9% per year, ARR 0.06, 95% CI 0.03–0.09; RRR 0.74, 95% CI 0.50–0.87), disabling stroke (5.6% vs. 1.7% per year; ARR 0.04, 95% CI 0.02–0.06), and vascular death or a primary event (11.8% vs. 6.4%). Use of low-intensity antithrombotic regimens have been less effective, and analyses of the optimal anticoagulation intensity for stroke prevention in atrial fibrillation have found that stroke risk substantially increased at INR levels < 2.0.[38,39]

Harms: In those with previous stroke or TIA, anticoagulation for atrial fibrillation compared with placebo increased the absolute rate of extracranial bleeding by 2.1 bleeds per 100 patient-years; the studies were too small to define the rate of intracranial hemorrhage (none occurred in the two RCTs). Major bleeding complications were more frequent with anticoagulation than with aspirin (ARs 0.9% per year with aspirin, 2.8% with anticoagulants, RRI 3.65, 95% CI 0.7–12).[33] In the primary prevention trials, the AR of major bleeding was 1% for placebo, 1% for aspirin, and 1.3% for warfarin. The AR of intracranial haemorrhage increased from 0.1% per year with control to 0.3% per year with warfarin.[35] The risk increased threefold in patients who had bled previously, and both bleeding and hemorrhagic stroke were more common in patients aged over 75 years. The risk of death after a major bleed ranged from 13% to 33% and the risk of morbidity in those who survived a major bleed was 15%. The risk of bleeding was associated with INR > 3, fluctuating INRs, and uncontrolled hypertension.

Comment: The apparent efficacy of warfarin in clinical trials may not translate into effectiveness in practice. First, most strokes in people randomized to warfarin occurred while the patients were not taking warfarin or were significantly underanticoagulated at the time of the event. Second, patients in the trials were highly selected, and on average <10% (range 3%–40%) of eligible patients were randomized. Many were excluded after assessments for the absence of contraindications and physicians' refusal to enter their patients into the study. Third, many of the studies were not double blinded, and some had lack of inter-rater agreement for soft neurological end points.[33,40] Finally, the frequent monitoring of warfarin treatment under trial conditions and motivation of patients/investigators was probably more than that seen in usual clinical practice. The best time to start anticoagulation after an ischemic stroke is unclear. For those in atrial fibrillation with high risk of stroke (those with prior stroke or TIA, all patients aged 75 years and over with diabetes or hypertension, and those with evidence of valve disease or heart failure), the benefit of anticoagulation is clear. For those with lower risk, the evidence is less clear cut; the harms of anticoagulation may outweigh the benefits. However, there is only weak evidence that aspirin substantially reduces the risk of stroke.

REFERENCES

1. Hankey GJ, Warlow CP. *Transient ischaemic attacks of the brain and eye*. London: WB Saunders, 1994.
2. Prospective Studies Collaboration. Cholesterol, diastolic blood pressure, and stroke: 13,000 strokes in 450,000 people in 45 prospective cohorts. *Lancet* 1995;346:1647–1653.
3. Eastern Stroke and Coronary Heart Disease Collaborative Research Group. Blood pressure, cholesterol, and stroke in eastern Asia. *Lancet* 1998;352:1801–1807.
4. Warlow CP, Dennis MS, van Gijn J, et al. Predicting recurrent stroke and other serious vascular events. In: *Stroke. A practical guide to management*. Oxford. Blackwell Science, 1996:545–552.
5. Antiplatelet Trialists' Collaboration. Collaborative overview of randomised trials of antiplatelet therapy – I: prevention of death, myocardial infarction, and stroke by prolonged antiplatelet therapy in various categories of patients. *BMJ* 1994;308:81–106.
6. Collins R, MacMahon S. Blood pressure, antihypertensive drug treatment and the risks of stroke and of coronary heart disease. *Br Med Bull* 1994;50:272–298.
7. PROGRESS Management Committee. Blood pressure lowering for the secondary prevention of stroke: rationale and design of PROGRESS. *J Hypertens* 1996;14(suppl 2):S41–46.
8. Gueyffier F, Boissel J-P, Boutitie F, et al. Effect of antihypertensive treatment in patients having already suffered from stroke: gathering the evidence. *Stroke* 1997; 28: 2557–2562.
9. PATS Collaborating Group. Post-stroke antihypertensive treatment study: a preliminary result. *Chinese Med J* 1995;108:710–717.
10. Rodgers A, MacMahon S, Gamble G, Slattery J, Sandercock P, Warlow C for the United Kingdom Transient Ischaemic Attack Collaborative Group. Blood pressure and risk of stroke in patients with cerebrovascular disease. *BMJ* 1996;313:147.
11. Neal B, Clark T, MacMahon S, Rodgers A, Baigent C, Collins R on behalf of the Antithrombotic Trialists' Collaboration. Blood pressure and the risk of recurrent vascular disease. *Am J Hypertension* 1998;11:25A–26A.
12. Hebert PR, Gaziano M, Hennekens CH. An overview of trials of cholesterol lowering and risk of stroke. *Arch Int Med* 1995;155:50–55.
13. Hebert PR, Gaziano JM, Chan KS, Hennekens CH. Cholesterol lowering with statin drugs, risk of stroke, and total mortality: an overview of randomized trials. *JAMA* 1997; 278:313–321.
14. Acheson J, Hutchinson EC. Controlled trial of clofibrate in cerebral vascular disease. *Atherosclerosis* 1972;15:177–183.
15. Anon. The treatment of cerebrovascular disease with clofibrate. Final report of the Veterans' Administration Cooperative Study of Atherosclerosis, neurology section. *Stroke* 1973;4:684-693.
16. Plehn JF, Davis BR, Sacks FM, Rouleau JL, Pfeffer MA, Bernstein V, et al for the CARE Investigators. Reduction of stroke incidence after myocardial infarction with pravastatin: the cholesterol and recurrent events (CARE) study. *Circulation* 1999; 99:216—223.
17. Scandinavian Simvastatin Survival Study Group. Randomised trial of cholesterol lowering in 4444 patients with coronary heart disease: the Scandinavian simvastatin survival study (4S). *Lancet* 1994;344:1383–1389.
18. Cholesterol Treatment Trialists' Collaboration. Protocol for a prospective collaborative overview of all current and planned randomized trials of cholesterol treatment regimens. *Am J Cardiol* 1995;75:1130–1134.
19. SALT Collaborative Group. Swedish aspirin low-dose trial (SALT) of 75 mg aspirin as secondary prophylaxis after cerebrovascular ischaemic events. *Lancet* 1991;338:1345–1349.
20. Juul-Möller S, Edvardsson N, Jahnmatz B, Rosen A, Sorenson S, Omblus R, for the Swedish Angina Pectoris Aspirin Trial (SAPAT) Group. Double-blind trial of aspirin in primary prevention of myocardial infarction in patients with stable chronic angina pectoris. *Lancet* 1992;340:1421-1425.
21. Diener HC, Cunha L, Forbes C, Sivenius J, Smets P, Lowenthal A. European stroke prevention study 2: dipyridamole and acetylsalicylic acid in the secondary prevention of stroke. *J Neurol Sci* 1996;143:1–13.
22. The Dutch TIA Study Group. A comparison of two doses of aspirin (30mg vs 283mg a day) in patients after a transient ischaemic attack or minor ischaemic stroke. *N Engl J Med* 1991; 325:1261–1266.
23. CAPRIE Steering Committee. A randomised, blinded, trial of clopidogrel versus aspirin in patients at risk of ischaemic events. *Lancet* 1996;348:1329–1339.
24. Sudlow C, Baigent C, on behalf of the Antithrombotic Trialists' Collaboration. Different

antiplatelet regimens in the prevention of vascular events among patients at high risk of stroke: new evidence from the antithrombotic trialists' collaboration. Seventh European Stroke Conference, Edinburgh, May, 1998. *Cerebrovascular Diseases* 1998;8(suppl 4):68.
25. Farrell B, Godwin J, Richards S, Warlow C. The United Kingdom transient ischaemic attack (UK-TIA) aspirin trial: final results. *J Neurol Neurosurg Psychiatry* 1991;54:1044–1054.
26. Liu M, Counsell C, Sandercock P. Anticoagulation versus no anticoagulation following non-embolic ischaemic stroke or transient ischaemic attack. (Cochrane Review). In: The Cochrane Library, Issue 2, 1998. Oxford: Update Software. Updated quarterly. (Search dates: 1995 to 1996, Primary sources: a wide range of electronic databases including MEDLINE 1996-1994, CRISP, CINAHL 1982-1996, BIOSIS, ADIS, SIGLE, Index of UK theses 1970 to 1994, and a manual search of selected journals.)
27. The Stroke Prevention in Reversible Ischaemia Trial (SPIRIT) Study Group. A randomised trial of anticoagulants versus aspirin after cerebral ischemia of presumed arterial origin. *Ann Neurol* 1997;42:857–865.
28. European Carotid Surgery Trialists' Collaborative Group. Randomised trial of endarterectomy for recently symptomatic carotid stenosis: final results of the MRC European carotid surgery trial. *Lancet* 1998;351:1379–1387.
29. North American Symptomatic Carotid Endarterectomy Trial Collaborators. Beneficial effect of carotid endarterectomy in symptomatic patients with high-grade carotid stenosis. *N Engl J Med* 1991;325:445–453.
30. Benavente O, Moher D, Pham B. Carotid endarterectomy for asymptomatic carotid stenosis: a meta-analysis. *BMJ* 1998;317:1477–1480 (search dates 1966 to 1998, primary sources MEDLINE, CCTR Ottawa Stroke Trials Register, Current Contents and hand searching).
31. Warlow CP, Dennis MS, van Gign J, et al, eds. *Stroke: a practical guide to management*. Oxford: Blackwell Science, 1996:547.
32. Brown MM, for the CAVATAS Investigators. Results of the carotid and vertebral artery transluminal angioplasty study (CAVATAS) [abstr]. *Cerebrovasc Dis* 1998;8(suppl 4):21.
33. Koudstaal P. Secondary prevention following stroke or transient ischaemic attack in patients with non-rheumatic atrial fibrillation: anticoagulant therapy versus control. (Cochrane Review) In: The Cochrane Library, Issue 2. Oxford: Update Software;1998. Updated quarterly. (Search dates: 1995 to 1996, Primary sources: a wide range of electronic databases including MEDLINE 1996-1994, CRISP, CINAHL 1982-1996, BIOSIS, ADIS, SIGLE, Index of UK theses 1970 to 1994, and a manual search of selected journals).
34. European Atrial Fibrillation Trial Study Group. Secondary prevention in non-rheumatic atrial fibrillation after transient ischaemic attack or minor stroke. *Lancet* 1993;342:1255–1262.
35. Atrial Fibrillation Investigators. Risk factors for stroke and efficacy of antithrombotic therapy in atrial fibrillation. *Arch Intern Med* 1994;154: 1449–1457.
36. Atrial Fibrillation Investigators. The efficacy of aspirin in patients with atrial fibrillation: analysis of pooled data from 3 randomized trials. *Arch Intern Med* 1997;157:1237–1240.
37. Stroke Prevention in Atrial Fibrillation Investigators. Adjusted-dose warfarin versus low-intensity, fixed-dose warfarin plus aspirin for high-risk patients with atrial fibrillation: stroke prevention in atrial fibrillation III randomised clinical trial. *Lancet* 1996;348:633–638.
38. The European Atrial Fibrillation Trial Study Group. Optimal oral anticoagulant therapy in patients with nonrheumatic atrial fibrillation and recent cerebral ischemia. *N Engl J Med* 1995;333:5–10.
39. Hylek EM, Skates SJ, Sheehan MA, Singer DE. An analysis of the lowest effective intensity of prophylactic anticoagulation for patients with nonrheumatic atrial fibrillation. *N Engl J Med* 1996;335:540–546
40. Green CJ, Hadorn DC, Bassett K, Kazanjian A. Anticoagulation in chronic non-valvular atrial fibrillation: a critical appraisal and meta-analysis. *Can J Cardiol* 1997;13:811–15.

Cathie Sudlow
Wellcome Research Fellow
in Clinical Epidemiology
University of Oxford
Oxford
UK

Colin Baigent
MRC Scientist
University of Oxford
Oxford
UK

Gord Gubitz
Clinical Research Fellow
Neurosciences Trials Unit
University of Edinburgh
Edinburgh
UK

Peter Sandercock
Reader in Neurology
University of Edinburgh
Edinburgh
UK

Gregory YH Lip
Consultant Cardiologist and Reader
in Medicine
City Hospital
Birmingham
UK

Competing interests: CS, CB, GG none declared. PS has received honoraria for lectures, funds for research, funds for members of his staff, and fees for single consultancies from Glaxo Wellcome, Boehringer Ingelheim, Sanofi/BMS. GYHL is UK Principal Investigator for the ERAFT Trial (Knoll) and has been reimbursed by various pharmaceutical companies for attending several conferences, running educational programmes and research projects.

TABLE 1 **Effects of cholesterol lowering on stroke: results of two systematic overviews of RCTs of nonstatin interventions and statins in the primary and secondary prevention of coronary artery disease*. (*See* text p. 117.)**

	Number of				Summary OR (95% CI) for active treatment vs. control	
Overview	**Trials**	**Participants**	**Strokes**	**Mean reduction in cholesterol %**	**Fatal or nonfatal stroke**	**Fatal stroke**
Nonstatin interventions[12]	11	36,000	435	11%	1.0 (0.8–1.2)	1.1 (0.8–1.6)
Statin interventions[13]	14	29,000	454	22%	0.71 (0.59–0.86)	1.17 (0.69–1.97)

*The findings of other published overviews were consistent with the results shown here.

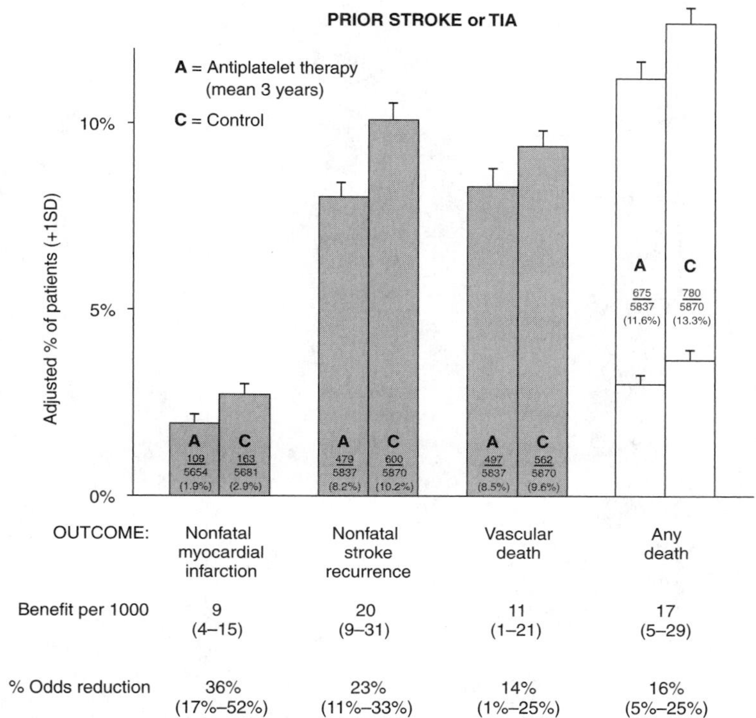

FIGURE 1 **Absolute effects of antiplatelet treatment on various outcomes in patients with a prior stroke or TIA: results of a systematic review.[5] The columns show the absolute risks over 3 years for each outcome; the error bars represent standard deviations. In the "any death" column nonvascular deaths are represented by lower horizontal lines. (*See* text p. 118.) Adapted with permission.[5]**

Glycemic control in diabetes

William H Herman, MD, MPH

QUESTIONS

INTERVENTIONS

Key Messages

- We found strong evidence that intensive compared with conventional treatment reduces the development and progression of microvascular and neuropathic complications in both type 1 and type 2 diabetes.
- Randomized controlled trials (RCTs) have found that intensive treatment causes hypoglycemia and weight gain without adverse impact on neuropsychological function or quality of life.
- We found no evidence that intensive treatment reduces adverse cardiovascular outcomes.
- Large RCTs have found that diabetic complications increase with HbA1c concentration above the nondiabetic range.

DEFINITION Diabetes mellitus is a group of metabolic diseases characterized by hyperglycemia (fasting plasma glucose ≈ 7.0 mM/L, or 2-hour post 75 g oral glucose load plasma glucose ≈ 11.1 mM/L, on two or more occasions). Intensive treatment is designed to achieve blood glucose values as close to the nondiabetic range as possible. The essential components of such treatment are education, counseling, monitoring, self-management, and pharmacologic treatment with insulin or oral antidiabetic agents to achieve specific glycemic goals.

INCIDENCE/ PREVALENCE Diabetes is diagnosed in approximately 5% of adults aged 20 years or over in the USA.[1] A further 2.7% have undiagnosed diabetes on the basis of a fasting glucose. The prevalence is similar in men and women, but diabetes is more common in many ethnic groups. The prevalence in people aged 40 to 74 years has increased over the past decade.

ETIOLOGY Diabetes results from deficient insulin secretion, decreased insulin action, or both. Many processes can be involved, ranging from autoimmune destruction of the β-cells of the pancreas to incompletely understood abnormalities that result in resistance to insulin action. Genetic factors are involved in both mechanisms. In type 1 diabetes, there is an absolute deficiency of insulin. In type 2 diabetes, insulin resistance and an inability of the pancreas to compensate are involved. Hyperglycemia sufficient to cause tissue damage can be present without clinical symptoms for many years before diagnosis.

PROGNOSIS Severe hyperglycemia causes numerous symptoms, including polyuria, polydipsia, weight loss, and blurred vision. Acute, life-threatening consequences of diabetes are hyperglycemia with ketoacidosis or the nonketotic hyperosmolar syndrome. There is increased susceptibility to certain infections. Long-term complications of diabetes include retinopathy (with potential loss of vision), nephropathy (leading to renal failure), peripheral neuropathy (increased risk of foot ulcers, amputation, and Charcot joints), autonomic neuropathy (gastrointestinal, sexual, and bladder dysfunction), and greatly increased risk of atheroma affecting large vessels (causing macrovascular complications of myocardial infarction, stroke, or peripheral vascular disease). The physical, emotional, and social impact of diabetes and the demands of intensive treatment also can create problems both for people with diabetes and their families.

AIMS To slow the development and progression of the microvascular and neuropathic complications of diabetes while minimizing adverse effects of treatment (hypoglycemia and weight gain) and maximizing quality of life.

OUTCOMES Quality of life; short-term burden of treatment; long-term clinical complications; risks and benefits of treatment. Both the development of complications in people who previously have been free of them and the progression of complications, are used as outcomes. Scales of severity are used to detect disease progression (e.g., 19 step scales of diabetic retinopathy; normoalbuminuria, microalbuminuria, and albuminuria for nephropathy; absence or presence of clinical neuropathy).

METHODS We searched MEDLINE and EMBASE in July 1998 for systematic reviews assessing the impact of control of blood glucose in people with diabetes that measured clinical outcomes of the type described above. Subsequent, relevant RCTs were also reviewed.

QUESTION What are the effects of intensive versus conventional glycemic control?

One systematic review and subsequent RCTs in people with both type 1 and type 2 diabetes have found that intensive treatment compared with conventional treatment reduces the development and progression of microvascular and neuropathic complications. Intensive treatment causes hypoglycemia and weight gain but does not seem to affect adversely neuropsychological function or quality of life. These trials and prospective observational studies have found no evidence that intensive treatment reduces adverse cardiovascular outcomes, but the confidence intervals were large, and a clinically important effect might still exist.

Benefits: **Microvascular and neuropathic complications:** We found one systematic review published in 1993 of 16 small RCTs comparing intensive versus conventional treatment in people with type 1 diabetes, with follow-up ranging from 8 to 60 months.[2] Subsequent longer-term RCTs have repeated and extended these findings, including the UK Prospective Diabetes Study (UKPDS) and the Diabetes Control and Complications Trial (DCCT). The main randomization group of UKPDS included 3867 newly diagnosed type 2 diabetes, with 2729 assigned to intensive therapy with sulfonylurea or insulin and 1138 assigned to diet control. Patients in both groups had adjustments made based on fasting glucose criteria and included starting insulin or sulfonylurea therapy in the latter group and adding metformin or insulin or intensifying insulin therapy in the former group. The intensive regimen resulted in a mean Hb1AC of 7.0% compared to 7.9% in the conventional group ($p < 0.001$), with a 25% risk reduction ($p = 0.0099$) in combined microvascular end point, including need for retinal photocoagulation. The key findings of reduced microvascular complications are consistent with DCCT and suggest that any therapeutic strategy (oral agents, insulin, or both) that reduce the glycosylated hemoglobin may be employed in patients with type 2 diabetes. UKPDS was not able to show any reduction in cardiovascular outcomes, diabetes-related mortality, or all-cause mortality.[3] The DCCT compared intensive versus conventional treatment over 6.5 years in 1441 people with type 2 diabetes.[4] Approximately half had no retinopathy and half had mild retinopathy. The Kumamoto study compared intensive versus standard treatment in 110 people with insulin-treated type II diabetes over 6 years.[5] Results of the DCCT and Kumamoto studies are shown in Table 1. The RR of retinopathy, nephropathy, and neuropathy were all reduced. **Cardiovascular outcomes:** In the DCCT, intensive treatment reduced the RR of any major macrovascular event from 0.8 to 0.5 events per 100 patient-years (RRR: 41%; 95% CI: 10%–68%).[4] In the Kumamoto study, the number of major cerebrovascular, cardiovascular, and peripheral vascular events in the intensive treatment group was half that of the conventional treatment group (0.6 vs. 1.3 events per 100 patient-years), but the event rates in this small trial were low and the results were not significant.[5]

Harms: **Hypoglycemia:** The systematic review found no consistent change in the risk of severe hypoglycemic reactions in six RCTs,[2] but the subsequent RCTs found increased risk of hypoglycemia with intensive treatment.[3–5] In the DCCT, the rates of severe hypoglycemic episodes (requiring help from someone else) were 0.6 episodes per patient-year in the intensive treatment group and 0.2 episodes per patient-year in the conventional treatment group.[4] On average, one extra severe hypoglycemic event occurred for every two people treated intensively for 1 year. In the Kumamoto study, the rate of hypoglycemia was lower and there was no significant difference between groups.[5] Over 6 years, six people in the intensive treatment group and four in the conventional treatment group had one or more mild hypoglycemic reactions. There were no episodes of coma, seizure, or severe hypoglycemia that required the assistance of another person. **Neuropsychological impairment:** The systematic review did not comment specifically on neuropsychological impairment.[2] However, one of the trials included in the review, the Stockholm Diabetes Intervention Study (SDIS), assessed cognitive impairment while comparing intensified versus standard treatment over 7.5 years in 102 people with type 1 diabetes, nonproliferative retinopathy, normal serum creatinine concentrations, and unsatisfactory blood glucose control.[6] After 3 years, it found no hypoglycemia associated cognitive impairment.[7] In the DCCT, intensive treatment did not affect neuropsychological performance.[8] In addition, people who had repeated episodes of hypoglycemia did not perform differently from people who did not have repeated episodes.[8] **Weight gain:** Four RCTs found more weight increase with intensive treatment than with standard treatment.[3,4,9] In the SDIS, weight remained stable in the conventional treatment group but body mass index increased by 5.8% in the intensive treatment group (95% CI: not presented; $p<0.01$).[9] In the DCCT, intensive treatment was associated with a 33% increase in the risk of developing a body weight more than 120% above the ideal (12.7 cases per 100 patient-years with intensive treatment versus 9.3 cases per 100 patient-years with conventional treatment). At 5 years, people treated intensively gained 4.6 kg more than people treated conventionally (CI not presented for weight data).[4] In the Kumamoto study, there was no significant increase in body mass index in either group from baseline to 6 years (intensive treatment group 20.5–21.2 kg/m^2; conventional treatment group 20.3–21.9 kg/m^2).[5] **Quality of life:** Only the DCCT looked at quality of life. It found that people undergoing intensive treatment did not suffer deterioration in the quality of their lives, even while the rigors of their diabetes care was increased.[10] The occurrence of severe hypoglycemia was not associated consistently with a subsequent increase in symptomatic distress or decline in diabetes-related quality of life. There was, however, a suggestion that in the primary prevention intensive treatment group, people who had repeated severe hypoglycemia (three or more events resulting in coma or seizure) tended to be at increased risk of measurable symptomatic distress.

Comment: None of the RCTs was designed to assess the impact of treatment on macrovascular disease. Major cardiovascular events were infrequent because the trials included relatively young people and follow-up was relatively short. As a result, the 95% CI for the effect on macrovascular events was wide.

QUESTION **What is the optimum target blood glucose?**

Large RCTs in people with type 1 and type 2 diabetes have found that the risk of the development or progression of complications increases progressively as HbA1c increases above the nondiabetic range.

Benefits: The DCCT found no HbA1c threshold below which there was no increased risk of the development or progression of complications.[11]

Harms: In the intensive treatment group, the absolute risk of severe hypoglycemia increased as HbA1c decreased.[11]

Comment: As HbA1c was reduced, there were continuing reductions in the RR of complications but there was a slower rate of increase in the risk of hypoglycemia.[11] The balance between benefits and harms of intensive treatment may be less favorable in children under 13 years of age or adults over 70 years of age, and in people with repeated severe hypoglycemia or unawareness of hypoglycemia. The benefit of intensive treatment is limited by the existence of advanced diabetes complications (e.g., blindness, end-stage renal disease, or cardiovascular disease), major comorbidity, and reduced life expectancy. The risk of intensive treatment is increased by a history of severe hypoglycemia or hypoglycemia unawareness, advanced autonomic neuropathy or cardiovascular disease, and impaired ability to detect or treat hypoglycemia (e.g., altered mental state, immobility, or lack of social support). For people likely to have limited benefit or increased risk with intensive treatment, less intensive goals for glycemic management should be negotiated, reflecting the individual's self-determined goals of care and willingness to make lifestyle modifications.

REFERENCES

1. Harris MI, Flegal KM, Cowie CC, et al. Prevalence of diabetes, impaired fasting glucose, and impaired glucose tolerance in US adults: the third national health and nutrition examination survey, 1988–1994. *Diabetes Care* 1998;21:518–524.
2. Wang PH, Lau J, Chalmers TC. Meta-analysis of effects of intensive blood glucose control on late complications of type I diabetes. *Lancet* 1993;341:1306–1309. (Search date 1991; primary sources MEDLINE 1966 to December 1991)
3. UK Prospective Diabetes Study Group: Intensive blood-glucose control with sulphonylureas or insulin compared with conventional treatment and risk of complications in patients with type 2 diabetes (UKPDS 33). *Lancet* 1998;352:837–853.
4. The Diabetes Control and Complications Trial Research Group. The effect of intensive treatment of diabetes on the development and progression of long-term complications in insulin-dependent diabetes mellitus. *N Engl J Med* 1993;329:977–986.
5. Ohkubo Y, Kishikawa H, Araki E, et al. Intensive insulin therapy prevents the progression of diabetic microvascular complications in Japanese patients with non-insulin-dependent diabetes mellitus: a randomized prospective 6-year study. *Diabetes Res Clin Pract* 1995;28:103–117.
6. Reichard P, Nilsson BY, Rosenqvist U. The effect of long-term intensified insulin treatment on the development of microvascular complications of diabetes mellitus. *N Engl J Med* 1993;329:304–309.
7. Reichard P, Berglund A, Britz A, Levander S, Rosenqvist U. Hypoglycaemic episodes during intensified insulin treatment: increased frequency but no effect on cognitive function. *J Intern Med* 1991;229:9–16.
8. The Diabetes Control and Complications Trial Research Group. Effects of intensive diabetes therapy on neuropsychological function in adults in the diabetes control and complications trial. *Ann Intern Med* 1996;124:379–388.
9. Reichard P, Berglund B, Britz A, Cars I, Nilsson BY, Rosenqvist U. Intensified conventional insulin treatment retards the microvascular complications of insulin-dependent diabetes mellitus (IDDM): the Stockholm diabetes intervention study (SDIS) after 5 years. *J Intern Med* 1991;230:101–108.

10. The Diabetes Control and Complications Trial Research Group. Influence of intensive diabetes treatment on quality-of-life outcomes in the diabetes control and complications trial. *Diabetes Care* 1996;19:195–203.

11. The Diabetes Control and Complications Trial Research Group. The absence of a glycemic threshold for the development of long-term complications: the perspective of the Diabetes Control and Complications Trial. *Diabetes* 1996;45:1289–1298.

William H Herman, MD, MPH
University of Michigan
Medical Center
Ann Arbor
Michigan
USA

Competing interests: None declared.

TABLE 1 **Risk (OR) for development or progression of microvascular and neuropathic complications with intensive versus conventional treatment (OR, NNT, and CIs all calculated from data in papers). (*See* text on p. 131.)**

	Systematic review[2]	DCCT[4]	Kumamoto[5]
Studies	16 RCTs	RCT	RCT
Diabetes type	Type 1	Type 1	Type 2
Number of participants	–	1441	110
Follow-up	8–60 months	6.5 years	6 years
Retinopathy			
Progression			
OR (95% CI)	0.49 (0.28–0.85)	0.39 (0.28–0.55)	0.25 (0.09 –0.65)
NNT (95% CI) over study duration	–	5 (4–7)	4 (3–11)
Development			
OR (95% CI)	–	0.22 (0.14–0.36)	–
NNT (95% CI) over study duration	–	6 (5–7)	–
Nephropathy			
Development or progression			
OR (95% CI)	0.34 (0.20–0.58)	0.50 (0.39–0.63)	0.26 (0.09–0.76)
NNT (95% CI) over study duration	–	7 (6–11)	5 (4–19)
Neuropathy			
Development or progression			
OR (95% CI)	–	0.36 (0.24–0.54)	
NNT (95% CI) over study duration	–	13 (11–18)	

Foot ulcers in diabetes

Dereck Hunt, MD, MSc, and Hertzel Gerstein, MD, MSc, FRCPC

QUESTIONS

INTERVENTIONS

Key Messages

- Randomized controlled trials (RCTs) have found that referring people with diabetes who are at high risk of developing foot ulcers to footcare clinic reduces the risk of foot ulcers and major amputation.
- We found limited evidence that total contact casting improves the healing of chronic noninfected diabetic foot ulcers.
- Three small RCTs have found that topical growth factors improve the rate of healing of chronic noninfected foot ulcers.
- We found limited evidence that systemic hyperbaric oxygen reduces the absolute risk of foot amputation in people with severe infected foot ulcers.
- We found limited evidence that therapeutic footwear decreases the recurrence of foot ulceration.
- We found limited evidence that patient education provided after acute foot complications decreases the risks of ulcer recurrence and major amputation.

DEFINITION Diabetic foot ulceration refers to full-thickness penetration of the dermis of the foot in a patient with diabetes. Nontraumatic lower-limb amputation refers to the surgical removal of all or part of the lower extremity. Minor amputations involve partial removal of a foot, including toe or forefoot resections. Major amputations refer to above- or below-knee amputations.

INCIDENCE/ PREVALENCE The annual incidence of foot ulcers among one US cohort of people with type 1 and 2 diabetes is 2.5%, and the prevalence over a 4-year study was 9.5% to 10.5%.[1] (See references 2–9 for further incidence and prevalence.)

ETIOLOGY Risk factors for foot ulcers and amputation include duration of diabetes, poor glycemic control, and the presence of microvascular complications (retinopathy, nephropathy, and neuropathy). The strongest predictors, however, are altered foot-sensation status and a history of a previous foot ulcer.[2–9]

PROGNOSIS Patients with diabetes are at risk of developing lower extremity complications. These include foot ulcers, infections, and vascular insufficiency. Lower-extremity amputation is indicated if complications are severe or do not improve with appropriate treatment. As well as affecting quality of life, these complications contribute significantly to the health care costs associated with diabetes. With appropriate screening, referral to a footcare clinic, and early treatment of complications, however, poor patient outcomes and chronic disability can be avoided. For patients with healed diabetic foot ulcers, the 5-year cumulative rate of ulcer recurrence and amputation is 66% and 12%, respectively.[10]

AIMS To prevent diabetic foot complications, including ulcers and amputations, and to improve ulcer healing and prevent amputations where ulcers already exist.

OUTCOMES Rates of development or recurrence of foot ulcers or major foot lesions; rate of amputation; time ulcers take to heal or the proportion healed in a given period; rates of hospital admission; rates of foot infection.

METHODS We searched MEDLINE and EMBASE in June 1998 for systematic reviews assessing the impact of interventions on foot ulcers and amputation in people with diabetes which measured clinical outcomes. Subsequent relevant RCTs were also reviewed.

QUESTION What are the effects of preventive and therapeutic interventions?

OPTION SCREENING AND REFERRAL TO FOOTCARE CLINIC

RCTs have found that screening for altered sensation and absent pedal pulses followed by referral to footcare clinics (for education, footwear, and podiatry) reduces the risk of foot ulcers and major amputation.

Benefits: We found no systematic reviews but found two RCTs. One RCT in 2001 people attending a general diabetes clinic compared usual care versus a diabetes screening and protection program.[11] People in the intervention group were screened for deficits in pedal pulses, light touch, and vibration sensation. Those with persistent abnormal findings were referred to the diabetic foot clinic if they had a history of a foot ulcer, were found to have a low ankle-brachial index (<0.75), or were noted to have foot deformities. The clinic provided podiatry and protective shoes for people as well as education regarding foot care. Follow-up 2 years after enrollment found that the number of people who had undergone major amputation was only one in the intervention group and 12 in the control group (RRR 92%; ARR 1.1%, 95% CI 0.4%–1.9%; NNT 91, 95% CI 53–250). Ninety-one people with diabetes would need to enter a screening and prevention program rather than receive usual care to prevent one additional major amputation in the following 2 years. A second RCT, including 352 people with type 2 diabetes attending a diabetes clinic, compared usual care versus a prevention program.[12] People in the intervention group received foot care education and reminders, and health care providers were reminded to examine participants' feet and discuss foot care. After 1 year, fewer people in the intervention arm than in the control arm were found to have serious foot lesions (baseline prevalence 2.9%; RRR 0.59, 95% CI 0–0.84).

Harms: None reported.

Comment: None.

OPTION TOTAL CONTACT CASTING

We found limited evidence from one small RCT that total contact casting compared with traditional dressing changes increases the likelihood and speed of healing of chronic noninfected diabetic foot ulcers. Total contact casting has not been compared directly with the use of topical growth factors.

Benefits: We found no systematic reviews but we found one RCT. This compared total contact casting versus traditional dressing changes in 40 people with diabetes and plantar foot ulcers but free of signs of infection or gangrene.[13] All participants were told to minimize weight bearing during treatment. Casts were applied by an experienced physical therapist, changed after 5 to 7 days and then every 2 to 3 weeks until healing occurred. Control participants were provided with accommodative footwear and crutches or a walker. They were instructed to complete wet to dry dressing changes 2 to 3 times daily. Ulcer healing occurred in 91% of people treated with total contact casting and 32% of people in the control group (absolute difference 59%, 95% CI 31%–87%; NNT 2, 95% CI 1–3). Two people would have to be treated with total contact casting rather than dressings for one additional ulcer to heal. Healing was quicker in people treated with total contact casting than controls (a mean of 42 days vs. 65 d). Five control participants were admitted to hospital because of infection and two required amputation. No participants in the total contact casting group required hospital admission.

Harms: In the RCT, three of 21 people treated with total contact casting developed fungal infections requiring topical treatment.[13] These events did not prevent continued casting.

Comment: Total contact casting is the application of a layer of plaster over the foot and lower leg designed to distribute pressure evenly over the entire plantar aspect of the foot to reduce exposure of plantar ulcers to pressure, even while walking. Soft tissue infections and osteomyelitis are contraindications to total contact casting. Other methods aimed at decreasing the pressure applied to plantar ulcers during walking, such as removable cast walkers, half shoes, healing sandals, and felted foam, have not been evaluated in RCTs.

OPTION TOPICAL GROWTH FACTORS

Three small RCTs on three separate products have found that topical growth factors improve the rate of healing of chronic, noninfected foot ulcers when compared with placebo. Topical growth factors have not been compared directly with total contact casting.

Benefits: We found no systematic review but found three RCTs. These compared topically applied growth factors versus placebo in people with diabetic foot ulcers who attended hospital outpatient clinics.[14–16] All participants were free of signs of infection or severe vascular compromise. All received wound debridement and were encouraged to avoid weight bearing on the affected limb. One RCT in 50 people found that treatment with neonatal cultured fibroblasts (weekly for 8 wk) achieved healing rates of 50% compared with 8% with placebo (RRR for nonhealing 0.46; ARR 0.42, 95% CI 0.05–0.80; NNT 2, 95% CI 1–20).[14] A second RCT in 65 people found that treatment with an arginine-glycine-aspartic (RGD) acid matrix (twice weekly for up to 10 wk) achieved healing rates of 35% versus 8% with placebo (RRR of nonhealing 0.29; ARR 0.27, 95% CI 0.06–0.48; NNT 4, 95% CI 2–15).[15] A third RCT in 118 people found that treatment with platelet derived growth factors (once daily for up to 20 wk) achieved healing rates of 48% compared with 25% with placebo (RRR of nonhealing 0.31; ARR 0.23, 95% CI 0.05–0.41; NNT 4, 95% CI 2–19).[14–16]

Harms: Adverse events were no more common in the intervention arm than in the control arm.

Comment: These therapeutic agents are not yet widely available, especially not in the US, and may be expensive. There has been little long-term follow-up of people treated with these growth factors.

OPTION SYSTEMIC HYPERBARIC OXYGEN

Two small RCTs have found that systemic hyperbaric oxygen reduces the absolute risk of foot amputation in people with severe infected foot ulcers, when compared with routine care.

Benefits: We found no systematic review but found two RCTs. These compared systemic hyperbaric oxygen treatment versus usual treatment in people with infected diabetic foot ulcers requiring hospital admission.[17,18] One RCT in 70 people with severe infected diabetic foot ulcers compared usual care (aggressive debridement, broad spectrum intravenous antibiotics, revascularization if indicated, and optimized glycemic control) versus usual care plus daily 90-minute sessions of systemic hyperbaric oxygen at 2.2 to 2.5 atmospheres. Participants either had full-thickness gangrene or abscess or a large infected ulcer that had not healed after 30 days. After 10 weeks, rates of major amputation were lower in the intervention group (8.6% vs. 33% in the control group; RRR 0.74, 95% CI 0.16–0.92; ARR 0.25, 95% CI 0.04–0.45; NNT 4, 95% CI 2–23).[17] A second RCT in 30 people with chronic infected foot ulcers compared usual treatment (including debridement, intravenous antibiotics, and optimized glycemic control) versus usual treatment plus four treatments with hyperbaric oxygen over 2 weeks. The risk of major amputation was lower in the intervention group, but the CI included zero (ARR 33%, 95% CI –1.6%–+68%).[18]

Harms: In the larger RCT[17] two people developed symptoms of barotraumatic otitis, but this did not cause an interruption of treatment.

Comment: None.

OPTION APPROPRIATE FOOTWEAR

We found limited evidence from one nonrandomized trial that therapeutic footwear, made according to the Towey guidelines, decreases recurrence of ulceration.

Benefits: We found no systematic review or RCTs but found one nonrandomized controlled trial.[19] Sixty-nine people with a previous diabetic foot ulcer were allocated alternately to either an intervention group in which patients received therapeutic shoes, or to a control group in which patients continued to wear their ordinary shoes. Therapeutic shoes were manufactured according to the Towey guidelines (super depth to fit customized insoles and toe deformities and made with soft thermoformable leather along with semi-rocker soles) and fitted with custom molded insoles. All participants received information on foot care and footwear. After 1 year, the AR of ulcer recurrence was 27% in the intervention group and 58% in the control group (RRR 0.53; ARR 0.31, 95% CI 0.07–0.55; NNT 3, 95% CI 2–14).

Harms: The trial did not document any adverse effects associated with use of the therapeutic shoes.[19]

Comment: Alternate allocation leaves open the possibility of bias and noncomparability of the two treatment groups.

OPTION EDUCATION

We found limited evidence from one nonrandomized trial that patient education provided after the management of acute foot complications decreases ulcer recurrences and major amputations.

Benefits: We found no systematic review or RCTs but found one nonrandomized controlled trial. This allocated 227 people according to their social security number, and evaluated the effect of providing a single 1-hour educational class focusing on diabetic foot complications and important components of foot care.[20] The participants initially presented because of a foot infection, a foot ulcer, or for assistance with issues related to the management of a previous amputation. Surgical treatment was provided for all people when necessary. Follow-up at 2 years demonstrated that people who had been allocated to the educational session had significantly fewer ulcer recurrences or major amputations. The AR of ulcer recurrence was 14.7% in the control group and 4.5% in the education group (RRR 0.69; ARR 0.10, 95% CI 0.04–0.16; NNT 10, 95% CI 6–26). The AR of major amputation was 10.2% in the control group and 2.8% in the education group (RRR 0.72; ARR 0.07, 95% CI 0.02–0.13; NNT 14, 95% CI 8–50).

Harms: None reported.

Comment: Allocation by social security number may introduce biases and could create noncomparable groups.

REFERENCES

1. Moss SE, Klein R, Klein BE. The prevalence and incidence of lower extremity amputation in a diabetic population. *Arch Intern Med* 1992;152:610–611.
2. Rith-Najarian SJ, Stolusky T, Gohdes DM. Identifying diabetic patients at high risk for lower-extremity amputation in a primary health care setting. *Diabetes Care* 1992;15:1386–1389.
3. Veves A, Murray HJ, Young MJ, Boulton AJ. The risk of foot ulceration in diabetic patients with high foot pressure: a prospective study. *Diabetologia* 1992;35:660–663.
4. Young MJ, Breddy JL, Veves, Boulton AJ. The prediction of diabetic neuropathic foot ulceration using vibration perception thresholds: a prospective study. *Diabetes Care* 1994;7:557–560.
5. Humphrey AR, Dowse GK, Thoma K, Zimmet PZ. Diabetes and nontraumatic lower extremity amputations. Incidence, risk factors, and prevention—a 12 year follow-up study in Nauru. *Diabetes Care* 1996;19:710–714.
6. Lee JS, Lu M, Lee VS, Russell D, Bahr C, Lee ET. Lower-extremity amputation: incidence, risk factors, and mortality in the Oklahoma Indian diabetes study. *Diabetes* 1993;42:876–882.
7. Lehto S, Ronnemaa T, Pyorala K, Laakso M. Risk factors predicting lower extremity amputations in patients with NIDDM. *Diabetes Care* 1996;19:607–612.
8. Moss SE, Klein R, Klein BE. Long-term incidence of lower-extremity amputations in a diabetic population. *Arch Fam Med* 1996;5:391–398.
9. Nelson RG, Gohdes DM, Everhart JE, et al. Lower-extremity amputations in NIDDM: 12 year follow-up study in Pima Indians. *Diabetes Care* 1988;11:8–16.
10. Apelqvist J, Larsson J, Agardh CD. Long-term prognosis for diabetic patients with foot ulcers. *J Intern Med* 1993;233:485–491.
11. McCabe CJ, Stevenson RC, Dolan AM. Evaluation of a diabetic foot screening and protection programme. *Diabet Med* 1998;15:80–84.
12. Litzelman DK, Slemenda CW, Langefeld CD, et al. Reduction of lower extremity clinical abnormalities in patients with non-insulin-dependent diabetes mellitus. *Ann Intern Med* 1993;119:36–41.
13. Mueller MJ, Diamond JE, Sinacore DR, et al. Total contact casting in treatment of diabetic plantar ulcers: controlled clinical trial. *Diabetes Care* 1989;12:384–388.
14. Gentzkow GD, Iwasaki SD, Hershon K, et al. Use of dermagraft, a cultured human dermis, to treat diabetic foot ulcers. *Diabetes Care* 1996;19:350–354.
15. Steed DL, Ricotta JJ, Prendergast JJ, et al. Promotion and acceleration of diabetic ulcer healing by arginine-glycine-aspartic acid (RGD) peptide matrix. *Diabetes Care* 1995;18:39–46.
16. Steed DL, and the Diabetic Ulcer Study Group. Clinical evaluation of recombinant human platelet-derived growth factor for the treatment of lower extremity diabetic ulcers. *J Vasc Surg* 1995;21:71–81.
17. Faglia E, Favales F, Aldeghi A, et al. Adjunctive systemic hyperbaric oxygen therapy in treatment of severe prevalently ischemic diabetic foot ulcer. *Diabetes Care* 1996;19:1338–1343.
18. Doctor N, Pandya S, Supe A. Hyperbaric oxygen therapy in diabetic foot. *J Postgrad Med* 1992;38:112–114.
19. Uccioli L, Faglia E, Monticone G, et al. Manufactured shoes in the prevention of diabetic foot ulcers. *Diabetes Care* 1995;18:1376–1378.
20. Malone JM, Snyder M, Anderson G, Bernhard VM, Holloway G, Bunt T. Prevention of amputation by diabetic education. *Am J Surg* 1989;158:520–524.

Dereck Hunt, MD, MSc
Clinical Scholar
McMaster University
Hamilton
Ontario
Canada

Hertzel Gerstein, MD, MSc, FRCPC
Associate Professor of Medicine
McMaster University
Hamilton
Ontario
Canada

Competing interests: None declared.

Gastroesophageal reflux disease

David A Katzka, MD

QUESTIONS

INTERVENTIONS

Key Messages

- One systematic review of randomzied controlled trials (RCTs) has found proton-pump inhibitors to be more effective than H_2-antagonists in both erosive and nonerosive esophagitis. One RCT has found no significant difference in the effectiveness of different proton-pump inhibitors.
- Surgical treatment has not been evaluated adequately in RCTs. Medical and surgical treatments have not been compared adequately.
- We found no RCTs evaluating whether patients with Barrett's esophagus benefit from medical or surgical treatment of their GERD.
- We found limited, conflicting evidence on the benefits of treating GERD in people with extra-esophageal manifestations of GERD (see Table 1).

DEFINITION Gastroesophageal reflux occurs when gastric contents enter the esophagus because of transient or chronic relaxation of the lower esophageal sphincter. Excessive reflux causes symptoms of GERD (heartburn, acid taste in the mouth). It can be divided into nonerosive esophagitis, in which endoscopy is normal, and erosive esophagitis, in which endoscopy shows inflammation and erosions.

INCIDENCE/ PREVALENCE Gastroesophageal reflux disease is common. Weekly heartburn occurs in up to 20% of people questioned in population surveys. Up to 10% of these will have erosive disease.

ETIOLOGY There are no clear predictive factors for GERD.

PROGNOSIS Gastroesophageal reflux disease is generally benign with little mortality. However, persistent symptoms can interfere with normal activities and cause considerable morbidity. Long-term retrospective data (up to 22 years) suggest that, in patients with an initially normal endoscopy, endoscopy tends to remain normal.[1] A small subset of patients develop strictures, Barrett's esophagus, adenocarcinoma, or extra-esophageal manifestations (Table 1).[2]

AIMS To relieve symptoms, to prevent complications in those with severe esophagitis, to control extra-esophageal manifestations, to minimize adverse effects of treatment, and to improve quality of life.

OUTCOMES Frequency and severity of symptoms; degree of esophagitis; esophageal pH (assessed by ambulatory monitoring); prevalence and severity of extra-esophageal manifestations; incidence of stricture, Barrett's esophagus, and adenocarcinoma. Symptoms do not correlate well with the extent of esophagitis; patients with Barrett's esophagus may have minimal symptoms, while those with severe symptoms may have no evidence of esophagitis.

METHODS *Clinical Evidence* search July 1998. Systematic reviews: MEDLINE (1988 to July 1998), EMBASE (1988 to July 1998), Cochrane Library (1988 issue 2). RCTs: MEDLINE (1995 to July 1998), EMBASE (1995 to July 1998), and Cochrane Controlled Clinical Trials Register (1966 to 1998). References found in key articles.

QUESTION What are the effects of treatment in erosive esophagitis?

OPTION PROTON-PUMP INHIBITORS VERSUS H_2-ANTAGONISTS

One systematic review of RCTs has found that proton-pump inhibitors are more effective than H_2-antagonists at healing erosive esophagitis and preventing recurrence. Short-term adverse effects are similar for both classes of drug and do not differ greatly from placebo. We found no good data on long-term risks of treatment or on possible long-term benefits, such as reduced risk of complications.

Benefits: One systematic review published in 1997 identified 43 single- and double-blind RCTs in 7635 participants comparing proton pump inhibitors versus H_2-antagonists.[3] **Healing:** The proportion of participants healed on endoscopic examination after 12 weeks was 83.6% (95% CI 79.1%–88.1%) for proton-pump inhibitors compared with 51.9% (95% CI 46.9%–56.9%) for H_2-antagonists, irrespective of drug dose or treatment duration. Proton-pump inhibitors provided the fastest overall healing rate with 11.7% healed per week (95% CI 10.7% to 12.6%), twice as fast as H_2-antagonists (5.9% healed per week, 95% CI 5.5%–6.3%) and four times faster than placebo (2.9% healed per week, (95% CI 2.4%–3.4%). Two of the RCTs added a prokinetic agent to the H_2-antagonist, but results still strongly favored the proton-pump inhibitor.[4,5] Doses of proton-pump inhibitors varied, not routinely exceeding 40 mg omeprazole or 30 mg lansoprazole. A cohort study in patients with esophagitis treated with omeprazole[6] found that higher doses were likely to have achieved even higher healing rates. **Preventing recurrence:** Three of the RCTs looked at recurrence rates. Two RCTs (one double-blind and one single-blind)[7,8] compared omeprazole versus ranitidine (with or without cisapride) in patients with endoscopically confirmed esophagitis who had already received omeprazole for 4 to 8 weeks. At 1 year, patients treated with daily omeprazole were significantly less likely to relapse than those on ranitidine. In the first RCT, 159 participants were randomized to omeprazole 20 mg daily, omeprazole 20 mg on three consecutive days a week (weekend omeprazole), or ranitidine 150 mg twice daily. At 12 months, a significantly greater proportion of patients treated with daily omeprazole remained in remission than those treated with either weekend omeprazole (reduction in absolute risk of relapse [ARR] 57%, 95% CI 42%–71%) or daily ranitidine (ARR 64%, 95% CI 50%–78%). There was no significant difference between weekend omeprazole and daily ranitidine treatments (ARR 7%, 95% CI –11% to +25%).[7] In the second RCT, 175 participants were randomized to omeprazole, ranitidine, or cisapride alone and in various combinations. At 12 months, patients on omeprazole were significantly more likely to be in remission than those on either ranitidine or cisapride alone (80% still in remission compared with ~50%). CIs were not reported.[8] **Preventing complications:** We found no RCTs that looked at possible longer-term benefits of medical treatment.

Harms: **Complications of inadequate treatment:** We found no RCTs that examined the course of incompletely treated GERD nor any good data on the natural history of inflammatory esophageal disease in general.[1] We also found no data on precisely what level of gastric acid suppression ensures adequate esophageal healing. **Short-term adverse effects:** In RCTs, neither proton-pump inhibitors nor H_2-antagonists have appreciably different rates of adverse effects compared with placebo. Most data on significant adverse effects come from case reports or uncontrolled trials. H_2-antagonists have been associated rarely with cytopenias, gynecomastia, liver function test abnormalities, and hypersensitivity reactions. Rare adverse effects of proton-pump inhibitors in people with GERD include liver function test abnormalities, increased small bowel bacterial counts, decreased (but not clinically important) vitamin B_{12} levels, cytopenias, and hypersensitivity reactions. **Long-term adverse effects:** We found no controlled trials with long-term follow-up on the safety of chronic use of H_2-antagonists. Chronic use of proton-pump inhibitors in the presence of *Helicobacter pylori* infection has been linked in two uncontrolled trials to atrophic gastritis after 3 to 5 years.[9,10] Among patients treated with omeprazole, none of whom had atrophic gastritis at baseline, atrophic gastritis developed in 18 of the 59 patients infected with *H. pylori* and two of the 46 patients who were not infected.[9] Of 14 patients with persistent *H. pylori* infection, six developed mild to severe atrophy in 5 years.[10]

Comment: None.

OPTION DIFFERENT PROTON-PUMP INHIBITORS

One RCT has found no significant difference between different proton-pump inhibitors in the healing of esophagitis.

Benefits: No systematic review. We found one good multicenter, double-blind RCT.[11] This compared 30 mg lansoprazole versus 20 mg omeprazole in patients with erosive esophagitis. At 8 weeks, healing had occurred in 87% and 82% of patients in the two groups. Relapse rates were not evaluated.

Harms: No differences in adverse effects were reported, but the data are limited.

Comment: It is not possible to generalize from this single study.

OPTION MEDICAL VERSUS SURGICAL TREATMENT

Medical and surgical treatment have not yet been compared adequately in RCTs. We found preliminary data suggesting that proton-pump inhibitors and fundoplication are about equally effective at healing. We found no good comparative data on prevention of relapse or complications.

Benefits: No systematic review. **Healing:** We found one RCT comparing medical versus surgical treatment in patients with complicated GERD (erosive esophagitis, Barrett's esophagus, stricture, or esophageal ulcer).[12] A total of 247 patients, mainly men, were randomized to continuous medical treatment (antacids, ranitidine, metoclopramide, or sucralfate), medical treatment for symptoms only, or open fundoplication. Patients were evaluated at 6 weeks (data on 201 patients available), 1 year (176 patients), and 2 years (106 patients). Those receiving fundoplication had significantly better results, measured by a symptom-based "activity index score" and grade of esophagitis than either medical treatment group ($p < 0.03$). **Preventing relapse:** The trial did not evaluate relapse rates. Data from uncontrolled trials on the long-term results of open fundoplication[13–15] suggest that up to 90% of patients continue to benefit 6 to 20 years after surgery in terms of relief of symptoms, reduced acid exposure on pH monitoring, and absence of inflammation on endoscopy. **Preventing complications:** We found no good data relating to this outcome.

Harms: In the RCT,[12] there were no operative deaths but operative and postoperative complications occurred in 15% and 18% of patients. From other studies, intraoperative complications include splenic trauma (0%–4%), viscus perforation (1%–2%), and, less commonly, abscess or inadvertent vagotomy. Immediate postoperative complications include pleural effusion, pulmonary embolism, or late abscess formation. Although morbidity is significant, mortality related to the surgery is usually less than 1%. Late adverse effects related to fundoplication include bloating, dysphagia, gastric herniation, or breakdown of the fundoplication. Reoperation is required in up to 15% of patients for either complications or failure.

Comment: Erosive esophagitis, stricture, and Barrett's esophagus are now known to require at least a proton-pump inhibitor for healing and maintenance of remission.[16–19] The use of only an H_2-antagonist in the trial cited here[12] may have been biased in favor of fundoplication. Preliminary data from one RCT suggest approximately equal treatment efficacy when comparing fundoplication to omeprazole for patients with erosive esophagitis at 3 year follow-up.[20] Individual patient characteristics may direct the clinician toward medical or surgical treatment. Some patients are refractory to proton-pump inhibitors[21] or have severe "mechanical" reflux requiring surgery. Some patients may be high-risk surgical candidates or have relative contraindications to reflux surgery (such as scleroderma, multiple prior laparotomies, or previous gastric surgery). Younger patients may prefer surgery to lifelong drug treatment. We found no studies addressing these issues.

OPTION DIFFERENT SURGICAL TECHNIQUES

We found no RCTs comparing surgical techniques.

Benefits: We found no RCTs comparing Nissen, Tope, or Dor fundoplication; Hill gastroplasty; nor RCTs comparing open versus laparoscopic approaches.

Harms: Inadequate data.

Comment: None.

QUESTION What are the effects of treatment in nonerosive esophagitis?

OPTION PROTON-PUMP INHIBITORS VERSUS H_2-ANTAGONISTS

RCTs have found proton-pump inhibitors to be more effective at relieving symptoms than H_2-antagonists, with or without prokinetic agents.

Benefits: We found no systematic review. We found at least 10 double-blind RCTs. The four best RCTs compared omeprazole 20 mg or 10 mg versus placebo,[22,23] 10 mg omeprazole versus cimetidine 800 mg daily,[24] 20 mg omeprazole versus 400 mg cimetidine,[25] and 20 or 10 mg omeprazole versus 40 (10 mg qid) cisapride.[26] In most trials, symptom relief was approximately twice as good with omeprazole. We found no good data on recurrence rates.

Harms: *See* p. 143.

Comment: None.

OPTION **SURGICAL TREATMENT**

We found no RCTs evaluating surgical treatment of nonerosive esophagitis.

Benefits: We found no RCTs comparing medical versus surgical treatment in patients with nonerosive esophagitis nor any comparing different surgical techniques.

Harms: Inadequate data.

Comment: Good long-term trials are needed comparing laparoscopic fundoplication with proton-pump inhibitors, taking into account symptom relief, adherence, prevention of complications, and adverse effects of treatment.

QUESTION **Does treatment for GERD reduce the risk of progression of Barrett's esophagus?**

We found no good evidence on the effects of treatment for GERD in people with Barrett's esophagus.

Benefits: We found no RCTs. Uncontrolled studies, looking at the long-term effect of either cimetidine,[27] ranitidine,[27] or fundoplication[28] in people with Barrett's esophagus found no effect. With the advent of proton-pump inhibitors, uncontrolled studies have found both regression[29] and no regression.[30,31] None of these studies followed more than 27 patients. Long-term studies on the effects of fundoplication on Barrett's esophagus suggest that effective fundoplication, as evaluated by ambulatory pH monitoring, symptoms, and endoscopy, may lead to regression, whereas failed procedures may cause progression and even dysplasia or carcinoma.[32,33] However, numbers of patients studied were again small.

Harms: We found no good data on harms of treatments for GERD in patients with Barrett's esophagus.

Comment: Few centers see enough patients with Barrett's esophagus to perform long-term RCTs. In addition, our poor understanding of the pathophysiology of Barrett's esophagus means that we do not know what end point of treatment for GERD (symptom relief, healing, elimination of acid reflux) may change the course of Barrett's metaplasia. It is also not clear whether progression can be measured endoscopically.[34,35] Only a long-term multicenter trial will be able to answer these important questions.

QUESTION **Does treatment for GERD alter outcome in patients with extra-esophageal manifestations of GERD?**

We found limited and conflicting evidence from RCTs in patients with asthma and symptoms of reflux. We found no RCTs that looked at effects of treatment on other extra-esophageal manifestations (see Table 1).

Benefits: No systematic review. **Asthma:** We found one RCT (double-blind placebo-controlled crossover design) comparing omeprazole 40 mg per day versus placebo in 25 patients with adult-onset asthma and symptoms of reflux.[36] The design included a washout and crossover period, and pulmonary function tests and symptoms were monitored. Patients treated with omeprazole had improved evening peak expiratory flow rate and reflux symptoms, but there was no significant difference in other parameters of lung function (forced expiratory volume in one second, forced vital capacity, histamine bronchial responsiveness, and daytime peak expiratory flow rate) or in asthmatic symptoms or treatment requirements. A prospective open-label cohort study evaluated omeprazole in patients with nonallergic asthma and reflux symptoms.[37] Mean asthma score improved in patients on omeprazole but not as significantly as pulmonary function studies. Abnormal proximal acid exposure on pH monitoring and a history of frequent regurgitation were good predictors of clinical response. We found two RCTs comparing H_2-antagonists versus placebo, one of which included a surgical treatment arm. The first was a double-blind crossover RCT of ranitidine 150 mg twice daily versus placebo in 48 asthma patients with abnormal pH monitoring.[38] This found no significant improvement in bronchial reactivity, lung function, or peak flow. The second randomized 90 patients with adult onset asthma and reflux to placebo, cimetidine, or fundoplication. This found significant improvement in pulmonary function tests and need for asthmatic medication with active treatment (surgery more so than cimetidine), whereas the placebo group worsened.[39] Both active treatments achieved long-term benefit (up to 6 years), the greatest being in the surgical group. One RCT in patients with GERD but without obvious lung disease found no improvement in pulmonary function after 1 year of either medical treatment or fundoplication.[40] **Other extra-esophageal manifestations:** We found no RCTs. Two prospective open label cohort studies of omeprazole in patients with chronic laryngitis found improvement.[41,42]

Harms: We found no good data on harms of treatment for GERD in these patients.

Comment: The link between extra-esophageal symptoms and GERD is by association rather than cause and effect; the symptoms are multifactorial, making it hard to prove that GERD is the primary cause. There was little standardization in these trials with regard to treatments used or patient characteristics. Before good RCTs can be performed, further research must first identify clear criteria for GERD as the cause of these syndromes.

REFERENCES

1. Isolauri J, Luostarinen M, Isolauri E, et al. The natural course of gastroesophageal reflux disease: 17–22 year follow-up of 60 patients. *Am J Gastroenterol* 1997;92:37–41.
2. Richter JE. Extraesophageal manifestations of gastroesophageal reflux disease. *Clinical Perspectives* 1998;1:28–39.
3. Chiba N, DeGara CJ, Wilkinson JM, Hunt RH. Speed of healing and symptom relief in grade II to IV gastroesophageal reflux disease: a meta-analysis. *Gastroenterology* 1997;112:1798–1810. (Search date July 1996; primary sources MEDLINE plus manual search of earlier issues of *Eur J Gastroenterol Hepatol*. Reference lists of retrieved articles searched.)
4. Richter JE, Sabesin SM, Kogut DG, Kerr RM, Wruble LD, Collen MJ. Omeprazole versus ranitidine or ranitidine/metoclopramide in poorly responsive symptomatic gastroesophageal reflux disease. *Am J Gastroenterol* 1996;91:1766–1772.
5. Robinson M, Decktor DL, Maton PN, et al. Omeprazole is superior to ranitidine plus metoclopramide in the short-term treatment of erosive esophagitis. *Aliment Pharmacol Ther* 1993;7:67–73.
6. Klinkenberg-Knol EC, Festen HP, Jansen JB, et al. Long-term treatment with omeprazole for refractory reflux esophagitis: efficacy and safety. *Ann Intern Med* 1994;121:161–167.
7. Dent J, Yeomans ND, Mackinnon M, et al. Omeprazole v ranitidine for prevention of relapse in reflux esophagitis: a controlled double blind trial of their efficacy and safety. *Gut* 1994;35: 590–598.
8. Vigneri S, Termini R, Leandro G, et al. A comparison of five maintenance therapies for reflux esophagitis. *N Engl J Med* 1995;333: 1106–1110.
9. Kuipers EJ, Lundell L, Klinkenberg-Knol EC, et al. Atrophic gastritis and Helicobacter pylori infection in patients with reflux esophagitis treated with omeprazole or fundoplication. *N Engl J Med* 1996;334:1018–1022.
10. Eissele R, Brunner G, Simon B, Solcia E, Arnold R. Gastric mucosa during treatment with lansoprazole: Helicobacter pylori is a risk factor for argyrophil cell hyperplasia. *Gastroenterology* 1997;112:707–717.
11. Hatlebakk JG, Berstad A, Carling L, et al. Lansoprazole versus omeprazole in short-term treatment of reflux oesophagitis. Results of a Scandinavian multicentre trial. *Scand J Gastroenterol* 1993;28(3):224–228.
12. Spechler SJ. Comparison of medical and surgical therapy for complicated gastroesophageal reflux disease in veterans. *N Engl J Med* 1992;326:786–792.
13. Martinez de Haro LF, Ortiz A, Parrilla P, et al. Long-term results of Nissen fundoplication in reflux esophagitis without strictures: clinical, endoscopic, and pH-metric evaluation. *Dig Dis Sci* 1992;37:523–527.
14. Bjerkeset T, Edna T-H, Fjosne U. Long-term results after 'floppy' Nissen/Rosetti fundoplication for gastroesophageal reflux disease. *Scand J Gastroenterol* 1992;27:707–710.
15. Luostarinen M, Isolauri J, Laitinen J, et al. Fate of Nissen fundoplication after 20 years: a clinical, endoscopical, and functional analysis. *Gut* 1993; 34:1015–1020.
16. Klinkenberg-Knoll EC, Festen HP, Jansen JB, et al. Long-term treatment with omeprazole for refractory reflux esophagitis: efficacy and safety. *Ann Intern Med* 1994;121:161–167.
17. Dent J, Yeomans ND, Mackinnon M, et al. Omeprazole v ranitidine for prevention of relapse in reflux esophagitis: a controlled double blind trial of their efficacy and safety. *Gut* 1994;35: 590–598.
18. Vigneri S, Termini R, Leandro G, et al. A comparison of five maintenance therapies for reflux esophagitis. *N Engl J Med* 1995;333:1106–1110.
19. Robinson M, Lanza F, Avner D, Haber M. Effective maintenance treatment of reflux esophagitis with low-dose lansoprazole: a randomized double blind placebo-controlled trial. *Ann Intern Med* 1996; 124:859–867.
20. Lundell L, Dalenback J, Hattlebakk J, et al. Omeprazole or antireflux surgery in the long term management of gastroesophageal reflux disease: results of a multicenter, randomized clinical trial. *Gastroenterology* 1998;114:A207.
21. Leite L, Johnston B, Just R, Castell DO. Persistent acid secretion during omeprazole therapy: a study of gastric acid profiles in patients demonstrating failure of omeprazole therapy. *Am J Gastroenterol* 1996;91:1527–1531.
22. Venables TL, Newland RD, Patel AC, et al. Maintenance treatment for gastroesophageal reflux disease: a placebo-controlled evaluation of 10 mg omeprazole once daily in general practice. *Scand J Gastroenterol* 1997;32:627–632.
23. Carlsson R, Dent J, Watts R, et al. Gastroesophageal reflux disease in primary care: an international study of different treatment strategies with omeprazole. *Eur J Gastroenterol Hepatol* 1998;10:119–124.
24. Bate CM, Green JR, Axon AT, et al. Omeprazole is more effective than cimetidine in the prevention of recurrence of GERD-associated heartburn and the occurrence of underlying esophagitis. *Aliment Pharmacol Ther* 1998;12:41–47.
25. Bate CM, Green JR, Axon AT, et al. Omeprazole is more effective than cimetidine for the relief of all grades of gastro-esophageal reflux disease-associated heartburn, irrespective of the presence or absence of endoscopic esophagitis. *Aliment Pharmacol Ther* 1997;11:755–763.
26. Galmiche JP, Barthelemy P, Hamelin B. Treating the symptoms of gastroesophageal reflux disease: a double-blind comparison of omeprazole and cisapride. *Aliment Pharmacol Ther* 1997;11: 765–773.
27. Sampliner RE, Garewal HS, Fennerty MB, Aickin M. Lack of impact of therapy on extent of Barrett's esophagus in 67 patients. *Dig Dis Sci* 1990;35:93–96.
28. Williamson WA, Ellis FH Jr, Gibb SP, Shahian DM, Aretz T. Effect of antireflux operation on Barrett's mucosa. *Ann Thorac Surg* 1990;49:537–542.
29. Gore S, Healey CJ, Sutton R, et al. Regression of columnar lined (Barrett's) esophagus with continuous omeprazole therapy. *Aliment Pharmacol Ther* 1993;7:623–628.
30. Sampliner RE. Effect of up to 3 years of high-dose lansoprazole on Barrett's esophagus. *Am J Gastroenterol* 1994;89:1844–1848.
31. Sharma P, Sampliner RE, Camargo E. Normalization of esophageal pH with high-dose proton pump inhibitor therapy does not result in regression of Barrett's esophagus. *Am J Gastroenterol* 1997;92:582–585.
32. Sagar PM, Ackroyd R, Hosie KB, et al. Regression and progression of Barrett's esophagus after antireflux surgery. *Br J Surg* 1995;82:806–810.
33. Csendes A, Braghetto I, Burdiles P, et al. Long-term results of classic antireflux surgery in 152

patients with Barrett's esophagus: clinical, radiologic, endoscopic, manometric and acid reflux test analysis before and late after operation. *Surgery* 1998;123:645–657.
34. Kim R, Baggott BB, Rose S, et al. Quantitative endoscopy: precise computerized measurement of metaplastic epithelial surface area in Barrett's esophagus. *Gastroenterology* 1995;108:360–366.
35. Sharma P, Morales TG, Bhattacharyya A, Garewal HS, Sampliner RE. Squamous islands in Barrett's esophagus: what lies underneath? *Am J Gastroenterol* 1998;93:332–335.
36. Teichtahl H, Kronborg IJ, Yeomans ND, Robinson P. Adult asthma and gastroesophageal reflux: the effects of omeprazole therapy on asthma. *Aust NZ J Med* 1996;26:671–676.
37. Harding SM, Richter JE, Guzzo MR, et al. Asthma and gastroesophageal reflux: acid suppressive therapy improves asthma outcome. *Am J Med* 1996;100:395–405.
38. Ekstrom T, et al. Effects of ranitidine treatment on patients with asthma and a history of gastroesophageal reflux: a double blind crossover study. *Thorax* 1989;44:19–23.
39. Larrain A, et al. Medical and surgical treatment of nonallergic asthma associated with gastroesophageal reflux. *Chest* 1991;99:1330–1335.
40. Spechler SJ, Gordon DW, Cohen J, Williford WO, Krol W. The effects of antireflux therapy on pulmonary function in patients with severe gastroesophageal reflux disease. Department of Veterans Affairs gastroesophageal reflux disease study group. *Am J Gastroenterol* 1995;90:915–918.
41. Kamel PL, Hanson D, Kahrilas PJ. Omeprazole for the treatment of posterior laryngitis. *Am J Med* 1994;96:321–326.
42. Hanson DG, Kamel PL, Kahrilas PJ. Outcomes of anti-reflux therapy in the treatment of chronic laryngitis. *Ann Otol Rhinol Laryngol* 1995;104: 550–555.

David A Katzka, MD
Associate Professor
Hospital of the University of Pennsylvania
Philadelphia
Pennsylvania

Competing interests: The author has received lecture fees from Astra, Janssen-Merck, and SmithKline Beecham.

TABLE 1 Extra-esophageal manifestations of gastroesophageal reflux disease.[2] **(*See* text p. 142, p. 147.)**

Pulmonary: asthma, chronic bronchitis, aspiration pneumonia, sleep apnoea, atelectasis, interstitial pulmonary fibrosis

Ear nose and throat: chronic cough, hoarseness, enamel erosion, halitosis, pharyngitis, subglottic stenosis, vocal cord inflammation, granuloma, possibly cancer

Other: noncardiac chest pain, chronic hiccups, nausea

Colorectal cancer

John Scholefield, ChM, FRCS

QUESTIONS

INTERVENTIONS

Beneficial

Surgery* 153
Colonoscopic polypectomy* . .152
Adjuvant chemotherapy in Dukes' type C colorectal cancer 151

Likely to be beneficial

Three- to five-yearly follow-up .152
Total mesorectal excision . . .153
Colonoscopy to detect metachronous cancers and polyps 152
Adjuvant chemotherapy in Dukes' type B colorectal cancer 151

Unlikely to be beneficial

Annual or biannual follow-up (no better than less frequent) . .152

To be covered in future issues of *Clinical Evidence*

Preoperative radiotherapy
Immunotherapy
Specialist versus generalist surgical care
Liver resection for metastases

*Not evaluated in RCTs

Key Messages

- Randomzied controlled trials (RCTs) have found that adjuvant chemotherapy improves 5-year survival by at least 5% in people with Dukes' type C tumors. The evidence of benefit in people with Dukes' type B tumors is less clear. We found no good data on harmful effects.
- We found limited evidence suggesting that annual or biannual follow-up is no better than three- to five-yearly follow-up in terms of detection of recurrence or survival. The potential harms of follow-up are poorly understood.
- Total mesorectal excision for rectal cancer has not yet been adequately evaluated in RCTs. Nonrandomized studies suggest that it may reduce the rate of recurrence.

DEFINITION Colorectal cancer is a malignant neoplasm arising from the lining (mucosa) of the large intestine (colon and rectum). Sixty percent of colorectal cancers occur in the rectum or sigmoid colon.

INCIDENCE/ PREVALENCE Colorectal cancer is the third most common malignancy in the developed world. It accounts for approximately 30,000 deaths per year in the UK and 60,000 deaths per year in the USA. Although the incidence of and mortality from colorectal cancer have generally been static for the past 40 years, recent evidence shows that the incidence of the disease is falling in both the UK and the USA.[1,2] Colon cancer affects almost equal proportions of men and women, most commonly between the ages of 60 and 80 years. Rectal cancer is more common in men.[1]

ETIOLOGY The pathogenesis of colorectal cancer is a multistep process involving genetic and environmental factors. The most important environmental factor is probably diet.[3]

PROGNOSIS Overall 5-year survival is approximately 50% and has remained largely unchanged over the past 40 years. Evidence is emerging from the USA and UK cancer registries that disease specific mortality is decreasing, but the reasons for this are unclear.[1,2] Surgery is undertaken with curative intent in over 80% of people, but approximately half will suffer recurrence without further treatment. In the UK, about a quarter of people with colorectal cancer present as emergencies with either intestinal obstruction or perforation.[4,5]

AIMS To remove the tumor in order to prevent bowel obstruction or perforation; to avoid creating a permanent stoma by restoring intestinal continuity wherever technically possible; to prevent or minimize metastasis; to minimize adverse effects of treatment and maximize quality of life.

OUTCOMES Survival, proportion of patients with permanent stoma, incidence of local recurrence, rates of metastasis, adverse effects of treatment, quality of life.

METHODS *Clinical Evidence* search for systematic reviews. Search for RCTs in Cochrane Library and on MEDLINE from 1966 to 1998 using key words: colorectal cancer, neoplasia, adjuvant chemotherapy, surgery, follow-up, recurrence. All RCTs were reviewed.

QUESTION What are the effects of adjuvant chemotherapy?

RCTs have found that adjuvant chemotherapy improves survival by at least 5% in people with Dukes' type B and C tumors. The evidence of benefit in people with Dukes' type B tumors is less clear. We found no good data on harmful effects.

Benefits: A systematic review published in 1997 identified 29 RCTs of adjuvant treatment in colorectal cancer (1673 people with Dukes' type C colon cancer and 695 with Dukes' type B or C rectal cancer).[6] This reported a small but significant improvement in overall survival (OR for death with adjuvant versus no adjuvant treatment 0.91, 95% CI

0.83–0.99), which translated into an overall improvement in 5-year survival of 5% for people with colon cancer and 9% for people with rectal cancer. Twenty-four of the 29 RCTs dated from before 1990. The data were less clear cut for Dukes' B than for Dukes' C type tumors, probably partly because of the smaller numbers of Dukes' type B tumors. The largest single RCT, a pooled analysis of three RCTs of adjuvant fluouracil and folinic acid in colon cancer,[7] showed a 10% survival advantage for Dukes' type C tumors at 3 years but no significant survival advantage for Dukes' type B tumors.

Harms: We found little good evidence on the adverse effects of chemotherapy or on its impact on quality of life, partly because of the many different regimens used. In the RCTs included in the systematic review,[6] the incidence of severe adverse effects (stomatitis, diarrhea, nausea, and leukopenia) with 5-fluorouracil and levamisole ranged from 10% to 30%, with life-threatening toxicity in approximately 5% of people. For every 10 people treated, up to three will experience an additional severe adverse effect. However, three studies reported deaths related to chemotherapy in nearly 2% of people with advanced disease.

Comment: A much larger RCT of the benefits and harms of adjuvant chemotherapy in Dukes' type B tumors is now under way in the UK (Kerr D, personal communication).

QUESTION What are the effects of routine follow-up for colorectal cancer?

We found limited evidence suggesting that nonintensive surveillance (colonoscopy and computed tomography [CT] every 3 to 5 years) is beneficial but that more intensive annual or biannual follow-up confers no additional benefit. Whether the interval between follow-up visits should be 3 or 5 years is currently uncertain. The potential harms of follow-up are poorly understood. Limited evidence suggests that follow-up is reassuring to most patients.

Benefits: We found no systematic review. We found two RCTs. One, in 1418 people who had undergone removal of adenomatous polyps, compared follow-up colonoscopy at 1 and 3 years versus 3 years only.[8] The proportion of participants in whom new polyps were detected was higher with more frequent follow-up (42% vs. 32%, RR of detection compared with less frequent follow-up 1.3, 95% CI 1.1–1.6). However, there was no significant difference in the proportion of detected polyps with advanced pathology (~3% in both groups, RR 1.0, 95% CI 0.5–2.2). The other RCT, in 325 people who had undergone curative resection for newly diagnosed colorectal cancer (Dukes' type A, B, or C), compared standard versus intensive follow-up. Standard follow-up comprised clinical review (history, examination, liver function tests, carcinoembryonic antigen, and fecal occult blood testing) every 3 months for 2 years, and every 6 months for 5 years thereafter or until a major end point was reached. Intensive follow-up comprised regular clinical review as above plus annual chest radiograph, CT scan of the liver, and colonoscopy. On completion of 5-years' follow-up, there was no significant difference in survival between the two groups. Yearly colonoscopy failed to detect any asymptomatic local recurrences.[9]

Harms: Presymptomatic diagnosis of incurable recurrent disease may increase patient anxiety and reduce quality of life. Invasive tests such as colonoscopy also carry risks. No data on these outcomes were reported in the trials.

Comment: An RCT in 212 people being followed up after treatment for colorectal cancer found that 78% were rather or very reassured by follow-up. However, follow-up had no effect on quality of life. Most patients said that they would still prefer follow-up even if it did not lead to earlier detection of recurrence.[10] Current follow-up regimens are haphazard in frequency and intensity. We found no evidence about whether follow-up should be discontinued in elderly people (aged > 75 years). This is important as many patients with colorectal cancer fall into this age group. In the UK, people over the age of 75 years are not routinely considered for chemotherapy because of the potential toxicity of therapy. We found no firm evidence to support this.

QUESTION **What are the effects of total mesorectal excision for rectal cancer?**

Total mesorectal excision for rectal cancer has not yet been evaluated adequately in RCTs. Nonrandomized studies suggest that it may reduce the rate of local recurrence.

Benefits: We found no systematic review or RCTs. We found several nonrandomized studies.[11–14] These are summarized in Table 1.

Harms: With conventional anterior resection, some of the rectum is retained. The removal of the entire rectum in total mesorectal excision necessitates a coloanal anastomosis. This results in impaired function, with increased stool frequency (median 4–5 per day versus 1–2 per day with techniques leaving a rectal stump). It also carries a higher incidence of anastomotic leakage (11%–15% vs. 8%–10%),[15] though this has never been evaluated in RCTs. In order to reduce the incidence of anastomotic leakage, many surgeons routinely use a temporary defunctioning stoma after total mesorectal excision.[11]

Comment: Rectal cancer surgery is more technically demanding than colon cancer resection. An increasing volume of data (but no RCTs) suggest that surgical technique is especially important in resecting rectal cancer.

REFERENCES

1. *Mortality statistics, cause, England and Wales 1993*. OPCS dh22. London: HMSO, 1995.
2. Miller BA, Ries LA, Hankey BF, et al. *Cancer statistics review 1973–1989*. Rockville (MD): National Institutes of Health, National Cancer Institute. Report No: NIH-NCI 92-2789.
3. Kune G, ed. *Causes and control of colorectal cancer: a model for cancer prevention*. Boston: Kluwer Academic Publishers, 1996.
4. Mella J, Biffen A, Radcliffe AG, Stamatakis JD, Steele RJ. Population-based audit of colorectal cancer management in two United Kingdom health regions. *Br J Surg* 1997;84:1731–1736.
5. Scholefield JH, Robinson MH, Mangham C, Hardcastle JD. Screening for colorectal cancer reduces emergency admissions. *Eur J Surg Oncol* 1998;24:47–50.
6. Dube S, Heyen F, Jenicek M. Adjuvant chemotherapy in colorectal carcinoma. Results of a meta analysis. *Dis Colon Rectum* 1997;40:35–41. (Search date January 1959 to June 1993; primary source MEDLINE.)
7. International Multicenter Pooled Analysis of Colon Cancer Trials (IMPACT) Investigators. Efficacy of adjuvant fluouracil and folinic acid in colon cancer. *Lancet* 1995;348:939–944.
8. Winawer SJ, Zauber AG, O'Brien MJ, et al. Randomised comparison of surveillance intervals after colonoscopic removal of newly diagnosed adenomatous polyps: the national polyp study workgroup. *N Engl J Med* 1993;328: 901–906.
9. Shoemaker D, Black R, Giles L, Toouli J. Yearly colonoscopy, liver CT and chest radiography do not influence 5 year survival of colorectal cancer patients. *Gastroenterology* 1998;114:7–14.

10. Stiggelbout AM, de Haes JC, Vree R, et al. Follow up of colorectal cancer patients: quality of life and attitudes towards follow up. *Br J Cancer* 1997;75:914–920.
11. MacFarlane JK, Ryall RD, Heald RJ. Mesorectal excision for rectal cancer. *Lancet* 1993;341: 457–460.
12. Enker WE, Thaler HT, Cranor ML, Polyak T. Total mesorectal excision in the operative treatment of carcinoma of the rectum. *J Am Coll Surg* 1995; 181:335–346.
13. Singh S, Morgan MB, Broughton M, Caffarey S, Topham C, Marks CG. A ten-year prospective audit of outcome of surgical treatment for colorectal carcinoma. *Br J Surg* 1995;82:1486–1490.
14. Arbman G, Nilsson E, Hallbook O, Sjodahl R. Local recurrence following total mesorectal excision for rectal cancer. *Br J Surg* 1996;83:375–379.
15. Karania ND, Corder AP, Bearn P, Heald RJ. Leakage from stapled low anastomosis after total mesorectal excision for carcinoma of the rectum. *Br J Surg* 1994;81:1224–1226.

John H Scholefield, ChM, FRCS
Reader in Surgery
University Hospital
Nottingham
UK

Competing interests: None declared.

TABLE 1 Effects of total mesorectal excision: results of nonrandomized studies. (See text p. 153.)

Study	Cancer stage (Dukes' type) No. of patients	Intervention	Recurrence at 5 years (95% CI) Local	Overall	Mortality (RRR of death by 5 years (95% CI))	Incidence of anastomotic leak (95% CI)
McFarlane et al.[11]	B (88) C (73)	TME	5% (0%–7.5%)	18% (10%–25%)	78% (68%–88%)	11% clinical 6.4% radiologic
Enker et al.[12]	B (99) C (147)	TME	7.3%	23%	74%	NA
Singh et al.[13]	A, B, and C (158 in total)	TME	8%	24%	60%	10%
Arbman et al.[14]	A (67) B (89) C (100)	TME	6% at 1 year	NA	NA	8% (57% stoma rate)
		Non-TME	14% at 1 year			9% (15% stoma rate)

TME, total mesorectal excision; NA, not applicable.

Common upper respiratory infections

Paul Glasziou, MBBS, PhD, and Chris Del Mar, MB, BChir, FRAGGP, FAFPHM

QUESTIONS

INTERVENTIONS

Key Messages

- Randomized controlled trials (RCTs) have found that antibiotics have no clinically significant effects in undifferentiated colds and minimal to modest effects in acute bronchitis, pharyngitis, and sinusitis. They can prevent nonsuppurative complications of β-hemolytic streptococcal pharyngitis, but in developed societies such complications are extremely rare.
- RCTs have found that β-agonists may reduce the duration of cough in acute bronchitis.
- One systematic review of RCTs has found that vitamin C may reduce the duration of symptoms in undifferentiated colds. However, the beneficial effect is small and may be explained by publication bias.
- We found no consistent evidence on the effects of zinc gluconate.

DEFINITION Upper respiratory tract infection comprises inflammation of the respiratory mucosa from the nose to the lower respiratory tree, not including the alveoli. In addition to systematic malaise, it causes localized symptoms that constitute several overlapping syndromes: sore throat (pharyngitis); rhinorrhoea (common cold); facial fullness and pain (sinusitis); and cough (bronchitis).

INCIDENCE/ PREVALENCE Upper respiratory tract infections, nasal congestion, throat complaints, and cough are responsible for 11% of general practice consultations in Australia.[1] Children on average suffer five such infections per year, and adults two to three infections annually.[1]

ETIOLOGY Infective agents include over 200 viruses (with 100 rhinoviruses) and several bacteria. Transmission is mostly through hand-to-hand contact, with subsequent passage to the nares or eyes, rather than, as commonly perceived, via droplets in the air.[2]

PROGNOSIS Upper respiratory tract infections are usually self-limiting. Although they cause little mortality or serious morbidity, upper respiratory tract infections are responsible for considerable discomfort, work loss, and medical costs. Clinical patterns are variable and overlap considerably between infective agents; in addition to nasal symptoms, half of sufferers experience sore throat and 40% experience cough. Symptoms peak within 1 to 3 days and generally clear by 1 week, although cough is often a persistent symptom.[2]

AIMS To relieve symptoms, to prevent suppurative and nonsuppurative complications of bacterial infection.

OUTCOMES Cure rate, duration of symptoms, incidence of complications, incidence of adverse effects of treatment.

METHODS We searched the Cochrane Library, MEDLINE and references of key articles up to 1998 for good systematic reviews and RCTs.

QUESTION What are the effects of treatment?

OPTION ANTIBIOTICS

RCTs have found that antibiotics have no clinically significant effects in undifferentiated colds and minimal to modest effects in acute bronchitis, pharyngitis, and sinusitis. They can prevent nonsuppurative complications of β-hemolytic streptococcal pharyngitis, but in developed societies such complications are extremely rare.

Benefits: **Colds:** We found no systematic review. A recent RCT in 314 people comparing amoxicillin with clavulanate (375 mg tid) versus placebo showed no overall difference in "cure" rates.[3] However, in the 61 patients (20%) who were found to have positive sputum cultures for *H. influenzae*, *M. catarrhalis*, or *S. pneumoniae*, there was a significant difference in recovery of 27% versus 4% at 5 days. If such people could be identified at first consultation, then treating four of these would result in one more recovery at five days. **Cough:** We found one systematic review[4] updated in 1997. This identified eight RCTs comparing doxycycline (four RCTs), erythromycin (three RCTs), and trimethoprim/sulfamethoxazole (one RCT) versus placebo in 750 patients (aged 8 to >65 years). Often, only outcome measures that were significant were reported explicitly, which may result in an optimistic bias. With this limitation in mind, people receiving antibiotics were less likely to report feeling unwell at a follow-up visit (OR 0.42, 95% CI 0.22–0.82). There was no significant difference in time to return to work or usual activities (WMD 0.74 days earlier; 95% CI 0.16–1.32). **Sore throat:** We found one systematic review[5] updated in 1998, which identified 18 controlled trials in 9189 people with sore throat. The combined effects from six studies showed a RRR for rheumatic fever of 0.28 (95% CI 0.19–0.40) and a trend for protection against acute glomerulonephritis with the use of antibiotics. Suppurative complications were also reduced: otitis media and peritonsillar abscess significantly (RR 0.23, 95% CI 0.12–0.45) (RR 0.19, 95% CI 0.08–0.47), and acute sinusitis nonsignificantly (RR 0.33, 95% CI 0.07–1.65). However, to prevent one case of otitis media would require 30 children or 145 adults suffering from sore throat to be treated. Antibiotics also shortened the duration of symptoms but by a mean of only approximately 8 hours overall; however, this benefit was greater in people who were culture positive for β-hemolytic streptococcus. **Sinusitis:** We found one systematic review[6] published in 1998, which identified six RCTs comparing antibiotics versus placebo in 761 people with sinusitis. It found antimicrobial agents (amoxicillin in three trials, other agents in three trials) to be effective in treating uncomplicated acute sinusitis. Although symptoms improved or disappeared in 69% of people on placebo, antibiotics almost halved this 31% clinical failure rate (RRR for treatment failure compared to placebo 46%, 95% CI 21%–63%). The same review analyzed comparative trials and showed no advantage of other antibiotics over amoxicillin.

Harms: Adverse effects such as nausea, vomiting, headache, skin rash, or vaginitis were more common on antibiotics than placebo—for example, in the bronchitis review the ARI for adverse effects was 6% (95% CI 0.1%–12%), or a rate of one extra adverse effect per 16 patients treated. As yet, there is no evidence of the size of the risk of antibiotic resistance or pseudomembranous colitis.

Comment: Because most upper respiratory tract infections are viral, the potential benefit from antibiotics is limited. Until rapid identification of those likely to benefit is possible, the modest effects seen in trials must be weighed against the adverse effects of antibiotics, the costs, and the potential for inducing antibiotic resistance.

OPTION β-AGONISTS

β-Agonists can reduce the duration of cough in acute bronchitis.

Benefits: We found no systematic review. Two RCTs in people with acute bronchitis have compared erythromycin versus the β-agonist albuterol.[7,8] In the first study, the numbers of patients not coughing at 7 days were 59% on liquid albuterol compared with 12% on erythromycin. In the second study the numbers not coughing were 39% (inhaled albuterol) compared with 9% (erythromycin). These ARRs of 47% and

30% mean two to three people would need to be treated for one fewer person coughing at the end of 1 week.

Harms: Short-term use of a β-agonist may cause tachycardia and anxiety.

Comment: The cough associated with acute bronchitis is self-limiting, and treatment is for symptomatic relief. Hence, it is important to consider the degree of disturbance caused and the patient's preferences and interpretation of the cough.

OPTION VITAMIN C

Vitamin C may provide a small benefit in people with upper respiratory tract infections.

Benefits: We found one systematic review[9–11] updated in 1997. This identified 30 RCTs comparing vitamin C versus placebo for prophylaxis and treatment of colds. Three RCTs used 1 g or more daily of vitamin C taken at the onset of symptoms. The duration of symptoms was reduced by half a day (WMD 0.55 days per cold episode, 95% CI 0.17–0.92), representing approximately 15% fewer symptom days per episode.

Harms: The studies of treatment found no difference in adverse effects potentially caused by vitamin C.

Comment: The beneficial effect reported in the review was small, and the authors concluded that it may be the result of publication bias.

OPTION ZINC GLUCONATE

There is a protocol for a Cochrane systematic review on zinc gluconate.[12] Existing trials are too heterogenous to give a meaningful summary at present.[13,14]

REFERENCES

1. Fry J, Sandler G. *Common diseases. Their nature, prevalence and care.* Dordrecht, The Netherlands: Kluwer Academic, 1993.
2. Lorber B. The common cold. *J Gen Intern Med* 1996;11:229–236.
3. Kaiser L, Lew D, Hirschel B, et al. Effects of antibiotic treatment in the subset of common-cold patients who have bacteria in nasopharyngeal secretions. *Lancet* 1996;347:1507–1510.
4. Becker L, Glazier R, McIsaac W, Smucny J. Antibiotics for acute bronchitis. (Cochrane Review). In: The Cochrane Library, Issue 2, 1998. Oxford: Update Software. Updated quarterly. Search date 1997. MEDLINE 1966-1996, EMBASE 1974-1996, Science Citation Index 1989 to 1996. Hand search of reference lists of relevant trials, textbooks, and review articles.
5. Del Mar CB, Glasziou PP. Antibiotics for the symptoms and complications of sore throat. (Cochrane Review) In: The Cochrane Library, Issue 2, 1998. Oxford: Update Software. Updated quarterly. Search date 1998. Index Medicus 1945–1965, MEDLINE 1966–1997, Cochrane Library 1997 issue 4. Hand search of reference lists of relevant articles.
6. de Ferranti SD, Ioannidis JP, Lau J, Anninger WV, Barza M. Are amoxycillin and folate inhibitors as effective as other antibiotics for acute sinusitis? A meta-analysis. *BMJ* 1998;317:632–637. Search date May 1998. MEDLINE (up to May 1998). Manual search of Excerpta Medica and recent abstracts for Interscience Conference on Antimicrobial Agents and Chemotherapy (1993–1997), and references of all trials, review articles, and special issues for additional studies.
7. Hueston WJ. A comparison of albuterol and erythromycin for the treatment of acute bronchitis. *J Fam Pract* 1991;33(5):476–480.
8. Hueston WJ. Albuterol delivered by metered-dose inhaler to treat acute bronchitis. *J Fam Pract* 1994;39(5):437–440.
9. Douglas RM, Chalker EB, Treacy B. Vitamin C for the common cold. (Cochrane Review) In: The Cochrane Library, Issue 2, 1998. Oxford: Update Software. Updated quarterly. Search details: Included all of the 30 trials that were included in an analysis by Hemila and Kleinjen[10,11].
10. Kleijnen J, ter Riet G, Knipschild PG. Vitamin C and the common cold; review of a megadoses literature [in Dutch]. *Ned Tijdschr Geneeskd*

1989;133(31):1532–1535.
11. Hemila H. Vitamin C and the common cold. *Br J Nutr* 1992;67:3–16.
12. Marshall I. Zinc in the treatment of the common cold (Protocol for a Cochrane Review). In: The Cochrane Library, Issue 1, 1999. Oxford: Update Software
13. Mossad SB, Mackmin ML, Medendorp SV, Mason P. Zinc gluconate lozenges for treating the common cold. *Ann Intern Med* 1996;125:81–88.
14. Mackmin ML, Piedmonte M, Calendine C, et al. Zinc gluconate lozenges for treating the common cold in children. *JAMA* 1998;279:1962–1967.

Paul Glasziou, MBBS, PhD
Assistant Professor in Clinical Epidemiology
University of Queensland Medical School
Herston
Australia

Chris Del Mar, MB, BChir, FRAGGP, FAFPHM
Professor of General Practice
University of Queensland
Brisbane
Australia

Competing interests: None declared.

Community-acquired pneumonia

Thomas J Marrie, MD

QUESTIONS

INTERVENTIONS

Key Messages

- A systematic review has found that, in patients with community-acquired pneumonia (CAP), there is no difference between most oral antibiotics, including amoxicillin and erythromycin, when local microbial sensitivities are taken into account.
- We found no strong evidence supporting new over older antibiotics in patients admitted to hospital or any particular combination of antibiotics in patients in intensive care.
- Randomized controlled trials (RCTs) found that, in immunocompetent patients, intravenous antibiotics were no more effective than oral antibiotics and actually prolonged length of stay in hospital.
- A systematic review of cohort studies, and recent RCTs, has found that influenza vaccine reduces risk of pneumonia and death in elderly people.
- A systematic review of RCTs has found that pneumococcal vaccination with currently available vacines does not protect against death or all-cause pneumonia but may protect young, fit adults against pneumococcal pneumonia.

DEFINITION Community-acquired pneumonia (CAP) is pneumonia contracted in the community, rather than in hospital.

INCIDENCE/ PREVALENCE In the northern hemisphere, CAP affects approximately 12/1000 people per year, particularly during winter and at the extremes of age (incidence:< 1 year of age 30–50/1000 per year; 15–45 years 1–5/1000 per year; 60–70 years 10–20/1000 per year; 71–85 years 50/1000 per year).[1–6]

ETIOLOGY Over 100 microorganisms have been implicated, but most cases are caused by *Streptococcus pneumoniae* (Table 1).[5,7] Susceptibility to penicillin varies considerably by geographic area.

PROGNOSIS Severity varies from mild to life-threatening illness within days of the onset of symptoms. One large review[8] found overall mortality to be 13.7%, ranging from 5.1% to 36.5% for patients requiring intensive care. The following prognostic factors were associated significantly with mortality: male sex (OR 1.3, 95% CI 1.2–1.4); pleuritic chest pain (OR 0.5, 95% CI 0.3–0.8); hypothermia (OR 5, 95% CI 2.4–10.4); systolic hypotension (OR 4.8, 95% CI 2.8–8.3); tachypnea (OR 2.9, 95% CI 1.7–4.9); diabetes mellitus (OR 1.3, 95% CI 1.1–1.5); neoplastic disease (OR 2.8, 95% CI 2.4–3.1); neurologic disease (OR 4.6, 95% CI 2.3–8.9); bacteremia (OR 2.8, 95% CI 2.3–3.6); leukopenia (OR 2.5, 95% CI 1.6–3.7); and multilobar radiographic pulmonary infiltrates (OR 3.1, 95% CI 1.9–5.1).

AIMS **Treatment:** To cure infection, to prevent death in seriously ill patients, to alleviate symptoms, to enable a return to normal activities, to prevent recurrence. **Prevention:** To prevent infection.

OUTCOMES Clinical cure, defined as return to premorbid health status; relief of symptoms; admission to hospital; complications (empyema, endocarditis, lung abscess); death; adverse effects of antibiotics (allergy, diarrhea, colitis); adverse effects of procedures (endotracheal intubation, central vascular lines).

METHODS *Clinical Evidence* search. Systematic reviews: MEDLINE (1966 to May 1998), EMBASE (1988 to May 1998). RCTs: MEDLINE (1995 to May 1998), EMBASE (1995 to May 1998), Cochrane Library (1966 to May 1998).

QUESTION Which antibiotics should be used in outpatients?

OPTION NEW VERSUS OLD ANTIBIOTICS

One systematic review has found that newer antibiotics have no advantage over older antibiotics such as broad-spectrum penicillins in outpatients with CAP.

Benefits: We found one systematic review published in 1994, which identified nine English language RCTs of oral antibiotics in outpatients with CAP. Five trials had fewer than 100 patients.[9] The antibiotics tested were amoxicillin with and without clavulanate; macrolides; first-, second-, and third-generation cephalosporins and quinolones. Cure or improvement occurred in over 90% of patients.

Harms: Antibiotics can cause allergic reactions (including anaphylaxis), rash, gastrointestinal intolerance (nausea, vomiting, diarrhea), vaginal or oral candidiasis, and *Clostridium difficile* diarrhea (including pseudomembranous colitis). The frequency of adverse effects varies with the antibiotic used.

Comment: None.

QUESTION **Which treatments should be used in patients admitted to hospital?**

OPTION **NEW VERSUS OLD ANTIBIOTICS**

RCTs found no difference in effectiveness between new and older antibiotics in patients admitted to hospital. However, most trials were small and were designed to show equivalence between treatments rather than superiority of one over another.

Benefits: We found no systematic review. **Second-generation cephalosporin versus broad-spectrum penicillin:** We found several RCTs, all of which were too small and/or too old to be reliable, given the changing sensitivity of organisms to antibiotics. **Quinolones versus high-dose amoxicillin:** We found one multicenter double-blind RCT comparing sparfloxacin versus amoxicillin in 329 inpatients in France, South Africa, and Switzerland.[10] Early failure (discontinuation of the drug on day 3, 4, or 5) occurred in 2.4% of the sparfloxacin group compared with 7.9% of the amoxicillin group (*p* value not given). In an intention-to-treat analysis, there was no significant difference in clinical cure rates (84% of patients on sparfloxacin compared with 85% of those on amoxicillin). **Quinolones versus second- and third-generation cephalosporins:** We found one double-blind RCT comparing levofloxacin versus intravenous ceftriaxone followed by oral cefuroxime in 226 patients, half of whom were inpatients. Treatment failure occurred in 3.5% on levofloxacin and 9.6% on cephalosporins (ARR 6.1%, 95% CI 1.3–10.7).[11]

Harms: *See* above.

Comment: Although penicillin-resistant and multidrug-resistant *S. pneumoniae* is commonly reported, it is hard to enroll patients with this infection in studies. One of the studies[10] was carried out in areas with a high prevalence of penicillin-resistant *S. pneumoniae*. However, only 8 of 135 isolates tested were resistant to penicillin and none showed high-level resistance.

OPTION **INTRAVENOUS VERSUS ORAL ANTIBIOTICS**

RCTs found that, in inpatients who were immunocompetent and were not suffering life-threatening illness, intravenous antibiotics were no more effective than oral antibiotics and increased length of stay in hospital.

Benefits: We found no systematic review. We found two RCTs comparing oral versus intravenous antibiotics in people admitted to hospital with CAP. The first included 541 participants with lower respiratory tract infections, two fifths of whom had chest radiographs that were compatible with pneumonia.[12] Patients were excluded if they had life-threatening infection or were immunocompromised. Patients were randomized to 7 days of treatment with oral amoxicillin with clavulanate, intravenous amoxicillin with clavulanate for 3 days followed by oral amoxicillin with clavulanate, or intravenous cefotaxime for 3 days followed by oral cefuroxime. At discharge there was no difference in cure rates or mortality among the three groups, but hospital stay was significantly shorter in those on oral treatment (group 1) than in those on intravenous treatment (groups 2 and 3) ($p<0.001$). The second RCT compared intravenous versus oral cefuroxime in 73 patients.[13] These patients were randomized to 2 days intravenous followed by 8 days of oral treatment, 5 days of each treatment, or 10 days of intravenous treatment. The only significant difference was in the length of hospital stay: 6, 8, and 11 days (no CI or *p* value was given).

Harms: None reported.

Comment: Intravenous antibiotics are required in patients who cannot take oral medication because of severe nausea or vomiting or who are bacteremic or in septicemic shock. A follow-up study in 96 patients admitted to hospital with CAP found that patients could be switched from intravenous to oral antibiotics when they had been afebrile for 8 hours, symptoms of cough and shortness of breath were improving, white blood counts were returning to normal, and they could tolerate oral medications.[14]

OPTION BOTTLE BLOWING

One RCT found slightly faster recovery in inpatients using this form of physiotherapy.

Benefits: We found no systematic review. We found one RCT in 145 inpatients with CAP.[15] Patients were randomized to three groups: early mobilization; early mobilization and encouragement to sit up 10 times a day and take 20 deep breaths; and early mobilization and encouragement to sit up 10 times a day and blow bubbles through a plastic tube for 20 breaths into a bottle containing 10 cm water. Mean hospital stay in the three groups was 5.3, 4.6, and 3.9 days ($p=0.01$ for early mobilization compared with bottle blowing).

Harms: None reported.

Comment: Neither patients nor clinicians could be blinded to the intervention. Note that this older technique is similar to the more common incentive spirometry.

QUESTION Which treatments should be used in patients receiving intensive care?

OPTION DIFFERENT COMBINATIONS OF ANTIBIOTICS

We found no good evidence supporting any particular antibiotic combination in this setting.

Benefits: We found no systematic review and no RCTs comparing one combination of antibiotics versus another in intensive care units.

Harms: Inadequate evidence.

Comment: The use of a combination of antibiotics is current best practice.

OPTION PROMPT VERSUS DELAYED ANTIBIOTIC TREATMENT

Retrospective studies found that prompt administration of antibiotics improved survival.

Benefits: We found no systematic review and no prospective studies. A multicenter retrospective review examined the medical records of over 14,000 people aged 65 years or older who were severely ill with CAP. It found that administering antibiotics within 8 hours of admission to hospital was associated with lower 30-day mortality (OR 0.90, 95% CI 0.75–0.96).[16] Another retrospective study examined outcome and time to start of treatment in 39 patients with serologically confirmed Legionnaires' disease.[17] For the 10 patients who died, the median delay between diagnosis of pneumonia and start of erythromycin was five days (range 1–10 days), and for those who survived it was one day (range 1–5 days) ($p<0.001$).

Harms: None reported.

Comment: This observation needs to be confirmed in a prospective study.

QUESTION What are the effects of preventive interventions?

OPTION INFLUENZA VACCINE

One systematic review of cohort studies, and recent RCTs, has found that influenza vaccination reduces the risk of influenza and death in elderly people.

Benefits: We found one systematic review published in 1995, which identified 20 cohort studies.[18] The pooled estimate for preventing pneumonia was an ARR of 0.53 (95% CI 0.35–0.66) and for preventing death 0.68 (95% CI and ARR of 0.56–0.76). Analysis of data from an administrative database of over 25,000 people aged 64 years or over suggested that influenza vaccination reduced the rate of admission to hospital for pneumonia and influenza by 48%–57% ($p<0.01$).[19] We found one double-blind RCT comparing split viron vaccine versus saline solution in over 1800 people aged 60 years or over.[20] At 5 months follow-up, the incidence of clinical influenza was significantly lower with the vaccine versus the placebo (2% vs. 3% RR 0.53, 95% CI 0.39–0.73). A double-blind RCT compared trivalent inactivated parenteral vaccine with or without intranasal live attenuated cold-adapted vaccine in 324 elderly residents of nursing homes. Live vaccine provided additional protection against influenza A (rates of documented influenza were 5.5% vs. 14.8%; vaccine protective efficacy [RRR] 0.6; 95% CI 0.18–0.82).[21]

Harms: Local adverse effects include pain and tenderness at the site of injection. Guillain–Barré syndrome is rare; it complicated 1 in

100,000 vaccinations during the national immunization program against swine influenza in the USA in 1976, during which 45 million people were vaccinated.[22] This excessive rate of Guillain–Barré syndrome has not occurred in any other year.

Comment: One RCT found that vaccination of health care workers in geriatric long-term care facilities reduced total patient mortality from 17% to 10% (OR compared with no vaccination 0.56, 95% CI 0.40–0.80).[23]

OPTION PNEUMOCOCCAL VACCINE

One systematic review of RCTs has found that pneumococcal vaccination with currently available vaccines does not protect against death or all-cause pneumonia but may protect young, fit adults against pneumococcal pneumonia.

Benefits: We found one systematic review, which identified nine RCTs with a total of 12 vaccine and control study groups.[24] In adults at low risk (immunocompetent, aged < 55 years, no other chronic medical conditions), vaccination protected against definitive pneumococcal pneumonia (positive *S. pneumoniae* cultures) (OR compared with no vaccine 0.34, 95% CI 0.24–0.48). Vaccination gave no significant protection against other outcomes (all-cause pneumonia, bronchitis, or death). Adults at high risk (those aged > 55 years, patients with one or more chronic medical conditions) or immunosuppressed patients did not benefit from the vaccine. We found two subsequent double-blind RCTs. The first compared a 23-valent pneumococcal capsular polysaccharide vaccine versus placebo in 691 middle-aged and elderly people who had been admitted to hospital for CAP. It found no significant protective effect against pneumococcal (RR 0.78, 95% CI 0.40–1.51) or all-cause pneumonia (RR 0.83, 95% CI 0.58–1.12).[25] The second RCT randomized over 2800 residents in a nursing home to receive either pneumococcal and influenza vaccines or influenza vaccine only.[26] All participants were followed for 3 years for the development of radiologically confirmed pneumonia. Pneumococcal etiology was defined serologically. No significant protection from pneumococcal pneumonia was found in the study group as a whole (vaccine efficacy [RRR] 0.15, 95% CI –0.43 to 0.50). However, there was significant protection in people with risk factors for contracting pneumonia: those who were immunocompromized; had received immunosuppressive treatment within one year before vaccination; had cancer, systemic connective tissue diseases, alcohol dependence, heart or lung disease; were institutionalized or permanently bedridden (RRR 59%, 95% CI 6%–82%).[26] Independent risk factors for a poor response to pneumococcal vaccine were malignancy (RR 2.64, $p = 0.01$) and daily use of angiotensin-converting–enzyme inhibitors (RR 4.16, $p = 0.0002$).

Harms: Discomfort at the site of the injection. No other harms reported.

Comment: A fifth of healthy elderly adults (mean age 71 years) do not mount an antibody response after vaccination.[27] New conjugate pneumococcal vaccines are being evaluated. These have been shown to be immunogenic in infants and have decreased the rate of carriage of resistant strains of *S. pneumoniae*.[28,29]

REFERENCES

1. Foy HM, Cooney MK, Allan I, Kenny GE. Rates of pneumonia during influenza epidemics in Seattle, 1964–1975. *JAMA* 1979;241:253–258.
2. Murphy TF, Henderson FW, Clyde WA, Collier AM, Denny FW. Pneumonia: an 11 year study in a pediatric practice. *Am J Epidemiol* 1981;113:12–21.
3. McConnochie KM, Hall CB, Barker WH. Lower respiratory tract illness in the first two years of life: epidemiologic patterns and costs in a suburban pediatric practice. *Am J Public Health* 1988;78:34–39.
4. Porath A, Schlaeffer F, Lieberman D. The epidemiology of community-acquired pneumonia among hospitalized adults. *J Infect* 1997;34:41–48.
5. Jokinen C, Heiskanen L, Juvonen H, et al. Incidence of community-acquired pneumonia in the population of four municipalities in eastern Finland. *Am J Epidemiol* 1993;137: 977–988.
6. Houston MS, Silverstein MD, Suman VJ. Risk factors for 30-day mortality in elderly patients with lower respiratory tract infection. *Arch Intern Med* 1997;157:2190–2195.
7. Bartlett JG, Mundy LM. Community-acquired pneumonia. *N Engl J Med* 1995;333:1618–1624.
8. Fine MJ, Smith MA, Carson CA, et al. Prognosis and outcomes of patients with community-acquired pneumonia: a meta-analysis. *JAMA* 1996;275:134–141.
9. Pomilla PV, Brown RB. Outpatient treatment of community-acquired pneumonia in adults. *Arch Intern Med* 1994;154:1793–1802. MEDLINE 1966 to 1994. English language only.
10. Aubier M, Verster R, Regamey C, Geslin P, Vercken J-B, and the Sparfloxacin European Study Group. Once-daily sparfloxacin versus high-dosage amoxicillin in the treatment of community-acquired, suspected pneumococcal pneumonia in adults. *Clin Infect Dis* 1998;26:1312–1320.
11. File TM Jr, Segreti J, Dunbar L, et al. A multicenter, randomized study comparing the efficacy and safety of intravenous and/or oral levofloxacin versus ceftriaxone and/or cefuroxime axetil in treatment of adults with community-acquired pneumonia. *Antimicrob Agents Chemother* 1997; 41:1965–1972.
12. Chan R, Hemeryck L, O' Regan M, Clancy L, Feely J. Oral versus intravenous antibiotics for community-acquired lower respiratory tract infection in a general hospital: open randomised controlled trial. *BMJ* 1995;310:1360–1362.
13. Siegel RE, Halperin NA, Almenoff PL, Lee A, Cashin R, Greene JG. A prospective randomized study of inpatient IV antibiotics for community-acquired pneumonia: the optimal duration of therapy. *Chest* 1996;110:965–971.
14. Ramirez JA, Ahkee S. Early switch from intravenous antimicrobials to oral clarithromycin in patients with community acquired pneumonia. *Infections in Medicine* 1997;14:319–323.
15. Bjorkqvist M, Wiberg B, Bodin L, Barany M, Holmberg H. Bottle-blowing in hospital-treated patients with community-acquired pneumonia. *Scand J Infect Dis* 1997;29:77–82.
16. Meehan TP, Fine MJ, Krumholz HM, et al. Quality of care, process, and outcomes in elderly patients with pneumonia. *JAMA* 1997;278:2080–2084.
17. Heath CH, Grove DI, Looke DF. Delay in appropriate therapy of legionella pneumonia associated with increased mortality. *Eur J Clin Microbiol Infect Dis* 1966;15:286–290.
18. Gross PA, Hermogenes AW, Sacks HS, Lau J, Levandowski RA. The efficacy of influenza vaccine in elderly persons: a meta-analysis and review of the literature. *Ann Intern Med* 1995;123:518–527. Search date not stated, primary sources MEDLINE.
19. Nichol KL, Margolis KL, Wuorenma J, Von Sternberg T. The efficacy and cost effectiveness of vaccination against influenza among elderly persons living in the community. *N Engl J Med* 1994;31:778–784.
20. Govaert TM, Thijs CT, Masurel N, Sprenger MJ, Dinant GJ, Knottnerus JA. The efficacy of influenza vaccination in elderly individuals: a randomized double-blind placebo-controlled trial. *JAMA* 1994;272:1661–1665.
21. Treanor JJ, Mattison HR, Dumyati G, et al. Protective efficacy of combined live intranasal and inactivated influenza A virus vaccines in the elderly. *Ann Intern Med* 1992;117:625–633.
22. Betts RF. Influenza virus p 1561. In: Mandell GL, Bennett JE, Dolin R, eds. *Principles and practice of infectious diseases*. 4th edn. New York: Churchill Livingston, 1995:1561.
23. Potter J, Stott DJ, Roberts MA, et al. Influenza vaccination of health care workers in long-term-care hospitals reduces the mortality of elderly patients. *J Infect Dis* 1997;175:1–6.
24. Fine MJ, Smith MA, Carson CA, et al. Efficacy of pneumococcal vaccination in adults: a meta-analysis of randomized controlled clinical trials. *Arch Intern Med* 1994;154:2666–2677. Search date 1991, primary sources MEDLINE, bibliographies of retrieved articles, and search for unpublished material by contact with key researchers and manufacturers.
25. Ortqvist A, Hedlund J, Burman L-A, et al, and Swedish Pneumococcal Vaccination Study Group. Randomised trial of 23-valent penumococcal capsular polysaccharide vaccine in prevention of pneumonia in middle-aged and elderly people. *Lancet* 1998;351:399–403.
26. Koivula I, Sten M, Leinonen M, Makela PH. Clinical efficacy of par pneumococcal vaccine in the elderly: a randomized, single-blind population-based trial. *Am J Med* 1997;103:281–290.
27. Rubins JB, Puri AKG, Loch J, et al. Magnitude, duration, quality and function of pneumococcal vaccine responses in elderly adults. *J Infect Dis* 1998;178:431–440.
28. Mbelle N, Wasas A, Huebner R, Kimura A, Chang I, Klugman K. Immunogenicity and impact on carriage of 9-valent pneumococcal conjugate vaccine given to infants in Soweto, South Africa. *Proceedings of the 37th Interscience Conference on Antimicrobial Agents and Chemotherapy*; 1997 September; Toronto. Herndon VA:ASM Press, 1997
29. Gesner M, Desiderio D, Kim M, et al. Streptococcus pneumoniae in human immunodeficiency virus type 1 infected children. *Pediatr Infect Dis J* 1994;13:697–703.

Tom Marrie, MD
Professor of Medicine
Dalhousie University
Halifax
Nova Scotia
Canada

Competing interests: The author has received funding from various drug companies, including Abbott, Janssen, Bayer, Glaxo Wellcome, Pfizer, and Smith-Kline-French.

TABLE 1 Causes of community-acquired pneumonia.* (*See* text p. 161.)

	North America (% of patients)*	United Kingdom (% of patients)†	Susceptibility‡
Streptococcus pneumoniae	20–60	60–75	25% penicillin resistant, sensitive to quinolones
Haemophilus influenzae	3–10	4–5	30% ampicillin resistant, sensitive to cephalosporins or amoxicillin/clavulanic acid
Staphylococcus aureus	3–5	1–5	Methicillin-resistant *S. aureus* rare as cause of CAP
Chlamydia pneumoniae	4–6	–	Sensitive to macrolides, tetracyclines, quinolones
Mycoplasma pneumoniae	1–6	5–18	Sensitive to macrolides, tetracyclines, quinolones
Legionella pneumophila	2–8	2–5	Sensitive to macrolides, tetracyclines, quinolones
Gram-negative bacilli	3–10	Rare	
Aspiration	6–10	–	
Viruses	2–15	8–16	

*Pooled data from 15 published reports from North America[7]; †Data from British Thoracic Society[4]; ‡Susceptibility data from recent studies.

Asthma

Paul O'Byrne, MB, FRCPI, FRCPC

QUESTIONS

INTERVENTIONS

Key Messages

- In people with mild, intermittent asthma, randomized controlled trials (RCTs) have found that regular use of short-acting inhaled β_2-agonists provides no additional clinical benefits and may worsen asthma control.
- In people with mild persistent asthma, RCTs have found that low doses of inhaled corticosteroids are more effective than placebo or β_2-agonists.
- In people with uncontrolled asthma, RCTs have found that adding long-acting inhaled β_2-agonists to inhaled corticosteroids improves symptoms and lung function, and reduces exacerbations. Regular use of long-acting β_2-agonists, when used in this way, has not been linked to deterioration in asthma control.
- In people with acute exacerbations of asthma, a systematic review of RCTs has found no difference in outcomes when β_2-agonists are delivered by spacer device/holding chamber or by nebulization.
- A systematic review of RCTs has found that oral corticosteroids taken at the start of an acute exacerbation reduce rates of admission and relapse. We found no good data on the optimal duration of treatment.

DEFINITION Asthma is characterized by dyspnea, cough, chest tightness, wheezing, variable airflow obstruction, and airway hyperresponsiveness. It can be classified into **mild intermittent asthma**—symptoms less than weekly with normal or near normal lung function; **mild persistent asthma**—symptoms more than weekly but less than daily with normal or near normal lung function; **moderate persistent asthma**—daily symptoms with mild to moderate variable airflow obstruction; and **severe asthma**—daily symptoms, frequent night time symptoms, and moderate to severe variable airflow obstruction. However, even patients with mild asthma can develop severe exacerbations if exposed to an appropriate stimulus.

INCIDENCE/ PREVALENCE The reported prevalence is increasing in all countries where this has been measured. Up to 10% of people have suffered an attack of asthma.[1]

ETIOLOGY Most people with asthma are atopic. In such people, exposure to certain stimuli (in particular, environmental allergens, occupational sensitizing agents, and respiratory viral infections)[2,3] initiate inflammation and structural changes in the airway. These cause airway hyperresponsiveness and variable airflow obstruction, which in turn cause most asthma symptoms.

PROGNOSIS In people with mild asthma, the prognosis is good and progression to severe disease is rare. However, as a group, people with asthma lose lung function faster than those without asthma, although less quickly than smokers.[4] People with persistent asthma can improve with current treatment. However, for reasons not clearly understood, a subset of people with asthma (possibly up to 5%) have severe disease, which responds poorly to conventional treatment. These people are at most risk of morbidity and death from asthma.

AIMS To minimize or eliminate symptoms, to achieve best possible lung function, to prevent exacerbations, to minimize the need for medication, to minimize adverse effects of treatment, and to educate people with asthma.

OUTCOMES Symptoms (daytime and nocturnal), lung function (peak expiratory flow rate [PEFR] and forced expiratory volume in 1 second [FEV_1]), need for rescue medication such as inhaled β_2-agonists, variability of flow rates, activities of daily living.

METHODS *Clinical Evidence* search, June and October 1998. All double-blind, placebo-controlled RCTs that were identified were reviewed.

QUESTION **In adults with mild intermittent asthma, what are the effects of intermittent versus regular use of short-acting, inhaled β_2-agonists?**

RCTs have found that regular use of short-acting inhaled β_2-agonists in people with mild intermittent asthma provides no additional clinical benefits and may worsen asthma control.

Benefits: No systematic review. We found several RCTs comparing regular versus as-needed inhaled salbutamol. The most recent included 255 people with mild intermittent asthma not previously taking inhaled corticosteroids.[5] At 16 weeks, there was no significant difference in symptoms, quality of life, air-flow obstruction, or frequency of exacerbations. However, people taking regular salbutamol used more of the drug than those taking it as needed (total salbutamol 9.3 vs. 1.6 puffs/day). They also experienced significantly worse variability in PEFR and methacholine responsiveness. An earlier RCT (a double-blind placebo-controlled crossover trial) in 64 evaluable patients found that people using regular fenoterol suffered deterioration in asthma control and increased frequency of exacerbations compared with those on intermittent treatment.[6] Inhaled corticosteroids did not seem to protect against the deterioration.

Harms: Two case control studies found increases in asthma mortality with overuse of inhaled short-acting β_2-agonists.[7,8] However, there is insufficient evidence to attribute causality, because it is possible that the overuse of β_2-agonists to treat frequent symptoms is simply a marker of severe, uncontrolled asthma, with affected individuals being at much greater risk of asthma death. Other RCTs have found that regular use of inhaled β_2-agonists is associated with transient rebound deterioration in airway hyperresponsiveness after stopping the medication[9] and increased allergen-induced bronchoconstriction.[10] Finally, tremor is commonly reported, although tolerance to this effect develops with more frequent use.[11]

Comment: None.

QUESTION **In people with mild persistent asthma, what are the effects of low doses of inhaled corticosteroids?**

RCTs have found that low doses of inhaled corticosteroids (250–500 μg of beclomethasone dipropionate or equivalent) are more effective than placebo or regular β_2-agonists in people with mild persistent asthma. We found no evidence of clinically important adverse effects in adults.

Benefits: **Versus placebo:** We found no systematic review. We found one RCT comparing low doses of inhaled budesonide versus placebo in 60 adults with mild asthma. This found significant improvement in lung function and symptoms and fewer exacerbations over the 4 months of the study.[12] **Versus β_2-agonists:** We found one systematic review, which identified five small RCTs in a total of 141 adults with mild persistent asthma.[13] The results suggested that use of inhaled corticosteroids was beneficial (overall weighted effect size for PEFR 0.59, 95% CI 0.32–0.84). One RCT not included in the review compared inhaled budesonide 1200 μg/d versus inhaled β_2-agonists in 103 mildly asthmatic adults followed for 2 years. It found persistent improvements in all outcomes for the duration of the study.[14]

Harms: Published studies have found no evidence that low doses of inhaled corticosteroids (<1000 μg/d of beclomethasone dipropionate or its equivalent) produce clinically important systemic effects in adults.[15] Although posterior subcapsular cataracts occur more frequently in people taking oral corticosteroids,[16] most studies in adults[17] provide no evidence that inhaled corticosteroids increase the risk once the confounding effect of oral corticosteroids is removed. However, a recent case control study suggests that, in older people, inhaled high-dose beclomethasone dipropionate is associated with a slightly greater risk of nuclear cataracts (RR 1.5, 95% CI 1.2–1.9) and posterior subcapsular cataracts (RR 1.9, 95% CI 1.3–2.8).[18] We found no published reports of an increased risk of osteoporosis or fractures. Inhaled corticosteroids can cause oral candidiasis, dysphonia, and bruising, but these are troublesome in fewer than 5% of people.[19,20]

Comment: The results of the systematic review should be interpreted with caution as the few small RCTs that were included did not consistently measure PEFR at the same time during the day nor report morning and evening PEFRs.[13] The case control study on cataract formation[18] did not stratify for the confounding effect of allergy, which is also a risk factor for cataract development.[21]

QUESTION **In people whose asthma is poorly controlled by inhaled corticosteroids, what are the effects of adding long-acting inhaled β_2-agonists?**

RCTs have found that, in people with uncontrolled asthma, adding regular doses of long-acting inhaled β_2-agonists to inhaled corticosteroids improves symptoms and lung function and reduces exacerbations. Regular use of long-acting β_2-agonists has not been linked to deterioration in asthma control.

Benefits: We found no systematic review. We found three RCTs of regular use of long-acting inhaled β_2-agonists. Two were in people whose asthma was uncontrolled on inhaled corticosteroids at doses of 400–1000 μg/d.[22,23] These found that adding twice daily salmeterol had a significantly greater beneficial effect on symptoms and lung function than doubling the dose of inhaled corticosteroid. The other RCT was in 850 people with moderately severe asthma. People who were given twice daily formoterol plus terbutaline as needed, in addition to low or moderate doses of inhaled budesonide, experienced significant improvements in symptoms, lung function, and exacerbations.[24] Exacerbations were reduced even more by a fourfold increase in the daily dosage of inhaled corticosteroid and further still by a combination of the higher-dose budesonide plus formoterol.

Harms: Several studies have found that people taking regular doses of long-acting inhaled β_2-agonists develop tolerance to their protection against bronchoconstriction.[25–27] Tremor can also occur. However, unlike short-acting inhaled β_2-agonists, regular use of long-acting inhaled β_2-agonists has not been linked to deterioration in asthma control.[6–8]

Comment: None.

QUESTION **How do spacer devices/holding chambers and nebulizers compare in the delivery of β_2-agonists?**

One systematic review of RCTs has found no difference in outcomes when β_2-agonists are delivered by holding chamber with metered-dose inhaler or by nebulization. The findings are limited to adults with mild to moderate asthma.

Benefits: We found one systematic review updated in 1998. This identified 13 RCTs comparing holding chambers plus metered-dose inhalers versus nebulization for the delivery of β_2-agonists. Participants were nonhospitalized adults and children with acute asthmatic exacerbations.[28] Results in adults and children were analyzed separately (for findings in children, see p. 501). In adults, there was no difference in rates of hospital admission (OR 1.12, 95% CI –0.45 to +2.76) or length of time spent in the emergency department (WMD 0.02 hours, 95% CI 0.40–0.44 hours). Nor was there any difference in PEFR or FEV_1, even when the three studies that included the most severely affected patients (e.g., those with $FEV_1 < 30\%$ predicted) were included (WMD for FEV_1 with the holding chamber compared with the nebulizer –1.5% predicted, 95% CI –8.28 to +5.28). Symptoms were measured on various scales, and the findings could not be combined.

Harms: There was no difference in pulse rates between the two methods (WMD with holding chamber compared with nebulizer 1.59% of baseline, 95% CI 5.51% to –2.43% of baseline).

Comment: Analysis showed no evidence of publication bias. The studies excluded people with life-threatening asthma, so the results should not be generalized beyond people with acute exacerbations of asthma.

QUESTION **In acute exacerbations, what are the effects of oral corticosteroids, and what is the optimal dose and duration of treatment?**

One systematic review of RCTs has found that a short course of systemic corticosteroids taken at the start of an acute exacerbation reduces rates of admission and relapse and reduces β_2-agonist use, without increasing adverse effects. We found no good data on the optimal dose or duration of treatment. The review found no difference between intramuscular and oral corticosteroids.

Benefits: **Rates of admission:** We found two systematic reviews. One, updated in 1997, identified seven RCTs in about 320 people comparing oral corticosteroids versus placebo (four trials), oral versus intramuscular corticosteroids (two trials), and intramuscular corticosteroids versus placebo (one trial). This found that systemic corticosteroids given at the time of an acute asthma exacerbation reduced hospital admissions in the first week by 65% in both adults and children (OR for admission compared to placebo 0.35, 95% CI 0.17–0.73).[29] This favorable effect was maintained over the first 21 days (OR 0.33, 95% CI 0.13–0.82). People receiving corticosteroids also had less need for β-agonists (WMD –3.3 activations/day, 95% CI –5.5 to –1.0). From these results, nine patients would need to be treated with systemic steroids rather than placebo to avoid one additional admission after an exacerbation of asthma. The review found no clear difference between intramuscular and oral corticosteroids. The other systematic review, published in 1992, identified five RCTs in 422 people comparing systemic corticosteroids versus placebo. This also indicated that early use of systemic corticosteroids reduced hospital admissions and relapses in both adults and children. (OR of admission in adults compared to placebo 0.47, 95% CI 0.27–0.79).[30] **Stopping treatment:** We found no systematic review. One RCT compared tapering of prednisolone over 1 week versus abrupt cessation in 35 people who were admitted to hospital with acute asthma. It found that a daily dose of 0.5 to 1 mg/kg for 10 days was effective when administered once daily for 10 days and could be stopped without tapering off once asthma control was reestablished.[31] **Optimal dose and duration of treatment:** We found no RCTs examining this question. The optimal duration of treatment will depend on the individual, the severity of the exacerbation, and the use of concomitant medications.

Harms: Systemic corticosteroids can cause the same unwanted effects in asthma as in other diseases, even when administered for a short time.

Comment: Owing to the small number of trials included in the reviews[29,30] and the small number of participants in each, no firm conclusions can be drawn regarding the effects of oral corticosteroids in different age groups and in people with different severities of asthma.

REFERENCES

1. Kaur B, Anderson HR, Austin J, et al. Prevalence of asthma symptoms, diagnosis, and treatment in 12–14 year old children across Great Britain (international study of asthma and allergies in childhood, ISAAC UK). *BMJ* 1998;316:118–124.
2. Duff AL, Platts-Mills TA. Allergens and asthma. *Pediatr Clin North Am* 1992;39:1277–1291.
3. Chan-Yeung M, Malo JL. Occupational asthma. *N Engl J Med* 1995;333:107–112.
4. Lange P, Parner J, Vestbo J, Schnohr P, Jensen G. A 15-year follow-up study of ventilatory function in adults with asthma. *N Engl J Med* 1998;339: 1194–1200.
5. Drazen JM, Israel E, Boushey HA, et al. Comparison of regularly scheduled with as-needed use of albuterol in mild asthma. Asthma clinical research network. *N Engl J Med* 1996;335: 841–847.
6. Sears MR, Taylor DR, Print CG, et al. Regular inhaled beta-agonist treatment in bronchial asthma. *Lancet* 1990;336: 1391–1396.
7. Spitzer WO, Suissa S, Ernst P, et al. The use of beta-agonists and the risk of death and near death from asthma. *N Engl J Med* 1992;326: 501–506.
8. Crane J, Pearce N, Flatt A, et al. Prescribed fenoterol and death from asthma in New Zealand, 1981–1983: case-control study. *Lancet* 1989;i:917–922.
9. Kerrebijn KF, van Essen-Zandvliet EE, Neijens HJ. Effect of long-term treatment with inhaled corticosteroids and beta-agonists on the bronchial responsiveness in children with asthma. *J Allergy Clin Immunol* 1987;79:653–659.
10. Cockcroft DW, McParland CP, Britto SA, Swystun VA, Rutherford BC. Regular inhaled salbutamol and airway responsiveness to allergen. *Lancet* 1993;342:833–837.
11. Ahrens RC. Skeletal muscle tremor and the influence of adrenergic drugs. *J Asthma* 1990,27: 11–20.
12. O'Byrne PM, Cuddy L, Taylor DW, Birch S, Morris J, Syrotiuk J. The clinical efficacy and cost benefit of inhaled corticosteroids as therapy in patients with mild asthma in primary care practice. *Canadian Respiratory Journal* 1996;3:169–175.
13. Hatoum HT, Schumock GT, Kendzierski DL. Meta-analysis of controlled trials of drug therapy in mild chronic asthma: the role of inhaled corticosteroids. *Ann Pharmacother* 1994;28:1285–1289. (Search date not given; primary sources MEDLINE).
14. Haahtela T, Jarvinen M, Kava T, et al. Comparison of a β_2 antagonist, terbutaline, with an inhaled corticosteroid, budesonide, in newly detected asthma. *N Engl J Med* 1991;325:388–392.
15. Barnes PJ, Pedersen S, Busse WW. Efficacy and safety of inhaled corticosteroids: new developments. *Am J Respir Crit Care Med* 1998;157: S1–53.
16. Weusten BL, Jacobs JW, Bijlsma JW. Corticosteroid pulse therapy in active rheumatoid arthritis. *Semin Arthritis Rheum* 1993;23:183–192.
17. Toogood JH, Markov AE, Baskerville JC, Dyson C. Association of ocular cataracts with inhaled and oral steroid therapy during long-term treatment of asthma. *J Allergy Clin Immunol* 1993;91: 571–579.
18. Cumming RG, Mitchell P, Leeder SR. Use of inhaled corticosteroids and the risk of cataracts. *N Engl J Med* 1997;337:8–14.
19. Toogood JH, Jennings B, Greenway RW, Chuang L. Candidiasis and dysphonia complicating beclomethasone treatment of asthma. *J Allergy Clin Immunol* 1980;65:145–153.
20. Roy A, Leblanc C, Paquette L, Ghezzo H, Cote J,

Cartier A, Malo JL. Skin bruising in asthmatic subjects treated with high doses of inhaled steroids: frequency and association with adrenal function. *Eur Respir J* 1996;9:226–231.
21. Eckerskorn U, Hockwin O, Müller-Breitenkamp R, Chen TT, Knowles W, Dobbs RE. Evaluation of cataract-related risk factors using detailed classification systems and multivariate statistical methods. *Dev Ophthalmol* 1987;15:82–91.
22. Greening AP, Ind PW, Northfield M, Shaw G. Added salmeterol versus higher-dose corticosteroid in asthma patients with symptoms on existing inhaled corticosteroid. *Lancet* 1994;344:219–224.
23. Woolcock AJ, Lundback B, Ringdal N, Jacques LA. Comparison of addition of salmeterol to inhaled steroids with doubling of the dose of inhaled steroids. *Am J Respir Crit Care Med* 1996;153: 1481–1488.
24. Pauwels RA, Lofdahl C-G, Postma DS, et al. Effect of inhaled formoterol and budesonide on exacerbations of asthma. *N Engl J Med* 1997;337:1405–1411.
25. Cheung D, Timmers MC, Zwinderman AH, Bel EH, Dijkman JH, Sterk PJ. Long-term effects of a long-acting beta 2-adrenoceptor agonist, salmeterol, on airway hyperresponsiveness in patients with mild asthma. *N Engl J Med* 1992;327:1198–1203.
26. O'Connor BJ, Aikman SL, Barnes PJ. Tolerance to the nonbronchodilator effects of inhaled beta2-agonists in asthma. *N Engl J Med* 1992;327: 1204–1208.
27. Nelson JA, Strauss L, Skowronski M, Ciufo R, Novak R, McFadden ER, Jr. Effect of long-term salmeterol treatment on exercise-induced asthma. *N Engl J Med* 1998;339:141–146.
28. Cates C. Holding chambers versus nebulisers for B agonist treatment of acute asthma. The Cochrane Library, Issue 1, 1999. Last substantive amendment 13 February 1998. Search date February 1998; primary sources, the Cochrane Airways Review Group register of trials, bibliographies of all included papers, authors of included studies, the Cochrane Controlled Trials Register.
29. Rowe BH, Spooner CH, Duchrame FM, Bratzlaff JA, Bota GW. The effectiveness of corticosteroids in the treatment of asthma: a meta-analysis of their effect on relapse following acute assessment. The Cochrane Library, Issue 3, 1998. Oxford: Update Software. (Search date 1997, primary sources Cochrane Airways Review Group Asthma and Wheeze RCT register.)
30. Rowe BH, Keller JL, Oxman AD. Effectiveness of steroid therapy in acute exacerbations of asthma: a meta-analysis. *Am J Emerg Med* 1992;10: 301–310. (Search date 1991; primary sources MEDLINE 1966–1991, Science Citation Index 1980–1990, review articles, textbooks, experts and primary authors.)
31. O'Driscoll BR, Kalra S, Wilson M, Pickering CA, Carroll KB, Woodcock AA. Double-blind trial of steroid tapering in acute asthma. *Lancet* 1993; 341:324–327.

Paul O'Byrne, MB, FRCPI, FRCPC
Professor of Medicine
McMaster University
Hamilton
Ontario
Canada

Competing interests: None declared.

Chronic obstructive pulmonary disease

Huib A M Kerstjens, MD, PhD

QUESTIONS

INTERVENTIONS

Key Messages

- To date, only two interventions—smoking cessation and long-term treatment with oxygen (in people with hypoxemia)—have been found to alter the long-term course of the disease.
- Randomized controlled trials (RCTs) found short-term benefits (as opposed to long-term effects on progression) from anticholinergic drugs, β_2-agonists, and oral steroids. The effects of anticholinergic drugs and β_2-agonists are not seen in all people with chronic obstructive pulmonary disease, and the two agents combined are slightly more effective than either alone.
- Adverse effects and the need for frequent monitoring of blood concentrations limit the usefulness of theophyllines.
- Data from one RCT provide no evidence that anticholinergic agents affect decline in lung function. Mucolytics have been shown to reduce the frequency of exacerbations but with a possible deleterious effect on lung function. β_2-Agonists, oral corticosteroids, and antibiotics have not been evaluated yet for their long-term effects.
- No other drug has been shown to affect progression of the disease or survival. However, there is some evidence from RCTs that maintenance treatment with inhaled corticosteroids may improve lung function.

DEFINITION Chronic obstructive pulmonary disease (COPD) is characterized by airflow obstruction caused by chronic bronchitis, emphysema, or both. Emphysema is defined as abnormal permanent enlargement of the air spaces distal to the terminal bronchioles accompanied by destruction of their walls and without obvious fibrosis. Chronic bronchitis is defined as chronic cough, mucus production, or both, for at least 3 months for at least 2 successive years where other causes of chronic cough have been excluded.[1]

INCIDENCE/ PREVALENCE COPD characteristically affects middle-aged and elderly people. It is one of the leading causes of morbidity and mortality worldwide. In the USA, it affects approximately 14 million people and is the fourth leading cause of death. Both morbidity and mortality are rising. Estimated prevalence in the USA has risen by 41% since 1982, and age-adjusted death rates rose by 71% between 1966 and 1985. This contrasts with the decline over the same period in age-adjusted mortality from all causes, which fell by 22%, and from cardiovascular diseases, which fell by 45%.[1]

ETIOLOGY COPD is a largely preventable disease. The main cause is exposure to cigarette smoke. COPD is rare in lifetime nonsmokers (reported in 5% in one large study[2]) in whom exposure to environmental tobacco smoke will explain at least some of the airways obstruction.[3] Other proposed etiologic factors include airway hyperresponsiveness,[4,5] ambient air pollution,[6] and allergy.[7]

PROGNOSIS The airflow obstruction in COPD is usually progressive in those who continue to smoke. This results in early disability and shortened survival. Smoking cessation reverts decline in lung function to values of nonsmokers.[8] Many patients will use medication chronically for the rest of their lives, with the need for increased doses and additional drugs during exacerbations.

AIMS To alleviate symptoms, to prevent exacerbations, to preserve optimal lung function, and to improve activities of daily living and quality of life.[9]

OUTCOMES Survival; short- and long-term changes in lung function (including changes in forced expiratory volume in one second [FEV_1]); exercise tolerance; frequency, severity, and duration of exacerbations; symptom scores for dyspnea; and quality of life. There are now two well-validated quality-of-life questionnaires for COPD.[10,11]

METHODS This review deals only with maintenance treatment in stable COPD, not with treatment of acute exacerbations. A *Clinical Evidence* search was performed in July 1998. Where we found no systematic reviews, we searched for RCTs. Because we were interested in maintenance treatment, we did not include single-dose or single-day cumulative-dose response trials.

QUESTION What are the short- and long-term effects of maintenance treatment in stable COPD?

OPTION INHALED ANTICHOLINERGIC DRUGS

Trials using a range of methods found that anticholinergic drugs achieve short-term bronchodilation and symptomatic relief in people with COPD. One large RCT found no evidence that maintenance treatment with inhaled anticholinergic drugs improved long-term prognosis in COPD.

Benefits: We found no systematic review. **Short-term treatment:** We found no major RCTs comparing ipratropium bromide versus placebo in COPD. The many small placebo-controlled trials used different end points. Most included at least some measure of airways obstruction and found a significant effect of ipratropium bromide.[12–15] **Maintenance treatment:** We found one RCT (Lung Health Study) in 5887 men and women smokers (aged 35–60 years) with spirometric signs of early COPD (FEV_1 75% predicted).[8] Three interventions were compared over a 5-year period: 1) usual care, 2) an intensive 12-session smoking cessation program combining behavior modification and use of nicotine gum, and 3) the same smoking intervention program plus ipratropium bromide three times daily. The addition of ipratropium bromide had no significant effect on decline in FEV_1. Decline in FEV_1 was significantly slower in participants who stopped smoking compared with the usual-care group.

Harms: In the Lung Health Study, serious adverse effects (cardiac symptoms, hypertension, skin rashes, and urinary retention) occurred in only 1.2% of patients on ipratropium bromide and 0.8% on placebo.[8] Dry mouth was the most common mild adverse effect. One RCT in 233 people with asthma or COPD found that continuous as opposed to as needed treatment with bronchodilators (both ipratropium bromide and fenoterol) resulted in faster decline in lung function.[16] This finding has not been replicated by others, including the much larger Lung Health Study.[8]

Comment: Over a 5-year period, there was no evidence that patients developed tachyphylaxis to the bronchodilating effect of ipratropium bromide.[8]

OPTION INHALED β_2-AGONISTS

RCTs found that short- and long-acting inhaled β_2-agonists achieve short term bronchodilation and symptomatic relief in many people with COPD. The effects of maintenance treatment with β_2-agonists on progression of the disease have not yet been adequately evaluated.

Benefits: We found no systematic review. **Short-term treatment:** We found many placebo-controlled RCTs of short-acting β_2-agonists in people with COPD. In general, these reported improved symptoms. Approximately half of the trials that looked at exercise capacity found improvements. β_2-Agonists achieved variable degrees of bronchodilatation in the smaller and shorter studies. One RCT in 985 people with severe COPD found a significant increase in lung function in up to half of patients.[17] The new long-acting inhaled β_2-agonists have been tested in single-dose and short-term studies. These suggest that their maximum effectiveness is comparable to short-acting β_2-agonists but with longer duration.[18,19] At least three RCTs of salmeterol have found significant improvements in symptoms and quality of life compared to placebo, even in the presence of only modest or no change in lung function.[20–22] **Maintenance treatment:** We found no RCTs looking at reduction of decline in lung function with inhaled β_2-agonists versus placebo.

Harms: In people with asthma, β_2-agonists have been linked to increased risk of death,[23] worsened asthma control, and deterioration in lung function. Similar data are not available for COPD. One RCT in 223 people with asthma or COPD found that continuous as opposed to as needed treatment with bronchodilators (ipratropium bromide as well as fenoterol) resulted in faster decline in lung function.[16] We found no other studies of β_2-agonists in COPD addressing this possibility. There are no systematic data on frequency of adverse effects of β_2-agonists in COPD. The most common immediate adverse effect is tremor, which is usually worse in the first few days of treatment. High doses of β_2-agonists can cause a fall in plasma potassium, dysrhythmias, and reduced arterial oxygen tension.[24]

Comment: Long-term placebo-controlled RCTs of β_2-agonists are difficult to perform because of clinicians' firmly held belief in their short-term benefits.

OPTION β_2-AGONISTS PLUS ANTICHOLINERGIC DRUGS

RCTs found that combining a β_2-agonist with an anticholinergic drug provided small additional bronchodilation compared with either drug alone.

Benefits: We found no systematic review. We found three large RCTs ($n = 534$, 195, and 652) comparing the addition of ipratropium to standard-dose inhaled β_2-agonists for approximately 90 days in people with stable COPD.[25–27] All three found significant improvements in FEV_1 of approximately 25% with the combination compared with either drug alone.

Harms: There were no significant increases in adverse effects.

Comment: None.

OPTION β_2-AGONISTS VERSUS ANTICHOLINERGICS

One systematic review of RCTs has found greater bronchodilator response with anticholinergic agents than β_2-agonists in people with COPD.

Benefits: **Short-term treatment:** Several RCTs have compared ipratropium bromide versus a β_2-agonist. They used a range of methodologies and have not been reviewed systematically. **Maintenance treatment:** A systematic review pooled data from seven RCTs ($n = 1445$) comparing ipratropium bromide versus various β_2-agonists for 90 days.[28] Lung function measurements were performed after withholding bronchodilators for at least 12 hours. There was a significantly greater mean improvement in FEV_1 with ipratropium bromide than with the β_2-agonists (28 mL vs. a 1 mL decrease, $p < 0.05$). A residual effect of the anticholinergic cannot be fully ruled out, limiting the interpretation of a favorable effect of anticholinergics on decline in lung function compared to β_2-agonists.

Harms: The adverse effects of β_2-agonists (tremor and dysrhythmias) are more frequent than those of anticholinergics.

Comment: It has been suggested that older people experience greater bronchodilator response with anticholinergics than with β_2-agonists, but this has not yet been adequately investigated.

OPTION THEOPHYLLINES

We found limited evidence from small RCTs for, at most, a small bronchodilatory effect of theophyllines in people with COPD. Adverse effects are frequent.

Benefits: We found no systematic review. **Short-term treatment:** A nonsystematic review, published in 1995, identified 11 small RCTs of theophyllines in people with COPD.[27] These reported changes in FEV_1 ranging from 0% to 20%, and equally varying effects on exercise capacity and symptoms with treatment periods ranging from 1 week to 2 months.[29] A formal meta-analysis has not been performed. **Maintenance treatment:** We found no long-term RCTs looking at effects of theophyllines on decline in lung function.

Harms: The therapeutic range for theophyllines is small. Blood concentrations of 15 to 20 mg/L are required for optimal effects. A wide range of adverse effects includes nausea, diarrhea, headache, irritability, seizures, and cardiac arrhythmias. These occur at highly variable blood concentrations and, in many people, within the therapeutic range. Dose must be adjusted individually according to smoking habits, infection, and other treatments.

Comment: Nonbronchodilator effects of theophylline have been investigated in laboratory settings, including effects on respiratory muscles and improved right ventricular function. Their clinical significance has not been established. Anti-inflammatory effects have been claimed in asthma, especially at lower dosages, but have not been tested for in COPD.

OPTION SYSTEMIC CORTICOSTEROIDS

One systematic review of short-term RCTs has found significant bronchodilatory effect compared with placebo in people with COPD. Long-term effects on lung function have not been investigated in an RCT and would have to be weighed against potentially serious adverse effects.

Benefits: **Short-term treatment:** We found one systematic review published in 1991, which identified 15 RCTs of oral steroids in stable COPD.[30] Duration of treatment was generally 2 to 4 weeks. Meta-analysis of data from the 10 RCTs that met all inclusion criteria found that approximately 20% improvement in baseline FEV_1 occurred significantly more often on oral corticosteroids than placebo (WMD in effect size 10%, 95% CI 2%–18%). When the other five RCTs were included, the difference in effect size was 11% (95% CI 4%–18%). **Maintenance treatment:** We found no long-term RCTs examining the effects of oral steroids on decline in lung function.

Harms: Many reviews have elaborated on the considerable potential harms of systemic corticosteroids. Perhaps the most important in this patient population are osteoporosis and induction of overt diabetes.

Comment: If longer term (> 2–4 weeks) use of oral steroids in COPD should be found to be useful, this would have to be weighed against substantial adverse effects. Moreover, it would be mandatory to compare the benefits and harms of these agents with the benefits and harms of inhaled steroids.

OPTION INHALED CORTICOSTEROIDS

Short-term studies have found no evidence of effects of inhaled steroids. The few fully published long-term studies found a small beneficial effect on lung function.

Benefits: **Short-term treatment:** We found no systematic review. We found 13 placebo-controlled RCTs.[31] Nine were short term (10 days to 10 weeks) and ranged in patient numbers from 10 to 127. All but one of these short-term studies showed no significant benefit in change of FEV_1 from use of inhaled steroids in COPD. None of the studies measuring airway hyperresponsiveness to histamine documented a change. **Maintenance treatment:** We found one systematic review, which identified three long-term placebo-controlled RCTs of inhaled steroids, with 15, 30, and 152 patients treated for 2 to 2.5 years.[32] At 2 years, people on inhaled steroids experienced a significantly greater improvement in prebronchodilator FEV_1 compared with placebo (WMD 34 mL/y, 95% CI 5–63 mL/y). There was no significant difference in postbronchodilator FEV_1 (WMD 39 mL/y, 95% CI –6 to 84 mL/y, $p = 0.095$), or in the frequency of exacerbations. A multicenter study, published since the search date for the systematic review, evaluated 6-months' treatment with fluticasone in 281 people with COPD.[33] This found a significant reduction in moderate and severe (but not mild) exacerbations and a small but significant improvement in lung function and 6-minute walking distance.

Harms: We found no good RCTs providing data on adverse effects of prolonged inhaled steroids in COPD, and interpretation of available studies is hampered by concomitant use of short bursts of oral steroids. Extrapolation from studies in people with asthma is of limited value because patients with COPD are generally at higher risk for osteoporosis because of age, menopausal status, inactivity, and cigarette smoking.[34]

Comment: Three large (~300, 750, and 950 patients) 2- to 3-year European multicenter RCTs of inhaled steroids in COPD have been completed recently, and full results, including valuable information on adverse effects, should be available soon (Pauwels RA, Burge PS, Vestbo J, personal communications). A large North American RCT is also under way (Buist AS, personal communication).

OPTION INHALED VERSUS ORAL STEROIDS

We found limited evidence from RCTs that oral prednisolone is more effective than inhaled beclomethasone in people with mild to moderate COPD.

Benefits: We found no systematic review. **Short-term treatment:** There have been at least three RCTs directly comparing oral prednisolone versus inhaled beclomethasone ($n = 12$, 83, and 107).[35–37] All were double-blind placebo-controlled crossover studies based on treatment periods of only 2 weeks. One found no significant difference between the number of participants responding to both, to either, or to one form of steroid only.[35] The other two trials found greater benefit from oral than inhaled steroids; lung function was significantly better after treatment with oral than inhaled steroids ($p < 0.01$),[36] and the proportion of participants responding to treatment was significantly higher ($p < 0.05$).[37] **Maintenance treatment:** We found no RCTs.

Harms: None of the RCTs reported adverse effects.

Comment: The smallest RCT[36] recruited only people known to be responsive to oral steroids and did not report the severity of COPD. The other two RCTs included people with COPD of more than 5-years' duration and FEV_1 < 70% predicted.[35,37] All studies excluded people with evidence of reversible airflow obstruction.

OPTION MUCOLYTIC DRUGS

One systematic review of RCTs has found that mucolytics have a modest beneficial effect on frequency and duration of exacerbations compared to placebo. The evidence also suggests a modest adverse effect on lung function.

Benefits: **Maintenance treatment:** We found one systematic review updated in 1998, which identified 15 double-blind placebo-controlled RCTs.[38] Mucolytics significantly reduced the number of exacerbations (WMD compared with placebo –0.105 exacerbations per month, 95% CI –0.11 to –0.10, $p < 0.001$) and days of disability (WMD –0.664 days per month, 95% CI –0.689 to –0.640). There was no significant difference in the number of days on antibiotics per month (WMD compared to placebo –0.677 days per month, 95% CI –0.710 to 0.644). Most of the trials were in people with mild COPD. The two trials in people with severe COPD (FEV_1 < 50%) found greater reductions in exacerbation frequency (WMD compared to placebo 0.142, CI not given). There was no significant difference between *N*-acetylcysteine and other mucolytics as a group.

Harms: The review found a small but significant reduction in lung function compared with placebo (WMD in FEV_1 compared with mucolytics –0.057 L, 95% CI –0.039 to –0.075 L; WMD in forced vital capacity –0.04 L, 95% CI –0.017 to –0.063 L).[38] The review did not include a separate analysis of the effect of *N*-acetylcysteine alone on decline in lung function. There was no difference between mucolytics and placebo in the total number of adverse events.[38] Adverse effects of *N*-acetylcysteine consist mainly of mild gastrointestinal complaints.

Comment: There was significant heterogeneity between the RCTs, and it was not possible to include symptom scores in the meta-analysis because these were not reported in a sufficiently coherent fashion. The theoretical antioxidant effect of *N*-acetylcysteine in slowing the decline in lung function has not been proved. It is currently the subject of a large European multicenter study (Dekhuijzen PNR, personal communication).

OPTION ANTIBIOTICS

The effects of antibiotics in maintenance treatment of stable COPD have not been evaluated in RCTs.

Benefits: **Maintenance treatment:** We found one systematic review published in 1995, which identified no RCTs of the use of antibiotics as maintenance treatment in stable COPD.[39]

Harms: The adverse effects of antibiotics vary greatly between agents and individuals.

Comment: None.

OPTION LONG-TERM OXYGEN TREATMENT

We found limited evidence from one RCT that long-term oxygen treatment improves survival in people with COPD and hypoxemia. Continuous treatment is more effective than nocturnal treatment.

Benefits: We found no systematic review. We found two RCTs on the effects of long-term domiciliary oxygen.[40,41] **Versus no oxygen:** One RCT compared oxygen for at least 15 hours per day versus no oxygen in 87 people aged under 70 years with hypoxemic COPD and congestive cardiac failure.[40] In men, rates of death were similar in the two groups for the first 500 days or so. After this time, rates of death were significantly lower on oxygen (12% vs. 29% per year, $p=0.04$) and remained constant over 5-years' follow-up. In women ($n=21$), rates of death on oxygen were significantly lower throughout the study ($p<0.05$). Long-term oxygen treatment seemed to slow the progress of respiratory failure in both men and women surviving longer than 500 days but not in those dying before this time. **Continuous versus nocturnal oxygen:** One RCT compared continuous versus nocturnal oxygen treatment in 203 people with hypoxemic COPD (FEV_1 $<70\%$ predicted) followed for a mean of 19.3 years. Overall risk of death was significantly higher on nocturnal treatment (RR versus continuous treatment 1.94, 95% CI 1.17–3.24, AR of death at one year 20.6% vs. 11.9%, and at 2 years 40.8% vs. 22.4%).[41]

Harms: No adverse effects of long-term oxygen have been reported. Administration is cumbersome and expensive.

Comment: None.

REFERENCES

1. Kerstjens HA, Brand PL, Postma DS. Risk factors for accelerated decline among patients with chronic obstructive pulmonary disease [review]. *Am J Respir Crit Care Med* 1996;154:S266–272.
2. American Thoracic Society. Standards for the diagnosis and care of patients with chronic obstructive pulmonary disease: ATS statement. *Am J Respir Crit Care Med* 1995;152:S77–121.
3. Whittemore AS, Perlin SA, DiCiccio Y. Chronic obstructive pulmonary disease in lifelong non-smokers: results from NHANES. *Am J Public Health* 1995;85:702–706.
4. Brunekreef B, Fischer P, Remijn B, van der Lende R, Schouten JP, Quanjer PH. Indoor air pollution and its effects on pulmonary function of adult non-smoking women: III passive smoking and pulmonary function. *Int J Epidemiol* 1985;14:227–230.
5. Rijcken B, Weiss ST. Longitudinal analyses of airway responsiveness and pulmonary function decline. *Am J Respir Crit Care Med* 1996;154: S246–249.
6. Dockery DW, Brunekreef B. Longitudinal studies of air pollution effects on lung function. *Am J Respir Crit Care Med* 1996;154:S250–256.
7. O'Connor GT, Sparrow D, Weiss ST. The role of allergy and non-specific airway hyperresponsiveness in the pathogenesis of chronic obstructive pulmonary disease: state of the art. *Am Rev Respir Dis* 1989;140:225–252.
8. Anthonisen NR, Connett JE, Kiley JP, et al. Effects of smoking intervention and the use of an inhaled anticholinergic bronchodilator on the rate of decline of FEV_1: the Lung Health Study. *JAMA* 1994;272:1497–1505.
9. Siafakas NM, Vermeire P, Pride NB, et al. Optimal assessment and management of chronic obstructive pulmonary disease (COPD): a consensus statement of the European Respiratory Society. *Eur Respir J* 1995;8:1398–1420.
10. Guyatt GH, Berman LB, Townsend M, Pugsley SO, Chambers LW. A measure of quality of life for clinical trials in chronic lung disease. *Thorax* 1987;42:773–778.
11. Jones PW, Quirk FH, Baveystock CM, Littlejohns P. A self-complete measure of health status for chronic airflow limitation: the St George's respiratory questionnaire. *Am Rev Respir Dis* 1992;145: 1321–1327.
12. Braun SR, McKenzie WN, Copeland C, Knignt L, Ellersieck M. A comparison of the effect of ipratropium bromide and albuterol in the treatment of chronic obstructive airway disease. *Arch Intern Med* 1989;149:544–547.
13. Higgins BG, Powell RM, Cooper S, Tattersfield AE. Effect of salbutamol and ipratropium bromide on airway calibre and bronchial reactivity in asthma and chronic bronchitis. *Eur Respir J* 1991;4: 415–420.
14. Ikeda A, Nishimura K, Koyama H, Izumi T. Bronchodilating effects of combined therapy with clinical dosages of ipratropium bromide and salbutamol for stable COPD: comparison with ipratropium bromide alone. *Chest* 1995;107: 401–405.
15. Ikeda A, Nishimura K, Koyama H, Izumi T. Comparative dose-response study of three anticholinergic agents and fenoterol using a metered dose inhaler in patients with chronic obstructive pulmonary disease. *Thorax* 1995;50:62–66.
16. van Schayck CP, Dompeling E, van Herwaarden CLA, et al. Bronchodilator treatment in moderate asthma or chronic bronchitis: continuous or on demand? A randomised controlled study. *BMJ* 1991;303:1426–1431.
17. Anthonisen NR, Wright EC, IPPB Trial Group. Bronchodilator response in chronic obstructive pulmonary disease. *Am Rev Respir Dis* 1986;133:814–819.
18. Grove A, Lipworth BJ, Reid P, et al. Effects of regular salmeterol on lung function and exercise capacity in patients with chronic obstructive airways disease. *Thorax* 1996;51:689–693.
19. Matera MG, Cazzola M, Vinciguerra A, et al. A comparison of the bronchodilating effects of salmeterol, salbutamol and ipratropium bromide in patients with chronic obstructive pulmonary disease. *Pulm Pharmacol* 1995;8:267–271.
20. Boyd G, Morice AH, Pounsford JC, Siebert M, Peslis N, Crawford C. An evaluation of salmeterol in the treatment of chronic obstructive pulmonary disease (COPD). *Eur Respir J* 1997;10:815–821.
21. Jones PW, Bosh TK. Quality of life changes in COPD patients treated with salmeterol. *Am J Respir Crit Care Med* 1997;155:1283–1289.
22. Ulrik CS. Efficacy of inhaled salmeterol in the management of smokers with chronic obstructive pulmonary disease: a single centre randomised, double blind, placebo controlled, crossover study. *Thorax* 1995;50:750–754.
23. Spitzer WO, Suissa S, Ernst P, et al. The use of β-agonists and the risk of death and near death from asthma. *N Engl J Med* 1992;326:501–506.
24. Hall IP, Tattersfield AE. Beta-agonists. In: Clark TJH, Godfrey S, Lee TH, eds. *Asthma*, 3rd ed. London: Chapman & Hall Medical, 1992: 341–365.
25. Combivent Inhalation Aerosol Study Group. In chronic obstructive pulmonary disease, a combination of ipratropium and albuterol is more effective than either agent alone: an 85-day multicenter trial. *Chest* 1994;5:1411–1419.
26. Levin DC, Little KS, Laughlin KR, et al. Addition of anticholinergic solution prolongs bronchodilator effect of beta 2 agonists in patients with chronic obstructive pulmonary disease. *Am J Med* 1996; 100:40S–48S.
27. Combivent Inhalation Solution Study Group. Routine nebulized ipratropium and albuterol together are better than either alone in COPD. *Chest* 1997;112:1514–1521.
28. Rennard SI, Serby CW, Ghafouri M, Johnson PA, Friedman M. Extended therapy with ipratropium is associated with improved lung function in patients with COPD: a retrospective analysis of data from seven clinical trials. *Chest* 1996;110:62–70.
29. Calverley PMA. Symptomatic bronchodilator treatment. In: Calverley PMA, Pride N, eds. *Chronic obstructive pulmonary disease*. London: Chapman & Hall, 1995:419–446.
30. Callahan CM, Dittus RS, Katz BP. Oral corticosteroid therapy for patients with stable chronic obstructive pulmonary disease: a meta-analysis. *Ann Intern Med* 1991;114:216–223.
31. Barnes PJ, Pedersen S, Busse WW. Efficacy and safety of inhaled corticosteroids: new developments. *Am J Respir Crit Care Med* 1998;157: S1–53.
32. van Grunsven PM, van Schayck CP, Derenne JP, et al. Long term effects of inhaled corticosteroids in chronic obstructive pulmonary disease: a meta-analysis. *Thorax* 1999;54:7–14.
33. Paggiaro PL, Dahle R, Bakran I, Frith L, Hollingworth K, Efthimou J. Multicentre randomised placebo-controlled trial of inhaled fluticasone propionate in patients with chronic obstructive pulmonary disease. *Lancet* 1998;351:773–780.

34. McEvoy CE, Niewoehner DE. Adverse effects of corticosteroid therapy for COPD: a critical review. *Chest* 1997;111:732–743.
35. Robertson AS, Gove RI, Wieland GA, Burge PS. A double-blind comparison of oral prednisolone 40 mg/day with inhaled belomethasone dipropionate 1500 μg/day in patients with adult onset chronic obstructive airways disease. *Eur J Respir Dis* 1986;69(suppl 146):565–569.
36. Shim CS, Williams MH. Aerosol beclomethasone in patients with steroid-responsive chronic obstructive pulmonary disease. *Am J Med* 1985; 78:655–658.
37. Weir DC, Gove RI, Robertson AS, Burge PS. Corticosteroid trials in non-asthmatic chronic airflow obstruction: a comparison of oral prednisolone and inhaled beclomethasone dipropionate. *Thorax* 1990;45:112–117.
38. Poole PJ, Black PN. Do mucolytics reduce the frequency of exacerbations in chronic bronchitis? In: The Cochrane Library, Issue 4, 1998. Oxford: Update Software. Search date 1998; primary sources MEDLINE, EMBASE, Cinahl, hand searching of respiratory journals and meeting abstracts 1980 to 1998.
39. Saint S, Bent S, Vittinghoff E, Grady D. Antibiotics in chronic obstructive pulmonary disease exacerbations: a meta-analysis. *JAMA* 1995;273:957–960.
40. Medical Research Council Working Party. Long term domiciliary oxygen therapy in chronic hypoxic cor pulmonale complicating chronic bronchitis and emphysema. *Lancet* 1981;i:681–686.
41. Nocturnal Oxygen Therapy Trial Group. Continuous or nocturnal oxygen therapy in hypoxemic chronic obstructive lung disease: a clinical trial. *Ann Intern Med* 1980;93:391–398.

Huib A M Kerstjens, MD, PhD
University Hospital Groningen
The Netherlands

Competing interests: The author has received funding from: Astra, the manufacturer of budesonide, terbutaline, formoterol; from Glaxo Wellcome, the manufacturer of beclomethasone, salbutamol, salmeterol; and from Boehringer Ingelheim, the manufacturer of fenoterol and ipratropium bromide.

Pulmonary tuberculosis

Alison Holmes and Paul Garner, MBBS, MD

QUESTIONS

INTERVENTIONS

To be covered in future issues of *Clinical Evidence*
Prevention in people without HIV infection

Key Messages

- No randomzied controlled trial (RCT) has found a difference in relapse rates between standard WHO short course chemotherapy (6 mo) and longer-term (8–9 mo) chemotherapy in people with pulmonary tuberculosis. Use of pyrazinamide in the first 2 months seems to speed up sputum clearance but makes no difference to relapse rates, and extending its use beyond the first 2 months confers no additional benefit.
- We found limited evidence suggesting no difference between daily and thrice-weekly short-course regimens. Reducing duration of treatment from 6 to 4 months results in higher relapse rates.
- We found no good evidence comparing regimens containing quinolones versus existing regimens.
- We found no good evidence comparing different drug regimens for multidrug-resistant tuberculosis.
- We found limited evidence suggesting that adherence to treatment may be improved by staff training, prompting mechanisms, cash incentives, health education, and direct patient observation. Sanctions for nonadherence to treatment have not been adequately evaluated.
- We found one RCT comparing the effect of directly observing patients while they take their treatment versus self-treatment at home. Nonrandomized tuberculosis strengthening programs, which include direct observation, have yielded improved adherence.

Pulmonary tuberculosis

DEFINITION Tuberculosis is caused by *Mycobacterium tuberculosis* and can affect many organs. Specific symptoms relate to site of infection and generally are accompanied by fever, sweats, and weight loss.

INCIDENCE/ PREVALENCE Approximately one third of the world's population is infected with *M. tuberculosis*. The organism kills more people than any other infectious agent. The WHO estimates that 95% of cases are in developing countries and that 25% of their avoidable deaths are caused by tuberculosis.[1]

ETIOLOGY Social factors that increase risk include poverty, overcrowding, homelessness, and inadequate health services. Medical factors include HIV or other immunosuppression.

PROGNOSIS Varies widely and depends on treatment.[2]

AIMS To cure tuberculosis, eliminate risk of relapse, reduce infectivity, avoid emergence of drug resistance, and prevent death.

OUTCOMES *M. tuberculosis* in sputum (smear examination and culture); symptoms; weight; rates of relapse.

METHODS We searched MEDLINE from 1966 to 1998 (key words: tuberculosis, pulmonary; trial, randomized controlled trial, controlled trial; isoniazid, pyrazinamide, rifampicin). We included all Cochrane systematic reviews and studies that were randomized or used alternate allocation, had over 300 patients, and had at least 1 years' follow up after completion of treatment.

QUESTION **What are the effects of different drug regimens in people with newly diagnosed pulmonary tuberculosis?**

OPTION **SHORT-COURSE CHEMOTHERAPY**

RCTs found no difference in relapse rates between WHO short-course chemotherapy (6 mo—*see* Glossary, p. 190) and longer term (8–9 mo) chemotherapy in people with pulmonary tuberculosis. Use of pyrazinamide in the first 2 months was found to speed up sputum clearance but made no difference to relapse rates. Extending the use of pyrazinamide beyond the first 2 months confered no additional benefit.

Benefits: We found no systematic review. Two RCTs, published in the mid-1980s, compared 6 versus 8 or 9 months' chemotherapy in a total of 1295 people with untreated, culture/smear positive pulmonary tuberculosis.[3,4] Participants were followed up for at least a year after treatment was completed. The trials were performed in the UK, and in East and Central Africa, and used different combinations of isoniazid, rifampicin, ethambutol, streptomycin, and pyrazinamide for initial (first 2 mo) and continuation treatment. Overall, there was no significant difference between short-course and longer regimens, and extending the use of pyrazinamide beyond the first 2 months did not improve cure rates. Sputum conversion was faster with regimens containing pyrazinamide, but there was no difference in relapse rates at 3 years' follow-up.[4] There was no difference between regimens using ethambutol or streptomycin as the fourth drug in the initial phase.[4] A 6-month regimen using rifampicin and isoniazid throughout was highly effective (relapse rate 2%) and significantly better than isoniazid used alone in the 4-month continuation phase (relapse rate 9%). When use of isoniazid alone was prolonged in a 6-month continuation phase, the relapse rate was not significantly better than with 4-months' continuation.[3]

Harms: In the largest trial, possible adverse reactions were reported in 24 of 851 patients (3%), with only six requiring modification of treatment.[3] Two patients in this study developed jaundice, one of whom died. **Pyrazinamide:** Adding pyrazinamide did not increase the incidence of hepatitis (4% with and without pyrazinamide).[4] However, mild adverse effects were more common, including arthralgia, skin rashes, flu-like symptoms, mild gastrointestinal disturbance, vestibular disturbance, peripheral neuropathy, and confusion. Arthralgia was the most common adverse effect, reported in approximately 0.7% of patients on pyrazinamide,[3,4] but was mild and never required modification of treatment.

Comment: In previously treated patients, the organisms may have acquired drug resistance, so WHO short-course chemotherapy may not be effective.

OPTION INTERMITTENT DOSING

The limited data we found provide no evidence of a difference between daily and thrice-weekly short-course regimens but do not exclude a clinically significant difference.

Benefits: One systematic review published in January 1999 identified one RCT comparing three-times-per-week versus daily chemotherapy for 6 months in 399 people with newly diagnosed pulmonary tuberculosis.[5] At 1 month after treatment was completed, there was no significant difference in rates of bacteriologic cure, defined as negative sputum culture (99.9% vs. 100%), or relapse (five patients vs. one patient). At least 12 cohort studies have found cure rates of 80% to 100% with thrice weekly regimens taken over 6 to 9 months.[5]

Harms: Intermittent treatment has the potential to contribute to drug resistance, but this was not shown in the studies.[5]

Comment: The number of people randomized was too small to exclude a clinically significant difference between the dosing regimens.

OPTION CHEMOTHERAPY FOR LESS THAN 6 MONTHS

We found limited evidence suggesting that reducing duration of treatment to less than 6 months results in unacceptably high relapse rates.

Benefits: We found one systematic review, including seven RCTs published between 1979 and 1989 of outpatients with newly diagnosed pulmonary tuberculosis.[6] The trials randomized 228 and 2020 people in India, Hong Kong, Singapore, and Germany, and compared a variety of shorter (minimum 2 mo) and longer (maximum 12 mo) drug regimens. Relapse rates were consistently higher after the shorter duration treatments.

Harms: There was little difference in adverse events or toxicity except in one trial. This found that patients given a 2-month regimen were less likely to change or discontinue drugs than those given a 12-month regimen. However, numbers were small (6/299 vs. 17/299).[6]

Comment: The treatments were given under ideal conditions. In clinical practice, relapse rates with shorter regimens are likely to be worse.

OPTION REGIMENS CONTAINING QUINOLONES

Regimens containing quinolones have not been compared adequately with existing regimens in people with tuberculosis.

Benefits: We found no systematic review. One RCT of 200 patients from Tanzania found no significant difference in the rate of treatment failure between a regimen containing ciprofloxacin and one not (RR of relapse at 6 months 16, 95% CI 0.94–278).[7] A relatively low dosage of ciprofloxacin was used (750 mg/d).

Harms: None reported.

Comment: Quinolones have good bactericidal activity in vitro. Some of the newer quinolones have enhanced antimycobacterial activity compared with ciprofloxacin.

QUESTION What are the effects of different drug regimens in people with multidrug-resistant tuberculosis?

Different drug regimens for multidrug-resistant tuberculosis have not been adequately compared.

Benefits: We found no systematic review and no RCTs comparing different regimens in people with multidrug-resistant tuberculosis.

Harms: Insufficient data.

Comment: Current clinical practice in multidrug-resistant tuberculosis is to include at least three drugs to which the particular strain of tuberculosis is sensitive, using as many bactericidal agents as possible. Patients are directly observed and managed by a specialized clinician.

QUESTION Which interventions improve adherence to treatment?

OPTION STAFF TRAINING

We found limited evidence suggesting that training of health staff improves adherence.

Benefits: We found one systematic review updated in November 1998.[8] This identified one RCT comparing intensive staff supervision versus routine supervision at centers in Korea performing tuberculosis extension activities. Centers were paired and randomized, and supervision was carried out by senior doctors. Higher completion rates were achieved with intensive supervision (RR 1.2, CIs not yet available as cluster effect not yet corrected for).

Harms: None reported.

Comment: The effect on adherence was modest, and we cannot yet say whether it was significant.

OPTION PROMPTING MECHANISMS

RCTs have found that prompting mechanisms improve adherence.

Benefits: We found one systematic review, which identified two RCTs.[8] The first compared reminder cards versus usual follow-up in people who did not collect their drugs after discharge from hospital. Those in the intervention group were more likely to complete their treatment (RR 1.2, 95% CI 1.1–1.4). The second trial in the USA compared the use of peer health advisers who met participants and went to the clinic with them. It found increased attendance at the first follow up appointment (RR vs. no intervention 1.4, 95% CI 1.1–1.8).

Harms: None.

Comment: Both were small studies from which it is not possible to generalize widely. Implementing prompting mechanisms in larger populations would require well-staffed and well-organized tuberculosis programs. It is not known whether the same effects would be observed in regional or national programs.

OPTION PATIENT INCENTIVES

RCTs have found that cash incentives improve adherence among people living in deprived circumstances.

Benefits: We found one systematic review,[8] which identified two RCTs, both from the USA. One, in homeless men, found that money ($5) improved attendance at the first appointment (RR 1.6, 95% CI 1.3–2.0). The other, in migrants, found that combining cash ($10) with health education improved attendance compared with usual care (RR 2.4, 95% CI 1.5–3.7).

Harms: None measured.

Comment: None.

OPTION HEALTH EDUCATION

The effects of health education alone on adherence have been poorly evaluated in the limited evidence we found.

Benefits: We found one systematic review,[8] which identified one RCT conducted in the USA. This compared education by a doctor at a clinic versus giving the participant a leaflet. It found no significant difference in the proportion of participants completing treatment, although numbers were small.

Harms: None measured.

Comment: The trial was probably too small to exclude an effect of health education. Other RCTs have evaluated health education as one part of a motivation package, such as nurses phoning patients every 3 months. This makes it difficult to evaluate the independent effects of education.

OPTION SANCTIONS

Sanctions for failure to adhere to treatment have not been evaluated adequately in the evidence we found.

Benefits: We found one systematic review, which identified no RCTs of sanctions.[8]

Harms: The use of sanctions may be ethically dubious because it reduces or removes patient choice.

Comment: In New York, the "locked hospital" was thought to have given credibility to the Department of Health's strategy for curing some patients.[9]

OPTION DIRECT PATIENT OBSERVATION

One RCT has found that directly observing patients as they take their drugs makes little difference to adherence. However, observational evidence suggests that tuberculosis strengthening programs, which usually include direct observation (often called directly observed therapy [DOT] short-course programs), can improve adherence.

Benefits: We found one systematic review,[8] which identified one RCT conducted in South Africa. This compared direct observation of patients versus self-administered treatment at home. It found no difference between the two strategies, although overall adherence in the study was low.

Harms: Potential harms include reduced cooperation between patient and doctor, removal of responsibility from patients, detriment to long-term sustainability of antituberculosis programs, and burden on health services to the detriment of care for other diseases. None of these have been investigated adequately.

Comment: Numerous observational studies have evaluated interventions described as DOT, but all were packages of interventions, including specific investment in antituberculosis programs (e.g., strengthened drug supplies; improved microscopy services, and numerous incentives, sanctions, and other co-interventions that were likely to influence adherence).[10] DOT is common in the US.

GLOSSARY

WHO short-course chemotherapy comprises 6-months' treatment, with four drugs in the first 2 months (isoniazid, rifampicin, pyrazinamide, and either ethambutol or intramuscular streptomycin), and two drugs in the subsequent 4 months (rifampicin and isoniazid).

REFERENCES

1. Global Tuberculosis Programme. *Treatment of tuberculosis*. Geneva: World Health Organization, 1997;WHO/TB/97.220.
2. Enarson D, Rouillon A. Epidemiological basis of tuberculosis control. In: Davis PD. *Clinical tuberculosis*, 2nd ed. London: Chapman and Hall Medical, 1998.
3. East and Central African/British Medical Research Council Fifth Collaborative Study. Controlled clinical trial of 4 short-course regimens of chemotherapy (three 6-month and one 8-month) for pulmonary tuberculosis. *Tubercle* 1983;64:153–166.
4. British Thoracic Society. A controlled trial of 6 months' chemotherapy in pulmonary tuberculosis, final report: results during the 36 months after the end of chemotherapy and beyond. *Br J Dis Chest* 1984;78:330–336.
5. Mwandumba HC, Squire SB. Intermittent dosing with drugs for tuberculosis (Cochrane Review). In: The Cochrane Library, Issue 1, 1999. Oxford: Update Software.
6. Gelband H. Less than six months treatment for TB. In: The Cochrane Library, Issue 3, 1999. Oxford: Update Software.
7. Kennedy N, Berger L, Curran J, et al. Randomized controlled trial of a drug regimen that includes ciprofloxacin for the treatment of pulmonary tuberculosis. *Clin Infect Dis* 1996;22:827–833.
8. Volmink J, Garner P. Promoting adherence to tuberculosis treatment (Cochrane Review). In: The Cochrane Library, Issue 1, 1999. Oxford: Update Software.
9. Fujiwara PI, Larkin C, Frieden TR. Directly observed therapy in New York City: history, implementation, results and challenges. *Tuberculosis* 1997;18:135–148.
10. Garner P. What makes DOT work? *Lancet* 1998; 352:1326–1327.

Alison Holmes
Senior Lecturer
Hammersmith Hospital
Imperial College
London
UK

Paul Garner, MBBS, MD
Senior Lecturer
Liverpool School of Tropical Medicine
Liverpool
UK

Competing interests: None declared.

Lung cancer

Alan J Neville, MBChB, MEd, MRCP, FRCPC

QUESTIONS

INTERVENTIONS

Key Messages

Non–small cell lung cancer

- Systematic reviews have found that cisplatin-based regimens are effective for non–small cell lung cancer. Other promising new drug treatments require further validation.
- Systematic reviews of randomized controlled trials (RCTs) have found that the combination of thoracic irradiation plus chemotherapy improves survival compared with radiotherapy alone in patients with unresectable stage 3 non–small cell lung cancer.
- Systematic reviews of RCTs have found that palliative chemotherapy improves 1-year survival in patients with stage 4 non–small cell lung cancer and may alleviate disease related symptoms. Effects on quality of life have not yet been adequately evaluated.

Small cell lung cancer

- We found no large-scale trials to affirm the best chemotherapy regimen for small cell lung cancer, although cisplatin-based chemotherapy is the current treatment standard.
- Systematic reviews of RCTs have found improved survival with chemotherapy plus radiation therapy compared with chemotherapy alone in patients with limited-stage small cell lung cancer. The optimal timing, dose, fractionation of radiation, and effects on quality of life require further evaluation.

- RCTs have found that prophylactic cranial irradiation reduces the incidence of brain metastases in limited-stage small cell lung cancer without improvement in survival and some evidence of cognitive impairment.
- We found no good evidence to determine the trade-off between reduced toxicity and shortened survival from using oral etoposide rather than combination chemotherapy for the palliative management of small cell lung cancer.

DEFINITION Lung cancer or bronchogenic carcinoma is an epithelial cancer, arising from the bronchial surface epithelium or bronchial mucous glands (Table 1).

INCIDENCE/ PREVALENCE Lung cancer is the leading cause of cancer death in both men and women, affecting approximately 100,000 men and 80,000 women annually in North America. Small cell lung cancer constitutes approximately 20% to 25% of all lung cancers, the remainder being non–small cell lung cancers, of which adenocarcinoma is now the most prevalent form.[1]

ETIOLOGY Smoking remains the major preventable risk factor, accounting for about 80% to 90% of all cases.

PROGNOSIS Lung cancer has an overall 5-year survival rate of 10% to 12%.[2] At the time of diagnosis, 10% to 15% of patients with lung cancer have localized disease. Of these, half will be alive at 5 years despite potentially curative surgery. Over half of patients have metastatic disease at the time of diagnosis. For those with initially unresectable non–small cell lung cancer, combined treatment with radiotherapy and chemotherapy followed by surgery has achieved modest improvements in 5-year survival.[2] Prognosis depends on the stage of disease. In patients with small cell cancer, those with limited-stage disease who undergo combined chemotherapy and mediastinal irradiation have a median survival of 18 to 24 months, whereas those with extensive-stage disease who are given palliative chemotherapy have a median survival of 10 to 12 months. One fifth of patients with small cell lung cancer present with central nervous system involvement, and half develop symptomatic brain metastases by 2 years. Of these, only half respond to palliative radiation and their median survival is less than 3 months. Patients with non–small cell cancer who undergo surgery have a 5-year survival of 60% to 80% for stage 1 disease and 25% to 50% for stage 2 disease.

AIMS To cure the disease, to prolong life, to improve quality of life, and to provide palliation.

OUTCOMES Survival, clinical response rates, disease-related symptoms, adverse effects of treatment, quality of life.

METHODS We searched MEDLINE and Cancerlit from 1980 to 1997. Articles were also found from citations in relevant articles. We reviewed all relevant systematic reviews and RCTs that met accepted quality criteria.

NON–SMALL CELL LUNG CANCER

QUESTION What are the effects of treatment?

OPTION THORACIC RADIATION PLUS CHEMOTHERAPY FOR UNRESECTABLE STAGE 3 NON–SMALL CELL LUNG CANCER

Systematic reviews of RCTs have found that the combination of thoracic irradiation plus chemotherapy improves survival compared with radiotherapy alone in patients with unresectable stage 3 non–small cell lung cancer. Effects on quality of life have not yet been adequately evaluated.

Benefits: Three systematic reviews using meta-analysis have compared thoracic irradiation plus chemotherapy versus radiotherapy alone[3–5] in unresected stage 3 non–small cell lung cancer. The first, published in 1995, analyzed 22 RCTs in a total of 3033 patients (range 48–353).[3] Pooled hazard ratio was 0.90 (95% CI 0.83–0.97), suggesting a 10% reduction in the risk of death and an absolute survival benefit from combined treatment of 3% at 2 years. The second review, also published in 1995, analyzed 14 RCTs (1887 patients). The addition of a cisplatin-based regimen to radiotherapy significantly reduced mortality at 1 and 2 years by 24% and 30% (pooled ORs for death compared with radiotherapy alone 0.76 [95% CI 0.6–0.9] and 0.70 [95% CI 0.5–0.9]).[4] Similar results were obtained in the third review, published in 1996.[5]

Harms: The reviews gave no data on the long-term adverse effects of treatment.

Comment: None.

OPTION VINCA ALKALOIDS WITH OR WITHOUT CISPLATIN IN STAGE 4 NON–SMALL CELL LUNG CANCER

RCTs have found conflicting results about the value of using vinca alkaloids plus cisplatin versus vinca alkaloids alone.

Benefits: We found no systematic review. At least two RCTs have looked at the effect of combining vinca alkaloids and cisplatin.[6,7] One, a multicenter RCT in 612 people which included people with stage 3 and 4 non–small cell lung cancer, compared vinorelbine alone, vinorelbine plus cisplatin, and vindesine plus cisplatin.[6] The combination of vinorelbine plus cisplatin achieved significantly higher median survival and clinical response rates than vinorelbine alone (median survival 40 vs. 31 weeks, $p=0.01$, clinical response rates 30% vs. 15%, $p<0.0001$) or vindesine plus cisplatin (median survival 40 vs. 32 weeks, $p=0.04$, clinical response 30% vs. 19%, $p<0.02$). There was no significant difference in median survival or response rate between vinorelbine alone and vindesine plus cisplatin. The other RCT compared vinorelbine alone versus vinorelbine plus cisplatin in 231 patients. This found no significant difference in survival.[7]

Harms: Adverse effects such as gastrointestinal toxicity and neuropathy were greater when cisplatin was given with the vinca alkaloid.

Comment: Although cisplatin-based regimens remain standard treatment for non–small cell lung cancer, paclitaxel, docetaxel, carboplatin, gemcitabine, and irinotecan are promising new agents for this disease.[2]

OPTION **CHEMOTHERAPY IN STAGE 4 NON–SMALL CELL LUNG CANCER**

Systematic reviews of RCTs have found that chemotherapy significantly prolongs 1-year survival in patients with stage 4 non–small cell lung cancer. Survival benefit is greatest with regimens containing cisplatin. One RCT found that chemotherapy reduced disease-related symptoms. However, effects on quality of life have not yet been adequately evaluated.

Benefits: Four systematic reviews have addressed survival in patients with stage 4 non–small cell lung cancer.[3,8–10] All found a significant survival benefit from chemotherapy. The largest review included 1190 patients from 11 RCTs and described individual patient data, providing the most accurate estimate of the treatment effect.[3] Overall, chemotherapy improved survival at 1 year. Benefit was most evident on subgroup analysis of regimens containing cisplatin, which showed a reduction in relative risk of death of 27% at 1 year (pooled hazard ratio 0.73, 95% CI 0.62–0.85).[3] Beyond 1 year, there was no survival benefit from chemotherapy. One multicenter RCT comparing different chemotherapy regimens found that chemotherapy reduced disease-related symptoms such as pain, cough, hemoptysis, and dyspnea.[6]

Harms: Universal alopecia and gastrointestinal and hematologic toxicity were reported in over half of patients treated with chemotherapy.[6]

Comment: For patients with stage 4 non–small cell lung cancer, treatment options consist of either chemotherapy or symptomatic care, including palliative radiation.

SMALL CELL LUNG CANCER

QUESTION **What are the effects of treatment?**

OPTION **STANDARD CHEMOTHERAPY VERSUS OTHER REGIMENS**

We found no good data from which to compare standard cisplatin- or doxorubicin-based chemotherapy with other chemotherapy regimens.

Benefits: We found no systematic review and no large-scale RCTs.

Harms: Except in patients with widespread extensive-stage disease, adverse effects of chemotherapy are of short duration. However, there are no good data comparing standard treatment with other regimens.[11]

Comment: Small cell lung cancer is relatively sensitive to chemotherapy. Standard treatment for both limited- and extensive-stage disease comprises four to six cycles of etoposide plus cisplatin or a regimen that alternates three cycles of etoposide plus cisplatin with three cycles of cyclophosphamide, doxorubicin, and vincristine.[11]

OPTION ADDITION OF THORACIC IRRADIATION TO CHEMOTHERAPY IN LIMITED-STAGE SMALL CELL LUNG CANCER

Systematic reviews of RCTs have found that the addition of thoracic irradiation improves survival in patients with limited-stage small cell lung cancer. The best timing, dose, and fractionation of radiation remain uncertain.

Benefits: Two systematic reviews, both published in 1992, have found that the addition of thoracic irradiation improves survival.[12,13] The first identified 13 RCTs in 2573 patients (range 52–426): 3-year survival was 15% with radiation compared with 10% with chemotherapy alone ($p = 0.001$).[12] The second identified 11 RCTs. Using data from nine of the RCTs, local control was achieved in 50% with radiation compared with 25% with chemotherapy alone (ARR 25%, 95% CI 16.5%–34.1%).[13] **Timing of radiation:** Questions remain over whether radiation should be concurrent with the chemotherapy (either early or late in the course), sequential, or alternating. We found no systematic review. The most impressive survival results favor early concurrent treatment. These derive from an RCT comparing radiation given during the second versus the sixth of six cycles of chemotherapy. Progression-free survival at 3 years was 26% (early) versus 19% (late), $p = 0.036$, and 5-year survival was 20% versus 11%, $p = 0.008$.[14] **Frequency, dose, and fractionation:** A recent RCT compared twice-daily thoracic radiation over 3 weeks versus once-daily irradiation over 5 weeks in patients given cisplatin and etoposide. Survival rates were 47% at 2 years and 26% at 5 years in the former group and 41% at 2 years and 16% at 5 years in the latter group ($p = 0.04$).[15]

Harms: The risk of treatment-related death was more than doubled among patients given thoracic irradiation compared to those receiving chemotherapy alone (OR 2.54, 95% CI 1.90–3.18).[13] The incidence of esophagitis was also higher in those treated with twice-daily irradiation.[15]

Comment: Interest in adding thoracic irradiation derives from the fact that local recurrence in the chest is a major cause of first treatment failure, which carries an extremely poor prognosis. Median survival in limited-stage disease has improved over the past 10 years from 14 to 16 months to 20 to 24 months. This may reflect the early use of radiation plus chemotherapy, rather than improvements in either modality alone.[14]

OPTION PROPHYLACTIC CRANIAL IRRADIATION IN LIMITED-STAGE SMALL CELL LUNG CANCER

RCTs have found that prophylactic cranial irradiation reduces the risk of brain metastases in patients with limited-stage small cell lung cancer, but there is no evidence of a beneficial effect on survival. Long-term cognitive dysfunction has been reported.

Benefits: We found no systematic review. Two reviews, which gave no details of their search methodology,[16,17] identified 12 published RCTs of prophylactic cranial irradiation in small cell lung cancer. Of these, six accepted only patients with limited-stage disease. Total dose of radiation and dose fraction varied across the 12 trials. All trials showed a significant reduction in the risk of developing brain metastases. In one, the incidence of brain metastases fell from 67% without prophylactic cranial irradiation to 40% with prophylactic cranial irradiation (RR 0.6) but there was no significant difference in survival at 2 years (AR of survival compared with treatment 29%, without treatment 21.5%, RR 0.9).[18]

Harms: Cognitive deficits are found before prophylactic cranial irradiation in many patients with small cell lung cancer, and follow-up 6 months after prophylactic cranial irradiation has found little additional deficit.[19] However, over the longer term, significant cognitive dysfunction has been reported.[19]

Comment: Because not all RCTs assessed this outcome, the clinical significance of cognitive impairment after prophylactic irradiation remains unknown.

OPTION ETOPOSIDE IN EXTENSIVE-STAGE SMALL CELL LUNG CANCER

RCTs have found that survival is worse with oral etoposide than with combination chemotherapy. Etoposide is less toxic in the short term but does not offer significantly better quality of life.

Benefits: We found no systematic review. Several RCTs have compared oral etoposide versus chemotherapy. One RCT in 155 patients with extensive-stage disease compared oral etoposide 100 mg/d for 5 days versus combination chemotherapy. One-year survival was significantly higher with chemotherapy than with etoposide (19.3% vs. 9.8% $p<0.05$). There was no significant difference in median survival (5.9 vs. 4.8 months) or quality of life.[20]

Harms: Acute nausea and vomiting were worse with combined intravenous chemotherapy, but there was no significant difference in overall quality of life.[20]

Comment: Because treatment of extensive-stage disease is palliative, and because age has been identified as a prognostic factor in small cell lung cancer, studies have looked at outcomes in elderly people with limited- and extensive-stage disease, and in patients of all ages with a poor prognosis. Although small cell lung cancer is relatively sensitive to chemotherapy, extensive-stage disease remains incurable. Median survival with treatment is 10 to 12 months, and as yet has been unaffected by the introduction of high-dose combination chemotherapy. Because of its lower toxicity, etoposide may be considered for elderly patients with extensive-stage disease or those with a poor prognosis.

REFERENCES

1. Travis WD, Travis LB, Devesa SS. Lung Cancer. *Cancer* 1995;75(1 Suppl):191–202.
2. Ihde DC, Pass HI, Glatstein E. Lung cancer. In: DeVita VT Jr, Hellman S, Rosenberg SA eds. *Cancer, principles and practice of oncology,* 5th ed. Philadelphia: Lippincott-Raven, 1997.
3. Non-Small Cell Lung Cancer Collaborative Group. Chemotherapy in non-small cell lung cancer: a meta-analysis using updated data on individual patients from 52 randomized clinical trials. *BMJ* 1995;311:899–909. (Search date 1995, primary sources MEDLINE, Cancer CD, plus hand search of meetings abstracts, bibliographies of books and specialist journals, and consultation of trials registers of National Cancer Institute, UK Coordinating Committee for Cancer Research, and the Union Internationale Contre le Cancer.)

4. Marino P, Cantoni A, Preatoni A. Randomized trials of radiotherapy alone versus combined chemotherapy and radiotherapy in stages IIIa and IIIb non small cell lung cancer. *Cancer* 1995;76:593–601. Search date 1995; primary sources MEDLINE, plus manual search of references of review articles and abstracts.
5. Pritchard RS, Anthony SP. Chemotherapy plus radiotherapy compared with radiotherapy alone in the treatment of locally advance, unresectable, non-small-cell lung cancer. *Ann Intern Med* 1996;125:723–729. Search date 1995; primary sources MEDLINE, plus manual search of references of review articles and abstracts.
6. Le Chevalier T, Brisgand D, Douillard J-Y, et al. Randomized study of vinorelbine and cisplatin versus vindesine and cisplatin versus vinorelbine alone in advanced non-small cell lung cancer: results of a European multicenter trial including 612 patients. *J Clin Oncol* 1994;12:360–367.
7. Depierre A, Chastang Cl, Quoix E, et al. Vinorelbine versus vinorelbine plus cisplatin in advanced non-small cell lung cancer: a randomized trial. *Ann Oncol* 1994;5:37–42.
8. Grilli R, Oxman AD, Julian JA. Chemotherapy for advanced non-small cell lung cancer: how much benefit is enough? *J Clin Oncol* 1993;11: 1866–1872. Search date 1991; primary source MEDLINE 1970–1991.
9. Souquet PJ, Chauvin F, Boissel JP, et al. Polychemotherapy in advanced non small cell lung cancer: a meta-analysis. *Lancet* 1993;342: 19–21. Search date not given. Manual and computerised search of medical journals. No further details.
10. Marino P, Pampallona S, Preatoni A, et al. Chemotherapy versus supportive care in advanced non-small cell lung cancer: results of a meta-analysis of the literature. *Chest* 1994;106: 861–865. Search date not given. MEDLINE and manual search of references from review articles and abstracts. No further details.
11. Murray N. New drugs for small cell lung cancer. *Oncology* 1997;9:38–42.
12. Pignon JP, Arriagada R, Ihde DC, et al. A meta-analysis of thoracic radiotherapy for small-cell lung cancer. *N Engl J Med* 1992;327:1618–1624. (Search date 1992, primary sources MEDLINE plus hand search of proceedings of key oncology meetings.)
13. Warde P, Payne D. Does thoracic irradiation improve survival and local control in limited-stage small cell carcinoma of the lung? A meta-analysis. *J Clin Oncol* 1992;10:890–895. (Search date not given; primary sources MEDLINE, Cancerline.)
14. Murray N, Coy P, Pater JL, et al. Importance of timing for thoracic irradiation in the combined modality treatment of limited-stage small cell lung cancer. *J Clin Oncol* 1993;11:336–344.
15. Turrisi AT III, Kim K, Blum R, et al. Twice-daily compared with once-daily thoracic radiotherapy in limited small cell lung cancer treated concurrently with cisplatin and etoposide. *N Engl J Med* 1999;340:265–271.
16. Glantz MJ, Choy H, Yee L. Prophylactic cranial irradiation in small cell lung cancer: rationale, results and recommendations. *Semin Oncol* 1997;24:477–483.
17. Gregor A. Prophylactic cranial irradiation in small cell lung cancer: is it ever indicated? *Oncology* 1998;12:19–24.
18. Arriagada R, Le Chevalier T, Borie F, et al. Prophylactic cranial irradiation for patient with small cell lung cancer in complete remission. *J Natl Cancer Inst* 1995;87:183–190.
19. Catane R, Schwade JG, Yarr I, et al. Follow-up neurological evaluation in patients with small cell lung carcinoma treated with prophylactic cranial irradiation and chemotherapy. *Int J Radiat Oncol Biol Phys* 1981;7:105–109.
20. Souhami RL, Spiro SG, Rudd RM, et al. Five day oral etoposide treatment for advanced small cell lung cancer: randomized comparison with intravenous chemotherapy. *J Natl Cancer Inst* 1997;89(8):577–580.

Alan Neville, MBChB, MEd, MRCP, FRCPC
Professor
McMaster University
Hamilton
Ontario
Canada

Competing interests: None declared.

TABLE 1 Staging lung cancer

Non–small cell lung cancer

Stage	**TNM**	**5-year survival %**
1	T1–T2, N0, M0	55–75
2	T1–T2, N1, M0	25–50
3A	T3, N0–N1, M0 T4, or any N3, M0	20–40 15–30
3B	T4, or any N3, M0	<5
4	Any M1	<5

Small cell lung cancer

Limited-stage disease Tumor confined to the same side of the chest, supraclavicular lymph nodes, or both.

Extensive-stage disease Defined as anything beyond.

Osteoarthritis

Paul Dieppe, BSc, MBBS, MD, FRCP, FFPHM, and Jiri Chard, MB

QUESTIONS

INTERVENTIONS

Key Messages

- We found no good evidence that nonsteroidal anti-inflammatory drugs (NSAIDs) are superior to simple analgesics, such as paracetamol (acetaminophen), or to suggest that any one of the many available NSAIDs has greater efficacy in relieving the pain of osteoarthritis.
- One systematic review of randomized controlled trials (RCTs) has found that topical agents provide pain relief in patients with osteoarthritis and offer a nontoxic alternative to systemic drug treatment. However, we found no evidence to indicate whether the prescribed agents are superior to cheap, nonprescription alternatives, or to other local treatments, such as heat or cold packs.
- We found little robust evidence on the effectiveness of nonmedicinal, noninvasive interventions, such as education and physical exercise, although two recent RCTs support findings from previous, weaker studies that both exercise and education may help reduce the burden of pain and disability for people with hip or knee osteoarthritis.

DEFINITION Osteoarthritis is a heterogeneous condition for which the prevalence, risk factors, expression, and prognosis vary according to the joint site involved. It most commonly affects hands, knees, hips, and spinal apophyseal joints. It usually is defined using pathologic or radiologic criteria, rather than clinical features, and is characterized by focal areas of damage to the cartilage surfaces of synovial joints associated with remodeling of the underlying bone and mild synovitis. When severe, this pathology results in characteristic joint-space narrowing, osteophyte formation, with visible subchondral bone changes on radiograph.

INCIDENCE/ PREVALENCE Varies according to site. Osteoarthritis is very common and one of the most important causes of pain and disability in older adults. Radiographic features are practically universal in at least some joints in people over the age of 60 years, but significant clinical disease probably affects only approximately 10% to 20% of this population.

ETIOLOGY Osteoarthritis is strongly related to age and is initiated by abnormalities in joint shape or injury. Progression is mediated by mechanical stress and by chemical dysregulation of synthesis and degradation of tissues.

PROGNOSIS We found little reliable quantitative data.

AIMS To reduce pain, stiffness, and disability; and to limit the risk of progressive joint damage, with minimal adverse effects.

OUTCOMES Frequency and severity of joint pain (particularly activity-related pain and night pain); stiffness; functional impairment and disability; quality of life. The Lequesne algofunctional index and the Western Ontario and McMaster Osteoarthritis Index (WOMAC) are two validated instruments for measuring disease-specific outcomes that are sensitive to change.[1,2]

METHODS Evidence was identified using two separate search strategies. The first was provided by *Clinical Evidence*; the second was designed while compiling a systematic review of interventions for osteoarthritis of the knee: MEDLINE, EMBASE, Cochrane, and BIDS Science Citation Index were searched. Studies were selected according to standard critical appraisal criteria.

QUESTION **How does systemic paracetamol (acetaminophen) compare with NSAIDs in relieving the symptoms of osteoarthritis?**

Systematic reviews of RCTs have found that simple analgesics and NSAIDs produce short-term pain relief in osteoarthritis. However, we found no good evidence that NSAIDs are superior to simple analgesics, such as paracetamol (acetaminophen), or that one NSAID is better than another.

Benefits: We found three systematic reviews of RCTs investigating analgesic and anti-inflammatory treatment in osteoarthritis of the hip[3] and knee.[4,5] These found no clear evidence for the superiority of NSAIDs over simple analgesics. They also found no difference in effectiveness between different NSAIDs, and no evidence that a person who does not respond to one NSAID might respond to another. **Individual agents:** Most of the literature consisted of short-term trials comparing different NSAIDs, most of which had design problems (see Comment). Small RCTs published in the early 1980s found that NSAIDs and paracetamol (acetaminophen) were both superior to placebo for short-term pain relief and global patient responses in osteoarthritis.[6,7] **Comparisons of NSAIDs and analgesics:** We found a few published comparisons of NSAIDs versus other analgesics. One trial compared naproxen versus paracetamol (acetaminophen) over 2 years in 178 people with knee osteoarthritis and found no significant difference between the two agents.[8] Another compared two doses of ibuprofen versus paracetamol in 184 people with osteoarthritis and concluded that there were no differences in the three treatment arms.[9] Twenty N-of-1 studies compared paracetamol (acetaminophen) versus diclofenac and concluded that whereas some patients were controlled adequately by paracetamol (acetaminophen) alone, others responded better to an NSAID.[10]

Harms: **Paracetamol (acetaminophen):** The main concern is liver damage when taken in overdose[11] or at lower doses in people with existing liver damage. **NSAIDs:** Indomethacin (and possibly other NSAIDs) may accelerate joint damage in osteoarthritis,[12] and there is a risk of gastrointestinal or renal damage in older people with osteoarthritis, particularly those with intercurrent disease. Case control data from several thousand people[13,14] indicate that the relative risk of gastrointestinal hemorrhage when taking any NSAID is around 4 to 5, the risk increasing with certain drugs and with increased doses. A subsequent meta-analysis ranked the risk from different drugs (Table 1)[15] and found it to be dose dependent. Risk cannot be calculated for more recently introduced NSAIDs because data are insufficient.

Comment: Despite the many studies of NSAID use in osteoarthritis, the evidence on efficacy remains poor and difficult to generalize. Most RCTs suffer from methodologic problems, including short duration, exclusion of older people and those with intercurrent disease or at risk of gastroinestinal and other drug complications, variable outcome measures, comparison of one drug with another rather than with placebo, and funding bias.[16,17] In the absence of clear evidence of the superiority of one type of treatment or product, other issues (e.g., safety [particularly the risk of gastrointestinal bleeding with NSAID use] and cost) should determine the choice of drug.

QUESTION What are the effects of topical agents?

We found limited evidence suggesting that topical agents provide some pain relief for osteoarthritis and are less toxic than systemic drug treatment. However, we found no evidence to indicate whether prescribed topical agents are superior to less expensive, nonprescription alternatives, or to other local treatment, such as heat or cold packs.

Benefits: **Topical NSAIDs:** We found one recent systematic review of 86 trials comparing topically applied agents containing NSAIDs versus placebo.[18] It found that these agents had a relative benefit of 2.0 (95% CI 1.5–2.7) for relief of chronic musculoskeletal pain (osteoarthritis and tendinitis). One good-quality RCT in 235 people with mild osteoarthritis of the knee compared topical piroxicam gel versus oral ibuprofen 1200 mg/d, and found no significant difference in pain relief between the two groups (60% good or excellent relief in the topical group, 64% in the systemic treatment group).[19] Another RCT in 119 people with osteoarthritis found diclofenac-hyaluronan gel to be more effective in relieving pain than placebo gel ($p = 0.057$).[20] **Capsaicin:** A nonsystematic meta-analysis of pooled data from three RCTs of topically applied capsaicin concluded that capsaicin cream was useful in osteoarthritis with an OR of 4.36 (95% CI 2.77–6.88) for pain relief.[21] A RCT in 70 people with osteoarthritis compared 0.025% capsaicin cream versus nonmedicated cream. Active treatment resulted in significantly greater pain reduction than placebo (no quantified estimates of benefit available).[22]

Harms: The main adverse effect of topical treatment is local skin irritation; systemic adverse effects were no more common than with placebo. There have been no reports of gastric or renal problems.

Comment: The evidence is poor, because most studies were short-term, included a mixture of patient groups, and compared different agents rather than controlled by placebo. There is no evidence available to indicate whether agents that contain NSAIDs or capsaicin are superior to simple rubefacients (anaesthetic creams) or to local applications, such as a hot pack. Note that these topical agents are not available in the US.

QUESTION What are the effects of education and physical therapy?

We found limited evidence from RCTs that both exercise and education reduce pain and disability in people with hip or knee osteoarthritis.

Benefits: A recent review concluded that more rigorous trial data were urgently needed to assess nonpharmacologic treatments, such as education and exercise, in osteoarthritis.[23] **Exercise:** One RCT examined the effects of a structured exercise program on self-reported disability in 439 people over 60 years of age with osteoarthritis of the knee randomized to one of three programs: an aerobic exercise program, a resistance exercise program, or a health education program.[24] The two exercise groups experienced significant but modest reductions in disability and pain in comparison to the education group. A review of all published trials of nonmedicinal and noninvasive treatments for hip and knee osteoarthritis concluded that, of seven modalities reviewed, exercise had the strongest evidence of benefit.[25] A review of the efficacy of one form of exercise treatment—aerobic exercises for osteoarthritis of the knee[26]—found only three admissible RCTs. It concluded that despite a favorable impression, the evidence currently available was inadequate. **Education:** We found one meta-analysis of 10 studies of patient education in arthritis.[27] It concluded that education provided additional benefits to those of medications, with an absolute pain reduction in osteoarthritis of 0.16 (95% CI –0.69 to +1.02). However, there was no significant effect on disability. A controlled trial of 211 people with osteoarthritis of the knee compared self-care education versus attention only. The self-care education group derived greater benefit on pain and disability over the 1-year duration of the study.[28]

Harms: We found no evidence of harm.

Comment: The evidence is poor, with few well-designed RCTs, and the participants in many trials were not representative of those in the general population.

REFERENCES

1. Dougados M, Devogelaer JP, Annefeldt M, et al. Recommendations for the registration of drugs used in the treatment of osteoarthritis. *Ann Rheum Dis* 1996;55:552–557.
2. Altman R, Brandt K, Hochberg M, et al. Design and conduct of clinical trials in patients with osteoarthritis: recommendations from a task force of the Osteoarthritis Research Society. *Osteoarthritis Cartilage* 1996;4:217–243.
3. Towheed T, Shea B, Wells G, Hochberg M. Osteoarthritis: a systematic review of randomized controlled trials of analgesia and anti-inflammatory therapy in osteoarthritis of the hip. Cochrane Review Group. 1997. Search date 1994; primary sources MEDLINE and Cochrane Library, Controlled Clinical Trials Register.
4. Watson MC, Brookes ST, Kirwan JR, Faulkner A. Osteoarthritis: the comparative efficacy of non-aspirin non-steroidal anti-inflammatory drugs for the management of osteoarthritis of the knee. Cochrane Review Group. 1996. Primary sources MEDLINE (search date January 1980 to December 1995); BIDS (search date 1996); EMBASE (search date 1996).
5. Towheed TE, Hochberg MC. A systematic review of randomized controlled trials of pharmacological therapy in osteoarthritis of the knee, with an emphasis on trial methodology. *Semin Arthritis Rheum* 1997;26:755–770.
6. Amadio P, Cummings DM. Evaluation of acetaminophen in the management of osteoarthritis of the knee. *Curr Ther Res Clin Exp* 1983;34:59–66.
7. Schubiger BI, Ciccolunghi SN, Tanner K. Once daily dose treatment with a non-steroidal anti-rheumatic drug (Diclofenac) in osteoarthrosis. *J Int Med Res* 1980;8:167–174.
8. Williams HJ, Ward JR, Egger MJ, et al. Comparison of Naproxen and acetaminophen in a 2-year study of treatment of osteoarthritis of the knee. *Arthritis Rheum* 1993;36:1196–1206.
9. Bradley JD, Brandt KD, Katz BP, Kalasinski LA, Ryan SI. Comparison of an anti-inflammatory dose of Ibuprofen, an analgesic dose of Ibuprofen, and acetaminophen in the treatment of patients with osteoarthritis of the knee. *N Engl J Med* 1991;325:87–91.
10. March L, Irwig L, Schwarz J, Simpson J, Chick C, Brooks P. N of 1 trials comparing a non-steroidal anti-inflammatory drug with paracetamol in osteoarthritis. *BMJ* 1994;309:1041–1046.
11. Hawton K, Ware C, Mistry H, et al. Why patients choose paracetamol for self poisoning and their knowledge of its dangers. *BMJ* 1995;310:164.
12. Huskisson EC, Berry H, Gishen P, Jubb RW, Whitehead J. Effects of anti-inflammatory drugs on the progression of osteoarthritis of the knee. *J Rheumatol* 1995;22;1941–1946.
13. Langman MJ. Non-steroidal anti-inflammatory drugs and peptic ulcer. *Hepatogastroenterology* 1992;39(suppl 1):37–39.
14. Garcia Rodriguez LA, Williams R, Derby LE, Dean AD, Jick H. Acute liver injury associated with non-steroidal anti-inflammatory drugs and the role of risk factors. *Arch Intern Med* 1994;154:311–316.
15. Henry D, Lim LL, Garcia Rodriguez LA, et al. Variability in risk of gastrointestinal complications with individual non-steroidal anti-inflammatory drugs: results of a collaborative meta-analysis. *BMJ* 1996;312:1563–1566.
16. Brandt KD. Nonsurgical management of osteoarthritis, with an emphasis on nonpharmacologic measures. *Arch Fam Med* 1995;4: 1057–1064.
17. Wollheim FA. Current pharmacological treatment of osteoarthritis. Drugs 1996;52(suppl 3):27–38.
18. Moore RA, Tramer MR, Carroll D, Wiffen PJ, McQuay HJ. Quantitative systematic review of topically applied non-steroidal anti-inflammatory drugs. *BMJ* 1998;316:333–338.
19. Dickson DJ. A double-blind evaluation of topical piroxicam gel with oral ibuprofen in osteoarthritis of the knee. *Curr Ther Res Clin Exp* 1991;49: 199–207.
20. Roth SH. A controlled clinical investigation of 3% diclofenac/2.5% sodium hyaluronate topical gel in the treatment of uncontrolled pain in chronic oral NSAID users with osteoarthritis. *Int J Tissue React* 1995;17:129–132.
21. Zhang WY, Po ALW. The effectiveness of topically applied capsaicin–a meta-analysis. *Eur J Clin Pharmacol* 1994;46:517–522.
22. Deal CL, Schnitzer TJ, Lipstein E, et al. Treatment of arthritis with topical capsaicin–a double-blind trial. *Clin Ther* 1991;13:383–395.
23. Balint G, Szebenyi B. Non-pharmacological therapies in osteoarthritis. *Baillieres Clin Rheumatol* 1997;11:795–815.
24. Ettinger WH Jr, Burns R, Messier SP, et al. A randomized trial comparing aerobic exercise and resistance exercise with a health education program in older adults with knee osteoarthritis. The Fitness Arthritis and Seniors Trial (FAST). *JAMA* 1997;277:25–31.
25. Puett DW, Griffin MR. Published trials of non-medicinal and non-invasive therapies for hip and knee osteoarthritis. *Ann Intern Med* 1994;121: 133–140.
26. La Mantia K, Marks R. The efficacy of aerobic exercises for treating osteoarthritis of the knee. *NZ J Physiother* 1995;23:23–30.
27. Superio-Cabuslay E, Ward MM, Lorig KR. Patient education interventions in osteoarthritis and rheumatoid arthritis: a meta-analytic comparison with non-steroidal anti-inflammatory drug treatment. *Arthritis Care Res* 1996;9:292–301.
28. Mazzuca SA, Brandt KD, Katz BP, Chambers M, Byrd D, Hanna M. Effects of self-care education on the health status of inner-city patients with osteoarthritis of the knee. *Arthritis Rheum* 1997; 40:1466–1474.

Paul Dieppe, BSc, MBBS, MD, FRCPC, FFPHM
Director
MRC Health Services Research Collaboration
University of Bristol
Bristol
UK

Jiri Chard, MB
Research Associate
MRC Health Services Research Collaboration
University of Bristol
Bristol
UK

Competing interests: None declared.

TABLE 1 **Estimated relative risk of gastrointestinal adverse effects with the use of individual NSAIDs (pooled data from 12 studies).[15]** **(See text p. 203.)**

Drug	Pooled RR	95% CI for pooled RR
Ibuprofen (low dose)*		1.0
Fenoprofen	1.6	1.0–2.5
Aspirin	1.6	1.3–2.0
Diclofenac	1.8	1.4–2.3
Sulindac	2.1	1.6–2.7
Diflunisal	2.2	1.2–4.1
Naproxen	2.2	1.7–2.9
Indomethacin	2.4	1.9–3.1
Tolmetin	3.0	1.8–4.9
Piroxicam	3.8	2.7–5.2
Ketoprofen	4.2	2.7–6.4
Azapropazone†	9.2	4.0–21.0

*Comparative data used low-dose ibuprofen as the reference control for calculating the relative risk of other drugs.
†Not available in US.

Rheumatoid arthritis

Maria E Suarez-Almazor, MD, MSc, PhD

QUESTIONS

INTERVENTIONS

To be covered in future issues of *Clinical Evidence*
Biological treatments (monoclonal antibodies, cytokines, cell receptors)
New drugs (leflunomide, mycophenolic acid, amiprilose)

Key Messages

- Systematic reviews of randomized controlled trials (RCTs) have found that early intervention with a DMARD improves outcome at 1 year.
- Most DMARDs have been shown to be more effective than placebo in reducing disease activity and joint inflammation, but the effect of prolonged treatment with DMARDs (for >1 year) has not been evaluated adequately.
- Systematic reviews of RCTs have found no evidence of a difference in effectiveness between most DMARDs, although auranofin seems to be the least effective.
- The effects of combined treatment with two or more DMARDs have not been evaluated adequately.
- Systematic reviews of RCTs have found that low-dose oral steroids relieve symptoms and may slow radiologic progression. However, long-term use carries the risk of serious adverse effects.

DEFINITION Rheumatoid arthritis is a chronic inflammatory disorder of unknown etiology. It is characterized by a chronic polyarthritis affecting primarily the peripheral joints and related periarticular tissues. It usually starts as an insidious symmetric polyarthritis, often with nonspecific systemic symptoms. Diagnostic criteria include arthritis lasting longer than 6 weeks, positive rheumatoid factor, and radiologic damage.[1]

INCIDENCE/ PREVALENCE Prevalence varies in different series from 0.5% to 1.5% of the population in industrialized countries.[2,3] Rheumatoid arthritis occurs more frequently in women than men (ratio 2.5 : 1).[2,3] The annual incidence in women was recently estimated at 36/100,000 and in men 14/100,000.[3]

AETIOLOGY The evidence suggests a multifactorial etiology in people with a genetic susceptibility.[4]

PROGNOSIS The course of rheumatoid arthritis is variable and unpredictable. Some patients experience flares and remissions and others a progressive course. Over the years, structural damage may occur, often leading to articular deformities and functional impairment. Approximately half of patients will be disabled or unable to work within 10 years.[5] Rheumatoid arthritis also shortens life expectancy.[6]

AIMS To relieve symptoms and to prevent or limit disease activity, joint inflammation, joint damage, and disability with minimal adverse effects.

OUTCOMES Number of swollen or tender joints; pain score; acute phase reactants such as erythrocyte sedimentation rate (ESR); functional status; patient and physician global assessments; radiologic progression; and rates of withdrawal from treatment.

METHODS *Clinical Evidence* search up to the end of 1998 for systematic reviews and RCTs that met acceptable criteria.

QUESTION What are the effects of DMARDs?

OPTION METHOTREXATE

One systematic review of short-term RCTs has found that methotrexate is more effective than placebo in reducing joint inflammation and improving functional status in people with rheumatoid arthritis, although adverse effects (mainly abnormal liver enzymes) cause up to a quarter of patients to withdraw from treatment. Its long-term effects have not yet been evaluated adequately. Systematic reviews of RCTs have found no consistent differences between methotrexate and other DMARDs.

Benefits: **Versus placebo:** We found one systematic review, which identified five placebo-controlled RCTs of low-dose methotrexate (usually < 20 mg/wk) for 12 to 18 weeks in 161 patients.[7] It found a significant improvement in the number of swollen and tender joints, pain score, physician and patient global assessment, and functional status. There was no significant difference in ESR. **Versus other DMARDs:** We found four other systematic reviews of RCTs.[8–11] These reported no consistent differences between methotrexate and other DMARDs. However, the magnitude of short-term improvement in disease activity appeared to be larger for methotrexate than for other DMARDs. A systematic review of observational studies comparing the effect of methotrexate with other DMARDs on radiologic progression found a significant benefit from methotrexate only when compared with auranofin.[12] No significant difference was observed between methotrexate and parenteral gold.

Harms: In the systematic review of placebo-controlled trials, 22% of patients on methotrexate withdrew because of adverse effects, most commonly liver enzyme abnormalities (11%).[7] Other common adverse effects were mucocutaneous, gastrointestinal, or hematologic. Pulmonary toxicity, hepatic fibrosis, and infections occur occasionally, even at the low dosages usually used in rheumatoid arthritis. Another systematic review found that concurrent administration of folic acid decreased the risk of gastrointestinal and mucocutaneous adverse effects with no adverse impact on the efficacy of methotrexate.[13] Although some studies reported an increased risk of tumors, the results have not been consistent.

Comment: Observational studies have found that patients are more likely to continue methotrexate than any other DMARD.[14–17]

OPTION ANTIMALARIALS

One systematic review of RCTs has found that hydrochloroquine is more effective than placebo in reducing disease activity and joint inflammation in people with rheumatoid arthritis. Older, poorer-quality RCTs also have found benefit from chloroquine compared with placebo. Two trials provided no evidence of a beneficial effect on functional status and radiologic progression. Systematic reviews of RCTs provide no evidence of a difference in effectiveness between antimalarials and other DMARDs.

Benefits: **Versus placebo:** We found one systematic review, which identified four placebo-controlled RCTs of hydrochloroquine given for 6–12 months in 371 patients.[18] It reported a significant improvement in the number of swollen and tender joints, pain score, physician and patient global assessment, and ESR. One trial measured functional status, and another evaluated radiologic progression. No significant differences were observed for these outcomes. Older trials, which were not included in the systematic review because of methodologic concerns, have also shown a beneficial effect of chloroquine compared with placebo.[18] **Versus other DMARDs:** We found four systematic reviews of RCTs.[8–11] These reported no significant differences between antimalarials and other DMARDs. Individual trials failed to show a consistent preference for any one drug, although some reported better results with D-penicillamine and sulfasalazine than with antimalarials. **Hydrochloroquine versus chloroquine:** We found no trials adequately comparing chloroquine versus hydroxychloroquine; one older trial included both drugs but did not report a direct comparison.

Harms: Antimalarials at currently recommended dosages seem to have limited toxicity. The systematic review of placebo-controlled trials found no difference in the number of withdrawals because of adverse effects on placebo and hydroxychloroquine.[18] **Ocular toxicity:** No patients discontinued treatment because of ophthalmologic adverse effects, and mild toxicity was reported in only one patient. Long-term observational studies have reported that the risk for ocular toxicity is low and seems to be higher with chloroquine than hydroxychloroquine.[19,20] The optimal frequency for eye examinations has not been established reliably; expert opinion ranges from every 6 months to 2 years. **Nonocular adverse effects:** The most common are gastrointestinal disturbances. Skin reactions and renal abnormalities occasionally occur. Mild neurological abnormalities include nonspecific symptoms such as vertigo and blurred vision. Cardiomyopathy and severe neurological disease are extremely rare.

Comment: Observational studies seem to show that the long-term effectiveness of antimalarials is lower than for methotrexate or parenteral gold, with most patients discontinuing treatment because of lack of efficacy.[14–16]

OPTION SULFASALAZINE

One systematic review of RCTs has found that sulfasalazine is more effective than placebo in reducing disease activity and joint inflammation in people with rheumatoid arthritis. Its effects on radiologic progression and functional status have not yet been evaluated adequately. Systematic reviews provide no evidence of a difference between sulfasalazine and other DMARDs.

Benefits: **Versus placebo:** We found one systematic review, which identified six placebo-controlled RCTs of sulfasalazine given for 6 months.[21] Analysis of data pooled from four trials in 252 patients found a significant improvement in the number of tender and swollen joints, pain score, and ESR. Only some trials included global assessments and evaluation of radiologic progression, with inconclusive results. None evaluated functional status. **Versus other DMARDs:** Several systematic reviews found no significant differences between sulfasalazine and other DMARDs. A RCT comparing sulfasalazine versus hydroxychloroquine found that sulfasalazine was significantly better in controlling radiologic damage, although progression occurred with both drugs.[22] However, hydroxychloroquine was given at a lower dose than usually is recommended.

Harms: Common adverse effects include gastrointestinal discomfort, rash, and liver enzyme abnormalities. More serious hematologic or hepatic toxicity is uncommon. Reversible leucopenia or agranulocytosis are occasionally observed. Treatment is discontinued for adverse effects less often than with other DMARDs, with the exception of antimalarials.

Comment: Observational studies have reported lower long-term efficacy of sulfasalazine compared with other DMARDs, such as methotrexate or parenteral gold, with most patients discontinuing treatment because of lack of efficacy.[17]

OPTION PARENTERAL GOLD

One systematic review of RCTs has found that parenteral gold is more effective than placebo in reducing disease activity and joint inflammation in people with rheumatoid arthritis. We also found evidence that parenteral gold may slow radiologic progression. We found no evidence on its effect on long-term functional status. Systematic reviews provide no evidence of a difference between parenteral gold and other DMARDs.

Benefits: **Versus placebo:** One systematic review, which identified four placebo-controlled RCTs of parenteral gold given for 6 months in 309 patients.[23] It found a significant improvement in the number of swollen joints, patient and physician global assessments, and ESR. Functional status was not evaluated. A systematic review of trials and observational studies, including radiologic assessment, found that parenteral gold decreased the rate of radiologic progression.[24] **Versus other DMARDs:** We found four systematic reviews of RCTs.[8–11] These reported no consistent differences between parenteral gold and other DMARDs. Parenteral gold was found in some trials to be more effective but also more toxic than its oral counterpart, auranofin. A few trials comparing parenteral gold versus methotrexate found no difference in short-term efficacy but increased toxicity with methotrexate.

Harms: In the systematic review of placebo-controlled trials, approximately 30% of the patients receiving gold discontinued treatment because of adverse effects, including dermatitis, stomatitis, proteinuria, and hematologic changes.[23] Life-threatening reactions, such as aplastic anemia or nephrotic syndrome, are rare.

Comment: Use of parenteral gold is limited mainly by toxicity.

OPTION AURANOFIN (ORAL GOLD)

We found limited evidence from RCTs that auranofin (oral gold) reduces disease activity and joint inflammation in people with rheumatoid arthritis. We found no evidence of its effect on radiologic progression or long-term functional status. We found limited evidence from direct comparisons that auranofin is less effective than other DMARDs.

Benefits: **Versus placebo:** We found no recent systematic review. Several RCTs found that auranofin was superior to placebo. **Versus other DMARDs:** Clinical trials comparing auranofin versus other DMARDs, such as antimalarials, found no consistent differences. However, a systematic review of RCTs published in 1992, concluded that auranofin was significantly less effective than other DMARDs.[9] A meta-analysis found auranofin to be less effective than parenteral gold in controlling disease activity.[25]

Harms: The major adverse effects of auranofin are diarrhea and gastrointestinal discomfort. Serious adverse effects, such as those associated with parenteral gold, are very rare with auranofin.

Comment: None.

OPTION MINOCYCLINE

We found limited evidence from RCTs that minocycline is more effective than placebo in controlling disease activity in people with rheumatoid arthritis. We found no evidence of its effect on radiologic progression or functional status. It has not been compared directly to other DMARDs.

Benefits: **Versus placebo:** We found no systematic review. Several placebo-controlled RCTs found that minocycline was superior to placebo in controlling disease activity.[26–28] **Versus other DMARDs:** We found no RCTs.

Harms: Adverse reactions include nausea, dyspepsia, photosensitivity, and vertigo. Serious adverse effects are rare.

Comment: The magnitude of the beneficial effects of minocycline seems to be moderate, similar to that observed with antimalarials or sulfasalazine. However, we found no direct comparisons with other DMARDs, and its precise place in the treatment of rheumatoid arthritis remains to be determined.

OPTION PENICILLAMINE

One systematic review of RCTs has found that D-penicillamine is effective compared with placebo in reducing disease activity and joint inflammation in people with rheumatoid arthritis. We found no evidence of its effect on radiologic progression or long-term functional status. Systematic reviews of RCTs have found no difference compared with other DMARDs. Common and potentially serious adverse effects limit its usefulness.

Benefits: **Versus placebo:** We found one systematic review, which identified six placebo-controlled RCTs of penicillamine.[29] It found significant improvement in the number of swollen joints and ESR. Only some of the studies evaluated global assessment and functional status, with inconclusive results. **Versus other DMARDs:** Systematic reviews of RCTs have found no consistent differences between penicillamine and other drugs,[8,9] although some trials have shown it to be superior to antimalarials.

Harms: Adverse effects are common and can be serious. Reactions include mucocutaneous reactions, altered taste, gastrointestinal reactions, proteinuria, hematologic effects, myositis, and autoimmune-induced disease.

Comment: The use of D-penicillamine is limited by the frequency of serious adverse reactions. Observational studies show that most patients discontinue the drug within 1 year.

OPTION AZATHIOPRINE

One systematic review of small RCTs has found that azathioprine is more effective than placebo in reducing disease activity in people with rheumatoid arthritis. We found no evidence of its effect on radiologic progression or long-term functional status. We found no evidence that it is superior to other DMARDs, and toxicity limits its usefulness.

Benefits: **Versus placebo:** We found one systematic review, which identified three placebo-controlled RCTs of azathioprine in 81 patients.[30] It reported a significant benefit from azathioprine. However, not all studies reported all outcomes, and some of the benefits were observed in only one trial. **Versus other DMARDs:** One RCT found azathioprine to be less effective than methotrexate. No other consistent differences between azathioprine and other DMARDs have been reported.

Harms: Nausea and abnormal liver enzymes are common adverse effects. Serious hematologic adverse reactions include leukopenia, thrombocytopenia, and anemia. Azathioprine is an immunosuppressive drug, and its use has been associated with increased risk of infection and tumors.

Comment: Because of its toxicity profile, azathioprine tends to be reserved for patients who have not responded to other DMARDs.

OPTION CYCLOPHOSPHAMIDE

One systematic review of small RCTs has found that cyclophosphamide is more effective than placebo in reducing disease activity and joint inflammation in people with rheumatoid arthritis. It also may reduce the rate of radiologic progression, but the evidence in this respect is limited. We found no evidence of its effect on long-term functional status. We found no evidence that it is more effective than other DMARDs. Severe toxicity limits its usefulness.

Benefits: **Versus placebo:** We found one systematic review, which identified three placebo-controlled RCTs of cyclophosphamide given for 6 months.[31] Pooled analysis of data from 70 patients showed a significant improvement in the number of tender and swollen joints. There was no significant difference in ESR. One trial reported radiologic progression, which appeared to be delayed in the cyclophosphamide group. **Versus other DMARDs:** Only a few trials have compared cyclophosphamide versus other DMARDs. These provide no good evidence of superiority.

Harms: Adverse effects include nausea, vomiting, alopecia, and amenorrhea. Severe reactions include leukopenia, thrombocytopenia, and anemia. Patients on cyclophosphamide are at increased risk of infections, such as herpes zoster. Prolonged use has been associated with increased risk of cancer.

Comment: Because of its cytotoxic effects, cyclophosphamide should be reserved for patients who have not responded to other DMARDs. Another related drug, chlorambucil, also has been used in severe rheumatoid arthritis unresponsive to other DMARDs.

OPTION CYCLOSPORIN

One systematic review of RCTs has found that cyclosporin reduces disease activity and joint inflammation, and improves functional status compared with placebo in people with rheumatoid arthritis. We found some evidence that it may decrease the rate of radiologic progression. Severe toxicity limits its usefulness.

Benefits: **Versus placebo:** We found one systematic review, which identified three RCTs of cyclosporin given for a minimum of 4 months.[32] It found a significant improvement in the number of tender and swollen joints and in functional status. Radiologic progression also was reduced. **Versus other DMARDs:** Only a few trials have compared cyclosporin with other DMARDs, such as methotrexate or antimalarials, with no clear evidence of superiority.

Harms: **Renal toxicity:** Patients may develop nephropathy, which can be irreversible, and hypertension. **Other adverse reactions:** These include nausea and dyspepsia, hypertrichosis, gingival hyperplasia, and hepatotoxicity. Cyclosporin has been associated with an increased risk of infections and tumors.

Comment: Cyclosporin should be reserved for patients with severe disease or those who do not respond to other less toxic DMARDs.

QUESTION Which DMARD is the treatment of choice?

We found no good evidence to suggest that one DMARD is more effective than another for initial treatment of rheumatoid arthritis, although auranofin seems to be the least effective. Penicillamine, azathioprine, cyclophosphamide, and cyclosporin are considered too toxic for first-line use. Trade-offs between efficacy, toxicity, costs, and patient preferences should be considered when choosing a DMARD for a given patient.

Benefits: We found two systematic reviews evaluating placebo-controlled RCTs of various DMARDs.[10,11] One found the efficacy of most drugs to be modest, with the overall risk of discontinuing treatment greater for the active drug than for placebo.[10] The other found no significant differences among most DMARDs compared with placebo; only methotrexate seemed slightly better for some outcomes, such as joint inflammation.[11] Two other systematic reviews compared the efficacy and toxicity of various DMARDs based on 66 trials with 117 treatment groups.[8,9] Results were pooled, "lumping" together all placebo groups from the different trials and all specific drug groups, providing a single summary measure for each drug. This approach has flaws (see Comment). Auranofin was significantly less effective than other drugs, although more effective than placebo. The differences between methotrexate, D-penicillamine, parenteral gold, and sulfasalazine were not significant and were clinically negligible. Parenteral gold had the highest withdrawal rate because of toxicity, whereas auranofin had the lowest withdrawal rate. Observational studies suggest that methotrexate has the greatest impact on disease activity and is more effective in the longer term.[14–17] It also acts faster than the other DMARDs, usually taking effect after 6 to 8 weeks.

Harms: The DMARDs most frequently prescribed as initial treatment are methotrexate, sulfasalazine, and antimalarials. These three drugs have a lower toxicity profile than others, although methotrexate may be more toxic than antimalarials or sulfasalazine.

Comment: The method of analysis used in the two systematic reviews mentioned above[8,9] removes the value of randomization, and the summary results cannot be truly considered as summary measures of RCTs. The approach recommended by the Cochrane Collaboration is to conduct various meta-analyses, one for each specific group of comparisons, and evaluate the effects of each drug within each group. The various interventions then can be compared by examining the magnitude of the effect sizes.

QUESTION **What are the effects of combining DMARDs?**

One systematic review of RCTs has found that combinations of certain DMARDs are more effective than individual drugs alone. However, the evidence remains conflicting and the balance between benefits and harms varies among combinations.

Benefits: We found one systematic review published in 1998, which identified 20 RCTs in 1956 people with rheumatoid arthritis. It concluded that many combinations of DMARDs may be useful.[33] Nine of the RCTs in 1240 people compared methotrexate plus another DMARD versus methotrexate or the other DMARD alone. A wide range of other DMARDs were included. The review found that methotrexate combined with most other DMARDs was more beneficial than treatment with a single drug.[33]

Harms: The toxicity of combination treatments depends on the drugs used. Potential synergistic interactions also should be considered. In some instances, combination treatment may be worse than using a single agent because of interactions between drugs.

Comment: An additional meta-analysis pooled data from RCTs comparing single versus combination drug treatment.[34] However, the analysis did not provide adequate data on specific combinations.

QUESTION **When should DMARDs be introduced?**

We found limited evidence from RCTs suggesting that people with active rheumatoid arthritis should start treatment with DMARDs early in the course of their disease.

Benefits: We found no systematic review. A RCT of 238 people with recently diagnosed rheumatoid arthritis compared early (within 1 year of symptom onset) versus delayed treatment with DMARDs.[35] Patients who received early treatment had significantly better outcomes at 12 months, including measures of disability, pain, joint inflammation, and ESR. No differences were observed in radiologic progression between the early and delayed groups. A prospective 3-year follow-up of 119 patients with early disease who participated in a placebo controlled trial of hydroxychloroquine found that a 9-month delay in instituting DMARD treatment had a significant detrimental effect on pain intensity and patient global well being.[36]

Harms: Apprxoimately 10% of people with rheumatoid arthritis experience a short illness that resolves and remains largely quiescent. Early treatment may expose them unnecessarily to adverse effects.

Comment: The only evidence on the effects of delaying treatment in patients with rheumatoid arthritis is from the trials discussed above. These suggest that, on average, it is more harmful to delay treatment. However, average results do not always apply to the individual patient. Careful consideration should be given to patients with mild or atypical rheumatoid arthritis, perhaps waiting to initiate treatment for a few more weeks until the clinical course is better defined.

QUESTION For how long should DMARDs be given?

We found no good evidence on which to base guidance on the optimum duration of treatment with DMARDs. Few trials have followed patients for more than 1 year, and most patients discontinue treatment with an individual drug within a few years because of toxicity or lack of effectiveness.

Benefits: We found one review of 122 controlled clinical trials and observational studies of DMARDs involving 16,071 patients. It found that 90% of the patients in clinical trials had been followed for 1 year or less.[37] Short-term clinical trials in patients with rheumatoid arthritis found beneficial effects for most of the DMARDs currently in use, but in the longer term the effectiveness of these drugs seems to decline. Observational studies have found that after a few years, most patients have discontinued the prescribed DMARD, either because of toxicity or lack of effectiveness.[14–17]

Harms: Serious adverse effects are common, limiting the long-term usefulness of DMARDs. Trials of longer duration may not be feasible because many patients will eventually receive a different or additional DMARD, contaminating the original groups.

Comment: It is difficult to evaluate the longer-term effects of individual DMARDs. Some studies have examined the effect of drug discontinuation, most often with parenteral gold or methotrexate. We found limited evidence that discontinuation of DMARD treatment, even for patients in remission, may result in a disease exacerbation or flare. Nevertheless, this will not be the case for every patient. Until better evidence is available, patients should be informed about possible harms from discontinuing treatment, which should be weighed against the risks of drug toxicity from prolonged treatment.

QUESTION What are the effects of low-dose oral corticosteroids?

Systematic reviews of RCTs have found benefit from both short- and longer-term (>3 mo) treatment with low-dose oral corticosteroids. Short-term treatment reduces disease activity and joint inflammation. Longer-term treatment may reduce radiologic progression while treatment continues. However, long-term use is associated with considerable adverse effects.

Benefits: **Versus placebo or nonsteroidal anti-inflammatory drugs (NSAIDs):** We found two systematic reviews. One compared short-term (weeks) treatment with low-dose prednisolone (≤15 mg/d) versus placebo or NSAIDs.[38] It found that, in the short term, prednisolone had a greater effect than placebo or NSAIDs in controlling disease activity. The other review evaluated longer-term treatment with corticosteroids (for at least 3 months).[39] One of the trials included in this review evaluated radiologic damage and found a significant decrease in the rate of progression in patients treated with prednisolone 7.5 mg/d compared with placebo over 2 years.[40] A follow-up study of patients in this trial found that joint destruction resumed after discontinuing the prednisolone.[41] **Versus chloroquine:** The second review found no significant difference between oral prednisone and chloroquine in improving disease activity.[39]

Harms: Serious long-term adverse effects of corticosteroids include hypertension, diabetes, osteoporosis, infections, gastrointestinal ulcers, obesity, and hirsutism. Observational studies of patients with rheumatoid arthritis have suggested that mortality may be increased by long-term treatment. However, many of these studies included patients receiving doses higher than those currently recommended (> 7.5 mg).

Comment: The decision to give a patient oral corticosteroids should balance the potential for increased comorbidity, which is affected by the patient's individual risk factors and the potential improvement in disease activity.

REFERENCES

1. Arnett FC, Edworthy SM, Bloch DA, et al. The American Rheumatism Association 1987 revised criteria for the classification of rheumatoid arthritis. *Arthritis Rheum* 1988;31:315–324.
2. Lawrence RC, Helmick CG, Arnett FC, et al. Estimates of the prevalence of arthritis and selected musculoskeletal disorders in the United States. *Arthritis Rheum* 1998;41:778–799.
3. Symmons DP, Barrett EM, Bankhead CR, Scott DG, Silman AJ. The incidence of rheumatoid arthritis in the United Kingdom: results from the Norfolk Arthritis Register. *Br J Rheumatol* 1994; 33:735–739.
4. Winchester R, Dwyer E, Rose S. The genetic basis of rheumatoid arthritis: the shared epitope hypothesis. *Rheum Dis Clin North Am* 1992;18: 761–783.
5. Yelin E, Henke C, Epstein W. The work dynamics of the person with rheumatoid arthritis. *Arthritis Rheum* 1987;30:507–512.
6. Mutru O, Laakso M, Isomäki H, Koota K. Ten year mortality and causes of death in patients with rheumatoid arthritis. *BMJ* 1985;290:1797–1799.
7. Suarez-Almazor ME, Belseck E, Shea B, Wells G, Tugwell P. Rheumatoid arthritis (RA): methotrexate vs. placebo. In: Tugwell P, Brooks P, Wells G, de Bie R, Bosi-Ferraz M, Gillespie W, eds. Musculoskeletal module of The Cochrane Database of Systematic Reviews. In: The Cochrane Library, Issue 3, 1998. Oxford: Update Software. Search date 1997; primary sources MEDLINE 1966 to July 1997; EMBASE 1988 to July 1997, Cochrane Controlled Trials Register searched up to 1997, and hand search of reference lists.
8. Felson DT, Anderson JJ, Meenan RF. The comparative efficacy and toxicity of second-line drugs in rheumatoid arthritis: results of two meta-analyses. *Arthritis Rheum* 1990;33:1449—1461. Search date 1989; primary sources MEDLINE 1966 to August 1989. Hand search of two key journals and reference lists.
9. Felson DT, Anderson JJ, Meenan RF. Use of short-term efficacy/toxicity trade-offs to select second-line drugs in rheumatoid arthritis: a meta-analysis of published clinical trials. *Arthritis Rheum* 1992;35:1117–1125. Search date 1990; primary sources MEDLINE 1966–December 1990. Hand search of 2 key journals and reference lists.
10. Gotzsche PC, Podenphant J, Olesen M, Halberg P. Meta-analysis of second-line antirheumatic drugs: sample size bias and uncertain benefit. *J Clin Epidemiol* 1992;45:587–594. Search date 1998; primary source MEDLINE September 1966 to 1988; hand searching of reference lists and drug companies contacted for unpublished trials.
11. Suarez-Almazor ME, Belseck E, Wells G, Shea B, Tugwell P. Meta-analyses of placebo controlled trials of disease-modifying antirheumatic drugs (DMARD) for the treatment of rheumatoid arthritis (RA). *Arthritis Rheum* 1998;41:S153. Search date not specified; primary sources MEDLINE and EMBASE.
12. Alarcon GS, Lopez-Mendez A, Walter J, et al. Radiographic evidence of disease progression in methotrexate treated and nonmethotrexate disease modifying antirheumatic drug treated rheumatoid arthritis patients: a meta-analysis. *J Rheumatol* 1992;19:1868–1873. Search date 1991; primary sources MEDLINE 1970 to May 1991. Handsearch of bibliographies and meetings abstract of the American College of Rheumatology 1988–1991.
13. Ortiz Z, Shea B, Suarez-Almazor ME, Moher D, Wells GA, Tugwell P. The efficacy of folic acid and folinic acid in reducing methotrexate gastrointestinal toxicity in rheumatoid arthritis: a meta-analysis of randomised controlled trials. *J Rheumatol* 1998;25;36–43. Search date 1996; primary sources MEDLINE 1966 to Dec 1996;

Hand search bibliographic references; Current Contents June 1996 to Dec 1996, and abstracts of selected rheumatology meetings and journals.
14. Wolfe F, Hawley DJ, Cathey MA. Termination of slow acting anti-rheumatic therapy in rheumatoid arthritis: a 14 year prospective evaluation of 1017 starts. *J Rheumatol* 1990;17:994–1002.
15. Pincus T, Marcum SB, Callahan LF. Longterm drug therapy for rheumatoid arthritis in seven rheumatology private practices: II. second line drugs and prednisone. *J Rheumatol* 1992;19:1885–1894.
16. Fries JF, Williams CA, Ramey D, Bloch DA. The relative toxicity of disease-modifying antirheumatic drugs. *Arthritis Rheum* 1993;36:297–306.
17. Suarez-Almazor ME, Soskolne CL, Saunders LD, Russell AS. Use of second-line drugs in the treatment of rheumatoid arthritis in Edmonton, Alberta: patterns of prescription and long-term effectiveness. *J Rheumatol* 1995;22:836–843.
18. Suarez-Almazor ME, Belseck E, Shea B, Homik J, Wells G, Tugwell P. Rheumatoid arthritis (RA): antimalarials vs. placebo. In: Tugwell P, Brooks P, Wells G, de Bie R, Bosi-Ferraz M, Gillespie W, eds. Musculoskeletal module of The Cochrane Database of Systematic Reviews. In: The Cochrane Library, Issue 3, 1998. Oxford: Update Software. Search date 1997; primary sources MEDLINE 1966 to July 1997; EMBASE 1988 to July 1997, Cochrane Controlled Trials Register searched up to 1997, and hand search of reference lists.
19. Finbloom DS, Silver K, Newsome DA, Gunkel R. Comparison of hydroxychloroquine and chloroquine use and the development of retinal toxicity. *J Rheumatol* 1985;12:692–694.
20. Easterbrook M. The ocular safety of hydroxychloroquine. *Semin Arthritis Rheum* 1993;23:62–67.
21. Suarez-Almazor ME, Belseck E, Shea B, Wells G, Tugwell P. Rheumatoid arthritis (RA): sulfasalazine vs. placebo. In: Tugwell P, Brooks P, Wells G, de Bie R, Bosi-Ferraz M, Gillespie W, eds. Musculoskeletal module of The Cochrane Database of Systematic Reviews. The Cochrane Library; Issue 3, 1998. Oxford: Update Software. Search date 1997; primary sources MEDLINE 1966 to July 1997; EMBASE 1988 to July 1997, Cochrane Controlled Trials Register searched up to 1997, and hand search of reference lists.
22. Van der Heijde DM, van Riel PL, Nuver-Zwart IH, Gribnau FW, van de Putte LB. Effects of hydroxychloroquine and sulphasalazine on progression of joint damage in rheumatoid arthritis. *Lancet* 1989;1:1036–1038.
23. Clark P, Tugwell P, Bennet K, et al. Meta-analysis of injectable gold in rheumatoid arthritis. In: Tugwell P, Brooks P, Wells G, de Bie R, Bosi-Ferraz M, Gillespie W, eds. Musculoskeletal module of The Cochrane Database of Systematic Reviews. The Cochrane Library, Issue 3, 1998. Oxford: Update Software. Search date 1997 primary sources MEDLINE 1966–July 1997 and hand search of reference lists and bibliographies in selected textbooks
24. Rau R. Does parenteral gold inhibit roentgen progression of chronic polyarthritis? *Z Rheumatol* 1996;55:307–318.
25. Berkey CS, Anderson JJ, Hoaglin DC. Multiple outcome meta-analysis of clinical trials. *Stat Med* 1996;15:537–557.
26. Kloppenburg M, Breedveld FC, Terwiel JP, Mallee C, Dijkmans BA. Minocycline in active rheumatoid arthritis: a double-blind, placebo-controlled trial. *Arthritis Rheum* 1994;37:629–636.
27. Tilley BC, Alarcon GS, Heyse SP, et al. Minocycline in rheumatoid arthritis: a 48-week, double-blind, placebo-controlled trial. MIRA trial group. *Ann Intern Med* 1995;122:81–89.
28. O'Dell JR, Haire CE, Palmer W, et al. Treatment of early rheumatoid arthritis with minocycline or placebo: results of a randomized, double-blind, placebo-controlled trial. *Arthritis Rheum* 1997; 40:842–848.
29. Suarez-Almazor ME, Belseck E, Shea B, Wells G, Tugwell P. Rheumatoid arthritis (RA): penicillamine versus placebo in RA. In: Tugwell P, Brooks P, Wells G, de Bie R, Bosi-Ferraz M, Gillespie W, eds. Musculoskeletal module of The Cochrane Database of Systematic Reviews. The Cochrane Library, Issue 1, 1999. Oxford: Update Software.
30. Suarez-Almazor ME, Belseck E, Shea B, Wells G, Tugwell P. Rheumatoid arthritis (RA): azathioprine versus placebo in RA. In: Tugwell P, Brooks P, Wells G, de Bie R, Bosi-Ferraz M, Gillespie W, eds. Musculoskeletal module of The Cochrane Database of Systematic Reviews. The Cochrane Library, Issue 1, 1999. Oxford: Update Software.
31. Suarez-Almazor ME, Belseck E, Shea B, Wells G, Tugwell P. Rheumatoid arthritis (RA): cyclophosphamide versus placebo in RA. In: Tugwell P, Brooks P, Wells G, de Bie R, Bosi-Ferraz M, Gillespie W, eds. Musculoskeletal module of The Cochrane Database of Systematic Reviews. The Cochrane Library, Issue 1, 1999. Oxford: Update Software. Search date 1997; primary sources MEDLINE 1966 to Dec 1997; EMBASE 1988 to Dec 1997, and hand search of reference lists.
32. Wells G, Haguenauer D, Shea B, Suarez-Almazor ME, Welch VA, Tugwell P. Rheumatoid arthritis (RA): cyclosporine vs placebo. In: Tugwell P, Brooks P, Wells G, de Bie R, Bosi-Ferraz M, Gillespie W, eds. Musculoskeletal module of The Cochrane Database of Systematic Reviews. The Cochrane Library, Issue 3, 1998. Oxford: Update Software. Search date 1997; primary sources MEDLINE 1966 to 1997and hand search of reference lists, consultation with experts.
33. Verhoeven AC, Boers M, Tugwell P. Combination therapy in rheumatoid arthritis: updated systematic review. *Br J Rheumatol* 1998;37:612–619. Search date 1992; primary sources MEDLINE. Handsearch of 5 rheumatology journals and meetings abstracts.
34. Felson DT, Anderson JJ, Meenan RF. The efficacy and toxicity of combination therapy in rheumatoid arthritis: a meta-analysis. *Arthritis Rheum* 1994; 37:1487–1491.
35. Van Der Heide A, Jacobs JW, Bijlsma JW, et al. The effectiveness of early treatment with 'second-line' antirheumatic drugs: a randomized, controlled trial. *Ann Intern Med* 1996;124:699–707.
36. Egsmose C, Lund B, Borg G, et al. Patients with rheumatoid arthritis benefit from early second line therapy: 5 year follow up of a prospective double blind placebo controlled study. *J Rheumatol* 1995;22:2208–2213.
37. Hawley DJ, Wolfe F. Are the results of controlled clinical trials and observational studies of second line therapy in rheumatoid arthritis valid and generalizeable as measures of rheumatoid arthritis outcomes? An analysis of 122 studies. *J Rheumatol* 1991;18:1008–1014.
38. Gotzsche PC, Johansen HK. Meta-analysis of short term low dose prednisolone versus placebo and non-steroidal anti-inflammatory drugs in rheumatoid arthritis. *BMJ* 1998;316:811–818. Search date 1997; primary sources MEDLINE 1966-Sept 1997; Cochrane Controlled Trials Register searched up to Sept 1997, and hand search of reference lists.
39. Criswell LA, Saag KG, Sems KM, et al. Rheumatoid arthritis (RA): Moderate-term low

dose corticosteroids. In: Tugwell P, Brooks P, Wells G, de Bie R, Bosi-Ferraz M, Gillespie W, eds. Musculoskeletal module of The Cochrane Database of Systematic Reviews. The Cochrane Library, Issue 1, 1999. Oxford: Update Software. Search date 1998; primary sources MEDLINE 1966 to May 1998; and hand search of selected journals

40. Kirwan JR. Arthritis and Rheumatism Council low dose glucocorticoid study group: the effect of glucocorticoids on joint destruction in rheumatoid arthritis. *N Engl J Med* 1995;333:142–146.
41. Hickling P, Jacoby RK, Kirwan JR, et al. Joint destruction after glucocorticoids are withdrawn in early rheumatoid arthritis. *Br J Rheumatol* 1998;37:930–936.

Maria E Suarez-Almazor, MD, MSc, PhD
Associate Professor of Public Health Sciences
University of Alberta
Edmonton
Canada

Competing interests: The author has been reimbursed by Sanofi-Winthrop, manufacturer of hydroxychloroquine, for attending a conference, and as a consultant in a study unrelated to this review.

Neck pain

Allan Binder, FRCP, MD

QUESTIONS

INTERVENTIONS

Key Messages

- We found little good-quality evidence. This highlights the need for prospective studies with standardized validation of diagnosis and good study design.

DEFINITION Neck pain will be considered in this review under the headings of uncomplicated pain, whiplash, and pain with radiculopathy. Patients commonly present with pain, limitation of movement, and, frequently, ill-defined neurologic symptoms affecting the upper limbs. However, they also can present with radiculopathy or myelopathy, sometimes with severe or intractable pain. Assessment should exclude serious pathology (e.g., inflammatory arthritis, polymyalgia rheumatica, or malignancy) and should attempt to distinguish the local cause of neck pain.

INCIDENCE/ PREVALENCE At least half of all people will develop neck pain at some stage in their lives.[1] Prevalence is highest in middle age. In the UK, neck pain accounts for approximately 15% of hospital-based physiotherapy; in Canada, 30% of chiropractic referrals are for neck pain.[2,3] Neck stiffness occurs in 30% of the 25- to 29-year-old working population in the US, rising to 50% in those over 45 years of age.[4]

ETIOLOGY The etiology of neck pain is poorly understood but believed to be multifactorial. Most uncomplicated pain is caused by poor posture, anxiety and depression, neck strain, or occupational or sport injuries. With chronic pain, mechanical and degenerative factors often referred to as cervical spondylosis become more evident, but the boundary between normal aging and cervical spondylosis is difficult to define. Some neck pain results from soft tissue trauma, most typically seen in whiplash syndrome. Rarely, disk prolapse and inflammatory, infective, or malignant conditions affect the cervical spine and present with neck pain with or without neurological features.

PROGNOSIS Neck pain is usually acute and self-limiting within days or weeks but can recur and become chronic. In some industries, neck-related disorders account for as much absenteeism as low-back pain.[5] The exact percentage of people in whom neck pain becomes chronic depends on etiology but is thought to be approximately 10%, similar to low-back pain. Whiplash-type injuries cause more severe disability and up to 40% of patients will suffer long-lasting symptoms, irrespective of treatment even after 15 years of continuous follow-up.[6] Factors associated with a poorer outcome following whiplash include neck stiffness before the injury and degenerative changes on radiographs at presentation.[7]

AIMS To reduce pain, to improve range of movement, and to prevent long-term disability.

OUTCOMES Pain; range of movement; function.

METHODS We searched MEDLINE, EMBASE, Chirolars, and the Cochrane database to identify English language articles from 1966 to 1998. Randomized controlled trials (RCTs) and other well-designed prospective studies were included, with particular emphasis on papers already evaluated for inclusion in previously published systematic reviews.

QUESTION **How effective are treatments for people with uncomplicated neck pain without severe neurological deficit?**

OPTION **PHYSICAL TREATMENTS**

We found insufficient evidence to support the use of most physical treatments—heat or cold, exercise, traction, electrotherapy, biofeedback, spray and stretch, acupuncture, and laser—in patients with uncomplicated neck pain without neurological deficit.

Benefits: We found one systematic review of 13 RCTs, including 760 patients without neurological deficit.[8] It found no significant benefit from any of the following physical treatments: heat or cold, exercise, traction, electrotherapy (pulsing electromagnetic field and transcutaneous electrical nerve stimulation), biofeedback, spray and stretch, acupuncture, and laser.[8] All studies included at least one physical treatment from those mentioned above. One RCT of 47 patients included in the review found a significant immediate benefit in pain reduction ($p < 0.05$) with active physiotherapy and exercise compared with passive treatment.[9]

Harms: We found no good data on harms. Incidence of serious adverse events seems to be low for all the physical treatments considered.

Comment: None.

OPTION **MANUAL TREATMENTS: MOBILIZATION AND MANIPULATION**

Two systematic reviews found possible but unproved benefit from manipulation and mobilization not requiring instrumentation or anesthesia.

Benefits: We found two systematic reviews that evaluated mobilization (defined as any manual treatment to improve joint function that does not involve high-velocity movement, anesthesia, or instrumentation) and chiropractic manipulation (the use of short- or long-lever high-velocity thrusts directed at one or more of the cervical spine joints that does not involve anesthesia or instrumentation).[10,11] **Mobilization:** One RCT (which was included in both systematic reviews) evaluated 30 patients with acute pain. It found no significant pain reduction with mobilization compared with analgesics, collar, or transcutaneous nerve stimulation.[12] However, the trial was too small to exclude a beneficial effect. Two other RCTs included patients with chronic neck lesions and found modest benefit from mobilization in the short term. The first of these compared mobilization plus analgesia versus less active physiotherapy plus analgesia in 63 patients.[13] It found significant pain reduction with mobilization in the 1st month but not thereafter; 83% of the mobilization group improved compared with 60% of the physiotherapy group ($p < 0.05$, unable to extract CIs from the report). The second RCT compared manual treatment (mobilization, manipulation, or both) versus physical treatment (heat, electrotherapy, ultrasound, shortwave diathermy), placebo (detuned shortwave diathermy or ultrasound), or usual medical care (analgesics, advice, home exercise, and bedrest) in 256 patients with chronic neck and back pain, 64 having chronic neck pain alone.[14] The study found significant benefit from manual treatment, which was sustained for 12 months. However, it was not possible to compare directly the effects of the two manual treatments, and more patients received manipulation. **Manipulation:** We found one nonsystematic meta-analysis (part of one of the systematic reviews[11]) of three RCTs in 155 patients with chronic pain. These compared manipulation versus diazepam,[15] anti-inflammatory drugs,[16] or usual medical care[14] (*see* above). This found that manipulation led to nonsignificant pain reduction at 3 weeks compared with the control groups (an improvement benefit of 12.6 mm on a 100-mm visual analog scale 95% CI 0.15–25.5), the difference just failing to reach significance ($p > 0.05$).[11] **Mobilization versus manipulation:** We found one RCT of 100 patients with mainly chronic neck pain that compared a single mobilization treatment versus a single manipulation treatment.[17] It found no significant difference between groups: immediate in pain was recorded in 69% of patients with mobilization and 85% with manipulation (RR of improvement in pain with manipulation compared with mobilization 1.23, $p = 0.05$ but corrects to $p = 0.16$ after adjusting for pretreatment differences between the groups). Patients in the manipulation group had improved range of movement, but the result was not significant.

Harms: **Mobilization:** Not well documented. There have been occasional reports of increased pain but no serious adverse effects or deaths. The risk is probably very low. **Manipulation:** Rare but serious adverse effects have been reported, including death and serious disability caused by vertebrobasilar and other strokes, dissection of the vertebral arteries, disk herniation, and other serious neurological complications. The estimated risk of serious adverse effects from case reports is 5 to 10 per 10 million manipulations.[11]

Comment: Although the complication rate is low, the potential for manipulation to cause death or permanent disability must be considered.

QUESTION How effective are treatments for whiplash injury?

RCTs have found electrotherapy to be more effective than placebo, early mobilization physiotherapy is more effective than immobilization, and return to normal activity is more effective than rest in people with acute whiplash injury. We found little good data on the management of chronic whiplash injury.

Benefits: **Physical treatments:** We found one RCT of 40 patients with acute whiplash that compared electrotherapy with a pulsing electromagnetic field (PEMF) versus a combination of analgesia and placebo PEMF.[18] Patients in the treatment group had significantly better pain relief ($p < 0.05$) after 4 weeks but not after 3 months. **Early mobilization versus immobilization or less active treatment:** We found two RCTs in 165 patients that compared early mobilization physiotherapy versus immobilization, analgesics, rest, and education.[19,20] Those in the mobilization groups had significantly better pain relief and improved range of movement at 4 and 8 weeks ($p < 0.01$). **Early resumption of normal activity versus immobilization and rest:** We found one single-blinded RCT of 201 patients presenting to an emergency department with acute whiplash that compared an "act as usual" group (advice plus anti-inflammatory drugs) versus an immobilization group (also given 14-days' sick leave).[21] The "act as usual" group did better for subjective symptoms, including pain during daily activities, neck stiffness, memory, concentration, and headache at 6 months but with no benefit for objective variables, such as neck range and length of sick leave. At 6 months, more than 10% of the "act as usual" group still had severe symptoms.

Harms: Not well documented, but early mobilization physiotherapy is not always well tolerated.[22]

Comment: The management of acute whiplash injury remains controversial and needs further investigation. To date, few studies have considered treatment for chronic whiplash, and many whiplash patients are included in general studies of chronic mechanical neck pain.

QUESTION How effective are treatments for neck pain with radiculopathy?

OPTION CONSERVATIVE TREATMENT VERSUS SURGERY FOR RADICULOPATHY

Conservative treatment and surgery have not yet been compared adequately in people with neck pain and radiculopathy.

Benefits: We found no systematic review. One nonblinded RCT of 81 patients with severe radicular symptoms of at least 3-months' duration (number with disk prolapse not stated) compared surgery versus physiotherapy or immobilization in a collar. Patients were reviewed at 12 months.[23] Although the "surgery" group had more rapid pain reduction ($p < 0.01$), there was no difference between the groups at 1-year follow-up.

Harms: No harms reported.

Comment: Conservative treatment warrants further assessment, particularly in patients considered to be poor risk candidates for surgery.

OPTION PERIRADICULAR AND/OR CERVICAL EPIDURAL STEROID INJECTION FOR RADICULOPATHY

Epidural steroid injection has not yet been evaluated adequately in people with neck pain and radiculopathy.

Benefits: We found no systematic review and no RCTs. One prospective study lacked a control group.[24]

Harms: Case reports have documented occasional complications, such as infection or bleeding after cervical epidural injection. The frequency of adverse events after different cervical injection techniques is unknown.

Comment: Well-designed RCTs comparing epidural versus conservative treatment or surgery are awaited.

REFERENCES

1. Brattberg G, Thorslund M, Wikman A. The prevalence of pain in a general population: the results of a postal survey in a county of Sweden. *Pain* 1989;37:215–222.
2. Hackett GI, Hudson MF, Wylie JB, et al. Evaluation of the efficacy and acceptability to patients of a physiotherapist working in a health centre. *BMJ* 1987;294:24–26.
3. Waalen D, White P, Waalen J. Demographic and clinical characteristics of chiropractic patients: a 5-year study of patients treated at the Canadian Memorial Chiropractic College. *J Can Chiropract Assoc* 1994;38:75–82.
4. Holt L. Frequency of symptoms for different age groups. In: Hirsch C, Sotterman Y (eds). *Cervical Pain.* New York: Pergamon Press. 1971:17–20.
5. Kvarnstrom S. Occurrence of musculoskeletal disorders in a manufacturing industry with special attention to occupational shoulder disorders. *Scand J Rehabil Med* 1983;suppl 8:1–114.
6. Squires B, Gargan MF, Bannister GC. Soft-tissue injuries of the cervical spine: 15 year follow-up. *J Bone Joint Surg Br* 1996;78:955–957.
7. Maimaris C, Barnes MR, Allen MJ. 'Whiplash injuries' of the neck: a retrospective study. *Injury* 1988;19:393–396.
8. Gross AR, Aker PD, Goldsmith CH, Peloso P. Conservative management of mechanical neck disorders. Part two: physical medicine modalities. In: Bombardier C, Nachemson A, Deyo R, et al, eds. Back review group for spinal module of The Cochrane Database of Systematic Reviews (updated 2 December 1997). In: The Cochrane Library, Issue 1, 1998. Oxford: Update Software. Updated quarterly.
9. Levoska S, Keinänen-Kiukaanniemi S. Active or passive physiotherapy for occupational cervicobrachial disorders? A comparison of two treatment methods with a 1-year follow-up. *Arch Phys Med Rehabil* 1993;74:425–430.
10. Aker PD, Gross AR, Goldsmith CH, Peloso P. Conservative management of mechanical neck pain: systematic overview and meta-analysis. *BMJ* 1996;313:1291–1296.
11. Hurwitz EL, Aker PD, Adams AH, Meeker WC, Shekelle PG. Manipulation and mobilization of the cervical spine: a systematic review of the literature. *Spine* 1996;21:1746–1760.
12. Nordemar R, Thörner C. Treatment of acute cervical pain: a comparative group study. *Pain* 1981; 10:93–101.
13. Brodin H. Cervical pain and mobilization. *Manual Medicine* 1985;2:18–22.
14. Koes BW, Bouter LM, van Mameren H, et al. Randomised clinical trial of manipulative therapy and physiotherapy for persistent back and neck complaints: results of one year follow up. *BMJ* 1992;304:601–605.
15. Sloop PR, Smith DS, Goldenberg E, Dore C. Manipulation for chronic neck pain: a double-blind controlled study. *Spine* 1982;7:532–535.
16. Howe DH, Newcombe RG, Wade MT. Manipulation of the cervical spine: a pilot study. *J R Coll Gen Pract* 1983;33:574–579.
17. Cassidy JD, Lopes AA, Yong-Hing K. The immediate effect of manipulation versus mobilization on pain and range of motion in the cervical spine: a randomised controlled trial. *J Manipulative Physiol Ther* 1992;15:570–575.
18. Foley-Nolan D, Moore K, Codd M, Barry C, O'Connor P, Coughlan RJ. Low energy high frequency pulsed electromagnetic therapy for acute whiplash injuries. A double blind randomised controlled study. *Scand J Rehab Med* 1992;24: 51–59.
19. Mealy K, Brennan H, Fenelon GC. Early mobilization of acute whiplash injuries. *BMJ* 1986;292: 656–657.
20. McKinney LA, Dornan JO, Ryan M. The role of physiotherapy in the management of acute neck sprains following road-traffic accidents. *Archives of Emergency Medicine* 1989;6:27–33.
21. Borchgrevink GE, Kaasa A, McDonagh D, Stiles TC, Haraldseth O, Lereim I. Acute treatment of whiplash neck sprain injuries: a randomised trial of treatment during the first 14 days after a car accident. *Spine* 1998;23:25–31.
22. Pennie BH, Agambar LJ. Whiplash injuries: a trial of early management. *J Bone Joint Surg Br* 1990; 72:277–279.
23. Persson LC, Carlsson CA, Carlsson JY. Long-lasting cervical radicular pain managed with surgery, physiotherapy, or a cervical collar: a prospective randomised study. *Spine* 1997;22:751–758.
24. Bush K, Hillier S. Outcome of cervical radiculopathy treated with periradicular/epidural corticosteroid injections: a prospective study with independent clinical review. *Eur Spine J* 1996;5: 319–325.

Allan Binder, FRCP, MD
Consultant Rheumatologist
Lister Hospital
Stevenage
UK

Competing interests: None declared.

Stress incontinence

Jason C Cooper, BSc, NBBF, MRCOG, MD, and Ash K Monga, MD

QUESTIONS

INTERVENTIONS

Key Messages

- One randomized controlled trial (RCT) found that postpartum pelvic floor muscle exercises reduced the risk of developing stress incontinence in the short term. The effect of antenatal exercises in preventing stress incontinence has not been assessed in RCTs.
- One systematic review of RCTs has found that pelvic floor muscle exercises and electrical stimulation of the pelvic floor muscle (an uncommon modality in the US) improve objective measures of stress incontinence.
- RCTs found no benefit from estrogen in postmenopausal women.
- One RCT found no difference between pelvic floor muscle exercises and α-adrenergic agonists.
- RCTs comparing different surgical procedures found that colposuspension and slings were the most effective approach, both in the short term and at 3-years' follow-up.

- We found limited evidence suggesting that endoscopic procedures are currently less effective than open procedures.
- We found no good evidence on how best to manage women in whom surgery has failed.

DEFINITION Urinary incontinence is defined as the involuntary loss of urine that is objectively demonstrable and is a social or hygienic problem.[1] There are two main types of urinary incontinence: stress incontinence and detrusor instability (*see* Glossary, p. 223), which together account for more than 80% of all cases of urinary incontinence. Urinary incontinence is eight times more common in women than in men.

INCIDENCE/ PREVALENCE Prevalence is increasing as the aging population expands. It is between 15% and 30% in people over 60 years of age and approaches 50% in institutionalized older persons.[2]

ETIOLOGY Despite paucity of data on the etiology of stress incontinence, observational, cohort, and epidemiologic studies implicate congenital alterations in connective tissue, pregnancy and childbirth, menopause, aging, obesity, race, chronic constipation, other causes of chronic raised intra-abdominal pressure, and pelvic surgery.[3] Psychological factors, bladder neck surgery, caffeine, and smoking may aggravate the condition. Other causes of urinary incontinence include urinary tract infection, immobility, loss of physical function and dexterity, dementia, and other conditions with impaired mental state.

PROGNOSIS Urinary incontinence affects an individual's physical, psychological, and social well being and reduces quality of life. The natural history has not been evaluated. The prognosis after treatment is probably better for stress incontinence than most other forms of urinary incontinence.

AIMS To improve or abolish urinary incontinence, and to restore normal social functioning and confidence, with minimal adverse effects.

OUTCOMES Objective demonstration of urinary loss by urodynamic investigation; subjective improvement in urinary loss; improvement in quality-of-life indicators; adverse effects of drug treatment; complications of surgical treatment.

SEARCH STRATEGY *Clinical Evidence* search to end of 1998, supplemented by a detailed hand search of relevant journals.

QUESTION What are the effects of preventive interventions?

OPTION PELVIC FLOOR EXERCISES

We found no evidence of sufficient quality on the effectiveness of antenatal pelvic floor exercises in the prevention of postpartum stress incontinence. One RCT found that postpartum pelvic floor exercises significantly reduced stress incontinence in the short term.

Benefits: We found no systematic review. **Antenatal pelvic floor exercises:** We found no RCTs. **Postnatal pelvic floor exercises:** We found one RCT published in abstract form, which compared instructed pelvic floor exercises plus bladder retraining versus routine postnatal exercises. Nearly 8000 women responded to a questionnaire survey 3 months after delivery. Of these, 749 who reported incontinence were randomized. At 12 months postpartum, the intervention group showed a significant reduction in stress incontinence (58% vs. 68%, $p=0.016$).[4]

Harms: None reported.

Comment: Large studies with common methodology are required to confirm these findings.

QUESTION What are the effects of nonsurgical treatments?

OPTION PELVIC FLOOR MUSCLE EXERCISES

One systematic review of RCTs has found that pelvic floor muscle exercises reduce the symptoms of stress incontinence, and that high-intensity exercise is more effective than low-intensity exercise.

Benefits: We found one systematic review, which identified 22 RCTs of conservative treatments for female stress incontinence.[5] Eleven RCTs were rejected because of poor methodology. Included trials had at least 50 participants in each group, appropriate randomization and blinding, less than 10% dropout rate, and relevant baseline and outcome measurements. Two RCTs compared pelvic floor muscle exercises versus no treatment. One found that the pelvic floor muscle exercise group were more likely to be dry or mildly incontinent than the no treatment group (61% vs. 3%).[6] After 3 months, the mean weekly frequency of incontinent episodes fell from 17.3 to 4.8 in the treatment group, whereas in the controls it increased from 23.1 to 25.3. The second RCT showed major decreases in frequency of incontinence episodes in the pelvic floor muscle exercise group with no change in the control group (54% vs. 6%).[7] A further RCT compared high- and low-intensity home-based pelvic floor muscle exercise programs and showed a greater rate of "cure or almost cure" for high-intensity exercise (60% vs. 17%). It also showed improvements in social and urodynamic parameters.[8]

Harms: None reported.

Comment: The main methodologic shortcomings were small sample size, lack of prestratification on prognostic determinants, lack of proper description of randomization, and inadequate blinding.

OPTION ELECTRICAL PELVIC FLOOR STIMULATION

One systematic review of RCTs has found that electrical stimulation of the pelvic floor reduces symptoms of stress incontinence.

Benefits: The systematic review[5] identified two RCTs comparing electrical and sham stimulation of the pelvic floor.[9,10] Electrical stimulation was associated with improvements in daily and weekly leakage episodes, pelvic floor muscle strength, and pad tests. In the first RCT,[9] voiding diaries indicated a 50% or greater improvement in 48% of subjects in the active group compared with only 13% in the sham group. The second RCT, in 14 women, also compared active versus sham electrical stimulation, but all participants also were treated with pelvic floor muscle exercises.[10] It found improvements in pelvic floor muscle strength and endurance and significantly reduced episodes of incontinence in the group receiving electrical stimulation. None of the group receiving electrical stimulation required further treatment compared with one third of those receiving sham treatment.

Harms: None reported.

Comment: There were considerable variations in the methodology for the use of electrical stimulation. Note that this modality is uncommon in the US.

OPTION ESTROGEN SUPPLEMENTATION IN POSTMENOPAUSAL WOMEN

RCTs have found no evidence that estrogen supplementation improves incontinence. The addition of an α-adrenergic agonist seems to improve objective measures.

Benefits: **Alone:** We found one systematic review on the treatment of female urinary incontinence, published in 1994, which identified six controlled and 17 uncontrolled trials of estrogen therapy.[11] It concluded that there was an overall subjective improvement in symptoms of incontinence, some objective improvement in maximal urethral closure pressure, but none in quantity of fluid loss. Two placebo-controlled RCTs have been published since, comprising 135 evaluable postmenopausal women with stress incontinence.[12,13] These found no significant difference between treated and placebo groups in the number of incontinent episodes at 3- to 6-months' follow-up. **Combined with an α-adrenergic agonist:** See below.

Harms: Adverse effects of long-term hormone replacement therapy include increased risk of breast cancer and thromboembolic disease. α-Adrenergic agonists should be used with care or not at all in women with hypertension, hyperthyroidism, or coronary heart disease or in those taking monoamine oxidase inhibitors.

Comment: The studies included clinically heterogeneous groups; the diagnostic criteria, therapeutic interventions and outcome assessments varied considerably.

OPTION α-ADRENERGIC AGONISTS (PHENYLPROPANOLAMINE)

One RCT found that the α-adrenergic agonist phenylpropanolamine was as effective as pelvic floor muscle exercises. A review of the literature concluded that combination with estrogen therapy in postmenopausal women improved objective measures of urinary incontinence more than estrogen alone.

Benefits: **Versus placebo:** We found no RCTs. **Versus pelvic floor muscle exercises:** We found one systematic review,[5] which identified one RCT of sufficient quality. This found no significant difference between pelvic floor muscle exercises and phenylpropanolamine (77% vs. 84% improvement). **Plus estrogen:** A review of the combination of oestrogen and phenylpropanolamine was published in 1995.[14] The authors did not state their search strategy. They reviewed two trials of combination therapy in 84 postmenopausal women, and concluded that frequency and nocturia improved more with combined treatment than with estrogen alone. Levels of significance were not given in the review. Stress incontinence improved subjectively in all groups but objectively only in the combined group. The authors concluded that the effect of phenylpropanolamine on α-adrenergic receptors in the urethra is probably potentiated by the concomitant use of estrogen replacement therapy in postmenopausal women.

Harms: *See* p. 230.

Comment: Limited data are available, which limits the ability to generalize.

OPTION **OTHER CONSERVATIVE INTERVENTIONS**

One systematic review has found no evidence of benefit from the use of intravaginal resistance devices or biofeedback.

Benefits: We found one systematic review,[5] which identified three RCTs of sufficient quality comparing pelvic floor muscle exercises alone and in combination with an intravaginal resistance device (one RCT) or biofeedback (two RCTs). These found no significant difference in the frequency of incontinence episodes per week.

Harms: None reported.

Comment: Vaginal cones, regulation of fluid intake, and weight loss have not yet been evaluated in RCTs of sufficient quality.

SURGICAL TREATMENT

QUESTION **How do the main surgical treatments for stress incontinence compare?**

OPTION **COLPOSUSPENSION, ANTERIOR COLPORRHAPY, NEEDLE SUSPENSION, SLINGS, AND DEVICES**

We found little good randomized evidence. From limited data, colposuspension and sling procedures seem to be the most successful surgical procedures for stress incontinence. We found no good comparative data on the harms of different procedures.

Benefits: We found one systematic review of the effectiveness of surgery for stress incontinence in women, published in 1996.[15] It identified 11 RCTs, 20 nonrandomized trials/prospective cohort studies, and 45 retrospective cohort studies of sufficient quality to be analyzed. **Colposuspension versus anterior colporraphy:** Four RCTs and 11 nonrandomized prospective studies found that colposuspension was more effective in curing and improving stress incontinence compared with anterior colporraphy at 1 year (Table 1).[15–19] Only one of the RCTs[16] was considered to have adequate power to examine this outcome. The benefits of colposuspension were sustained for at least 5 years, whereas those of anterior colporraphy seemed to diminish rapidly. **Colposuspension versus needle suspension:** Three RCTs and 10 nonrandomized studies compared colposuspension versus needle-suspension procedures.[15,16,19,20] Two RCTs and two nonrandomized studies reported a higher success rate for colposuspension, whereas one RCT and eight nonrandomized studies found no significant difference. **Colposuspension versus slings:** The systematic review[21] found no RCTs. Fewer than 150 women have ever been included in prospective studies. One small RCT published since the review found that paravaginal repair was less effective than colposuspension in curing stress incontinence.[22] **Anterior colporraphy versus needle suspension:** Three RCTs and five nonrandomized prospective studies found no difference in the effectiveness of anterior colporraphy and needle-suspension procedures.[16,18,19] **Injectable devices and artificial sphincters:** We found no RCTs.

Harms: Reported complications of surgery include urinary retention, frequency, and urgency. However, we found no good data on the frequency of complications.

Comment: A review published in 1997 identified 282 articles with acceptable outcome data (as determined by an expert panel, rejection encompassing such points as being published only in abstract form, lack of original data, or inadequate follow-up).[21] Combined data from the 282 included articles gave cure rates of 84% for retropubic suspensions, 65%–79% for transvaginal suspensions, 61%–85% for anterior repairs, and 82%–83% for paravaginal sling procedures. The authors concluded that at 48 months' follow-up, retropubic suspensions (colposuspension) and slings were more effective than anterior colporraphy or needle suspension. No differentiation was made between primary and secondary procedures. Studies suffered from lack of standardization on definition, severity, and diagnosis of stress incontinence. Information on detrusor instability, prior surgery, quality-of-life measurements, surgical technique, length of follow-up, and external validity often were not available. Of great concern is a cohort study of 259 patients who underwent the Stamey endoscopic bladder neck suspension; at 10-year follow-up, a success rate of only 6% was achieved with this procedure. If this is borne out by further research, then needle suspension cannot be recommended.

QUESTION How do endoscopic and open procedures compare?

We found limited evidence suggesting that open procedures are currently superior.

Benefits: Two poor-quality RCTs found that laparoscopic colposuspension was less effective than the open procedure.[23,24]

Harms: We found no good comparative data on harms.

Comment: None.

QUESTION What effective treatments are available if primary surgery fails?

This question has not yet been addressed adequately in RCTs.

Benefits: We found two systematic reviews.[15,25] These found no RCTs and both commented on the paucity of data and the misleading influence of confounding variables. The first review, published in 1994, identified 213 articles supplying information on 20,481 surgical procedures.[25] Objective results were available for 1439 women undergoing a primary procedure and 555 women undergoing a repeat procedure. Case series and cohort studies found that secondary surgery was less effective than primary surgery, but the confidence intervals were wide and overlapping (Table 2). We found no evidence on the role of nonsurgical interventions, such as pelvic floor exercises and devices, when primary surgery fails. Prospective case series found that injectable agents,[26] colposuspension, and slings were effective.[15,25]

Harms: We found no good comparative data on harms.

Comment: More data are required.

GLOSSARY[27]

Anterior colporrhaphy (anterior repair) A surgical procedure involving repair of the anterior vaginal wall, intended to provide support to the urethra and bladder neck. This procedure is performed through the vagina and is used to treat urinary incontinence due to hypermobility of the urethra and/or bladder neck.
Colposuspension (retropubic) A class of surgical procedures (e.g., Burch, Marshall–Marchetti–Krantz) conducted through a low abdominal incision, intended to move the lower urinary tract into the retropubic space.
Electrical pelvic floor stimulation A small device is placed into the vagina or anus or is attached to the perianal surface, delivering electrical stimulation to the levator ani and the external urethral and anal sphincters. This stimulation causes reflexive inhibition of the detrusor muscle of the urinary bladder and thus helps prevent urinary incontinence.
Needle suspension The general name for a group of surgical procedures (e.g., Peyrera, Stamey, Raz) wherein urinary incontinence is treated by providing support to the urethra and/or bladder neck. These procedures are characterized by the use of sutures passed through the vagina through small suprapubic skin incisions.
Paravaginal repair A type of surgical repair procedure used to treat urinary incontinence wherein the endopelvic fascia are reattached to the pelvic wall.
Pessary/vaginal cone A device placed within the vagina to provide support to the anterior and/or posterior vaginal walls and to treat vaginal prolapse and occasionally urinary incontinence.
Slings A type of surgical procedure used to treat urinary incontinence wherein a sling of ligamentous tissue or artificial material is used to support the urethra and/or bladder neck. This procedure is performed through the vagina, the abdomen, or both and is most often performed on patients who have poor success with other procedures.
Stress incontinence Diagnosed when, in the absence of a detrusor contraction, the pressure inside the bladder exceeds the pressure in the urethra.
Detrusor instability Diagnosed when the detrusor muscle contracts, spontaneously or on provocation, during the filling phase, while the patient is attempting to inhibit micturition.

REFERENCES

1. Abrams P, Blaivas JG, Stanton SL, Andersen J. Standardisation of terminology of lower urinary tract function. *Scand J Urol Nephrol* 1988;114 (suppl):5–19.
2. Thom D. Variation in testimates of urinary incontinence prevalence in the community: effects of differences in definition, population characteristics, and study type.
3. Handa VL, Harris TA, Ostergard DR. Protecting the pelvic floor: obstetric management to prevent incontinence and pelvic organ prolapse. *Obstet Gynecol* 1996;88:470–478.
4. Gladzener CMA, Lang G, Wilson PD, Herbison GP, MacArthur C, Gee H. Postnatal incontinence: a

multicentre randomised controlled trial of conservative treatment. *Br J Obstet Gynaecol* 1998;105 (suppl 117):47.
5. Berghamans LCM, Hendriks HJM, Bo K, Hay-Smith EJ, de Ble RA, van Waalwijk van Doorn ES. Conservative treatment of stress urinary incontinence in women, a systematic review of randomised controlled trials. *Br J Urol* 1998;82: 181–191. (Search date 1980 to March 1997; primary sources MEDLINE, Excerpta Medica, Cochrane field in therapies and rehabilitation.)
6. Lagro-Janssen TLM, Debruyne FMJ, Smits AJA, Van Weel C. Controlled trial of pelvic floor exercises in the treatment of urinary stress incontinence in general practice. *Br J Gen Pract* 1991;41:445–449.
7. Burns PA, Pranekoff K, Nochajski TH, et al. Comparison of effectiveness of biofeedback and pelvic muscle exercise treatment in stress incontinence in older community dwelling women. *J Gerontol* 1993;48:M167–174.
8. Bo K, Hagan RH, Kvarstein B, Jorgensen J, Larsen S. Pelvic floor muscle exercise for the treatment of female stress incontinence: III. Effects of two difference degrees of pelvic floor muscle exercises. *Neurourol Urodyn* 1990;9:489–502.
9. Sand PK, Richardson DA, Staskin DR, et al. Pelvic floor electrical stimulation in the treatment of genuine stress incontinence: a multicentre placebo controlled trial. *Am J Obstet Gynecol* 1995;173:72–79.
10. Blownan C, Pickles C, Emery S, et al. Prospective double blind controlled trial of intensive physiotherapy with and without stimulation of the pelvic floor in the treatment of genuine stress incontinence. *Physiotherapy* 1991;77: 661–664.
11. Fantl JA, Cardozo LD, McClish DK. Estrogen therapy on the management of urinary incontinence in post-menopausal women: a meta-analysis. *Obstet Gynecol* 1994;83:12–18. (Search date January 1969 to June 1992; primary sources English language articles found in Excerpta Medica, Biosis, and MEDLINE.)
12. Fantl JA, Bump RC, Robinson D, McClish DK, Wyman JF and the Continence Program for Women Research Group. Efficacy of estrogen supplementation in the treatment of urinary incontinence. *Obstet Gynecol* 1996;88:745–749.
13. Jackson S, Shepherd A, Abrams P. Does oestrogen supplementation improve the symptoms of postmenopausal urinary stress incontinence? A double blind placebo controlled trial. *Neurourol Urodyn* 1997;16:350–351.
14. Cardozo LD, Kelleher CJ. Sex hormones, the menopause and urinary problems. *Gynecol Endocrinol* 1995;9:75–84.
15. Black NA, Downs SH. The effectiveness of surgery for stress urinary incontinence in women: a systematic review. *Br J Urol* 1996;78:497–510. (Search strategy: English and non-English articles found in MEDLINE (1966 to June 1995), Embase (1980 to June 1995), Science Citation Index (1980 to June 1995), British Library Information Index (1995) together with information from informed experts.)
16. Bergman A, Koonings PP, Ballard CA.. Primary stress incontinence and pelvic relaxation: prospective randomised comparison of three different operations. *Am J Obstet Gynecol* 1989;161:97–101.
17. Klarskov P, Jepsen PV, Dorph S. Reliability of voiding colp-cysto-urethrography in female urinary stress incontinence before and after treatment. *Acta Radiol* 1988;29:685–688.
18. Bergman A, Ballard CA , Koonings PP. Comparison of three different surgical procedures for stress urinary incontinence: a prospective randomized study. *Am J Obstet Gynecol* 1989;160:1102–1106.
19. Elia G, Bergman A. Prospective randomised comparison of three surgical procedures for stress urinary incontinence: a five year follow up. *Neurourol Urodyn* 1994;13:498–500.
20. German KA, Kynaston H, Weight S, Stephenson TP. A prospective randomised trial comparing a modified needle suspension procedure for the vagina and obturator shelf procedure for genuine stress incontinence. *Br J Urol*, 1994;74:188–190.
21. Leach GE, Dmochowski RR, Appell RA, et al. Female stress urinary incontinence clinical guidelines panel summary report on surgical management of female stress urinary incontinence. *J Urol* 1997;158:875–880.
22. Colombo M, Milani R, Vitobello D, Maggioni A. A randomised comparison of Burch colposuspension and abdominal paravaginal defect repair for female stress urinary incontinence. *Am J Obstet Gynecol* 1996;175:78–84.
23. Su TH, Wang K-G, Hsu C-Y, Wei H-J, Hong B-K. Prospective comparison of laparoscopic and traditional colposuspensions in the treatment of genuine stress incontinence. *Acta Obstet Gynecol Scand* 1997;76:576–582.
24. Burton G. A three year prospective randomised urodynamic study comparing open and laparoscopic colposuspension. *Neurourol Urodyn* 1997;16:353–354.
25. Jarvis GJ. Surgery for genuine stress incontinence. *Br J Obstet Gynaecol* 1994;101:371–374. (Search strategy: hand searching of 16 scientific journals from 1970 to 1994 for surgical procedures used in treating stress incontinence.)
26. Monga AK, Stanton SL. Urodynamics: prediction, outcome and analysis of mechanism for cure of stress incontinence by periurethral collagen. *Br J Obstet Gynaecol* 1997;104:158–162.
27. Fantl JA, Newman DK, Colling J, et al. *Urinary Incontinence in Adults: Acute and Chronic Management. Clinical Practice Guideline No. 2, 1996 Update.* Rockville, MD: USDHHS Public Health Service, Agency for Health Care Policy and Research. AHCPR Publication No. 96-0682. Mar 1996.

Jason C Cooper, BSc, NBBF, MRCOG, MD
Consultant Gynaecologist
City General Hospital
Stoke on Trent
Staffordshire
UK

Ash K Monga, MD
Consultant Urogynaecologist
Princess Anne Hospital
Southampton
UK

Competing interests: None declared.

TABLE 1 **Results of RCTs comparing colposuspension versus anterior colporraphy and needle suspension.[16] (*See* text p. 231.)**

Procedure	Number of patients	Follow-up (years)	% cure (95% CI)
Study 1[17]			
Colposuspension	101	1	87 (81–94)
Anterior colporraphy	99		70 (60–79)
Study 2[18]			
Colposuspension	19	1	25
Anterior colporraphy	15		0
Study 3[19]			
Colposuspension	38	1	89 (75–97)
Anterior colporraphy	35		65 (47–80)
Study 4[20]			
Colposuspension	127*	5	82
Anterior colporraphy			37
Study 1[17]			
Colposuspension	101	1	87 (81–94)
Needle suspension	98		67 (59 to 78)
Study 2[21]			
Colposuspension	24	1–3.7	71 (49–87)
Needle suspension	26		58 (37–77)
Study 3[20]			
Colposuspension	127*	5	82
Needle suspension			43

*Available information does not specify numbers of patients in each group.

TABLE 2 **Objective success rates for primary and secondary surgery.[25] (*See* text p. 233.)**

Procedure	All patients (%)	Those undergoing primary surgery (% [95% CI])	Those undergoing secondary surgery (% [95% CI])
Anterior colporraphy	72	68 (63–73)	–
Colposuspension	84	90 (88–92)	83 (76–89)
Needle suspension	70	87 (75–97)	86 (72–100)
Sling	85	94 (89–99)	86 (82–90)

Recurrent cystitis

Lisa D Chew, MD, and Stephan D Fihn, MD, MPH

QUESTIONS

INTERVENTIONS

Key Messages

- Consistent evidence from randomized controlled trials (RCTs) have found that antibiotic prophylaxis (either continuous or postcoital), using nitrofurantoin, a quinolone, trimethoprim, or trimethoprim-sulfamethoxazole (TMP-SMZ) reduces infection rates in women with high rates of recurrent urinary tract infections (at least two per year).
- One RCT has found that intermittent patient-administered treatment (taken at the onset of symptoms) is less effective at preventing recurrent infection than continuous antibiotic prophylaxis in women with high rates of infection (at least two per year), but most infections in the self-treatment group responded to a single dose.
- An observational study has found that long-term prophylaxis is likely to benefit women with a baseline rate of more than two infections per year over many years. However, long-term treatment has not yet been evaluated in RCTs.
- In women who experience recurrent, uncomplicated urinary tract infections, we found no evidence to support routine investigation of the urinary tract with excretory urography, ultrasonography, cystoscopy, or voiding cystourethrography. No specific subgroups of women who clearly would benefit from investigation have yet been defined adequately.

DEFINITION Cystitis is an infection of the lower urinary tract causing dysuria, frequency, urgency, hematuria, or suprapubic pain. Pyuria and bacteriuria are almost always present. The presence of fever, flank pain, nausea, or vomiting suggests pyelonephritis. Recurrent cystitis may be either a reinfection (after successful eradication of infection) or a relapse after inadequate treatment.

INCIDENCE/ PREVALENCE The incidence of cystitis among premenopausal sexually active women is 0.5 to 0.7 infections per person year.[1] Between one and two fifths of women will experience cystitis during their lifetime. Of those, 20% will develop recurrence, almost all of which (90%) will be caused by reinfection rather than relapse. Rates of infection fall during the winter months.[2]

ETIOLOGY Cystitis is caused by uropathogenic bacteria in the fecal flora that colonize the vaginal and periurethral introitus and ascend the urethra into the bladder. Prior infection, sexual intercourse, and exposure to vaginal spermicide are risk factors for developing cystitis.[3,4]

PROGNOSIS There is little evidence on the long-term effects of untreated cystitis. One study found that progression to upper urinary tract infection was infrequent, and that most cases of cystitis regressed spontaneously, although symptoms sometimes persisted for several months.[5] Women with a baseline rate of more than two infections per year, over many years, are likely to continue to suffer from recurrent infections.[6]

AIMS To prevent recurrent infection in women predisposed to frequent infections, with minimal adverse effects.

OUTCOMES Rate of infection based on urine culture and symptoms.

METHODS We searched MEDLINE from 1970 to 1998. We reviewed all systematic reviews and RCTs comparing different forms of prophylaxis or comparing prophylaxis versus placebo in nonpregnant women with a history of recurrent urinary tract infection. We excluded studies in populations consisting mainly of men or pregnant women.

QUESTION **Which interventions prevent further recurrence in women experiencing at least two infections per year?**

OPTION **CONTINUOUS ANTIBIOTIC PROPHYLAXIS**

RCTs have found that continuous antibiotic prophylaxis using trimethoprim, TMP-SMZ, nitrofurantoin, cefaclor, or a quinolone reduces rates of urinary tract infection in nonpregnant women. There is no good evidence of any difference between continuous regimens, nor between continuous and postcoital regimens.

Benefits: We found no systematic review. We found seven RCTs comparing different regimens for continuous antibiotic prophylaxis lasting 6 to 12 months in women with high rates of recurrent urinary tract infection (at least two episodes per year)[7–13] (Table 1). Three of the RCTs included a placebo or no treatment arm.[7–9] All found significantly lower rates of infection with active treatment (nitrofurantoin, ciprofloxacin, norfloxacin, or trimethoprim, TMP-SMZ), but CIs were not given. **Versus each other:** Five RCTs compared different regimens.[7,10–13] The comparative evidence for individual drugs is too limited to draw conclusions. **Versus postcoital prophylaxis:** One RCT compared daily versus postcoital treatment with ciprofloxacin in 135 women. There was no significant difference in rates of infection, but a CI was not given[8].

Harms: Rates of side effects in these studies ranged from 7% to 40% for trimethoprim; 0% to 40% for nitrofurantoin; 5% for cefaclor; 7% to 21% for norfloxacin; and 13% for ciprofloxacin.[7–9,11–13] The most common adverse effects for all agents were gastrointestinal symptoms, rash, and yeast vaginitis.

Comment: Many of the studies were not placebo controlled or blinded and had small study populations. Despite the small study sizes, however, differences in infection rates with and without prophylaxis were significant. Adjustments were not made for confounding factors such as frequency of sexual intercourse.

OPTION POSTCOITAL PROPHYLAXIS

RCTs have found that taking nitrofurantoin, a quinolone, trimethoporin, or TMP-SMZ within 2 hours after sexual intercourse significantly reduces the rates of infection in women with recurrent urinary tract infection. There is no evidence of any difference between postcoital and continuous antibiotic regimens.

Benefits: We found no systematic review. We found four RCTs of postcoital antibiotic regimens, evaluated over 6 to 14 months, in women with high rates of recurrent urinary tract infection (at least two episodes per year)[8,14–16] (Table 2). Treatment was to be taken within 2 hours after sexual intercourse. **Versus placebo or no treatment:** All trials found a significant reduction in rates of infection with active treatment (TMP-SMZ, nitrofurantoin, or a quinolone). **Versus daily prophylaxis:** One RCT compared daily versus postcoital treatment with ciprofloxacin in 135 women.[8] There was no significant difference in rates of infection.

Harms: Rates of adverse effects were TMP-SMZ 18%; ciprofloxacin 6%; and nitrofurantoin <1%.[8,14–16] The most common adverse effects for all agents were gastrointestinal symptoms, rash, and yeast vaginitis.

Comment: Only one of the studies was placebo controlled and blinded.[14] Adjustments were not made for confounding factors such as frequency of sexual intercourse.

OPTION SELF-TREATMENT

One RCT found that intermittent patient-administered treatment (taken at the onset of symptoms) is an effective alternative management strategy but less effective than continuous antibiotic prophylaxis in women with high rates of infection (at least two per year).

Benefits: We found no systematic review. We found one RCT using a crossover design in 38 nonpregnant women with two or more culture-documented urinary tract infections in the previous 12 months.[17] This compared continuous antibiotic prophylaxis with TMP-SMZ (40 mg/200 mg) versus a self-administered single dose of TMP-SMZ (40 mg/200 mg) to be taken at the onset of symptoms of cystitis. The self-treatment group was given enough tablets for four single treatments. Infection rates were 0.22/year with continuous prophylaxis compared to 2.2/year with self-administered treatment. In the self-treatment group, 85% of infections responded to a single dose.

Harms: There were no significant differences with regard to adverse effects between continuous antibiotic prophylaxis versus self-administered treatment.

Comment: The trial showed that the women were able to diagnose their own infections accurately from symptoms (positive predictive value 92%).[17]

OPTION LONG-TERM ANTIBIOTIC PROPHYLAXIS

Long-term antibiotic prophylaxis (>12 months) has not yet been evaluated adequately in RCTs.

Benefits: We found no systematic review or RCTs.

Harms: A cohort study followed 51 nonpregnant women receiving prophylaxis over 112 patient years with trimethoprim, TMP-SMZ, or nitrofurantoin. Antibiotic prophylaxis was highly effective in preventing cystitis and pyelonephritis without significant adverse effects, even when used for as long as 5 years. The development of bacterial resistance from continuous antibiotic prophylaxis was rare; however, the number of TMP-SMZ–resistant organisms increased during the latter part of the study.[2]

Comment: The RCTs of prophylactic antibiotic regimens, either continuous or postcoital, included only women with a high baseline rate of infection (at least two episodes per year). Although there is some evidence that antibiotic resistance is rare, the decision to initiate long-term prophylaxis should take this possibility into account.

QUESTION Which women with recurrent infections should undergo investigation for urinary tract abnormalities?

OPTION CYSTOSCOPY, UROGRAPHY, CYSTOGRAPHY, AND ULTRASONOGRAPHY

Evidence is limited, and no specific subgroups of women who clearly would benefit from investigation have yet been defined adequately.

Benefits: We found no systematic review or RCTs. Two older, cross-sectional studies[18,19] and one prospective study[20] examined the yield of routine excretory urography in women with recurrent urinary tract infections. Among the 421 women studied, urography was normal in 88%, showed anatomic variants in approximately 6%, and was abnormal in approximately 5%. None of the abnormalities detected were correctable or thought to be causally related to infection. In two of the studies,[19,20] cystoscopy also detected no clinically important abnormalities. In a more recent cross-sectional study, 186 women were selected nonrandomly from a larger group of 475 women with recurrent urinary tract infections because the referring physician suspected an underlying problem.[21] Of these, 21% had an abnormality reported on cystoscopy, excretory urography, ultrasonography, or voiding cystourethrography. Results from this study are difficult to interpret because there was no standard protocol for evaluation and results were collected retrospectively.

Harms: None of the studies had a sample size large enough to report accurately the incidence of adverse effects in this age group. Excretory urography with iodinated dye can cause anaphylactoid reactions and renal dysfunction. Cystoscopy can cause bleeding and other complications depending on the type of procedure and anesthesia used. Ultrasonography has no known adverse effects.

Comments: The reported rates of detection of abnormalities are likely to be overestimates because the studies took place in a specialist urology unit.

REFERENCES

1. Hooton TM, Scholes D, Hughes JP, et al. A prospective study of risk factors for symptomatic urinary tract infection in young women. *N Engl J Med* 1996;335:468–474.
2. Stamm WE, McKevitt M, Roberts PL, White NJ. Natural history of recurrent urinary tract infections in women. *Rev Infect Dis* 1991;13:77–84.
3. Fihn SD, Latham RH, Roberts P, Running K, Stamm WE. Association between diaphragm use and urinary tract infection. *JAMA* 1985;254:240–245.
4. Fihn SD, Boyko EJ, Normand EH, et al. Association between use of spermicide-coated condoms and *Escherichia coli* urinary tract infection in young women. *Am J Epidemiol* 1996;144: 512–520.
5. Mabeck CE. Treatment of uncomplicated urinary tract infection in non-pregnant women. *Postgrad Med J* 1972;48: 69–75.
6. Stamm WE, Counts GW, McKevitt M, Turck M, Holmes KK. Urinary prophylaxis with trimethoprim and trimethoprim-sulfamethoxazole: efficacy, influence on the natural history of recurrent bacteriuria and cost control. *Rev Infect Dis* 1982;4:450–455.
7. Stamm WE, Counts GW, Wagner KF, et al. Antimicrobial prophylaxis of recurrent urinary tract infections: a double-blind placebo-controlled trial. *Ann Intern Med* 1980;92:770–775.
8. Melekos MD, Asbach HW, Gerharz E, Zarakovitis IE, Weingaertner K, Naber KG. Post-intercourse versus daily ciprofloxacin prophylaxis for recurrent urinary tract infections in premenopausal women. *J Urol* 1997;157:935–939.
9. Nicolle LE, Harding GK, Thompson M, Kennedy J, Urias B, Ronald AR. Prospective, randomized, placebo-controlled trial of norfloxacin for the prophylaxis of recurrent urinary tract infection in women. *Antimicrob Agents Chemother* 1989;33: 1032–1035.
10. Brumfitt W, Smith GW, Hamilton-Miller JM, Gargan RA. A clinical comparison between macrodantin and trimethoprim for prophylaxis in women with recurrent urinary infection. *J Antimicrob Chemother* 1985;16:111–120.
11. Raz R, Boger S. Long-term prophylaxis with norfloxacin versus nitrofurantoin in women with recurrent urinary tract infection. *Antimicrob Agents Chemother* 1991;35:1241–1242.
12. Brumfitt W, Hamilton-Miller JM, Smith GW, Al-Wali W. Comparative trial of norfloxacin and macrocrystalline nitrofurantoin (Macrodantin) in the prophylaxis of recurrent urinary tract infection in women. *Q J Med* 1991;81:811–820.
13. Brumfitt W, Hamilton-Miller JM. A comparative trial of low-dose cefaclor and macrocrystalline nitrofurantoin in the prevention of recurrent urinary tract infection. *Infection* 1995;23:98–102.
14. Stapleton A, Latham RH, Johnson C, Stamm WE. Postcoital antimicrobial prophylaxis for recurrent urinary tract infection: a randomized, double-blind placebo-controlled trial. *JAMA* 1990;264:703–706.
15. Pfau A, Sacks TG. Effective postcoital quinolone prophylaxis of recurrent urinary tract infection in women. *J Urol* 1994; 152:136–138.
16. Pfau A, Sacks T, Englestein D. Recurrent urinary tract infections in premenopausal women: prophylaxis based on an understanding of the pathogenesis. *J Urol* 1983;129: 1153–1157.
17. Wong ES, McKevitt M, Running K, Counts GW, Turck M, Stamm WE. Management of recurrent urinary tract infections with patient-administered single-dose therapy. *Ann Intern Med* 1985;102:302–307.
18. Fair WR, McClennan BL, Jost RG. Are excretory urograms necessary in evaluating women with urinary tract infection? *J Urol* 1979;121:313–315.
19. Engel G, Schaeffer AJ, Grayhack JT, Wendel EF. The role of excretory urography and cystoscopy in the evaluation and management of women with recurrent urinary tract infection. *J Urol* 1980;123:190–191.
20. Fowler JE Jr, Pulaski ET. Excretory urography, cystography, and cystoscopy in the evaluation of women with urinary tract infection: a prospective study. *N Engl J Med* 1981;304: 462–465.
21. Nickel JC, Wilson, J, Morales A, Heaton J. Value of urologic investigation in a targeted group of women with recurrent urinary tract infections. *Can J Surg* 1991;34:591–594.

Lisa D Chew, MD
Acting Instructor of Obstetrics and Gynecology
University of Washington
Harborview Medical Center
Seattle
Washington
USA

Stephan D Fihn, MD, MPH
Professor of Medicine and of Health Services
University of Washington
Seattle
Washington
USA

Competing interests: None declared.

TABLE 1 Continuous antimicrobial prophylactic regimens for recurrent urinary tract infections: results of RCTs. (See text p. 237.)

Study	Total number of participants	Regimen	Duration of prophylaxis (months)	Infections per patient year	*p* value
Stamm et al[7] (placebo controlled RCT) 1980	60	Placebo	6	2.80	
		TMP-SMZ (40 mg/200 mg) at bedtime		0.15	<0.001 (placebo vs. drug treatment)
		Nitrofurantoin 100 mg at bedtime		0.14	
		Trimethoprim 100 mg at bedtime		0	
Melekos et al[8] (open RCT) 1997	135	Without prophylaxis	12	3.62–3.66	
		Ciprofloxacin 125 mg postcoital		0.043	<0.0001
		Ciprofloxacin 125 mg/d		0.031	
Nicolle et al[9] (placebo controlled RCT) 1989	30	Placebo	12	1.6	
		Norfloxacin 200 mg at bedtime		0	<0.001
Brumfitt et al[10] (open RCT) 1985	72	Trimethoprim 100 mg at bedtime	12	1.00	
		Nitrofurantoin 100 mg bedtime		0.17	<0.05
Raz et al[11] (open RCT) 1991	94	Norfloxacin 200 mg at bedtime	6	0.04	
		Nitrofurantoin 50 mg at bedtime		0.60	0.05
Brumfitt et al[12] (open RCT) 1991	88	Norfloxacin 200 mg at bedtime	12	0.002	Not reported
		Nitrofurantoin 100 mg at bedtime		0.003	
Brumfitt et al[13] (open RCT) 1995	97	Cefaclor 250 mg at bedtime	12	0.006	Not reported
		Nitrofurantoin 50 mg at bedtime		0.006	

TMP-SMZ, trimethoprim-sulfamethoxazole.

TABLE 2 Postcoital regimens for recurrent urinary tract infections: results of RCTs. **(See text p. 238.)**

Study	Total number of participants	Regimen	Duration of prophylaxis (months)	Infections per patient-year	*p* value
Stapleton et al[14] (placebo-controlled RCT) 1990	27	Placebo	6	3.6	
		Postcoital TMP-SMZ (40 mg/20 mg)		0.3	0.0001
Pfau et al[15] (open RCT) 1994	33	Without prophylaxis	14	6.13	
		Postcoital prophylaxis with either		0.02	0.0000
		Ofloxacin 100 mg			
		Norfloxacin 200 mg			
		Ciprofloxacin 125 mg			
Melekos et al[8] (open RCT) 1997	135	Without prophylaxis	12	3.62–3.66	
		Ciprofloxacin 125 mg/d		0.031	<0.0001
		Ciprofloxacin 125 mg postcoital		0.043	
Pfau et al[16] (open RCT) 1983	56	Without prophylaxis	12	4.6	
		Postcoital prophylaxis with either			<0.001
		TMP-SMZ 80 mg/400 mg		0	
		Nitrofurantoin 50–100 mg		0.1	

TMP-SMZ, trimethoprim-sulfamethoxazole.

Acute pyelonephritis in women

Lisa D Chew, MD, and Stephan D Fihn, MD, MPH

QUESTIONS

INTERVENTIONS

Key Messages

- Randomized controlled trials (RCTs) consistently found that oral antibiotic treatment with trimethoprim-sulfamethoxazole (TMP-SMZ), amoxicillin-clavulanic acid, or a fluoroquinolone (ciprofloxacin, norfloxacin, levofloxacin, or lomefloxacin) is effective in healthy female outpatients.
- We found limited evidence that intravenous antibiotics are effective in women admitted to hospital with uncomplicated infection but that ampicillin should not be used alone to treat infection with *Escherichia coli* because of antimicrobial resistance.
- We found no well-designed trials comparing newer intravenous antibiotics with older standard regimens.
- We found no direct evidence comparing the inpatient and outpatient management of acute uncomplicated pyelonephritis in nonpregnant women.

DEFINITION Acute pyelonephritis, or upper urinary tract infection, is an infection of the kidney, characterized by dysuria, fever, flank pain, nausea, and vomiting. Pyuria is almost always present, and white blood cell casts occasionally are seen on urine microscopy. Uncomplicated infection occurs in an otherwise healthy individual without underlying comorbidity. Complicated infection occurs in patients with structural or functional urinary tract abnormalities or comorbid diseases.

INCIDENCE/ PREVALANCE In the USA, there are 250,000 cases/year.[1] Worldwide prevalence and incidence are unknown.

ETIOLOGY Pyelonephritis is most commonly caused when bacteria in the bladder ascend the ureters and invade the renal parenchyma. In some cases, this results in bacteremia.

PROGNOSIS Patients can be divided into those requiring parenteral treatment in hospital and those able to take oral antibiotics and without signs of sepsis who can be managed at home. With prompt diagnosis and treatment, the prognosis is good. Comorbidity (e.g., renal disease, diabetes mellitus, and immunosuppression) may worsen prognosis, with a potential increase in risk of sepsis and death, but there are no good long-term data for such patients.

AIMS To reduce the duration and severity of symptoms, and to prevent or minimize potential complications (sepsis, metastatic infection, renal impairment, renal abscess), with minimum adverse effects.

OUTCOMES Urine culture after treatment; signs and symptoms of infection.

METHODS We performed a MEDLINE search from 1970 to 1998 using the MeSH terms pyelonephritis, upper urinary tract infection, hospitalization, outpatient therapy, and oral antibiotics. We included RCTs and systematic reviews that focused on the inpatient and outpatient management of acute uncomplicated pyelonephritis in nonpregnant women. We excluded studies that were primarily of men, pregnant women, and patients with complicated infections. All studies were reviewed by both authors.

QUESTION What are the effects of treatments?

OPTION ORAL ANTIBIOTICS

One systematic review of RCTs has found that oral antibiotic treatment with TMP-SMZ, amoxicillin-clavulanic acid, or a fluoroquinolone (ciprofloxacin, norfloxacin, levofloxacin, and lomefloxacin) is effective in healthy women with acute pyelonephritis who are able to take oral treatment and who lack signs of sepsis.

Benefits: We found one systematic review published in 1992, which identified nine RCTs comparing oral antibiotics in 470 men and nonpregnant women with acute pyelonephritis (Table 1).[2] Five trials were in outpatients and four in inpatients. The studies were conducted in the USA, Europe, and Peru. All included more women than men, and most excluded patients with complicating factors such as structural abnormalities of the urinary tract, comorbid illnesses, pregnancy, or signs of possible sepsis. All except one found no significant difference in rates of early cure (negative urine culture within 7–10 days), and six of the nine studies found no significant difference in rates of late cure (negative urine culture 2–4 weeks or more after stopping treatment). However, several of the individual studies were too small to rule out a difference between antibiotic regimens. We found two good RCTs published since the systematic review. A multicenter RCT in 47 outpatients with acute uncomplicated pyelonephritis compared oral lomefloxacin 400 mg/d versus oral TMP-SMZ 160 mg/800 mg twice daily, both for 14 days.[3] At 5 to 9 days, there was a significantly higher rate of bacteriologic eradication on lomefloxacin (100%) compared with TMP-SMZ (88.9%, $p=0.05$) but no significant difference in clinical cure rates. At 4 to 6 weeks, there were no significant differences. The other RCT compared 10 days of levofloxacin 250 mg/d versus 10 days of ciprofloxacin 500 mg twice daily or 14 days of lomefloxacin 400 mg/d in 186 outpatients (87% women) with acute uncomplicated pyelonephritis.[4] There was no significant difference in rates of early cure (defined as a negative urine culture 5–9 days after treatment, which occurred in 94% on each of the three drugs) or microbiologic relapse at long-term follow-up.

Harms: Adverse effects were reported in 12% of patients on lomefloxacin and 17% taking TMP-SMZ.[3] The most frequent adverse effects were skin reactions. Three patients taking TMP-SMZ withdrew from treatment: one patient because of dermatitis and one because of hepatocellular damage. There were no withdrawals because of adverse events in patients taking lomefloxacin.[3] Adverse effects were reported in 2% of patients on levofloxacin, 8% on ciprofloxacin, and 5% on lomefloxacin.[4] Gastrointestinal symptoms were common with both ciprofloxacin and levofloxacin, whereas rash was the commonest adverse effect with lomefloxacin. One of the 186 patients discontinued treatment (lomefloxacin) because of adverse effects.[4]

Comment: Calculated cure rates from the systematic review are likely to overestimate rates that would be achieved in clinical practice because many patients were excluded, including those who did not adhere to treatment, experienced adverse effects, or had growth of a resistant bacteria on initial culture. Although ampicillin and amoxicillin have cure rates comparable with other antibiotics, they are not recommended in pyelonephritis because of high rates of ampicillin resistance. Some centers are encountering increasing resistance to TMP-SMZ by common urinary tract pathogens, so local susceptibility data should dictate antimicrobial choice. Resistance to fluoroquinolone among community isolates remains uniformly low.

OPTION PARENTERAL ANTIBIOTICS

One RCT found that TMP-SMZ or ampicillin combined with gentamicin are effective and well tolerated in women admitted to hospital with acute uncomplicated pyelonephritis. There are no well-designed trials comparing newer antibiotics with these standard regimens. Because of the high rates of ampicillin-resistant *E. coli,* ampicillin should not be used alone.

Benefits: We found no systematic review, but one RCT of 85 women admitted to hospital for acute uncomplicated pyelonephritis. This compared intravenous ampicillin 1 g every 6 hours with intravenous TMP-SMZ 160 mg/800 mg every 12 hours, initiated before culture results were known.[5] Both regimens were combined with gentamicin and followed by oral treatment with either ampicillin or TMP-SMZ. *E. coli* was the sole micro-organism isolated from the urine in 91% of patients. Fourteen of the 42 women (32%) treated with ampicillin and gentamicin were infected with ampicillin-resistant isolates and were withdrawn from the study. No women allocated to TMP-SMZ required a change of treatment, and there were no other treatment failures in either group.

Harms: Adverse effects vary by agent. In the above study,[5] adverse effects that may have been a result of treatment were reported equally in the two groups (33% ampicillin; 32% TMP-SMZ). Common adverse effects with ampicillin include rash, diarrhea, and vaginitis; with TMP-SMZ, they included nausea, vomiting, and vaginitis. There are no figures available on the rates of these adverse effects. One patient from each group discontinued treatment because of adverse effects.[5]

Comment: Although uropathogenic organisms may be sensitive to certain agents (e.g., quinolones, cephalosporins, and broad spectrum β-lactams), there are no adequately designed RCTs comparing those agents with standard treatment. The choice of empiric antibiotics should take into account the setting, medical history of the patient, Gram stain of the urine, previous infecting organism, and the local antibiotic sensitivity of pathogenic organisms.

OPTION INPATIENT VERSUS OUTPATIENT MANAGEMENT

We found no direct evidence comparing inpatient and outpatient management of acute, uncomplicated pyelonephritis in nonpregnant women. RCTs found that outpatient treatment of mild to moderate acute uncomplicated pyelonephritis with oral antibiotics is safe and effective in women without underlying illnesses. However, these findings cannot be applied reliably to patients with severe pyelonephritis or to those with underlying diseases (e.g., diabetes, renal insufficiency, and immunosuppression) until studies including such patients have found similar results.

Benefits: We found no systematic review and no RCTs comparing outpatient with inpatient management of acute uncomplicated pyelonephritis in nonpregnant women. Evidence summarized above, from a systematic review[2] and two subsequent RCTs,[3,4] shows that oral treatment with TMP-SMZ, amoxicillin-clavulanic acid, or a fluoroquinolone (ciprofloxacin, norfloxacin, levofloxacin, and lomefloxacin) is effective in healthy adults with mild to moderate acute pyelonephritis who are able to take oral treatment and who lack signs of sepsis.

Harms: None reported.

Comment: Studies of outpatient management excluded patients with comorbid illness.[2] The systematic review[2] also identified one RCT comparing oral with intravenous cephalosporins in 72 pregnant women admitted to hospital with uncomplicated acute pyelonephritis. This found no significant difference in early cure rates (nearly 90% for both groups).

REFERENCES

1. Stamm WE, Hooton TM, Johnson JR, et al. Urinary tract infection: from pathogenesis to treatment. *J Infect Dis* 1989;15:400–406.
2. Pinson AG, Philbrick JT, Lindbeck GH, Schorling JB. Oral antibiotic therapy for acute pyelonephritis: a methodologic review of the literature. *J Gen Intern Med* 1992;7:544–553. (Search date 1991; primary sources MEDLINE 1965 to 1990, Current Contents 1990 to 1991.)
3. Mouton Y, Ajana F, Chidiac C, Capron MH, Home P, Masquelier AM. A multicenter study of lomefloxacin and trimethoprim/sulfamethoxazole in the treatment of uncomplicated acute pyelonephritis. *Am J Med* 1992;92:87S–90S.
4. Richard GA, Klimberg IN, Fowler CL, Callery-D'Amico S, Kim SS. Levofloxacin versus ciprofloxacin versus lomefloxacin in acute pyelonephritis. *Urology* 1998;52:51–55.
5. Johnson JR, Lyons MF, Pearce W, et al. Therapy for women hospitalized with acute pyelonephritis: a randomized trial of ampicillin versus trimethoprim-sulfamethoxazole for 14 days. *J Infect Dis* 1991;163:325–330.

Lisa D Chew, MD
Acting Instructor of Medicine and Obstetrics and Gynecology
University of Washington
Harborview Medical Center
Seattle
Washington
USA

Stephan D Fihn, MD, MPH
Professor of Medicine and of Health Services
University of Washington
Seattle
Washington
USA

Competing interests: None declared.

TABLE 1 **Oral antibiotic treatment for acute pyelonephritis: results of RCTs.**[2] (See text p. 245.)

Study number	Oral antibiotic regimens	Total number of patients	Early cure* rates (%)	Late cure* rates (%)	*p* value
1	Amoxicillin 500 mg three times daily for 14 days	16	–	94	NS
	TMP-SMZ (160 mg/800 mg) twice daily for 14 days	12	–	92	
2	Norfloxacin 400 mg twice daily for 10 days	14	100	86	NS
	TMP-SMZ (160 mg/800 mg) twice daily for 10 days	10	100	90	
3	Ampicillin 500 mg four times daily for 10 days	8	88	–	NS
	Cefaclor 250 mg twice daily for 10 days	6	67	–	
4	Norfloxacin 400 mg twice daily for 7 days or longer	3	67	–	NS
	TMP-SMZ (160 mg/800 mg) twice daily for 7 days or longer	12	92	–	
5	Amoxicillin-clavulanic acid 250 mg/125 mg three times daily for 10 days	54	94	85	0.02 for late cure;
	TMP-SMZ (160 mg/800 mg) twice daily for 10 days	50	82	64	NS for early cure
6	Ampicillin 500 mg four times daily for 2 or 6 weeks	17	100	47	0.004 for late cure;
	TMP-SMZ (160 mg/800 mg) twice daily for 2 or 6 weeks	22	100	91	NS for early cure
7	Amoxicillin 2000 mg one-time dose then 1000 mg twice daily for 9 days	22	100	100	NS
	Amoxicillin 750 mg three times daily for 12 days	23	96	87	
8	Cefetamet 2000 mg daily or 1000 mg twice daily for 10–15 days	28	93	79	NS
	Cefadroxil 1000 mg twice daily for 10–15 days	22	73	52	
9	Norfloxacin 400 mg twice daily for 14 days	76	91	82	<0.0001 for both
	Cefadroxil 1000 mg twice daily for 14 days	75	59	44	early and late cures

Table adapted with permission from Pinson AG, Philbrick JT, Lindbeck GH, et al.[2] NS, not significant. *Early cure: negative urine culture within 7–10 days of starting treatment; Late cure: negative urine culture 2–4 weeks or more after stopping treatment.

Bacterial vaginosis

M Riduan Joesoef, MD, PhD, and George P Schmid, MD, MSc

QUESTIONS

INTERVENTIONS

Key Messages

- Bacterial vaginosis may resolve spontaneously but is associated with complications in pregnancy.
- **In nonpregnant women** Randomized controlled trials (RCTs) have found that oral and intravaginal administration of anti-anaerobic agents are equally effective. There are fewer side effects with intravaginal treatment. Limited evidence suggests that oral metronidazole for 1 week may be more effective than a single dose.
- **In women about to undergo surgical abortion** there is limited evidence that treating bacterial vaginosis reduces the risk of pelvic inflammatory disease. Effects of treatment before other gynecologic procedures have not yet been evaluated.
- **In pregnant women** who have previously delivered a premature infant, we found limited evidence from RCTs that treating bacterial vaginosis with oral anti-anaerobic agents reduces the risk of premature delivery. Limited evidence from RCTs suggests no benefit from intravaginal administration or from treating bacterial vaginosis in pregnant women with no previous his-

tory of premature delivery.

- Infection recurs in approximately one third of women. RCTs have found no reduction in recurrence rates from treating male sexual partners.

DEFINITION Bacterial vaginosis is a microbial disease characterized by an alteration in the bacterial flora of the vagina, from a predominance of *Lactobacillus* species to high concentrations of anaerobic bacteria. The clinical diagnosis requires three out of four signs: the presence of clue cells; a homogenous discharge that adheres to the vaginal walls; pH of vaginal fluid > 4.5; and a "fishy" amine odor of the vaginal discharge before or after addition of 10% potassium hydroxide. Half of women with bacterial vaginosis have no symptoms. Those with symptoms have an excessive white to gray or malodorous, vaginal discharge; the odor may be noticeable particularly during sexual intercourse.

INCIDENCE/PREVALENCE Bacterial vaginosis is the most prevalent infectious cause of vaginitis, being approximately twice as common as candidiasis.[1] Prevalences of 10% to 61% have been reported among unselected women from diverse care settings.[2] Limited incidence data are available, but one study found that over a 2-year period 50% of women using an intrauterine device had at least one episode, as did 20% of women using oral contraceptives.[3] Bacterial vaginosis is particularly prevalent in lesbians.[4]

ETIOLOGY The cause of the alteration of vaginal flora is not fully understood. Risk factors include new or multiple sexual partners[1,3,5] and early age of sexual debut,[6] but bacterial vaginosis is not a sexually transmitted disease. No causative micro-organism has been shown to be transmitted from men to women. Use of an intrauterine device[3] and douching[5] also have been reported as risk factors, and it appears to be most common around the time of menses.[7]

PROGNOSIS Bacterial vaginosis has a variable and poorly understood course. Without treatment, symptoms may persist or resolve, both in pregnant and nonpregnant women. After treatment, recurrences occur in approximately one third of women. Bacterial vaginosis is associated with complications of pregnancy [low birth weight, preterm birth, preterm labor, premature rupture of the membranes (6.3% of women with bacterial vaginosis vs. 4.2% of women without bacterial vaginosis OR 1.4 95% CI 1.1–1.8,[6] other studies reported OR from 1.5–6.9); late miscarriage, chorioamnionitis (48% vs. 22%; OR 2.6, 95% CI 1.0–6.6); endometritis (8.2% vs. 1.5%; OR 5.6, 95% CI 1.8–17.2); and endometritis after normal delivery, caesarean section (55% vs. 17%; OR 5.8, 95% CI 3.0–10.9)], and surgery to the genital tract.[6,8] It also has been reported to enhance HIV transmission.[9]

AIMS To alleviate symptoms and to prevent complications relating to childbirth, termination of pregnancy, and gynecologic surgery.

OUTCOMES Clinical or microbiologic cure rates usually after 1 to 2 weeks or 4 weeks of completing treatment.

METHODS We searched MEDLINE (bacterial vaginosis, nonspecific vaginosis, clindamycin, metronidazole) from 1988 through September 1998.

In addition, we used information from drug manufacturers. For each study, we assessed study design, study population, treatment, outcome measures, reported findings, and potential biases.

QUESTION **What are the effects of treating nonpregnant women with symptomatic bacterial vaginosis?**

RCTs have found no difference in effectiveness of oral versus intravaginal administration of anti-anaerobic agents. Intravaginal administration lessens the risk of systemic adverse effects. Limited evidence suggests no difference between oral clindamycin and oral metronidazole. Regardless of the route of administration or type of anti-anaerobic agent used, symptoms recur after treatment in over one third of women.

Benefits: **Oral versus intravaginal administration:** We found one systematic review, which identified five RCTs comparing oral and intravaginal formulations of metronidazole and clindamycin.[10] Three RCTs recruited symptomatic nonpregnant women with bacterial vaginosis and two RCTs recruited symptomatic or asymptomatic nonpregnant women with bacterial vaginosis. Cumulative cure rates 5 to 10 days after completing treatment were 86% for oral metronidazole (500 mg tid for 7 days), 85% for clindamycin vaginal cream (5 g at qn for 7 consecutive days), and 81% for metronidazole vaginal gel (5 g tid for 5 days). Four weeks after completing treatment, the cumulative cure rates were 78% for oral metronidazole, 82% for clindamycin vaginal cream, and 71% for metronidazole vaginal gel. **Different oral regimens:** An earlier systematic review found four RCTs comparing metronidazole 500 mg twice daily for 7 days versus a single 2-g dose of metronidazole. Cumulative cure rates 3 to 4 weeks after completing treatment were 82% and 62%, respectively ($p < 0.05$).[8] We found only one RCT comparing metronidazole versus clindamycin. This randomized 144 symptomatic nonpregnant women to either oral clindamycin 300 mg twice daily for 7 days or metronidazole 500 mg twice daily for 7 days. It found no significant difference (cure rates within 7–10 days of starting treatment 94% versus 96%, respectively). However, one third of patients were lost to follow-up.[11] **Recurrence:** In 30% of women, bacterial vaginosis recurred after 12 weeks of treatment with clindamycin vaginal cream.[12] No well-studied long-term maintenance regimen for recurrent bacterial vaginosis has been reported.

Harms: A quarter to two thirds of participants in the trials[8] experienced adverse effects from oral metronidazole, including mild to moderate nausea/dyspepsia, unpleasant metallic taste, headache, and dizziness. Infrequent side effects from oral clindamycin included heartburn, nausea, vomiting, diarrhea, constipation, headache, dizziness, and vertigo. No data on frequency were available from the trial reports. Intravaginal clindamycin has been associated, rarely, with mild to severe colitis[13] and with vaginal candidiasis. Yeast vulvovaginitis may be less common with intravaginal than with oral metronidazole (4% for intravaginal[14] versus 8%–22% for oral[15]).

Comment: Intravaginal administration of the drug reduces systemic absorption, and reduces the systemic side effects. However, some women prefer to take oral medication because it is more convenient to use and less messy.

QUESTION What are the effects of treating pregnant women?

RCTs suggest that oral metronidazole (alone or with erythromycin) or clindamycin may reduce the risk of preterm birth, premature rupture of membranes, and low birth weight. Effects on other complications associated with bacterial vaginosis in pregnancy have not been evaluated in RCTs. Benefit was confined to women with a previous history of premature delivery, but the number of such high-risk women in the studies was small. Limited evidence suggests no benefit from intravaginal administration. Good data provide no evidence that treatment is teratogenic.

Benefits: We found no systematic review. We found five RCTs. These looked at only three of the clinical sequelae of bacterial vaginosis in pregnancy: preterm birth, premature rupture of membranes, and low birth weight, and did not always separate symptomatic from asymptomatic women.[16–20] **Oral treatment versus placebo:** One RCT, in 80 high-risk pregnant women with bacterial vaginosis, compared oral metronidazole (250 mg tid for 7 days) versus placebo. It reported a reduction of preterm birth (< 34 weeks of gestation, 5% vs. 11%, $p > 0.05$; < 37 weeks, 18% vs. 39%, $p < 0.05$), of low birth weight (< 2500 g, 14% vs. 33%, $p < 0.05$), and of premature rupture of membranes (5% vs. 33%, $p < 0.05$).[16] Another RCT, involving 857 pregnant women, compared treatment (initial treatment at 24 weeks of gestation with oral metronidazole 400 mg bid for 2 days, followed by the same regimen for those with persistent bacterial vaginosis at 29 weeks of gestation) versus placebo.[20] It reported a reduction of preterm birth (< 37 weeks of gestation, 9% vs. 42%, OR = 0.14, 95% CI 0.01–0.84) among high-risk pregnant women ($n = 46$), but not among low-risk women. A third RCT, involving 624 pregnant women with bacterial vaginosis, compared oral metronidazole 250 mg three times a day for 7 days plus erythromycin 333 mg three times a day for 14 days versus placebo.[17] Women with persistent bacterial vaginosis 2 to 4 weeks after completion of initial treatment received the same regimen again. This reported a reduction of preterm birth (< 37 weeks of gestation, 39% vs. 57%, $p < 0.05$) in high-risk women. **Intravaginal treatment versus placebo:** Two further RCTs in a total of 810 pregnant women compared intravaginal clindamycin cream 5 g at bedtime for 7 consecutive days versus placebo. They reported no significant difference in risk of preterm birth, low birth weight, or premature rupture of membranes.[18,19]

Harms: Metronidazole crosses the placenta readily, but a recent meta-analysis of six prospective studies and one retrospective study of metronidazole in 1336 pregnant women found no evidence for teratogenicity.[21]

Comment: Two of the RCTs included only small numbers of high-risk women: 80[16] and 46.[20] The third RCT[17] had the following limitations: bacterial vaginosis was treated with both oral metronidazole and erythromycin, making it unclear what metronidazole alone would achieve; the bacterial vaginosis aspect of the trial was a post hoc analysis; and the study population comprised black, lower-socioeconomic urban patients who might not be representative of the overall US population. Preliminary findings from a large RCT of anti-anaerobic treatment in pregnant women in the USA indicates no such benefit from oral treatment.[22] The effectiveness of oral as opposed to intravaginal metronidazole may be caused by a systemic effect on subclinical intrauterine infection.

QUESTION Does treating male partners prevent recurrence?

RCTs have found that, in women with one steady male sexual partner, treating the partner with an anti-anaerobic agent does not reduce the woman's risk of recurrence.

Benefits: We found no systematic review. We found four RCTs on treating sex partners of women with one steady partner.[11,23–25] Two RCTs (348 couples) used two single doses of 2 g metronidazole at 1 and 3 days and found no significant difference in recurrence rates between women whose sexual partners had been treated and those who had received placebo.[24,25] The third, in 140 couples, compared treating the partner with a single dose of 2 g metronidazole versus placebo.[23] Clinical cure rates were not significantly different. Cure rates defined by the Gram stain were significantly different at 4 weeks after treatment (RR and CI were not calculable from the report) but not at 8 weeks. The fourth RCT, in 139 couples, compared treating the partner with clindamycin hydrochloride capsules 150 g four times a day for 7 days versus placebo.[12] Recurrence rates within 3 months from diagnosis were not significantly different.

Harms: No harmful effects were reported in the trials.

Comment: The lack of effectiveness of both metronidazole and clindamycin suggests that anaerobes are unlikely to be the sole pathogenic agents in the association of bacterial vaginosis with sexual intercourse.

QUESTION What are the effects of treating women before gynecologic procedures?

In women with bacterial vaginosis who are about to undergo surgical abortion, we found limited evidence suggesting that oral metronidazole reduces the risk of pelvic inflammatory disease. The effects of treatment before other gynecologic procedures, including insertion of intrauterine devices, have not yet been evaluated in RCTs.

Benefits: We found no systematic review. We found one RCT. This compared oral metronidazole 500 mg three times daily for 10 days versus placebo in 174 women with bacterial vaginosis who were about to undergo surgical abortion.[26] Among 174 evaluable women, 3.8% in the metronidazole group developed pelvic inflammatory disease versus 12.2% in the placebo group ($p < 0.05$). RR and CI were not calculable from the report.

Harms: The trial reported no harmful effects.

Comment: Although bacterial vaginosis is associated with an increased risk of endometritis after cesarean section and of vaginal cuff cellulitis after abdominal hysterectomy,[27,28] no RCTs have evaluated treatment of bacterial vaginosis before such procedures. Bacterial vaginosis also has been associated with use of an intrauterine contraceptive device,[3] but no RCTs have evaluated whether treatment of bacterial vaginosis before insertion of such devices reduces the incidence of infective complications or pelvic inflammatory disease.

REFERENCES

1. Barbone F, Austin H, Louv WC, Alexander WJ. A follow-up study of methods of contraception, sexual activity, and rates of trichomoniasis, candidiasis, and bacterial vaginosis. *Am J Obstet Gynecol* 1990;163:510–514.
2. Mead PB. Epidemiology of bacterial vaginosis. *Am J Obstet Gynecol* 1993;169:446–449.
3. Avonts D, Sercu M, Heyerick P, Vandermeeren I, Meheus A, Piot P. Incidence of uncomplicated genital infections in women using oral contraception or an intrauterine device: a prospective study. *Sex Transm Dis* 1990;17:23–29.
4. Berger BJ, Kolton S, Zenilman JM, et al. Bacterial vaginosis in lesbians: a sexually transmitted disease. *Clin Infect Dis* 1995;21:1402–1405.
5. Hawes SE, Hillier SL, Benedetti J, et al. Hydrogen peroxide-producing lactobacilli and acquisition of vaginal infections. *J Infect Dis* 1996;174:1058–1063.
6. Hillier SL, Nugent RP, Eschenbach DA, et al. Association between bacterial vaginosis and preterm delivery of a low-birth-weight infant. *N Engl J Med* 1995;333:1737–1742.
7. Schwebke JR, Morgan SC, Weiss HL. The use of sequential self-obtained vaginal smears for detecting changes in the vaginal flora. *Sex Transm Dis* 1997;24:236–239.
8. Joesoef MR, Schmid GP. Bacterial vaginosis: review of treatment options and potential clinical indications for therapy. *Clin Infect Dis* 1995; 20(suppl 1):S72–79.
9. Sewankambo N, Gray RH, Wawer MJ, et al. HIV-1 infection associated with abnormal vaginal flora morphology and bacterial vaginosis. *Lancet* 1997;350:546–550.
10. Joesoef MR, Schmid GP, Hillier SL. Bacterial vaginosis: review of treatment options and potential clinical indications for therapy. *Clin Infect Dis* 1999;28 (suppl 1):S57–S65.
11. Greaves WL, Chungafung J, Morris B, Haile A, Townsend JL. Clindamycin versus metronidazole in the treatment of bacterial vaginosis. *Obstet Gynecol* 1988;72:799–802.
12. Colli E, Landoni M, Parazzini F. Treatment of male partners and recurrence of bacterial vaginosis: a randomised trial. *Genitourin Med* 1997;73:267–270.
13. Trexler MF, Fraser TG, Jones MP. Fulminant pseudomembranous colitis caused by clindamycin phosphate vaginal cream. *Am J Gastroenterol* 1997;92:2112–2113.
14. Hillier SL, Lipinski C, Briselden AM, Eschenbach DA. Efficacy of intravaginal 0.75% metronidazole gel for the treatment of bacterial vaginosis. *Obstet Gynecol* 1993;81:963–967.
15. Schmitt C, Sobel JD, Meriwether C. Bacterial vaginosis: treatment with clindamycin cream versus oral metronidazole. *Obstet Gynecol* 1992;79: 1020–1023.
16. Morales WJ, Schorr S, Albritton J. Effect of metronidazole in patients with preterm birth in preceding pregnancy and bacterial vaginosis: a placebo-controlled, double-blind study. *Am J Obstet Gynecol* 1994;171:345–349.
17. Hauth JC, Goldenberg RL, Andrews WW, DuBard MB, Copper RL. Midtrimester treatment with metronidazole plus erythromycin reduces preterm delivery only in women with bacterial vaginosis [abstract]. *Am J Obstet Gynecol* 1995;172:253.
18. Joesoef MR, Hillier SL, Wiknjosastro G, et al. Intravaginal clindamycin treatment for bacterial vaginosis: effects on preterm delivery and low birth weight. *Am J Obstet Gynecol* 1995;173: 1527–1531.
19. McGregor JA, French JI, Jones W, et al. Bacterial vaginosis is associated with prematurity and vaginal fluid mucinase and sialidase: results of a controlled trial of topical clindamycin cream. *Am J Obstet Gynecol* 1994;170:1048–1060.
20. McDonald HM, O'Loughlin JA, Vigneswaran R, et al. Impact of metronidazole therapy on preterm birth in women with bacterial vaginosis flora (Gardnerella vaginalis): a randomized, placebo controlled trial. *Br J Obstet Gynaecol* 1998;104: 1391–1397.
21. Burtin P, Taddio A, Ariburnu O, Einarson TR, Koren G. Safety of metronidazole in pregnancy: a meta-analysis. *Am J Obstet Gynecol* 1995;172:525–529.
22. Klebanoff M, Carey JC, NICHD MFMU Network. Metronidazole did not prevent preterm birth in asymptomatic women with bacterial vaginosis. *Am J Obstet Gynaecol* 1999;180(part 2):52 (abstract).
23. Mengel MB, Berg AO, Weaver CH, et al. The effectiveness of single-dose metronidazole therapy for patients and their partners with bacterial vaginosis. *J Fam Pract* 1989;28:163–171.
24. Vejtorp M, Bollerup AC, Vejtorp L, et al. Bacterial vaginosis: a double-blind randomized trial of the effect of treatment of the sexual partner. *Br J Obstet Gynecol* 1988;95:920–926.
25. Moi H, Erkkola R, Jerve F, et al. Should male consorts of women with bacterial vaginosis be treated? *Genitourin Med* 1989;65:263–268.
26. Larsson PG, Platz-Christensen JJ, Thejls H, Forsum U, Pahlson C. Incidence of pelvic inflammatory disease after first-trimester legal abortion in women with bacterial vaginosis after treatment with metronidazole: a double-blind, randomized study. *Am J Obstet Gynecol* 1992;166:100–103.
27. Soper DE, Bump RC, Hurt WG. Bacterial vaginosis and trichomoniasis vaginitis are risk factors for cuff cellulitis after abdominal hysterectomy. *Am J Obstet Gynecol* 1990;163:1016–1023.
28. Watts D, Krohn M, Hillier S, Eschenbach D. Bacterial vaginosis as a risk factor for postcesarean endometritis. *Obstet Gynecol* 1990;75:52–58.

M Riduan Joesoef, MD, PhD
Medical Epidemiologist
National Center for HIV, STD, and TB Prevention
Atlanta
Georgia
USA

George P Schmid, MD, MSc
Medical Epidemiologist
National Center for HIV, STD and TB Prevention
Atlanta
Georgia
USA

Competing interests: None declared.

Premenstrual syndrome

K M Wyatt, PhD, P W Dimmock, PhD, and P M S O'Brien, MD, FRCOG

QUESTIONS

INTERVENTIONS

Key Messages

- Randomized controlled trials (RCTs) have found SSRIs and prostaglandin inhibitors to be effective in overall relief of premenstrual symptoms. Antidepressants and ovulation suppression with danazol and GnRH analogues are also effective but have significant adverse effects, including the masculinizing adverse effects of danazol and the "menopausal" adverse effects of GnRH analogues.
- We found limited evidence suggesting that estrogen, vitamin B_6, evening primrose oil, and exercise also may be beneficial.
- RCTs have found that bromocriptine is effective for the treatment of breast symptoms and diuretics are effective for bloatedness and swelling. Both treatments are associated with adverse effects.
- We found no good evidence to support the use of progesterone or oral contraceptives.
- Most treatments have not been evaluated adequately in RCTs.

DEFINITION A woman has premenstrual syndrome (PMS) if she complains of regularly recurring psychological or somatic symptoms (or both) which occur specifically during the luteal phase of the menstrual cycle and which resolve by the end of menstruation (Table 1).[1]

INCIDENCE/ PREVALENCE Premenstrual symptoms occur in 95% of all women of reproductive age; severe, debilitating symptoms occur in approximately 5% of women.[1]

ETIOLOGY The etiology remains unknown.[2] Current research suggests that hormonal and other (possibly neuroendocrine) factors contribute.[3] There seems to be an enhanced sensitivity to progesterone, possibly caused by a deficiency of serotonin.[3]

PROGNOSIS Except after the removal of the ovaries, it is likely that symptoms will recur when treatment is stopped.

AIMS To improve or eliminate physical and psychological symptoms; to minimize the impact on normal functioning, interpersonal relationships, and quality of life; to minimize adverse effects of treatment.

OUTCOMES Symptom severity. There is no consensus on how this should be assessed. A review of PMS outcome measures found 65 different questionnaires or scales, measuring 199 different symptoms or signs (Table 1).[4]

METHODS We used the search strategy of the Cochrane Collaboration's menstrual disorders and subfertility group.[5] A well-controlled study should 1) show the existence of PMS before treatment by prospectively administered, validated scales; 2) include a prerandomization placebo cycle to exclude women who have a nonspecific response; and 3) contain sufficient cycles to allow for symptom variability between cycles. Few studies fulfilled these criteria. The wide range of diagnostic scales, outcome criteria, and dosing regimens made comparison between trials difficult. Detailed numerical analysis for each intervention awaits full systematic review.

QUESTION What are the effects of drug treatments?

HORMONAL

OPTION PROGESTERONE

Evidence from RCTs is conflicting.

Benefits: We found no systematic review. We identified 12 RCTs,[6–17] four of which found progesterone to be more effective than placebo (two trials gave progesterone as a suppository[9,14] and two as oral micronized progesterone[11,16]) and eight trials (seven gave progesterone as a suppository and one as an intramuscular injection[12]) found no benefit over placebo.

Harms: Some trials reported adverse effects, such as abdominal pain,[10] nausea,[10,11,14] headache,[14] vaginal pruritus,[14] dizziness,[11] drowsiness,[11] excessive bleeding,[10,14] and dysmenorrhea.[10,14]

Comment: There is no direct evidence to support the theory of progesterone deficiency or the use of progesterone to treat PMS.

OPTION PROGESTOGENS (SYNTHETIC PROGESTERONE-LIKE DRUGS)

Evidence from RCTs is conflicting.

Benefits: We found no systematic review. We identified seven RCTs comparing dydrogesterone versus placebo.[18–24] Three trials[20,22,24] reported a significant improvement with dydrogesterone for some premenstrual symptoms. The remaining four showed no therapeutic effect.[18,19,21,23] Three trials compared medroxyprogesterone acetate versus placebo.[25–27] Two of these[25,27] found an improvement in women taking the drug, whereas the third found no difference.

Harms: The most commonly reported adverse effects were nausea, breast discomfort, headache, and menstrual irregularity.

Comment: The progestogen most commonly used as a treatment for PMS is dydrogesterone, which is not available in the US. Medroxyprogesterone acetate is used occasionally as it suppresses ovulation. However, there is no evidence to show that it is effective. Paradoxically, progestogens seem to induce PMS symptoms during hormone replacement therapy.

OPTION ESTROGEN

Limited evidence from RCTs suggests benefit.

Benefits: We found no systematic review. Of the three RCTs identified in which estrogen was compared with placebo, one[28] (using oral conjugated equine estrogens) found no effect. Estradiol (given as a transdermal patch or subcutaneous implant) improved overall premenstrual symptoms.[29,30] One trial found estradiol gel to be an effective treatment for premenstrual migraine.[30]

Harms: Adverse effects included breast discomfort, nausea, weight gain, headache, and skin pigmentation (in the patch trial).[29]

Comment: The studies suggest that suppression of the ovarian cycle with estrogen can eliminate PMS. To avoid endometrial hyperplasia and adenocarcinoma, a 12-day progestogen course is needed every 28 days. Many adverse effects result from the direct effects of this progestogen. If progestogen is given locally (levonorgestrel intrauterine device or progesterone gel), thus avoiding systemic effects, resurgence of PMS theoretically may be avoided. No evidence for this exists from adequately controlled trials.

OPTION DANAZOL

RCTs have found danazol to be of some benefit but with notable adverse effects and long-term risks associated with masculinization.

Benefits: We found no systematic review. Of the seven RCTs identified,[31–37] five found that danazol given continuously was significantly better than placebo. In two trials in which danazol was given in the luteal phase only,[35,37] one found it to be better than placebo in treating overall premenstrual symptomatology[35] whereas the other, larger trial[37] found it to be better at treating premenstrual breast pain only.

Harms: Danazol has important adverse effects and long-term risks associated with its continued use. Although osteoporosis does not appear to be a risk, masculinizing effects can be notable; they extend not only to the effects on the voice, hirsutism, and weight gain but possibly to more subtle effects on plasma lipids, with consequent impact on the risk of cardiovascular disease.

Comment: Danazol has been prescribed as a treatment for PMS as it suppresses the ovarian cycle in most patients.

OPTION GNRH ANALOGUES

RCTs have found benefit from GnRH analogues. GnRH analogues should be given for a maximum of 6 months because of the risk of osteoporosis, which limits their usefulness. Treatment may be extended when "add back" treatment is included.

Benefits: We found no systematic review. We found eight trials,[38–45] which compared GnRH analogues versus placebo. Seven of the trials showed an improvement with the drug over placebo. The other reported no difference between drug and placebo, as all patients improved on either treatment.[40] In two of these trials, "add back" therapy with estrogen and medroxyprogesterone also was given.[42,43] Both found the treatment significantly better than placebo.

Harms: Adverse effects of GnRH analogues alone, other than osteoporosis, include hot flushes,[39,41] night sweats,[39] decreased libido, pruritus, nausea,[41] and bronchospasm.

Comment: A true double-blind controlled trial of GnRH analogues would be hard to conduct because patients receiving these agents will experience amenorrhea, unblinding the active treatment arm of the study.

OPTION BROMOCRIPTINE

RCTs have found that bromocriptine relieves breast tenderness, although side effects are common.

Benefits: We found no systematic review. In a survey of 14 trials,[46] there was no evidence to show that bromocriptine was effective in treating PMS, although it seems effective in treating premenstrual mastalgia. One RCT[47] subsequent to that survey also found it be effective for breast tenderness and edema.

Harms: The use of bromocriptine is associated with a high incidence of adverse effects, including nausea,[47–50] dizziness,[47,49,50] headache,[47] weight gain,[47] and swelling.[47]

Comment: None.

OPTION **ORAL CONTRACEPTIVES**

Limited and conflicting evidence from RCTs shows little benefit.

Benefits: We found no systematic review. We found four RCTs[51–54] comparing oral contraceptives versus placebo. Three found no improvement over placebo, with one reporting improvement in premenstrual breast pain and bloating.[53]

Harms: A notable proportion of women develop PMS-like symptoms for the first time when taking the oral contraceptive pill. Few adverse effects are mentioned in the trials.

Comment: A large amount of anecdotal evidence suggests that oral contraceptives are beneficial in PMS. Continuous combined regimens (those without a week's break) should, in theory, suppress ovulation and provide symptom relief, but there are no published trials on such regimens.

NONHORMONAL DRUGS

OPTION **DIURETICS**

RCTs have found diuretics to improve symptoms relating to breast tenderness and bloatedness.

Benefits: No systematic review. Six RCTs[12,25,54–58] have used spironolactone. Five found an improvement in premenstrual symptoms compared with placebo (particularly those associated with bloatedness/breast tenderness) and one found no difference between drug and placebo. Two other trials used metolazone[59] and chlorthalidone.[60] Metolazone was effective for physical and somatic symptoms, whereas chlorthalidone was not effective.

Harms: Adverse effects include nausea,[56] dizziness,[25] palpitations,[58] excess diuresis,[59] and weakness.[59]

Comment: Diuretics have been prescribed widely in the belief that many of the symptoms of PMS are the direct consequence of fluid retention, although there is little evidence of water retention in most women with PMS.

OPTION **PROSTAGLANDIN INHIBITORS**

RCTs have found benefit for a range of symptoms but not for premenstrual breast pain.

Benefits: We found no systematic review. Of the five RCTs identified using mefenamic acid,[61–65] all reported an improvement on drug versus placebo for a variety of premenstrual symptoms but not for premenstrual breast pain. One trial used naproxen sodium and found it to be effective for physical premenstrual symptoms.[66]

Harms: Adverse effects include nausea,[61] gastrointestinal disturbances,[62] and rashes.[62,63]

Comment: The prostaglandin inhibitor mefenamic acid has been used extensively in the treatment of menstrual problems and has been proposed as a treatment for PMS.

PSYCHOTROPIC DRUGS

OPTION ANTIDEPRESSANTS/ANXIOLYTICS

RCTs have found benefit for one or more symptoms of PMS, but a proportion of women stop treatment because of adverse effects.

Benefits: We found no systematic review. We found nine adequately controlled trials of antidepressants/anxiolytic drugs for PMS. All reported some positive effects on one or more PMS symptom. Three trials used tricyclic antidepressants (clomipramine[67,68] or nortriptyline[69]) and six trials used anxiolytics (alprazolam[16,70–73] or buspirone[74]). Lithium was also assessed but was found to be ineffective.[75]

Harms: There were problems with compliance in all of these trials, arising from adverse effects, such as drowsiness,[68,69,73,76] nausea,[68,73] anxiety,[69,73] and headache.[73]

Comment: Although there may be some benefit from the use of antidepressants/anxiolytics in PMS, this must be weighed carefully against the adverse effects.

OPTION SELECTIVE SEROTONIN-REUPTAKE INHIBITORS (SSRIs)

One systematic review of RCTs has found major improvement in overall symptoms of PMS for women taking SSRIs.

Benefits: We found one preliminary systematic review[76] published in 1998, which identified 10 RCTs in 601 women with PMS. There was a significant improvement in overall premenstrual symptoms for women taking SSRIs compared with those on placebo (overall WMD –0.15, 95% CI –0.09 to –0.21, which corresponds to OR 1.88, 95% CI 1.48–2.40, in favour of SSRIs). SSRIs used in the trials were fluoxetine ($n=6$), fenfluramine ($n=1$), sertraline ($n=2$), and fluvoxamine ($n=1$).

Harms: Adverse effects commonly reported were headache, nervousness, insomnia, drowsiness/fatigue, sexual dysfunction, and gastrointestinal disturbances.[76]

Comment: Fenfluramine[77] was included as it has a similar action to SSRIs, being a serotonin-releasing agent with reuptake inhibition. It has been withdrawn from the US market.

QUESTION What are the effects of nutritional supplements?

OPTION VITAMIN B_6

A systematic review of poor-quality RCTs has found benefit with vitamin B_6 for overall symptoms.

Benefits: We found one systematic review[78] published in 1998, which found no high-quality RCTs. It identified nine RCTs in 940 women with PMS comparing vitamin B_6 (either as a single supplement or as part of a multivitamin supplement) versus placebo. The pooled OR was 2.32 (95% CI 1.95–2.54) in favor of vitamin B_6 for treating overall PMS symptomatology. There was no dose-related response.

Harms: High doses (> 200 mg/d) are associated with peripheral neuropathy, which is reversible on cessation of treatment.[78]

Comment: None of these trials met the established criteria for a systematic review.[78]

OPTION EVENING PRIMROSE OIL

Evening primrose oil is likely to be of benefit. However, it has not yet been evaluated adequately in RCTs.

Benefits: We found one systematic review[79] published in 1996, which identified eight placebo-controlled trials. The authors concluded that, although the properly controlled studies showed a small beneficial effect of evening primrose oil in PMS, the low numbers of women in the trials meant that there was no evidence to support its use in PMS.

Harms: Few adverse effects. There are rare reports of evening primrose oil causing seizures in people with epilepsy.

Comment: Evening primrose oil is one of the most popular "self-help" remedies for PMS, although, as with many complementary medications, the purity of the product cannot be guaranteed.

OPTION MINERAL SUPPLEMENTS

Mineral supplements have not yet been evaluated adequately in women with PMS.

Benefits: We found no systematic review. Two trials have been identified that used magnesium as a supplement for relieving PMS symptoms; one trial found an improvement in overall PMS symptoms versus placebo[80] while the other found no effect.[81] One RCT looked at the effect of calcium[82] and found it to be effective for water retention and pain (breast tenderness and swelling, headaches, and abdominal cramps).

Harms: None reported.

Comment: None.

QUESTION What are the effects of behavioral treatment?

OPTION COGNITIVE BEHAVIORAL TREATMENT

Limited evidence from RCTs is conflicting.

Benefits: We found no systematic review. Four trials have been identified which compared cognitive treatment versus a dummy treatment or placebo. Two trials[83,84] comparing dydrogesterone versus coping skills versus relaxation found cognitive treatment to be more effective than the other intervention, and the other two found there to be no improvement over placebo.[15,85]

Harms: None reported.

Comment: None.

OPTION EXERCISE

RCTs have found that exercise improves symptoms of PMS.

Benefits: We found no systematic review. Three controlled studies[86–88] have found that moderate aerobic exercise was effective in reducing PMS symptoms.

Harms: None reported.

Comment: None.

OPTION RELAXATION TREATMENT

Relaxation treatment has not yet been evaluated properly in women with PMS.

Benefits: We found no systematic review. Two published controlled studies[84,89] have looked at relaxation treatment by itself versus keeping a daily chart of symptoms versus reading leisure material and keeping a daily chart of symptoms as a treatment for PMS with mixed results. One study found relaxation treatment efficacious in treating physical and emotional symptoms associated with PMS, whereas the other found no overall benefit.

Harms: None mentioned.

Comment: Most studies of relaxation techniques have used them as an adjunct to other treatment.

QUESTION What are the effects of surgical treatment?

OPTION HYSTERECTOMY WITH OR WITHOUT OOPHORECTOMY

RCTs have found that hysterectomy and oophorectomy are curative but are rarely appropriate except for very severe symptoms. Hysterectomy alone seems to reduce symptoms, but the evidence is limited because of the difficulty in providing true controls.

Benefits: We found no systematic review. We identified two trials[90,91] in which PMS symptoms were relieved following hysterectomy without bilateral oophorectomy and two trials[92,93] in which PMS symptoms were relieved after hysterectomy with bilateral oophorectomy.

Harms: Potential risks include those associated with major surgery.

Comment: Although surgery is rarely used to manage PMS, it may be indicated if there are co-existing gynecologic problems.[94]

OPTION LAPAROSCOPIC BILATERAL OOPHORECTOMY

This has not yet been evaluated adequately.

Benefits: We found no systematic review or RCTs.

Harms: Insufficient evidence.

Comment: After oophorectomy, estrogen replacement would be required and, hence, the cyclical progesterone treatment would still be needed to protect the endometrium from hyperplasia and carcinoma. This would restimulate PMS in many women.

OPTION ENDOMETRIAL ABLATION

This has not been evaluated in women with PMS. There is no rationale for endometrial ablation, because a "menotoxin" has not yet been demonstrated.

Benefits: We found no systematic review or RCTs.

Harms: Insufficient evidence.

Comment: Studies claiming that endometrial ablation may relieve symptoms of PMS have been in the context of menorrhagia, and thus women were not randomized on the basis of the complaint of PMS.

REFERENCES

1. O'Brien PM. *Premenstrual syndrome*. London: Blackwell Science, 1987.
2. O'Brien PM. Helping women with premenstrual syndrome. *BMJ* 1993;307:1471–1475.
3. Rapkin AJ, Morgan M, Goldman L, Brann DW, Simone D, Mahesh VB. Progesterone metabolite allopregnanolone in women with premenstrual syndrome. *Obstet Gynecol* 1997;90:709–714.
4. Budeiri DJ, Li Wan Po A, Dornan JC. Clinical trials of treatments of premenstrual syndrome: entry criteria and scales for measuring treatment outcomes. *Br J Obstet Gynaecol* 1994;101:689–695.
5. Cochrane Menstrual Disorders and Subfertility Group. Search strategy for specialist registrar (Collaborative Review Groups) In: The Cochrane Library, Issue 4. Oxford: Update Software, 1998.
6. Baker ER, Best RG, Manfredi RL, Demers LM, Wolf GC. Efficacy of progesterone vaginal suppositories in alleviation of nervous symptoms in patients with premenstrual syndrome. *J Assist Reprod Genet* 1995;12:205–209.
7. Maddocks S, Hahn P, Moller F, Reid RL. A double-blind placebo-controlled trial of progesterone vaginal suppositories in the treatment of premenstrual syndrome. *Am J Obstet Gynecol* 1986;154: 573–581.
8. Freeman E, Rickels K, Sondheimer SJ, Polansky M. Ineffectiveness of progesterone suppository treatment for premenstrual syndrome. *JAMA* 1990;264:349–353.
9. Andersch B, Hahn L. Progesterone treatment of premenstrual tension: a double blind study. *J Psychosom Res* 1985;29:489–493.
10. Sampson GA. Premenstrual syndrome: a double-blind controlled trial of progesterone and placebo. *Br J Psychiatry* 1979;135:209–215.
11. Dennerstein L, Spencer-Gardner C, Gotts G, Brown JB, Smith MA, Burrows GD. Progesterone and the premenstrual syndrome: a double blind crossover trial. *BMJ (Clin Res Ed)* 1985;90: 1617–1621.
12. Smith SL. Mood and the menstrual cycle. In: Sachar EJ, ed. *Topics in psychoendocrinology*. New York: Grune & Stratton, 1975:19–58.
13. Van der Meer YG, Benedek-Jaszmann LJ, Van Loenen AC. Effect of high-dose progesterone on the pre-menstrual syndrome; a double blind crossover trial. *J Psychosom Obstet Gynaecol* 1983;24:220–222.
14. Magill PJ. Investigation of the efficacy of progesterone pessaries in the relief of symptoms of premenstrual syndrome: progesterone study group. *Br J Gen Pract* 1995;45:589–593.
15. Corney RH, Stanton R, Newell R. Comparison of progesterone, placebo and behavioural psychotherapy in the treatment of premenstrual syndrome. *J Psychosom Obstet Gynaecol* 1990;11: 211–220.
16. Freeman EW, Rickels K, Sondheimer SJ, Polansky M. A double-blind trial of oral progesterone, alprazolam, and placebo in treatment of severe premenstrual syndrome. *JAMA* 1995;274:51–57.

17. Richter MA, Haltvick R, Shapiro SS. Progesterone treatment of premenstrual syndrome. *Current Therapeutic Research* 1984;36:850.
18. Sampson GA, Heathcote PR, Wordsworth J, Prescott P, Hodgson A. Premenstrual syndrome. A double-blind cross-over study of treatment with dydrogesterone and placebo. *Br J Psychiatry* 1988;153:232–235.
19. Dennerstein L, Morse C, Gotts G, et al. Treatment of premenstrual syndrome: a double-blind trial of dydrogesterone. *J Affect Disord* 1986;11:199–205.
20. Kerr GD, Day JB, Munday MR, Brush MG, Watson M, Taylor RW. Dydrogesterone in the treatment of the premenstrual syndrome. *Practitioner* 1980; 224:852–855.
21. Hoffmann V, Pedersen PA, Philip J, Fly P, Pedersen C. The effect of dydrogesterone on premenstrual symptoms: a double-blind, randomized, placebo-controlled study in general practice. *Scand J Prim Health Care* 1988;6:179–183.
22. Haspels AA. A double blind, placebo controlled multi-centre study of the efficacy of dydrogesterone (Duphaston). In: Van Keep PA, Utian WH, eds. *The premenstrual syndrome*. Lancaster: MTP Press, 1980:81–92.
23. Williams JGC, Martin AJ, Hulkenberg-Tromp A. PMS in 4 European countries: part 2. a double blind controlled study of dydrogesterone. *Br J Sex Med* 1983;10:8–18.
24. Coppen AJ, Milne HB, Outram DH, Weber JCP. Dytide, norethisterone and placebo in the premenstrual syndrome. *Clinical Trials Journal* 1969; 6:33–35.
25. Hellberg D, Claesson B, Nilsson S. Premenstrual tension: a placebo-controlled efficacy study with spironolactone and medroxyprogesterone acetate. *Int J Gynaecol Obstet* 1991;34:243–248.
26. Jordheim O. The premenstrual syndrome: clinical trials of treatment with a progestogen combined with a diuretic compared with both a progestogen alone and with a placebo. *Acta Obstet Gynecol Scand* 1972;51:77–80.
27. West CP. Inhibition of ovulation with oral progestins: effectiveness in premenstrual syndrome. *European Journal of Obstetrics and Gynecology and Reproductive Biology* 1990;34:119–128.
28. Dhar V, Murphy BE. Double-blind randomized crossover trial of luteal phase estrogens (Premarin) in the premenstrual syndrome (PMS). *Psychoneuroendocrinology* 1990;15:489–493.
29. Watson NR, Studd JW, Savvas M, Garnett T, Baber RJ. Treatment of severe premenstrual syndrome with oestradiol patches and cyclical oral norethisterone. *Lancet* 1989;2:730–732.
30. de Lignieres B, Vincens M, Mauvais-Jarvis P, et al. Prevention of menstrual migraine by percutaneous oestradiol. *BMJ* 1986;293:1540.
31. Gilmore DH, Hawthorn RJ, Hart DM. Danol for premenstrual syndrome: a preliminary report of a placebo-controlled double-blind study. *J Int Med Res* 1985;13:129–130.
32. Halbreich U, Rojansky N, Palter S. Elimination of ovulation and menstrual cyclicity (with danazol) improves dysphoric premenstrual syndromes. *Fertil Steril* 1991;56:1066–1069.
33. Watts JF, Butt WR, Logan ER. A clinical trial using danazol for the treatment of premenstrual tension. *Br J Obstet Gynaecol* 1987;94:30–34.
34. Deeny M, Hawthorn R, McKay HD. Low dose danazol in the treatment of the premenstrual syndrome. *Postgrad Med J* 1991;67:450–454.
35. Sarno AP, Miller EJ, Lundblad EG. Premenstrual syndrome: beneficial effects of periodic, low-dose danazol. *Obstet Gynecol* 1987;70:33–36.
36. Hahn PM, Van Vugt DA, Reid RL. A randomized, placebo-controlled, crossover trial of danazol for the treatment of premenstrual syndrome. *Psychoneuroendocrinology* 1995;20:193–209.
37. O'Brien PMS, Abukhalil IEH. Randomised controlled trial of the management of premenstrual syndrome and premenstrual mastalgia using luteal phase only danazol. *Am J Obstet Gynecol* [In press]
38. Freeman EW, Sondheimer SJ, Rickels K. Gonadotropin-releasing hormone agonist in the treatment of premenstrual symptoms with and without ongoing dysphoria: a controlled study. *Psychopharmacol Bull* 1997;33:303–309.
39. Brown CS, Ling FW, Andersen RN, Farmer RG, Arheart KL. Efficacy of depot leuprolide in premenstrual syndrome: effect of symptom severity and type in a controlled trial. *Obstet Gynecol* 1994;84: 779–786.
40. Helvacioglu A, Yeoman RR, Hazelton JM, Aksel S. Premenstrual syndrome and related hormonal changes. Long-acting gonadotrophin releasing hormone agonist treatment. *J Reprod Med* 1993; 38:864–870.
41. Muse KN, Cetel NS, Futterman LA, Yen SC. The premenstrual syndrome. Effects of "medical ovariectomy". *N Engl J Med* 1984;311:1345–1349.
42. Mortola JF, Girton L, Fischer U. Successful treatment of severe premenstrual syndrome by combined use of gonadotrophin-releasing hormone agonist and estrogen/progestin. *J Clin Endocrinol Metab* 1991;72:252A–252F.
43. Mezrow G, Shoupe D, Spicer D, Lobo R, Leung B, Pike M. Depot leuprolide acetate with estrogen and progestin add-back for long-term treatment of premenstrual syndrome. *Fertil Steril* 1994;62: 932–937.
44. Hammarback S, Backstrom T. Induced anovulation as treatment of premenstrual tension syndrome: a double-blind cross-over study with GnRH-agonist versus placebo. *Acta Obstet Gynecol Scand* 1988; 67:159–166.
45. West CP, Hillier H. Ovarian suppression with the gonadotrophin-releasing hormone agonist goserelin (Zoladex) in management of the premenstrual tension syndrome. *Hum Reprod* 1994;9:1058–1063.
46. Andersch B. Bromocriptine and premenstrual symptoms: a survey of double blind trials. *Obstet Gynecol Surv* 1983;38:643–646.
47. Ylostalo P. Cyclical or continuous treatment of the premenstrual syndrome (PMS) with bromocriptine. *European Journal of Obstetrics and Gynecology and Reproductive Biology* 1984;17:337–343.
48. Ylostalo P, Kauppila A, Puolakka J, Ronnberg L, Janne O. Bromocriptine and norethisterone in the treatment of premenstrual syndrome. *Obstet Gynecol* 1982;59:292–298.
49. Graham JJ, Harding PE, Wise PH, Berriman H. Prolactin suppression in the treatment of premenstrual syndrome. *Med J Aust* 1978;2:18–20.
50. Kullander S, Svanberg L. Bromocriptine treatment of the premenstrual syndrome. *Acta Obstet Gynecol Scand* 1979;58:375–378.
51. Cullberg J. Mood changes and menstrual symptoms with different gestagen/estrogen combinations: a double blind comparison with a placebo. *Acta Psychiatr Scand Suppl* 1972; 236:1–86.
52. Morris NM, Udry JR. Contraceptive pills and day-by-day feelings of well-being. *Am J Obstet Gynecol* 1972;113:763–765.
53. Graham CA, Sherwin BB. A prospective treatment study of premenstrual symptoms using a triphasic oral contraceptive. *J Psychosom Res* 1992;36: 257–266.
54. Silbergeld S, Brast N, Noble EP. The menstrual cycle: a double blind study of symptoms, mood

and behaviour and biochemical variables using Enovid and placebo. *Psychosom Med* 1971;33:411–428.
55. Wang M, Hammarback S, Lindhe BA, Backstrom T. Treatment of premenstrual syndrome by spironolactone: a double-blind, placebo-controlled study. *Acta Obstet Gynecol Scand* 1995;74:803–808.
56. Burnet RB, Radden HS, Easterbrook EG, McKinnon RA. Premenstrual syndrome and spironolactone. *Aust NZ J Obstet Gynaecol* 1991;31:366–368.
57. Vellacott ID, Shroff NE, Pearce MY, Stratford ME, Akbar FA. A double-blind, placebo-controlled evaluation of spironolactone in the premenstrual syndrome. *Current Medical Research Opinion* 1987;10:450–456.
58. O'Brien PM, Craven D, Selby C, Symonds EM. Treatment of premenstrual syndrome by spironolactone. *Br J Obstet Gynaecol* 1979;86:142–147.
59. Werch A, Kane RE. Treatment of premenstrual tension with metolazone: a double-blind evaluation of a new diuretic. *Current Therapeutic Research: Clinical and Experimental* 1976; 19:565–572.
60. Mattsson B, von Schoultz B. A comparison between lithium, placebo and a diuretic in premenstrual tension. *Acta Psychiatr Scand Suppl* 1974;255:75–84.
61. Mira M, McNeil D, Fraser IS, Vizzard J, Abraham S. Mefenamic acid in the treatment of premenstrual syndrome. *Obstet Gynecol* 1986;68:395–398.
62. Jakubowicz DL, Godard E, Dewhurst J. The treatment of premenstrual tension with mefenamic acid: analysis of prostaglandin concentrations. *Br J Obstet Gynaecol* 1984;91:78–84.
63. Wood C, Jakubowicz D. The treatment of premenstrual symptoms with mefenamic acid. *Br J Obstet Gynaecol* 1980;87:627–630.
64. Gunston KD. Premenstrual syndrome in Cape Town. Part II: a double-blind placebo-controlled study of the efficacy of mefenamic acid. *S Afr Med J* 1986;70:159–160.
65. Budoff PW. *No more menstrual cramps and other good news*. New York: GP Putman & Sons, 1980.
66. Facchinetti F, Fioroni L, Sances G, Romano G, Nappi G, Genazzani AR. Naproxen sodium in the treatment of premenstrual symptoms: a placebo-controlled study. *Gynecol Obstet Invest* 1989;28:205–208.
67. Sundblad C, Hedberg MA, Eriksson E. Clomipramine administered during the luteal phase reduces the symptoms of premenstrual syndrome: a placebo-controlled trial. *Neuropsychopharmacology* 1993;9:133–145.
68. Sundblad C, Modigh K, Andersch B, Eriksson E. Clomipramine effectively reduces premenstrual irritability and dysphoria: a placebo-controlled trial. *Acta Psychiatr Scand* 1992;85:39–47.
69. Harrison WM, Endicott J, Nee J. Treatment of premenstrual depression with nortriptyline: a pilot study. *J Clin Psychiatry* 1989;50:136–139.
70. Schmidt PJ, Grover GN, Rubinow DR. Alprazolam in the treatment of premenstrual syndrome: a double-blind, placebo-controlled trial. *Arch Gen Psychiatry* 1993;50:467–473.
71. Harrison WM, Endicott J, Rabkin JG, Nee JC, Sandberg D. Treatment of premenstrual dysphoria with alprazolam and placebo. *Psychopharmacol Bull* 1987;23:150–153.
72. Smith S, Rinehart JS, Ruddock VE, Schiff I. Treatment of premenstrual syndrome with alprazolam: results of a double- blind, placebo-controlled, randomized crossover clinical trial. *Obstet Gynecol* 1987;70:37–43.
73. Harrison WM, Endicott J, Nee J. Treatment of premenstrual dysphoria with alprazolam: a controlled study. *Arch Gen Psychiatry* 1990;47:270–275.
74. Rickels K, Freeman E, Sondheimer S. Buspirone in treatment of premenstrual syndrome. *Lancet* 1989;1:777.
75. Singer K, Cheng R, Schou M. A controlled evaluation of lithium in the premenstrual tension syndrome. *Br J Psychiatry* 1974;124:50–51.
76. Dimmock PW, Wyatt KM, O'Brien PMS. Treatment of premenstrual syndrome with serotonin re-uptake inhibitors: a systematic review. *Br J Obstet Gynaecol* 1998;105 (suppl 17):104. Search Date 1998 (before July); primary sources: MEDLINE (1966 to May 1998), Psychlit (1974 to 1996), CINAHL (1982 to May 1998).
77. FitzGerald M, Malone KM, Li S, et al. Blunted serotonin response to fenfluramine challenge in premenstrual dysphoric disorder. *Am J Psychiatry* 1997;154:556–558.
78. Wyatt KM, Dimmock PW, O'Brien PMS. Vitamin B6 therapy - a systematic review of its efficacy in premenstrual syndrome. *Br J Obstet Gynaecol* 1998;105 suppl.17:104. Search Date 1998 (before July); primary sources: MEDLINE (1966 to May 1998), Psychlit (1974 to 1996), CINAHL (1982 to May 1998).
79. Budeiri D, Li Wan Po A, Dornan JC. Is evening primrose oil of value in the treatment of premenstrual syndrome? *Control Clin Trials* 1996;17:60–68. Search Date July 1997; primary sources: Science Citation Index (1987 to July 1993), MEDLINE (1966 to July 1993), Dissertation Abstracts (1964 to July 1992), companies who marketed evening primrose oil were approached for any published or unpublished trials.
80. Facchinetti F, Borella P, Sances G, Fioroni L, Nappi RE, Genazzani AR. Oral magnesium successfully relieves premenstrual mood changes. *Obstet Gynecol* 1991;78:177–181.
81. De Souza MC, Walker AF, Bolland KM, Robinson PA. A synergistic effect of magnesium and vitamin B6 supplementation for the relief of symptoms of the premenstrual syndrome (PMS). *Proc Nutr Soc* 1996;56:75a.
82. Thys-Jacobs S, Ceccarelli S, Bierman A, Weisman H, Cohen MA, Alvir J. Calcium supplementation in premenstrual syndrome: a randomized crossover trial. *J Gen Intern Med* 1989;4:183–189.
83. Kirkby RJ. Changes in premenstrual symptoms and irrational thinking following cognitive - behavioural coping skills training. *J Consult Clin Psychol* 1994;62:1026–1032.
84. Morse C, Dennerstein L, Farrell E, Varnavides K. A comparison of hormone therapy, coping skills training and relaxation for the relief of premenstrual syndrome. *J Behav Med* 1991;14:469–489.
85. Christensen AP, Oei TP. The efficacy of cognitive behaviour therapy in treating premenstrual dysphoric changes. *J Affect Disord* 1995;33:57–63.
86. Prior JC, Vigna Y, Alojada N. Conditioning exercise decreases premenstrual symptoms. A prospective controlled three month trial. *Eur J Appl Physiol* 1986;55:349–355.
87. Lemos D. The effects of aerobic training on women who suffer from premenstrual syndrome. *Dissertation Abstracts International* 1991;52:563.
88. Bibi KW. The effects of aerobic exercise on premenstrual syndrome symptoms. *Dissertation Abstracts International* 1995;56:6678.
89. Goodale IL, Domar AD, Benson H. Alleviation of premenstrual syndrome symptoms with the relaxation response. *Obstet Gynecol* 1990;75: 649–655.
90. Metcalf MG, Braiden V, Livesey JH, Wells JE. The premenstrual syndrome: amelioration of symptoms after hysterectomy. *J Psychosom Res* 1992; 36:569–584.
91. Osborn M, Gath D. Psychological and physical

determinants of premenstrual symptoms before and after hysterectomy. *Psychol Med* 1990;20: 565–572.
92. Casper RF, Hearn MT. The effect of hysterectomy and bilateral oophorectomy in women with severe premenstrual syndrome. *Am J Obstet Gynecol* 1990;162:105–109.
93. Casson P, Hahn PM, Van Vugt DA, Reid RL. Lasting response to ovariectomy in severe intractable premenstrual syndrome. *Am J Obstet Gynecol* 1990;162:99–105.
94. Shaw RW, Soutter WP, Stanton SL. *Gynaecology*. New York: Churchill Livingstone, 1997.

KM Wyatt, PhD
Non-Clinical Lecturer in Reproductive Endocrinology

PW Dimmock, PhD
Research Scholar

PMS O'Brien, MD, FROCG
Professor and Head of Department

North Staffordshire NHS Trust &
School of Postgraduate Medicine Keele University
Stoke-on-Trent
UK

Competing interests: None declared.

TABLE 1 Commonly reported symptoms in women with PMS.[4] **(See text p. 257.)**

Psychological symptoms	Irritability, depression, crying/tearfulness, anxiety, tension, mood swings, lack of concentration, confusion, forgetfulness, social withdrawal, restlessness, sadness/blues, loneliness, change in libido
Behavioral symptoms	Fatigue, dizziness, sleep/insomnia, decreased efficiency, accident prone, increased energy, tiredness, temper outbursts/anger, social withdrawal
Physical symptoms	Headache/migraine, breast tenderness/soreness/breast pain/breast swelling (collectively known as premenstrual mastalgia), back pain, abdominal cramps, generalized pain, dizziness, fatigue, weight gain, abdominal bloating or swelling, edema of extremities (arms and legs), water retention
Appetite symptoms	Increased appetite, food cravings, nausea

Menorrhagia

Kirsten Duckitt, MA, MBBChir, MRCOG

QUESTIONS

INTERVENTIONS

Key Messages

- Medical treatments for menorrhagia preserve fertility, although some also may be contraceptive. Symptoms usually return once treatment has stopped.
- Systematic reviews of randomized controlled trials (RCTs) have found that NSAIDs and tranexamic acid reduce menstrual blood loss. NSAIDs also alleviate dysmenorrhea. Similarly good evidence shows danazol to be effective, but unacceptable side effects occur in two fifths of women.
- RCTs of ethamsylate are conflicting but suggest at most a small reduction in menstrual blood flow.
- Neither oral nor intrauterine progestogens have been compared with placebo. A systematic review of RCTs has found little benefit from oral progestogens given in the luteal phase, but one small RCT found that a longer treatment cycle (for 3 weeks out of 4) reduced menstrual blood loss. Three small RCTs evaluating the levonorgestrel-releasing IUD found no significant difference compared with norethisterone and less effectiveness than endometrial resection.
- Hysterectomy and endometrial destruction are suitable only for women who have completed childbearing. A systematic review of RCTs found high levels of patient satisfaction after both procedures but significantly higher levels after hysterectomy.
- Hysterectomy causes major and minor complications in approximately one third of women. Between 30% to 90% of women will experience continued bleeding after endometrial destruction, although in most cases this is light. One in four to five women will require reoperation. RCTs comparing resection versus medical treatments are conflicting.

- The oral contraceptive pill, GnRH analogues, dilatation and curettage, and myomectomy have not yet been evaluated adequately in the treatment of menorrhagia.

DEFINITION Menorrhagia is defined as heavy but regular menstrual bleeding. Idiopathic ovulatory menorrhagia is regular heavy bleeding in the absence of recognizable pelvic pathology or a general bleeding disorder. Objective menorrhagia is taken to be a total menstrual blood loss of 80 mL or more per menstruation.[1] Subjectively, menorrhagia may be defined as a complaint of regular excessive menstrual blood loss occurring over several consecutive cycles in a woman of reproductive years.

INCIDENCE/ PREVALENCE In the UK, one in 20 women aged 30 to 49 years consults her general practitioner each year with menorrhagia.[2]

ETIOLOGY Idiopathic ovulatory menorrhagia is thought to be caused by disordered prostaglandin production within the endometrium.[3] Prostaglandins also may be implicated in menorrhagia associated with uterine fibroids, adenomyosis, or the presence of an intrauterine contraceptive device. Fibroids have been reported in 10% of women with moderately heavy menstrual loss (80–100 mL) and 40% of those with severe menstrual loss (> 200 mL).[4]

PROGNOSIS Menorrhagia limits normal activities[5,6] and causes iron-deficient anemia in two thirds of women proved to have objective menorrhagia.[1] One in five women in the UK[7] and one in three women in the USA[8] will have a hysterectomy before 60 years of age; menorrhagia is the main presenting problem in at least half of these women.[9] Approximately half of women who have a hysterectomy for menorrhagia have a normal uterus removed.[10]

AIMS To reduce menstrual bleeding, improve quality of life, and prevent or correct iron-deficient anemia.

OUTCOMES Menstrual blood flow (assessed objectively or subjectively); hemoglobin concentration; quality of life; patient satisfaction; incidence of drug adverse effects; incidence of postoperative complications.

METHODS *Clinical Evidence* search July 1998, plus individual searches for each intervention using MEDLINE (1966 to 1998, including foreign language publications), EMBASE (1974 to 1998), and the Cochrane Library up to issue 3, 1998. Reference lists of nonsystematic reviews and studies obtained from the initial search were examined, and recent issues of key journals were hand searched. There was no systematic attempt to search the "gray literature" (conference abstracts, theses, unpublished trials). Published systematic reviews were used where available. Otherwise, all identified and relevant RCTs were reviewed. Where possible, reductions in menstrual blood loss are presented in terms of WMD because menstrual loss is a continuous variable. However, individual trials often report percentage reduction in menstrual blood loss compared with either placebo or an alternative treatment or with pretreatment menstrual blood loss. Whether or not a particular percentage reduction in menstrual blood loss is considered clinically important will depend on the pretreatment menstrual loss and the individual woman's perception of acceptable menstrual loss.

QUESTION **What are the effects of medical treatments?**

OPTION **NONSTEROIDAL ANTI-INFLAMMATORY DRUGS**

A systematic review of RCTs has found that NSAIDs, with the exception of ibuprofen, significantly reduce menstrual blood loss compared with placebo. Another systematic review of RCTs found no difference in effectiveness between mefenamic acid and naproxen. A systematic review of a few small RCTs found no difference between NSAIDs and other medical treatments. NSAIDs have the additional advantage of relieving dysmenorrhea in three quarters of women.

Benefits: **Versus placebo:** We found one systematic review published in 1998, which identified 12 RCTs comparing NSAIDs (mefenamic acid, naproxen, meclofenamic acid, ibuprofen, and diclofenac) versus placebo in 313 women with menorrhagia.[11] All NSAIDs tested, except ibuprofen, reduced menstrual blood loss compared with placebo. Treatment was taken only during menstruation, but doses varied depending on the specific drug. The mean reduction in menstrual blood loss compared with placebo ranged from 23 mL (mefenamic acid) to 74 mL (diclofenac). When all the NSAIDs were combined, the weighted mean difference compared with placebo was a reduced blood loss of 35 mL (95% CI 27–43). **Versus other NSAIDs and other drugs:** We found one systematic review published in 1998,[12] which identified 16 RCTs comparing different NSAIDs and NSAIDs versus other drugs. This found no significant difference between mefenamic acid and naproxen. It also found, in the few small studies suitable for evaluation, no significant difference between NSAIDs and oral progestogens given in the luteal phase, the combined oral contraceptive pill, or a progesterone releasing intrauterine contraceptive device.

Harms: Commonly reported adverse effects were headaches and gastrointestinal disturbances, including indigestion, nausea, vomiting, and diarrhea. They occurred in at least half of women taking NSAIDs in the RCTs that reported data on adverse effects, but similar adverse effects were also found in placebo cycles.

Comment: NSAIDs have the additional benefit of relieving dysmenorrhea. A systematic review published in 1984 identified 51 RCTs and found that three quarters of women with dysmenorrhea reported significant pain relief with NSAIDs.[13] A more recent systematic review[14] published in 1998 found that naproxen, ibuprofen, and mefenamic acid were all significantly better than placebo in relieving dysmenorrhea (RRs for each drug versus placebo: 3.17, 95% CI 2.72–3.65; 2.41, 95% CI 1.58–3.68; and 2.03, 95% CI 1.65–2.48, respectively).

OPTION TRANEXAMIC ACID

A systematic review of RCTs found that tranexamic acid significantly reduces menstrual blood loss compared with placebo. Small individual RCTs found that tranexamic acid was significantly more effective than mefenamic acid, ethamsylate, flurbiprofen, diclofenac, and norethisterone. Leg cramps occurred in one third of women. The possible increased risk of thromboembolism has not been confirmed in long-term follow-up studies.

Benefits: **Versus placebo:** We found one systematic review published in 1998, which identified five RCTs in 153 women with menorrhagia. These compared tranexamic acid (250 to 500 mg qid during menstruation) versus placebo.[11] There was a significant reduction in mean menstrual blood loss compared with placebo (WMD 52 mL, graphic plot in published report shows significant difference). Few studies measured patient satisfaction. **Versus other drugs:** The systematic review identified but did not analyze several RCTs comparing tranexamic acid versus other drugs.[11] These found that tranexamic acid was significantly more effective than mefenamic acid, ethamsylate, flurbiprofen, diclofenac, and norethisterone. One of the only RCTs to look at quality of life (in 46 women)[15] found that tranexamic acid reduced limitations to social activities and sex life significantly more than norethisterone.

Harms: Nausea and leg cramps occur in one third of women taking tranexamic acid. Isolated case reports have suggested a risk of thromboembolism, but a large population-based study over 19 years found this to be no higher than expected in the normal population.[16]

Comment: Unlike the NSAIDs, tranexamic acid has no effect on dysmenorrhea. Note that tranexamic acid is not available in the US.

OPTION ETHAMSYLATE

We found limited evidence suggesting no notable benefit from ethamsylate. A systematic review of RCTs found a small reduction in menstrual blood loss compared to baseline, with minimal side effects. Limited evidence from one RCT found that ethamsylate is less effective than tranexamic or mefanamic acid.

Benefits: We found one systematic review published in 1995, which identified four RCTs comparing ethamsylate versus placebo (one trial), mefenamic acid (one trial), amincaproic acid (one trial), and mefenamic acid plus tranexamic acid (one trial).[17] Most results were presented as comparison with baseline. The review concluded that ethamsylate achieved an overall reduction in menstrual blood loss compared to baseline of 13.1% (95% CI 10.9%–15.3%), which may not be clinically significant. The individual trials reported conflicting results. Two found that ethamsylate 500 mg four times daily during menstruation decreased menstrual blood loss compared to baseline by 7% and 20% (CIs not reported), whereas one of the others found that the same dosage had no significant effect. In contrast, the only placebo-controlled trial (22 women) found that ethamsylate reduced menstrual blood loss by 50% compared to baseline in women with "primary menorrhagia" and by 19% in women using intrauterine contraceptive devices. Only one trial gave direct comparative results rather than comparison with baseline.[18] This found that both tranexamic acid and mefanamic acid were significantly more effective than ethamsylate (WMD in menstrual loss with tranexamic acid compared with ethamsylate 97 mL, 95% CI 54–140 mL, and with mefenamic acid versus ethamsylate 51 mL, 95% CI 6–96 mL).

Harms: Adverse effects (e.g., nausea, headaches, and dizziness) were reported in the trials, but no more so than for the comparative drugs; they were seldom the cause for study withdrawals.

Comment: The individual trials differed in their methods. Two included women using intrauterine contraceptive devices as well as women with "idiopathic" menorrhagia and did not require a menstrual blood loss of more than 80 mL before entry. The other two studies looked only at women with a pretreatment menstrual blood loss greater than 80 mL. The placebo-controlled trial may not be comparable with the other trials; it did not use the normally accepted alkaline hematin method to determine menstrual blood loss, and the women started ethamsylate 5 days before the expected start of their period, instead of on day 1 as in the other trials. Note that ethamsylate is not available in the US.

OPTION DANAZOL

A systematic review of RCTs found that danazol reduced menstrual blood flow compared with placebo. Individual RCTs found that danazol was as or more effective compared with luteal phase oral progestogens, mefenamic acid, naproxen, or the pill. Unacceptable adverse effects occur in 40% of women.

Benefits: **Versus placebo:** We found one systematic review published in 1998, which identified three RCTs comparing danazol (200 mg/d continuously for 2–3 months) versus placebo in 127 women with menorrhagia.[11] It found a significant reduction in menstrual blood loss compared with placebo (WMD 108 mL, CIs presented graphically). **Versus other drugs:** Several RCTs have found no difference or greater effectiveness with danazol compared with luteal phase oral progestogens, mefenamic acid, naproxen, or the pill.[19–22]

Harms: The main disadvantage of danazol is its adverse effects, which are dose related. In one comparative RCT,[19] adverse effects occurred in three quarters of those given danazol 200 mg/d compared with one third of those given mefenamic acid; 40% of these adverse effects were deemed unacceptable. An average weight gain of 2 to 4 kg occurs in approximately one quarter of women after 3-months' treatment. Other adverse effects, which together occur in approximately half of women, include androgenic effects, such as acne, seborrhoea, hirsutism, voice changes, and general complaints (e.g., irritability, musculoskeletal pains, and tiredness). Hot flushes and breast atrophy can sometimes occur. Most of these adverse effects are reversible on stopping treatment.

Comment: Women must be advised to use barrier methods of contraception because of potential virilization of a fetus if pregnancy occurs while on treatment.

OPTION COMBINED ORAL CONTRACEPTIVE PILL

The combined oral contraceptive pill has not yet been evaluated adequately in the treatment of menorrhagia.

Benefits: We found one systematic review published in 1998[23] and one small RCT comparing the combined oral contraceptive pill versus danazol, mefenamic acid, or naproxen in 38 women. There was no significant difference between any of the interventions. A 30-μg estrogen pill significantly reduced menstrual blood loss from baseline by 43% in 12 women. A series of 164 women given a 50-μg estrogen pill reported a 53% reduction in menstrual blood loss compared to baseline.[24] Two longitudinal case control studies found that women on the pill were less likely than those not taking the pill to experience heavy menstrual bleeding or anemia.[25,26]

Harms: Minor adverse effects are common and include nausea, headache, breast tenderness, changes in bodyweight, hypertension, changes in libido, and depression. A change of preparation may help.

Comment: The oral contraceptive pill has the advantage of reducing symptoms of dysmenorrhea and providing effective contraception.

OPTION ORAL PROGESTOGENS

We found no studies comparing oral progestogens with placebo in menorrhagia. A systematic review of RCTs has found little benefit from oral progestogens given in the luteal phase, but one small RCT found that a longer treatment cycle reduced menstrual blood loss.

Benefits: **Versus placebo:** We found no placebo-controlled RCTs. **Versus other drugs:** We found one systematic review published in 1995[17] that identified four comparative RCTs. Results were presented as comparison with baseline. The review found that norethisterone (days 15–26 or 19–26) had no significant effect on menstrual loss from baseline (WMD –3.6%, 95% CI –6.1 to –1.1). Only two of the RCTs gave direct comparative data. These found norethisterone to be less effective than danazol[20] and as effective as mefenamic acid.[27] An RCT published since the systematic review compared a longer treatment cycle of norethisterone (days 5–25) versus a progestogen-releasing intrauterine contraceptive device in 22 women with regular heavy menstrual bleeding who were given norethisterone.[22] Menstrual blood loss was reduced by 87% from baseline after three treatment cycles. There was no significant difference in change from baseline between norethisterone and the intrauterine device. The trial also reported a significant reduction from baseline in mood swings and breast tenderness after 3-months' treatment.

Harms: Adverse effects were reported in one third to one half of women but were not usually serious. They consisted mainly of headache, breast tenderness, premenstrual symptoms, and gastrointestinal disturbances. In the trial of the longer treatment cycle,[28] only 44% of women said they liked the treatment "well" or "very well," and only 22% elected to continue with treatment after the 3 months of the study.

Comment: The large number of dropouts (27%) in the norethisterone arm of one RCT[28] may make the findings less valid.

OPTION INTRAUTERINE PROGESTOGENS

We found no studies comparing progestogen-releasing intrauterine devices with placebo. Three small RCTs evaluating the levonorgestrel-releasing intrauterine device found no significant difference compared with norethisterone and less effectiveness compared with endometrial resection.

Benefits: We found no systematic review or placebo-controlled trials. **Progesterone-releasing intrauterine contraceptive device:** We found one RCT comparing a progesterone-releasing intrauterine contraceptive device (65 μg/d) versus danazol, mefenamic acid, or norethisterone in women with objectively proven menorrhagia.[22] The RCT found a significant reduction in menstrual blood loss from baseline. No data were presented on direct comparisons between treatments. **Levonorgestrel-releasing intrauterine contraceptive device:** We found three recent RCTs comparing an intrauterine contraceptive device releasing 20 μg/d of levonorgestrel (85 women) versus either norethisterone (days 5–26),[28] endometrial resection,[29] or existing treatment while on the waiting list for a hysterectomy.[30] There was no significant difference compared to 3 weeks of oral norethisterone,[28] but the intrauterine device reduced menstrual loss from baseline significantly less than did endometrial resection (79% vs. 89% from baseline, CIs not reported).[29] Menstrual blood loss was reduced by 79% to 94% compared with baseline in two of these trials.[28,29] In the other RCT, menstrual disturbance scores were decreased significantly compared with baseline for all groups of activities (general wellbeing, work performance, physical activity, sex life, leisure time activity) in the levonorgestrel group after 6 months.[30] After 6 months of treatment, 64% of women on levonorgestrel had canceled their hysterectomy compared with 14% of those receiving existing treatment.[30] Patient satisfaction ranged from 64%[28] to 85%.[29]

Harms: Progesterone-releasing intrauterine contraceptive devices (marketed as Progestasert) were withdrawn in the UK after concerns about unacceptably high rates of associated ectopic pregnancies. They are still used in the USA and France but have a short lifespan of 12 to 18 months. No current data are available on rates of ectopic pregnancy. Most of the adverse effects in the women using a levonorgestrel-releasing intrauterine contraceptive device were typical of progestogens (bloating, weight gain, breast tenderness), suggesting that the action of levonorgestrel is not always restricted to the uterine cavity. These adverse effects occurred in 56% of women in one RCT.[29] The other main adverse effect was irregular, although not usually heavy, bleeding. RCTs looking at the contraceptive effect of levonorgestrel-releasing intrauterine contraceptive devices in younger women found that, during the first few months of use, the total number of bleeding days (including menstrual bleeding, intermenstrual bleeding, and spotting) increased in most women.[31] However, by 12 months, most women bled lightly for only 1 day per month, whereas approximately 15% were amenorrheic.[32] It is not yet known whether these figures can be extrapolated into the older age group of women with menorrhagia.

Comment: The trial comparing the intrauterine device with no existing treatment in women on a waiting list for hysterectomy is weakened by the lack of placebo controls.[30] Long-term follow-up is required on women with menorrhagia to assess continuation rates, patient satisfaction, and whether surgical treatment is avoided or just postponed.

OPTION GONADOTROPHIN-RELEASING–HORMONE (GnRH) ANALOGUES

We found no RCTs evaluating GnRH analogues in menorrhagia.

Benefits: No systematic review. We found no RCTs. A few small nonrandomized studies have looked at GnRH analogues in menorrhagia. Others have looked at their effects in women with fibroids or on thinning the endometrium before ablation or resection. Observational studies in women with menorrhagia[33,34] found that GnRH analogues caused amenorrhea in most women, but pretreatment levels of menstrual blood loss returned after stopping treatment, although this sometimes took several weeks.

Harms: Adverse effects are mainly caused by reduced oestrogens. Hormone replacement to counteract the hypo-estrogenism has been tried with only limited success in reducing hot flushes.[35] Bone demineralization occurs in most women after 6-months treatment but is reversible after stopping treatment.[36] Contraception is not guaranteed.[37]

Comment: GnRH analogues are approved for use in the management of endometriosis and before surgery for fibroids but not for menorrhagia.

QUESTION If medical treatment fails, what are the effects of surgical treatments?

OPTION DILATATION AND CURETTAGE

Dilatation and curettage has not been evaluated adequately in women with menorrhagia.

Benefits: We found no systematic review or RCTs comparing dilatation and curettage versus no treatment. The only study[38] to measure blood loss before and after dilatation and curettage found a reduction in menstrual blood loss immediately after the procedure, but losses returned to previous levels or higher by the second menstrual period.

Harms: The procedure has small but real risks of morbidity with the possibility of uterine perforation and cervical laceration,[39] and the usual risks of general anesthesia.

Comment: Dilatation and curettage still plays a part in the investigation of menorrhagia.

OPTION ENDOMETRIAL DESTRUCTION (RESECTION OR LASER ABLATION)

One systematic review of RCTs has found that, although patient satisfaction is high after endometrial destruction, it is significantly lower than after hysterectomy. Between 30% to 90% of women treated with endometrial destruction will experience continued bleeding, although in most cases this is light. One in four to five women will require reoperation. Endometrial destruction has several short-term advantages over hysterectomy: shorter operating time, fewer complications, faster recovery, and less need for analgesia.

Benefits: **Versus hysterectomy:** We found one systematic review published in 1998, which identified five RCTs and related follow up studies in 708 premenopausal women comparing either endometrial resection or laser ablation versus hysterectomy.[11] Outcomes included subjective reports of bleeding, patient satisfaction, reoperation rate, operating time, length of hospital stay, postoperative complications, duration of analgesia, and time to resume normal activities (Table 1). Average follow-up ranged from 1 to 2.8 years. The five RCTs were consistent in their findings. Of the women treated with endometrial resection or laser ablation, 13% to 64% experienced no further menstrual bleeding, compared with 100% of those treated with hysterectomy. However, most women who did not become amenorrhoic after endometrial resection or laser ablation experienced only light bleeding. One in four to five women (23%) who were treated with resection or laser ablation underwent reoperation (either repeat resection or hysterectomy) within 2 years. High levels of patient satisfaction were reported for both procedures in all trials, but meta-analysis found patient satisfaction to be significantly higher for hysterectomy than for resection or ablation, both at 12 months (OR 2.17, 95% CI 1.14–4.12) and 24 months (OR 3.10, 95% CI 1.61–5.96).[11] This corresponds to a relative risk of being satisfied after endometrial resection or ablation compared with hysterectomy of 0.88 at 24 months (CIs not reported). Nine women would need to undergo hysterectomy rather than resection or ablation for one more woman to be happier with the result (NNT 9, 95% CI 6–18). **Resection versus laser ablation:** We found no systematic review. We found one RCT[40] comparing resection versus laser ablation in 372 women with menorrhagia. This found no significant differences in operative complications, recovery, satisfaction rates, relief of symptoms, or need for further treatment. **Resection versus medical treatment:** We found no systematic review. We found two RCTs,[29,41] which gave conflicting results. One found no significant difference in controlling menstrual blood loss or in patient satisfaction between a levonorgestrel-releasing intrauterine contraceptive device and endometrial resection.[29] The other found that patient satisfaction was significantly lower among women treated with one of a variety of medical treatments (not including a levonorgestrel-releasing intrauterine contraceptive device) rather than endometrial resection (27% vs. 76%).[41] However, the women in this study had already failed to benefit from medical management and may differ from women newly presenting with menorrhagia.

Harms: Intraoperative complications include uterine perforation, hemorrhage, and fluid overload from the distension medium. Immediate postoperative complications include infection, hemorrhage and, rarely, bowel injury. Complication rates in the five RCTs described above ranged from 0% to 15%. A large prospective survey of 10,686 women undergoing endometrial destructive procedures in the UK[42] found an immediate complication rate of 4.4%. Intraoperative emergency procedures were performed in 1.26% and two procedure-related deaths occurred.

Comment: These are good-quality RCTs with results that should be able to be generalized widely. The prospective survey gives a good indication of what happens when the procedure is in widespread use outside the possibly artificial situation of a randomized trial. RCTs of other methods of endometrial destruction are underway.

OPTION MYOMECTOMY

Myomectomy has not yet been evaluated adequately in women with menorrhagia.

Benefits: We found no systematic review. **Open or laparoscopic myomectomy:** We found no RCTs or other studies that measured menstrual blood loss in women with menorrhagia. **Hysteroscopic myomectomy:** We found one study[43] that reported objective measures of menstrual blood loss. This included only four women whose sole complaint was menorrhagia. Mean menstrual blood loss (assessed preoperatively and at 3 and 6 months postoperatively) was significantly reduced from 261 mL at baseline to 76 mL at 3 months and 57 mL at 6 months. There was also a significant reduction in pain scores and menstrual duration, despite the fact that the fibroids removed measured only 1 to 4 cm.

Harms: Intraoperative complications for hysteroscopic myomectomy are similar to those encountered for endometrial destructive procedures that use a hysteroscope. The main complication of open myomectomy is hemorrhage, making a hysterectomy necessary.

Comment: RCTs are needed that use objective assessment of menstrual blood loss. This is especially important when evaluating surgical procedures because of the greater difficulty in blinding participants and researchers.

OPTION HYSTERECTOMY

Hysterectomy is the only certain way to stop all menstrual loss. Major and minor complications occur in about one third of women.

Benefits: We found no systematic review. **Versus endometrial resection or laser ablation:** See p. 276 and Table 1. **Different techniques:** We found a few small RCTs in a total of 334 women comparing abdominal, vaginal, or laparoscopic hysterectomy.[44–48] They reported no difference in effectiveness or complication rates. However, operating and recovery times varied.

Harms: Large population-based analyses stratified by age show a mortality after hysterectomy for nonmalignant conditions of 1 in 2000 in women under 50 years of age.[49] In the five RCTs included in the systematic review comparing hysterectomy with endometrial resection or ablation,[11] complication rates for hysterectomy were 32% overall (2% for vaginal and 46%–47% for abdominal hysterectomy). A large, prospective cohort study of hysterectomy for nonmalignant conditions[50] reported combined major and minor complication rates of 25% for vaginal hysterectomy and 43% for abdominal hysterectomy. Most of these were because of fever.

Comment: None.

REFERENCES

1. Hallberg L, Hogdahl A, Nilsson L, Rybo G. Menstrual blood loss — a population study: variation at different ages and attempts to define normality. *Acta Obstet Gynecol Scand* 1966;45: 320–351.
2. Vessey MP, Villard-Mackintosh L, McPherson K, Coulter A, Yeates D. The epidemiology of hysterectomy: findings in a large cohort study. *Br J Obstet Gynaecol* 1992;99:402–407.
3. Smith SK, Abel MH, Kelly RW, Baird DT. A role for prostacyclin (PGI_2) in excessive menstrual bleeding. *Lancet* 1981;i:522–524.
4. Rybo G, Leman J, Tibblin R. Epidemiology of menstrual blood loss. In: Baird DT, Michie EA, eds. *Mechanisms of menstrual bleeding*. New York: Raven Press, 1985:181–193.
5. Alexander DA, Naji AA, Pinion SB, et al. Randomised trial comparing hysterectomy with endometrial ablation for dysfunctional uterine bleeding: psychiatric and psychosocial aspects. *BMJ* 1996;312:280–284.
6. Coulter A, Peto V, Jenkinson C. Quality of life and patient satisfaction following treatment for menorrhagia. *Fam Pract* 1994;11:394–401.
7. Coulter A, McPherson K, Vessey M. Do British women undergo too many or too few hysterectomies? *Soc Sci Med* 1988;27:987–994.
8. Pokras R, Hufnagel VG. *Hysterectomy in the United States, 1965–84.* Washington DC: Public Health Service, 1987:87–1753.
9. Coulter A, Kelland J, Long A. The management of menorrhagia. *Effective Health Care Bulletin* 1995;9:1–14.
10. Clarke A, Black N, Rowe P, Mott S, Howle K. Indications for and outcome of total abdominal hysterectomy for benign disease: a prospective cohort study. *Br J Obstet Gynaecol* 1995;102: 611–620.
11. Working Party of the National Health Committee New Zealand. *Guidelines for the management of heavy menstrual bleeding*. Wellington: Ministry of Health, 1998. (Available from The Ministry of Health, 133 Molesworth Street, PO Box 5013, Wellington, New Zealand.) (Search date 1996; primary sources MEDLINE, EMBASE, Current Contents, Biological Abstracts, Social Sciences Index, Psych Lit, CINAHL.)
12. Lethaby A, Augood C, Duckitt K. Nonsteroidal anti-inflammatory drugs vs either placebo or any other medical treatment for heavy menstrual bleeding (menorrhagia) (Cochrane Review). In: The Cochrane Library, 1998. Oxford: Update Software. Cochrane Register of Controlled Trials.
13. Owen PR. Prostaglandin synthetase inhibitors in the treatment of primary dysmenorrhoea. *Am J Obstet Gynecol* 1984;148:96–103. Search date January 1982; primary sources MEDLINE 1974 to 1982.
14. Zhang WY, Li Wan Po A. Efficacy of minor analgesics in primary dysmenorrhoea: a systematic review. *Br J Obstet Gynaecol* 1998;105:780–789. (Search date 1997; primary sources MEDLINE, EMBASE, Science Citation Index, reference lists of retrieved RCTs and review articles, communication with the manufacturers.)
15. Preston JT, Cameron IT, Adams EJ, Smith SK. Comparative study of tranexamic acid and norethisterone in the treatment of ovulatory menorrhagia. *Br J Obstet Gynaecol* 1995;102: 401–406.
16. Rybo G. Tranexamic acid therapy is effective treatment in heavy menstrual bleeding: clinical update on safety. *Therapeutic Advances* 1991;4:1–8.
17. Coulter A, Kelland J, Peto V, Rees MC. Treating menorrhagia in primary care. An overview of drug trials and a survey of prescribing practice. *Int J Technol Assess Health Care* 1995;11:456–471. (Search date not given; primary sources MEDLINE, EMBASE.)
18. Bonnar J, Sheppard BL. Treatment of menorrhagia during menstruation: randomised controlled trial of ethamsylate, mefenamic acid, and tranexamic acid. *BMJ* 1996;313:579–582.
19. Dockeray CJ, Sheppard BL, Bonnar J. Comparison between mefenamic acid and danazol in the treatment of established menorrhagia. *Br J Obstet Gynaecol* 1989;96:840–844.
20. Higham JM, Shaw RW. A comparative study of danazol, a regimen of decreasing doses of danazol, and norethindrone in the treatment of objectively proven unexplained menorrhagia. *Am J Obstet Gynecol* 1993;169:1134–1139.
21. Fraser IS, McCarron G. Randomized trial of 2 hormonal and 2 prostaglandin-inhibiting agents in women with a complaint of menorrhagia. *Aust NZ J Obstet Gynaecol* 1991;31:66–70.
22. Cameron IT, Leask R, Kelly RW, Baird DT. The effects of danazol, mefenamic acid, norethisterone and a progesterone-impregnated coil on endometrial prostaglandin concentrations in women with menorrhagia. *Prostaglandins* 1987; 34:99–110.
23. Iyer V, Farquhar C, Jepson R. The effectiveness of oral contraceptive pills versus placebo or any other medical treatment for menorrhagia. (Cochrane Review). In: The Cochrane Library, 1998. Oxford: Update Software. (Search date 1997; primary sources Cochrane Register of Controlled Trials.)
24. Nilsson L, Rybo G. Treatment of menorrhagia. *Am J Obstet Gynecol* 1971;5:713–720.

25. Ramcharan S, Pellegrin FA, Ray RM, Hsu J. The Walnut Creek contraceptive drug study — a prospective study of the side effects of oral contraceptives. Volume III, an interim report: a comparison of disease occurrence leading to hospitalization or death in users and nonusers of oral contraceptives. *J Reprod Med* 1980;25:345–372.
26. Royal College of General Practitioners. *Oral Contraceptives and Health*. London: Pitman Medical, 1974.
27. Cameron IT, Haining R, Lumsden MA, Thomas VR, Smith SK. The effects of mefenamic acid and norethisterone on measured menstrual blood loss. *Obstet Gynecol* 1990;76:85–88.
28. Irvine GA, Campbell-Brown MB, Lumsden MA, Heikkila A, Walker JJ, Cameron IT. Randomised comparative study of the levonorgestrel intrauterine system and norethisterone for the treatment of idiopathic menorrhagia. *Br J Obstet Gynaecol* 1998;105:592–598.
29. Crosignani PG, Vercellini P, Mosconi P, Oldani S, Cortesi I, De Giorgi O. Levonorgestrel-releasing intrauterine device versus hysteroscopic endometrial resection in the treatment of dysfunctional uterine bleeding. *Obstet Gynecol* 1997;90:257–263.
30. Lahteenmaki P, Haukkamaa M, Puolakka J, et al. Open randomised study of use of levonorgestrel releasing intrauterine system as alternative to hysterectomy. *BMJ* 1998;316:1122–1126.
31. Long-acting progestogen-only contraception. *Drug Ther Bull* 1996;34:93–96.
32. Luukkainen T. The levonorgestrel-releasing IUD. *Br J Fam Plann* 1993;19:221–224.
33. Gardner RL, Shaw RW. LHRH analogues in the treatment of menorrhagia. In: Shaw RW, ed. *Dysfunctional uterine bleeding*. Carnforth: Parthenon Press, 1990:149–159.
34. Shaw RW, Fraser HM. Use of a superactive luteinizing hormone-releasing hormone (LHRH) agonist in the treatment of menorrhagia. *Br J Obstet Gynaecol* 1984;91:913–916.
35. Thomas EJ, Okuda KJ, Thomas NM. The combination of a depot gonadotrophin releasing hormone agonist and cyclical hormone replacement therapy for dysfunctional uterine bleeding. *Br J Obstet Gynaecol* 1991;98:1155–1159.
36. Eldred JM, Haynes PJ, Thomas EJ. A randomized double blind placebo controlled trial of the effects on bone metabolism of the combination of nafarelin acetate and norethisterone. *Clin Endocrinol* 1992;37:354–359.
37. Pickersgill A, Kingsland CR, Garden AS, Farquharson RG. Multiple gestation following gonadotrophin releasing hormone therapy for the treatment of minimal endometriosis. *Br J Obstet Gynaecol* 1994;101:260–262.
38. Haynes PJ, Hodgson H, Anderson AB, Turnbull AC. Measurement of menstrual blood loss in patients complaining of menorrhagia. *Br J Obstet Gynaecol* 1977;84:763–768.
39. Smith JJ, Schulman H. Current dilatation and curettage practice: a need for revision. *Obstet Gynecol* 1985;65:516–518.
40. Bhattacharya S, Cameron IM, Parkin DE, et al. A pragmatic randomised comparison of transcervical resection of the endometrium with endometrial laser ablation for the treatment of menorrhagia. *Br J Obstet Gynaecol* 1997;104:601–607.
41. Cooper KG, Parkin DE, Garratt AM, Grant AM. A randomised comparison of medical and hysteroscopic management in women consulting a gynaecologist for treatment of heavy menstrual loss. *Br J Obstet Gynaecol* 1997;104:1360–1366.
42. Overton C, Hargreaves J, Maresh M. A national survey of the complications of endometrial destruction for menstrual disorders: the MISTLETOE study. Minimally invasive surgical techniques — laser, endothermal or endoresection. *Br J Obstet Gynaecol* 1997;104:1351–1359.
43. Broadbent JAM, Magos AL. Menstrual blood loss after hysteroscopic myomectomy. *Gynaecological Endoscopy* 1995;4:41–44.
44. Phipps JH, John M, Nayak S. Comparison of laparoscopically assisted vaginal hysterectomy and bilateral salpingo-oophorectomy with conventional abdominal hysterectomy and bilateral salpingo-oophorectomy. *Br J Obstet Gynaecol* 1993; 100:698–700.
45. Raju KS, Auld BJ. A randomised prospective study of laparoscopic vaginal hysterectomy versus abdominal hysterectomy each with bilateral salpingo-oophorectomy. *Br J Obstet Gynaecol* 1994;101:1068–1071.
46. Richardson RE, Bournas N, Magos AL. Is laparoscopic hysterectomy a waste of time? *Lancet* 1995;345:36–41.
47. Summitt RL, Jr, Stovall TG, Lipscomb GH, Ling FW. Randomized comparison of laparoscopy-assisted vaginal hysterectomy with standard vaginal hysterectomy in an outpatient setting *Obstet Gynecol* 1992;80:895–901.
48. Langebrekke A, Eraker R, Nesheim B, Urnes A, Busund B, Sponland G. Abdominal hysterectomy should not be considered as primary method for uterine removal. *Acta Obstet Gynecol Scand* 1996;75:404–407.
49. Carlson KJ. Outcomes of hysterectomy. *Clin Obstet Gynecol* 1997;40:939–946.
50. Dicker RC, Greenspan JR, Strauss LT, et al. Complications of abdominal and vaginal hysterectomy among women of reproductive age in the United States: the collaborative review of sterilization. *Am J Obstet Gynecol* 1982;144:841–848.

Kirsten Duckitt, MA, MBBChir, MRCOG
Former Research Fellow
Royal College of Obstetrics and Gynaecologists
London
UK

Competing interests: None declared.

TABLE 1 **Hysterectomy versus endometrial resection/laser ablation: results of meta-analysis of five RCTs.[11] (OR or RR and CIs not reported). (*See* text p. 276.)**

	Endometrial resection/ laser ablation	Hysterectomy
Cessation of menstrual blood loss	13%–64%	100%
Patient satisfaction	78%–85%	89%–96%
Quality of life	48%	73%
Improvement in menstrual symptoms	79%–90%	95%–96%
Operating time	30–45 minutes	45–67 minutes
Complications	0.15%	15%–47%
Recovery time	2–3 weeks	8–11 weeks
Need for analgesia	16%–39%	99%
Repeat surgery	23%	0

Infertility

Kirsten Duckitt, MA, MBBChir, MRCOG

QUESTIONS

INTERVENTIONS

Key Messages

- In women with infertility caused by ovulation disorders, a systematic review of randomized crossover trials has found that clomiphene increases the chances of becoming pregnant. However, clomiphene has not been directly compared with other interventions in women with ovulation disorders. Randomized controlled trials (RCTs) have compared follicle-stimulating hormone, human menopausal gonadotrophin, and laparoscopic ovarian drilling. These found no difference in pregnancy rates. None of these interventions has been compared directly with placebo in women with ovulation disorders.

- In women with tubal infertility, none of the main interventions (selective salpingography and tubal catheterization, tubal surgery, *in vitro* fertilization) has been evaluated adequately in RCTs.
- In women with infertility caused by endometriosis, systematic reviews of cohort studies have found that pregnancy rates are higher with surgical than medical treatment. *In vitro* fertilization has not been evaluated adequately in this context.
- In couples with male factor infertility, a systematic review of RCTs has found that intrauterine insemination achieves higher pregnancy rates than intracervical insemination or natural intercourse. Intracytoplasmic sperm injection plus *in vitro* fertilization has not been evaluated adequately. Donor insemination achieves live birth rates of approximately 10% in women with no evidence of reduced fertility or in whom problems with fertility have been corrected.
- In couples with unexplained infertility, we found no evidence to support the use of clomiphene. A systematic review of RCTs found that intrauterine insemination achieves higher pregnancy rates than timed intercourse, especially when ovarian stimulation with gonadotrophins is also used. Gamete intrafallopian transfer has not been tested in an RCT against no treatment in couples with unexplained infertility. Limited comparisons with other treatments (ovarian hyperstimulation and *in vitro* fertilization) found no difference in pregnancy rates.
- Interventions involving ovarian stimulation carry the risk of multiple pregnancy and ovarian hyperstimulation syndrome. The risk of each varies with the type of ovarian stimulation used. Moderate to severe ovarian hyperstimulation complicates 4% of ovulation induction cycles and up to 10% of all *in vitro* fertilization cycles. Multiple pregnancy occurs in 29% of women with polycystic ovaries when conventional (as opposed to low-dose) regimens of gonadotrophins are used.

DEFINITION Normal fertility has been defined as achieving a pregnancy within 2 years by regular sexual intercourse.[1] However, many define infertility as the failure to conceive after 1 year of unprotected intercourse. Infertility can be primary (in couples who have never conceived) or secondary (in couples who have previously conceived). Infertile couples include those who are sterile (who will never achieve a natural pregnancy) and those who are subfertile (who should eventually achieve a pregnancy).

INCIDENCE/ PREVALENCE Although there is no evidence of a major change in prevalence of infertility, many more couples are seeking help than previously. Currently, approximately one in seven couples in industrialized countries will seek medical advice for infertility.[2] Rates of primary infertility vary widely between countries, ranging from 10% in Africa to approximately 6% in North America and Europe.[1] Reported rates of secondary infertility are less reliable.

ETIOLOGY Nearly one third of cases of infertility are unexplained. The rest are caused by ovulatory failure (27%), low sperm count or quality (19%), tubal damage (14%), endometriosis (5%), and other causes (5%).[3]

PROGNOSIS In developed countries, 80% to 90% of couples attempting to conceive are successful after 1 year, and 95% after 2 years.[3] The chances of becoming pregnant vary with the cause and duration of infertility, the woman's age, the couple's previous pregnancy history,[4,5] and the availability of different treatment options. For the first 2 to 3 years of unexplained infertility, cumulative conception rates remain high (27%–46%) but decrease with increasing age of the woman and duration of infertility. The background rates of spontaneous pregnancy in infertile couples can be calculated from longitudinal studies of infertile couples who have been observed without treatment.[4]

AIMS To achieve the delivery of one healthy baby, to reduce the distress associated with infertility, and to help couples come to terms with childlessness if treatments fail or are unavailable.

OUTCOMES Rates of pregnancy, live birth, miscarriage, and multiple pregnancy; incidence of ovarian hyperstimulation syndrome; couples' satisfaction with services and treatments; couples' acceptance of childlessness if treatment is unsuccessful. Ovulation is an intermediate outcome. A large number of pregnancies in infertile couples will occur spontaneously without treatment.[4] Effectiveness of treatments for infertility should be assessed on the basis of pregnancy rates over and above the spontaneous pregnancy rates. Otherwise the impacts of treatments will be overestimated.

METHODS For each subject, I searched MEDLINE (CD Ovid version) from January 1966 to March 1998, including foreign language publications; EMBASE from 1974 to March 1998; and the Cochrane Library up to Issue 3, 1998. I also searched reference lists of nonsystematic review articles and studies obtained from the initial search, hand searched recent journals in the Royal College of Obstetricians and Gynaecologists library, and contacted experts. I made no systematic attempt to search the "grey literature" (conference abstracts, theses, unpublished trials). Published systematic reviews and meta-analyses were used where available. In their absence, I reviewed all RCTs that addressed the specified intervention with pregnancy as an outcome. Good-quality RCTs are uncommon in the field of infertility, especially for assisted reproductive techniques, such as *in vitro* fertilization, gamete intrafallopian transfer, and intracytoplasmic sperm injection. In their absence, the best evidence comes from comparing data from large retrospective case series with what is known of outcomes in untreated couples. In the field of infertility, RCTs with a crossover design have been shown to overestimate the treatment effect, because pregnancies occurring in the first half of the trial will remove participants from the second half.[6] Crossover trials were included in some systematic reviews where no or very few RCTs using a parallel group design were available. Ideally, only data from the first half of the trial before crossover should be used.

QUESTION **What are the effects of treatments for infertility caused by ovulation disorders?**

OPTION CLOMIPHENE

A systematic review of randomized crossover trials has found that clomiphene increases the likelihood of pregnancy in oligo-ovulatory women. The suggestion of an increased risk of ovarian cancer with prolonged use has not been confirmed. The incidence of multiple pregnancy (mostly with twins) is increased. Clomiphene has not been compared to other treatments for ovulation disorders.

Benefits: **Versus placebo:** A systematic review updated in 1996[7] identified three double-blind crossover RCTs comparing 50 to 200 mg clomiphene versus placebo in 217 cycles in oligo-ovulatory women. Pregnancy was over three times more likely per treatment cycle with clomiphene than placebo (OR 3.41, 95% CI 1.23–9.48). **Versus tamoxifen:** No systematic review. We found three studies comparing clomiphene versus tamoxifen in 102 anovulatory or oligo-ovulatory women: one RCT with a parallel-group design,[8] one with an alternate-cycles design,[9] and one observational study.[10] Data on pregnancy rates were limited to fewer than 30 pregnancies in two small studies.[8,10]

Harms: **Ovarian cancer:** Eleven cases of ovarian cancer were detected in a cohort of 3837 infertile women.[11] A nested case control study found a sevenfold increase in risk of ovarian cancer in women using clomiphene citrate for 12 or more cycles (RR 7.2, 95% CI 1.2–43.9), which increased to 11-fold when adjusted for gravidity at enrolment (RR 11.1, 95% CI 1.5–82.3). The association was present for both gravid and nulligravid women and for infertile women with both ovulatory disorders and infertility from other causes. Since then, no other studies have found an association between clomiphene and ovarian cancer.[12–15] **Multiple pregnancy:** Multiple pregnancy occurs in 2% to 13% of women with all causes of infertility taking clomiphene, compared with a spontaneous multiple pregnancy rate of approximately 1% to 2% of women in North American and European populations.[16,17] In a 1-year survey in the UK,[18] 25 of the 44 triplet pregnancies reported were attributable to clomiphene. Clomiphene was also implicated in two of the eight sets of quads and quints reported. **Ovarian hyperstimulation syndrome:** Clomiphene tends to cause only mild ovarian hyperstimulation that does not require treatment.

Comment: Clomiphene was first introduced in the 1960s, and all the trials took place in the 1970s before more recent quality standards for RCTs were established.

OPTION GONADOTROPHINS

A systematic review of RCTs has found no difference in pregnancy rates between human menopausal gonadotrophin and urinary follicle-stimulating hormone or laparoscopic ovarian drilling. However, compared to follicle-stimulating hormone, human menopausal gonadotrophin carries greater risk of ovarian hyperstimulation syndrome. Gonadotrophins have not been compared with placebo or with clomiphene. The suggestion of an increased risk of ovarian cancer is unproven.

Benefits: **Versus placebo:** We found no RCTs. **Versus clomiphene:** We found no RCTs. **Human menopausal gonadotrophin versus follicle-stimu-**

lating hormone: A systematic review updated in 1996 identified six RCTs, three of which used crossover designs. The RCTs compared human menopausal gonadotrophin versus purified urinary follicle-stimulating hormone in 182 women with clomiphene-resistant polycystic ovary syndrome.[19] There was no significant difference in pregnancy rates (37% vs. 27%, OR for pregnancy versus follicle stimulating hormone 0.66, 95% CI 0.35–1.24). **Urinary versus recombinant follicle-stimulating hormone:** We found no systematic review. A recent multicenter RCT comparing recombinant versus urinary follicle stimulating hormone in 172 women with clomiphene-resistant normogonadotrophic anovulation found no significant difference in pregnancy rates; however, a significantly lower total dose and shorter duration of recombinant follicle-stimulating hormone achieved ovulation.[20] **Versus laparoscopic ovarian drilling:** *See* below.

Harms: **Ovarian cancer:** A case control study of 200 Israeli women with ovarian cancer and 408 area-matched controls found that women with noninvasive ovarian tumors were over three times more likely to have been exposed to any ovulation induction agents (adjusted OR 3.52, 95% CI 1.23–10.09), particularly to human menopausal gonadotrophin (adjusted OR 9.38, 95% CI 1.66–52.08).[14] Women with invasive ovarian tumors were no more likely to have been exposed to any ovulation induction agents. **Multiple pregnancy:** Multiple pregnancy occurs in 29% of women with polycystic ovaries when conventional regimens of gonadotrophins are used to induce ovulation.[21] **Ovarian hyperstimulation:** The risk of moderate to severe ovarian hyperstimulation was lower with follicle stimulating hormone than with human menopausal gonadotrophin (OR compared with human menopausal gonadotrophin 0.20, 95% CI 0.09–0.46).[19] **Urinary versus recombinant follicle-stimulating hormone:** No significant difference in the risk of multiple pregnancy or ovarian hyperstimulation syndrome.[20]

Comments: The avoidance of gonadotrophins may reduce the risk of multiple pregnancy and ovarian hyperstimulation syndrome. Recombinant follicle-stimulating hormone is not derived from human tissues. A systematic review comparing recombinant and urinary follicle-stimulating hormone in *in vitro* fertilization/intracytoplasmic sperm injection cycles will be available soon (Daya S, personal communication).

OPTION LAPAROSCOPIC OVARIAN DRILLING

One systematic review of RCTs has found no significant difference in pregnancy rates between laparoscopic ovarian drilling and gonadotrophins.

Benefits: We found one systematic review updated in 1998, which identified two RCTs (one using a crossover design) in 112 women with anovulatory clomiphene-resistant polycystic ovary syndrome, comparing laparoscopic ovarian drilling versus gonadotrophins.[22] These found no significant difference in pregnancy rates (OR 0.72, 95% CI 0.29–1.78).

Harms: Laparoscopic drilling incurs the risks and morbidity of the laparoscopy under general anesthesia, postoperative adhesion formation, and the as yet theoretical long-term risk of premature ovarian failure. However, it carries no increased risk of multiple pregnancy.

Comment: Two more RCTs are in progress (Bayran N, Farquhar C, personal communication).

OPTION **PULSATILE GONODOTROPHIN-RELEASING HORMONE**

Pulsatile gonadotrophin-releasing hormone has not yet been evaluated adequately in women with infertility caused by ovulation disorders.

Benefits: We found no systematic review or RCTs. Case series in 256 anovulatory women with hypogonadotrophic hypogonadism undergoing 1043 treatment cycles[23–25] found cumulative pregnancy rates of 59% to 73% at 6 months and 81% to 92% at 12 months. Only one series reported live birth rate; this was 65.4% after 12 treatment cycles.[23]

Harms: A retrospective analysis in 229 cycles in 71 women of pulsatile gonadotrophin-releasing hormone versus gonadotrophins alone found no significant difference in multiple pregnancy rates after six cycles.[26] However, 75% of the multiple pregnancies in the gonadotrophin group were triplets or higher-order multiple pregnancies, whereas all those in the gonadotrophin-releasing hormone group were twins.

Comment: Pulsatile gonadotrophin-releasing hormone is used in women with anovulation caused by low serum gonadotrophins and estrogen concentrations. This is a well-defined condition, so the evidence (although only from case series) can be generalized to all women with hypogonadotrophic hypogonadism.

QUESTION **What are the effects of treatment for tubal infertility?**

OPTION **SELECTIVE SALPINGOGRAPHY/TUBAL CATHETERIZATION**

Selective salpingography and tubal catheterization have not yet been evaluated adequately in RCTs. Nonrandomized studies found that, if used in isolated proximal tubal obstruction, these procedures reduced the need for tubal surgery or *in vitro* fertilization in some women.

Benefits: We found no RCTs. A nonsystematic review published in 1994 identified 11 case series in 479 women with bilateral proximal tubal obstruction undergoing selective salpingography and tubal catheterization. Tubal patency was achieved in 82% and intrauterine pregnancy in 24%.[27] A prospective observational study[28] followed 43 women with bilateral proximal tubal obstruction and 33 control women undergoing reversal of tubal sterilization. Those in whom tubal catheterization was unsuccessful went on to have microsurgical resection and anastomosis. Cumulative pregnancy rates at 12 months were 68% with successful tubal catheterisation, 56% with microsurgery, and 29% in the control group.

Harms: Tubal perforation, which does not seem to be clinically important, occurred in 2% and ectopic pregnancy in 3% of women undergoing selective salpingography and tubal catheterization.[27]

Comment: None of the published studies included an untreated group, so it is not possible to give the treatment-related pregnancy rate over and above the spontaneous pregnancy rate. Tubal patency and pregnancy without treatment have been reported in women diagnosed with bilateral proximal tube obstruction.[29]

OPTION TUBAL SURGERY

Tubal surgery has not been rigorously investigated. Limited evidence suggests that surgical division of tubal adhesions improves pregnancy rates, and that laparoscopic techniques offer no benefit over open microsurgical techniques. However, these data precede recent improvements in case selection and laparoscopic training. RCTs of current practice are needed. No RCTs have compared tubal surgery with *in vitro* fertilization.

Benefits: **Versus *in vitro* fertilization:** We found no systematic review or RCTs. Case series of tubal surgery have been compared with large databases of couples undergoing *in vitro* fertilization. These found that tubal surgery was as effective as *in vitro* fertilization in women with filmy adhesions, mild distal tubal occlusion, or proximal obstruction.[30–35] Success rates with tubal surgery depend on the severity and site of disease. The best figures from surgery in women with distal tubal occlusion are live birth rates of 20% to 30%[30,36,37] with rates of up to 60% reported for the less common proximal occlusion.[38,39] **Different types of tubal surgery:** We found one systematic review[40] updated in 1998, which identified eight RCTs and 14 nonrandomized trials looking at all aspects of infertility surgery. It concluded that 1) pregnancy rates were higher with microsurgery for adhesiolysis plus salpingostomy than with macrosurgery and with adhesiolysis than with no treatment; 2) pregnancy rates were no different with laparoscopic than with open microsurgical adhesiolysis or with a carbon dioxide laser for adhesiolysis, salpingostomy, or reversal of sterilization than with standard techniques; and 3) total and intrauterine pregnancy rates were lower with laparoscopic than with open microsurgical salpingostomy. However, this last conclusion was based on four trials reported between 1987 and 1991.

Harms: Tubal surgery involves general anesthesia and admission to hospital, although the laparoscopic approach reduces hospital stay and recovery time. There is a risk of ectopic pregnancy caused by preexisting tubal damage; rates of 7% to 9% have been reported compared with 1% to 3% with *in vitro* fertilization.[41,42] *In vitro* fertilization carries the risk of multiple pregnancy and ovarian hyperstimulation syndrome (see below).

Comment: If successful, tubal surgery allows women to have more pregnancies without further medical intervention and without the risks associated with *in vitro* fertilization.[43]

OPTION *IN VITRO* FERTILIZATION

Two RCTs found improved pregnancy and live birth rates with immediate compared with delayed *in vitro* fertilization. Data from *in vitro* fertilization databases suggest higher pregnancy rates compared with expected spontaneous pregnancy rates without treatment,[4,44] but a large trial or meta analysis is needed to prove a beneficial effect of treatment over and above no treatment or other interventions.

Benefits: We found no systematic review. We found two RCTs comparing immediate versus delayed *in vitro* fertilization in 598 infertile couples with all causes of infertility. The delayed group served as untreated controls for at least 6 months. One RCT found increased rates of live birth in the immediate compared with the delayed group (11.6% vs. 4.9%, RR of live birth 2.36, 95% CI 1.03–5.66).[45] The other RCT found an increase in crude and cumulative pregnancy rates in the immediate compared with the delayed group, but the effect was significant only in women with severe bilateral tubal disease.[46] **Versus tubal surgery:** *See* above. In all causes of infertility, *in vitro* fertilization gives live birth rates per cycle of 15% in the UK and 20% in the USA.[5] If three to five cycles of *in vitro* fertilization are possible, 59% to 77% of women with tubal infertility will become pregnant, which is better than the best outcomes from tubal surgery.[47]

Harms: **Multiple pregnancy:** Multiple pregnancy rates were not reported in the RCTs mentioned above. However, of the 5538 live births following *in vitro* fertilization in the UK in 1995 to 1996, 32% were multiple, including 230 (4.2%) sets of triplets and five sets of quads (Human Fertilisation and Embryology Authority database). In the UK, the number of embryos that can be replaced is restricted to three. In the USA, where there are no such restrictions, 7939 deliveries included 36.6% multiple births, 7% of which were triplets and above. **Ovarian hyperstimulation syndrome:** Severe ovarian hyperstimulation syndrome occurs in 0.5% to 2% of all *in vitro* fertilization cycles.[48] Ovarian hyperstimulation syndrome rates were not reported in the RCTs above.

Comment: Similar clinics, ostensibly using the same methods, report different success rates. In the UK, the live birth rates per cycle vary from 0% to 28% with an average of 15%.[44] The equivalent average figure in the USA is nearly 20%,[49] but again results vary widely.[50] In the UK, larger centers (≥200 cycles per year) report slightly higher live birth rates than smaller centers (15.7% per cycle started compared with an average of 12.7%).[5] Such a difference has not been reported consistently in the USA. The success of *in vitro* fertilization is influenced by age, duration of infertility, and previous pregnancy history. Pregnancy rates are highest between the ages of 25 and 35 years but decline steeply after 35 years.[5]

QUESTION What are the effects of treatment for infertility associated with endometriosis?

OPTION DRUG-INDUCED OVARIAN SUPPRESSION

One systematic review of RCTs has found no significant difference in pregnancy rates between drugs that induce ovarian suppression and either placebo or danazol in women with endometriosis. Ovarian suppression is less effective than surgical treatment.

Benefits: We found one systematic review updated in 1996, which identified 13 RCTs.[51] **Versus placebo:** Five RCTs compared ovulation suppression agents (medroxyprogesterone acetate, gestrinone, combined oral contraceptive pills, and gonadotrophin-releasing hormone analogues) versus placebo in 244 women with visually diagnosed endometriosis who had been attempting conception for over 12 months. There was no significant difference in pregnancy rates (OR for pregnancy compared with placebo 0.83, 95% CI 0.50–1.39). **Versus danazol:** Eight RCTs compared ovulation suppression versus danazol in 658 similar women. There was no significant difference in pregnancy rates (OR compared with danazol 1.20, 95% CI 0.85–1.68). **Versus surgery:** *See* below.

Harms: Drugs that cause ovulation suppression can have important adverse effects, such as weight gain, hot flushes, and osteoporosis. Adverse effects of danazol are dose related. An average weight gain of 2 to 4 kg is common with 3-months' treatment. Other adverse effects, include androgenic effects such as acne, seborrhoea, hirsutism, voice changes, and general complaints (e.g., irritability, musculoskeletal pains, and tiredness). Hot flushes and breast atrophy can sometimes result. Most of these adverse effects are reversible on stopping treatment. Treatment using ovulation suppression also can waste valuable time for women who are trying to get pregnant, because the opportunity for spontaneous conceptions is lost during treatment.

Comment: None of the RCTs in the systematic review used a crossover design, but co-intervention with clomiphene and other infertility drugs was a concern in three of the trials.

OPTION SURGICAL TREATMENT

Systematic reviews of cohort studies have found that surgery is more effective than ovarian suppression in women with infertility related to endometriosis and that there is no significant difference in pregnancy rates between open and laparoscopic surgery. No RCTs have compared surgery with *in vitro* fertilization in women with endometriosis.

Benefits: **Versus placebo or ovarian suppression:** We found two systematic reviews published in 1993 and 1994,[52,53] which together identified 21 cohort studies and one quasi-randomized trial in a total of 3879 women with all stages of endometriosis. Interventions were laparoscopic or open surgery versus medical treatment or no treatment. Surgical treatment produced a two-fifths increase in pregnancy rate compared with medical treatment or no treatment (RR 38%, 95% CI 28%–48%), but there was no significant difference between laparoscopic and open surgery (RR 0.93, 95% CI 0.84–1.02). In women with mild or minimal endometriosis, analysis of pooled data found that laparoscopic surgery achieves higher pregnancy rates than danazol or no treatment (OR 2.7, 95% CI 2.1–3.5). **Versus diagnostic laparoscopy:** We found one RCT published since the systematic reviews. This compared laparoscopic surgery (ablation or resection of endometriosis) versus diagnostic laparoscopy in 341 infertile women with minimal or mild endometriosis. The group undergoing laparoscopic surgery had an absolute increase of 13% in the probability of a pregnancy occurring within 36 weeks and lasting longer than 20 weeks (RR 1.7, 95% CI 1.2–2.6, NNT 9, 95% CI 5–33).[54]

Harms: The risks and morbidity of surgery under general anesthesia and of postoperative adhesion formation have to be balanced against the adverse effects of treatments involving ovarian suppression or stimulation. A multicenter series of 29,966 diagnostic and operative gynecologic laparoscopies[55] found a mortality of 3.33 per 100 000 laparoscopies, and a complication rate of 3.20 per 1000.

Comment: In the RCT described above,[54] 14% of the women who received surgery for their endometriosis also had periadnexal adhesions lysed, which may have increased their fecundity.

OPTION ***IN VITRO* FERTILIZATION**

Retrospective studies suggest that *in vitro* fertilization achieves similar rates of pregnancy in women with endometriosis as in those with other causes of infertility. There is no evidence from which to evaluate whether *in vitro* fertilization is better than drug-induced ovarian suppression or surgery for women with moderate or severe endometriosis.

Benefits: We found no systematic review or RCTs. We reviewed two retrospective studies of women undergoing *in vitro* fertilization. These compared pregnancy rates in those with endometriosis and those with other causes of infertility.[56,57] There were no significant differences in pregnancy rates for different stages of endometriosis or for endometriosis compared to other causes of infertility.

Harms: As with *in vitro* fertilization for tubal infertility.

Comment: There is a need for properly controlled prospective studies that present their results for different stages of endometriosis using a validated classification system. Comparisons with assisted reproductive techniques also are required.

MALE INFERTILITY

OPTION **INTRAUTERINE INSEMINATION**

A systematic review of RCTs has found that intrauterine insemination more than doubles the chance of pregnancy compared with intracervical insemination or natural intercourse in couples with male infertility.

Benefits: We found one systematic review published in 1997, which identified 10 RCTs (2082 treatment cycles) comparing intrauterine insemination versus intracervical insemination or natural intercourse.[58] In couples reported as having male infertility, intrauterine insemination more than doubled the pregnancy rate compared with intracervical insemination or timed natural intercourse (OR 2.20, 95% CI 1.43–3.39). Pregnancy rate per cycle was 6.5% with intrauterine insemination versus 3.1% with intracervical insemination or timed natural intercourse.

Harms: Apart from the risks of ovarian hyperstimulation syndrome and multiple pregnancy associated with ovarian stimulation, intrauterine insemination may increase the likelihood of infection and may be associated with some discomfort. However, data from RCTs are scarce.

Comment: A systematic review on intrauterine insemination in male infertility is expected soon (Cohlen B, personal communication).

OPTION INTRACYTOPLASMIC SPERM INJECTION PLUS *IN VITRO* FERTILIZATION

This combination has not been tested rigorously in RCTs.

Benefits: **Versus *in vitro* fertilization alone:** We found no systematic review. We found one RCT[59] and data from a review of the UK Human Fertilisation and Embryology Authority database adjusted for age and other factors.[5] These found that, when the sperm was normal and another (female) factor was the cause of the infertility, intracytoplasmic sperm injection plus *in vitro* fertilization achieved no significant increase in pregnancy rates compared with *in vitro* fertilization alone. Pregnancy was reported in 31% with *in vitro* fertilization and 32.8% with *in vitro* fertilization plus intracytoplasmic sperm injection in 116 women with tubal infertility.[59] Live birth was reported in 20% of cases,[44] but this was not over and above spontaneous rates.

Harms: Although conflicting reports of congenital abnormality in children born after intracytoplasmic sperm injection suggest no increase over background rates of abnormality[60], major birth defects may be twice as likely and minor defects may be 50% more likely.[61] There also has been a suggestion that chromosomal defects may be more likely.[62]

Comment: The data on congenital and chromosome abnormalities with intracytoplasmic sperm injection are being revised constantly as experience increases.

OPTION *IN VITRO* FERTILIZATION VERSUS GAMETE INTRAFALLOPIAN TRANSFER

One small RCT found no difference between *in vitro* fertilization and gamete intrafallopian transfer in male infertility.

Benefits: We found no systematic review. We reviewed one RCT in 14 couples with male infertility.[63] This found no difference in pregnancy rates.

Harms: *See* above.

Comment: None.

OPTION DONOR INSEMINATION

Analysis of data from large databases has found live birth rates of approximately 10% with donor insemination in women without evidence of reduced fertility or in whom problems with fertility have been corrected. No RCTs have compared donor insemination with other treatments for male infertility.

Benefits: We found no systematic review. No RCTs have compared donor insemination versus no treatment or versus other interventions for male infertility. However, such comparisons may be inappropriate, because for many couples donor insemination is not an acceptable option. Data are available from large databases, but it is sometimes unclear whether ovarian stimulation was used also. The live birth rate per cycle in the UK Human Fertilisation and Embryology Authority database (based on 7136 women) was 9%.[44] Similar rates are reported from the French donor insemination database (23,700 women over 4 years), with a mean pregnancy rate of 10.3% per cycle,[64] and the Sheffield database (343 women, 980 treatment cycles), with an 11.3% overall live birth rate.[65]

Harms: Few adverse effects are reported if ovarian stimulation is not used. Couples must come to terms with the fact that the child is not the man's genetic offspring.

Comment: RCTs have tended to concentrate on comparisons between different techniques of donor insemination. Some RCTs have found that introduction of the sperm is more effective via intrauterine than intracervical insemination.[3] A systematic review of donor insemination comparing intrauterine with intracervical insemination has just been published and will be reviewed in the next issue of *Clinical Evidence*.[66]

UNEXPLAINED INFERTILITY

OPTION CLOMIPHENE

One systematic review of RCTs (mainly using crossover designs) provides no support for the use of clomiphene in couples with unexplained infertility.

Benefits: We found one systematic review updated in 1996,[67] which identified five placebo-controlled RCTs, four using crossover designs, in women with unexplained infertility (458 cycles). This found a significant benefit in pregnancy rates (OR of pregnancy per cycle versus placebo 2.5, 95% CI 1.35–4.62). When only cycles before crossover were included (which was only possible from the data from three of these trials), the positive effect increased (OR 5.01, 95% CI 1.75–14.31). Since the review, another RCT using a parallel-group design[68] in 33 women with unexplained infertility found significantly higher pregnancy rates in spontaneous cycles compared with clomiphene cycles. When added to the review, the combined OR for pregnancy compared with placebo/no treatment fell to 1.4 with a CI that crossed unity, showing no benefit from clomiphene in women with unexplained infertility (Collins J, personal communication). This negative finding was consolidated by a systematic review of 22 RCTs in couples with all causes of infertility, which found no independent effect of clomiphene versus no ovarian stimulation.[69]

Harms: *See* p. 284.

Comment: The RCTs were generally of poor quality, and it is possible that, if a further RCT was published, the direction of the overall effect found with meta-analysis could change again. The review highlighted important differences between the trials: two included women with surgically treated endometriosis, one included only couples with primary infertility, and one included couples with a short duration of infertility (median of 28 months). Three of the trials included co-intervention with intrauterine insemination or cervicovaginal insemination. The trials also differed in their design (four were crossover trials) and in the quality of randomization (only one used properly concealed randomization). The additional RCT[68] also lacked a secure method of randomization. A large double-blind RCT without co-interventions in a well-defined group of couples with unexplained infertility is needed to clarify the role of clomiphene in unexplained infertility.

OPTION INTRAUTERINE INSEMINATION

Systematic reviews have found that, in couples with unexplained infertility receiving follicle-stimulating hormone, intrauterine insemination increases the rate of pregnancy compared with timed intercourse. Two reviews found that intrauterine insemination doubles the rate of pregnancy, whereas a third found that the apparent benefit disappears when intrauterine insemination is compared with intercourse timed favorably rather than late.

Benefits: We found three systematic reviews. The first, published in 1997, identified eight RCTs (number of treatment cycles not stated) comparing intrauterine insemination versus timed intercourse in couples with unexplained infertility receiving follicle-stimulating hormone.[69] In stimulated cycles, intrauterine insemination more than doubled the likelihood of pregnancy compared with timed intercourse (OR 2.37, 95% CI 1.43–3.90). The review also assessed the independent effects of follicle-stimulating hormone, clomiphene, and intrauterine insemination across 22 trials in couples with all causes of infertility. The likelihood of pregnancy was more than doubled with follicle-stimulating hormone (OR 2.35, 95% CI 1.87–2.94), and nearly trebled with intrauterine insemination (OR 2.82, 95% CI 2.18–3.66). Clomiphene did not increase the chances of pregnancy compared with no ovarian stimulation. The second review, published in 1998, identified seven RCTs (980 treatment cycles) comparing intrauterine insemination versus timed intercourse in couples with unexplained infertility (both interventions in addition to ovarian stimulation with gonadotrophins).[70] In stimulated cycles, intrauterine insemination achieved nearly twice the rate of pregnancy (20%) compared with timed intercourse (11.4%) (OR 1.84, 95% CI 1.30–2.62). The third systematic review, published in 1997, identified seven RCTs comparing intrauterine insemination versus timed intercourse or intracervical insemination (one RCT) in couples with unexplained infertility (934 treatment cycles).[58] Four RCTs used gonadotrophins, two used clomiphene, and three used no ovarian stimulation. When all cycles were combined, pregnancy rates were higher with intrauterine insemination (OR compared with intracervical insemination or timed intercourse 1.47, 95% CI 0.98–2.21). However, when the authors included only cycles in which natural intercourse was timed favorably rather than late, the beneficial effect of intrauterine insemination disappeared (unstimulated cycles, OR versus intracervical insemination or timed intercourse 0.92, 95% CI 0.23–3.64; stimulated cycles, OR 0.97, 95% CI 0.51–1.86). The addition of ovarian stimulation with gonadotrophins to any of the three interventions increased the overall pregnancy rates from 9.0% to 19.3%, suggesting that 11 women would need to receive ovarian stimulation in addition to one of the other interventions in order to achieve one additional pregnancy (NNT 11, 95% CI 6–37). **Versus gamete intrafallopian transfer:** *See* below.

Harms: Apart from the risks of ovarian hyperstimulation syndrome and multiple pregnancy associated with the ovarian stimulation (*see* above), intrauterine insemination may increase the likelihood of infection and may be associated with some discomfort. However, data from RCTs are scarce.

Comment: Only three of the RCTs were common to all three systematic reviews. One of the reviews[70] scored the included studies for validity. The scores ranged from 49% to 70% when 100% was taken as the ideal study.

OPTION GAMETE INTRAFALLOPIAN TRANSFER

Gamete intrafallopian transfer has not been tested rigorously against no treatment in couples with unexplained infertility. RCTs comparing it with other treatments (intrauterine insemination, timed intercourse, and *in vitro* fertilization) found no difference.

Benefit: **Versus no treatment:** We found no systematic review or RCTs. A prospective cohort study reported pregnancy rates in couples with unexplained infertility before and after gamete intrafallopian transfer. It found that gamete intrafallopian transfer was more effective than no treatment.[71] **Versus intrauterine insemination or timed intercourse:** We found no systematic review. We reviewed three RCTs in 283 couples with unexplained infertility. The first compared gamete intrafallopian transfer versus ovarian stimulation plus either timed intercourse or timed cervical donor insemination.[72] It found no significant difference. Of the other two RCTs, one found higher pregnancy rates with gamete intrafallopian transfer than with ovarian stimulation plus intrauterine insemination,[73] the other found no difference.[74] **Versus *in vitro* fertilization:** *See* below.

Harms: Potential harms include the risks attributable to general anesthesia and laparoscopy. Multiple pregnancy rates vary with the number of oocytes transferred.

Comment: Gamete intrafallopian transfer, unlike *in vitro* fertilization, gives no diagnostic information regarding fertilization, and involves a laparoscopy and general anesthetic, both of which are usually avoided with *in vitro* fertilization. Success rates decrease with increasing age.[75,76]

OPTION *IN VITRO* FERTILIZATION

Limited evidence from RCTs found no difference in pregnancy rates between *in vitro* fertilization and gamete intrafallopian transfer in unexplained infertility.

Benefits: We found no systematic review. We reviewed two RCTs in 155 couples with unexplained infertility.[63,77] Neither found a significant difference between gamete intrafallopian transfer and *in vitro* fertilization.

Harms: *See* above.

Comment: The RCTs were too small to rule out a beneficial effect.

Table 1 summarizes the comparative success rates of all treatments for infertility reviewed in this article.

GLOSSARY

Gamete intrafallopian transfer (GIFT) The process of placing a mixture of sperm and oocytes into the fallopian tube, usually at the time of laparoscopy. Fertilization of the oocytes then takes place in the tube. Oocytes are obtained in a fashion similar to IVF.

In vitro fertilization (IVF) The process of fertilizing the oocyte with sperm in the laboratory. Oocytes usually are obtained transvaginally with ultrasound guidance after ovarian stimulation with gonadotropins to increase the number of follicles.

Intracytoplasmic sperm injection (ICSI) A process by which a single sperm is mechanically injected directly into the oocyte using a special microscope. A sperm is isolated and placed into a micropipette, which is used to puncture the zone pelucida and oocyte membrane. The technique is used in conjunction with IVF to treat couples when the male has a very low sperm count.

Laparoscopic ovarian drilling A surgical technique used to reduce the number of ovarian stromal cells that produce androgens. During laparoscopy, a laser or electrocautery probe is passed through the ovarian cortex and into the stroma of the ovary. The stroma cells are then ablated. This process is usually repeated in many sites on the ovary.

Ovarian hyperstimulation syndrome A life-threatening syndrome characterized by sever ovarian enlargement accompanied by fluid shifts from the intravascular space to the peritoneal, pleural, and pericardial cavities.

REFERENCES

1. European Society for Human Reproduction and Embryology. Guidelines to the prevalence, diagnosis, treatment and management of infertility, 1996. *Hum Reprod* 1996;11:1775–1807.
2. Schmidt L, Munster K. Infertility, involuntary infecundity, and the seeking of medical advice in industrialized countries 1970–1992: a review of concepts, measurements and results. *Hum Reprod* 1995;10:1407–1418.
3. Effective Health Care. The management of subfertility. *Effective Health Care Bulletin* 1992;3:13. (Date of search and primary sources not stated.)
4. Collins JA, Burrows EA, Wilan AR. The prognosis for live birth among untreated infertile couples. *Fertil Steril* 1995;64:22–28.
5. Templeton A, Morris JK. In vitro fertilisation — factors affecting outcome. In: Templeton A, Cooke ID, O'Brien PMS, eds. *35th RCOG study group evidence-based fertility treatment*. London: RCOG Press, 1998.
6. Khan KS, Daya S, Collins JA, Walter SD. Empirical evidence of bias in infertility research: overestimation of treatment effect in crossover trials using pregnancy as the outcome measure. *Fertil Steril* 1996;65:939–945.
7. Hughes E, Collins J, Vandekerckhove P. Clomiphene citrate vs placebo for ovulation induction in oligo- amenorrhoiec women. (Cochrane Review) In: The Cochrane Library, Issue 3, 1998. Oxford: Update Software. (Date of search not stated, relevant trials were identified from the Cochrane subfertility group's register of controlled trials.)
8. Buvat J, Buvat-Herbaut M, Marcolin G, Ardaens-Boulier K. Antiestrogens as treatment of female and male infertilities. *Horm Res* 1987;28:219–229.
9. Messinis IE, Nillius SJ. Comparison between tamoxifen and clomiphene for induction of ovulation. *Acta Obstet Gynecol Scand* 1982;61:377–379.
10. Gerhard I, Runnebaum B. Comparison between tamoxifen and clomiphene therapy in women with anovulation. *Arch Gynecol* 1979;227:279–288.
11. Rossing MA, Daling JR, Weiss NS, Moore DE, Self SG. Ovarian tumours in a cohort of infertile women. *N Engl J Med* 1994;331:771–776.
12. Parazzini F, Negri E, La Vecchia C, Moroni S, Franceschi S, Crosignani PG. Treatment for infertility and risk of invasive epithelial ovarian cancer. *Hum Reprod* 1997;12:2159–2161.
13. Mosgaard BJ, Lidegaard O, Kjaer SK, Schou G, Andersen AN. Infertility, fertility drugs, and invasive ovarian cancer: a case-control study. *Fertil Steril* 1997;67:1005–1012.
14. Shushan A, Paltiel O, Iscovich J, Elchalal U, Peretz T, Schenker JG. Human menopausal gonadotrophin and the risk of epithelial ovarian cancer. *Fertil Steril* 1996;65:13–18.
15. Venn A, Watson L, Lumley J, Giles G, King C, Healy D. Breast and ovarian cancer incidence after infertility and in vitro fertilisation. *Lancet* 1995;346:995–1000.
16. Dunn A, Macfarlane A. Recent trends in the incidence of multiple births and associated mortality in England and Wales. *Arch Dis Child Fetal Neonatal Ed* 1996;75:F10–19.
17. State-specific variation in rates of twin births — United States, 1992–1994. *MMWR Morb Mortal Wkly Rep* 1997;46:121–125.
18. Levene MI, Wild J, Steer P. Higher multiple births and the modern management of infertility in Britain. British Association of Perinatal Medicine. *Br J Obstet Gynaecol* 1992;99:607–613.
19. Hughes E, Collins J, Vandekerckhove P. Ovulation induction with urinary follicle stimulating hor-

mone vs human menopausal gonadotrophin for clomiphen-citrate–resistant polycystic ovary syndrome.(Cochrane Review) In: The Cochrane Library, Issue 3, 1998. Oxford: Update Software. (Date of search not stated, relevant trials were identified from the Cochrane subfertility group's register of controlled trials.)

20. Coelingh-Bennink HJ, Fauser BC, Out HJ. Recombinant follicle-stimulating hormone (FSH; Puregon) is more efficient than urinary follicle stimulating hormone (Metrodin) in women with clomiphene-resistant, normogonadotrophic, chronic anovulation: a prospective, multicenter, assessor-blind, randomized, clinical trial. European Puregon collaborative anovulation study group. *Fertil Steril* 1998;69:19–25.
21. Wang CF, Gemzell C. The use of human gonadotrophins for the induction of ovulation in women with polycystic ovarian disease. *Fertil Steril* 1980;33:479–486.
22. Farquhar C, Vandekerckhove P, Arnot M, Lilford R. Polycystic ovary syndrome: laparoscopic "drilling" by diathermy or laser for ovulation induction in patients with anovulatory polycystic ovarian syndrome. (Cochrane Review) In: The Cochrane Library, Issue 3, 1998. Oxford: Update Software, 1998. (Date of search not stated, relevant trials were identified from the Cochrane menstrual disorders and subfertility group's register of controlled trials.)
23. Balen AH, Braat DD, West C, Patel A, Jacobs HS. Cumulative conception and live birth rates after the treatment of anovulatory infertility: safety and efficacy of ovulation induction in 200 patients. *Hum Reprod* 1994;9:1563–1570.
24. Braat DD, Schoemaker R, Schoemaker J. Life table analysis of fecundity in intravenously gonadotropin-releasing hormone-treated patients with normogonadotropic and hypogonadotropic amenorrhea. *Fertil Steril* 1991;55:266–271.
25. Filicori M, Flamigni C, Dellai P, et al. Treatment of anovulation with pulsatile gonadotropin-releasing hormone: prognostic factors and clinical results in 600 cycles. *J Clin Endocrinol Metab* 1994;79: 1215–1220.
26. Martin KA, Hall JE, Adams JM, Crowley WF, Jr. Comparison of exogenous gonadotropins and pulsatile gonadotropin-releasing hormone for induction of ovulation in hypogonadotropic amenorrhea. *J Clin Endocrinol Metab* 1993;77:125–129.
27. Thurmond AS. Pregnancies after selective salpingography and tubal recanalization. *Radiology* 1994;190:11–13.
28. Ransom MX, Garcia AJ. Surgical management of cornual-isthmic tubal obstruction. *Fertil Steril* 1997;68:887–891.
29. Marana R. Proximal tubal obstruction: are we overdiagnosing and overtreating? *Gynaecological Endoscopy* 1992;1:99–101.
30. Winston RM, Margara RA. Microsurgical salpingostomy is not an obsolete procedure. *Br J Obstet Gynaecol* 1991;98:637–642.
31. Filippini F, Darai E, Benifla JL, et al. Distal tubal surgery: a critical review of 104 laparoscopic distal tuboplasties. *J Gynecol Obstet Biol Reprod* 1996;25:471–478.
32. Donnez J, Casanas-Roux F. Prognostic factors of fimbrial microsurgery. *Fertil Steril* 1986;46: 200–204.
33. Tomazevic T, Ribic-Pucelj M, Omahen A, Colja B. Microsurgery and in-vitro fertilization and embryo transfer for infertility resulting from pathological proximal tubal blockage. *Hum Reprod* 1996;11: 2613–2617.
34. Wu CH, Gocial B. A pelvic scoring system for infertility surgery. *Int J Fertil* 1988;33:341–346.
35. Oelsner G, Sivan E, Goldenberg M, Carp HJ, Admon D, Mashiach S. Should lysis of adhesions be performed when in-vitro fertilization and embryo transfer are available? *Hum Reprod* 1994;9:2339–2341.
36. Singhal V, Li TC, Cooke ID. An analysis of factors influencing the outcome of 232 consecutive tubal microsurgery cases. *Br J Obstet Gynaecol* 1991;98:628–636.
37. Marana R, Quagliarello J. Distal tubal occlusion: microsurgery versus in vitro fertilization: a review. *Int J Fertil* 1988;33:107–115.
38. Marana R, Quagliarello J. Proximal tubal occlusion: microsurgery versus IVF: a review. *Int J Fertil* 1988;33:338–340.
39. Patton PE, Williams TJ, Coulam CB. Results of microsurgical reconstruction in patients with combined proximal and distal tubal occlusion: double obstruction. *Fertil Steril* 1987;47:670–674.
40. Watson A, Vandekerchove P, Lilford R. Techniques for tubal surgery. (Cochrane Review) In: The Cochrane Library, Issue 3, 1998. Oxford: Update Software. (Date of search not stated, relevant trials were identified from the Cochrane menstrual disorders and subfertility group's register of controlled trials.)
41. Holst N, Maltau JM, Forsdahl F, Hansen LJ. Handling of tubal infertility after introduction of in vitro fertilization: changes and consequences. *Fertil Steril* 1991;55:140–143.
42. Vilos GA, Verhoest CR, Martin JS, Botz C. Economic evaluation of in vitro fertilization-embryo transfer and neosalpingostomy for bilateral tubal obstruction. *Journal of the Society of Obstetricians and Gynaecologists of Canada* 1998;20:139–147.
43. Gillett WR, Clarke RH, Herbison GP. First and subsequent pregnancies after tubal surgery: evaluation of the fertility index. *Fertil Steril* 1997;68: 1033–1042.
44. Human Fertilisation and Embryology Authority. *Sixth Annual Report 1997*. London: HFEA, 1998.
45. Jarrell J, Labelle R, Goeree R, Milner R, Collins J. In vitro fertilization and embryo transfer: a randomized controlled trial. *Online J Curr Clin Trials* 1993.
46. Soliman S, Daya S, Collins J, Jarrell J. A randomized trial of in vitro fertilization versus conventional treatment for infertility. *Fertil Steril* 1993;59:1239–1244.
47. Benadiva CA, Kligman I, Davis O, Rosenwaks Z. In vitro fertilization versus tubal surgery: is pelvic reconstructive surgery obsolete? *Fertil Steril* 1995;64:1051–1061.
48. Brinsden PR, Wada I, Tan SL, Balen A, Jacobs HS. Diagnosis, prevention and management of ovarian hyperstimulation syndrome. *Br J Obstet Gynaecol* 1995;102:767–772.
49. Centers for Disease Control and Prevention. US Department of Health and Human Services. 1995 *Assisted Reproductive Technology Success Rates*. National Summary and Fertility *Clinic Reports* 1997;1–23.
50. Chapko KM, Weaver MR, Chapko MK, Pasta D, Adamson GD. Stability of in vitro fertilization-embryo transfer success rates from the 1989,1990, and 1991 clinic-specific outcome assessments. *Fertil Steril* 1995;64:757–763.
51. Hughes E, Fedorkow DM, Collins J, Vandekerckhove P. Ovulation suppression versus placebo in the treatment of endometriosis. (Cochrane Review) In: The Cochrane Library, Issue 3, 1998. Oxford: Update Software. (Date of search not stated, relevant trials were identified from the cochrane subfertility group's register of controlled trials.)
52. Adamson GD, Pasta DJ. Surgical treatment of endometriosis-associated infertility: meta-analysis compared with survival analysis. *Am J Obstet Gynecol* 1994;171:1488–1505. Primary sources MEDLINE 1966 to 1992; Science Citation Index

January 1986 to December 1989; abstracts from scientific meetings 1986 to 1992; experts contacted and bibliographies of relevant trials handsearched.
53. Hughes EG, Fedorkow DM, Collins J. A quantitative overview of controlled trials in endometriosis-associated infertility. *Fertil Steril* 1993;59: 963–970. Primary sources MEDLINE 1966 to 1992; Science Citation Index January 1986 to December 1989; abstracts from scientific meetings 1986 to 1992; experts contacted and bibliographies of relevant trials handsearched.
54. Marcoux S, Maheux R, Berube S. Laparoscopic surgery in infertile women with minimal or mild endometriosis. *N Engl J Med* 1997;337:217–222.
55. Chapron C, Querleu D, Bruhat M, et al. Surgical complications of diagnostic and operative gynaecological laparoscopy: a series of 29,966 cases. *Hum Reprod* 1998;13:867–872.
56. Olivennes F, Feldberg D, Liu H-C, Cohen J, Moy F, Rosenwaks Z. Endometriosis: a stage by stage analysis — the role of in vitro fertilization. *Fertil Steril* 1995;64:392–398.
57. Geber S, Paraschos T, Atkinson G, Margara M, Winston RML. Results of IVF in patients with endometriosis: the severity of the disease does not affect outcome or the incidence of miscarriage. *Hum Reprod* 1995;10:1507–1511.
58. Ford WCL, Mathur RS, Hull MGR. Intrauterine insemination: is it an effective treatment for male factor infertility? *Balliere's Clin Obstet Gynecol* 1997;11(4):691–710. (Date of search not stated, primary sources MEDLINE, BIDS and manual scanning of leading reproductive journals.)
59. Aboulghar MA, Mansour RT, Serour GI, Amin YM, Kamal A. Prospective controlled randomized study of in vitro fertilization versus intracytoplasmic sperm injection in the treatment of tubal factor infertility with normal semen parameters. *Fertil Steril* 1996;66:753–756.
60. Bonduelle M, Legein J, Buyesse A, et al. Prospective follow-up study of 423 children born after intracytoplasmic sperm injection. *Hum Reprod* 1996;11:1558–1564.
61. Kurinczuk J, Bower C. Birth defects in infants conceived by intracytoplasmic sperm injection: an alternative interpretation. *BMJ* 1997;315: 1260–1266.
62. Van Steirteghem A. Intracytoplasmic sperm injection. *Balliere's Clin Obst Gynaecol* 1997;11:725–738.
63. Leeton J, Rogers P, et al. A controlled study between the use gamete intrafallopian transfer (GIFT) and in vitro fertilization and embryo transfer in the management of idiopathic and male infertility. *Fertil Steril* 1987;48:605–607.
64. Le Lannou D, Lansac J. Artificial procreation with frozen donor sperm: the French experience of CECOS. In: Barratt CLR, Cooke ID, eds. *Donor insemination*. Cambridge: CUP, 1993;152–169.
65. Cooke ID. Donor insemination – timing and insemination method. In: Templeton A, Cooke ID, O'Brien PMS, eds. *35th RCOG Study Group evidence-based fertility treatment*. London: RCOG Press, 1998.
66. O'Brien P, Vandekerckhove P. Intra-uterine versus cervical insemination of donor sperm for subfertility (Cochrane Review). In: The Cochrane Library, Issue 1, 1999. Oxford: Update Software.
67. Hughes E, Collins J, Vandekerckhove P. Clomiphene citrate vs placebo or no treatment in unexplained subfertility. (Cochrane Review) In: The Cochrane Library, Issue 3, 1998. Oxford: Update Software. (Date of search not stated, relevant trials were identified from the Cochrane menstrual disorders and subfertility group's register of controlled trials.)
68. Fujii S, Fukui A, Fukushi Y, Kagiya A, Sato S, Saito Y. The effects of clomiphene citrate on normally ovulatory women. *Fertil Steril* 1997;68:997–999.
69. Hughes EG. The effectiveness of ovulation induction and intrauterine insemination in the treatment of persistent infertility: a meta-analysis. *Hum Reprod* 1997;12:1865–1872. (Date of search not stated, relevant trials were identified from the Cochrane menstrual disorders and subfertility group's register of controlled trials.)
70. Zeyneloglu HB, Arici A, Olive DL, Duleba AJ. Comparison of intrauterine insemination with timed intercourse in superovulated cycles with gonadotrophins: a meta-analysis. *Fertil Steril* 1998;69:486–491. (Date of search 1966—1997; primary sources MEDLINE and hand search of bibliographies of relevant publications and review articles.)
71. Murdoch AP, Harris M, Mahroo M, Williams M, Dunlop W. Is GIFT (gamete intrafallopian transfer) the best treatment for unexplained infertility. *Br J Obstet Gynaecol* 1991;98:643–647.
72. Hogerzeil HV, Spiekerman JCM, de Vries JWA, de Schepper G. A randomized trial between GIFT and ovarian stimulation for the treatment of unexplained infertility and failed artificial insemination by donor. *Hum Reprod* 1992;7:1235–1239.
73. Murdoch AP, Harris M, Mahroo M, Williams M, Dunlop W. Gamete intrafallopian transfer (GIFT) compared with intrauterine insemination in the treatment of unexplained infertility. *Br J Obstet Gynaecol* 1991;98:1107–1111.
74. Wessels PHX, Cronje HS, Oosthuizen AP, Trumpelmann MD, Grobler S, Hamlett DK. Cost-effectiveness of gamete intrafallopian transfer in comparison with induction of ovulation with gonadotrophins in the treatment of female infertility: a clinical trial. *Fertil Steril* 1992;57:163–167.
75. Rombauts L, Dear M, Breheny S, Healy DL. Cumulative pregnancy and live birth rates after gamete intra-fallopian transfer. *Hum Reprod* 1997;12(6):1338–1342.
76. Society for Assisted Reproductive Technology and the American Society for Reproductive Medicine. Assisted reproductive technology in the United States and Canada: 1995 results generated from the American Society for Reproductive Medicine/Society for Assisted Reproductive Technology Registry. *Fertil Steril* 1998;69:389–398.
77. Ranieri M, Beckett VA, Marchant S, Kinis A, Serhal P. Gamete intra-fallopian transfer or in-vitro fertilization after failed ovarian stimulation and intrauterine insemination in unexplained infertility. *Hum Reprod* 1995;10:2023–2026.
78. Meirow D, Schenker JG. Appraisal of GIFT. *Eur J Obstet Gynecol Reprod* 1995;58:59–65.
79. RCOG Infertility Guideline Group. The management of infertility in secondary care. London: RCOG, 1998. Primary sources MEDLINE, EMBASE, Cochrane Library, handsearching major journals.

Kirsten Duckitt, MA, MBBChir, MRCOG
Former research Fellow
Royal College of Obstetrics and Gynaecology
London
UK

Competing interests: None declared.

TABLE 1 Comparative success rates of treatments for infertility: evidence from RCTs and analysis of database data

Treatment	Live birth rates	Pregnancy rates	Adverse effects
ALL CAUSES OF INFERTILITY			
IVF (per treated cycle)	UK 15%, US 20%[5]	59%–77% (with 3–5 treatment cycles) [47]	Ectopic pregnancy: 1%–3%[41,42]
GIFT (per cycle) (not including tubal infertility)	23%[78]		MP 25%[78]
INFERTILITY CAUSED BY OVULATION DISORDERS			
Clomiphene to induce ovulation in amenorrheic women (cumulative rate after 11 cycles of treatment)		90%.[3] 3 times more likely than with placebo[7]	Risk of ovarian cancer, unproved. MP: 2%–13%, mostly twins.[16,17] OHSS: infrequent and mild
Gonadotrophins to induce ovulation in clomiphene-resistant PCOS (cumulative rate after 4 months of treatment)		27%–40%[3,19] FSH 27%[19]	Risk of ovarian cancer, unproved. MP: 29%[21] OHSS: 4%
Laparoscopic drilling (cumulative rate 1–2 years after treatment)		48%[22,79]	Risks of laparoscopy, general anesthesia, and adhesions. Risk of premature ovarian failure unproved
TUBAL INFERTILITY			
Tubal surgery for distal occlusion (cumulative rate 2 years after surgery)	20%–30%[30,36,37]		Risks of general anesthesia. Ectopic pregnancy: 7%–9%[41,42]
Tubal surgery for proximal occlusion (cumulative rate)	40%–60%[38,39]		
Reversal of female sterilisation (cumulative rate 1–2 years after surgery)			

Continued overleaf

Continued

INFERTILITY ASSOCIATED WITH ENDOMETRIOSIS			
Surgery (per cycle)		13%–38%†[52–54]	Risks of surgery and general anesthesia (for laparoscopic surgery, mortality 3.33/100 000, complication rate 3.2/1000)[55]
MALE INFERTILITY			
IUI ± ovarian stimulation (per cycle)		6.5%[58]	
ICSI plus IVF (per cycle)	20%[5]		
Donor insemination* (per cycle)	9%–12%[44,64,65]		No adverse effects if no ovarian stimulation is given, but child is not male partner's genetic offspring
UNEXPLAINED INFERTILITY			
IUI ± ovarian stimulation (per cycle)		9%–12% without stimulation 19%–20% with stimulation[58,70]	

*Using frozen donor sperm in women without female factor or with corrected female factor; †Over spontaneous rate; MP, multiple pregnancy; OHSS, ovarian hyperstimulation syndrome; IUI, intrauterine insemination; IVF, *in vitro* fertilization; ICSI, intracytoplasmic sperm injection; GIFT, gamete intrafallopian transfer; PCOS, polycystic ovary syndrome.

Breast cancer

Mike Dixon, MD, Alan Rodger, MB, ChB, FRCSEd, FRCR, FRANZCR, and Stephen Johnston, MBBS, MA, MRCP, PhD

QUESTIONS

INTERVENTIONS

See Glossary, p. 309

Key Messages

- Systematic reviews have found that, as long as all local disease is excised, more extensive surgery is not associated with better outcomes in early invasive breast cancer. More extensive local resection in breast-conserving surgery gives worse cosmetic results.
- Randomized controlled trials (RCTs) have found that radiotherapy after breast-conserving surgery for early invasive disease reduces the risk of isolated local recurrence but does not increase 10-year survival.

- A systematic review has found that similar rates of survival and local recurrence are achieved with breast conserving surgery plus radiotherapy as with mastectomy.
- A systematic review has found that radiotherapy to the chest wall after mastectomy reduces the risk of local recurrence by approximately two thirds and the risk of death from breast cancer at 10 years by 6% but that it has no effect on overall 10-year survival.
- A systematic review has found that adjuvant chemotherapy reduces rates of recurrence and improves survival for women with early breast cancer.
- A systematic review has found that adjuvant tamoxifen taken for up to 5 years reduces the chance of recurrence and death in pre- and postmenopausal women with estrogen-receptor–positive tumors irrespective of age, menopausal status, nodal involvement, or the addition of chemotherapy. Tamoxifen slightly increases the risk of endometrial cancer but has no overall effect on non–breast cancer mortality.
- A systematic review has found that ovarian ablation significantly improves long-term survival in women aged under 50 years with early breast cancer.
- One RCT found that adding combined chemotherapy to tamoxifen improved survival.

DEFINITION Invasive breast cancer can be separated into three main groups: early or operable breast cancer, locally advanced disease, and metastatic breast cancer. Women with early or operable breast cancer have disease that apparently is restricted to the breast and sometimes to local lymph nodes and can be removed surgically. Although these women do not have overt metastases at the time of staging, they remain at risk of local recurrence and of metastatic spread. They can be divided into those with tumors less than 4 cm in length or multifocal cancers that can be treated by mastectomy and those with tumors greater than 4 cm in length or unifocal cancers that can be treated by breast-conserving surgery. Locally advanced breast cancer is characterized by matted lymph nodes or involvement of the skin or chest wall. Ductal carcinoma *in situ* (DCIS) is a noninvasive tumor characterized by the presence of malignant cells in the breast ducts but with no evidence that they breach the basement membrane, thereby invading into periductal connective tissues.

INCIDENCE/ PREVALENCE Breast cancer affects one in 12 women in the UK and causes 21,000 deaths per year. Prevalence is approximately five times higher, with over 100,000 women living with breast cancer at any one time.

ETIOLOGY The risk of breast cancer increases with age, doubling every 10 years up to the menopause. Risk factors include an early age at menarche, older age at menopause, older age at birth of first child, family history, atypical hyperplasia, alcohol, radiation exposure, oral contraceptive use, and postmenopausal hormone replacement therapy. Risk in different countries varies fivefold.

PROGNOSIS Tumor size, axillary node status, histologic grade and estrogen-receptor status provide the most significant prognostic information. Seventy percent of women with operable disease are alive 5 years after diagnosis and treatment. Risk of recurrence is highest through the first 5 years, but the risk remains even 15 to 20 years after surgery. Those with node-positive disease have a 50% to 60% chance of recurrence within 5 years compared with 30% to 35% for node-negative disease.

Adjuvant systemic drug treatment is given to most women to eliminate micrometastatic disease remaining after surgery.

AIMS To improve survival, to prevent local or regional node recurrence, to obtain prognostic information on the type and extent of tumor and the status of the axillary lymph nodes, to optimize cosmetic results and minimize psychosocial impact, to minimize adverse effects of treatment, and to maximize quality of life.

OUTCOMES Survival; rates of local and regional recurrence; rates of mastectomy after breast conserving treatment; rates of development of metastases; cosmetic outcomes; quality of life; incidence of adverse effects of treatment, including upper limb lymphoedema.

METHODS *Clinical Evidence* search, July 1998. All systematic reviews and RCTs that were identified were reviewed.

QUESTION What are the effects of radiotherapy to the breast after breast conserving surgery for ductal carcinoma *in situ*?

We found limited evidence that radiotherapy reduces the risk of local recurrence and invasive carcinoma but makes no difference to survival.

Benefits: We found no systematic review. One RCT found no difference in survival at 8 years but a significant reduction in risk of local recurrence if radiotherapy is given (12.1% vs. 26.8%).[1] (Risk of recurrent DCIS 8.2% vs. 13.4%, $p = 0.007$; risk of invasive carcinoma 3.9% vs. 13.4%, $p < 0.0001$.)

Harms: We found no comparative evidence on harms.

Comment: Several large ongoing RCTs are evaluating the role of radiotherapy and tamoxifen in all grades of ductal carcinoma *in situ*. One recent RCT found that the addition of tamoxifen to radiotherapy after surgery resulted in a decreased incidence of invasive or noninvasive cancer in the ipsilateral or contralateral breast over 5 years than radiotherapy and placebo after surgery (8.2% vs. 13.4%; $p = 0.0009$).[2]

QUESTION Is the extent of surgery related to outcome in early invasive breast cancer?

Systematic reviews of RCTs have found that more extensive surgery is not associated with better outcomes, providing that all local disease is excised. The more extensive the local resection in breast conserving surgery is, the worse the final cosmetic result.

Benefits: **Comparisons between supraradical, radical, and total mastectomy:** We found one systematic review of five RCTs that compared supraradical versus radical mastectomy, radical versus total mastectomy, and supraradical versus total mastectomy in 2090 women with operable breast cancer.[3] It found no significant difference in risk of death over 10 years (RRR with more extensive compared with less extensive surgery 0.02, 95% CI –0.04 to 0.08). **Comparisons between radical, total, and simple mastectomy:** The systematic review included four RCTs comparing radical versus simple mastectomy (three trials) and total versus simple mastectomy (one trial) in 1296 women with operable breast cancer.[3] Meta-analysis found no significant difference in risk of death over 10 years (RRR for more extensive compared with less extensive surgery 0.02, 95% CI –0.05 to +0.09). **Mastectomy versus breast conservation:** We found two systematic reviews. The first identified nine RCTs in 4981 women potentially suitable for breast conserving treatment.[3] All participants received postoperative radiotherapy. Meta-analysis found no significant difference in risk of death over 10 years (RRR for breast conservation compared with mastectomy 0.02, 95% CI –0.05 to +0.09). Rates of local recurrence were adequately reported in six trials in 3107 women; there was no significant difference (RRR for mastectomy compared with breast conservation 0.04, 95% CI –0.04 to +0.12). The second systematic review analyzed data on 10-year survival from six RCTs comparing breast conservation versus mastectomy.[4] Meta-analysis of data from five of the trials showed no significant difference in the risk of death at 10 years (OR compared with mastectomy 0.91, 95% CI 0.78–1.05). The sixth trial used a much lower dose of radiotherapy after breast conservation. Most benefit from breast conservation was seen in women with positive lymph nodes, the overall survival benefit being limited to those trials in which node-positive women who underwent mastectomy did not receive regional radiotherapy: when > 50% of node-positive women in both the mastectomy and breast conservation arms received adjuvant nodal radiotherapy, both arms had similar survival rates; when < 50% of node-positive women in both arms received adjuvant nodal radiotherapy, survival was better with breast conservation (OR compared with mastectomy 0.69, 95% CI 0.49–0.97). **Different extents of local excision in breast conservation:** Only one RCT has been performed ($n = 705$) comparing lumpectomy versus quadrantectomy.[5] There were significantly more breast recurrences with lumpectomy (7%) than quadrantectomy (2%), but a major factor associated with local recurrence in the lumpectomy group was incomplete excision[6] (*see* Comment). In a subset of 148 women, there was a significantly higher rate of poor cosmetic outcome with quadrantectomy (RR compared with lumpectomy 3.11, 95% CI 1.2–8.1).[5] No RCTs have compared wide local excision (complete excision microscopically) with quadrantectomy.

Harms: More extensive surgery results in greater mutilation and adverse psychosocial impact. Between 60% to 90% of women having breast conservation had an excellent or good cosmetic result (median 83%, 95% CI 67%–87%).[5,7–15] The single most important factor influencing cosmetic outcome is the volume of tissue excised; the larger the amount of tissue excised is, the worse the cosmetic result.[7] Only isolated small studies have shown no correlation between the extent of surgical excision and cosmesis.[13]

Comment: The link between completeness of excision and local recurrence after breast conservation has been evaluated in 16 centers. In 13 of these, incomplete excision was associated with an increased RR of local recurrence compared with complete excision of between 1.7- and 9-fold (median RRI 3.4, 95% CI 2.6–4.6).[6] The three centers that have not reported increased rates of local recurrence after incomplete excision gave much higher doses of local radiotherapy (65–72 Gy). Two centers also used re-excision, and women with involved margins had only focal margin involvement.

QUESTION **What are the effects of radiotherapy after breast-conserving surgery for early invasive disease?**

One systematic review of RCTs found that radiotherapy reduced the risk of isolated local recurrence and loss of breast but did not increase 10-year survival. Similar rates of survival and local recurrence were achieved with breast-conserving surgery plus radiotherapy as with mastectomy.

Benefits: **Versus breast-conserving sugery alone:** We found one systematic review, which identified four RCTs ($n=381–1450$) comparing surgery plus radiotherapy versus surgery alone.[3] All four trials began before 1985 and used megavoltage X-ray radiation. Pooled data from trials that reported sites of local recurrence ($n=781$) found that radiotherapy reduced the odds of isolated local recurrence by 75% (OR 0.25, 95% CI 0.16–0.34). Even a trial limited to "good prognosis disease" (tumor ≤2 cm, node negative) found a significant reduction in local relapse rate with radiotherapy at 5 years: relapse rate with radiotherapy 2.3% (95% CI 1%–4.3%) compared with no radiotherapy 18.4% (95% CI 12.5%–24.2%).[16] In that trial, unpublished 10-year data found that radiotherapy reduced local recurrence rates (8.5% vs. 24%) and rates of breast loss (8% vs. 16%). One subsequent RCT ($n=585$) also found after 6 years that the proportion of women free of locoregional disease with breast conservation was higher with radiotherapy (93.8% vs. 81.3%).[17] Pooled data from all four trials found no difference in 10-year survival (OR 0.12 vs. 0.09, $p>0.1$). **Versus mastectomy:** The systematic review identified nine RCTs ($n=4891$) comparing breast radiotherapy after breast conserving surgery versus simple or modified radical mastectomy in women with invasive breast cancer. It that found no difference in survival rates at 10 years (22.9% vs. 22.9%; no CIs quoted) or in local recurrence (6.2% vs. 5.9% from pooled data from six trials, $n=3107$).[3]

Harms: We found few strong study designs that addressed harms. One RCT found no evidence that arm lymphoedema was increased by radiotherapy to the breast.[16] Experience suggests that acute adverse effects include tiredness, skin erythema (with occasional desquamation), and, rarely, acute radiation pneumonitis (<1%) or pericarditis. **Late toxicity and noncancer mortality:** Radiotherapy is known to cause pigmentation and, less commonly, telangiectasia, subcutaneous fat and breast parenchyma fibrosis, rib osteitis with radionecrosis (fracture is unusual), and heart and lung fibrosis. We found no evidence about the effect of radiotherapy to the breast on death from heart disease. Studies assessing cosmetic results mainly have been retrospective, using poorly validated outcomes. The effects of social, psychological, and financial disruptions from attending for 5 to 6 weeks of radiotherapy have not been addressed clearly in studies, because comparisons are usually made with mastectomy or breast conserving surgery without radiotherapy. There is an extremely low reported incidence of radiation-induced malignancy, usually soft tissue sarcomas, in the irradiated breast.

Comment: Although few in number, the four trials are of high quality with consistent results. Their results, as well as those from retrospective case series, suggest that prognostic factors for local recurrence after breast-conserving surgery include positive margins, an extensive intraduct component, younger age, lymphovascular invasion, histologic grade, and chemotherapy. The only consistent independent risk factor is avoidance of radiotherapy.

QUESTION **What are the effects of radiotherapy after mastectomy for invasive breast cancer?**

One systematic review has found that radiotherapy to the chest wall after mastectomy reduces the risk of local recurrence by approximately two thirds and the risk of death from breast cancer at 10 years by 6%, but that it has no effect on 10-year survival.

Benefits: We found one systematic review of 32 RCTs (1962–1985) comparing mastectomy versus mastectomy followed by radiotherapy to the chest wall. Five trials were of mastectomy alone, $n=4541$; four of mastectomy and axillary sampling, $n=3286$; and 23 of mastectomy and axillary clearance, $n=6699$. The review found that radiotherapy reduced local recurrence by two thirds and breast cancer mortality by 6% (OR 0.94, 95% CI 0.88–1.00), but found no difference in overall survival (OR 0.98, 95% CI 0.93–1.03).[3] Two subsequent trials in high-risk women receiving adjuvant chemotherapy after mastectomy compared irradiation to the chest wall and peripheral lymphatics versus no radiotherapy.[18,19] They found that radiotherapy reduced locoregional relapse rates by 56% (RR 0.44, 95% CI 0.26–0.77)[18] and from 58% to 14%.[19] One found that survival at 10 years was increased from 45% (95% CI 42%–48%) to 54% (95% CI 51%–58%) with the addition of radiotherapy.[19] The other, smaller trial[18] found a 29% reduction in mortality at 15 years for the radiotherapy group (RR 0.71, CI 0.51–0.99), although when these results were pooled with the results of the previous review,[3] no significant difference in overall mortality was detected (RRR of death 0.04; OR 0.96, 95% CI 0.91–1.01).[20] We found no evidence that the RRR of local recurrence is affected by age, nodal status, receptor status, tumor grade, or tumor size nor that the effect of radiotherapy on mortality varies significantly with extent of surgery, type of radiotherapy (megavoltage or orthovoltage), the years the trials commenced or completed recruitment, or whether systemic drug treatment was administered.[20]

Harms: The RCTs and systematic review included in a consensus document (mainly of women undergoing breast-conserving surgery or mastectomy with variation in radiotherapy techniques, doses, and fractionation)[21] reported severe acute adverse effects to be acute pneumonitis (0.7%–7.0%) and pericarditis (0%–0.3%),[21] and long-term adverse effects to be significant arm edema (1% without axillary dissection), radionecrotic rib fracture (1.1%–1.5%), and brachial plexopathy (0%–1.8%).[21] The risk and severity of adverse effects increase with volume irradiated, total dose received, dose per fraction, previous surgery (e.g., axillary dissection), and radiotherapy techniques that cause overlap in irradiated tissues. The systematic review found an increased risk of non–breast cancer death of 24% (OR 1.24, 95% CI 1.09–1.43).[3] One systematic review of 10 RCTs[22] found that the excess of non–breast cancer deaths after chest wall radiotherapy was caused by cardiac deaths resulting from the radiotherapy, but recent trials[18,19] with data beyond 10 years did not show an excess of cardiac deaths.

Comment: The trials in the large systematic review[3] were heterogeneous, in part because they began when trial methods were less developed. They varied in randomization processes, areas irradiated, use of systemic treatment, radiotherapy doses, fractionation, and treatment schedules. We found little strong evidence to identify which women should have postmastectomy radiotherapy to prevent local recurrence. A review[20] of retrospective data[23–25] found that extent of axillary node involvement, larger tumor size, higher histologic grade, presence of lymphovascular invasion, and involvement of tumor margins reduced the chance of successful treatment.

QUESTION What are the effects of adjuvant systemic treatment?

OPTION ADJUVANT COMBINATION CHEMOTHERAPY

One systematic review has found that adjuvant chemotherapy reduces rates of recurrence and improves survival for women with early breast cancer. The benefit seems to be independent of nodal or menopausal status, although the absolute improvements are greater in those with node-positive disease and probably are greater in younger women. The review found no evidence of a survival advantage from additional months of polychemotherapy (two or more drugs), nor did RCTs find survival advantage from increased and reduced dosages of polychemotherapy. Regimens containing anthracycline may improve outcomes modestly compared with the standard cyclophosphamide, methotrexate, and 5-fluorouracil (CMF) regimen.

Benefits: **Versus no chemotherapy:** We found one systematic review, published in 1998. This identified 47 RCTs (18,000 women) comparing prolonged combination chemotherapy versus no chemotherapy.[26,27] It found that the treatment group had significantly reduced rates of recurrence (women aged under 50 years, OR 0.65, 95% CI 0.61–0.69; women aged 50–69 years, OR 0.80, 95% 0.72–0.88), and death from all causes (women aged under 50 years, OR 0.73, 95% CI 0.68–0.78; women aged 50–69 years, OR 0.89, 95% CI 0.86–0.92). Rates of recurrence were similar for women with node-negative and node-positive disease. Ten-year survival according to nodal and menopausal status is summarized in Table 1. **Duration of treatment:** The systematic review identified 11 RCTs ($n=6104$) that compared longer regimens (doubling the duration of chemotherapy from between 4–6 months to 8–12 months) versus shorter regimens. It found no additional benefit from longer duration.[27] **Different doses:** Several RCTs did not find significant improvement from enhanced dose regimens,[28] whereas others found effectiveness approaching untreated controls when suboptimal doses were used.[29] **Anthracycline regimens:** The systematic review identified 11 RCTs ($n=5942$) comparing regimens containing anthracycline (including the drugs doxorubicin or 4-epidoxorubicin) versus the standard CMF regimen.[27] It found a significant reduction in recurrence rates in those on anthracycline regimens ($p=0.006$), and a modest but significant improvement in 5-year survival (69%–72%; $p=0.02$).

Harms: **Acute adverse effects:** Adverse effects include nausea and vomiting, hair loss, bone marrow suppression, fatigue, and gastrointestinal disturbance. Prolonged chemotherapy is more likely to be associated with lethargy and hematologic toxicity (anemia and neutropenia), whereas anthracycline regimens cause complete hair loss. **Long-term adverse effects:** Fertility and ovarian function may be affected permanently by chemotherapy, especially in women aged over 40 years (although for some women with hormone-dependent cancer, reduced ovarian function may contribute to the benefit of adjuvant treatment). Other potential long-term risks include induction of second cancers (especially hematologic malignancies, although the risk is very low) and cardiac impairment with cumulative anthracycline dosages. Provided the cumulative dose of doxorubicin does not exceed 300 to 350 mg/m^2, the risk of congestive heart failure is less than 1%.

Comment: The absolute benefits of these regimens need to be balanced against their toxicity for different types of women. Trials are under way of high-dose chemotherapy with haematologic support (bone marrow transplantation or peripheral stem cell support) in women with high-risk disease (> 10 positive lymph nodes),[30] although a recent RCT failed to show survival advantage for high-dose treatment.[31] New and highly active cytotoxic agents, such as the taxanes, are being examined with anthracyclines either in combination or sequence. Alternating sequences of cytotoxic agents may prove an effective way of circumventing acquired drug resistance and, thus, enhancing the efficacy of a regimen such as the Milan regimen of single-agent anthracycline followed by standard CMF chemotherapy.[32]

OPTION TAMOXIFEN

One systematic review has found that adjuvant tamoxifen taken for up to 5 years reduced the chance of recurrence and death in postmenopausal women and in women with estrogen-receptor–positive tumors irrespective of age, menopausal status, nodal involvement, or the addition of chemotherapy. Five years of treatment seems better than shorter durations, but available evidence does not find benefit associated with prolongation beyond 5 years. Tamoxifen carries a slightly increased risk of endometrial cancer but has no overall effect on non–breast cancer mortality.

Benefits: We found one systematic review of 55 RCTs (37,000 women) comparing adjuvant tamoxifen versus placebo.[26,33] It found that 5 years of adjuvant tamoxifen had similar effect on recurrence and long-term survival in all age groups irrespective of menopausal status or age. For women over 50 years of age (usually postmenopausal), tamoxifen reduced the annual chance of recurrence by 29% and of death from any cause by 20%. **Estrogen-receptor status:** Five-years' tamoxifen treatment reduced the rate of recurrence more in women with estrogen-receptor–positive than with estrogen-receptor–negative tumors (50% vs. 6%), and reduced risk of 10-year recurrence in women with node-positive more than in women with node-negative disease (14.9% vs. 15.2%). **Duration of treatment:** It found significantly greater reduction of recurrence with increasing duration of adjuvant tamoxifen ($p < 0.00001$), corresponding to a 26% proportional reduction in death for 5 years of tamoxifen use compared with

12% for 1-year usage. Table 2 presents findings on absolute improvement in 10-year survival from 5 years of tamoxifen. One RCT comparing 5 and 2 years of treatment found similar results.[34] The benefits and risks of prolonged treatment beyond 5 years are unclear. In the largest trial[35] in the systematic review,[33] 1153 women who had completed 5 years of tamoxifen were randomized to either placebo or 5 more years of tamoxifen. Disease-free survival after 4 years of further follow-up was greater for those switched to placebo rather than continued tamoxifen (92% vs. 86%, $p=0.003$), although this did not affect overall survival. Other studies have shown no detriment in continuing tamoxifen beyond 5 years but equally have failed to show further improvement.[36]

Harms: Evidence suggests a small but significant increased risk of endometrial cancer. One systematic review found an increased hazard ratio of 2.58 (95% CI 2.23–2.93) for any duration of tamoxifen usage.[33] For 5 years of tamoxifen treatment, this resulted in a cumulative risk over 10 years of two deaths (95% CI 0–4) per 1000 women. There was no evidence of an increased incidence of other cancers nor of deaths not related to breast cancer (i.e., cardiac or vascular), although one extra death per 5000 women was attributed to pulmonary embolus. Bone loss was found in premenopausal women (1.4% bone loss per year[37]) but not in postmenopausal women because of tamoxifen's partial agonist effects. There were mixed effects on cardiovascular risk, with significant reductions in low-density lipoprotein cholesterol associated with a reduced incidence of myocardial infarction in some studies, but an increased risk of thrombosis. Overall, no effect has been found on mortality not related to breast cancer (hazard ratio 1.02, 95% CI 0.88 to 1.16).[33]

Comment: The effect of adjuvant tamoxifen on reduced recurrence and improved survival may be the reason for improved mortality.[38] The risk-to-benefit ratio may vary among different patient groups, with estrogen-receptor–negative women deriving little benefit. Even in estrogen-receptor–positive women, any benefit on breast cancer could be offset with prolonged treatment (beyond 5 years) by drug resistance and adverse effects on the endometrium. Two multicenter trials of tamoxifen duration are in progress (aTTom and ATLAS), although because of concerns regarding long-term toxicity with tamoxifen (see above) and in the absence of further definitive data, current practice outside the setting of a clinical trial has been to recommend tamoxifen for 5 years.[39] The effect on estrogen-receptor–positive tumors emphasizes the importance of estrogen-receptor measurement. For women with completely estrogen-receptor–negative disease, the overall benefit of adjuvant tamoxifen needs further research.

OPTION COMBINED CHEMOTHERAPY AND ENDOCRINE TREATMENT

One RCT found that adding combined chemotherapy to tamoxifen improved survival.

Benefits: We found one RCT of 2306 women with lymph node-negative, estrogen-receptor–positive early breast cancer that compared tamoxifen alone versus tamoxifen plus CMF chemotherapy.[40] It found that adding chemotherapy to tamoxifen caused a further absolute improvement in disease-free survival of approximately 5% (95% CI not available, $p=0.006$) and in survival of approximately 3% ($p=0.03$).

Harms: Adding CMF chemotherapy to tamoxifen was associated with a greater incidence of grade 3/4 neutropenia (9% vs. 0%), ~grade 2 nausea (35.2% vs. 3.7%), moderate/severe alopecia (35.6% vs. 0.4%), and thromboembolism/phlebitis (7.5% vs. 2.1%).[39]

Comment: None.

OPTION **OVARIAN ABLATION**

One systematic review has found that ovarian ablation significantly improves long-term survival in women aged under 50 years with early breast cancer.

Benefits: We found one systematic review of 12 RCTs ($n=2102$) with at least 15 years follow-up in premenopausal women comparing ovarian ablation by irradiation or surgery versus no ablation.[40] There was a significant improvement in both recurrence free survival (45% vs. 39%, $p=0.0007$) and overall survival (52.4% vs. 46.1%, $p=0.001$). Benefit was independent of nodal status.

Harms: We found no good evidence on long-term adverse effects. Concerns exist about the late sequelae of ovarian ablation, especially the effect on bone mineral density and cardiovascular risk. The acute adverse effects are likely to be menopausal symptoms.

Comment: Five of the trials compared ovarian ablation plus chemotherapy versus chemotherapy alone.[41] In these, the absolute benefit of ablation was smaller than in trials of ovarian ablation alone. It may be that cytotoxic chemotherapy itself suppresses ovarian function, making the effect of ablation difficult to detect in combined trials. When only premenopausal women were considered in the absence of chemotherapy, there was a 27% improvement in the odds of recurrence-free survival. Trials are under way of reversible oophorectomy using gonadotrophin-releasing–hormone analogues, which would allow preservation of fertility in younger women with estrogen-receptor–positive tumors.

GLOSSARY

Breast-conserving surgery Surgery that can consist of lumpectomy (minimal free margins), wide local excision (wider free margins), or segmental or quadrant resection (usually with very wide free margins).
Radiotherapy Part of initial local and regional treatment. In early stage disease it may be an adjunct to surgery; in locally advanced disease (T4;N2) it may be the sole locoregional treatment. It may be delivered to the breast or postmastectomy chest wall as well as to the lymphatic areas of the axilla, supraclavicular fossa, or internal mammary node chain.
Total mastectomy Removal of breast.
Radical mastectomy Removal of breast and pectoralis major and minor muscles and axillary contents.

Supraradical mastectomy Removal of breast, pectoralis major and minor muscles, axillary contents, and internal mammary chain of nodes.
Lumpectomy Gross tumor excision.
Quadrantectomy Tumor excised with at least 2 cm of normal surrounding breast tissue and with a segment of breast tissue from the periphery of the breast to the nipple.
Combination chemotherapy Two or more cytotoxic drugs given intravenously every 3–4 weeks for 4–6 months.
Tamoxifen A nonsteroidal anti-estrogen taken as daily oral tablets, usually for between 2–5 years.
Ovarian ablation Surgical, medical, or radiation-induced suppression of ovarian function in premenopausal women.

REFERENCES

1. Fisher B, Dignam J, Wolmark N, et al. Lumpectomy and radiation therapy for the treatment of intraductal breast cancer: findings from the National Surgical Adjuvant Breast and Bowel Project B-17. *J Clin Oncol* 1998;16:441–452.
2. Fisher B, Dignam J, Wolmark N, et al. Tamoxifen in treatment of intraductal breast cancer: National Surgical Adjuvant Breast and Bowel Project B-24 randomized controlled trial. *Lancet* 1999;353:1993–2000.
3. Early Breast Cancer Trialists' Collaborative Group. Effects of radiotherapy and surgery in early breast cancer: an overview of the randomised trials. *N Engl J Med* 1995;333:1444–1455. (Not a systematic review; selected group of trialists who conducted trials that began before 1985).
4. Morris AD, Morris RD, Wilson JF, et al. Breast conserving therapy versus mastectomy in early stage breast cancer: a meta-analysis of 10 year survival. *Cancer Journal from Scientific American* 1997;3:6–12. Primary source MEDLINE search date 1996 to 1995.
5. Sacchini V, Luini A, Tana S, et al. Quantitative and qualitative cosmetic evaluation after conservative treatment for breast cancer. *Eur J Cancer* 1991;27:1395–1400.
6. Smitt MC, Nowels KW, Zdeblick MJ et al. The importance of the lumpectomy surgical margin status in long-term results of breast conservation. *Cancer* 1995;76(2):259–267.
7. Wazer DE, DiPetrillo T, Schmidt-Ullrich R, et al. Factors influencing cosmetic outcome and complication risk after conservative surgery and radiotherapy for early-stage breast carcinoma. *J Clin Oncol* 1992;10:356–363.
8. Abner AL, Recht A, Vicini FA, et al. Cosmetic results after surgery, chemotherapy and radiation therapy for early breast cancer. *Int J Radiat Oncol Biol Phys* 1991;21:331–338.
9. Dewar JA, Benhamou S, Benhamou E, et al. Cosmetic results following lumpectomy axillary dissection and radiotherapy for small breast cancers. *Radiother Oncol* 1988;12:273–280.
10. Rochefordiere A, Abner A, Silver B, et al. Are cosmetic results following conservative surgery and radiation therapy for early breast cancer dependent on technique? *Int J Radiat Oncol Biol Phys* 1992;23:925–931.
11. Sneeuw KC, Aaronson N, Yarnold J, et al. Cosmetic and functional outcomes of breast conserving treatment for early stage breast cancer 1: comparison of patients' ratings, observers' ratings and objective assessments. *Radiother Oncol* 1992;25:153–159.
12. Ash DV, Benson EA, Sainsbury JR et al. Seven year follow-up on 334 patients treated by breast conserving surgery and short course radical postoperative radiotherapy: a report of the Yorkshire breast cancer group. *Clin Oncol* 1995;7:93–96.
13. Lindsey I, Serpell JW, Johnson WR, Rodger A. Cosmesis following complete local excision of breast cancer. *Aust NZ J Surg* 1997;67:428–432.
14. Touboul E, Belkacemi Y, Lefranc JP, et al. Early breast cancer: influence of type of boost (electrons vs iridium-192 implant) on local control and cosmesis after conservative surgery and radiation therapy. *Radiother Oncol* 1995;34:105-113.
15. Halyard MY, Grado GL, Schomberg PJ, et al. Conservative therapy of breast cancer: the Mayo Clinic experience. *Am J Clin Oncol* 1996;19: 445–450.
16. Liljegren G, Holmberg L, Adami HO, Westman G, Graffman S, Bergh J for the Uppsala- Orebro Breast Cancer Study Group. Sector resection with or without postoperative radiotherapy for stage I breast cancer: five year results of a randomised trial. *J Natl Cancer Inst* 1994;86:717–722.
17. Forrest AP, Stewart HJ, Everington D, et al on behalf of the Scottish Cancer Trials Breast Group. Randomised controlled trial of conservation therapy in breast cancer: 6 year analysis of the Scottish trial. *Lancet* 1996;348:708–713.
18. Ragaz J, Jackson SM, Le N, et al. Adjuvant radiotherapy and chemotherapy in node-positive premenopausal women with breast cancer. *N Engl J Med* 1997;337:956–962.
19. Overgaard M, Hansen PS, Overgaard J, et al. Postoperative radiotherapy in high-risk premenopausal women with breast cancer who receive adjuvant chemotherapy. *N Engl J Med* 1997;337:949–955.
20. Ghersi D, Simes J. Draft report of effectiveness of postmastectomy radiotherapy and risk factors for local recurrence in early breast cancer. Report to NHMRC National Breast Cancer Centre, Sydney, 1998.
21. Steering Committee on Clinical Practice Guidelines for the Care and Treatment of Breast Cancer. A Canadian consensus document. *Can Med Assoc J* 1998;158(suppl 3):S1–S84)
22. Cuzick J, Stewart H, Rutqvist L, et al. Cause-specific mortality in long term survivors of breast cancer who participated in trials of radiotherapy. *J Clin Oncol* 1994;12:447–453.
23. O'Rourke S, Galea MH, Morgan D, et al. Local recurrence after simple mastectomy. *Br J Surg* 1994;81:386–389.
24. Fowble B, Gray R, Gilchrist K, Goodman RL, Taylor S, Tormey D. Identification of a subgroup of patients with breast cancer and histologically

positive axillary nodes who may benefit from postoperative radiotherapy. *J Clin Oncol* 1988;6:1107–1117.
25. Houghton J, Baum M, Haybittle JL. Role of radiotherapy following total mastectomy in patients with early breast cancer: the closed trials working party of the CRC breast cancer trials group. *World J Surg* 1994;18:117–122.
26. Early Breast Cancer Trialists' Collaborative Group. Systemic treatment of early breast cancer by hormonal, cytotoxic or immune therapy. *Lancet* 1992;339:71–85.
27. Early Breast Cancer Trialists' Group. Polychemotherapy for early breast cancer: an overview of the randomised trials. *Lancet* 1998; 352:930–942. (Not a systematic review; selected group of trialists who conducted trials that began before 1990.)
28. Fisher B, Anderson S, Wickerham DL, et al. Increased intensification and total dose of cyclophosphamide in a doxorubicin-cyclophosphamide regimen for the treatment of primary breast cancer: findings from national surgical adjuvant breast and bowel project B-22. *J Clin Oncol* 1997;15:1858–1869.
29. Wood WC, Budman DR, Korzun AH. Dose and dose intensity of adjuvant chemotherapy for stage II, node-positive breast carcinoma. *N Engl J Med* 1994;330:1253–1259.
30. Peters WP, Ross M, Vredenburgh JJ, et al. High-dose therapy and autologous bone marrow support as consolidation after standard-dose adjuvant chemotherapy for high-risk primary breast cancer. *J Clin Oncol* 1993;11:1132–1143.
31. Rodenhuis S, Richel DJ, van der Wall E, et al. Randomised trial of high-dose chemotherapy and haemopoietic progenitor-cell support in operable breast cancer with extensive axillary lymph-node involvement. *Lancet* 1998;352:515–521.
32. Bonadonna G, Zambetti M, Valagussa P. Sequential or alternating doxorubicin and CMF regimens in breast cancer with more than three positive nodes. *JAMA* 1995;273:542–547.
33. Early Breast Cancer Trialists' Collaborative Group. Tamoxifen for early breast cancer: an overview of the randomised trials. *Lancet* 1998;351:1451–1467. (Not a systematic review; selected group of trialists who conducted trials that began before 1990.)
34. Swedish Breast Cancer Cooperative Group. Randomised trial of two versus five years of adjuvant tamoxifen for post-menopausal early stage breast cancer. *J Natl Cancer Inst* 1996;88:1543–1549.
35. Fisher B, Dignam J, Bryant J, et al. Five versus more than five years of tamoxifen therapy for breast cancer patients with negative lymph nodes and estrogen receptor-positive tumours. *J Natl Cancer Inst* 1996;88:1529–1542.
36. Stewart HJ, Forrest AP, Everington D, et al. Randomised comparison of 5 years of adjuvant tamoxifen with continuous therapy for operable breast cancer. *Br J Cancer* 1996;74:297-299.
37. Powles TJ, Hickish T, Kanis JA, Tidy A, Ashley S. Effect of tamoxifen on bone mineral density measured by dual-energy x-ray absorptiometry in healthy premenopausal and postmenopausal women. *J Clin Oncol* 1996;14:78–84.
38. Beral V, Hermon C, Reeves G, Peto R. Sudden fall in breast cancer death rates in England and Wales. *Lancet* 1995;345:1642–1643.
39. Swain SM. Tamoxifen: the long and short of it. *J Natl Cancer Inst* 1996;88:1510–1512.
40. Fisher B, Dignam J, Wolmark N, et al. Tamoxifen and chemotherapy for lymph node-negative, estrogen receptor-positive breast cancer. *J Natl Cancer Inst* 1997;89:1673–1682.
41. Early Breast Cancer Trialists' Group. Ovarian ablation in early breast cancer: overview of the randomised trials. *Lancet* 1996;348:1189–1196. (Not a sytemtatic review; selected group of trialists who conducted trials that began before 1985.)

Mike Dixon, MD
Honorary Senior Lecturer in Surgery
Western General Hospital
Edinburgh
UK

Alan Rodger, MBChB, FRCSEd, FRCR, FRANZCR
Professor of Radiation Oncology
William Buckland Radiotherapy Centre
The Alfred Hospital
Melbourne
Australia

Stephen Johnston, MBBS, MA, MRCP, PhD
Senior Lecturer in Medical Oncology
The Royal Marsden NHS Trust
London
UK

Competing interests: None declared.

TABLE 1 **Ten-year survival with combination chemotherapy versus placebo, according to nodal and age/menopausal status: results of a systematic review of RCTs.[27,28] (*See text p. 306.*)**

	Control (%)	Chemo-therapy (%)	Absolute benefit (%)	SD (%)	Significance (two sided)
Age <50 years					
Node positive	41.4	53.8	+12.4	2.4	$p<0.00001$
Node negative	71.9	77.6	+5.7	2.1	$p=0.02$
Age 50–69 years					
Node positive	46.3	48.6	+2.3	1.3	$p=0.002$
Node negative	64.8	71.2	+6.4	2.3	$p=0.005$

TABLE 2 **Ten-year survival in women treated with tamoxifen for 5 years compared with control patients: results of a systematic review of RCTs.[26,33] (*See text p. 307.*)**

	Control (%)	Chemo-therapy (%)	Absolute benefit (%)	SD (%)	Significance (two sided)
Node positive	50.5	61.4	+10.9	2.5	$p<0.00001$
Node negative	73.3	78.9	+5.6	1.3	$p<0.00001$

Eczema

Carolyn Charman, BM, BCh, MA(Cantab), MRCP

QUESTIONS

INTERVENTIONS

To be covered in future issues of *Clinical Evidence*
Prevention in predisposed children
Avoidance of provoking factors
Other topical treatments (emollients, ichthammol and tar, bandaging techniques)
PUVA
Oral treatments (antibiotics, antihistamines, systemic immunosuppressants)
Alternative treatments (evening primrose oil, Chinese herbal medicine)
Psychological approaches

Key Messages

- Small randomized controlled trials (RCTs) have found that topical corticosteroids provide symptomatic relief and are safe in the short term. We found little good information on their long-term adverse effects or on effects (if any) on the natural history of atopic eczema.
- We found limited evidence suggesting that the routine addition of antimicrobial agents to topical steroid preparations provides no additional benefit.
- We found limited evidence that control of house dust mite reduces severity of symptoms, especially in patients with positive mite RAST scores and in children, but only if very low levels are achieved. Bedding covers were found to be the most effective control method.
- We found insufficient evidence that dietary manipulation in adults or children reduces the severity of symptoms.
- We found insufficient evidence that either prolonged breast feeding or maternal dietary manipulation during lactation protects against the development of eczema in infants with a family history of atopy.

DEFINITION	Atopic eczema (atopic dermatitis) is an inflammatory skin disease, characterized by an itchy erythematous poorly demarcated skin eruption, which has a predilection for the skin creases.[1]
INCIDENCE/ PREVALENCE	It affects 9% to 12% of children in the US,[2] and 2% to 3% of adults. Prevalence has increased substantially over the past 30 years,[3] possibly because of environmental and lifestyle changes.
ETIOLOGY	Etiology is believed to be multifactorial. Recent interest has focused on the role of air borne allergens (house dust mites, pollen, animal dander), outdoor pollution, climate, diet, and prenatal/early-life factors such as infections.
PROGNOSIS	Although there is currently no cure, various interventions exist to control symptoms. Atopic eczema can be expected to clear in 60% to 70% of children by their early teens, although relapses may occur.
AIMS	To reduce the risk of atopic eczema in predisposed infants and children; to minimize the impact of the disease on quality of life.
OUTCOMES	Severity of symptoms (pruritus, sleep disturbance) and signs (erythema, oozing/crusting, lichenification, cracking, edema/papulation, excoriation, and dryness); quality of life; area of skin involvement.
METHODS	Systematic reviews and controlled clinical trials were located by searching the Cochrane Library (1998), Best Evidence (1998), MEDLINE (1966 to 1998), and EMBASE (1988 to 1998). We included all RCTs that met *Clinical Evidence* quality criteria. Because of the limited studies available for many questions, we included some with methodologic shortcomings but have mentioned specifically any problems in the text. Trials used a range of atopic eczema scoring systems, including SCORAD, six-area six-sign atopic dermatitis severity score (SASSAD), Rajka and Langeland scoring system, and dermatology life quality index.

TREATMENT

QUESTION What are the effects of treatment in adults and children?

OPTION TOPICAL STEROIDS

Small short-term placebo-controlled RCTs have found that topical corticosteroids applied for 2 to 4 weeks improve atopic eczema. We found little good information on their long-term effects. No systemic effects have been reported in short-term RCTs or in one longer-term cohort study. Volunteer studies found that potent topical steroid preparations cause skin thinning after twice daily application for 6 weeks, although skin thickness returns to normal within 4 weeks of stopping treatment. Topical steroids provide symptomatic relief while used, but their effect, if any, on the natural history of atopic eczema is unknown.

Benefits: No systematic review. **Versus placebo:** We found nine RCTs (double-blind vehicle-controlled studies) comparing topical steroids versus placebo cream (vehicle) in patients with atopic eczema. Three RCTs included patients with nonatopic forms of eczema, and another three did not specify the type of eczema. The three remaining RCTs all found substantial improvement with steroid compared with placebo (Table 1).[4–6] **Versus each other:** We found 11 further double-blind RCTs comparing a variety of topical steroids with each other (no placebo) in children and adults with atopic eczema. These showed significant improvements in 41% to 97% of patients after 2 to 6 weeks of treatment.

Harms: No serious systemic effects or cases of skin atrophy were reported in these short term RCTs, nor in a longer cohort study in 14 prepubertal children.[7] Minor adverse effects such as burning, stinging, irritation, folliculitis, hypertrichosis, contact dermatitis, and pigmentary disturbances occurred in less than 10% of patients. **Skin thinning:** We found no RCTs looking at skin thinning in patients with atopic eczema. Four small RCTs in healthy volunteers ($n = 12$) used ultrasound to evaluate skin thickness.[8–11] Skin thinning occurred with three preparations (triamcinolone acetonide 0.1%, clobetasol 17-propionate 0.05%, and betamethasone 17-valerate 0.1%) after twice daily application for 6 weeks but reversed within 4 weeks of stopping treatment.

Comment: The RCTs used different clinical scoring systems, making it difficult to compare results.

OPTION TOPICAL ANTIMICROBIAL/STEROID COMBINATIONS

Two RCTs have found that these agents have no benefit over topical steroids alone in improving the clinical signs and symptoms of atopic eczema. Only one of the trials used patients with clinically infected eczema.

Benefits: We found no systematic review. **Versus topical steroid alone:** We found two RCTs comparing topical antimicrobial/steroid combinations versus topical steroid alone in patients with atopic dermatitis.[12,13] These trials found no significant difference in the improvement in clinical signs and symptoms with hydrocortisone acetate/fusidic acid compared with hydrocortisone (186 participants) or betamethasone/fusidic acid compared with betamethasone (60 participants) after treatment for 2 weeks and 1 week. **Versus each other:** We found four further RCTs (34–207 patients) comparing different topical steroid/antimicrobial preparations with each other in clinically infected eczema (atopic eczema not specified).[14–17] These found no significant difference between the various preparations with respect to improvement in clinical signs and symptoms. However, patients treated with acetate/fusidic acid showed a more rapid clinical response than those treated with miconazole/hydrocortisone, and bacteriologic responses to betamethasone and acetate/fusidic acid were superior to those with betamethasone/clioquinol and miconazole/hydrocortisone.

Harms: Minor adverse effects comprising itching, stinging, burning, and irritation were reported in less than 2% of patients.

Comment: Only the second study specified a degree of infection in most participants at recruitment. This study also included patients with contact dermatitis in the overall analysis, and the use of left/right comparisons within individual participants may have reduced any observed beneficial effect of combination therapy due to systemic absorption of the antimicrobial agent.[13] In practice, topical antimicrobial/steroid combinations usually are reserved for clinically infected eczema. Note that these combinations are not used in the US.

OPTION CONTROL OF HOUSE DUST MITE

Based on the results of a single small RCT, extreme reduction in dust levels (achieved with mattresses covered with Gore-Tex, acaricidal spraying, and high-filtration vacuuming) may reduce eczema severity score. However, it is impossible to say from this evidence how many patients might benefit and for how long. The clinical relevance of the reduced severity score is uncertain. Bedding covers seem to be the most effective intervention for reducing levels in the home (Table 2).

Benefits: We found no systematic review. We found three controlled trials, one of which did not mention randomization. A double-blind RCT in 48 atopic patients (24 adults and 24 children >7 years of age, skin prick and radioallergosorbent test [RAST] status not specified) compared Gore-Tex bed covers, benzyltannate spray, and high-filtration vacuuming versus cotton bedcovers, placebo spray, and standard vacuum cleaners. After 6 months there was a significantly greater reduction in eczema severity scores on active treatment compared with placebo (mean difference in severity score [maximum 108 units] = 4.3 units, 95% CI 1.3–7.3). This was associated with a 98% reduction in mean mattress dust load compared with 16% in the placebo group ($p = 0.002$) and a 91% and 76% reduction in the concentration of bedroom and living-room carpet mite allergen Der *p* 1 compared with 89% and 38% in the placebo group ($p = 0.94$ and 0.27).[20] A double-blind RCT using natamycin or placebo spray with or without vacuuming in 20 atopic dermatitis patients (aged 12–47 years) with positive skin prick and RAST tests to house dust mite showed no correlation between improvement in clinical score and lowered mite numbers. However, the study was small and the maximum reduction in mite numbers in mattresses was only 68%.[21] A controlled trial (randomization not mentioned) in patients with atopic eczema showed induction of an itch-free period and prolonged remission in 30 patients with positive-mite RAST scores after 3 to 4 weeks in a "clean room" with reduced dust levels (Der *p* 1 levels were not measured). Neither an itch-free period nor prolonged remission were seen in the 11 patients with negative RAST scores treated in a similar environment or in the 10 controls with positive-mite RAST scores treated in a common hospital room.[22]

Harms: No harmful effects were reported in the trials.

Comment: Additional small uncontrolled studies have suggested a beneficial effect of mite reduction measures on symptoms, although mite or allergen levels were not quantified. The use of bedding covers seems to be the simplest and most effective measure to reduce house dust mite levels in the home (Table 2).

OPTION **DIETARY MANIPULATION**

We found insufficient evidence to recommend dietary manipulation such as exclusion of egg and cow's milk in children with atopic eczema; such intervention should be reserved for highly motivated patients with eczema unresponsive to conventional treatment. We found no good evidence that dietary manipulation alters the severity of eczema in adults.

Benefits: **In infants:** We found one systematic review that identified one small RCT in 17 breast-fed infants with atopic eczema. This looked at the effect of excluding allergenic foods, such as eggs and cow's milk, from the mother's diet. It found no effect on eczema severity.[23] However, soya milk, which is potentially allergenic itself, was used as a cow's milk substitute in this trial. **In children:** We found no systematic review. We found two RCTs (double-blind crossover) evaluating the effects of an egg-and-milk-exclusion diet in unselected children with eczema. Both used potentially allergenic soya-based milk substitute during the trial period.[24,25] One (40 children aged 2–8 years) found a significant improvement in eczema severity (14/20 treated children improved compared with 1/20 controls).[24] The other (40 children and young adults) showed no effect.[25] Double-blind placebo-controlled food challenges have been used to identify patients with food allergy, but the clinical relevance of positive reactions (which may comprise gastrointestinal, respiratory, or cutaneous symptoms) to subsequent eczema control is unclear. In three studies, double-blind placebo-controlled food challenges caused immediate hypersensitivity reactions in 63% of children ($n = 320$) with moderate to severe atopic eczema, and in 33% to 39% of children ($n = 211$) with mild to severe atopic eczema. Egg, milk, and peanut accounted for 67% to 78% of the reactions. The effect of subsequent dietary elimination was studied in only 27 of these children. This showed a greater improvement in patients on exclusion diets than in non–randomly selected controls, using a crude scoring system.[26] Only one RCT (in 85 children) has looked at a "few foods diet," in which all but a handful of foods are excluded. This failed to show a beneficial effect on eczema severity. **In adults:** We found no systematic review. We found one RCT (double-blind crossover) that had analyzed adults separately. This found no significant improvement in eczema severity with an egg-and-milk-exclusion diet in 18 adults, although potentially allergenic soya milk was used as a cow's milk substitute.[25]

Harms: Calcium, protein, and calorie deficiency are risks of dairy-free diets in children.

Comment: The clinical relevance to patients of the changes in severity scores obtained in many studies is unknown. We have not included studies looking at the role of food additives, fatty acid supplementation, or trace elements in eczema.

PREVENTION IN PREDISPOSED INFANTS

QUESTION What are the effects of preventive interventions?

OPTION PROLONGED BREAST FEEDING

We found limited observational evidence suggesting that exclusive breast feeding for at least 5 months reduces the risk of eczema in infants with a family history of atopy.

Benefits: We found no systematic review or RCTs. One 17-year prospective cohort study of 236 healthy infants found that those who were breast fed exclusively for more than 6 months had a significantly lower prevalence of eczema at 1 year (all infants) and 3 years (infants with a family history of atopy) than those breast fed for less than 1 month and weaned onto cow's milk formula.[27] Infants who were intermittently breast fed for 2 to 6 months showed no reduction in the prevalence of eczema. Two prospective studies[28,29] compared prevalence of eczema in exclusively breast fed infants and in non–breast fed infants. Non–breast fed infants were randomized to different formulas. In infants with a family history of atopy, those who were exclusively breast fed for an average of 5 months had a significantly lower prevalence of eczema at 18 months compared with non–breast fed infants randomized to soya or cow's milk, but not compared with those randomized to whey hydrolysate or casein hydrolysate. One further prospective study showed a significantly lower incidence of eczema at 3 years in infants breast fed for 6 to 13 months (with or without milk supplements) compared with those fed conventional adapted formula but a comparable incidence to those fed hydrolysed milk formulas. Some studies found no beneficial effect of breast feeding, but all had methodologic problems.

Harms: We found no evidence of harms associated with prolonged breast feeding.

Comment: Much of the available evidence suffers from methodologic difficulties, such as selection and information bias, short duration of breast feeding, and inadequate control for confounding factors (e.g., introduction of supplemental milk or solid foods). Prolonged self-selected breast feeding may be associated with unknown protective factors, leading to bias.

OPTION MATERNAL DIETARY RESTRICTION DURING LACTATION

Maternal dietary restriction during lactation may protect against the development of eczema in infants with a family history of atopy, but we found insufficient evidence to recommend such restrictions routinely.

Benefits: We found one systematic review that identified three RCTs.[30] These found a lower prevalence of eczema in breast fed infants whose mothers took antigen-avoidance diets compared with those on normal diets during lactation.

Harms: None reported.

Comment: Methodologic shortcomings in all three trials argue for caution in applying these results.[30]

REFERENCES

1. Williams HC, Burney PG, Pembroke AC, Hay RJ. The UK working party's diagnostic criteria for atopic dermatitis. III. Independent hospital validation. *Br J Dermatol* 1994;131:406–416.
2. Schultz-Larsen F, Hanifin JM. Secular change in the occurrence of atopic dermatitis. *Acta Derm Venereol Suppl (Stockh)* 1992;176:7–12.
3. Williams HC. Is the prevalence of atopic dermatitis increasing? *Clin Exp Dermatol* 1992;17:385–391.
4. Lawlor F, Black AK, Greaves M. Prednicarbate 0.25% ointment in the treatment of atopic dermatitis: A vehicle-controlled double-blind study. *Journal of Dermatological Treatment* 1995;6:233–235.
5. Roth HL, Brown EP. Hydrocortisone valerate. Double-blind comparison with two other topical steroids. *Cutis* 1978;21:695–698.
6. Maloney JM, Morman MR, Stewart DM, et al. Clobetasol propionate emollient 0.05% in the treatment of atopic dermatitis. *Int J Dermatol* 1998;37:142–144.
7. Patel L, Clayton PE, Addison GM, Price DA, David TJ. Adrenal function following topical steroid treatment in children with atopic dermatitis. *Br J Dermatol* 1995;132:950–955.
8. Kerscher MJ, Hart H, Korting HC, Stalleicken D. In vivo assessment of the atrophogenic potency of mometasone furoate, a newly developed chlorinated potent topical glucocorticoid as compared to other topical glucocorticoids old and new. *Int J Clin Pharmacol Ther* 1995;33:187–189.
9. Kerscher MJ, Korting HC. Comparative atrophogenicity potential of medium and highly potent topical glucocorticoids in cream and ointment according to ultrasound analysis. *Skin Pharmacol* 1992;5:77–80.
10. Kerscher MJ, Korting HC. Topical glucocorticoids of the non-fluorinated double-ester type. *Acta Derm Venereol (Stockh)* 1992;72:214–216.
11. Korting HC, Vieluf D, Kerscher M. 0.25% prednicarbate cream and the corresponding vehicle induce less skin atrophy than 0.1% betamethasone-17-valerate cream and 0.05% clobetasol-17-propionate cream. *Eur J Clin Pharmacol* 1992;42:159–161.
12. Ramsay CA, Savoie JM, Gilbert M, et al. The treatment of atopic dermatitis with topical fusidic acid and hydrocortisone acetate. *J Eur Acad Dermatol Venereol* 1996;7(suppl 1):S15–22.
13. Hjorth N, Schmidt H, Thomsen K. Fusidic acid plus betamethasone in infected or potentially infected eczema. *Pharmatherapeutica* 1985;4:126–131.
14. Hill VA, Wong E, Corbett MF, Menday AP. Comparative efficacy of betamethasone/clioquinol (Betnovate-C) cream and betamethasone/fusidic acid (Fucibet) cream in the treatment of infected hand eczema. *Journal of Dermatological Treatment* 1998;9:15–19.
15. Poyner TF, Dass BK. Comparative efficacy and tolerability of fusidic acid/hydrocortisone cream (Fucidin H cream) and miconazole/hydrocortisone cream (Daktacort cream) in infected eczema. *J Eur Acad Dermatol Venereol* 1996;7(suppl 1):S23–30.
16. Meenan FOC. A double-blind comparative study to compare the efficacy of Locoid C with Tri-Adcortyl in children with infected eczema. *Br J Clin Pract* 1988;42:200–202.
17. Jaffe GV, Grimshaw JJ. A clinical trial of hydrocortisone/potassium hydroxyquinolone sulphate (Quinocort) in the treatment of infected eczema and impetigo in general practice. *Pharmatherapeutica* 1986;4:628–636.
18. Owen S, Morganstern M, Hepworth J, Woodcock A. Control of house dust mite antigen in bedding. *Lancet* 1990;335:396–397.
19. Nishioka K, Yasueda H, Saito H. Preventative effect of bedding encasement with microfine fibers on mite sensitization. *J Allergy Clin Immunol* 1998;101:28–32.
20. Tan B, Weald D, Strickland I, Friedmann PS. Double-blind controlled trial of effect of house dust-mite allergen avoidance on atopic dermatitis. *Lancet* 1996;347:15–18.
21. Colloff MJ, Lever RS, McSharry C. A controlled trial of house dust mite eradication using natamycin in homes of patients with atopic dermatitis: effect on clinical status and mite populations. *Br J Dermatol* 1989;121:199–208.
22. Sanda T, Yasue T, Oohashi M, Yasue A. Effectiveness of house dust-mite allergen avoidance through clean room therapy in patients with atopic dermatitis. *J Allergy Clin Immunol* 1992;89:653–657.
23. Kramer MS. Maternal antigen avoidance during lactation for infants with atopic eczema. In: Neilson JP, Crowther CA, Hodnett ED, Hofmeyr GJ, eds. *Pregnancy and childbirth module*. The Cochrane Library, Issue 1, 1998. Oxford: Update Software. Updated quarterly. (Search date 1995, primary sources: the Cochrane Pregnancy and Childhood Review Group strategy: MEDLINE, hand search selected journals, conference proceedings, survey of unpublished trials.)
24. Atherton DJ, Sewell M, Soothill JF, Wells RS, Chilvers CE. A double-blind controlled crossover trial of an antigen avoidance diet in atopic eczema. *Lancet* 1978;1:401–403.
25. Neild VS, Marsden RA, Bailes JA, Bland JM. Egg and milk exclusion diets in atopic eczema. *Br J Dermatol* 1986;114:117–123.
26. Sampson HA, McCaskill CC. Food hypersensitivity and atopic dermatitis: evaluation of 113 patients. *J Pediatr* 1985;107:669–675.
27. Saarinen UM, Kajosaari M. Breast-feeding as prophylaxis against atopic disease: prospective follow-up study until 17 years old. *Lancet* 1995;346:1065–1069.
28. Chandra RK. Five year follow up of high risk infants with a family history of allergy who were exclusively breast-fed or fed partial whey hydrolysate, soy, and conventional cow's milk formulas. *J Pediatr Gastroenterol Nutr* 1997;24:380–388.
29. Chandra RK, Puris S, Hamed A. Influence of maternal diet during lactation and use of formula feeds on development of atopic eczema in high risk infants. *BMJ* 1989;299:228–230.
30. Kramer MS. Maternal antigen avoidance during lactation in women at high risk for atopic offspring. In: Neilson JP, Crowther CA, Hodnett ED, Hofmeyr GJ, eds. *Pregnancy and childbirth module*. The Cochrane Library, Issue 1, 1998. Oxford: Update Software. Updated quarterly. (Search date 1995, primary sources: the Cochrane Pregnancy and Childhood Review Group strategy: MEDLINE, hand search selected journals, conference proceedings, survey of unpublished trials.)

Carolyn Charman, BM, BCh, MA(Cantab), MRCP
Research Fellow in Dermatology
Queen's Medical Centre
Nottingham
UK

Competing interests: None declared.

TABLE 1 **Topical steroids versus placebo in atopic eczema: results of RCTs.[4–6]* (*See* text p. 314.)**

	Number of participants (age in years)	Outcome
Prednicarbate ointment, 0.25% twice daily for 4 weeks.[5]	51 (18–60)	Reduced dermatitis: 87% active treatment, 8% controls; significantly reduced patient-assessed pruritis on active treatment
Hydrocortisone valerate cream, 0.2% three times daily for 2 weeks.[6]	20 (2–75)	Excellent or better: 75% active treatment, 20% controls
Clobetasol propionate cream, 0.05% twice daily for 4 weeks.[7]	81 (~12)	Good, excellent, or clear: 82% active treatment, 29% controls

*Confidence intervals not reported.

TABLE 2 **Methods for reducing house dust mite levels: results of controlled trials. (*See* text p. 316.)**

Methods	Results*
Mattress, pillow and duvet covers (microporous or polyurethane coated)	Very effective (3 RCTs)[18–20]; dust mite allergen levels 1%–25% of control levels after 3–12 months; 44%–98% reduction in dust load after 3 months
Washing bedding at 55°C	Effective (2 CCTs); reduces levels of dust mite allergen by > 95% and kills 100% of mites
Removal of carpets and curtains	Unknown
Acaricides (e.g. benzyl benzoate)	Conflicting results from RCTs—better when used on carpets than on mattresses; effect may be short lived
Intensive vacuuming	Small effect on mite levels in mattresses (1 RCT, 1 CCT) but not correlated with improvement in symptoms, possibly because conventional rather than high-filtration cleaners may increase levels of airborne mite allergens, which may aggravate atopic disease (1 RCT in 16 rooms)
Air filters and dehumidifiers	Conflicting results from RCTs

*Trials have tended to use a combination of control measures, making it difficult to see which measures were responsible for beneficial effects.

Herpes labialis

Graham Worrall, MBChB, MD, BDS, FRCS, FDSRCS

QUESTIONS

INTERVENTIONS

Key Messages

- Randomized controlled trials (RCTs) have found that oral acyclovir marginally reduces the duration of symptoms and pain of first-time and recurrent herpes labialis. It may be harmful in nursing and pregnant women.
- RCTs found that oral acyclovir taken prophylactically may reduce the frequency and severity of attacks, but optimal timing is uncertain.
- Except for one RCT of topical acylovir used early in an attack, which showed a small reduction in the duration of symptoms, we found no evidence for the effectiveness of topical treatments.

DEFINITION Herpes labialis is a mild self-limiting infection with herpes simplex virus type 1 (HSV-1 and occasionally HSV type 2). It causes pain and blistering on the lips and perioral area; fever and constitutional symptoms are rare. Most people have no warning of an attack, but some experience a recognizable prodrome.

INCIDENCE/ PREVALENCE Herpes labialis accounts for approximately 1% of primary care consultations in the UK each year; 20% to 40% of the population has experienced cold sores at some time.[1]

ETIOLOGY Herpes labialis is caused by HSV-1. After the primary infection, which usually occurs in childhood, the virus is thought to remain latent in the trigeminal ganglion[2] and a variety of factors (e.g., exposure to bright sunlight, fatigue, or psychological stress) can precipitate a recurrence.

PROGNOSIS In most people, herpes labialis is a mild self-limiting illness. Recurrences are usually shorter and less severe than the initial attack. Healing is usually complete in 7 to 10 days without scarring.[3] Rates of reactivation are unknown. Herpes labialis can cause serious illness in immunocompromised patients.

AIMS To reduce the frequency and severity of recurrent attacks; to speed healing of lesions; and to reduce pain; with minimal adverse effects.

OUTCOMES Severity of symptoms; time to healing; rate of recurrence; adverse effects.

METHODS MEDLINE and FAMLI databases were searched from 1980. Keywords were "herpes labialis," "treatment," "prevention," "prophylaxis," "controlled trial," and "effectiveness." Only articles relating to clinical care of patients were selected. Fifteen trials[4–18] were found and were assessed for methodologic strength using the methods of Sackett et al.[19]

QUESTION **What are the effects of treatment for the first attack of herpes labialis?**

OPTION **TOPICAL/ORAL ANTIVIRAL AGENTS**

We found no good evidence for the effectiveness of topical agents on the duration or severity of symptoms of the first attack of herpes labialis. Limited evidence from small RCTs suggests that oral acyclovir may marginally reduce duration of pain and time to healing (Table 1).

Benefits: We found no systematic review. **Topical antiviral agents:** We found no RCTs. **Oral antiviral agents:** We found two small RCTs that found an effect.[4,5] A double-blind RCT in 20 children having their first attack compared oral acyclovir 200 mg five times per day versus placebo.[4] Mean duration of pain was reduced from 5.0 to 4.3 days, and mean duration of excess salivation was reduced from 5.0 to 3.3 days ($p<0.05$). An RCT in 72 children aged 16 years with gingivostomatitis of less than 3-days' duration compared oral acyclovir 15 mg/kg five times per day for 7 days versus placebo. Time to healing was reduced from 10 to 4 days, a mean reduction of 6 days (95% CI 4–8 days).[5] We found no RCTs in adults.

Harms: Topical acyclovir causes rash, pruritus, and irritation in some people, but no more frequently in trials than placebo.[6,7] Oral acyclovir is excreted in breast milk and is not recommended for nursing mothers. It also has caused head and tail abnormalities in fetal rats and is not recommended for use during pregnancy. There have been no recorded cases of teratogenicity in humans.

Comment: Research in this area is difficult because people do not usually consult clinicians until after they have had several attacks of cold sores.

QUESTION **Do antiviral agents taken at the beginning or during a recurrent attack reduce the duration or severity of symptoms?**

We found mainly small RCTs of topical and oral antiviral agents, which reported mixed results.

Benefits: No systematic review. **Topical antiviral agents:** Trials of acyclovir cream have produced mixed results.[6–12] The largest RCT (double blind) in 2209 patients given penciclovir cream 2-hourly for 4 days or placebo found healing times were reduced by 0.7 days and duration of pain by 0.6 days (CIs could not be calculated from the published report).[11] **Other topical treatments:** Small short-duration trials have studied the effects of idoxuridine, foscarnet sodium, zinc glycerolate powder, topical zinc sulphate, topical interferon-β, topical undecylenic acid, betadine paint, lomaherpan cream, melissa officinalis extract, and n-docosanol cream. None had sufficient power to draw conclusions. **Oral antiviral agents:** We found two RCTs. A double-blind RCT in 174 adults with recurrent herpes labialis compared oral acyclovir 400 mg five times a day for 5 days versus placebo.[16] Taken early in the attack (when the patient first experienced tingling), oral acyclovir led to a reduction in duration of symptoms from 12.5 to 8.1 days (CIs could not be calculated from the published report). If treatment was initiated later (when the vesicular rash appeared) there was no benefit compared with placebo. A second double-blind RCT in 149 people compared oral acyclovir within 12 hours of onset of symptoms versus placebo.[17] Oral acyclovir reduced healing time by 0.98 days and duration of pain by 0.04 days ($p < 0.05$).

Harms: As above.

Comment: We found no RCTs comparing early versus delayed intervention, so no firm conclusions about timing of treatment can be drawn.

QUESTION **What are the effects of antiviral preventive agents taken as prophylaxis?**

OPTION **ORAL/TOPICAL ANTIVIRAL AGENTS**

We found limited evidence from RCTs that prophylactic oral acyclovir may reduces the frequency and severity of attacks. It is not clear whether

prophylaxis should be continuous or restricted to high-risk periods. We found no good evidence about topical antiviral agents.

Benefits: No systematic review. **Topical antiviral agents:** We found no good-quality RCTs. **Oral antiviral agents:** We found three double-blind placebo-controlled RCTs. The first, in 147 American skiers with a history of herpes labialis precipitated by ultraviolet light, concluded that those given prophylactic oral acyclovir (200 mg five times a day for 5 days beginning 7 days before UV exposure) suffered fewer attacks and shorter duration of symptoms ($p < 0.05$).[13] The second, in 239 Canadian skiers, found no significant difference between acyclovir 800 mg twice a day, starting the day before exposure to ultraviolet light for 3 to 7 days compared with placebo.[15] The third, in 20 people with recurrent herpes labialis, found that acyclovir 400 mg twice a day for 4 months led to 53% fewer clinical recurrences (0.85 vs. 1.80, ARR 0.95, 95% CI 0.26–1.64) and 71% fewer virus culture positive recurrences ($p = 0.05$).[14]

Harms: As above

Comment: The existing trials of topical antiviral agents are probably too small to exclude a beneficial effect.

OPTION SUNSCREEN

One randomized, crossover trial found significant reduction in herpes recurrence from UVB light with sunscreen.

Benefits: We found one randomized, double-blind, crossover trial that compared sunscreen versus placebo in 38 people exposed to UVB light. It found that sunscreen significantly reduced recurrence of herpes labialis (71% with placebo, 0% with sunscreen).[18]

Harms: None reported.

Comment: None.

REFERENCES

1. Hodgkin K. *Towards earlier diagnosis: a guide to general practice.* London: Churchill Livingstone 1973:129.
2. Baringer SR, Swoveland P. Recovery of herpes simplex virus from human trigeminal ganglions. *N Engl J Med* 1973;288:648–650.
3. Baker C, Crumpacker CS, Schnipner LE. The natural history of recurrent facial-oral infections with the herpes simplex virus. *J Infect Dis* 1978;138: 897–905.
4. Ducoulombier H, Cousin J, DeWilde A, et al. La stomato-gingivite herpetique de l'enfant: essai a contolle aciclovir versus placebo. *Ann Pediatr* 1988;35:212–216.
5. Amir J, Harel L, Smetana Z, Varsano I. Treatment of herpes simplex gingivostomatitis with aciclovir in children: a randomised double blind placebo controlled trial. *BMJ* 1997;314:1800–1803.
6. Raborn GW, McGaw WT, Grace M, Percy J, Samuels S. Herpes labialis treatment with acyclovir 5% modified aqueous cream: a double-blind randomized trial. *Oral Surg Oral Med Oral Pathol* 1989;67:676–679.
7. Fiddian AP, Ivanyi L. Topical acyclovir in the management of recurrent herpes labialis. *Br J Dermatol* 1983;109:321–326.
8. Van Vloten WA, Swart RNJ, Pot F. Topical acyclovir therapy in patients with recurrent orofacial herpes simplex infections. *J Antimicrob Chemother* 1993;12(suppl B):89–93.
9. Shaw M, King M, Best JM. Failure of acyclovir ointment in treatment of recurrent herpes labialis. *BMJ* 1985;291:7–9.
10. Spruance SL, Schnipper LE, Overall JC. Treatment of herpes simplex labialis with topical acyclovir in polyethylene glycol. *J Infect Dis* 1982; 146:85–90.
11. Spruance SL, Rea TL, Thoming C, Tucker R, Saltzman R, Boon R. Penciclovir cream for the treatment of herpes simplex labialis. *JAMA* 1997;277:1374–1379.
12. Raborn GW, McGraw WT, Grace MG, Houle L. Herpes labialis treatment with acyclovir 5 per cent ointment. *Scientific Journal*

1989;55:135–137.
13. Spruance SL, Hamil ML, Hoge WS, Davis LG, Mills J. Acyclovir prevents reactivation of herpes labialis in skiers. *JAMA* 1988;260:1597–1599.
14. Rooney JF, Straus SE, Mannix ML, et al. Oral acyclovir to suppress frequently recurrent herpes labialis: a double-blind, placebo controlled trial. *Ann Intern Med* 1993;118:268–272.
15. Raborn GW, Martel AY, Grace MG, McGaw WT. Oral acyclovir in prevention of herpes labialis: a randomized, double-blind, multicentered clinical trial. *Oral Surg Oral Med Oral Pathol Oral Radiol Endod* 1998;85:55–59.
16. Spruance SL, Stewart JC, Rowe NH, et al. Treatment of recurrent herpes simplex labialis with oral acyclovir. *J Infect Dis* 1990;161:185–190.
17. Raborn WG, McGraw WT, Grace M, Tyrell LD, Samuels SM. Oral acyclovir and herpes labialis: a randomized, double-blind, placebo-controlled study. *J Am Dental Assoc* 1987;115:38–42.
18. Rooney JF, Bryson Y, Mannix ML, Dillon M, et al. Prevention of ultraviolet-light-induced herpes labialis by sunscreen. *Lancet* 1991;338:1419–1422.
19. Sackett DL, Haynes RB, Tugwell P. *Clinical epidemiology: a basic science for physicians.* Boston, Massachusetts: Little, Brown & Co 1985;171–197.

Graham Worrall, MBChB, MD, BDS, FRCS, FDSRCS
Associate Professor of Family Medicine
Memorial University of Newfoundland
Whitbourne
Canada

Competing interests: None declared.

Head lice

Ian F Burgess, MPhil, MSc, BSc, FRES

QUESTIONS

INTERVENTIONS

Key Messages

- We found limited evidence suggesting that treatments using chemical insecticides are effective. No serious adverse effects have been reported.
- We found no evidence in support of combing or alternative treatments.

DEFINITION Head lice are obligate ectoparasites of socially active humans. They infest the scalp, causing itching, and attach their eggs to the shaft of the hair. Head lice infestation can be diagnosed only by finding living lice. Eggs glued to hairs, whether hatched (nits) or unhatched, do not constitute sufficient evidence for an active infection because eggs may retain a viable appearance for weeks after death.

INCIDENCE/ PREVALENCE We found no incidence studies and no recent published prevalence data from any developed country. Anecdotal reports suggest that prevalence has increased in the past 4 to 5 years in most communities in Britain and North America.

ETIOLOGY Observational studies indicate that infections occur most frequently in school-age children, although there is no proof of a link with school attendance. We found no evidence to support the modern myth that lice prefer clean hair to dirty hair.

PROGNOSIS The infection is essentially harmless, although sensitization reactions to louse saliva and feces may result in localized irritation and erythema, and secondary infection of scratches. Lice have been identified as primary mechanical vectors of scalp pyoderma,[1] caused by streptococci and staphylococci usually found on the skin. The psychological reaction to lice infections greatly outweighs their clinical significance.

AIMS To eliminate infestation by killing or removing all head lice and their eggs.

OUTCOMES Treatment success, given as percentage of patients completely cleared of head lice. A clinically significant difference between treatments would be a more than 20% difference in the proportion of patients successfully treated. There are no commonly agreed standardised criteria for judging treatment success. Trials use different methods, and many do not state the method used.

METHODS The evidence for this review was derived from a search performed by the Cochrane Infectious Diseases Group at the Liverpool School of Tropical Medicine, for a systematic review compiled in July 1998.[2] The trials discussed were those selected for that review based on a new protocol published in the Cochrane Library in September 1998.

QUESTION **What are the effects of treatment for head lice?**

OPTION **INSECTICIDE-BASED PHARMACEUTICAL PRODUCTS**

We found few randomized controlled trials (RCTs) of adequate quality, employing sufficiently rigorous inclusion criteria, to show efficacy. A recent systematic review selected three trials, showing activity for permethrin and malathion against placebo and equivalence between synergized pyrethrins and permethrin. An earlier meta-analysis found permethrin more effective than lindane. All studies had flaws that could be avoided in future trials.

Benefits: We found one meta-analysis of seven RCTs involving 1808 people and 11 insecticide products.[3] Interventions included lindane, carbaryl, malathion, permethrin, and other pyrethroids in various vehicles. Only permethrin produced clinically significant differences in the rate of treatment success. Analysis was based largely on two studies, both comparing lindane 1% shampoo versus permethrin 1% cream rinse. Permethrin was found to be more effective. RR of treatment failure was reduced by 94.9% at 7 days and 92.3% at 14 days (95% CI 8.0–28.8 for permethrin compared with lindane, at 14 days, NNT to prevent one additional treatment failure at 14 days 6.3). A subsequent systematic review set new criteria for RCTs and rejected all but three trials on methodologic grounds.[2] It excluded both studies on which the earlier meta-analysis was based. Placebo-controlled trials of permethrin 1% cream rinse (63 participants) and malathion 0.5% alcoholic lotion (115 participants) gave an RRR of treatment failure for permethrin compared with placebo of 100% (95% CI 26.3–10 724, NNT 1.1) and an RRR of treatment failure for malathion compared to placebo of 83.3% (95% CI 7.0–93.3, NNT 2.2) both at 7 days after treatment. At 14 days after treatment, permethrin 1% gave an RRR of treatment failure of 96.4% compared with placebo (95% CI 38.5–5209.8, NNT 1.1). Comparison of synergised pyrethrin 0.16% mousse with permethrin 1% cream rinse (47 participants) gave an RRR of 89.5% (95% CI 4%–25.7%, NNT 9.5) after 6 days. All three trials were conducted in developing countries where insecticide treatment products were not otherwise regularly available.

Harms: Only minor adverse effects, possibly related to formulation, have been reported for most insecticides, with the exception of lindane for which there is an extensive literature of reported effects related to overdosing in the treatment of scabies and by ingestion in the treatment of head lice. Although lindane has been shown to pass transdermally during treatment of head lice,[4] there are no reports of adverse effects in this setting. Despite concern in the public press about the organophosphate malathion, there have been no confirmed reports of adverse effects when used therapeutically.

Comment: Most trials were old and of poor quality. No RCT has yet addressed the possibility that a pediculicide's formulation might affect its activity, and studies have used different vehicles and concentrations of insecticide. Studies *in vitro* suggest that other components in products, such as terpenoids and solvents, may contribute more than the named insecticide.[5] Lice in several countries have now developed resistance to one or more insecticides.[6–8] Failure to recognize this can lead to multiple dosing of individuals without therapeutic effect. Note that malathion is not available in the US.

OPTION — MECHANICAL REMOVAL OF LICE OR VIABLE EGGS BY COMBING

Combing has not yet been adequately evaluated.

Benefits: We found no systematic review. Neither combing to remove lice nor nit combing to remove viable eggs have been evaluated formally in RCTs or cohort studies. We found two RCTs comparing different pediculicides in combination with nit combing,[9,10] but neither included a noncombing control group.

Harms: None known apart from discomfort.

Comment: Anecdotal reports indicate success is related to time spent on combing and the skill of the operator.

OPTION HERBAL AND "AROMATHERAPY" TREATMENTS

We found no good evidence on the effects of these alternative treatments.

Benefits: We found no systematic review. Neither herbal nor aromatherapy treatments have been formally evaluated in RCTs or cohort studies.

Harms: None known, but toxicology studies have been limited.

Comment: Reported successes may be caused by concurrent combing or vehicle activity. These alternative treatments are not common in the US.

REFERENCES

1. Taplin D, Meinking TL. Infestations. In: Schachner LA, Hansen RC eds. *Pediatric Dermatology*, vol 2. New York: Churchill Livingstone, 1995:1347–1367.
2. Dodd C. Head lice treatment. The Cochrane Library (in press). Search date: April/May 1998; primary sources: CCTR, MEDLINE, EMBASE, BIDS SC, BIOSIS, Toxline.
3. Vander Stichele RH, Dezeure EM, Bogaert MG. Systematic review of clinical efficacy of topical treatments for head lice. *BMJ* 1995;311: 604–608. Search date March 1995; primary sources MEDLINE, International Pharmaceutical Abstracts, Science Citation Index.
4. Ginsburg CM, Lowry W. Absorption of gamma benzene hexachloride following application of Kwell shampoo. *Pediatr Dermatol* 1983;1:74–76.
5. Burgess I. Malathion lotions for head lice: a less reliable treatment than commonly believed. *Pharmaceutical Journal* 1991;247:630–632.
6. Rupes V, Moravec J, Chmela J, et al. A resistance of head lice (*Pediculus capitis*) to permethrin in Czech Republic. *Centr Eur J Public Health* 1995; 1:30–32.
7. Burgess IF, Brown CM, Peock S, et al. Head lice resistant to pyrethroid insecticides in Britain. *BMJ* 1995; 311:752.
8. Mumcuoglu KY, Hemingway J, Miller J, et al. Permethrin resistance in the head louse *Pediculus capitis* from Israel. *Med Vet Entomol* 1995;9:427–447.
9. Bainbridge C, Neibart SI, Hassman D, et al. An evaluator-blinded comparative study of the clinical effectiveness of a pyrethrin-based pediculicide with combing vs a permethrin-based pediculicide with combing. 27th Conference of the National Association of School Nurses, New Mexico, 1995.
10. Clore ER, Longyear LA. A comparative study of seven pediculicides and their packaged nit combs. *J Pediatr Health Care* 1993;7:55–60.

Ian F Burgess, MPhil, MSc, BSc, FRES
Medical Entomology Centre
Cambridge
UK

Competing interests: The author has received consultancy fees from all major producers of pediculides and several smaller companies.

Chronic plaque psoriasis

Luigi Naldi, MD

QUESTIONS

INTERVENTIONS

Key Messages

- We found no good evidence on the effects of heliotherapy, lifestyle change, dietary supplements, or psychotherapy (including techniques aimed at reducing stress, e.g., biofeedback and hyponosis).
- We found topical treatments to have been evaluated only in the short term, with few comparative randomized controlled trials (RCTs). We found no good evidence on the value of maintenance treatment with topical treatments or on methods for assessing patients' preferences and satisfaction.
- RCTs have found that ultraviolet B phototherapy and psoralen plus ultraviolet A (PUVA) are effective in the clearance and long-term maintenance of psoriasis, but long-term treatment carries the risk of squamous cell carcinoma.
- RCTs have found that cyclosporine clears psoriasis, but we found little evidence on its value as maintenance treatment. Toxicity makes treatment unacceptable to many patients.
- We found limited evidence on the long-term effects of other systemic treatments (acitretin, methotrexate, and fumaric acid derivatives) and no comparative RCTs.

DEFINITION Psoriasis is a chronic inflammatory skin disease characterized by well-demarcated erythematous scaly patches on the extensor surfaces of the body and scalp (chronic plaque psoriasis). The lesions may itch, sting, and occasionally bleed. Dystrophic nail changes are common, occurring in more than a third of patients, and psoriatic arthropathy occurs in 1% to 3% of patients (this figure concerns psoriatic patients sampled in the general population; hospital-based series may provide much higher estimates). Varieties of psoriasis include guttate (i.e., disseminate small round eruptive lesions more frequently observed among children and young adults), inverse, pustular (i.e., lesions predominantly involving body folds rather than extensor surfaces), and erythrodermic psoriasis (i.e., generalized erythema and desquamation). The disease waxes and wanes with wide variations between and within individual patients. This discussion is limited to treatment options for chronic plaque psoriasis.

PREVALENCE Psoriasis affects 1% to 2% of the general population. It is believed to be less frequent among African and Asian populations but convincing epidemiologic data are lacking.[1]

ETIOLOGY Genetic and environmental factors are both important. About one third of patients have a family history of the disease, but physical trauma, acute infection, and selected medications (e.g., lithium slats and beta-adrenergic blockers) commonly are viewed as triggers. A few observational studies have linked the onset or relapse of psoriasis with stressful life events and personal habits, including cigarette smoking and, less consistently, alcohol consumption; others have found an association of psoriasis with body mass index and an inverse association with the intake of fruit and vegetables.

PROGNOSIS We found no long-term prognostic studies. With the exception of erythrodermic and acute generalized pustular psoriasis (severe conditions affecting less than 1% of psoriatic patients and requiring intensive hospital care), psoriasis is not known to affect mortality; however, it may substantially affect the quality of life.[2] At present, there is no cure for psoriasis.

AIMS To achieve short-term suppression of symptoms and long-term modulation of disease severity with minimal adverse effects and to improve the patient's quality of life. At present there is no cure for psoriasis.

OUTCOMES State of lesions over time; use of treatments; duration of remission; patient satisfaction and autonomy; disease-related quality of life. We found no documented evidence that clinical activity scores, such as the psoriasis area severity index (PASI), are reliable proxies for these outcomes. Many clinical studies fail to provide explicit criteria for severity.[3]

METHODS *Clinical Evidence* search July 1998, updated July 1999. In addition, we hand searched a number of dermatologic and medical journals* for the years 1976 to 1996 as a project of the European Dermatoepidemiology Network. **Journal of Investigative Dermatology, British Journal of Dermatology, Dermatology, Acta Dermo-*

Venereologica, Archives of Dermatology, Journal of the American Academy of Dermatology, Annales de Dermatologie et de Vénéréologie, Giornale Italiano di Dermatologia e Venereologia, Hautarzt, British Medical Journal, Lancet, Journal of the American Medical Association, New England Journal of Medicine.

QUESTION What are the effects of nondrug treatments?

Because several trigger and perpetuating factors for psoriasis have been recognized, including physical trauma, acute infections, smoking, diet, and stress, there is good reason to believe that disease severity could be modulated by nonpharmacologic interventions. However, we found no good evidence on the effects of nonpharmacologic measures in psoriasis. A few interventions have been tested in small RCTs.

Benefits: **Heliotherapy:** We found no systematic review. We found one RCT, which used a 2-year cross over design to compare 4 weeks of supervised heliotherapy versus no intervention in 95 patients.[4] The study documented a highly significant alleviation of psoriasis at the end of heliotherapy and a 30% reduction in routine treatment usage score in the year following heliotherapy. **Fish oil supplementation:** We found no systematic review. We found several RCTs, which reported conflicting results. The largest RCT involving 145 patients showed no benefit from fish oil compared with corn oil.[5] **Stress reduction:** We found no systematic review. We found two small RCTs, the largest one involving 51 patients.[6] These suggested that a psychological intervention aimed at reducing stress may improve psoriasis. The largest study found slight but significant changes in psoriasis activity scores. **Thermal baths:** We found no RCTs. **Acupuncture:** We found no systematic review. We found one RCT involving 56 patients. It found no significant difference between classic acupuncture and sham (placebo) acupuncture.[7]

QUESTION What are the effects of topical treatment?

OPTION EMOLLIENTS AND KERATOLYTICS

Emollients and keratolytics are well established in the treatment of psoriasis but have been evaluated in only a few small RCTs.

Benefits: We found no systematic review of emollients and keratolytics in general. We found five small RCTs. The largest, in 43 people, found that emollients temporarily improved psoriasis when combined with ultraviolet B radiation.[8] One systematic review identified four RCTs of capsaicin, an alkaloid derived from *Solanaceae* plants (*see* Comment), in 245 patients.[9] It found a beneficial effect on itching, scaling, and erythema. However, there was significant heterogeneity in the rate differences in individual trials.

Harms: Local irritation and contact dermatitis have been reported.

Comment: Emollients and keratolytics are usually used as an adjunct to other treatment modalities. Capsaicin is not an established treatment for psoriasis.

OPTION TARS

Tars are well established in the treatment of psoriasis but have been evaluated in only a few small RCTs.

Benefits: We found no systematic review. We found only one small RCT in 18 patients, which found that tar was more effective that the emollient base alone in improving disease activity scores.[10] Four small RCTs found conflicting results on the added efficacy of coal tar when combined with ultraviolet B exposure and dithranol (the Ingram regimen).

Harms: Smell, staining, and burning are the main adverse effects of coal tar.

Comment: None.

OPTION DITHRANOL

Dithranol is well established in the treatment of psoriasis. The best evidence for the effect of dithranol concerns its use in the Ingram regimen (see Combination regimens and Glossary).

Benefits: **Versus placebo:** We found no systematic review. We found two small RCTs that reported dithranol was better than placebo in improving psoriasis. **Conventional versus short-contact treatment:** A survey of published studies (search date: 1989; primary sources: MEDLINE, Index Medicus, Excerpta Medica) identified 22 small RCTs comparing conventional dithranol treatment versus dithranol short-contact treatment (shorter contact time at higher concentrations).[11] These found no evidence of differences but were too small to rule out clinically important differences.

Harms: Smell, staining, and burning are the main adverse effects of dithranol.

Comment: Because few trials looked at patient satisfaction, the conclusion that short-contact treatment is easier and more convenient for the patient at home compared with conventional dithranol treatment should be regarded cautiously.

OPTION TOPICAL STEROIDS

RCTs have found that topical steroids improve psoriasis in the short term.

Benefits: We found no systematic review. **Clearance:** More than 30 short-term, mainly small vehicle-controlled RCTs, frequently involving within-patient comparisons, found that topical mid-to-high-potency steroids temporarily improved psoriatic lesions. The study duration was usually no longer than 8 weeks, and improvement was judged mainly in terms of reduced erythema and scaling. The largest parallel group RCTs evaluated the more recently developed molecules, such as mometasone. **Maintenance:** Of the RCTs reviewed, only one addressed the maintenance value of steroids. In this trial, 90 patients who had one target area cleared or nearly cleared of psoriasis with betamethasone dipropionate, were randomized to either placebo or steroid use once a week.[12] At 6 months, the disease was successfully controlled (maintenance of clearance in the target area) in 60% of the patients in the active and 20% in the placebo group. **Occlusive dressings:** Eleven small RCTs, most using patients as their own controls, have found that occlusive polythene or hydrocolloid dressings may enhance clinical activity.

Harms: Topical steroids may cause striae and atrophy. These adverse effects increase with clinical potency and occlusion. Continuous use and occlusion may lead to adrenocortical suppression,[13] whereas case reports suggest that severe flares of the disease may occur on withdrawal. Diminishing clinical response with repeated use (tachyphylaxis) has been described, but we found no estimates of the frequency of this effect.

Comment: Because only maintenance value within the target area was assessed in the RCT described above,[9] the results cannot be generalized to clinical practice.

OPTION VITAMIN D DERIVATIVES

RCTs and long-term uncontrolled studies have found that calcipotriol improves plaque psoriasis compared with placebo and that it is at least as effective as topical steroids, coal tars, and dithranol.

Benefits: We found no systematic review. **Versus placebo:** More than 15 RCTs found that calcipotriol controls mild to moderately severe plaque psoriasis. In the largest of these trials ($n=277$), 70% of those assigned to calcipotriol showed an improvement of approximately 75% in the severity index (judged as a major outcome of treatment) compared with 19% of those in the vehicle treated group (RRR 63%, 95% CI 50%–75%).[14] Long-term uncontrolled studies found that treatment gains were maintained in approximately 70% of patients for as long as the treatment was continued.[15] **Versus topical steroids:** In four short-term comparative RCTs, the largest are involving 345 people, calcipotriol was either as effective or a little more effective than topical steroids.[16] **Versus dithranol short-contact treatment:** In four RCTs, the largest one involving 478 people, calcipotriol was either as effective as or a little more effective than dithranol short-contact treatment.[17] **Versus coal tar:** Two RCTs, the largest one involving 122 people, found that calcipotriol was more effective than coal tar.[18] **With other treatments:** Four RCTs, the largest one involving 169 patients, found that combining calcipotriol with topical steroids provided better clearance and maintenance.[19]

Harms: Perilesional irritation from calcipotriol has been reported in as many as 25% of patients, with the face and intertriginous areas being more susceptible. Hypercalcemia and hypercalciuria are dose-related adverse effects. On the short term, the combination of topical steroid may reduce the incidence of skin irritation.[20]

Comment: Limitation of the dosage to 100 g/wk is recommended.

OPTION TOPICAL RETINOIDS

RCTs have found that tazarotene, an acetylenic retinoic acid–receptor–specific retinoid, improves plaque psoriasis compared with placebo.

Benefits: We found no systematic review. **Clearance:** These vehicle-controlled RCTs found that tazarotene was effective in plaque psoriasis. The largest involved 324 patients of whom 318 were evaluable. Clinical response was judged as good, excellent, or completely cleared in 60% on tazarotene 0.1%, 50% on tazarotene 0.05%, and 30% on vehicle control, after 12 weeks of treatment (RRR for tazarotene 0.1% compared with placebo 43%, 95% CI 30%–60%).[21] One RCT in 275 evaluable patients found that tazarotene was nearly as effective in clearing psoriasis as the high-potency steroid flucinonide.[22]

Harms: Some degree of perilesional irritation is reported in most patients. One RCT in 300 patients, examining combined mid- or high-potency steroid versus placebo over 12 weeks found that treatment reduced the incidence of acute adverse effects.[23]

Comment: Tazarotene is contraindicated in women who are, or are intending to become, pregnant because it is potentially teratogenic.

QUESTION What are the effects of treatment with ultraviolet light?

OPTION PHOTOTHERAPY

RCTs have found that phototherapy improves psoriasis in the short term and when used as maintenance treatment.

Benefits: We found no systematic review. We found two small RCTs using precise radiometric data that reported phototherapy with erythematogenic doses of ultraviolet B radiation (290–320 nm) improves moderately severe psoriasis.[24,25] In one RCT, ultraviolet B radiation was compared with PUVA treatment in 183 patients with moderate to severe psoriasis. Clearance rates were 81% (95% CI 73%–89%) with ultraviolet B compared with 88% (95% CI 82%–94%) with PUVA.[26] Subgroup analysis found that ultraviolet B radiation was significantly less effective in patients with more than 50% body involvement. **Maintenance:** One RCT addressed the maintenance value of ultraviolet B phototherapy after initial clearing. Of the 165 patients enrolled, 104 (63%) were cleared of their symptoms. More than 50% were still clear 181 days after initial clearing in the maintenance group (weekly treatment) compared with 28% in the control group. RRR for relapsing at 181 days was 33% (95% CI 8%–59%).[27] **Narrow-band versus broad-band phototherapy:** We found only three small short-term self-control RCTs, the largest one involving 23 patients.[28]

Harms: Ultraviolet B exposure may increase photo-aging and the risk of skin cancer. A recent systematic review (search date: 1996; primary sources: MEDLINE, Biosis, Online Contents) concluded that it was unlikely that the excess risk of non-melanoma skin cancer associated with ultraviolet B exposure exceeds 2% per year.[29]

Comment: The advantage of narrow-band ultraviolet B phototherapy over conventional broad-band phototherapy in terms of efficacy and safety remains to be largely defined.

OPTION PUVA TREATMENT

RCTs have found effective clearance and long-term maintenance with PUVA. Long-term treatment carries the risk of squamous cell carcinoma, reported in a quarter of patients.

Benefits: We found no systematic review. We found 17 RCTs. **Clearance:** One RCT[30] compared PUVA treatment versus an inpatient Ingram regimen (see Glossary) in 224 patients with at least 10% of body surface area involved. It found clearance rates of 91% with PUVA compared with 82% with the Ingram regimen. **Maintenance:** The largest RCT, in 1005 patients whose psoriasis had been cleared by PUVA treatment, found that maintenance treatment reduced relapse. At 18 months follow-up, 62% of patients in the nontreatment schedule had flares compared with 27% in the once-a-week maintenance schedule and 34% of patients in the once-every-three-weeks maintenance schedule.[31] RRR for relapse on the once-a-week schedule versus no treatment was 56% (95% CI 44%–68%). **Different regimens:** At least eight small RCTs have looked at various combinations of ultraviolet radiation and systemic or topical treatments, including ultraviolet A plus 5-methoxypsoralen, ultraviolet A plus bathwater-delivered psoralen, and psoralen plus ultraviolet B. These found no significant difference from conventional PUVA treatment, but the trials are likely to have been too small to exclude a clinically significant difference.

Harms: The best evidence concerning chronic toxicity comes from an ongoing study of more than 1300 patients who first received PUVA treatment in 1975.[32,33] The study has documented a dose-dependent increased risk for squamous cell carcinoma, basal cell carcinoma, and possibly malignant melanoma as compared with the general population. Findings concerning nonmelanoma skin cancer have been repeated by a recent meta-analysis (search date: 1998; primary sources: MEDLINE, Healthstar, AIDSLINE, CANCERLIT) of eight additional studies. Premature photo-aging is another expected adverse effect. After less than 15 years, approximately one quarter of patients exposed to 300 or more treatments of PUVA had at least one squamous cell carcinoma of the skin. The risk was particularly high for patients with skin types I and II. If patients wear UVA opaque glasses for 24 hours after psoralen ingestion, the risk for cataract development seems to be negligible.

Comment: PUVA treatment needs close monitoring for acute toxicity and cutaneous carcinogenic effects.

OPTION COMBINATION REGIMENS

Of the two most established combination regimens, the Ingram regimen has been found in one RCT to be nearly as effective as PUVA therapy in clearing moderate to severe psoriasis. We found no good evidence on the effectiveness of the Goeckerman treatment.

Benefits: We found no systematic review. **Ingram regimen (see Glossary):** In one RCT, 224 patients with at least 10% of the body surface area involved were treated with either an inpatient Ingram regimen or PUVA treatment. Dithranol was used at a concentration 0.01% to 1.0%.

Clearance rates were 82% (95% CI 77%–89%) with the Ingram regimen compared with 91% (95% CI 86%–96%) with PUVA.[30] Five small RCTs, the largest one involving 53 people, gave conflicting results on the added efficacy of dithranol when combined with ultraviolet B exposure.[35] However, the trials were too small to rule out a clinically important difference. **Goeckerman treatment:** We found no good evidence on the combination of coal tar and ultraviolet B radiation in the Goeckerman regimen. **Other combinations:** Two RCTs found benefit from the combination of calcipotriol with ultraviolet B radiation or PUVA treatment.[36,37]

Harms: Adverse effects vary with the treatments being combined. Local irritation occurs frequently.

Comment: None.

QUESTION What are the effects of systemic treatment?

OPTION ORAL RETINOIDS (ETRETINATE AND ACITRETIN)

We found limited evidence suggesting that oral retinoids achieve complete clearance in a small proportion of patients with plaque psoriasis. We found no good evidence relating to its value as maintenance treatment. Adverse effects and the risk of teratogenicity will make retinoids unacceptable to some.

Benefits: We found no systematic review (although there has been one in psoriatic arthropathy).[38] **Versus placebo:** We found eight RCTs, the largest one involving 291 people, comparing etretinate (0.2–1.2 mg/kg/d) versus placebo or conventional treatment in patients with severe psoriasis.[39] These reported wide differences in treatment effects, with clearance occurring in 15% to 90% of patients. Such striking differences may be explained by different entry criteria, outcome measures, or treatment schedules. The high dropout rates in most RCTs called for an intention-to-treat analysis, which was rarely performed. **Versus each other:** Etretinate and acitretin (0.5–1.0 mg/kg/d) have been compared in four RCTs. The largest, in 168 people, reported similar therapeutic effects but a higher rate of mucocutaneous adverse effects with acitretin.[40] **With other treatments:** Nine RCTs found that the combination of PUVA or ultraviolet B and retinoids speed up the response and, by doing so, reduce the cumulative ultraviolet exposure or retinoid dosage.[41] One RCT, in 135 people, found a higher clearance rate for the combination of acitretin and calcipotriol compared with acitretin alone.[42] **Different types of psoriasis:** In subgroup analyses and at least two small RCTs, pustular and erythrodermic psoriasis seem to be more responsive to etretinate or acitretin than plaque psoriasis.[43,44] **Maintenance:** We found only one small RCT (*n* = 36) of 1-year duration supporting the maintenance value of etretinate over placebo, after clearance has been reached by PUVA.[45]

Harms: Most patients experience mucocutaneous adverse effects, such as dry skin, cheilitis, and conjunctivitis. Increases in serum cholesterol and triglyceride levels occur in approximately one half of patients.

Low-grade hepatotoxicity is observed in approximately 1% of patients treated with etretinate.[46] Occasionally, acute hepatitis as a purported idiosyncratic hypersensitivity reaction may occur. Radiographic evidence of extraspinal tendon and ligament calcifications has been documented. In one cohort study, one quarter of 956 patients treated with etretinate attributed a joint problem or its worsening to the drug.[47] Etretinate is a known teratogen and may be detected in the plasma for 2 to 3 years after stopping treatment. It is now known that acitretin can undergo esterification to etretinate.

Comment: Women of childbearing potential should use effective contraception for 1 month before etretinate treatment, throughout treatment, and following discontinuation for a still indefinite time. The manufacturer has replaced etretinate with acitretin, and etretinate is no longer available in the US.

OPTION METHOTREXATE

We found only one small RCT evaluating methotrexate for the treatment of skin lesions in psoriasis. Nonrandomized data suggest that clearance can be maintained as long as treatment is continued. Half of patients relapse within 6 months of stopping treatment. Long-term treatment carries the risk of serious adverse effects, especially liver fibrosis, which is reported in approximately one third of patients.

Benefits: We found no systematic review (although there has been one in psoriatic arthropathy).[38] **Clearance:** We found two small RCTs primarily dealing with psoriatic arthropathy. One of the two trials provided data on skin lesions and documented improvement compared with placebo.[47] **Maintenance:** We found no RCTs. In an uncontrolled series of 113 patients with severe psoriasis, maintenance treatment with low-dose methotrexate (weekly dose not to exceed 15 mg), provided satisfactory control of skin lesions in as many as 81% of patients (mean treatment duration 8 years). Treatment was discontinued in 33 patients because of adverse effects. When treatment was stopped, 45% of patients experienced a full relapse within 6 months.[48]

Harms: In the uncontrolled case mentioned above,[48] treatment was stopped in 33 of 113 patients because of adverse effects. The most serious acute reaction, particularly in elderly people, is dose-related myelosuppression. In the long term, major adverse events include liver fibrosis and pulmonary toxicity. According to a meta-analysis, approximately 28% of patients (95% CI 24%–32%) on chronic methotrexate treatment for psoriasis and rheumatoid arthritis may progress to histologic grade 1 or higher on liver biopsy, whereas 5% may develop advanced liver disease (histologic grade IIIB or IV).[49] The risk is dose related and increases with increased alcohol consumption. A limitation of the meta-analysis was the lack of untreated control groups. Methotrexate-associated pulmonary disease has been described as an acute interstitial pneumonitis.[50] Adverse pulmonary effects are usually considered much rarer in psoriasis than in rheumatoid arthritis, but there is a lack of published evidence to support this claim. Several drug interactions (e.g., with sulfonamides) that increase methotrexate toxicity have been described. Methotrexate may represent an independent risk factor for developing squamous cell carcinoma in patients exposed to PUVA treatment because it appears to double the risk of the tumor.[32] A higher risk of lymphoproliferative diseases in long-term users is suggested by a few case reports. Based on data from a large case series (n = 248), the cumulative incidence of lymphoma is not expected to be remarkably higher than 1%.[51]

Comment: Patients should undergo close monitoring for liver toxicity[52] and be advised to limit their consumption of alcohol. The most reliable test of liver damage remains needle biopsy of the liver. It is rare for life-threatening liver disease to develop with the first 1.0 to 1.5 g of methotrexate.

OPTION CYCLOSPORINE AND OTHER IMMUNOSUPPRESSIVE DRUGS

RCTs have found that cyclosporine clears psoriasis, especially at higher doses, although toxicity is high and causes many patients on continuous long-term treatment to withdraw. Data on the use of other immunosuppressive drugs, such as tachrolimus, remain inconclusive.

Benefits: We found no systematic review. **Clearance:** Six dose-finding and placebo-controlled RCTs found that cyclosporine was effective in temporarily controlling psoriasis. In a pooled analysis based on five European placebo-controlled RCTs using individual data from 457 patients, success (activity score reduction ≥75%) was achieved in 24%, 52%, and 88% of patients treated with an initial cyclosporine dose of 1.25, 2.5–3, and 5 mg/kg/d, respectively.[53] The large majority of patients experience a relapse within weeks after stopping treatment. One RCT (n = 309) found that a more rapid response was produced by a microemulsion formulation compared with the usual oil-in-water emulsion.[54] **Maintenance:** Two RCTs have assessed different maintenance schedules.[55,56] In one study, 61 patients who had achieved clearance during an induction phase were randomized to 1.5 or 3.0 mg/kg/d cyclosporine or placebo.[55] At 4-months' follow-up, 57% of the 3 mg/kg group had no relapses compared with 21% and 5% of the 1.5-mg/kg and placebo groups, respectively. RRR for the 3-mg/kg schedule was 55% (95% CI 30%–80%). **Versus other treatments:** One RCT compared cyclosporine 2.5 mg/kg/d versus etretinate 0.5 mg/kg/d in 210 patients. After 10 weeks of treatment, 47% of the patients on cyclosporine and 10% on etretinate showed a reduction of more than 80% in skin involvement.[57] **Different types of psoriasis:** One small RCT (n = 58) suggests that low-dose (1–2 mg/kg/d) cyclosporine may be effective as maintenance treatment in palmoplantar pustulosis.[58]

Harms: **Long-term toxicity:** In a follow-up study of 122 consecutive patients treated for several months at a dose not exceeding 5 mg/kg/d, 104 patients discontinued treatment.[59] Of these, 55 stopped treatment because of adverse effects, which included renal dysfunction in 34 (28%) patients and hypertension in 23 (19%) patients.

Comment: Renal function should be monitored. The long-term safety profile has yet to be defined.

OPTION FUMARIC ACID DERIVATIVES

We found limited evidence of short-term effectiveness but high rates of acute adverse effects. We found no evidence relating to its value as maintenance treatment. At variance with practice in some European countries, fumaric acid is not an established treatment for psoriasis in the US.

Benefits: We found no systematic review. We found 5 RCTs. In the largest RCT ($n = 100$), a response ranging from slight to complete was observed in 71% of patients treated with esters of fumaric acid (maximum dose of 1290 mg ester mixture per day) compared with 18% in the placebo group.[60]

Harms: The safety profile is poorly defined. Acute adverse effects, including flushing and gastrointestinal symptoms, have been reported in as many as 75% of patients.[60] Eosinophilia is commonly observed and there are a few case reports of drug induced tubular nephropathy.[61]

Comment: The largest RCT had a high dropout rate (48%).

GLOSSARY

Ingram regimen Consists of a daily coal tarbath, ultraviolet B irradiation, and dithranol.
Goekerman treatment Consists of a daily application of coal tar followed by ultraviolet B radiation.

REFERENCES

1. Naldi L. Psoriasis. In: Williams HC, Strachan DP, eds. *The challenge of dermato-epidemiology*. Boca Raton: CRC Press, 1997.
2. O'Neill P, Kelly P. Postal questionnaire study of disability in the community associated with psoriasis. *BMJ* 1996;313: 919–921.
3. Petersen LI, Kristensen JK. Selection of patients for psoriasis clinical trials: a survey of the recent dermatological literature. *Journal of Dermatology Treatment* 1992;3:171–176.
4. Snellman E, Aromaa A, Jansen CT, et al. Supervised four-week heliotherapy alleviates the long-term course of psoriasis. *Acta Derm Venereol* 1993;73:388–392.
5. Soyland E, Funk J, Rajka G, et al. Effect of dietary supplementation with very-long-chain n-3 fatty acids in patients with psoriasis. *N Engl J Med* 1993;328:1812–1816.
6. Zachariae R, Oster H, Bjerring P, Kragballe K. Effects of psychologic intervention on psoriasis: a preliminary report. *J Am Acad Dermatol* 1996;34:1008–1015.
7. Jerner B, Skogh M, Vahlquist A. A controlled trial of acupunture in psoriasis: no convincing effect. *Acta Derm Venereol* 1997;77:154–156.
8. Berne B, Blom I, Spangberg S. Enhanced response of psoriasis to UVB therapy after pretreatment with a lubrificating base. *Acta Derm Venereol* 1990;70:474–477.
9. Zhang WY, Li Wan Po A. The effectiveness of topically applied capsaicin. a meta-analysis. *Eur J Clin Pharmacol* 1994;46:517–522. Search date 1994, primary sources BIDS, MEDLINE.
10. Kanzler MH, Gorsulowsky DC. Efficacy of topical 5% liquor carbonis detergens vs. its emollient base in the treatment of psoriasis. *Br J Dermatol* 1993;129:310–314.
11. Naldi L, Carrel CF, Parazzini F, et al. Development of anthralin short-contact therapy in psoriasis: survey of published clinical trials. *Int J Dermatol* 1992;31:127–130.
12. Katz HI, Prawer SE, Medansky RS, et al. Intermittent corticosteroid maintenance treatment of psoriasis: a double-blind multicenter trial of augmented betamethasone dipropionate ointment in a pulse dose treatment regimen. *Dermatologica* 1991;183:269–274.
13. Wilson L, Williams DI, Marsh SD. Plasma corticosteroid levels in outpatients treated with topical steroids. *Br J Dermatol* 1973;88:373–380.
14. Highton A, Quell J. Calcipotriene ointment 0.005% for psoriasis: a safety and efficacy study. Calcipotriene study group. *J Am Acad Dermatol* 1995;32:67–72.
15. Ramsay CA, Berth-Jones J, Brundin G, et al. Long-term use of topical calcipotriol in chronic plaque psoriasis. *Dermatology* 1994;189:260–264.
16. Kragballe K, Gjertsen BT, De Hoop D, et al. Double-blind, right/left comparison of calcipotriol and bethamethasone valerate in treatment of psoriasis vulgaris. *Lancet* 1991;337:193–196.
17. Berth-Jones J, Chu AC, Dodd WAH, et al. A multicentre, parallel-group comparison of calcipotriol ointment and short-contact therapy in chronic plaque psoriasis. *Br J Dermatol* 1992;127: 266–271.
18. Pinheiro N. Comparative effects of calcipotriol ointment (50 micrograms/g) and 5% coal tar/2% allantoin/0.5% hydrocortisone cream in treating plaque psoriasis. *Br J Clin Pract* 1997;51:16–19.
19. Ruzicka T, Lorenz B. Comparison of calcipotriol monotherapy and a combination of calcipotriol and betamethasone valerate after 2 weeks' treatment with calcipotriol in the tropical therapy

of psoriasis vulgaris: a multicentre, double-bind, randomised study. *Br J Dermatol* 1998;138: 254–258.

20. Kragballe K, Barnes L, Hamberg K, et al. Calcipotriol cream with or without concurrent topical corticosteroid in psoriasis. Tolerability and efficacy *Br J Dermatol* 1998;139:649–654.
21. Weinstein GD, Krueger GG, Lowe NJ, et al. Tazarotene gel, a new retinoid, for topical therapy of psoriasis: vehicle-controlled study of safety, efficacy, and duration of therapeutic effect. *J Am Acad Dermatol* 1997;37:85–92.
22. Lebwohl M, Ast E, Callen JP, et al. Once-daily tazarotene gel versus twice-daily fluocinonide cream in the treatment of plaque psoriasis. *J Am Acad Dermatol* 1998;38:705–711.
23. Lebwohl MG, Breneman DL, Goffe BS, et al. Tazarotene 0.1% gel plus corticosteroid cream in the treatment of plaque psoriasis. *J Am Acad Dermatol* 1998;39:590–596.
24. Fisher T. UV-light treatment of psoriasis. *Acta Derm Venereol* 1976;56:473–479.
25. Parrish JA. Treatment of psoriasis with long-wave ultraviolet light. *Arch Dermatol* 1977;113: 1525–1528.
26. Boer J, Hermans J, Schothorst AA, Suurmond D. Comparison of phototherapy (UVB) and photochemotherapy (PUVA) for clearing and maintenance therapy of psoriasis. *Arch Dermatol* 1984: 120:52–57.
27. Stern RS, Armstrong RB, Anderson TF, et al. Effect of continued ultraviolet B phototherapy on the duration of remission of psoriasis. a randomized study. *J Am Acad Dermatol* 1986; 15:546–552.
28. Storbeck K, Holzle E, Schurer N, et al. Narrow-band UVB (311 nm) versus conventional broad-band UVB with and without dithranol in phototherapy for psoriasis. *J Am Acad Dermatol* 1993;28:227–231.
29. Pieternel CM, Pasker-de-Jong M, Wielink G, et al. Treatment with UV-B for psoriasis and non-melanoma skin cancer. A systematic review of the literature. *Arch Dermatol* 1999;135:834–840.
30. Rogers S, Marks J, Shuster S, Vella-Briffa D, Warin A, Greaves M. Comparison of photochemotherapy and dithranol in the treatment of chronic plaque psoriasis. *Lancet* 1979;i:455–458.
31. Melski JW, Tanenbaum L, Parrish JA, et al. Oral methoxsalen photochemotherapy for the treatment of psoriasis. A cooperative clinical trial. *J Invest Dermatol* 1977;68:328–325.
32. Stern RS, Laird N. The carcinogenic risk of treatments for severe psoriasis. Photochemotherapy follow-up study. *Cancer* 1994;73:2759–2764.
33. Stern RS, Nichols KT, Vakeva LH. Malignant melanoma in patients treated for psoriasis with methoxsalen (psoralen) and ultraviolet A radiation. *N Engl J Med* 1997;336:1041–1045.
34. Stern RS, Lunder EJ. Risk of squamous cell carcinoma and methoxsalen (psoralen) and UV-A radiation (PUVA). A meta-analysis. *Arch Dermatol* 1998;134:1582–1585.
35. Paramsothy Y. Effect of UVB therapy and a coal tar bath on short contact dithranol treatment for psoriasis. *Br J Dermatol* 1988;118:783–789.
36. Kragballe K. Combination of topical calcipotriol (MC 903) and UVB radiation for psoriasis vulgaris. *Dermatologica* 1990;181:211–214.
37. Frappaz A, Thivolet J. Calcipotriol in combination with PUVA: a randomized double-blind placebo study in severe psoriasis. *Eur J Dermatol* 1993;3:351–354.
38. Jones G, Crotty M, Brooks P. Psoriatic arthritis. An overview of therapy and toxicity. Cochrane Library 1998, issue 2. Search date 1995, primary sources MEDLINE, Excerpta Medica.
39. Orfanos CED, Goerz A. Orale Psoriasis-therapie mit einem neuen aromatischen Retinoid (Ro 10-9359). Eine multizentrische kontrollierte Studie an 291 Patienten in der Bundesrepublik. *Dtsch Med Wochenschr* 1978;103:195–199.
40. Kragballe K, Jansen CT, Bjerke JR, et al. A double-blind comparison of acitretin and etretinate in the treatment of severe psoriasis. Results of a Nordic multicentre study. *Acta Derm Venereol* 1989;69:35–40.
41. Ruzicka T, Sommerburg C, Braun-Falco O, et al. Efficiency of acitretin in combination with UV-B in the treatment of severe psoriasis. *Arch Dermatol* 1990;126:482–486.
42. van der Kerkhof PC, Cambazard F, Hutchinson PE, et al. The effect of addition of calcipotriol ointment (50 micrograms/g) to acitretin therapy in psoriasis. *Br J Dermatol* 1998;138:84–89.
43. Lassus A, Lauharanta J, Juvakoski T, Kanerva L. Efficacy of etretinate (Tigason) in clearing and prevention of relapse of palmoplantar pustulosis. *Dermatologica* 1983;166:215–219.
44. White SI, Puttick L, Marks JM. Low-dose etretinate in the maintenance of remission of palmoplantar pustular psoriasis. *Br J Dermatol* 1986;115:577–582.
45. Dubertret L, Chastang C, Beylot C, et al. Maintenance treatment of psoriasis by Tigason: a double-blind randomized clinical trial. *Br J Dermatol* 1985;113:323–330.
46. Stern RS, Fitzgerald E, Ellis CN, et al. The safety of etretinate as long-term therapy for psoriasis. Results of the etretinate follow-up study. *J Am Acad Dermatol* 1995;33:44–52.
47. Wilkens RF, Williams HJ, Ward JR, et al. Randomized, double-blind, placebo controlled trial of low-dose pulse methotrexate in psoriatic arthritis. *Arthritis Rheum* 1984;27:376–381.
48. Van Dooren-Greebe RJ, Kuijpers AL, Mulder J, et al. Methotrexate revisited: effects of long-term treatment of psoriasis. *Br J Dermatol* 1994;130: 204–210.
49. Whiting-O'Keefe QE, Fye KH, Sack KD. Methotrexate and histologic hepatic abnormalities. *Am J Med* 1991;90:711–716. Search date and primary sources not stated.
50. Cottin B, Tebib J, Souquet PJ, Bernard JP. Pulmonary function in patients receiving long-term low-dose methotrexate. *Chest* 1996;109:933–938.
51. Nyfors A, Jensen H. Frequency of malignant neoplasms in 248 long-term methotrexate-treated psoriatics. A preliminary study. *Dermatologica* 1983;167:260–261.
52. Roenigk HH, Auerbach R, Maibach H, Weinstein G, Lebwohl M. Methotrexate in psoriasis: consensus conference. *J Am Acad Dermatol* 1998;38:478–485.
53. Timonen P, Friend D, Abeywickrama K, et al. Efficacy of low-dose cyclosporine A in psoriasis: results of dose finding studies. *Br J Dermatol* 1990;122 (suppl 36):33–39.
54. Koo J for the OLP302 Study Group. A randomized double-blind study comparing the efficacy, safety and optimal dose of two formulations of cyclosporin. Neoral and Sandimmun, in patients with severe psoriasis. *Br J Dermatol* 1998;139:88–95.
55. Shupack J, Abel E, Bauer E, et al. Cyclosporine as maintenance therapy in patients with severe psoriasis. *J Am Acad Dermatol* 1997;36:423–432.
56. Ellis CN, Fradin MS, Hamilton TA, Voorhees JJ.

Duration of remission during maintenance cyclosporine therapy for psoriasis. *Arch Dermatol* 1995;131:791–795.

57. Mahrle G, Schulze HJ, Fraber L, et al. Low-dose short-term cyclosporine versus etretinate in psoriasis: improvement of skin, nail, and joint involvement. *J Am Acad Dermatol* 1995;32:78–88.
58. Erkko P, Granlund H, Remitz A, et al. Double-blind placebo-controlled study of long-term low-dose cyclosporin in the treatment of palmoplantar pustulosis. *Br J Dermatol* 1998;139:997–1004.
59. Grossman RM, Chevret S, Abi-Rached J, Blanchet F, Dubertret L. Long-term safety of cyclosporine in the treatment of psoriasis. *Arch Dermatol* 1996;132:623–629.
60. Altmeyer PJ, Matthes U, Pawlak F, et al. Antipsoriatic effect of fumaric acid derivatives. Results of a multicenter double-blind study in 100 patients. *J Am Acad Dermatol* 1994;30:977–981.
61. Mrowietz U, Shristophers E, Altmeyer P. Treatment of psoriasis with fumaric acid esters: Results of a prospective multicentre study. *Br J Dermatol* 1998;138:456–460.

Luigi Naldi, MD
Dermatologist
Ospedali Riuniti
Bergamo
Italy

Competing interests: The research activities of the Italian Group for Epidemiological Research in Dermatology, which is coordinated by the author, have been partly supported by grants from Glaxo Wellcome, Roche, Novartis, Schering, and Schering-Plough.

Leg ulcers

E Andrea Nelson, BSc, RN, Nicky Cullum, PhD, and
June E Jones, MSc, BA, RGN, CertEd, NDN, PGD

QUESTIONS

INTERVENTIONS

Key Messages

- Randomized controlled trials (RCTs) have found that compression heals venous leg ulcers more effectively than no compression and that the addition of intermittent pneumatic compression further accelerates healing.
- Limited evidence suggests that recurrence rates are lower with higher compression pressures.
- The effects of occlusive and nonocclusive dressings compared with simple dressings have not yet been evaluated adequately in RCTs.
- Limited evidence suggests that oral pentoxyfylline or flavonoids may accelerate healing but that neither stanozolol nor rutoside decrease recurrence rates.
- Neither ultrasound nor vein surgery has yet been evaluated adequately.
- Flavonoids and rutoside are nonprescription herbal preparations that may not be familiar to US practitioners.

DEFINITION Definitions of leg ulcers vary, but the following is widely used: loss of skin on the leg or foot that takes more than 6 weeks to heal. Some definitions exclude ulcers confined to the foot whereas others include ulcers on the whole of the lower limb. This section deals with ulcers of venous origin in people without concurrent diabetes mellitus, arterial insufficiency, or rheumatoid arthritis.

PREVALENCE Between 1.5 and 3 people per 1000 have active leg ulcers, and prevalence increases with age to approximately 20 per 1000 in people over 80 years.[1] Data obtained in the 1960s in Michigan revealed a prevalence of active or healed venous ulcers of 0.1% and 0.3% for men and women, respectively. Among those aged 60 to 69 years, the respective values were 0.6% and 2.1%.[2]

ETIOLOGY Leg ulceration is strongly associated with venous disease. However, approximately one fifth of people with leg ulceration have arterial disease, either alone or in combination with venous problems, which may require specialist referral.[1] Venous ulcers (also known as varicose or stasis ulcers) are caused by venous reflux or obstruction, both of which lead to poor venous return and venous hypertension.

PROGNOSIS People with leg ulcers have a poorer quality of life than age-matched controls, because of pain, odor, and reduced mobility.[3] In the UK, audits have shown wide variation in the types of care (hospital inpatient care, hospital clinics, outpatient clinics, home visits), in the treatments used (topical agents, dressings, bandages, stockings), in healing rates, and in recurrence rates (26%–69% in 1 year).[4,5]

AIMS To promote healing, to reduce recurrence, to improve quality of life.

OUTCOMES Ulcer area; number of ulcers healed; number of ulcer-free limbs; recurrence rates; number of new ulcer episodes; number of ulcer free weeks or months; number of people who are ulcer free; number of dressing/bandage changes; quality of life.

METHODS We used the search strategy for the Cochrane Wounds Group: search date June 1998, primary sources Cochrane Library, MEDLINE, EMBASE, Cinahl. We included RCTs with clinically important and objective outcomes: proportion of wounds healed, healing rates, incidence of new or recurring wounds, infection, and quality of life. Many of the trials did not provide useful information on the characteristics of participants. Most researchers seem to have regarded leg ulcers as venous in origin if other major causes (arterial disease, rheumatoid arthritis, diabetes mellitus) had been ruled out, and this approach reflects common clinical practice. Participants in trials reflect those seen in large epidemiologic studies.

TREATMENT

QUESTION **What are the effects of treatments?**

OPTION **COMPRESSION**

One systematic review of RCTs has found that compression heals venous leg ulcers more effectively than no compression. Multilayered, high-compression, elastic systems containing rubber or Lycra (e.g., four-layer bandages), Unna's boot, high-compression stockings, and European short-stretch bandages are all effective. We found insufficient evidence to recommend any particular type of compression.

Benefits: **Compression versus no compression:** We found one recent systematic review, which identified six RCTs in 260 patients comparing compression versus no compression.[6] It found that compression (e.g., short-stretch bandages, double-layer bandage, and Unna's boot) healed venous leg ulcers more effectively than no compression (e.g., dressing alone). The trials were heterogeneous, using different forms of compression in different settings and patient populations, and results were therefore not pooled. However, the results were consistently in favor of compression. **Elastic versus nonelastic multilayer compression:** The systematic review identified three RCTs (273 patients) comparing elastomeric multilayer high-compression bandages versus nonelastomeric multilayer compression.[6] Meta-analysis found an increase in the proportion of patients healing with the elastomeric regimen (RRI for healing 54%, 95% CI 19%–100%).[6] Five patients would need to be treated with elastomeric rather than nonelastomeric multilayer compression for one more to heal (NNT 5, 95% CI 3–12) (Table 1). **Multilayer high-compression versus short-stretch systems (those containing no elastic fibers):** Three small RCTs (120 patients) found no difference between multilayer high-compression and short-stretch systems (RRI for healing 1%, 95% CI –60% to +34%).[6] The lack of power in these small studies means that a difference cannot be excluded. **Multilayer high-compression versus single-layer bandage:** The systematic review identified four trials (280 patients) comparing multilayer high compression versus a single layer of bandage.[6] Meta-analysis found a relative increase in the proportion of ulcers healing of 41% (95% CI 11%–80%) associated with multilayered compression (NNT 6, 95% CI 4–18) (Table 1).

Harms: High levels of compression applied to limbs with insufficient arterial supply, or inexpert application of bandages, can lead to tissue damage and, at worst, amputation.[7] Complication rates are rarely reported in trials.

Comment: Patients suitable for high compression are those with clinical signs of venous disease (ulcer in the gaiter region—from the upper margin of the malleolus to the bulge of the gastrocnemius, peri-ulcer pigmentation, or eczema), no concurrent diabetes mellitus or rheumatoid arthritis, and adequate arterial supply to the foot as determined by ankle/brachial pressure index. The precise ankle/brachial pressure index below which compression is contraindicated is often quoted as 0.8; however, many trials use the higher cutoff of 0.9.[6] Effectiveness is likely to be influenced by the ability of those applying the bandage to generate safe levels of compression. Bandages may be applied by the patient, their caregiver, nurse, or doctor. There are no comparisons of healing rates between specialist and non-specialist application of compression. Training improves bandaging techniques among nurses.[8] Bandages containing elastomeric fibers such as Lycra and rubber can be applied weekly because they maintain their tension over time. Bandages made of wool or cotton or both, such as short stretch bandages, may need to be reapplied more frequently because they do not maintain their tension. Note that these bandages are not commonly used in the US.

OPTION INTERMITTENT PNEUMATIC COMPRESSION

Three small RCTs have found that intermittent pneumatic compression in conjunction with compression bandages accelerates ulcer healing.

Benefits: We found one systematic review, which identified two RCTs (67 patients) comparing intermittent pneumatic compression in conjunction with compression (bandages or stockings) versus compression alone.[6] An additional RCT (53 patients) has been subsequently published.[9] The three RCTs were sufficiently similar to pool results, giving a relative increase in the proportion of ulcers healing of 69% associated with intermittent pneumatic compression (95% CI 21%–144%) (NNT 4, 95% CI 2–10) (Table 1).

Harms: No harmful effects have been reported.

Comment: Availability may vary widely between health care settings. Treatment can be delivered in the home, in outpatient clinics, or in the hospital ward. Clinical trials have evaluated its use for 1 hour twice a week and 3 to 4 hours per day. The optimal duration and pattern of pressure has yet to be determined. Treatment requires the patient to rest for 1 to 4 hours daily, which may impact on quality of life.

OPTION DRESSINGS AND TOPICAL AGENTS

We found no firm evidence on the effects of occlusive and nonocclusive dressings, topical agents, or antimicrobial agents compared with simple primary dressings such as gauze. Given the small sample sizes and lack of replication available, trials provide no evidence of benefit rather than firm evidence of a lack of benefit.

Benefits: **Simple low-adherent dressings versus occlusive or semi-occlusive dressings:** An ongoing systematic review has identified 16 RCTs that compared occlusive (e.g., hydrocolloids) or semi-occlusive dressings (e.g., foam, film, alginates) versus simple dressings (e.g., paraffin-tulle, knitted viscose dressings).[10] Nine of the trials compared hydrocolloid dressings versus simple dressings, and a pooled analysis of seven of these (714 patients) found no evidence of benefit. Two comparisons of foam dressings versus simple dressings, two of film dressings versus simple dressings, and one comparing an alginate versus a simple dressing failed to find evidence of benefit.[10] However, the trials were not of sufficient size (range 10–132 participants, median 60) to detect anything other than a very large difference in effectiveness. **Topical agents versus inert comparators:** The same systematic review identified 16 RCTs comparing topical agents (e.g., growth factors, cell suspensions, oxygen free-radical scavengers) versus either placebo preparations or standard care in the treatment of venous leg ulcers.[10] There was insufficient evidence to recommend any topical agent. The studies were small (range 9–233 participants, median 45) and heterogeneous, and therefore could not be pooled. **Antimicrobial agents versus placebo or standard care:** We found one systematic review, which identified 14 RCTs comparing antimicrobial agents versus either placebo agents or standard care.[11] The trials were small (range 25–153 participants, median 56.5), of poor quality, and no firm conclusions could be drawn.

Harms: It is unlikely that low-adherent primary wound dressings would cause harm, although iodine-containing dressings may affect thyroid function if used over large surface areas for extended periods.[12] People with venous leg ulcers exhibit a high rate (50%–85%) of contact sensitivity to preservatives, perfumes, and dyes; therefore, simple products should be used where possible.[13]

Comment: Simple primary dressings maintain a moist environment beneath compression bandages by preventing loss of moisture from the wound.[14] There are significant differences in cost between simple low-adherent dressings and the alternatives.

OPTION THERAPEUTIC ULTRASOUND

We found insufficient evidence of the effects of therapeutic ultrasound in the treatment of venous leg ulcers.

Benefits: We recently completed a systematic review (search date June 1998, primary sources Cochrane Library, MEDLINE, EMBASE, Cinahl), which identified seven RCTs comparing therapeutic ultrasound versus no ultrasound or sham ultrasound for venous leg ulcers.[15–21] A meta-analysis of the four trials with similar interventions and outcomes (201 patients) suggested a benefit associated with ultrasound (relative increase in proportion of ulcers healed 43%, 95% CI −2% to +111%).

Harms: No harmful effects have been reported.

Comment: Further research is needed to confirm the results of this meta-analysis. This intervention is not common in the US.

OPTION DRUG TREATMENTS

We found limited evidence suggesting that oral pentoxyfylline or flavonoids accelerates the healing of venous leg ulcers.

Benefits: **Pentoxyfylline:** We found no systematic review. We found two RCTs comparing pentoxyfylline (400 mg tid) versus placebo in venous leg ulcers. One trial reported accelerated healing and one trial reported no significant difference.[22–23] Meta-analysis of these two trials shows a relative increase in the proportion of ulcers healing of 48% (95% CI 14%–94%) (NNT 6, 95% CI 3–16) (Table 1). **Flavonoids:** One RCT compared a flavonoid versus placebo in venous leg ulcers. This concluded that 1000 mg (900 mg diosmin and 100 mg flavonoids expressed as hesperidin) increased the rate of complete healing of ulcers that were initially < 10 cm in diameter (relative increase in proportion of ulcers healed 150%, 95% CI 9%–485%, NNT 5, 95% CI 3–50).[24] (Table 1).

Harms: In one trial of pentoxyfylline versus placebo, 45% of patients receiving pentoxyfylline and 33% of those receiving placebo reported adverse effects, such as depression, dyspepsia, vomiting, and diarrhea.[23] Adverse effects of flavonoids, such as gastrointestinal disturbances, were reported in 10% of patients.[24]

Comment: None.

OPTION VEIN SURGERY

We found insufficient evidence of the effects of vein surgery on ulcer healing.

Benefits: We found no systematic review. One RCT (47 patients) compared vein surgery (perforator ligation) versus no surgery or surgery plus skin grafting.[25] There was no difference in the proportion of ulcers healed after 1 year or the rate of ulcer healing. The trial was small and therefore unable to rule out a beneficial effect.

Harms: Vein surgery carries the usual risks of surgery and anesthesia.

Comment: Several operative approaches are commonly used, including perforator ligation, saphenous vein stripping, and a combination of both procedures.

PREVENTING RECURRENCE

QUESTION What are the effects of interventions to prevent recurrence?

OPTION COMPRESSION

We found limited evidence from one RCT suggesting that class 3 compression reduces recurrence rates compared with class 2 (see Comment) but is less well tolerated by patients.

Benefits: We found one systematic review, which identified no trials comparing compression stockings versus no compression.[6] It identified two RCTs comparing different types of compression. One trial compared two brands of class 2 stockings in 166 patients and found no difference in recurrence rates.[26] The larger trial (300 patients) compared recurrence rates under class 2 and class 3 stockings.[27] It reported a relative reduction in recurrence at 3 to 5 years of 34% associated with class 3 stockings compared with class 2 stockings (NNT 9, 95% CI 5–236) (Table 1); however, compliance was higher with the class 2 stockings.

Harms: The application of high compression to limbs with reduced arterial supply may result in tissue damage and, at worst, ischemia and amputation.[7]

Comment: Compression stockings are classified according to the magnitude of pressure exerted at the ankle; the UK classification states that class 2 stockings are capable of applying 18 to 24 mm Hg pressure, and class 3 is capable of applying 25 to 35 mm Hg pressure at the ankle. Stockings are palliative rather than curative because they cannot correct permanently the underlying venous hypertension responsible for ulceration. Therefore, patients are advised to wear compression stockings for life. It seems to be good practice to reassess arterial supply regularly because patients might develop arterial disease and, hence, be at risk of pressure necrosis caused by their compression stockings. Other measures designed to reduce leg edema, such as resting with the leg elevated, may be useful.

OPTION SYSTEMIC DRUGS

We found insufficient evidence on the effects of systemic drugs on ulcer recurrence.

Benefits: We found one systematic review of drugs in the prevention of leg ulcer recurrence. This identified two RCTs and concluded that there was no evidence that stanozolol or rutoside decreased recurrence rates.[6] One trial, of stanozolol versus placebo in 60 patients, found no significant difference in recurrence rates (17% vs. 20%). The other trial, of rutoside versus placebo in 138 patients, found no significant difference in recurrence rates (32% vs. 34%).

Harms: Stanozolol is an anabolic steroid, and patients therefore require close monitoring, particularly of liver function. Tolerance of rutosides is reported to be good.[28]

Comment: None.

OPTION VEIN SURGERY

We found insufficient evidence on the effects of vein surgery on ulcer recurrence.

Benefits: We found one systematic review, which identified one poorly controlled RCT (30 patients) comparing surgery plus compression stockings versus compression stockings alone for prevention of recurrence.[6] It reported a reduced rate of recurrence when surgery was carried out in addition to the use of elastic stockings (5% vs. 24%; relative reduction in recurrence 79%, 95% CI 20%–97%).

Harms: Vein surgery carries the usual risks of surgery and anesthesia.

Comment: The results of this small, poorly controlled trial should be interpreted with caution.

REFERENCES

1. Callam MJ, Ruckley CV, Harper DR, et al. Chronic ulceration of the leg: extent of the problem and provision of care. *BMJ* 1985;290:1855–1856.
2. Coon WW, Willis PW III, Keller JB. Venous thromboembolism and other venous disease in the Tecumseh community health study. *Circulation* 1973;48:839–846.
3. Roe B, Cullum N, Hamer C. Patients' perceptions of chronic leg ulceration. In: Cullum N, Roe B, eds. *Leg ulcers: nursing management.* Harrow: Scutari, 1995:125–134.
4. Roe B, Cullum N. The management of leg ulcers:

current nursing practice In: Cullum N, Roe B, eds. *Leg ulcers: nursing management.* Harrow: Scutari, 1995:113–124.
5. Vowden KR, Barker A, Vowden P. Leg ulcer management in a nurse-led, hospital-based clinic. *Journal of Wound Care* 1997;6:233–236.
6. Cullum N, Fletcher A, Semlyen A, Sheldon TA. Compression therapy for venous leg ulcers. *Quality in Health Care* 1997;6:226–231. [Searched until 1997.]
7. Callam MJ, Ruckley CV, Dale JJ, Harper DR. Hazards of compression treatment of the leg: an estimate from Scottish surgeons. *BMJ* 1987;295:1382.
8. Nelson EA, Ruckley CV, Barbenel J. Improvements in bandaging technique following training. *Journal of Wound Care* 1995;4: 181–184.
9. Schuler JJ, Maibenco T, Megerman J, Ware M, Montalvo J. Treatment of chronic venous leg ulcers using sequential gradient intermittent pneumatic compression. *Phlebology* 1996;11:111–116.
10. Bradley M, Nelson EA, Cullum N, Petticrew, M Torgerson D, Sheldon T. Dressings and topical agents for healing of chronic wounds: a systematic review. *NHS Health Technology Assessment Report* [In press]. (Searched until October 1997, primary sources Cochrane Library, MEDLINE, EMBASE, Cinahl.)
11. O'Meara S, Cullum N, Majid M, Sheldon T. A systematic review of systemic and topical antimicrobial agents used in the treatment of chronic wounds. *NHS Health Technology Assessment Report* [In press]. (Searched until October 1997, primary sources Cochrane Library, MEDLINE, EMBASE, Cinahl.)
12. Thomas S. *Wound management and dressings.* London: Pharmaceutical Press, 1990.
13. Cameron J, Wilson C, Powell S, Cherry G, Ryan T. Contact dermatitis in leg ulcer patients. *Ostomy Wound Management* 1992;38(9):8, 10–11.
14. Wu P, Nelson EA, Reid WH, Ruckley CV, Gaylor JD. Water vapour transmission rates in burns and chronic leg ulcers: influence of wound dressings and comparison with in vitro evaluation. *Biomaterials* 1996;17:1373–1377.
15. Callam MJ, Dale JJ, Ruckley CV, Harper DR. Trial of ultrasound in the treatment of chronic leg ulceration. In: Negus D, Jantet G, eds. *Phlebology '85*. London: John Libbey, 1986:625–626.
16. Dyson M, Franks C, Suckling J. Stimulation of healing of varicose ulcers by ultrasound. *Ultrasonics* 1976;14:232–236.
17. Eriksson SV, Lundeberg T, Malm M. A placebo controlled trial of ultrasound therapy in chronic leg ulceration. *Scand J Rehabil Med* 1991;23: 211–213.
18. Lundeberg T, Nordstrom F, Brodda-Jansen G, Eriksson SV, Kjartansson J, Samuelson UE. Pulsed ultrasound does not improve healing of venous ulcers. *Scand J Rehabil Med* 1990;22:195–197.
19. Peschen M, Vanscheidt W. Low frequency ultrasound of chronic venous leg ulcers as part of an out-patient treatment. In: Cherry GW, Gottrup F, Lawrence JC, eds. *Proceedings of the 5th European Conference on Advances in Wound Management*. London: Macmillan Magazines, 1996:271.
20. Roche C, West J. A controlled trial investigating the effect of ultrasound on venous ulcers referred from general practitioners. *Physiotherapy* 1984;70:475–477.
21. Weichenthal M, Mohr P, Stegmann W, Eckhard W, Breitbart MD. Low-frequency ultrasound treatment of chronic venous leg ulcers. *Wound Repair and Regeneration* 1997;5:18–22.
22. Dale JJ, Ruckley CV, Harper DR, Gibson B, Nelson EA, Prescott RJ. A factorial trial of drugs, dressings and bandages in the treatment of leg ulcers. In: Cherry GW, Gottrup F, Lawrence JC, eds. *Proceedings of the 5th European Conference on Advances in Wound Management*. London: Macmillan Magazines, 1995:193–194.
23. Colgan MP, Dormandy JA, Jones PW, Schraibman IG, Shanik DG, Young RA. Oxpentifylline treatment of venous ulcers of the leg. *BMJ* 1990;300:972–975.
24. Guilhou JJ, Dereure O, Marzin L, et al. Efficacy of Daflon 500 mg in venous leg ulcer healing: a double-blind, randomized, controlled versus placebo trial in 107 patients. *Angiology* 1997;48:77–85.
25. Warburg FE, Danielsen L, Madsen SM, et al. Vein surgery with or without skin grafting versus conservative treatment for leg ulcers. *Acta Dermatol Venereol* 1994;74:307–309.
26. Franks P, Oldroyd M, Dickson D, et al. Risk factors for leg ulcer recurrence: a randomised trial of two types of compression stocking. *Age Ageing* 1995;24:490–494.
27. Harper DR, Nelson E, Gibson B, et al. A prospective randomised trial of class 2 and class 3 elastic compression in the prevention of venous ulceration. *Phlebology* 1995;10(suppl 1):872–873.
28. Taylor HM, Rose KE, Twycross RG. A double-blind clinical trial of hydroxyethylrutosides in obstructive arm lymphoedema. *Phlebology* 1993;8(suppl 1):22–28.

E Andrea Nelson, BSc, RN
Nicky Cullum, PhD
Centre for Evidence Based Nursing
Department of health studies
University of York
York
UK

June E Jones, MSc, BA, RGN, CertEd, NDN, PGD
Clinical Nurse Specialist
Southport and Fornby community services NHS trust
Southport
UK

Competing interests: AN has been reimbursed for attending symposia by Smith and Nephew, and Convatec; JJ has been reimbursed for attending symposia by 3M and Convatec.

TABLE 1 NNTs for interventions

Intervention	NNT (95% CI)
Elastomeric multilayer compression vs. nonelastomeric multilayer compression bandages	5 (3–12)
Multilayer high-compression vs. single-layer compression bandages	6 (4–18)
Intermittent pneumatic compression plus compression bandages vs. compression bandages alone	4 (2–10)
Pentoxyfylline 400 mg tid vs. placebo	6 (3–16)
Class 3 vs. class 2 compression hosiery for prevention of recurrence	9 (5–236)

Pressure sores

Nicky Cullum, PhD, E Andrea Nelson, BSc, RN, and Jane Nixon, BSc, MA

QUESTIONS

INTERVENTIONS

Key Messages

Prevention

- One systematic review of randomized controlled trials (RCTs) has found that foam alternatives to the standard hospital foam mattress reduce the incidence of pressure sores in people at high risk.
- The relative merits of alternating and constant low pressure, and of the different alternating-pressure devices, are unclear.
- RCTs have found the use of pressure-relieving overlays on operating tables to reduce the incidence of pressure sores.
- We found insufficient evidence on the effects of seat cushions, constant-low-pressure devices, regular repositioning ("turning"), sheepskins, topical lotions, or dressings.

Treatment

- Systematic reviews of RCTs have found that air-fluidized support and low-air-loss beds may improve healing rates and that hydrocolloid dressings are more effective than gauze soaked in saline or hypochlorite solution.
- We found no good evidence on the effects of other types of dressings, debridement, surgery, nutritional supplementation, electrotherapy, or ultrasound on healing rates of pressure sores.

DEFINITION Pressure sores (also known as pressure ulcers, bed sores, and decubitus ulcers) may present as persistently hyperemic, blistered, broken, or necrotic skin and may extend to underlying structures, including muscle and bone. Whether blanching and nonblanching erythema constitute pressure sores remains controversial.

INCIDENCE/ PREVALENCE Methodologies used to determine the incidence of pressure sores vary among studies. Incidences range from 2.7% to 29.0% in hospitals and from 1.9% to 28.0% in skilled-care facilities and nursing homes.[1,2]

ETIOLOGY Pressure sores are caused by unrelieved pressure, shear, or friction, and are most common below the waist and at bony prominences, such as the sacrum, heels, and hips. They occur in all health care settings. Increased age, reduced mobility, and impaired nutrition emerge consistently as risk factors. However, the relative importance of these and other factors is uncertain.[3]

PROGNOSIS The presence of pressure sores has been associated with a two- to fourfold increased risk of death in elderly people or patients in intensive care.[4,5] However, pressure sores are a marker for underlying disease severity and other comorbidities rather than an independent predictor of mortality.[4] Pressure sores vary considerably in size and severity.

AIMS To prevent pressure sore formation, to heal existing pressure sores, and to improve quality of life.

OUTCOMES Incidence and severity of pressure sores; rate of change of area and volume; time to heal. Interface pressure recorded at various anatomic sites is a surrogate outcome sometimes used in studies of preventive interventions; it has not yet been linked to clinical outcomes.

METHODS We searched the Specialist Trials Register of the Cochrane Wounds Group, which is compiled by searching 19 electronic databases including MEDLINE (1966 to June 1998), CINAHL, BIDS, and EMBASE, and hand searching journals and conference proceedings. We reviewed all RCTs that used objective clinical outcome measures. For many trials, we could not be sure that pressure sore size was evenly distributed between groups at baseline. Unequal distribution of wound size at baseline will impact on all measures of wound healing. Ideally, studies of treatment should stratify randomization by initial wound area and be of sufficient size to ensure even distribution of baseline wound size. Many of the studies performed by manufacturers were in healthy people who are not representative of clinical subjects, and these studies have been excluded.

PREVENTION

QUESTION **What are the effects of interventions aimed at preventing pressure sores?**

OPTION **PRESSURE-RELIEVING SURFACES**

One systematic review of RCTs has found that foam alternatives (e.g., eggcrate mattresses) to the standard hospital foam mattress reduce the incidence of pressure sores in people at high risk. Foam alternatives use foam of varying densities, often within the same mattress, and are sometimes sculptured. There is no obvious "best" foam alternative. The relative merits of alternating and constant low pressure, and of the different alternating-pressure devices, are unclear. Seat cushions and low-tech constant-low-pressure devices have not yet been evaluated adequately. Limited evidence from one RCT suggests that low-air-loss beds reduce the incidence of pressure sores in intensive care. RCTs have found that the use of pressure-relieving overlays on operating tables reduces the incidence of pressure sores.

Benefits: We found one systematic review published in 1995[6] and several subsequent RCTs. **Foam alternatives versus standard hospital mattress:** The systematic review[6] identified three RCTs, and another RCT has been published since.[7] The trials indicated that using various foam alternatives to the standard hospital mattress reduced the relative risk of sores by 73% (95% CI 62%–81%); NNT to prevent one additional sore 4 (95% CI 3–6). **Different foam alternatives:** Four RCTs[7–9] (JE Santy, MK Butler, JD Whyman, unpublished data) have compared different foam alternatives. One reported a relative reduction in the risk of pressure sores of 58% (95% CI 10%–82%) associated with using a five section foam and fiber replacement compared with a 4-inch-thick dimpled foam overlay (NNT 3, 95% CI 2–25).[9] The other studies were of insufficient power to distinguish between the foam alternatives. **Cushions:** The systematic review identified only one small RCT in 62 people comparing different types of seat cushion for preventing pressure sores. It found no significant difference. **Low-tech constant-low-pressure supports:** The systematic review identified six RCTs,[6] and two more have been published since.[10,11] Most were too small or flawed to allow conclusions. **Low-air-loss beds:** The systematic review identified one RCT in 98 people in intensive care.[6] This found a relative reduction in risk of developing a new sore of 317% (95% CI 97%–826%) on low-air-loss beds compared with a standard intensive care unit bed (NNT 3, 95% CI 2–5). **Alternating pressure:** The systematic review[6] identified eight RCTs involving 11 comparisons of constant-low-pressure devices versus alternating-pressure devices in the prevention of pressure sores. A further RCT has been conducted since (Raurent S, Third European Conference for Nurse Managers, 1997). Most studies were too small to exclude a clinically important difference. Three found no significant difference between an inexpensive Silicore overlay and an alternating-pressure overlay in neurologic and elderly orthopedic patients. Another trial reported a significant reduction in the incidence of pressure sores for patients on an alternating-pressure device versus a standard foam mattress (RRR 68%, 95% CI

28%–86%; NNT 11, 95% CI 6–34). In two others, the incidence of pressure sores was significantly reduced when alternating rather than constant low pressure was used. The relative merits of the different alternating-pressure devices are unclear. **Pressure-relieving overlays on the operating table:** No systematic review. We identified three RCTs. The first compared a viscoelastic polymer pad versus a standard table in people undergoing elective major general, gynecologic, or vascular surgery. It reported a significant reduction in the incidence of postoperative pressure sores with the polymer pad (RRR 48%, 95% CI 17%–68%; NNT 11, 95% CI 6–36).[12] The other two RCTs compared an alternating system used both during and after surgery versus a gel pad during surgery and a standard mattress postoperatively. They reported a significant reduction in the incidence of pressure sores with the alternating system (RRR 80%, 95% CI 35%–94%; NNT 16, 95% CI 9–48) (Beckrich K, personal communication).

Harms: There is no direct or indirect evidence of harm arising from use of pressure-relieving beds, mattresses, overlays, and cushions.

Comment: Studies have tended to be small and of poor quality, and few comparisons have been undertaken more than once. There may be a 100-fold difference in purchase cost between low-tech foam alternatives and high-tech replacement beds.

OPTION OTHER PREVENTIVE INTERVENTIONS

We found no evidence that regular repositioning ("turning"), sheepskins, topical lotions, or dressings are effective. However, this may represent a lack of evidence rather than a lack of benefit from these interventions.

Benefits: We found one systematic review published in 1995[6] and no subsequent RCTs. **Repositioning/turning:** The systematic review identified three RCTs of regular manual repositioning.[6] These were small and found no significant difference between experimental and control groups. No RCTs have evaluated the impact of positioning patients in different ways. **Sheepskin:** The systematic review identified one small trial of sheepskin overlays.[6] This was inconclusive and of poor quality. **Topical lotions and dressings:** We found one RCT of sufficient quality that was not identified in the systematic review.[13] This compared a lotion containing hexachlorophene versus one containing cetrimide in 120 participants and found no significant difference in skin condition.

Harms: We found no direct or indirect evidence of harm arising from repositioning, sheepskin, topical applications, or dressings.

Comment: The RCTs were small and of poor quality, and few comparisons have been undertaken more than once.

TREATMENT

QUESTION **What are the effects of treatment?**

OPTION **PRESSURE-RELIEVING SURFACES**

One systematic review of RCTs has found that air-fluidized support and low-air-loss beds improve healing rates. Seat cushions have not been evaluated adequately.

Benefits: We found one systematic review published in 1995.[6] **Air-fluidized supports:** The systematic review identified four RCTs comparing air fluidized support versus standard care. In two trials in hospital patients, standard care involved use of pressure-relieving surfaces, such as alternating-pressure mattresses, regular changes of position, sheepskin or gel pads, and limb protectors. Both trials reported that air-fluidized support was more effective in healing established sores. A third RCT, in 97 people being cared for at home, found no significant difference. However, this trial had a high withdrawal rate. The fourth RCT was small and involved patients who had undergone plastic surgery to repair pressure sores. It found no significant difference between air-fluidized support and dry flotation. **Low-air-loss beds:** The systematic review[6] identified two RCTs. Both reported that low-air-loss beds were more effective than foam. We found no RCTs comparing low air loss versus alternating pressure or air-fluidized supports. **Seat cushions:** We found one RCT in 25 people published since the systematic review. This reported no significant difference between seat cushions using dry flotation compared with alternating pressure.[14]

Harms: We found no direct or indirect evidence of harm arising from air-fluidized support, low-air-loss beds, or repositioning.

Comment: Patients are unable to move into and out of bed independently while using an air-fluidized bed, and this limits the type of patient for whom it is suitable. Air-fluidized support has been evaluated in a range of settings, including surgical and medical wards and home care. Thus, the evidence could be widely generalized to people with pressure sores. The trials were of varying quality. Low-air-loss beds have been evaluated in a range of acute and elderly care settings, but one of the two trials was of poor quality.

OPTION **OTHER TREATMENTS**

Limited evidence from a systematic review of RCTs suggests that hydrocolloid dressings are more effective than gauze soaked in saline or hypochlorite solution. We found no good evidence on the effects of other types of dressings, debridement, surgery, nutritional supplementation, electrotherapy, or ultrasound on healing rates of pressure sores.

Benefits: **Hydrocolloid and gauze dressings:** We performed a systematic review of dressings and topical agents for pressure sores (*see* Methods), which identified 28 RCTs. Most were small, of poor quality, and inconclusive. Meta-analysis of five RCTs in 287 patients[15–19] indicated that hydrocolloid dressings significantly improved the healing rate of pressure sores compared with gauze soaked in saline or hypochlorite (relative improvement in the rate of healing 61%, 95% CI 26%–108%; NNT 5, 95% CI 4–11). **Other dressings:** Twelve of the RCTs identified in the systematic review compared hydrocolloid versus other dressings, such as foam. All were too small and most were too flawed to allow conclusions to be drawn. **Debridement:** A systematic review, completed in 1998, found no RCTs that compared the impact of debridement versus no debridement on wound healing.[20] It identified 32 RCTs comparing different debriding agents, but these were small, included a range of wounds, and many were unique comparisons. The authors concluded that there was insufficient evidence to promote the use of any particular debriding agent over another. **Surgery:** We found no RCTs evaluating surgical treatments for pressure sores. **Nutritional supplements:** We found two RCTs of ascorbic acid supplementation for healing pressure sores. A small trial in surgical patients with pressure sores[21] reported that ascorbic acid supplementation (500 mg twice daily vs. placebo) improved healing rates. A larger trial in 88 participants found no significant difference in healing rates between those receiving ascorbic acid 500 mg bid and those receiving 10 mg twice daily.[22] We found no RCTs of the effects of parenteral nutrition or hyperalimentation on wound healing. **Electrotherapy:** We found four RCTs comparing electrotherapy versus sham treatment.[23–26] The trials were of varying quality. Overall they suggested that electrotherapy improved healing of pressure sores, but confirmatory research is needed. **Ultrasound:** We found three RCTs comparing the effects of ultrasound versus sham or standard treatment on pressure sore healing.[27–29] All found no difference, but they were too small to rule out a beneficial effect.

Harms: We found no reports of harms arising from these treatments.

Comment: Overall, the evidence relating to these treatments is poor.

REFERENCES

1. Frantz RA. Measuring prevalence and incidence of pressure ulcers. *Adv Wound Care* 1997;10: 21–24.
2. Burd C, Lungemo DK, Olson B, et al. Epidemiology of pressure ulcers in a skilled-care facility. *J Geriatr Nurs* 1992;18:29–39.
3. Allman RM. Pressure ulcer prevalence, incidence, risk factors, and impact. *Clin Geriatr Med* 1997;13:421–436.
4. Thomas DR, Goode PS, Tarquine PH, Allman RM. Hospital acquired pressure ulcers and risk of death. *J Am Geriatr Soc* 1996;44:1435–1440.
5. Clough NP. The cost of pressure area management in an intensive care unit. *Journal of Wound Care* 1994;3:33–35.
6. Cullum N, Deeks JJ, Fletcher AW, Sheldon TA, Song F. Preventing and treating pressure sores. *Quality in Health Care* 1995;4:289–297. Primary sources Medline (1966 to February 1999); Cinahl (February 1995); handsearching of five journals.
7. Collier ME. Pressure-reducing mattresses. *Journal of Wound Care* 1996;5:207–211.
8. Bliss MR. Preventing pressure sores in elderly patients: a comparison of seven mattress overlays. *Age Ageing* 1995;24:297–302.
9. Vylhidal SK, Moxness D, Bosak KS, Van Meter, Bergstrom N. Mattress replacement or foam overlay? A prospective study on the incidence of pressure ulcers. *Appl Nurs Res* 1997;10: 111–120.
10. Takala J, Varmavuo S, Soppi E. Prevention of pressure sores in acute respiratory failure: a randomised controlled trial. *Clinical Intensive Care* 1996;7:228–235.
11. Cooper PJ, Gray DG , Mollison J. A randomised controlled trial of two pressure reducing surfaces. *Journal of Wound Care* 1998;7:374–376.
12. Nixon J, McElvenny D, Mason S, Brown J, Bond S. A sequential randomised controlled trial comparing a dry visco-elastic polymer pad and standard operating table mattress in the prevention of postoperative pressure sores. *Int J Nurs Stud* 1998;35(4):193–203.
13. van der Cammen TJ, O'Callaghan U, Whitefield M. Prevention of pressure sores. A comparison of new and old pressure sore treatments. *Br J Clin Pract* 1987;41:1009–1011.
14. Clark M, Donald IP. A randomised controlled trial comparing the healing of pressure sores upon two pressure-redistributing seat cushions. Improving Clinical Outcomes Through Education. *Proceedings of the 7th European Conference on Advances in Wound Management.* November

18–20, 1997; Harrogate, UK. London: EMAP Healthcare, 1998:122–125.
15. Barrois B. Comparison of Granuflex and medicated paraffin gauze in pressure sores. *Proceedings of the 2nd European Conference on Advances in Wound Management*. London: Macmillan, 1993: 209.
16. Alm A, Hornmark AM, Fall PA, et al. Care of pressure sores: a controlled study of the use of a hydrocolloid dressing compared with wet saline gauze compresses. *Acta Derm Venereol Suppl* 1989;149:1–10.
17. Colwell JC, Foreman MD, Trotter JP. A comparison of the efficacy and cost-effectiveness of two methods of managing pressure ulcers. *Decubitus* 1993;6(4):28–36.
18. Xakellis GC, Chrischilles EA. Hydrocolloid versus saline-gauze dressings in treating pressure ulcers: a cost-effectiveness analysis. *Arch Phys Med Rehabil* 1992;73:463–469.
19. Gorse GJ, Messner RL. Improved pressure sore healing with hydrocolloid dressings. *Arch Dermatol* 1987;123:766–771.
20. Bradley M, Cullum N, Sheldon T. The debridement of chronic wounds: a systematic review. *NHS HTA Report*. In press. (Search undertaken of 19 electronic databases including MEDLINE and EMBASE up until June 1998.)
21. Taylor TV, Rimmer S, Day B, Butcher J, Dymock IW. Ascorbic acid supplementation in the treatment of pressure sores. *Lancet* 1974;2:544–546.
22. ter Riet G, Kessels AG, Knipschild PG. Randomized clinical trial of ascorbic acid in the treatment of pressure ulcers. *J Clin Epidemiol* 1995;48:1453–1460.
23. Salzberg CA, Cooper Vastola SA, Perez F, Viehbeck MG, Byrne DW. The effects of non-thermal pulsed electromagnetic energy on wound healing of pressure ulcers in spinal cord-injured patients: a randomized, double-blind study. *Ostomy Wound Management* 1995;41(3):42–48.
24. Wood JM, Evans PE 3rd, Schallreuter KU, et al. A multicenter study on the use of pulsed low-intensity direct current for healing chronic stage II and stage III decubitus ulcers. *Arch Dermatol* 1993; 129:999–1009.
25. el-Zeky F. Efficacy of high voltage pulsed current for healing of pressure ulcers in patients with spinal cord injury. *Physical Therapy* 1991;71: 433–442.
26. Kloth LC, Feedar JA. Acceleration of wound healing with high voltage, monophasic, pulsed current. *Physical Therapy* 1988;68:503–508.
27. McDiarmid T. Ultrasound in the treatment of pressure sores. *Physiotherapy* 1985;February: 66–70.
28. ter Riet G, Kessels AG, Knipschild P. Randomised clinical trial of ultrasound treatment for pressure ulcers. *BMJ* 1995;310:1040–1041.
29. Nussbaum EL, Biemann I, Mustard B. Comparison of ultrasound/ultraviolet-C and laser for treatment of pressure ulcers in patients with spinal cord injury. *Physical Therapy* 1994;74: 812–825.

Nicky Cullum, PhD
Reader
E Andrea Nelson, BSc, RN
Research Fellow
Centre for Evidence Based Nursing
Department of Health Studies
University of York
York
UK

Jane Nixon, BSc, MA
Head of Nursing Research and Practice Development
Leeds Teaching Hospitals NHS Trust
St James's University Hospital
Leeds
UK

Competing interests: AN has received lecture fees and expenses from Convatec and Smith and Nephew for speaking at symposia; JN has received lecture fees and expenses from Central Medical Supplies, UK, for speaking at symposia.

Genital warts

D J Wiley, PhD, and Karl R Beutner, MD, PhD

QUESTIONS

INTERVENTIONS

Key Messages

- Only five treatments have been compared with placebo. Podofilox, imiquimod, and intralesional interferon have been found to be significantly more effective in the clearance of warts compared with placebo, but data on recurrence are lacking. Placebo-controlled randomized controlled trials (RCTs) of topical interferon give conflicting results, and those of systemic interferon show no evidence of benefits.
- We found no clear evidence that one treatment is superior to another.
- Topical 5-fluorouracil, and bi- and trichloroacetic acid have not been evaluated adequately.
- We do not know whether treatment of external genital warts decreases infectivity, and the preventive effects of condoms have not been evaluated adequately.

DEFINITION External genital warts are benign epidermal growths on the external perianal and perigenital region. There are four morphologic types: condylomatous, keratotic, papular, and flat warts.

INCIDENCE/ PREVALENCE In 1996, external and internal genital warts accounted for over 180,000 initial visits to private physicians' offices in the USA, approximately 60,000 fewer than were reported for 1995.[1] In the USA, 1% of sexually active men and women between the ages of 18 and 49 years are estimated to have external genital warts.[2]

ETIOLOGY External genital warts are caused by the human papillomavirus (HPV). Although more than 70 HPVs have been identified, most external genital warts among immunocompetent patients are caused by HPV types 6 and 11.[3,4] HPV infection and, more specifically, external genital warts are sexually transmissible diseases.

PROGNOSIS The factors that influence recurrence, recrudescence, and reinfection are not fully understood. However, evidence from clinical trials shows that recurrences are frequent and may necessitate repeated treatment. Without treatment, external genital warts may remain unchanged, may increase in size or number, or may completely resolve. They rarely, if ever, progress to cancer.[5] Juvenile laryngeal papillomatosis, a rare and sometimes life-threatening condition, occurs in children of women with a history of genital warts. Its rarity makes it hard to design studies that can evaluate whether treatment in pregnant women alters the risk.[6,7]

AIMS To eliminate symptomatic warts from the external genitalia, to prevent recurrence, and to avoid sequelae, with minimal adverse effects.

OUTCOMES Wart clearance (generally accepted as complete eradication of warts from the treated area); recurrence; sequelae; adverse effects of treatment; quality of life; transmission. Few clinical trials have included enough participants to evalute whether treatment alters recurrence rates. Selection biases and inadequate power may account for the high variability in recurrence rates across studies.

METHODS We searched MEDLINE and other proprietary databases from 1985 to 1996. We also performed selected MEDLINE searches for manuscripts published before 1985 and after 1996. Other data came from abstract booklets, conference proceedings, references identified from bibliographies of pertinent articles and books, and manufacturers of therapeutic agents. This review is limited to RCTs, unless no RCTs were found for a particular treatment. This limitation may have biased the review in favor of newer and heavily marketed treatments.

QUESTION What are the effects of nonsurgical treatments?

OPTION PODOFILOX (PODOPHYLOTOXIN)

RCTs have found that podofilox is more effective than placebo.

Benefits: We found no systematic review. **Versus placebo:** Data from seven placebo-controlled RCTs in a total of 709 men and women found wart clearance within 16 weeks of treatment in 58% to 77% of participants.[8–14] Clearance was between 2.0 (95% CI 0.9–4.3)[9] and 48 (95% CI 3.0–773)[8] times more likely with podofilox than with placebo. **Recurrence rates:** RCTs of 0.5% cream or solution found recurrence rates ranging from 4% (1 of 25)[15] to 33% (8 of 24).[9] One RCT of 0.5% podofilox solution as prophylaxis against recurrence of external genital warts in 57 participants initially treated in an open-label study showed fewer recurrences among placebo-treated participants.[16] **Versus podophyllin:** Four RCTs have compared podofilox versus podophyllin.[17–20] These found no significant difference in wart clearance (RRs of clearance with podophyllin vs. podofilox 0.7, 95% CI 0.4–1.1[18]; 0.8, 95% CI 0.4–1.8[17]; 0.8, 95% CI 0.7–1.0[19]; 1.7, 95% CI 0.9–3.2[20]).

Harms: Safety during pregnancy is unknown. Podofilox does not contain the mutagenic flavonoid compounds (quercetin and kaempherol) that are contained in podophyllin resin preparations.[21] Local inflammation or irritation, erosion, burning, pain, and itching are reported by most investigators. Balanoposthitis,[22,23] dyspareunia, bleeding, scarring, and insomnia are reported uncommonly.[8] One large RCT reported burning and inflammation in three quarters of treated patients and bleeding in one quarter.[12] Although infrequent, preputial tightening has been reported.[17]

Comment: RCTs examined the efficacy of podofilox solutions more often than cream preparations, but cream or gel preparations may be easier to apply than solutions. These and other application differences may cause variable efficacy and effectiveness.

OPTION IMIQUIMOD

RCTs have found that imiquimod is more effective than placebo.

Benefits: We found no systematic review. **Versus placebo:** We reviewed two placebo-controlled RCTs in a total of 642 men and women (Table 1). Wart clearance within 3 months occurred twice as often with 1% cream as placebo (RR 1.9, 95% CI 1.1–3.3);[24] 37% to 56% of treated participants showed wart clearance compared with 0% to 14% on placebo.[24,25] **Recurrence rates:** No recurrences were reported on 1% cream, but recurrences were reported in 13% to 19% of participants treated with 5% cream.[24,25] This compared with 10% among placebo-treated participants in one study.[24]

Harms: Local itching, erythema, and burning have been reported in more than 15% of participants and irritation, tenderness, ulceration, and pain in fewer than 10%.[25]

Comment: None.

OPTION CRYOTHERAPY

RCTs have found that cryotherapy is as effective as podophyllin, trichloroacetic acid, and electrosurgery. It has not been compared with placebo. Cryotherapy has been used successfully in pregnancy.

Benefits: We found no published systematic review and no placebo-controlled RCTs. We reviewed six RCTs: two compared cryotherapy plus interferon versus cryotherapy alone[26,27]; the other four compared cryotherapy versus podophyllin,[28] trichloroacetic acid,[29,30] or electrosurgery.[28,31] **Clearance:** Four of these reported 63% to 88% clearance 3 months or more after cryotherapy.[28–31] These studies show that podophyllin acts more slowly than cryotherapy. Although one study found that cryotherapy was more effective than podophyllin after six treatments (RR of wart clearance compared to podophyllin: 1.9, 95% CI 1.4–2.6), there was no significant difference in wart clearance 3 months after treatment (RR 1.4, 95% CI 0.9–2.2).[28] Similarly, others found no significant difference between cryotherapy and trichloroacetic acid at the end of treatment or 3 months later (RR 1.1, 95% CI 0.8–1.5, and RR 0.9, 95% CI 0.8–1.1).[29,30] However, cryotherapy was slightly less effective than electrosurgery (RRs of wart clearance with electrosurgery vs. cryotherapy at the end of treatment and 3 months after: 1.2, 95% CI 1.1–1.3, and 1.4, 95% CI 1.0–2.0).[28,31] **Recurrence rates:** There was no significant difference in recurrence rates between cryotherapy and electrosurgery (21% vs. 22%).[28]

Harms: Discomfort, ulceration, and scabbing were reported in nearly one fifth of participants on cryotherapy.[28,30] One RCT reported local infection in one of 86 participants on cryotherapy compared with none of 149 participants on podophyllin resin or electrosurgery.[28]

Comment: One case series of 34 pregnant women who received three or fewer treatments showed no subsequent infection or premature rupture of membranes.[32]

OPTION PODOPHYLLIN RESIN

RCTs have found that podophyllin resin is as effective as most other treatments but is less effective than surgical excision. It has not been compared directly with placebo.

Benefits: We found no systematic review and no placebo-controlled RCTs. We reviewed 12 RCTs: four compared podophyllin versus podofilox,[17–20] one versus cryotherapy,[28] one versus electrosurgery,[28] three with and without interferon,[33–35] one with and without trichloroacetic acid,[36] two versus surgical excision,[37,38] and two comparing alternate doses of podophyllin.[36,39] **Clearance:** Complete wart clearance was no different with podophyllin than with podofilox (RRs 0.7, 95% CI 0.4–1.1[18]; 0.8, 95% CI 0.4–1.8[17]; 0.8, 95% CI 0.7–1.0[19]; 1.7, 95% CI 0.9–3.2[20]) nor when cryotherapy or electrosurgery were compared to podophyllin 3 months after treatment (RR for both comparison treatments: 1.4, 95% CI 0.9–2.1).[28] Although one RCT found that podophyllin and intralesional interferon together were more effective than podophyllin alone 3 weeks after treatment (RR of wart clearance: 2.0, 95% CI 1.1–3.6), no difference was observed at 11 weeks (RR 2.3 95% CI 0.9–5.8).[34] However, podophyllin was less effective than surgical excision in two trials (RRs 0.3, 95% CI 0.2–0.7; and 0.5, 95% CI 0.2–0.9).[37,38] **Recurrence rates:** Recurrences were more frequent on podophyllin (reported in 60%–65% vs. 19%–29% after surgery).[37,38]

Harms: Pain, erythema, irritation, and tenderness were reported in 3% to 17% of participants treated with podophyllin in eight of these trials.[17,18,20,28,33,34,37,38] Skin burns (1%–3%[37,38]), bleeding (4%[37]), and erosion or ulcerations (1%[18]–11%[33]) were also reported. Fecal incontinence (4%[37]) and preputial tightening (1%[17]) were reported rarely.

Comment: Safety during pregnancy is unknown. Podophyllin may contain mutagenic flavonoid compounds, quercetin, and kaempherol.[21]

OPTION BI- AND TRICHLOROACETIC ACID

We found inadequate evidence to evaluate the efficacy of bi- and trichloroacetic acid.

Benefits: We found no systematic review and no placebo-controlled RCTs. We reviewed two RCTs comparing trichloroacetic acid versus cryotherapy in 192 participants. These found no significant difference between treatments (RRs of wart clearance with trichloroacetic acid vs. cryotherapy: 1.1, 95% CI 0.8–1.5; and 0.9, 95% CI 0.8–1.1).[29,30] We also reviewed one RCT in 73 people comparing trichloracetic acid plus podophyllin versus podophyllin alone.[36] Participants were followed for 3 months. There was no significant difference in wart clearance between the two groups.

Harms: Insufficient data are available for comment on possible harms.

Comment: Small numbers of participants and inadequate study designs make it nearly impossible to evaluate effectiveness. In pregnant women, only case series are available: 31 of 32 pregnant women showed wart clearance and 2 of 31 showed recurrence.[40] We cannot evaluate adverse effects of trichloroacetic acid in pregnancy from these data.

OPTION TOPICAL INTERFERON

We found evidence from RCTs to be limited and conflicting.

Benefits: We found no systematic review. **Versus placebo:** We reviewed two placebo-controlled RCTs in 163 men and women. Complete wart clearance 4 weeks after treatment was reported in 6% and 90% of participants on interferon compared with 3% and 20% on placebo.[11,41] One third of participants in the first study had cleared their warts by 16 weeks after treatment.[41] Recurrence could not be evaluated from these data. **Versus podofilox:** One RCT also compared topical interferon versus podofilox.[11] Interferon was slightly more effective than podofilox approximately 4 weeks after treatment (RR compared with podofilox: 1.5, 95% CI 1.0–2.1).[11]

Harms: Local burning and itching (39%) was reported in one study,[41] and fever, headache, and itching were reported in 18% of interferon-treated patients in the other.[11]

Comment: Differences in the RCTs' findings may be attributable to the preparations used; one preparation was incorporated into a methyl cellulose aqueous base,[41] and the other was instilled into a cream base.[11]

OPTION INTRALESIONAL INJECTION OF INTERFERON

RCTs have found that intralesional injection of interferon is more effective than placebo.

Benefits: We found no systematic review. We reviewed seven placebo-controlled trials,[42–49] two of which treatment was randomized to lesions rather than patients,[45,47] and one RCT comparing interferon plus podophyllin versus podophyllin alone[34] in a total of 1000 men and women. Doses and follow-up intervals varied. Complete wart clearance was reported in 17% to 63% of participants on intralesional interferon within 8 to 20 weeks of treatment. **Versus placebo:** In studies using 1 MU/mL, intralesional interferon was between 2 (95% CI 0.8–4.6)[46] and 3.5 (95% CI 1.4–8.8)[43] times more likely to achieve complete wart clearance than placebo. **Added to podophyllin:** Although one RCT found that podophyllin and intralesional interferon together were more effective than podophyllin alone 3 weeks after treatment (RR 2.0 95% CI 1.1–3.6), no difference was observed at 11 weeks (RR 2.3 95% CI 0.9–5.8).[34]

Harms: Flu-like symptoms (dizziness, fever, malaise, myalgia, nausea and vomiting, headache, and pain) were reported in 0% to 100% of participants. Seven of the eight studies reported local irritation and one reported hypopigmentation among the treated individuals. Several studies reported a fall in white blood cell counts,[34,42–44,46–49] thrombocytopenia (1%),[42] and raised serum aspartate transaminase concentrations (6%)[34] in patients on interferon.

Comment: None.

OPTION SYSTEMIC INTERFERON

RCTs have found that systemic interferon is no more effective than placebo and is associated with a range of adverse effects.

Benefits: We found no systematic review. We reviewed 15 RCTs in 1943 men and women: six placebo-controlled trials, two trials that compared systemic interferon versus podophyllin or diathermocoagulation, and seven trials that evaluated its use with one or more adjunct therapies.[26,27,50–62] Fourteen of the trials reported wart clearance within 3 months of treatment in 17% to 67% of participants. However, in four trials that compared systemic interferon with placebo, we found no significant difference in rates of wart clearance.[51–56] One study found that patients taking systemic interferon showed greater wart clearance than placebo-treated patients that was statistically significant at 8 weeks of follow-up, but no difference was detected 12 months after treatment.[55] Recurrence rates varied from 9% to 69%.[26,52,53]

Harms: Flu-like symptoms were reported at variable frequencies; headache, fatigue and malaise, myalgia, nausea and vomiting, fever, chills, and dizziness were reported in 0.5% to 100% of participants on interferon.[26,27,50–58,60,61,63,64] Anaphylactic reaction was noted in 2% of participants in one RCT,[58] leukopenia in 6% to 28% in eight RCTs,[53,60,61,] thrombocytopenia in 3% to 4% in two RCTs,[53,61] and raised liver enzymes were noted in as few as 3% in two RCTs.[53,63]

Bronchospasm and depression were rarely reported (in 1 of 97 participants for each symptom in one trial).[26]

Comment: None.

OPTION TOPICAL 5-FLUOROURACIL

Topical 5-fluorouracil has not yet been evaluated adequately in the treatment of external genital warts.

Benefits: We found no systematic review or RCTs. We reviewed data from three case series in 224 men and women treated with 1% and 5% cream and solution preparations in various doses.[65–67] Wart clearance was reported in 10% to 50% of participants within 3 months of treatment. Only one study reported recurrence rates based on data from only 20 of its 49 participants; recurrences were noted in 10.[66]

Harms: One study of 1% solution reported minor local and urinary meatus erosions in 48% and 5% of participants, vulvar irritation (10%), burning (10%), and dysuria (4%).[67]

Comment: 5-fluorouracil has teratogenic and mutagenic properties. Safety in pregnancy is not known. Exposure to 5-fluorouracil during pregnancy has been reported rarely, with no untoward outcomes.[68,69]

QUESTION What are the effects of surgical treatments?

OPTION ELECTROSURGERY

Limited evidence from RCTs suggests that electrosurgery is more effective than interferon. It has not been compared directly with no treatment.

Benefits: We found no systematic review. **Clearance:** We reviewed three RCTs comparing electrosurgery versus interferon, cryotherapy, or podophyllin resin in 482 men and women.[28,31,58] We found no RCTs versus no or sham treatment. Complete wart clearance was reported in 61% to 94% of participants 3 to 6 weeks after treatment. Electrosurgery was more effective than intramuscular or subcutaneous interferon (RRs 3.3, 95% CI 1.8–5.9; RR 6.9, 95% CI 2.8–17.1).[58] Although one RCT found that electrosurgery was more effective than podophyllin resin 4 weeks after treatment, this difference disappeared after 3 months (RR after 4 weeks: 2.3, 95% CI 1.7–3.0, and after 3 months 1.4, 95% CI 0.9–2.1).[28] Two studies found that electrosurgery was slightly more effective than cryotherapy within 3 to 4 weeks of treatment (RRs 1.2, 95% CI 1.1–1.3 and RR 1.4, 95% CI 1.0–2.0).[28,31] However, when followed for a longer period, no difference between electrosurgery and cryotherapy was observed at 3 months (RRs 1.0, 95% CI 0.8–1.2).[28] **Recurrence rates:** One trial reported recurrences in 22% of participants on electrosurgery versus 21% on cryotherapy and 44% on podophyllin resin.[28]

Harms: Pain and local irritation have been reported in 17% of treated participants.[28]

Comment: No study compared electrosurgery versus no treatment.

OPTION SURGICAL EXCISION

Evidence from RCTs suggests that surgical (scissor) excision is as effective as laser surgery and more effective than podophyllin. It has not been compared directly with no treatment.

Benefits: We found no systematic review. **Clearance:** We reviewed three RCTs comparing surgical excision versus carbon dioxide laser[70] or podophyllin.[37,38] We found no RCTs versus no treatment. Within 1 year of treatment, complete wart clearance was reported in 35% to 72% of participants treated with surgical excision. Surgery was more effective than podophyllin (RRs for wart clearance with podophyllin vs. surgery: 0.3, 95% CI 0.2–0.7; and 0.5, 95% CI 0.2–0.9).[37,38] There was no significant difference in rates of wart clearance between conventional and laser surgery (RR with laser compared with conventional surgery 1.2, 95% CI 0.6–2.4). **Recurrence rates:** Recurrences occurred in 19% to 29% of excision treated participants versus 60% to 65% of their podophyllin-treated comparison groups.[37,38] When time to recurrence was measured, the rates for conventional and laser therapies were not significantly different.[70]

Harms: All surgically treated participants experienced pain, whereas scar formation (9%)[70] and bleeding (37%)[37] were infrequently reported.

Comment: No study compared surgical/scissor excision with no treatment.

OPTION LASER SURGERY

Limited evidence from one RCT suggests no difference in wart clearance or recurrence rates between laser and conventional surgery. Laser surgery has not been compared directly with no treatment.

Benefits: We found no systematic review and no RCT versus no or sham treatment. We reviewed three RCTs in 285 men and women that evaluated laser surgery plus interferon versus laser alone[60–62] and 1 RCT in 50 people that compared laser surgery versus conventional surgical excision.[70] **Clearance:** Complete wart clearance was reported in 23% to 52% of participants within 36 months of laser surgery. This did not differ significantly from clearance after conventional surgery (RR of clearance with laser compared with conventional surgery: 1.2, 95% CI 0.6–2.4).[70] **Recurrence rates:** Recurrences were reported in 60% to 77% of participants given laser surgery.[60,62,70] Again, when time to recurrence was measured, the rates for conventional and laser therapies were not significantly different.[70]

Harms: Local scar formation was reported in 28% of participants after laser surgery versus 9% after conventional surgery. This difference was not significant ($p > 0.2$).[70] Postoperative pain was reported equally in both groups.

Comment: No studies compared laser surgery versus no treatment. Laser surgery has been evaluated in two case series, including 47 pregnant women.[40,71] These reported premature rupture of membranes in 2/32 participants, prolonged rupture of membranes in 1/32, the need for postoperative suprapubic catheterization in 7/32, pyelonephritis in 1/32, prolonged healing time in 1/52, and rectal perforation with secondary abscess in 1/52.

QUESTION **Does treatment of external genital warts prevent transmission?**

We do not know whether treatment truly decreases the infectivity of clinically diagnosed external genital warts. Controlled studies to examine the secondary attack rate for treated and untreated patients have not been conducted.

QUESTION **Do condoms prevent transmission of external genital warts?**

In the context of external genital warts, the preventive effects of condoms have not been evaluated adequately.

Benefits: We found no RCTs or nonrandomized cohort studies evaluating whether condoms or other barrier contraceptive methods prevent HPV infection.

Harms: None reported.

Comment: Penetrative intercourse may not be required for transmission of HPV infection, and it is unclear whether sexual contact with infected and uninfected perigenital tissues is sufficient to cause external genital warts.

REFERENCES

1. US Department of Health and Human Services, Public Health Service. Division of STD Prevention. *Sexually Transmitted Disease Surveillance*. Atlanta: Centers for Disease Control and Prevention, 1996.
2. Koutsky LA, Galloway DA, Holmes KK. Epidemiology of genital human papillomavirus infection. *Epidemiolog Rev* 1988;10:122–163.
3. Gissmann L, zur Hausen H. Partial characterization of viral DNA from human genital warts (condylomata acuminata). *Int J Cancer* 1980;25:605–609.
4. Gissmann L, Boshart M, Durst M, Ikenberg H, Wagner D, zur Hausen H. Presence of human papillomavirus in genital tumors. *J Invest Dermatol* 1984;83(suppl 1):26s–28s.
5. IARC Working Group on Evaluation of Carcinogenic Risks to Humans. *IARC monographs on the evaluation of carcinogenic risks to humans: human papillomaviruses*. Lyon, France: World Health Organization, International Agency for Research on Cancer, 1995.
6. Bonnez W, Kashima HK, Leventhal B, et al. Antibody response to human papillomavirus (HPV) type 11 in children with juvenile-onset recurrent respiratory papillomatosis (RRP). *Virology* 1992;188:384–387.
7. Hallden C, Majmudar B. The relationship between juvenile laryngeal papillomatosis and maternal condylomata acuminata. *J Reprod Med* 1986;31:804–807.
8. Beutner KR, Conant MA, Friedman-Kien AE, et al. Patient-applied podofilox for treatment of genital warts. *Lancet* 1989;i:831–834.
9. Greenberg MD, Rutledge LH, Reid R, Berman NR, Precop SL, Elswick RK, Jr. A double-blind, randomized trial of 0.5% podofilox and placebo for the treatment of genital warts in women. *Obstet Gynecol* 1991;77:735–739.
10. Kirby P, Dunne A, King D, Corey L. Double-blind randomized clinical trial of self-administered podofilox solution versus vehicle in the treatment of genital warts. *Am J Med* 1990;88:465–469.
11. Syed TA, Khayyami M, Kriz D, et al. Management of genital warts in women with human leukocyte interferon-alpha vs podophyllotoxin in cream: a placebo-controlled, double-blind, comparative study. *J Mol Med* 1995;73:255–258.
12. Tyring S, Edwards L, Cherry LK, et al. Safety and efficacy of 0.5% podofilox gel in the treatment of anogenital warts. *Arch Dermatol* 1998;134: 33–38.
13. Von Krogh G, Hellberg D. Self-treatment using a 0.5% podophyllotoxin cream of external genital condylomata acuminata in women. A placebo-controlled, double-blind study. *Sex Transm Dis* 1992;19:170–174.
14. Von Krogh G, Szpak E, Andersson M, Bergelin I. Self-treatment using 0.25%–0.50% podophyllotoxin-ethanol solutions against penile condylomata acuminata: a placebo-controlled comparative study. *Genitourin Med* 1994;70:105–109.
15. Syed TA, Lundin S, Ahmad SA. Topical 0.3% and 0.5% podophyllotoxin cream for self-treatment of condylomata acuminata in women: a placebo-controlled, double-blind study. *Dermatology* 1994;189:142–145.
16. Bonnez W, Elswick RK, Jr, Bailey-Farchione A, et al. Efficacy and safety of 0.5% podofilox solution in the treatment and suppression of anogenital

warts. *Am J Med* 1994;96:420–425.
17. Edwards A, Atma-Ram A, Thin RN. Podophyllotoxin 0.5% v podophyllin 20% to treat penile warts. *Genitourin Med* 1988;64:263–265.
18. Hellberg D, Svarrer T, Nilsson S, Valentin J. Self-treatment of female external genital warts with 0.5% podophyllotoxin cream (Condyline) vs weekly applications of 20% podophyllin solution. *Int J STD AIDS* 1995;6:257–261.
19. Kinghorn GR, McMillan A, Mulcahy F, Drake S, Lacey C, Bingham JS. An open, comparative, study of the efficacy of 0.5% podophyllotoxin lotion and 25% podophyllotoxin solution in the treatment of condylomata acuminata in males and females. *Int J STD AIDS* 1993;4:194–199.
20. Lassus A, Haukka K, Forsstrom S. Podophyllotoxin for treatment of genital warts in males: a comparison with conventional podophyllin therapy. *Eur J Sex Transm Dis* 1984;2:31–33.
21. Petersen CS, Weismann K. Quercetin and kaempherol: an argument against the use of podophyllin? *Genitourin Med* 1995;71:92–93.
22. Von Krogh G. Topical self-treatment of penile warts with 0.5% podophyllotoxin in ethanol for four or five days. *Sex Transm Dis* 1987;14:135–140.
23. Von Krogh G. Penile condylomata acuminata: an experimental model for evaluation of topical self-treatment with 0.5–1.0% ethanolic preparations of podophyllotoxin for three days. *Sex Transm Dis* 1981;8:179–186.
24. Edwards L, Ferenczy A, Eron L, et al. Self-administered topical 5% imiquimod cream for external anogenital warts. *Arch Dermatol* 1998;134: 25–30.
25. Beutner KR, Spruance SL, Hougham AJ, Fox TL, Owens ML, Douglas JM, Jr. Treatment of genital warts with an immune-response modifier (imiquimod). *J Am Acad Dermatol* 1998;38(2 pt 1):230–239.
26. Eron LJ, Alder MB, O'Rourke JM, Rittweger K, DePamphilis J, Pizzuti DJ. Recurrence of condylomata acuminata following cryotherapy is not prevented by systemically administered interferon. *Genitourin Med* 1993;69:91–93.
27. Handley JM, Horner T, Maw RD, Lawther H, Dinsmore WW. Subcutaneous interferon alpha 2a combined with cryotherapy vs cryotherapy alone in the treatment of primary anogenital warts: a randomised observer blind placebo controlled study. *Genitourin Med* 1991;67:297–302.
28. Stone KM, Becker TM, Hadgu A, Kraus SJ. Treatment of external genital warts: a randomised clinical trial comparing podophyllin, cryotherapy, and electrodesiccation. *Genitourin Med* 1990;66:16–19.
29. Abdullah AN, Walzman M, Wade A. Treatment of external genital warts comparing cryotherapy (liquid nitrogen) and trichloroacetic acid. *Sex Transm Dis* 1993;20:344–345.
30. Godley MJ, Bradbeer CS, Gellan M, Thin RN. Cryotherapy compared with trichloroacetic acid in treating genital warts. *Genitourin Med* 1987;63: 390–392.
31. Simmons PD, Langlet F, Thin RN. Cryotherapy versus electrocautery in the treatment of genital warts. *Br J Venereal Dis* 1981;57:273–274.
32. Bergman A, Bhatia NN, Broen EM. Cryotherapy for treatment of genital condylomata during pregnancy. *J Reprod Med* 1984;29:432–435.
33. Condylomata International Collaborative Study Group. A comparison of interferon alfa-2a and podophyllin in the treatment of primary condylomata acuminata. *Genitourin Med* 1991;67: 394–399.
34. Douglas JM Jr, Eron LJ, Judson FN, et al. A randomized trial of combination therapy with intralesional interferon alpha 2b and podophyllin versus podophyllin alone for the therapy of anogenital warts. *J Infect Dis* 1990;162:52–59.
35. Potkul RK, Lancaster WD, Kurman RJ, Lewandowski G, Weck PK, Delgado G. Vulvar condylomas and squamous vestibular micropapilloma. Differences in appearance and response to treatment. *J Reprod Med* 1990;35: 1019–1022.
36. Gabriel G, Thin RN. Treatment of anogenital warts. Comparison of trichloracetic acid and podophyllin versus podophyllin alone. *Br J Venereal Dis* 1983;59:124–126.
37. Jensen SL. Comparison of podophyllin application with simple surgical excision in clearance and recurrence of perianal condylomata acuminata. *Lancet* 1985;ii:1146–1148.
38. Khawaja HT. Podophyllin versus scissor excision in the treatment of perianal condylomata acuminata: a prospective study [see comments]. *Br J Surg* 1989;76:1067–1068.
39. Simmons PD. Podophyllin 10% and 25% in the treatment of ano-genital warts: a comparative double-blind study. *Br J Venereal Dis* 1981; 57:208–209.
40. Schwartz DB, Greenberg MD, Daoud Y, Reid R. Genital condylomas in pregnancy: use of trichloroacetic acid and laser therapy. *Am J Obstet Gynecol* 1988;158(6 pt 1):1407–1416.
41. Keay S, Teng N, Eisenberg M, Story B, Sellers PW, Merigan TC. Topical interferon for treating condyloma acuminata in women. *J Infect Dis* 1988;158:934–939.
42. Eron LJ, Judson F, Tucker S, et al. Interferon therapy for condylomata acuminata. *N Engl J Med* 1986;315:1059–1064.
43. Friedman-Kien AE, Eron LJ, Conant M, et al. Natural interferon alfa for treatment of condylomata acuminata. *JAMA* 1988;259:533–538.
44. Friedman-Kien A. Management of condylomata acuminata with Alferon N injection, interferon alfa-n3 (human leukocyte derived). *Am J Obstet Gynecol* 1995;172(4 pt 2):1359–1368.
45. Monsonego J, Cessot G, Ince SE, Galazka AR, Abdul-Ahad AK. Randomised double-blind trial of recombinant interferon-beta for condyloma acuminatum. *Genitourin Med* 1996;72:111–114.
46. Reichman RC, Oakes D, Bonnez W, et al. Treatment of condyloma acuminatum with three different interferons administered intralesionally: a double-blind, placebo-controlled trial. *Ann Intern Med* 1988;108:675–679.
47. Scott GM, Csonka GW. Effect of injections of small doses of human fibroblast interferon into genital warts: a pilot study. *Br J Venereal Dis* 1979;55:442–445.
48. Vance JC, Bart BJ, Hansen RC, et al. Intralesional recombinant alpha-2 interferon for the treatment of patients with condyloma acuminatum or verruca plantaris. *Arch Dermatol* 1986;122:272–277.
49. Welander CE, Homesley HD, Smiles KA, Peets EA. Intralesional interferon alfa-2b for the treatment of genital warts. *Am J Obstet Gynecol* 1990;162:348–354.
50. Armstrong DK, Maw RD, Dinsmore WW, et al. A randomised, double-blind, parallel group study to compare subcutaneous interferon alpha-2a plus podophyllin with placebo plus podophyllin in the treatment of primary condylomata acuminata. *Genitourin Med* 1994;70:389–393.
51. Armstrong DK, Maw RD, Dinsmore WW, et al. Combined therapy trial with interferon alpha-2a and ablative therapy in the treatment of anogenital warts. *Genitourin Med* 1996;72:103–107.
52. Condylomata International Collaborative Study Group. Recurrent condylomata acuminata treat-

ed with recombinant interferon alfa-2a: a multicenter double-blind placebo-controlled clinical trial. *JAMA* 1991;265:2684–2687.
53. Condylomata International Collaborative Study Group. Recurrent condylomata acuminata treated with recombinant interferon alpha-2a: a multicenter double-blind placebo-controlled clinical trial. *Acta Derm Venereol* 1993;73:223–226.
54. Gall SA, Constantine L, Koukol D. Therapy of persistent human papillomavirus disease with two different interferon species. *Am J Obstet Gynecol* 1991;164(1 pt 1):130–134.
55. Olmos L, Vilata J, Rodriguez Pichardo A, Lloret A, Ojeda A, Calderon MD. Double-blind, randomized clinical trial on the effect of interferon-beta in the treatment of condylomata acuminata. *Int J STD AIDS* 1994;5:182–185.
56. Reichman RC, Oakes D, Bonnez W, et al. Treatment of condyloma acuminatum with three different interferon-alpha preparations administered parenterally: a double-blind, placebo-controlled trial. *J Infect Dis* 1990;162:1270–1276.
57. Condylomata International Collaborative Study Group. A comparison of interferon alfa-2a and podophyllin in the treatment of primary condylomata acuminata. *Genitourin Med* 1991;67: 394–399.
58. Benedetti Panici P, Scambia G, Baiocchi G, Perrone L, Pintus C, Mancuso S. Randomized clinical trial comparing systemic interferon with diathermocoagulation in primary multiple and widespread anogenital condyloma. *Obstet Gynecol* 1989;74(3 pt 1):393–397.
59. Bonnez W, Oakes D, Bailey-Farchione A, et al. A randomized, double-blind, placebo-controlled trial of systemically administered interferon-alpha, -beta, or -gamma in combination with cryotherapy for the treatment of condyloma acuminatum. *J Infect Dis* 1995;171:1081–1089.
60. Condylomata International Collaborative Study Group. Randomized placebo-controlled double-blind combined therapy with laser surgery and systemic interferon-alpha 2a in the treatment of anogenital condylomata acuminatum. *J Infect Dis* 1993;167:824–829.
61. Petersen C, Bjerring P, Larsen J, et al. Systemic interferon alpha-2b increases the cure rate in laser treated patients with multiple persistent genital warts: a placebo-controlled study. *Genitourin Med* 1991;67:99–102.
62. Reid R, Greenberg MD, Pizzuti DJ, Omoto KH, Rutledge LH, Soo W. Superficial laser vulvectomy. V. Surgical debulking is enhanced by adjuvant systemic interferon. *Am J Obstet Gynecol* 1992;166:815–820.
63. Kirby PK, Kiviat N, Beckman A, Wells D, Sherwin S, Corey L. Tolerance and efficacy of recombinant human interferon gamma in the treatment of refractory genital warts. *Am J Med* 1988;85:183–188.
64. Reichman RC, Micha JP, Weck PK, et al. Interferon alpha-n1 (Wellferon) for refractory genital warts: efficacy and tolerance of low dose systemic therapy. *Antiviral Res* 1988;10(1-3):41–57.
65. Haye KR. Treatment of condyloma acuminata with 5 per cent. 5-fluorouracil (5-FU) cream [Letter]. *Br J Venereal Dis* 1974;50:466.
66. Krebs H. Treatment of extensive vulvar condylomata acuminata with topical 5-fluorouracil. *South Med J* 1990;83:761–764.
67. Von Krogh G. The beneficial effect of 1% 5-fluorouracil in 70% ethanol on therapeutically refractory condylomas in the preputial cavity. *Sex Transm Dis* 1978;5:137–140.
68. Dreicer R, Love RR. High total dose 5-fluorouracil treatment during pregnancy. *Wis Med J* 1991; 90:582–583.
69. Van Le L, Pizzuti DJ, Greenberg M, Reid R. Accidental use of low-dose 5-fluorouracil in pregnancy. *J Reprod Med* 1991;36:872–874.
70. Duus BR, Philipsen T, Christensen JD, Lundvall F, Sondergaard J. Refractory condylomata acuminata: a controlled clinical trial of carbon dioxide laser versus conventional surgical treatment. *Genitourin Med* 1985;61:59–61.
71. Kryger-Baggesen N, Falck Larsen J, Hjortkjaer Pedersen P. CO_2 laser treatment of condylomata acuminata. *Acta Obstet Gynecol Scand* 1984;63:341–343.

DJ Wiley, PhD
Assistant professor in residence
School of Nursing, Primary Care
University of California, Los Angeles
Los Angeles, California
USA

Karl R Beutner, MD, PhD
Department of Dermatology
University of California, San Francisco
San Francisco, California
USA

Competing interests: DJW has been a consultant to 3M Pharmaceuticals. KRB has been a consultant, investigator, speaker for and has organized educational events for 3M Pharmaceuticals and Watson Pharmaceuticals.

Genital herpes

Anna Wald, MD

QUESTIONS

INTERVENTIONS

Key Messages

- Randomized controlled trials (RCTs) have found that 1) oral antiviral treatment reduces the duration of symptoms, lesions, and viral shedding in first and recurrent episodes of genital herpes; and that 2) daily treatment reduces the rate of recurrence.
- RCTs have found no significant difference in effectiveness or adverse effects between acyclovir, valacyclovir, and famciclovir.
- Interventions to prevent sexual transmission have not yet been assessed adequately in RCTs.
- The highest risk of mother to baby transmission is in women newly infected with genital herpes in late pregnancy. Interventions aimed at preventing infection in late pregnancy (e.g., serologic screening and counseling) have not been evaluated.
- The effect of abdominal delivery on mother to baby transmission has not been evaluated. The procedure carries the risk of excess maternal morbidity and mortality.
- Limited evidence from RCTs suggests that antiviral treatment may reduce the number of pregnant women with genital lesions at term. Because women with genital lesions at term are usually offered abdominal deliveries, antiviral treatment may reduce the rate of abdominal delivery.

DEFINITION Genital herpes is an infection with herpes simplex virus (HSV) type 1 or 2 (HSV-1 or HSV-2), causing ulceration in the genital area. HSV infections can be defined on the basis of virologic and serologic findings. Types of infection include: first-episode primary infections—HSV in a person without prior HSV-1 or HSV-2 antibodies; first-episode nonprimary infections—HSV-2 in a person with prior HSV-1 antibodies; and first recognized recurrence—HSV-2 (or HSV-1) in a person with prior HSV-2 (or HSV-1) antibodies. Recurrent genital herpes is caused by reactivation of latent HSV.

PREVALENCE Genital herpes infections are among the most common sexually transmitted diseases. Seroprevalence studies show that 22% of adults in the USA have HSV-2 infection;[1] a UK study showed that 23% of adults attending sexual medicine clinics and 7.6% of blood donors in London had antibodies to HSV-2.[2]

ETIOLOGY Both HSV-1 and HSV-2 can cause a first episode of genital infection, but HSV-2 is more likely to cause recurrent disease.[3] Most people with HSV-2 infection are not aware that they have genital herpes because their symptoms are mild. However, these people serve as a source of new infections to sexual partners and newborns.[4,5]

PROGNOSIS The sequelae of HSV infection include neonatal HSV, opportunistic infections in immunocompromised people, recurrent genital ulceration, and psychosocial morbidity. HSV-2 infection is associated with an increased risk of HIV transmission and acquisition. The most common neurologic complications are aseptic meningitis (reported in ~25% of women during primary infection) and urinary retention. The risk of neonatal infection is high (41%, 95% CI 26–56) in babies born to women who acquire infection near the time of labor[6,7] and low (<3%) in women with established infection, even in those who suffer recurrence at term. Approximately 15% of neonatal infections result from postnatal transmission from oral lesions.

AIMS To reduce the morbidity of the first episode, to reduce the risk of recurrent disease after a first episode, and to prevent further transmission.

OUTCOMES Severity and duration of symptoms; healing time; duration of viral shedding; rates of recurrence; psychosocial morbidity; rates of transmission; adverse effects of treatment.

METHODS We searched MEDLINE from 1992 to 1998 using the terms herpes simplex virus, valacyclovir, famciclovir, cidofovir, trifluridine, and neonatal herpes. Preliminary results of clinical trials published in the abstracts of the Interscience Conference on Antimicrobial Agents and Chemotherapy and International Society for STD Research were also included. Experts in the field and makers of antiviral drugs were contacted to identify completed studies that were undergoing peer review but have not yet been published.

QUESTION What are the effects of antiviral treatment in people with a first episode of genital herpes?

RCTs have found that oral antiviral treatment decreases the duration of lesions, symptoms, and viral shedding and prevents neurologic complications in patients with first-episode genital herpes. It is more convenient than intravenous and more effective than topical treatment. Limited data provide no evidence that oral antiviral treatment reduces the rate of recurrence compared with placebo. RCTs have found no significant difference between acyclovir, valacyclovir, and famciclovir.

Benefits: We found no systematic review. **Immediate effects:** We found several RCTs (> 350 men and women) of oral acyclovir for the treatment of first episode genital herpes. Compared with placebo, acyclovir 200 mg five times a day decreased the duration of viral shedding (2 vs. 10 days), pain (5 vs. 7 days), time to healing of lesions (8 vs. 14 days), and prevented formation of new lesions. Neurologic complications (aseptic meningitis and urinary retention) also were reduced. Numbers were small so no firm estimates of effectiveness were available.[8–12] **Different regimens:** In an international trial of 643 healthy adults with first-episode genital herpes, valacyclovir 1000 mg twice daily was compared with acyclovir 200 mg five times a day for 10 days.[13] No significant differences were noted between the two medications in any clinical or virologic variables. Another RCT evaluated three different doses of famciclovir (125 mg, 250 mg, or 500 mg tid) versus acyclovir 200 mg five times a day in 951 adults with first-episode genital herpes.[14] No significant differences were found. **Recurrence rates:** A meta-analysis of two placebo-controlled RCTs in 61 participants showed no significant difference in time to recurrence or frequency of recurrence between those given acyclovir and those given placebo.[15]

Harms: Adverse effects (mostly headache and nausea) were rare and occurred with similar frequency on acyclovir, valacyclovir, famciclovir, and placebo.

Comment: Intravenous and topical acyclovir also have been studied. Oral acyclovir is more convenient than intravenous and more effective than topical preparations.[16]

QUESTION What interventions reduce the impact of recurrence?

OPTION ANTIVIRAL TREATMENT AT THE START OF RECURRENCE

RCTs have found that oral antiviral treatment taken at the start of a recurrence reduces the duration of lesions, symptoms, and viral shedding in patients with recurrent genital herpes.

Benefits: We found no systematic review. Several RCTs in more than 650 healthy adults with recurrent genital herpes were identified in a nonsystematic review published in 1990.[17] These evaluated 5 days of oral acyclovir 200 mg five times a day or 800 mg twice a day, initiated at the first sign of recurrence. Compared with placebo, treatment decreased viral shedding (1 vs. 2 days) and duration of lesions (5 vs. 6 days). An

RCT in 987 people with recurrent genital herpes compared patient initiated valacyclovir 500 mg or 1000 mg twice daily for 5 days versus placebo. Valacyclovir decreased the episode duration (4 vs. 6 days), viral shedding (2 vs. 4 days), and increased the rate of aborted recurrences (31% vs. 21%).[18] An RCT of famciclovir (125–500 mg bid) versus placebo in 467 people with recurrent genital herpes found a significant reduction in the duration of lesions (5 vs. 4 days) and viral shedding (3 vs. 2 days).[19] Differences were significant for all doses of famciclovir ($p < 0.01$). Two RCTs in 1939 patients found no significant difference between valacyclovir and acyclovir.[20,21]

Harms: Adverse effects (mostly headache and nausea) were rare and occurred with similar frequency on acyclovir, valacyclovir, famciclovir, and placebo.

Comment: The benefit was greater if the patient initiated treatment at the first symptom or sign of a recurrence.[22] People with recurrent herpes can learn to recognize recurrences early and should have an adequate supply of medication at home.

OPTION DAILY MAINTENANCE ANTIVIRAL TREATMENT

RCTs have found that daily maintenance treatment with oral antiviral agents reduces the frequency of recurrences and viral shedding in patients with genital herpes. Daily treatment also may improve psychosocial function.

Benefits: We found no systematic review. **Recurrence rates:** Several RCTs were identified in a nonsystematic review published in 1990.[17] These compared daily treatment with varying doses of acyclovir versus placebo for prevention of recurrences in people with genital herpes. Most participants had a history of frequent recurrences (six or more per year). Daily acyclovir reduced the recurrence rate by 74% to 93%, and recurrences were shorter than those that occur without treatment (3.5 vs. 5 days).[17] Of 210 adults who completed 5 years of continuous treatment with acyclovir 400 mg twice daily, 53% to 70% were free of recurrence each year.[23] The first year of this study was a double-blind placebo-controlled RCT in 1146 adults. Those on acyclovir had significantly fewer recurrences during the first year (1.7 vs. 12.5, $p < 0.0001$). Two RCTs evaluated daily valacyclovir.[24,25] In a 1-year study of 1479 adults, 40% to 50% of persons who received valacyclovir 500 mg or 1000 mg once daily, valacyclovir 250 mg twice daily, or acyclovir 400 mg twice daily were recurrence free compared with 5% of persons who received placebo. Two RCTs evaluated daily famciclovir for up to 1 year in adults with frequently recurring genital herpes.[26,27] In a 1-year study of 455 adults treated with varying doses of famciclovir, the median time to first recurrence was 11 months for famciclovir 250 mg twice daily and 1.5 months for placebo recipients. **Viral shedding:** One RCT has evaluated the effect of daily maintenance treatment on viral shedding in women with recently acquired genital HSV-2 infection. Participants obtained swabs for viral cultures daily for 70 days while receiving acyclovir 400 mg twice daily or placebo.[28] Viral shedding was reduced by 95% on days with reported lesions and by 94% on days without lesions. **Psychosocial morbidity:** We found no RCTs that assessed this outcome. The effect of daily acyclovir on psychosocial morbidity has been assessed in a prospective observational study of 102 men and women with frequently recurring genital herpes.[29] Patients were asked questions assessing mental health and psychosocial function. The levels of anxiety and depression fell from 63% to 26% in 80% of patients who completed 3 months of acyclovir treatment.

Harms: Daily treatment with acyclovir, famciclovir, and valacyclovir was well tolerated. Patients on acyclovir have been followed for up to 7 years, and on famciclovir and valacyclovir for up to 1 year. Nausea and headache were infrequent, and patients rarely discontinued treatment because of adverse effects. Whether daily maintenance treatment increases high-risk sexual behavior has not been studied. There is no evidence that daily treatment with acyclovir results in emergence of acyclovir-resistant HSV during or after cessation of treatment in healthy adults.[30]

Comment: Although continuous treatment is safe, discussion of cessation of treatment is reasonable on an annual basis, because some patients experience less frequent recurrences with time or experience less distress during the recurrences. Several effective dosages have been studied: most patients prefer once- or twice-daily regimens. Patients with frequent recurrences may benefit from twice-daily treatment.

OPTION PSYCHOTHERAPY

The effects of psychotherapy on the rate of genital herpes recurrences has not yet been studied adequately.

Benefits: We found one systematic review published in 1993, which identified six studies of psychotherapeutic interventions in 69 participants (4 studies had < 10 participants).[31] Interventions varied from hypnotherapy and progressive muscle relaxation to cognitive therapy and multidimensional psychosocial intervention. In the largest study, 31 patients with four or more recurrences per year were randomly assigned to psychosocial intervention, social support, or waiting list. Subjects receiving psychosocial intervention had significantly lower recurrence rates (6 per year) compared with the pretreatment frequency (11 per year), and to the other groups (11 per year).

Harms: No adverse effects were noted.

Comment: Small numbers of patients, inadequate controls, and subjective and retrospective assessment of recurrence frequency at baseline limit the usefulness of these studies. Controlled studies that include prospective clinical evaluation of disease activity are needed.

QUESTION What interventions prevent transmission of HSV?

OPTION CONDOMS, ANTIVIRAL TREATMENT, AND IMMUNIZATION

The effectiveness of these interventions in preventing HSV transmission has not been studied adequately.

Benefits: **Condoms:** We found no RCTs. In a prospective cohort study of 144 couples in the United States discordant for HSV-2 infection, use of condoms or diaphragms was associated with lower rate of HSV-2 acquisition, 5.7% vs. 13.6% ($p=0.2$).[32] **Antiviral treatment:** No RCTs have looked at rates of transmission. However, RCTs have shown that daily antiviral treatment decreases the frequency of clinical and subclinical viral shedding (see above). There is no direct evidence that treatment reduces HSV transmission in serologically discordant couples. **Immunization:** No effective vaccines are currently available.

Harms: As for individual interventions.

Comment: Controlled studies of condoms for prevention of HSV-2 transmission are unlikely to be done. Because HSV reactivates over a wide genital area, condoms may offer less protection for genital herpes than for STDs characterized by urethral or cervical discharge.

OPTION ABDOMINAL DELIVERY

The effect of abdominal delivery on the risk of neonatal herpes is uncertain. The procedure carries the risk of excess maternal morbidity and mortality.

Benefits: No RCTs have assessed the benefit of abdominal deliveries. In the Netherlands, women with recurrent genital herpes at delivery have been allowed vaginal birth since 1987. This policy has not resulted in an increase of neonatal herpes: 26 cases from 1981 to 1986 and 19 cases from 1987 to 1991.[7]

Harms: Abdominal delivery is associated with significant maternal morbidity and mortality. The number of maternal deaths caused to prevent one neonatal death from HSV has been estimated as 0.57.[33] The estimated cost of the excess abdominal deliveries is $2.5 million US per case of neonatal HSV averted.

Comment: Countries vary in their approach to obstetric management of women with recurrent genital herpes at delivery. Abdominal deliveries are done in the USA and the UK in women with genital lesions at term, with attendant maternal and financial costs. The risk of neonatal infection is high (41%, 95% CI 26–56) in babies born to women who acquire infection near the time of labor[6,7] and low (<3%) in women with established infection, even in those who suffer recurrence at term. Most women who acquire infection towards the end of pregnancy are undiagnosed and most cases of neonatal HSV infection are acquired from women without a history of genital herpes. The available evidence suggests that prevention of neonatal HSV should focus on preventing infection in late pregnancy.

OPTION ANTIVIRAL TREATMENT DURING PREGNANCY

We found limited evidence from a systematic review of RCTs that acyclovir reduces the rate of abdominal deliveries in women with first or recurrent episodes of genital HSV during pregnancy. The risk of rare adverse events has not been studied adequately.

Benefits: We found one systematic review published in 1998. This identified three studies, including two RCTs, of daily acyclovir versus placebo near term in 210 pregnant women with genital herpes.[7] Dose and duration of acyclovir and populations enrolled differed in each study. Abdominal delivery was performed in women with genital lesions at labor. All three studies found lower rates of abdominal delivery in women treated with acyclovir: 8% vs. 34% ($p=0.02$), 13% vs. 33% ($p=0.03$), and 13% vs. 25% ($p=0.2$).

Harms: No adverse effects for women or newborns were reported.

Comment: The number of women was small, and rare events (e.g., an increase in asymptomatic viral shedding or acyclovir-related obstructive uropathy in the newborns) would be difficult to detect.

OPTION **SEROLOGIC SCREENING AND COUNSELING DURING PREGNANCY**

Neither serologic screening with type-specific assays to identify women at risk for HSV acquisition in late pregnancy nor counseling to avoid genital-genital and oral-genital contact in late pregnancy has been evaluated.

REFERENCES

1. Fleming DT, McQuillan GM, Johnson RE, et al. Herpes simplex virus type 2 in the United States, 1976 to 1994. *N Engl J Med* 1997;337:1105–1111.
2. Cowan FM, Johnson AM, Ashley R, Corey L, Mindel A. Antibody to herpes simplex virus type 2 as serological marker of sexual lifestyle in populations. *BMJ* 1994;309:1325–1329.
3. Benedetti J, Corey L, Ashley R. Recurrence rates in genital herpes after symptomatic first-episode infection. *Ann Intern Med* 1994;121:847–854.
4. Mertz GJ, Schmidt O, Jourden JL, et al. Frequency of acquisition of first-episode genital infection with herpes simplex virus from symptomatic and asymptomatic source contacts. *Sex Transm Dis* 1985;12:33–39.
5. Whitley RJ, Kimberlin DW, Roizman B. Herpes simplex viruses. *Clin Infect Dis* 1998;26:541–553; quiz 554–555.
6. Brown ZA, Selke SA, Zeh J, et al. Acquisition of herpes simplex virus during pregnancy. *N Engl J Med* 1997;337:509–515.
7. Smith J, Cowan FM, Munday P. The management of herpes simplex virus infection in pregnancy. *Br J Obstet Gynaecol* 1998;105:255–260.
8. Nilsen AE, Aasen T, Halsos AM, et al. Efficacy of oral aciclovir in treatment of initial and recurrent genital herpes. *Lancet* 1982;ii:571–573.
9. Corey L, Fife K, Benedetti JK, et al. Intravenous aciclovir for the treatment of primary genital herpes. *Ann Int Med* 1983;98:914–921.
10. Mertz G, Critchlow C, Benedetti J, et al. Double-blind placebo-controlled trial of oral aciclovir in the first episode genital herpes simplex virus infection. *JAMA* 1984;252:1147–1151.
11. Mindel A, Adler MW, Sutherland S, Fiddian AP. Intravenous aciclovir treatment for primary genital herpes. *Lancet* 1982;i:697–700.
12. Bryson YJ, Dillon M, Lovett M, et al. Treatment of first episodes of genital herpes simplex virus infections with oral aciclovir: a randomized double-blind controlled trial in normal subjects. *N Engl J Med* 1983;308:916–921.
13. Fife KH, Barbarash RA, Rudolph T, Degregorio B, Roth R. Valaciclovir versus aciclovir in the treatment of first-episode genital herpes infection: results of an international, multicenter, double-blind randomized clinical trial. *Sex Transm Dis* 1997;24:481–486.
14. Loveless M, Harris W, Sacks S. Treatment of first episode genital herpes with famciclovir. *Programs and abstracts of the 35th Interscience Conference on Antimicrobial Agents and Chemotherapy.* San Francisco, California, 1995.
15. Corey L, Mindel A, Fife KH, Sutherland S, Benedetti J, Adler MW. Risk of recurrence after treatment of first episode genital herpes with intravenous aciclovir. *Sex Trans Dis* 1985;12:215–218.
16. Corey L, Benedetti J, Critchlow C, et al. Treatment of primary first-episode genital herpes simplex virus infections with aciclovir: results of topical, intravenous and oral therapy. *J Antimicrob Chemother* 1983;12(suppl B):79–88.
17. Stone K, Whittington W. Treatment of genital herpes. *Rev Infect Dis* 1990;12(suppl 6):S610–619.
18. Spruance S, Trying S, Degregorio B, et al. A large-scale, placebo-controlled, dose-ranging trial of peroral valaciclovir for episodic treatment of recurrent herpes genitalis. *Arch Intern Med* 1996;156:1729–1735.
19. Sacks SL, Aoki FY, Diaz-Mitoma F, Sellors J, Shafran SD. Patient-initiated, twice-daily oral famciclovir for early recurrent genital herpes: a randomized, double-blind multicenter trial. *JAMA* 1996;276:44–49.
20. Bodsworth NJ, Crooks RJ, Borelli S, et al. Valaciclovir versus aciclovir in patient-initiated treatment of recurrent genital herpes: a randomized, double-blind clinical trial. *Genitourin Med* 1997;73:110–116.
21. Tyring SK, Douglas JM, Spruance SL, et al. A randomized, placebo-controlled comparison of oral valaciclovir and aciclovir in immunocompetent patients with recurrent genital herpes infections. *Arch Dermatol* 1998;134:185–191.
22. Reichman RC, Badger GJ, Mertz GJ, et al. Treatment of recurrent genital herpes simplex

infections with oral aciclovir: a controlled trial. *JAMA* 1984;251:2103–2107.
23. Goldberg L, Kaufman R, Kurtz T, et al. Continuous five-year treatment of patients with frequently recurring genital herpes simplex virus infection with aciclovir. *J Med Virol* 1993;S1:45–50.
24. Patel R, Bodsworth NJ, Wooley P, et al. Valaciclovir for the suppression of recurrent genital HSV infection: a placebo controlled study of once-daily therapy. *Genitourin Med* 1997;73: 105–109.
25. Reitano M, Tyring S, Lang W, et al. Valaciclovir for the suppression of recurrent genital herpes simplex virus infection: a large-scale dose range finding study. *J Infect Dis* 1998;178:603–610.
26. Mertz GJ, Loveless MO, Levin MJ, et al. Oral famciclovir for suppression of recurrent genital herpes simplex virus infection in women: a multicenter, double-blind, placebo-controlled trial. *Arch Intern Med* 1997;157:343–349.
27. Diaz-Mitoma F, Sibbald RG, Shafran SD, et al. Oral famciclovir for the suppression of recurrent genital herpes: a randomized controlled trial. *JAMA* 1998;280:887–892.
28. Wald A, Zeh J, Barnum G, Davis LG, Corey L. Suppression of subclinical shedding of herpes simplex virus type 2 with aciclovir. *Ann Intern Med* 1996;124:8–15.
29. Carney O, Ross E, Ikkos G, Mindel A. The effect of suppressive oral aciclovir on the psychological morbidity associated with recurrent genital herpes. *Genitourin Med* 1993;69:457–459.
30. Fife KH, Crumpacker CS, Mertz GJ, et al. Recurrence and resistance patterns of herpes simplex virus following cessation of ≥6 years of chronic suppression with aciclovir. *J Infect Dis* 1994;169:1338–1341.
31. Longo D, Koehn K. Psychosocial factors and recurrent genital herpes: a review of prediction and psychiatric treatment studies. *Int J Psychiatry Med* 1993;23:99–117.
32. Mertz GJ, Benedetti J, Ashley R, Selke SA, Corey L. Risk factors for the sexual transmission of genital herpes. *Ann Intern Med* 1992;116: 197–202.
33. Randolph A, Washington A, Prober C. Cesarean delivery for women presenting with genital herpes lesions. *JAMA* 1993;270:77–82.

Anna Wald, MD
Assistant Professor of Medicine and Epidemiology
University of Washington
Seattle
Washington
USA

Competing interests: The author has received a fee from Glaxo Wellcome, SmithKline Beecham, Wyeth Lederly Vaccines and Pediatrics, Bristol Myers Squibb for research support, and from Glaxo Wellcome and SmithKline Beecham for consultancy.

Scabies

Godfrey Walker, MD, and Paul Johnstone, BM, MRCGP, MFPHM

QUESTIONS

INTERVENTIONS

To be covered in future issues of *Clinical Evidence*
Cleanliness and washing with soap
Frequent washing of clothing and bed linen
Treating crusted scabies

Key Messages

- One systematic review of mainly small randomized controlled trials (RCTs) has found that topical permethrin and gamma-benzene hexachloride are effective in the treatment of scabies. However, gamma-benzene hexachloride has been linked to rare reports of serious adverse effects.
- We found limited evidence suggesting that crotamiton is safe but less effective than permethrin.
- We found that other topical agents (malathion, benzyl benzoate, and sulfur compounds) have not been evaluated adequately in RCTs. Malathion achieves cure rates of over 80%, but its safety has not been assessed adequately.
- We found that oral ivermectin had not been assessed adequately in RCTs. It is known to be safe in adults from its use in onchocerciasis, but its safety in children and elderly people is uncertain.

DEFINITION Scabies is an infestation of the skin by the mite *Sarcoptes scabiei*.[1] Typical sites of infestation are skin folds and flexor surfaces. In adults, the most common sites are between the fingers and on the wrists, although infection may manifest in elderly people as a diffuse truncal eruption. In infants and children, the face, scalp, palms, and soles often are affected as well.

INCIDENCE/ PREVALENCE Scabies is a common public health problem with an estimated prevalence of 300 million cases worldwide, mostly affecting people in developing countries where prevalence can exceed 50%.[2] In industrialized countries it is more common among institutionalized communities. Case studies suggest that epidemic cycles occur every 7 to 15 years and that these partly reflect the population's immune status.

ETIOLOGY Scabies is particularly common where there is social disruption, overcrowding with close body contact, and limited access to water.[3] Young children, immobilized elderly people, people with HIV/AIDS, and other medically and immunologically compromised individuals are predisposed to infestation and have particularly high mite counts.[4]

PROGNOSIS Scabies is not life threatening, but the severe persistent itch and secondary infections may be debilitating. Occasionally, crusted scabies develops, which is resistant to routine treatment and can be a source of continued reinfestation and can spread to others.

AIMS To eliminate the scabies mites and ova from the skin, to cure pruritus (itching), to prevent reinfestation, and to prevent spread to other people.

OUTCOMES Number of visible burrows and papular and vesicular eruptions; presence of mites, ova, or fecal pellets in skin scrapings under a magnifying lens or microscope; pruritus. Outcomes should be assessed 28 to 30 days after start of treatment, which is the time it takes for lesions to heal and for any eggs and mites to reach maturity if treatment fails.

METHODS In performing a systematic review,[5] we used standardized strategies to search for all RCTs of pharmaceutical preparations, both topical and oral, using the Cochrane Controlled Trials Register, MEDLINE, EMBASE, and direct approaches to pharmaceutical companies and experts in the field. The most recent searches were completed in June 1998. We included all the relevant RCTs that we found. Of the four trials between different topical treatments that we identified, three used gamma-benzene hexachloride (lindane) as one of the comparators. Gamma-benzene hexachloride has been off the market in the UK since 1995 because of concern about possible adverse effects.

QUESTION What are the effects of topical treatment?

OPTION **PERMETHRIN**

One systematic review of RCTs has found that permethrin is effective in the treatment of scabies with a parasitic cure rate of approximately 90%. Two small trials found that it was more effective than crotamiton. A larger trial found no difference compared with gamma-benzene hexachloride, although nontrial data suggest that permethrin is less toxic.

Benefits: We found one systematic review,[5] which identified four RCTs.[6–9] **Permethrin versus crotamiton:** Two RCTs,[6,7] in a total of 194 adults and children, compared topical permethrin versus crotamiton. Permethrin was associated with significantly higher clinical cure rates in both studies (OR for failed clinical cure with permethrin vs. crotamiton 0.21, 95% CI 0.10–0.47).[5] Only one of the RCTs evaluated parasitic cure rates.[7] This also showed permethrin to be significantly more effective (OR for failed parasitic cure with permethrin compared with crotamiton 0.21, 95% CI 0.08–0.53). The same RCT found no significant difference in patients' reports of pruritus (OR for itch persistence with permethrin compared with crotamiton 0.38, 95% CI 0.12–1.19).[7] **Permethrin versus gamma-benzene hexachloride:** The systematic review [5] found three RCTs[6,8,9] comparing permethrin versus gamma-benzene hexachloride, all using the same drug concentrations. Two trials in a total of 152 adults and children found permethrin to be more effective than gamma-benzene hexachloride.[6,9] The largest trial, with 467 participants,[8] showed no significant difference between the two treatments (OR for failed parasitic cure with permethrin compared with gamma-benzene hexachloride 0.68, 95% CI 0.34–1.36). This trial also reported patient assessed outcome, with a result in favor of permethrin (OR for itch persistence with permethrin compared with gamma-benzene hexachloride 0.65, 95% CI 0.44–0.96).

Harms: One RCT[8] reported five serious adverse effects, two in the permethrin group (rash and possible diarrhea) and three in the gamma-benzene hexachloride group (pruritic rash, papules, and diarrhea). Other evidence suggests an excellent safety record for permethrin. During 1990 to 1995, six adverse events were reported per 100,000 units distributed in the USA (one central nervous system adverse effect reported per 500,000 units distributed).[10] Resistance to permethrin seems to be rare.[10]

Comment: None

OPTION **GAMMA-BENZENE HEXACHLORIDE**

One systematic review of RCTs has found that gamma-benzene hexachloride is effective in the treatment of scabies, but its use is constrained by rare reports of convulsions and other adverse effects.

Benefits: We found one systematic review,[5] which identified three RCTs comparing gamma-benzene hexachloride versus other topical agents.[6,8,9] **Gamma-benzene hexachloride versus crotamiton:** One RCT[6] in 100 adults and children found no significant difference in clinical cure rates (OR for failed clinical cure with crotamiton vs. gamma-benzene hexachloride 0.41, 95% CI 0.15–1.10). **Gamma-benzene hexachloride versus permethrin:** Three RCTs[6,8,9] all used the same drug concentrations. Two small trials found permethrin to be more effective than gamma-benzene hexachloride.[6,9] A larger trial of 467 adults and children[8] found no significant difference between the two treatments (OR for failed parasitic cure with permethrin vs. gamma-benzene hexachloride 0.68, 95% CI 0.34–1.36). This trial also reported patient-assessed outcome, with a result in favor of permethrin (OR for itch persistence with permethrin vs. gamma-benzene hexachloride 0.65, 95% CI 0.44–0.96).

Harms: The RCTs reported no severe adverse effects. Case reports and data from the WHO collaborating center for international drug monitoring include reports of rare severe adverse effects (e.g., convulsions and aplastic anemia), particularly when gamma-benzene hexachloride is applied in people with extensive skin disease and in children.[11,12] Summary reports from 47 countries suggest that gamma-benzene hexachloride is more toxic than other preparations. The number of convulsions reported in patients on benzyl benzoate were four, crotamiton one, gamma-benzene hexachloride 38, malathion two, and permethrin six; deaths reported on benzyl benzoate were zero, crotamiton one, gamma-benzene hexachloride one, malathion zero, and permethrin five.[13] Resistance has been reported in many countries.[14]

Comment: The evidence linking gamma-benzene hexachloride with convulsions is suggestive but not conclusive. Summary reports are influenced by the extent to which the products are used for the treatment of scabies and other infestations and the quality of reporting. The safety data need summarizing from trials and observational studies, particularly with regard to additional risks in pregnant women and infants.

OPTION CROTAMITON

One systematic review of RCTs found crotamiton to be as effective as gamma-benzene hexachloride but less effective than permethrin. Severe adverse effects are rare.

Benefits: We found one systematic review,[5] which identified two RCTs comparing crotamiton versus other topical agents.[6,7] **Crotamiton versus permethrin:** Two RCTs[6,7] in 194 adults and children found permethrin to be significantly more effective in clinical cure (OR for failed clinical cure with permethrin vs. crotamiton 0.21, 95% CI 0.10–0.47; OR for failed parasitic cure 0.21, 95% CI 0.08–0.53). One RCT[7] found no significant difference in patients' reports about relief of pruritus (OR for itch persistence with permethrin vs. crotamiton 0.38, 95% CI 0.12–1.19). **Crotamiton versus gamma-benzene hexachloride:** One RCT[6] found no significant difference in clinical cure rates (OR for failed clinical cure with permethrin vs. crotamiton 0.41, 95% CI 0.15–1.10).

Harms: We found limited data on the toxicity of crotamiton, but reports of serious adverse effects are rare.[1] There have been a few reports of resistance.[11]

Comment: None.

OPTION **MALATHION**

Malathion has not been evaluated in RCTs. Cure rates of over 80% have been reported in case series.

Benefits: We found one systematic review,[5] which identified no RCTs comparing malathion against any other drug treatments. Several case series suggest that malathion is effective in curing infestation with scabies, with a cure rate at 4 weeks of over 80%.[15,16]

Harms: No important adverse events have been reported.

Comment: The safety data need summarizing from trials and observational studies, particularly with regard to additional risks in pregnant women and infants.

OPTION **BENZYL BENZOATE**

Benzyl benzoate has not been adequately evaluated in RCTs. Cure rates of about 50% have been reported in nonrandomized trials.

Benefits: We found one systematic review,[5] which identified only one small RCT in 44 adults and children comparing benzyl benzoate versus oral ivermectin.[17] This found no difference between the two treatments (*see* later under systemic drug treatments). Nonrandomized trials suggest benzyl benzoate is of variable effectiveness (as low as 50%).[18–20]

Harms: Approximately one quarter of people treated with benzyl benzoate report a transient increase in pruritus and dermatitis.[17]

Comment: The low cure rate may be related to the concentration of the preparation and the resistance of the mite to benzyl benzoate.

OPTION **SULFUR**

Sulfur has not been evaluated adequately in RCTs.

Benefits: We found no RCTs comparing sulfur with other preparations.

Harms: The use of sulfur is associated with increased local irritation in approximately one quarter of cases.[11]

Comment: None

QUESTION **What are the effects of systemic treatment?**

OPTION **IVERMECTIN**

Ivermectin has not been evaluated adequately in RCTs. Experience of its use in onchocerciasis suggests that it is safe in adults, but no such experience exists for children, and there have been reports of increased risk of death in elderly people.

Benefits: We found one systematic review,[5] which identified only two RCTs. **Ivermectin versus placebo:** One RCT[21] in 55 young adults and children aged over 5 years found oral ivermectin significantly more effective than placebo at 7 days (clinical cure rates 23/29 on ivermectin and 4/26 on placebo, OR for clinical failure at 7 days with ivermectin versus placebo 0.08, 95% CI 0.03–0.23). **Ivermectin versus benzyl benzoate:** One RCT[17] in 44 adults and children found no significant difference in clinical cure rates in 16/23 on ivermectin and 10/21 on benzyl benzoate at 30 days.

Harms: The two RCTs were too small to give adequate data on harms.[17,21] Ivermectin has been used widely in adults with onchocerciasis, and even with repeated doses, serious adverse effects have been rare.[22,23] There are no good data on its safety in children. An increased risk of death has been reported among elderly people with scabies in a long-term care facility.[24] Whether this was caused by ivermectin or interactions with other scabicides (including gamma-benzene hexachloride and permethrin) or with other treatments (e.g., psychoactive drugs) was not clear. Others reported no such complications in its use in elderly patients.[25]

Comment: Systemic treatment may be more acceptable and cost effective in deprived communities in developing countries where privacy to apply topical treatments may be limited. More systematic information is required on adverse effects, particularly among children and elderly people. Case series suggest that ivermectin is effective when included in the treatment of hyperkeratotic crusted scabies (also known as Norwegian scabies)[26,27] and in people with concomitant HIV disease.[4]

REFERENCES

1. Meinking TL, Taplin D. Infestations. In: Schachner LA, Hansen RC, eds. *Pediatric dermatology*. New York: Churchill Livingston, 1995: 1347–1392.
2. Stein DH. Scabies and pediculosis. *Curr Opin Pediatr* 1991;3:660–666.
3. Green M. Epidemiology of scabies. *Epidemiol Rev* 1989;11:126–150.
4. Meinking TL, Taplin D, Hermida JL, Pardo R, Kerdel FA. The treatment of scabies with ivermectin. *N Engl J Med* 1995;333:26–30.
5. Walker GJA, Johnstone PW. Treating scabies. In: The Cochrane Library, Issue 1, 1988. Oxford: Update Software. 1997. Primary sources MEDLINE 1966 to 1997, EMBASE 1974 to 1997, records of military trials from UK, USA, Russia and specialist register of the Cochrane Diseases Group.
6. Amer M, El-Gharib I. Permethrin versus crotamiton and lindane in the treatment of scabies. *Int J Dermatol* 1992;31:357–358.
7. Taplin D, Meinking TL, Chen JA, Sanchez R. Comparison of crotamiton 10% cream (Eurax) and permethrin 5% cream (Elimite) for the treatment of scabies in children. *Pediatr Dermatol* 1990;7:67–73.
8. Schultz MW, Gomez M, Hansen RC, et al. Comparative study of 5% permethrin cream and 1% lindane lotion for the treatment of scabies. *Arch Dermatol* 1990;126:167–170.
9. Taplin D, Meinking TL, Porcelain SL, Castiliero PM, Chen JA. Permethrin 5% dermal cream: a new treatment for scabies. *J Am Acad Dermatol* 1986;15:995–1001.
10. Meinking TL, Taplin D. Safety of permethrin vs lindane for the treatment of scabies. *Arch Dermatol* 1996;132:959–962.
11. Elgart ML. A risk-benefit assessment of agents used in the treatment of scabies. *Drug Saf* 1996;14:386–393.
12. McLeod WA. Acute lindane poisoning [letter]. *Can Med Assoc J* 1978;118:123,125.
13. Abstracted from WHO Collaborating Centre for International Drug Monitoring, Uppsala, Sweden. Reported adverse reactions to ectoparasiticodes, including scabicides, insecticides and repellants. January 1998. It should be noted "that the information is not homogenous at least with respect to origin or likelihood that the pharmaceutical product caused the adverse reaction and that the information does not represent the opinion of the World Health Organisation".
14. Brown S, Belcher J, Brady W. Treatment of ectoparasitic infections: review of the English-language literature. *Clin Infect Dis* 1995;20(suppl 1):S104–109.
15. Hanna NF, Clay JC, Harris JRW. *Sarcoptes scabiei* infestation treated with malathion liquid. *Br J Venereal Dis* 1978;54:354.
16. Thianprasit M, Schuetzenberger R. Prioderm lotion in the treatment of scabies. *Southeast Asian J Trop Med Public Health* 1984;15: 119–121.
17. Glaziou P, Cartel JL, Alzieu P, Briot C, Moulia-Pelat JP, Martin PMV. Comparison of ivermectin and benzyl benzoate for treatment of scabies. *Trop Med Parasitol* 1993;44:331–332.
18. Burgess I, Robinson RJF, Robinson J, Maunder

JW, Hassan Z. Aqueous malathion 0.5% as a scabicide: clinical trial. *BMJ* 1986;292:1172.
19. Kaur GA, Nadeswary K. Field trials on the management of scabies in Jengka Triangle, Pahang. *Med J Malaysia* 1980;35:14–21.
20. Haustein UF, Hlawa B. Treatment of scabies with permethrin versus lindane and benzyl benzoate. *Acta Derm Venereol (Stockh)* 1989;69:348–351.
21. Macotela-Ruiz E, Pena-Gonzalez G. Tratamiento de la escabiasis con. ivermectina por via oral. *Gac Med Mex* 1993;129:201–205.
22. Pacque M, Munoz B, Greene BM, White AT, Dukuly Z, Taylor HR. Safety of and compliance with community-based ivermectin therapy. *Lancet* 1990;335:1377–1380.
23. De Sole G, Remme J, Awadzi K, et al. Adverse reactions after large-scale treatment of onchocerciasis with ivermectin: combined results from eight community trials. *Bull World Health Organ* 1989;67:707–719.
24. Barkwell R, Shields S. Deaths associated with ivermectin treatment of scabies. *Lancet* 1997; 349:1144–1145.
25. Diazgranados JA, Costa JL. Deaths after ivermectin treatment. *Lancet* 1997;349:1698.
26. Sullivan JR, Watt G, Barker B. Successful use of ivermectin in the treatment of endemic scabies in a nursing home. *Australas J Dermatol* 1997;38:137–140.
27. Aubin F, Humbert P. Ivermectin for crusted (Norwegian) scabies. *N Engl J Med* 1995;332: 612.

Godfrey Walker, MD
WHO Adviser in Reproductive Health
UNFPA Country Support Team for Central and South Asia
Kathmandu
Nepal

Paul Johnstone, BM, MRCGP, MFPHM
Consultant in Public Health Medicine
Berkshire Health Authority
Reading
UK

Competing interests: None declared.

Gonorrhea

John S Moran, MD, MPH

QUESTIONS

INTERVENTIONS

Key Messages

- One systematic review of patients with uncomplicated gonococcal infection found that single-drug regimens using selected fluoroquinolones, selected cephalosporins, or spectinomycin are highly effective and safe. Resistance to penicillins, sulfonamides, and tetracyclines is now widespread.
- We found few data on treatment in pregnant women. Available data show no difference in effectiveness compared with nonpregnant women and, despite concerns about safety, no adverse effects on pregnancy outcome.
- We found no trials evaluating currently accepted treatment of disseminated gonococcal infection, but no treatment failures have been reported.
- Dual treatment for *Neisseria gonorrhoeae* and *Chlamydia trachomatis* is based on theory and expert opinion rather than evidence from clinical trials. The balance between benefits and harms will vary with the prevalence of co-infection in each population.
- The choice of the most appropriate antigonococcal regimen cannot be based on the results of randomized controlled trials (RCTs) alone. Data from other sources, such as studies of antimicrobial susceptibility and adverse drug effect surveillance programs, also must be considered.

DEFINITION Gonorrhea is caused by infection with *N. gonorrhoeae*. In men, uncomplicated urethritis is the commonest manifestation, with dysuria and urethral discharge. Less typically, signs and symptoms are mild and indistinguishable from chlamydial urethritis. In women, the commonest manifestation is cervicitis, which produces symptoms (e.g., vaginal discharge, lower abdominal discomfort, and dyspareunia) in only half of cases. Co-infection with chlamydia is reported in 20% to 40% of patients.[1]

INCIDENCE Between 1975 and 1997, the incidence of reported gonorrhea in the USA fell by 74%. In 1996, the incidence of reported gonococcal infection in the USA was 24/100,000 people,[1] and in England, 44/100,000 people aged 15 to 64 years were treated for gonorrhea at genitourinary medicine clinics.[2] In poor communities, rates may be higher: the estimated incidence in people aged 15 to 59 years living in three inner-London boroughs in 1996 was 138/100,000 women and 292/100,000 men.[3] Rates are highest in younger people. In the USA in 1997, incidence was highest in women aged 15 to 19 years (718/100,000) and men aged 20 to 24 years (532/100,000).[1]

ETIOLOGY Most infections result from penile-vaginal, penile-rectal, or penile-pharyngeal contact. An important minority of infections are transmitted from mother to child during birth. Less common are ocular infections among older children and adults as a result of sexual exposure, poor hygiene, or the medicinal use of urine.

PROGNOSIS In most men, symptoms are severe enough to cause them to seek treatment, but an estimated 1% to 3% of infected men remain asymptomatic. In many women, the lack of readily discernible signs or symptoms of cervicitis means that infections go unrecognized and untreated. An unknown proportion of untreated infections cause local complications, including epididymitis, lymphangitis, periurethral abscess, bartholinitis, and urethral stricture, or spread to cause salpingitis and perihepatitis. Manifestations of disseminated gonococcal infection include petechial or pustular skin lesions, asymmetrical arthralgias, tenosynovitis or septic arthritis, and, rarely, meningitis or endocarditis.

AIMS To relieve symptoms, to avoid complications, and to prevent further transmission.

OUTCOMES Cure rates (percentage of positive cultures 3 to 7 days after treatment).

METHODS *Clinical Evidence* search for systematic reviews using MEDLINE 1966 to May 1998, EMBASE 1988 to May 1998 (key words gonorrhea and *N. gonorrhoeae* infections), plus search of references of key articles and books. Studies were excluded if they defined possible treatment failures as "reinfections," if they did not use end points based on microbiologic cure, or if they were based on drug regimens unlikely to be of general use (e.g., those using antibiotic regimens to which resistance is now widespread or that are expensive or toxic).[4] Uncontrolled trials were included on the grounds that, in the case of antibiotic treatment for gonorrhea, the effects of biases are small compared with the effect of treatment and also that restricting this review to randomized studies would introduce a bias in favor of heavily marketed drugs and against generic drugs.

QUESTION **What are the effects of treatments for uncomplicated infections in men and nonpregnant women?**

One systematic review found that modern antimicrobial agents other than penicillin and tetracycline achieve cure rates of 97% or better. Cure rates are lower (80% or worse) for pharyngeal infection. Most regimens cause few adverse effects. Resistance is now widespread to penicillins, tetracyclines, and sulfonamides.

Benefits: **Uncomplicated urogenital, rectal, and pharyngeal infections:** We found one systematic review published in 1995. This included all interpretable studies published from 1981 to 1993 that used a single-dose regimen based on an antimicrobial other than a β-lactamase–sensitive penicillin or a tetracycline.[5] The data comprised 24,383 evaluable patients or infections, 96.7% of which were cured (based on culture results). When specified, sites of infection included the cervix, urethra, rectum, and pharynx. Comparison of cure rates by site of infection showed that cure rates were over 95% for all sites except the pharynx, for which they were approximately 80%.[6] **Eye infections:** We found no systematic review or RCTs. In the only recent published study of the treatment of gonococcal conjunctivitis, all of the 12 participants responded well to a single 1-g dose of ceftriaxone.[7]

Harms: Single-dose regimens using fluoroquinolones, third-generation and extended-spectrum cephalosporins, or spectinomycin are all safe and generally well tolerated. The most important adverse effects are rare hypersensitivity reactions. Minor adverse effects are most troublesome for the 800-mg cefixime regimen,[8,9] and the 2-g azithromycin regimen[10]; both cause frequent gastrointestinal upset. The ceftriaxone and spectinomycin regimens require intramuscular injection. One large observational cohort study of azithromycin, cefixime, ciprofloxacin, and ofloxacin "in everyday use" found few serious adverse effects, and the investigators concluded that the drugs were acceptably safe antimicrobial agents when used in general medical practice.[11] Quinolones are contraindicated for children aged under 17 years because they cause arthropathy in animals. No evidence of joint toxicity has been observed in clinical use, even with prolonged multiple-dose regimens used for the management of children with cystic fibrosis.[12–16] Resistance is now widespread for all penicillins, sulfonamides, and tetracyclines, but has not been reported widely for fluoroquinolones, third-generation and extended-spectrum cephalosporins, or spectinomycin.

Comment: There is good agreement between antigonococcal activity of antimicrobials *in vitro* and their efficacy in clinical trials. The large number of patients evaluated in a range of settings make the results able to be generalized. Single-dose regimens make adherence more likely.

QUESTION **What are the effects of treatments for uncomplicated infections in pregnant women?**

Limited evidence from one RCT suggests that treatment in pregnancy is safe and effective. Serious adverse effects of antigonococcal treatment in pregnancy outcome have not been reported.

Benefits: We found two RCTs of the treatment of gonococcal infection during pregnancy, only one of which has been published in full. This included 267 pregnant women with positive cultures for gonorrhea. Various antibiotic regimens (amoxicillin and probinecid, spectinomycin, ceftriaxone, and cefixime) were compared. All achieved high eradication rates (89%–97%). There was no evidence of significant differences between regimens: ceftriaxone 250 mg cured 95.2% (95% CI 89.2–98.5) of rectal and urogenital infections and 100% (54.1–100) of pharyngeal infections; spectinomycin 2 g cured 97.0% (95% CI 91.5–99.4) of rectal and urogenital infections and 83.3% (95% CI 35.9–99.6) of pharyngeal infections.[17]

Harms: The RCT reported vomiting after treatment in only one of the 267 women.[17] Little other information on adverse effects was available. Quinolones cause arthropathy in animals, but no adverse effects of quinolones on pregnancy outcome have been reported in humans. A single multicenter, prospective, controlled study of 200 exposed women found no evidence of adverse effects.[18] There is no evidence that the nonquinolone regimens listed above are less safe or less well tolerated by pregnant women than by men or nonpregnant women.

Comment: Pregnant women are expected to respond to gonorrhea treatment as well as nonpregnant women do and are therefore rarely included in clinical trials.

QUESTION **What are the effects of treatments for disseminated gonococcal infection?**

We found no recent trials evaluating treatment for disseminated gonococcal infection. There have been no reports of treatment failure with accepted treatment using injectable cephalosporins and quinolones.

Benefits: We found no systematic review and no studies of the treatment of disseminated gonococcal infection published in the past 10 years. Although no published data prove the efficacy of currently accepted treatment with injectable cephalosporins and quinolones, there have been no reports of treatment failures.

Harms: We found no reports of adverse effects of these drugs in this context.

Comment: None.

QUESTION **What are the effects of dual treatment for *N. gonorrhoeae* and *C. trachomatis*?**

Dual treatment with an antimicrobial effective against *C. trachomatis* is based on theory and expert opinion rather than evidence. The balance between benefits and harms from controlled trials will vary with the prevalence of co-infection in each population.

Benefits: Routine dual treatment has been advocated and implemented for the past 10 years and is believed to have two potential benefits. First, it is believed to have contributed to the decline in the prevalence of genital chlamydia infection. We found no good data to support this belief, and other factors (including widespread screening for asymptomatic chlamydia infection and changes in sexual behavior), which also have impacted on the prevalence of chlamydia, make it hard to attribute secular trends to a single cause. Secondly, routine dual treatment is believed to retard the spread of resistant gonococcal strains. Limited data from case reports support this belief.

Harms: Harms of dual treatment are also more theoretical than observed. Treatment for chlamydia can cause mild gastrointestinal distress, and there is the possibility that using a second drug could stimulate the emergence or spread of resistance in *Neisseria* or other bacteria.

Comment: In the past, chlamydia testing was often unavailable, expensive, time consuming, and not highly sensitive, and dual treatment with a tetracycline such as doxycycline was safe and inexpensive. Chlamydia testing now has become more widely available, more affordable, quicker, and more sensitive, and the prevalence of chlamydia has fallen in some populations. Nevertheless, chlamydia is still found among 20% to 40% of people with gonorrhea in many clinics.[1] Where rates of co-infection are low, clinicians may prefer to test for chlamydia rather than treat presumptively. Presumptive treatment is important in people who may not return for test results.

REFERENCES

1. Division of STD Prevention, Centers for Disease Control and Prevention: *Sexually Transmitted Disease Treatment Guidelines*. Atlanta: US Department of Health and Human Sciences, Public Health Services; 1998.
2. Division of STD prevention. *Sexually transmitted diseases surveillance, 1996.* US Department of Health and Human Services. Atlanta: Centers for Disease Control and Prevention, 1997.
3. CDSC. Sexually transmitted disease quarterly report: gonorrhoea in England and Wales. *Commun Dis Rep Wkly* 1997;7:225–227.
4. Low N, Daker-White G, Barlow D, Pozniak Al. Gonorrhoea in inner London: results of a cross-sectional study. *BMJ* 1997;314:1719–1723.
5. Moran JS, Levine WC. Drugs of choice for the treatment of uncomplicated gonococcal infections. *Clin Infect Dis* 1995; 20(Suppl 1):S47–65.
6. Moran JS. Treating uncomplicated *Neisseria gonorrhoeae* infections: is the anatomic site of infection important? *Sex Transm Dis* 1995;22(1): 39–47.
7. Haimovici R, Roussel TJ. Treatment of gonococcal conjunctivitis with single-dose intramuscular ceftriaxone. *Am J Ophthalmol* 1989;107:511–514.
8. Handsfield HH, McCormack WM, Hook EW III, Douglas JM, Covino JM, Verdon MS, et al. The Gonorrhea Treatment Study Group. A comparison of single-dose cefixime with ceftriaxone as treatment for uncomplicated gonorrhea. *N Engl J Med* 1991;325:1337–1341.
9. Megran DW, LeFebvre K, Willets V, Bowie WR. Single-dose oral cefixime versus amoxicillin plus probenecid for the treatment of uncomplicated gonorrhea in men. *Antimicrob Agents Chemother* 1990;34:355–357.
10. Handsfield HH, Dalu ZA, Martin DH, Douglas JM Jr, McCarty JM, Schlossberg D, Azithromycin Gonorrhea Study Group. Multicenter trial of single-dose azithromycin vs. ceftriaxone in the treatment of uncomplicated gonorrhea. *Sex Transm Dis* 1994;21:107–111.
11. Wilton LV, Pearce GL, Mann RD. A comparison of ciprofloxacin, norfloxacin, ofloxacin, azithromycin and cefixime examined by observational cohort studies. *Br J Clin Pharmacol* 1996;41:277–284.
12. Green SD. Indications and restrictions of fluoroquinolone use in children. *Br J Hosp Med* 1996; 56:420–423.
13. Grenier B. Use of fluoroquinolones in children. An overview. *Adv Antimicr Antineopl Chemother* 1992;11-2:135–140.
14. Schaad UB. Use of quinolones in children and articular risk. *Arch Pediatr* 1996;3:183–184.
15. Hampel B, Hullmann R, Schmidt H. Ciprofloxacin in pediatrics: worldwide clinical experience based on compassionate use. Safety report. *Pediatr Infect Dis J* 1997;16: 127–129; discussion 160–162.
16. Warren RW. Rheumatologic aspects of pediatric cystic fibrosis patients treated with fluoroquinolones. *Pediatr Infect Dis J* 1997;16: 118–122; discussion 123–126.
17. Cavenee MR, Farris JR, Spalding TR, Barnes DL, Castaneda YS, Wendel GD. Treatment of gonorrhea in pregnancy. *Obstet Gynecol* 1993;81: 33–38.
18. Loebstein R, Addis A, Ho E, Andreou R, Sage S, Donnenfeld AE, et al. Pregnancy outcome following gestational exposure to fluoroquinolones: a multicenter prospective controlled study. *Antimicrob Agents Chemother* 1998;42: 1336–1339.

John S Moran, MD, MPH
STD advisor
HIV/AIDS Prevention Project
US Agency for International Development
Jakarta, Indonesia
and Medical Epidemiologist
Centres for Disease Control and Prevention
USA

Competing interests: None declared.

TABLE 1 **Reported resistance of *N. gonorrhoeae* to antimicrobials**

Sulfonamides	Widespread
Penicillins	Widespread
Tetracyclines	Widespread
Third-generation cephalosporins (e.g., ceftriaxone, cefixime)	None reported
Spectinomycin	Rare
Quinolones	Parts of Asia and Australia: widespread US: decreased susceptibility to ciprofloxacin reported in only 0.5% of isolates in 1997, and only five (0.1%) were resistant[2]; no increase since 1995 UK: rare reports of imported fluoroquinolone-resistant *N. gonorrhoeae*

Partner notification

Catherine Mathews, MSc, Nicol Coetzee, MD, Sally Guttmacher, PhD, and Merrick Zwarenstein, MBBch, MSc

QUESTIONS

INTERVENTIONS

See Glossary, p. 396

Key Messages

- We found little evidence on the acceptability of various strategies of partner notification to index patients and partners.
- We found no sound evidence of the effects of partner notification on the relationship between patient and partners and, in particular, on the precipitation of violence, abuse, and abandonment of the patient or partner.
- Thus, in the few studies where there is evidence that a partner notification strategy increases the number of infected partners who are notified or treated, it is not possible to weigh these benefits against harms.
- We found no studies comparing the effects of an intervention across different patient groups, such as patients with different diseases or combinations of diseases or patients from different settings.
- The few randomzied controlled trials (RCTs) that have compared different partner notification strategies found that provider referral is more effective than patient referral in HIV and chlamydia infections and that, in patients with gonorrhea or syphilis, there is no significant difference between provider and contract referral.

DEFINITION Partner notification is a process whereby the sex partners of people with a diagnosis of sexually transmitted infection are informed of their exposure to infection. The main methods are patient referral and contract referral (see Glossary, p. 386)

RATIONALE A large proportion of people infected with sexually transmitted infections will have neither symptoms nor signs of infection. For example, 22% to 68% of men with gonorrhea, who were identified through partner notification, were asymptomatic.[1] Partner notification is one of the two strategies to reach such individuals, the other strategy being screening. Managing infection in people with more than one current sexual partner will have the greatest impact on the spread of sexually transmitted infections.[2]

AIMS To prevent complications of infection in the partner, to prevent transmission to others, to prevent reinfection of the index patient, and to identify social networks of individuals practicing risky sexual behaviors.

OUTCOMES Partners identified; partners notified; partners presenting for care; partners tested positive; partners treated; rates of reinfection in the index patient; incidence of sexually transmitted diseases in the population; harms to patient or partner, such as domestic violence and abuse; ethical outcomes (patient autonomy vs. beneficence).

METHODS *Clinical Evidence* search, July 1998. We included RCTs that compared at least two alternative partner notification strategies and in which randomization was appropriate; patient follow-up was greater than 80%; participants were analyzed in the groups to which they were assigned; and the groups were similar at the start of the trial. The outcome used in this summary was the absolute difference between the ratio of partners identified, notified, presenting for care, testing positive, or treated per index case.

QUESTION **What are the effects of various partner notification strategies in different groups of patients?**

OPTION **IN PEOPLE WITH HIV INFECTION**

For HIV infection, we found moderately strong evidence that provider referral results in more partners being notified than patient referral.

Benefits: A systematic review[3] published in 1994 found only one RCT, and we found no RCTs published since the review. **Provider versus patient referral:** The RCT compared provider versus patient referral. It was conducted at three public health departments in North Carolina in 162 people who had tested positive for HIV.[4] Of those approached, the 46% who agreed to participate in the study were mostly men (69%) and, of these, most were homosexual or bisexual (76%). Provider referral significantly increased the likelihood that partners would be notified; 50% of identified partners were notified in the provider referral group versus 7% in the patient referral group (ARR of non-notification with provider rather than patient referral 0.43, 95% CI 0.34–0.52). Thus, only two index patients would have to be offered provider referral, compared with using patient referral, for one additional partner to be notified (NNT 2, 95% CI 2–3). **Contract referral:** This has not yet been evaluated in people with HIV infection. One group in the USA tried to compare contract referral with provider referral, but contamination between the comparison groups made this impossible. The results were therefore analyzed as a cohort study without comparison groups, in which all patients were assigned to provider referral.[5] The study included 1070 index patients, who reported having had 8633 partners in the past year. Of these partners, 1035 were successfully located of whom 248 had previously tested positive for HIV, 560 were tested by the disease intervention specialist, 69 refused testing, and 158 were located by record search only. Of the 560 partners tested, 122 tested positive. **Rates of disclosure:** A descriptive study[6] of 276 patients attending for initial primary care for HIV infection in the USA found that 40% of the respondents had not disclosed their HIV status to all partners over the preceding 6 months. Those with more than one partner were significantly less likely to disclose to all partners. Only 42% of the nondisclosers reported that they used condoms all the time, which indicates that many partners were at risk of HIV infection. Another descriptive study conducted in the USA[7] showed that, even after repeated individual counseling of index patients with HIV infection and a 6-month opportunity to disclose HIV status, 30% of index patients had not informed any of their past partners and 29% had not informed any of their present partners.

Harms: Reluctance to notify partners suggests expectation of harms from doing so. These and other potential harms are poorly understood.

Comment: The number of partners notified is an intermediate outcome. The number of infections in partners that are prevented or treated has not been evaluated. Thus, the true benefits and harms of HIV partner notification are unknown.

OPTION — IN PEOPLE WITH GONORRHEA AND CHLAMYDIA

Two RCTs have found that, for patients with gonorrhea, contract referral was no better at identifying partners with positive culture than patient referral. For patients with chlamydia, provider referral increases the proportion of partners notified and positive partners detected per index patient compared with patient referral.

Benefits: A systematic review[3] identified two RCTs of patients with gonorrhea and one of patients with nongonococcal urethritis. We found no subsequent studies that met our inclusion criteria. **Gonorrhea:** The two RCTs compared patient and contract referral in 2085 people with gonorrhea (personal communication).[8] A meta-analysis found no significant difference in the proportion of partners with positive gonorrhea culture per index patient (ARR 0.05, 95% CI –0.10 to +0.21). **Chlamydia:** The RCT in patients with nongonococcal urethritis compared patient and provider referral in 678 patients.[9] It found that provider referral significantly increased the proportion of partners assessed per index patient (ARR for nonassessment 0.52, 95% CI 0.44–0.59). In this study, provider referral also resulted in a significant increase in the proportion of partners with positive culture per index patient (ARR 0.06, 95% CI 0.02–0.10). Provider referral was six times as costly per partner with positive culture. Provider referral would have to be offered to two index patients with nongonococcal urethritis for one additional partner to be assessed (NNT 2, 95% CI 1.7–2.3) and to 17 index patients to identify one additional partner with a positive culture (NNT 17, 95% CI 10–50). These findings are likely to underestimate the effectiveness of patient referral, because partners referred by the index patients may have been assessed elsewhere.

Harms: These are poorly understood.

Comment: A cohort study in 265 urban, adolescent girls attending a clinic in Alabama, USA,[10] found that patients with gonorrhea or chlamydia who are given the choice are about as likely to choose provider referral as patient referral. For each partner, index patients chose either provider referral (by telephone or letter) or patient referral (with a contact slip).

OPTION IN PEOPLE WITH SYPHILIS

We found good evidence from one large RCT that provider referral was no more effective than contract referral, when patients receiving the contract referral option were given only two days in which to notify their partners. We found no RCTs evaluating patient referral.

Benefits: We found only one large, recent RCT.[11] This included 1966 patients diagnosed with syphilis in three states of the USA. It compared the proportion of partners per index patient who were located, tested, tested positive, and treated, using three types of referral process: 1) contract referral (index patients were given two days to notify partners themselves, before disease intervention specialists would notify them); 2) provider referral (immediate notification by an intervention specialist); and 3) provider referral with the option of a blood test (immediate notification by an intervention specialist who had the option of performing a blood test if he or she thought that the partner would not seek medical attention despite being notified of exposure). In the three groups: 1.2, 1.1, and 1.1 partners per index patient were located; 0.92, 0.87, and 0.86 were tested; and 0.67, 0.61, and 0.62 were treated. There was no substantial difference in cost.

Harms: These are poorly understood.

Comment: In this trial, the investigators had no way of determining whether the disease intervention specialists began actively seeking partners in the contract referral group before waiting two days. The use of disease intervention specialists is an approach that may not be able to be generalized outside the USA.

QUESTION What can be done to improve the effectiveness of patient referral?

One RCT has found that the addition of telephone reminders and contact cards may improve patient referral compared with counseling alone. Other methods (e.g., educational videos for index patients) have not yet been evaluated using strong study designs.

Benefits: Different methods for improving the effectiveness of patient referral have been investigated in a controlled manner only with gonococcal and chlamydial infections. A systematic review published in 1994[3] identified two published and one unpublished RCT. We found no studies published subsequently that met our inclusion criteria. One published RCT compared the use of counseling plus referral cards and telephone follow-up of the index case versus counseling alone in 65 patients from a university clinic in the USA.[12] The referral card was to be given to the partner or to be used in preparing to speak to the partner. It contained the index patient's diagnosis to facilitate treatment of the partner and a message exhorting the partner to seek treatment. The addition of referral cards and telephone follow-up significantly increased the number of partners presenting for care per partner identified (ARR for failure to present 0.34, 95% CI 0.13–0.56) for 25% less cost per partner traced. A referral card and telephone follow-up would have to be offered to only three index patients for one additional partner to present for care (NNT 3, 95% CI 2–8). The trial also evaluated the addition of a $3 incentive to the referral card. This had no effect (at three times the cost) on the number of partners presenting for care. The other published RCT[9] found that there was no difference between patient referral using nurses (who did not ask for partners' names and gave referral letters) and disease intervention specialists (who took partners' names but no contact details) in terms of the number of partners with positive cultures that were identified (RR 0.001, 95% CI –0.03 to +0.03). The unpublished RCT, which also was conducted in the USA in people with gonococcal and chlamydial infections, investigated the use of information pamphlets compared with a routine counseling interview.[3] Providing index patients with information pamphlets was slightly less effective than the interview, and it significantly reduced the number of partners presenting for care per index patient (ARR for failing to present –0.05, 95% CI –0.07 to –0.03). The two strategies were equally effective (and costly) in terms of the number of partners identified with a positive culture per index patient.

Harms: None reported.

Comment: The use of contact cards seems to be an intervention easily generalized to other settings, whereas the use of telephone reminders may not be possible in developing countries.

QUESTION **Does the type of health professional make any difference to the effectiveness of provider or contract referral?**

We found no strong evidence about the effects of employing different categories of health professional for provider or contract referral.

Benefits: Two observational studies have been conducted—one comparing the effects of trained interviewers versus routine providers[13]; the other comparing the effect of physicians, midwives, and nurses versus social workers.[14] However, we are unable to ascertain the selection biases present in these studies. One RCT[9] included in a systematic review[3] found no difference between disease intervention specialists (who asked for partners' names) and sexually transmitted disease nurses (who did not ask for names) in terms of the number of partners with positive cultures that were identified.

Harms: These are poorly understood.

Comment: The RCT combined two interventions: different health professionals and asking for partners' names, either of which may have affected the results.[9]

QUESTION **Do patient preferences make a difference?**

We found no RCTs comparing outcomes achieved by giving patients a choice between patient and provider or contract referral versus assigning them to one or the other group.

GLOSSARY

Provider referral, when third parties (usually health service personnel) notify partners identified by index patients.
Patient referral, when health service personnel encourage index patients to inform their partners directly of their possible exposure to sexually transmitted infections.
Contract referral (also referred to as conditional referral), when index patients are encouraged to inform their partners, with the understanding that health service personnel will notify those partners who do not visit the health service within a contracted time period.

REFERENCES

1. Holmes KK, Mardh PA, Sparling PF, Weisner PJ, eds. *Sexually transmitted diseases*, 2nd ed. New York: McGraw-Hill, 1990:1083.
2. Fenton KA, Peterman TA. HIV partner notification: taking a new look. *AIDS* 1997;11:1535–1546.
3. Oxman AD, Scott EA, Sellors JW, et al. Partner notification for sexually transmitted diseases: an overview of the evidence. *Can J Public Health* 1994;85:541–547. Search date not provided. Primary sources MEDLINE, EMBASE, SciSearch, hand searching of five key journals, personal contact with 80 key experts.
4. Landis SE, Schoenbach VI, Weber DJ, et al. Results of a randomized trial of partner notification in cases of HIV infection in North Carolina. *N Engl J Med* 1992;326:101–106.
5. Toomey KE, Peterman TA, Dicker LW, Zaidi AA, Wroten JE, Carolina J. Human immunodeficiency virus partner notification. *Sex Transm Dis* 1998; 25:310–316.
6. Stein MD, Freedberg KA, Sullivan LM, et al. Sexual ethics: disclosure of HIV-positive status to partners. *Arch Intern Med* 1998;158: 253–257.
7. Perry SW, Card CAL, Moffatt M, Ashman T, Fishman B, Jacobsberg LB. Self-disclosure of HIV infection to sexual partners after repeated counseling. *AIDS Educ Prev* 1994;6:403–411.
8. Potterat JJ, Rothenberg R. The case-finding effectiveness of self-referral system for gonorrhea: a preliminary report. *Am J Public Health* 1977;67: 174–176.
9. Katz BP, Danos CS, Quinn TS, et al. Efficiency and cost-effectiveness of field follow-up for patients with chlamydia trachomatis infection in a sexually transmitted diseases clinic. *Sex Transm Dis* 1988;15:11–16.
10. Oh MK, Boker JR, Genuardi FJ, Cloud GA, Reynolds J, Hodgens JB. Sexual contact tracing outcome in adolescent chlamydial and gonococcal cervicitis cases. *J Adolesc Health* 1996;18: 4–9.
11. Peterman TA, Toomey KE, Dicker LW, Zaidi AA, Wroten JE, Carolina J. Partner notification for syphilis: a randomized, controlled trial of three approaches. *Sex Transm Dis* 1997;24:511–518.
12. Montesinos L, Frisch LE, Greene BF, Hamilton M. An analysis of and intervention in the sexual transmission of disease. *J Appl Behav Anal* 1990;23:275–284.
13. Alary M, Joly JR, Poulin C. Gonorrhea and chlamydial infection: comparison of contact tracing performed by physicians or by a specialized service. *Can J Public Health* 1991;82:132–134.
14. Eitrem R, Erenius M, Meeuwisse A. Contact tracing for genital Chlamydia trachomatis in a Swedish county. *Sex Transm Dis* 1998;25: 433–436.

Catherine Mathews, MSc
Senior Scientist
Health Systems Research Division
Centre for Epidemiological Research
South African Medical Research Council
South Africa

Nicol Coetzee, MD
Senior Lecturer and Consultant
Department of Community Health
University of Cape Town
South Africa

Sally Guttmacher, PhD
Professor
Department of Health Studies
New York University
USA

Merrick Zwarenstein, MBBCh, MSc
Head
Health Systems Research Division
Centre for Epidemiological Research
South African Medical Research Council
South Africa

Competing interests: None declared.

Erectile dysfunction

Michael O'Leary, MD, MPH

QUESTIONS

INTERVENTIONS

*Not adequately evaluated in RCTs

Key Messages

- Yohimbine and sildenafil both have been shown to be effective compared with placebo in randomized controlled trials (RCTs). They have not been compared directly. Indirect comparison of placebo-controlled trials suggest that yohimbine is less effective but safer.
- RCTs have found that prostaglandin E1 (alprostadil) is effective in 30% to 80% of men and more effective when administered by intracavernosal injection than intraurethrally. For both methods, patient adherence in the long term is poor.
- Neither vacuum devices nor penile prostheses have been evaluated adequately in RCTs.

DEFINITION Erectile dysfunction has largely replaced the term "impotence." It is defined as the persistent inability to obtain or maintain sufficient rigidity of the penis to allow satisfactory sexual performance.

INCIDENCE/ PREVALENCE There is little good epidemiologic information, but current normative data suggest that age is the variable most strongly associated with erectile dysfunction and that up to 30 million men in the USA may be affected.[1] Even among men in their 40s, nearly 40% report at least occasional difficulty obtaining or maintaining erection, whereas this approaches 70% in 70-year-olds.

ETIOLOGY It is now believed that approximately 80% of cases of erectile dysfunction have an organic etiology, the rest being psychogenic in origin. Erectile problems fall into three categories: failure to initiate; failure to fill (caused by insufficient arterial inflow into the penis to allow engorgement and tumescence, owing to vascular insufficiency); and failure to store, owing to veno-occlusive dysfunction.

PROGNOSIS In erectile dysfunction of organic etiology, treatment is almost always symptomatic. We found no good data on prognosis in untreated organic erectile dysfunction.

AIMS To restore satisfactory erections with minimal adverse effects.

OUTCOMES Patient and partner self-report of satisfaction; sexual function; adverse effects of treatment.

METHODS MEDLINE was searched to the end of 1998. All systematic reviews and RCTs were reviewed.

QUESTION What are the effects of treatments for erectile dysfunction?

OPTION YOHIMBINE

RCTs have found that yohimbine is effective compared with placebo. Yohimbine has not yet been directly compared with other oral or local treatments. Mild, transient adverse effects are reported in up to a third of men.

Benefits: We found one systematic review published in 1998. This identified seven RCTs (11–100 participants with erectile dysfunction defined variously as organic, psychogenic, and of unknown cause) comparing the α-blocker yohimbine versus placebo.[2] Duration of treatment ranged from 2 to 10 weeks, and outcomes varied from self-reported improvement in sexual function to objective tests of penile rigidity. The RCTs found positive responses in 34% to 73% of men on yohimbine compared with 9% to 28% on placebo (OR for positive response with treatment compared with placebo 3.85, 95% CI 2.22–6.67).

Harms: Adverse events were reported in 10% to 30% of men receiving yohimbine and were generally mild, including agitation, anxiety, headache, mild increase in blood pressure, and gastrointestinal upset.

Comment: The end points in some of these trials were subjective and can be questioned. Yohimbine must be taken three times a day for at least 1 month before potential benefit is realized. Although yohimbine may be only moderately effective, its adverse effect profile is good, which makes it a reasonable option particularly in men with cardiovascular risk factors, although care should be taken about its effects on blood pressure.

OPTION SILDENAFIL

RCTs have found that sildenafil is effective compared with placebo. It has not yet been compared directly with other treatments for erectile dysfunction. Mild, transient adverse effects are reported in up to one fifth of men, and deaths have been reported in men on concomitant treatment with oral nitrates. Long-term safety is unknown.

Benefits: We found no systematic review. The most cited report compared sildenafil versus placebo.[3] It involved two different evaluations in 861 men aged 20 to 87 years with erectile dysfunction of all causes for 3 to 5 years. In the first evaluation, 532 men were randomized to receive either placebo or 25, 50, or 100 mg sildenafil approximately 1 hour before planned sexual activity, but not more than once per day, for 24 weeks. In the second evaluation, 329 different men were randomized to placebo or sildenafil in an escalating dose up to 100 mg for 12 weeks, followed by open-label treatment for a further 32 weeks. Sixty-nine percent of all attempts at sexual intercourse were successful for men taking sildenafil compared with 22% for those on placebo ($p < 0.001$) (CIs were not quoted in the report.) Efficacy increased with increasing dose and did not vary according to the cause of erectile dysfunction.

Harms: Headache, flushing, and dyspepsia were reported in 6% to 18% of men taking sildenafil.[3] Another article reported specifically on adverse effects of sildenafil. It summarized results from a series of double-blind placebo-controlled RCTs in a total of 4274 men aged 19 to 87 years with a broad spectrum of erectile dysfunction for more than 6 months and a mean of 5 years. All participants were treated for up to 6 months, and 2199 received open-label treatment for up to another year.[4] Headache, flushing, and dyspepsia were reported in 7% to 16% of men taking sildenafil compared with 1% to 4% taking placebo. Similar proportions in both groups discontinued treatment (~2.4%). An important contraindication of sildenafil is concomitant treatment with oral nitrates. This combination results in precipitous hypotension. To date, approximately 60 deaths have been reported to the US Food and Drug Administration in men who had been given prescriptions for sildenafil. However, it is not known whether any were attributable directly to the drug. Long-term (>1 year) safety of sildenafil is unknown, but growing clinical experience suggests that it is safe and efficacious when given under appropriate conditions.

Comment: Sildenafil is intended to be taken as required approximately 1 hour before sexual activity, making it likely to be a more convenient option than yohimbine. We found no data on patient satisfaction or adherence.

OPTION INTRAURETHRAL PROSTAGLANDIN E1

RCTs have found that intraurethral administration of prostaglandin E1 (alprostadil) leads to satisfactory erection in approximately 40% of men. Approximately one third of men suffer penile ache, which causes many to discontinue treatment. Intraurethral prostaglandin E1 has not yet been compared directly to either intracavernosal or oral drug treatment.

Benefits: We found no systematic review. One double-blind RCT began by testing the response to intraurethral alprostadil in 1511 men aged 27 to 88 who had erectile dysfunction of organic etiology for at least 3 months. In clinic testing, 66% (996 men) had erections sufficient for intercourse. These men were randomized to intraurethral alprostadil or placebo for use at home.[5] Over 3 months, those given alprostadil were more likely to report having successful sexual intercourse (64.9% vs. 18.6% on placebo, $p<0.001$) and at least one orgasm (63.6% vs. 23.6% on placebo, $p<0.001$). Subsequent RCTs, published only in abstract form, found slightly lower efficacies of 30% to 48% on alprostadil.

Harms: The most common adverse effect was mild to moderate penile ache, occurring in approximately one third of men.[5] This caused many men to discontinue treatment. There have been no reports of priapism, penile fibrosis, or other serious adverse events.

Comment: Intraurethral agents may be considered as second-line treatment, particularly in men who have not benefited from oral treatment.

OPTION INTRACAVERNOSAL PROSTAGLANDIN E1

RCTs have found that intracavernosal injection of prostaglandin E1 (alprostadil) leads to satisfactory erection in approximately 80% of men, but long-term adherence is poor. Intracavernosal prostaglandin E1 has not yet been compared directly with either intraurethral or oral drug treatment.

Benefits: We found no systematic review. The largest study was a multicenter trial in 1128 men aged 20 to 79 years with all causes of erectile dysfunction.[6] Heavy smokers and men with uncontrolled hypertension or diabetes were excluded. Nearly 300 men were randomly assigned to double-blind doses of placebo or 2.5, 5, 10, or 20 μg of alprostadil. Injections were given and outcome was assessed by an investigator or research nurse. None of the 59 men who received placebo had a response. There were significant differences in response between all doses and placebo; there was also a significant dose-response relationship. The remaining 884 men, including 52 who had taken part in the dose-response study, were enrolled in a single-blind dose-escalation study (201 men) and an uncontrolled open-label flexible-dose study to assess efficacy, safety, and feasibility of self-injection at home (683 men). Of the 13,762 injections for which men recorded their response, nearly 90% were followed by satisfactory sexual activity. **Versus vacuum devices:** An RCT with crossover compared intracavernosal self-injections versus vacuum devices in 50 men with erectile dysfunction, 44 of whom completed the study.[7] Outcome was assessed by questionnaire to patients and their partners after 15 uses for each device, and couples were followed for 18 to 24 months.

There was no significant difference in the ability to achieve an erection suitable for intercourse. However, the ability to attain orgasm was significantly better with injection ($p<0.05$). On a scale of 1 to 10, overall satisfaction was significantly better when using injections, both for patients (6.5 vs. 5.4, $p<0.05$) and partners (6.5 vs. 5.1, $p<0.05$). Younger men (<60 years) and those with shorter duration of erectile dysfunction (<12 months) favored injections ($p<0.05$).

Harms: Penile pain was reported by half of the men in the study of efficacy and safety of alprostadil injection, and priapism (prolonged erection for >4 hours) was reported by 1%.[6] There was no significant difference in the frequency of adverse events between vacuum devices and injections.[7]

Comment: Most men can be taught to inject themselves using small-gauge needles. In the RCT comparing injections and vacuum devices,[7] 80% of the 44 couples who completed the study were still using one or other treatment after 18 to 24 months.

OPTION VACUUM DEVICES

Vacuum devices have not been evaluated adequately in RCTs. One small RCT found that they were as effective as intravenous injections.

Benefits: We found no systematic review. **Versus intravenous injections:** *See* comment.

Harms: Insufficient data.

Comment: Vacuum devices may be less popular with patients than injections because only the distal portion of the penis becomes firm,[7] but generally they are presumed to be safe.

OPTION PENILE PROSTHESES

Penile prostheses have not been evaluated formally in RCTs. Usually they are considered only after less-invasive treatments have failed. Anecdotal evidence suggests that they have a high success rate.

Benefits: We found no RCTs. Anecdotal evidence suggests that patient satisfaction is high, but good studies are lacking.

Harms: A recent study found the morbidity of penile prostheses to be 9% (surgical revision 7%, mechanical failure 2.5%). Infection rates were between 2% and 7%.[8]

Comment: None.

REFERENCES

1. Feldman HA, Goldstein I, Hatzichristov DG, Krane RJ, McKinlay JB. Impotence and its medical and psychosocial correlates: results of the Massachusetts male aging study. *J Urol* 1994;151:54–61.
2. Ernst E, Pittler MH. Yohimbine for erectile dysfunction: a systemic review and meta-analysis of randomized clinical trails. *J Urol* 1998;159:433–436.
3. Goldstein I, Lue TF, Padma-Nathan H, Rosen RC, Steers WD, Wicker PA, for the Sildenafil Study Group. Oral sildenafil in the treatment of erectile dysfunction. *N Engl J Med* 1998;338: 1397–1404.
4. Morales A, Gingell C, Collins M, Wicker PA, Osterloh IH. Clinical safety of oral sildenafil cit-

rate (Viagra) in the treatment of erectile dysfunction. *Int J Impot Res* 1998;10:69–74.
5. Padma-Nathan H, Hellstrom WJ, Kaiser FE, et al, for the Medicated Urethral System for Erection (MUSE) Study Group. Treatment of men with erectile dysfunction with transurethral alprostadil. *N Engl J Med* 1997;336:1–7.
6. PGE_1 Study Group. Prospective, multicenter trials of efficacy and safety of intracavernosal alprostadil (prostaglandin E_1) sterile powder in men with erectile dysfunction. *N Engl J Med* 1996;334: 873–877.
7. Soderdahl DW, Thrasher JB, Hansberry KL, et al. Intracavernosal drug induced erection therapy vs external vacuum device in the treatment of erectile dysfunction. *Br J Urol* 1997;79:952–957.
8. Goldstein I, Newman L, Baum N, et al. Safety and efficacy outcome of Mentor Alpha 1 inflatable penile prosthesis implantation for impotence treatment. *J Urol* 1997;157:833–839.

Michael O'Leary, MD, MPH
Associate professor in urological surgery
Harvard Medical School
Boston
Massachusetts
USA

Competing interests: The author has been paid by Pfizer for several lectures.

Chronic prostatitis

Jeffrey A Stern, MD, and Anthony J Schaeffer, MD

QUESTIONS

INTERVENTIONS

Key Messages

In men with chronic bacterial prostatitis

- Antimicrobial drugs have not been evaluated adequately. Retrospective cohort studies report cure rates of 0% to 90% depending on the drug used and the duration of treatment. The limited evidence available suggests that quinolones are more effective than trimethoprim-sulfamethoxazole (TMP-SMZ).
- We found no good evidence that local injection of antimicrobial agents is more effective than oral or parenteral antimicrobial treatment.
- Limited evidence from one randomized controlled trial (RCT) suggests that adding α-blockers to antimicrobial treatment may improve outcome and reduce recurrence.
- Transurethral resection and radical prostatectomy have not yet been evaluated adequately. Very limited evidence from retrospective cohort studies suggests transurethral resection may cure some men with refractory chronic bacterial prostatitis.

In men with chronic abacterial prostatitis

- Limited evidence from one RCT suggests that α-blockers may ameliorate symptoms.
- Thermotherapy, prostatic massage, sitz baths, and biofeedback have not yet been evaluated formally.

DEFINITION *Chronic bacterial prostatitis* is characterized by a positive culture of expressed prostatic secretions. It can be symptomatic (recurrent urinary tract infection, suprapubic, lower back, or perineal pain), asymptomatic, or associated with minimal urgency, frequency, and dysuria. *Chronic abacterial prostatitis* is characterized by pelvic or perineal pain, often associated with urinary urgency, nocturia, weak urinary stream, frequency, dysuria, hesitancy, dribbling after micturition, interrupted flow, and inflammation (white cells) in prostatic secretions. Symptoms also can include suprapubic, scrotal, testicular, penile, or lower back pain or discomfort. In the absence of inflammation in prostatic secretions, these pain symptoms are referred to as prostadynia.

INCIDENCE/ PREVALENCE A community-based study estimated that 9% of men have a diagnosis of chronic prostatitis at any one time.[1] Another study found that, of men with genitourinary symptoms, 8% presenting to urologists and 1% presenting to primary care physicians are diagnosed with chronic prostatitis.[2] Most cases of chronic prostatitis are abacterial. Acute bacterial prostatitis, although easy to diagnose and treat, is rare.

ETIOLOGY Organisms commonly implicated in bacterial prostatitis include *Escherichia coli*, other gram-negative *Enterobacteriaciae*, occasionally *Pseudomonas* species, and rarely gram-positive enterococci. The cause of abacterial prostatitis is unclear, but autoimmunity may be involved.[3]

PROGNOSIS A recent study found that chronic abacterial prostatitis had an impact on quality of life similar to that found with angina, Crohn's disease, or after a myocardial infarction.[4]

AIMS To relieve symptoms and eliminate infection where present, with minimum adverse effects.

OUTCOMES Symptom improvement (symptom scores, bother scores); quality of life; urodynamics; rates of bacteriologic cure (clearance of previously documented organisms from prostatic secretions).

METHODS We searched MEDLINE up to July 1998. No systematic reviews were available on prostatitis. We reviewed all relevant RCTs that were identified.

QUESTION What are the effects of treatments for chronic bacterial prostatitis?

OPTION ANTIMICROBIAL DRUGS

Antimicrobial drugs have not been evaluated adequately in men with chronic bacterial prostatitis. Retrospective cohort studies report cure rates (clearing prostatic secretions of previously documented organisms) of 0% to 90% depending on the drug used and the duration of treatment. The limited evidence available suggests that quinolones are more effective than TMP-SMZ.

Benefits: **TMP-SMZ:** We found no systematic review and no RCTs. A nonsystematic review identified 10 retrospective cohort studies in 135 men with bacteriologically confirmed prostatitis treated with TMP-SMZ 160 mg/800 mg twice daily for 10 to 140 days.[5] The studies reported bacteriologic cure rates of 0% to 67%. Cure was achieved in over 30% when men were treated for at least 90 days. **Quinolones:** We found no systematic review or RCTs. A review summarized three retrospective cohort studies in 106 men treated with norfloxacin 400 mg twice daily for 10, 28, and 174 days.[6] The studies reported cure rates of 64% to 88%. We also found six retrospective cohort studies in 141 men treated with ciprofloxacin 250 to 500 mg twice daily for 14 to 259 days, with cure rates of 60% to 75%.

Harms: The studies of TMP-SMZ did not report adverse effects. In the other studies, toxicity from quinolones was rare. Late relapse (6–12 months after treatment) was common.

Comment: The higher cure rates with quinolones may be explained by greater penetration into the prostate.[7] We reviewed only studies that used standard methods to localize infection to the prostate.[8]

OPTION LOCAL INJECTION OF ANTIMICROBIALS

We found no good evidence that local injection of antimicrobial agents is more effective than oral or parenteral antimicrobial treatment.

Benefits: We found no systematic review and no RCTs. One cohort study included 24 men with refractory chronic bacterial prostatitis.[9] All patients had a long history of recurrent prostatitis with relapse soon after discontinuation of antimicrobial treatment. An antimicrobial solution (160 mg gentamicin plus 3 g cefazolin) was injected directly into the prostate via the perineum. Seventeen men achieved remission for at least 6 months after one or two infiltrations, six needed several procedures to achieve remission, and one did not respond. Eradication of infection was eventually achieved after an unstated period in 15 men.

Harms: Although it was not reported in this study, infection must be a concern in this invasive procedure.

Comment: RCTs are needed to compare local injection versus systemic antimicrobial treatment.

OPTION α-BLOCKERS

Limited evidence from one RCT suggests that adding α-blockers to antimicrobial treatment may improve outcome and reduce recurrence in men with chronic bacterial prostatitis.

Benefits: We found no systematic review. We found one RCT of α-blockers in 270 men with bacterial or abacterial prostatitis or prostadynia.[10] Those randomized to receive α-blockers were given either 1 to 2 mg terazosin daily or 2.5 mg alfuzosin once or twice daily. Antimicrobials were given to all men with positive culture of expressed prostatic secretions and to half of those with inflammatory expressed prostatic secretions. Of men with bacterial prostatitis, those given α-blockers and antimicrobials had significantly higher rates of clinical improvement and significantly lower rates of recurrence (assessed by culture of expressed prostatic secretions) compared with those given antimicrobials alone ($p=0.019$). The report did not provide figures for RR or CI.

Harms: No adverse effects of α-blockers were reported in this study.

Comment: None.

OPTION TRANSURETHRAL RESECTION

Transurethral resection of the prostate has not yet been evaluated adequately in men with chronic bacterial prostatitis. Very limited evidence from retrospective cohort studies suggests that it may cure some men with refractory chronic bacterial prostatitis.

Benefit: We found no systematic review, RCTs, or prospective cohort studies. One retrospective cohort study reported 40% to 50% cure rates in 50 men with chronic prostatitis treated with transurethral resection. However, proof of bacterial prostatitis was not shown in many cases.[11]

Harms: Long-term morbidity rates of transurethral resection are low. A trial in men with benign prostatic hypertrophy found no difference in the incidence of impotence or urinary incontinence with transurethral resection or watchful waiting.[12]

Comment: Complications such as prostatic calculi seem to be reasonable indications for surgery in chronic bacterial prostatitis refractory to antimicrobial treatment. However, most of the inflamed tissue in chronic prostatitis is in the peripheral zone, from which the ducts typically empty into the urethra distal to the verumontanum.[13] Thus, tissue distal to the verumontanum would need to be resected, substantially increasing the risk of urinary incontinence.

OPTION RADICAL PROSTATECTOMY

Radical prostatectomy is a treatment of last resort. Its use in men with chronic prostatitis has not been evaluated formally.

Benefits: We found no RCTs. We found one report of radical prostatectomy in two young men whose refractory bacterial prostatitis caused relapsing hemolytic crises and paroxysmal nocturnal hemoglobinuria.[14]

Harms: Radical prostactectomy can cause impotence (9% to 75% depending upon age)[15] and varying degrees of stress urinary incontinence (8%).[16]

Comment: None.

QUESTION What are the effects of treatments for chronic abacterial prostatitis?

OPTION α-BLOCKERS

Limited evidence from one RCT suggests that α-blockers may ameliorate symptoms in men with nonbacterial prostatitis.

Benefits: We found no systematic review. We found one RCT of α-blockers in 270 men with bacterial or abacterial prostatitis or prostadynia.[10] Those randomized to receive α-blockers were given either 1 to 2 mg terazosin daily or 2.5 mg alfuzosin once or twice daily. Antimicrobials were given to all men with positive culture of expressed prostatic secretions and to half of those with inflammatory expressed prostatic secretions. Of men with abacterial prostatitis, those given α-blockers had significantly lower rates of symptomatic recurrence compared with those given either no treatment or antimicrobials ($p=0.0007$). The report did not provide figures for RR or CI.

Harms: No adverse effects of α-blockers were reported.[10]

Comment: None.

OPTION TRANSURETHRAL MICROWAVE THERMOTHERAPY

Thermotherapy has not been evaluated adequately in abacterial prostatitis. One small RCT suggests that it may ameliorate symptoms.

Benefits: We found no systematic review. We found one RCT comparing transurethral microwave thermotherapy versus sham treatment in 20 men.[17] Participants were assessed blindly using a symptom severity index and symptom frequency questionnaire. Seven of the 10 men in the treatment group were said to have improved significantly over a mean of 21-months' follow-up compared with only one of the 10 men in the sham group.

Harms: Four men complained of transient (resolved in 3 weeks) adverse reactions, including hematuria (two), urinary tract infection (one), impotence (one), urinary retention (one), urinary incontinence (one), and premature ejaculation (one).

Comment: The trial used only changes in clinical symptoms to determine efficacy. Thermotherapy caused persistent elevation of leukocytes in the urine prostatic fluid, which could indicate tissue damage.

OPTION OTHER INTERVENTIONS

Prostatic massage, sitz baths, and biofeedback (training the patient to contract and relax the pelvic floor muscles to interrupt the myofascial pain attacks) have not yet been evaluated formally in men with nonbacterial prostatitis.

REFERENCES

1. Roberts RO, Lieber MM, Rhodes T, et al. Prevalence of a physician-assigned diagnosis of prostatitis: the Olmsted County study of urinary symptoms and health status among men. *Urology* 1998;51:578–584.
2. Collins MM, Stafford, RS, O'Leary MP, Barry MJ. How common is prostatitis? A national survey of physician visits. *J Urol* 1998;159:1224–1228.
3. Alexander RB, Brady F, Ponniah S. Autoimmune prostatitis: evidence of T cell reactivity with normal prostatic proteins. *Urology* 1997;50: 893–899.
4. Wenninger K, Heiman JR, Rothman I, Berghuis JP, Berger RE. Sickness impact of chronic nonbacterial prostatitis and its correlates. *J Urol* 1996;155: 965–968.
5. Hanus PM, Danzinger LH. Treatment of chronic bacterial prostatitis. *Clin Pharm* 1988;3:49–55.
6. Naber KG, Sorgel F, Kees F, et al. Norfloxacin concentration in prostatic adenoma tissue (patients) and in prostatic fluid in patients and volunteers. 15th International Congress of Chemotherapy, Landsberg. In: Weidner N, Madsen PO, Schiefer HG, eds. *Prostatitis: etiopathology, diagnosis and therapy.* New York: Springer Verlag, 1987.
7. Cox CE. Ofloxacin in the management of complicated urinary tract infections, including prostatitis. *Am J Med* 1989;87(suppl 6c):61–68.
8. Meares EM, Stamey TA. Bacteriologic localization patterns in bacterial prostatitis and urethritis. *Invest Urol* 1968;5:492–518.
9. Baret L, Leonare A. Chronic bacterial prostatitis: 10 years of experience with local antibiotics. *J Urol* 1998;140:755–757.
10. Barbalias GA, Nikiforidis G, Liatsikos EN. Alpha-blockers for the treatment of chronic prostatitis in combination with antibiotics. *J Urol* 1998;159: 883–887.
11. Smart CJ, Jenkins JD, Lloyd RS. The painful prostate. *Br J Urol* 1975;47:861–869.
12. Wasson JH, Reda DJ, Bruskewitz RC, et al. A comparison of transurethral surgery with watchful waiting for moderate symptoms of benign prostatic hyperplasia. *N Engl J Med* 1995;332: 75–79.
13. McNeal JE. Regional morphology and pathology of the prostate. *Am J Clin Pathol* 1968;49: 347–357.
14. Davis BE, Weigel JW. Adenocarcinoma of the prostate discovered in 2 young patients following total prostatovesiculectomy for refractory prostatitis. *J Urol* 1990;144:744–745.
15. Quinlan DM, Epstein JI, Carter BS, Walsh PC. Sexual function following radical prostatectomy: influence of preservation of neurovascular bundles. *J Urol* 1991;145:998–1002.
16. Steiner MS, Morton RA, Walsh PC. Impact of anatomical radical prostatectomy on urinary continence. *J Urol* 1991;145:512–515.
17. Nickel J, Sorensen R. Transurethral microwave thermotherapy for nonbacterial prostatitis: a randomized double-blind sham controlled study using new prostatitis specific assessment questionnaires. *J Urol* 1996;155:1950–1955.

Jeffrey A Stern, MD
Anthony J Schaeffer, MD
Northwestern University Medical School
Chicago
Illinois
USA

Competing interests: None declared

Benign prostatic hyperplasia

Michael Barry, MD, and Claus Roehrborn, MD

QUESTIONS

INTERVENTIONS

Key Messages

- Randomized controlled trials (RCTs) have found that both α-blockers and 5α-reductase inhibitors are more effective than placebo in improving lower urinary tract symptoms in men with benign prostatic hyperplasia. One RCT found that α-blockers were more effective than 5α-reductase inhibitors in men not selected for having large prostates. Neither drug has been compared directly with surgical treatment.
- We found limited evidence from one RCT that TURP is more effective than watchful waiting in improving symptoms and reducing complications and that it does not increase the risk of erectile dysfunction or incontinence.
- TURP has not yet been compared adequately with medical treatments or to newer, less-invasive techniques.
- RCTs have found that TUMT is more effective than sham treatment at reducing symptoms. Weaker data provide no evidence of any difference in short-term symptom relief between TURP and TUMT, but one RCT found that TURP was more effective than TUNA in men with benign prostatic hyperplasia.

DEFINITION Benign prostatic hyperplasia (BPH) is characterized by lower urinary tract symptoms (urinary frequency, urgency, a weak and intermittent stream, needing to strain, a sense of incomplete emptying, and nocturia) and can lead to complications, including acute urinary retention.

INCIDENCE/ PREVALENCE Estimates of the prevalence of BPH range between 10% to 30% for men in their early 70s, depending on how BPH is defined.[1]

ETIOLOGY BPH is a histologic process. The mechanisms by which it causes symptoms and complications are poorly defined.[2] The best documented risk factors are increasing age and functioning testes.[3]

PROGNOSIS Community- and practice-based studies suggest that men with lower urinary tract symptoms can expect slow progression over time.[4,5] However, symptoms can wax and wane without treatment. In men with symptoms of BPH, rates of acute urinary retention range from 1% to 2% per year.[5–7]

AIMS To reduce or alleviate lower urinary tract symptoms, to prevent complications, and to minimize the adverse effects of treatment.

OUTCOMES Burden of lower urinary tract symptoms; rates of acute urinary retention and prostatectomy; incidence of adverse effects of treatment. Symptoms are measured using the validated International Prostate Symptom Score (IPSS), which includes seven questions quantifying symptoms on an overall scale from 0 to 35, with higher scores representing more frequent symptoms.[8] Older studies used a variety of symptom assessment instruments, which makes comparisons difficult.

METHODS This review is based on ongoing MEDLINE searches and prospective journal hand searches by the Patient Outcomes Research Team for Prostatic Diseases (Agency for Health Care Policy and Research grant number HS08397).

QUESTION What are the effects of medical treatment?

OPTION α-BLOCKERS

RCTs have found that α-blockers are more effective than placebo in improving lower urinary tract symptoms in men with a diagnosis of BPH. One RCT found that α-blockers were more effective in improving symptoms than 5α-reductase inhibitors in men not selected for having larger prostates. α-Blockers have not been compared directly with surgical treatment.

Benefits: We found no systematic review. **Versus placebo:** Many RCTs have found that α-blockers are significantly more effective than placebo in reducing lower urinary tract symptoms.[9] The largest trial compared terazosin at doses of up to 10 mg/d for a year versus placebo in 2084 men with BPH. Treatment achieved a significantly greater mean drop in the IPSS (–7.6 points from baseline vs. –3.7 with placebo,

95% CI of difference –5.5 points to –3.3 points).[10] The effect of α-blockers on complications of BPH is poorly documented. **Versus each other:** We found two RCTs comparing different α-blockers.[11,12] The larger trial compared tamsulosin versus alfuzosin in 282 men and found no significant difference in the change in symptom score from baseline.[11] **Versus 5α-reductase inhibitors:** One RCT compared finasteride versus an α-blocker or both treatments in 1229 men with a diagnosis of BPH.[13] Terazosin was superior to finasteride at reducing symptoms. The difference in mean IPPS scores at 1 year was 2.9 points. There was no difference between treatment with both agents and with terazosin alone.

Harms: Theoretically, "uroselective" α-blockers such as tamsulosin should cause fewer adverse effects, but in a large RCT dizziness was still more common with tamsulosin than placebo.[14] In the RCT comparing tamsulosin versus alfuzosin, adverse effect profiles were similar. Overall, dizziness was seen in 7%, asthenia in 2%, and postural hypotension in 2%.[11] **Versus 5α-reductase inhibitors:** In the trial comparing terazosin versus finasteride, dizziness was seen in approximately 25% of men on terazosin, asthenia in 15%, rhinitis in 8%, and postural hypotension in 8%, while sexual dysfunction was more common in men taking finasteride.[13]

Comment: Men with severe symptoms can expect the largest absolute fall in their symptom scores with medical treatment.[10,14] Prazosin, alfuzosin, terazosin, and doxazosin lower blood pressure and may be used in some men to treat both hypertension and BPH.[15] Men who cannot safely tolerate any decrease in blood pressure because of co-existent medical problems or other medications may be treated best with uroselective tamsulosin.[16,17]

OPTION 5α-REDUCTASE INHIBITORS

RCTs have found that 5α-reductase inhibitors are more effective than placebo in improving lower urinary tract symptoms and reducing complications in men with BPH, especially in men with larger prostates. One RCT found that 5α-reductase inhibitors were less effective at improving symptoms than α-blockers. They have not been compared directly with surgical treatment.

Benefits: **Versus placebo:** We found two systematic reviews. The first, published in 1996, identified six RCTs of the 5α-reductase inhibitor finasteride. Treatment significantly reduced symptom scores compared with placebo (difference in symptom score –0.9 points, range of score 0–30 points, 95% CI –1.2 to –0.6).[18] The beneficial effect over placebo was greatest in men with larger prostates (~40 g). The second systematic review, published in 1997, identified three placebo-controlled RCTs of finasteride. Treatment reduced the 2-year risk of acute urinary retention requiring catheterization from 2.7% to 1.1% (NNT 62), of progression to prostatectomy from 6.5% to 4.2% (NNT 44), and of either event from 7.5% to 4.9% (NNT 38).[19] A subsequent RCT compared finasteride 5 mg/d versus placebo in 3040 men with enlarged prostates and symptoms of BPH.[7] After 4 years of treatment, finasteride reduced symptoms significantly more than placebo (difference in symptom score –1.6 points, range of score 0–34 points, 95% CI

–2.5 to –0.7). However, the risk of acute urinary retention was reduced from 6.6% to 2.8% (NNT 26), of prostatectomy from 8.3% to 4.2% (NNT 24), and of either event from 13.2% to 6.6% (NNT 15). A follow-up report found a greater effect among men with higher concentrations of prostate specific antigen at baseline (3.3–12.0 ng/mL), reflecting larger prostates. In this subgroup, the risk of either acute urinary retention or prostatectomy dropped from 19.9% to 8.3% (NNT 9, albeit with a broad CI).[20] **Versus 5α-reductase inhibitors:** We found one RCT (see p. 411).[13]

Harms: The most common attributable adverse effects of finasteride in the first year were decreased libido (6%), impotence (8%), and decreased ejaculate (4%). After the first year of treatment, adverse effects were less common.[7] Finasteride reduced concentrations of prostate specific antigen by an average of 50% (individual responses were highly variable). However, use of finasteride for up to 4 years did not change the rate of detection of prostate cancer relative to placebo.[7] **Versus 5α-reductase inhibitors:** *See* p. 411.

Comment: The larger systematic review[18] found that finasteride was more effective in men with larger prostates. However, the difference in mean decrease in symptom score from baseline between men with the smallest and largest prostates was only approximately 1 point. Men with severe symptoms can expect the largest absolute fall in their symptom scores with medical treatment.[10,15]

QUESTION What are the effects of surgical treatments?

OPTION TRANSURETHRAL RESECTION (TURP)

We found limited evidence from one RCT that TURP is more effective than watchful waiting in improving symptoms and reducing complications, and does not increase the risk of erectile dysfunction or incontinence. TURP has not yet been compared adequately with medical treatments or to newer, less invasive techniques such as laser ablation and electrovaporization.

Benefits: We found no systematic review of RCTs. **Versus watchful waiting:** One RCT compared TURP versus watchful waiting in 556 men with moderate symptoms of BPH.[21] Symptoms were reduced to a significantly greater degree with TURP, and the risk of predefined treatment failure over approxiamtely 3 years was reduced from 17.0% to 8.2% (NNT 11). The major categories of treatment failure reduced by TURP were acute urinary retention, development of a large bladder residual (> 350 mL), and deterioration to a severe symptom level. After 5 years, the failure rate was reduced from 21.0% to 10.0% (NNT 9), and 36% of men assigned to watchful waiting had crossed over to surgery.[22] **Versus less invasive techniques:** We found no systematic review. Several small short-term RCTs have found either no difference between TURP and either laser ablation and electrovaporization[23,24] or that TURP achieves better symptom relief.[25,26] Long-term durability of symptom relief and effect on the incidence of complications of BPH have not yet been evaluated adequately. **Versus TUMT and TUNA:** *See* below.

Harms: Administrative data suggest that mortality in the 30 days after TURP for BPH ranges from 0.4% for men aged 65 to 69 years to 1.9% for men aged 80 to 84 years and that it has been falling in recent years.[27] In a synthesis of nonexperimental studies, TURP for BPH was associated with immediate surgical complications in 12% of cases, bleeding requiring intervention in 2%, erectile dysfunction in 14%, retrograde ejaculation in 74%, and incontinence in approximately 5%.[28–30] Claims data suggest a reoperation rate, implying a need for retreatment, of approximately 1% per year.[27] However, in the only comparative trial, men randomized to prostatectomy did not seem to have a greater burden of erectile dysfunction or incontinence than men assigned to watchful waiting.[21,22] Laser prostatectomy and electrovaporization require less hospital time and seem to cause fewer short-term adverse effects and less bleeding than TURP.[23,25]

Comment: Rapid changes in techniques and few controlled trials make comparisons between TURP and newer techniques difficult.

OPTION TRANSURETHRAL MICROWAVE THERMOTHERAPY (TUMT)

RCTs have found that TUMT is more effective than sham treatment at reducing symptoms of BPH. Weaker data provide no evidence of a difference in short-term symptom relief between TUMT and TURP.

Benefits: We found no systematic review. **Versus sham treatment:** Several small- to medium-sized RCTs have compared TUMT versus sham treatment. In the largest trial ($n=220$), the IPSS dropped from 23.6 at baseline to 12.7 points with active treatment after 6 months, 5.0 points more than with sham treatment. The difference between active and sham treatments at 6 months was significant ($p<0.05$).[31] **Versus TURP:** Two small trials with follow-up to 2.5 years found no difference in symptom relief between TUMT and TURP.[32,33]

Harms: Adverse effects of TUMT vary among trials but seem to include the need for catheterization for more than 1 week (8% vs. 2% with sham treatment),[34] persistent irritative symptoms (22% vs. 8%),[31] hematuria (14% vs. 1%),[31] and sexual dysfunction (mostly hematospermia and other ejaculatory abnormalities, 29% vs. 1%).[31]

Comment: Most RCTs were too small to exclude a clinically important difference between groups. The long-term effects of treatment have not been evaluated adequately.

OPTION TRANSURETHRAL NEEDLE ABLATION (TUNA)

We found limited evidence from one RCT that TURP is more effective than TUNA in men with BPH, although TUNA caused fewer adverse effects.

Benefits: We found no systematic review. **Versus TURP:** We found one RCT comparing TUNA versus TURP in 121 men.[35] The mean IPSS dropped from 24.7 to 11.1 points at 1 year with TUNA, 2.4 points fewer than the decrease following TURP.[35] Benefit at 1 year was significantly greater with TURP than with TUNA (IPPS 11.1 with TUNA vs. 8.3 with TURP, $p=0.04$).

Harms: Compared with TURP, TUNA caused less retrograde ejaculation (38% vs. 0%) and bleeding (100% vs. 32%).[35]

Comment: TUNA uses radiofrequency energy via two intraprostatic electrodes to generate heat to coagulate prostate tissue, again in the outpatient setting. Anesthesia requirements vary in reported studies. The long-term effects of treatment have not been evaluated adequately.

REFERENCES

1. Bosch JL, Hop WC, Kirkels WJ, Schroder FH. Natural history of benign prostatic hyperplasia: appropriate case definition and estimation of its prevalence in the community. *Urology* 1995; 46(suppl A):34–40.
2. Barry MJ, Adolfsson J, Batista JE, et al. Committee 6: measuring the symptoms and health impact of benign prostatic hyperplasia and its treatments. In: Denis L, Griffiths K, Khoury S, et al, eds. *Fourth International Consultation on BPH, Proceedings*. Plymouth, UK: Health Publication Ltd, 1998:265–321.
3. Oishi K, Boyle P, Barry MJ, et al. Committee 1: Epidemiology and natural history of benign prostatic hyperplasia. In: Denis L, Griffiths K, Khoury S, et al, eds. *Fourth International Consultation on BPH, Proceedings*. Plymouth, UK: Health Publication Ltd, 1998:23–59.
4. Jacobsen SJ, Girman CJ, Guess HA, Rhodes T, Oesterling JE, Lieber MM. Natural history of prostatism: longitudinal changes in voiding symptoms in community dwelling men. *J Urol* 1996; 155:595–600.
5. Barry MJ, Fowler Jr FJ, Bin L, Pitts III JC, Harris CJ, Mulley Jr AG. The natural history of patients with benign prostatic hyperplasia as diagnosed by North American urologists. *J Urol* 1997;157: 10–15.
6. Jacobsen S, Jacobson D, Girman C, et al. Natural history of prostatism: risk factors for acute urinary retention. *J Urol* 1997;158:481–487.
7. McConnell J, Bruskewitz R, Walsh P, et al. The effect of finasteride on the risk of acute urinary retention and the need for surgical treatment among men with benign prostatic hyperplasia. *N Engl J Med* 1998;338:557–563.
8. Barry MJ, Fowler FJ Jr, O' Leary MP, et al. The American Urological Association symptom index for benign prostatic hyperplasia. *J Urol* 1992; 148:1549–1564.
9. Chapple CR, Andersson K, Bono V, et al. Committee 12: Alpha blockers in the treatment of BPH. 2. Alpha blockers clinical results. In: Denis L, Griffiths K, Khoury S, et al, eds. *Fourth International Consultation on BPH, Proceedings*. Plymouth, UK: Health Publication Ltd, 1998:610–632.
10. Roehrborn CG, Oesterling JE, Auerbach S, et al. The Hytrin community assessment trial study: a one-year study of terazosin versus placebo in the treatment of men with symptomatic benign prostatic hyperplasia. *Urology* 1996;47:159–168.
11. Buzelin J, Fonteyne E, Kontturi M, Witjes W, Khan A. Comparison of tamsulosin with alfuzosin in the treatment of patients with lower urinary tract symptoms suggestive of bladder outlet obstruction (symptomatic benign prostatic hyperplasia). *Br J Urol* 1997;80:597–605.
12. Lee E, Lee C. Clinical comparison of selective and non-selective alpha 1 α-adrenoreceptor antagonists in benign prostatic hyperplasia: studies on tamsulosin in a fixed dose and terazosin in increasing doses. *Br J Urol* 1997;80: 606–611.
13. Lepor H, Williford WO, Barry MJ, et al. The efficacy of terazosin, finasteride, or both in benign prostatic hyperplasia. Veterans' Affairs cooperative studies benign prostatic hyperplasia study group. *N Engl J Med* 1996;335:533–539.
14. Mobley D, Dias N, Levenstein M. Effects of doxazosin in patients with mild, intermediate, and severe benign prostatic hyperplasia. *Clin Ther* 1998;20:101–109.
15. Kaplan S, Kaplan N. Alpha-blockade: monotherapy for hypertension and benign prostatic hyperplasia. *Urology* 1996;48:541–550.
16. Lepor H, for the Tamsulosin Investigator Group. Phase III multicenter placebo-controlled study of tamsulosin in benign prostatic hyperplasia. *Urology* 1998;51:892–900.
17. Abrams P, Schulman C, Vaage S, for the European Tamsulosin Study Group. Tamsulosin, a selective alpha 1c-adrenoceptor antagonist: a randomized, controlled trial in patients with benign prostatic 'obstruction' (symptomatic BPH). *Br J Urol* 1995; 76:325–336.
18. Boyle P, Gould AL, Roehrborn CG. Prostate volume predicts outcome of treatment of benign prostatic hyperplasia with finasteride: meta-analysis of randomized clinical trials. *Urology* 1996;48: 398–405.
19. Andersen J, Nickel J, Marshall V, Schulman C, Boyle P. Finasteride significantly reduces acute urinary retention and need for surgery in patients with symptomatic benign prostatic hyperplasia. *Urology* 1997;49:839–845.
20. Roehrborn CG, McConnell JD, Lieber M, et al. Serum prostate-specific antigen concentration is a powerful predictor of acute urinary retention and the need for surgery in men with clinical benign prostatic hypoplasia. *Urology* 1999;53: 473–480.
21. Wasson J, Reda D, Bruskewitz R, et al. A comparison of transurethral surgery with watchful waiting for moderate symptoms of benign prostatic hyperplasia. *N Engl J Med* 1995;332:75–79.
22. Flanigan RC, Reda DJ, Wasson JH, Anderson RJ, Abdellatif M, Bruskewitz RC. Five year outcome of surgical resection and watchful waiting for men with moderately symptomatic benign prostatic hyperplasia: a Department of Veterans' Affairs cooperative study. *J Urol* 1998;160: 12–17.
23. Shokeir A, Al-Sisi H, Farage Y, El-Maaboud M, Saeed M, Mutabagani H. Transurethral prostatectomy: a prospective randomized study of conventional resection and electrovaporisation in benign prostatic hyperplasia. *Br J Urol* 1997;80: 570–574.
24. Kaplan S, Laor E, Fatal M, Te A. Transurethral resection of the prostate versus transurethral electrovaporization of the prostate: a blinded, prospective comparative study with 1-year followup. *J Urol* 1998;159:454–458.
25. Cowles RS 3rd, Kabalin JN, Childs S, et al. A prospective randomized comparison of transurethral resection to visual laser ablation of the prostate for the treatment of benign prostatic

hyperplasia. *Urology* 1995;46:155–160.
26. Kabalin JN, Gill HS, Bite G, Wolfe V. Comparative study of laser versus electrocautery prostatic resection: 18-month followup with complex urodynamic assessment. *J Urol* 1995;153:94–97; discussion 97–98.
27. Lu-Yao GL, Barry MJ, Chang CH, Wasson JH, Wennberg JE, and the Prostate PORT. Transurethral resection of the prostate among medicare beneficiaries in the United States: time trends and outcomes. *Urology* 1994;44: 692–699.
28. McConnell JD, Barry MJ, Bruskewitz RC, et al. Direct treatment outcomes – complications. *Benign prostatic hyperplasia: diagnosis and treatment. Clinical Practice Guideline, Number 8.* Rockville, Maryland: Agency for Health Care Policy and Research, Public Health Service, US Department of Health and Human Services, 1994:91–98.
29. McConnell JD, Barry MJ, Bruskewitz RC, et al. Direct treatment outcomes – sexual dysfunction. *Benign prostatic hyperplasia: diagnosis and treatment. Clinical Practice Guideline, Number 8.* Rockville, Maryland: Agency for Health Care Policy and Research, Public Health Service, US Department of Health and Human Services, 1994:99–103.
30. McConnell JD, Barry MJ, Bruskewitz RC, et al. Direct treatment outcomes – urinary incontinence. *Benign prostatic hyperplasia: diagnosis and treatment. Clinical Practice Guideline, Number 8.* Rockville, Maryland: Agency for Health Care Policy and Research, Public Health Service, US Department of Health and Human Services, 1994:105–106.
31. Roehrborn C, Preminger G, Newhall P, et al. Microwave thermotherapy for benign prostatic hyperplasia with the Dornier Urowave: results of a randomized, double-blind, multicenter, sham-controlled trial. *Urology* 1998;51:19–28.
32. D'ancona F, Francisca E, Witjes W, Welling L, Debruyne F, De La Rosette J. Transurethral resection of the prostate vs high-energy thermotherapy of the prostate in patients with benign prostatic hyperplasia: long-term results. *Br J Urol* 1998; 81:259–264.
33. Ahmed M, Bell T, Lawrence WT, Ward JP, Watson GM. Transurethral microwave thermotherapy (Prostatron version 2.5) compared with transurethral resection of the prostate for the treatment of benign prostatic hyperplasia: a randomized, controlled, parallel study. *Br J Urol* 1997;79:181–185.
34. Larson T, Blute M, Bruskewitz R, Mayer R, Ugarte R, Utz W. A high-efficiency microwave thermoablation system for the treatment of benign prostatic hyperplasia: results of a randomized, sham-controlled, prospective, double-blind, multicenter clinical trial. *Urology* 1998;51:731–742.
35. Bruskewitz R, Issa M, Roehrborn C, et al. A prospective, randomized 1-year clinical trial comparing transurethral needle ablation to transurethral resection of the prostate for the treatment of symptomatic benign prostatic hyperplasia. *J Urol* 1998;159:1588–1594.

Michael Barry, MD
Medical Practitioner
Evaluation Center
Massachusetts General Hospital
Boston
Massachusetts
USA

Claus G Roehrborn, MD
Department of Urology
Southwestern Medical School
Dallas
Texas
USA

Competing interests: None declared.

Localized prostate cancer

Timothy J Wilt, MD, MPH, and Michael K Brawer, MD

QUESTIONS

INTERVENTIONS

Key Messages

In men with clinically localized disease

- The data we found do not provide clear evidence for the superiority of any one treatment, including androgen deprivation. However, limited data from one randomized controlled trial (RCT) suggest that radical prostatectomy may reduce recurrence compared with radiation treatment.
- We found limited data from RCTs suggesting that radical prostatectomy or external-beam radiation may not improve survival or reduce the risk of metastatic disease or need for palliative treatment compared with watchful waiting.
- External-beam radiation, brachytherapy, and cryosurgery have not been compared with watchful waiting in RCTs.
- We found no RCTs addressing the question of whether androgen deprivation should be offered to asymptomatic men in whom raised concentrations of prostate specific antigen are detected after primary treatment or during watchful waiting.

In men with locally advanced disease

- We found limited evidence from RCTs suggesting that androgen deprivation initiated at diagnosis improves survival and reduces the risk of major complications compared with treatment deferred until disease progression.
- A systematic review found that adding androgen deprivation to radiation treatment improves survival compared with radiation alone.
- We found no good evidence that radiation alone is beneficial for survival.

DEFINITION Prostatic cancer can be staged according to two systems: the tumor, node, metastasis (TNM) classification system; and the American urologic staging system (*see* Table 1). Nonmetastatic prostate cancer can be divided into clinically localized disease and advanced disease.

INCIDENCE/ PREVALENCE Prostate cancer is the most common nondermatologic malignancy worldwide and the second leading cause of cancer death in men in the USA.[1] It caused an estimated 184,500 new cases and 39,200 deaths in 1998.[2] For a 50-year-old man with a life expectancy of 25 years, the lifetime risk of microscopic prostate cancer is approximately 42%, the risk of clinically evident prostate cancer is 10%, and that of fatal prostate cancer is 3%.[3]

ETIOLOGY Risk factors include age, family history of prostate cancer, black race, and possibly higher dietary fat intake.

PROGNOSIS The chance that men with well to moderately differentiated, palpable, clinically localized prostate cancer will remain free of symptomatic progression is 70% at 5 years and 40% at 10 years.[4] The risk of symptomatic disease progression is higher in men with poorly differentiated prostate cancer.[5] Morbidity from local or regional disease progression includes hematuria, bladder obstruction, and lower extremity edema. Despite widespread testing for prostate specific antigen and increased rates of radical prostatectomy and radiation, population based studies show that rates of death from prostate cancer in the USA have declined by only approximately 1/100,000 men since 1992.[6,7] Regions of the USA that have experienced the greatest decreases in mortality are those with the lowest rates of testing for prostate specific antigen and treatment with radical prostatectomy or radiation.[7] Countries with low rates of testing and treatment do not have consistently higher age-adjusted rates of death from prostate cancer than countries, such as the USA, with high rates of testing and treatment.

AIMS To prevent premature death and disability while minimizing adverse effects of treatment.

OUTCOMES Survival; time to progression; response in terms of symptoms and signs; quality of life; adverse effects of treatment.

METHODS We searched for systematic reviews and RCTs using the search strategy of the Department of Veterans' Affairs Cochrane Review Group on Prostatic Diseases (Cochrane Library and MEDLINE to end 1998). We reviewed all systematic reviews and RCTs that were identified.

QUESTION **What are the effects of treatment in men with clinically localized prostate cancer?**

OPTION **WATCHFUL WAITING**

We found no direct evidence from RCTs that watchful waiting improves length or quality of life in men with clinically localized prostate cancer compared with other management strategies.

Benefits: We found two systematic reviews.[1,8] In men managed by watchful waiting, prospective cohort studies report 15-year disease-free survival of 80%, ranging from 95% for well-differentiated to 30% for poorly differentiated cancers.[9,10] **Versus early androgen deprivation:** We found no RCTs. **Versus radical prostatectomy:** We found one RCT[11] (see below).

Harms: Expectant management does not remove a cancer that may progress and cause death or disability.

Comment: There is approximately a 10-year lead time between the detection of cancers by raised concentrations of prostate specific antigen and detection by digital rectal examination or the development of symptoms. This means that outcomes are likely to be similar in men with palpable tumors who are followed for 15 years and in men whose tumors are detected because of raised concentrations of prostate specific antigen who are followed for 25 years.

OPTION RADICAL PROSTATECTOMY

Limited data from RCTs provide no evidence that radical prostatectomy improves outcome compared with watchful waiting. It may reduce the risk of metastases compared with external-beam radiation. Radical prostatectomy carries the risks of major surgery and of sexual and urinary dysfunction.

Benefits: We found two systematic reviews.[1,8] **Versus watchful waiting:** One RCT has compared radical prostatectomy versus watchful waiting in 142 men with clinically localized prostate cancer. After a median follow-up of 23 years (range 19–27 years) no difference in survival was detected between the two groups (median survival 10.6 years with prostatectomy versus 8 years with watchful waiting, no CI quoted).[11] **Versus external-beam radiation:** One RCT compared radical prostatectomy versus external-beam radiation in 97 evaluable men with clinically localized prostate cancer. Men receiving radiation had an increased risk of metastases (four "treatment failures" with prostatectomy versus 17 with radiation).[12]

Harms: Fatal complications have been reported in 0.5% to 1% of men treated with radical prostatectomy and may exceed 2% in men aged 75 years and over.[13] Nearly 8% of men over 65 years of age suffered major cardiopulmonary complications within 30 days of operation. The incidence of other adverse effects of surgery was over 80% for sexual dysfunction, 30% for urinary incontinence requiring pads or clamps to control wetness, 18% for urethral stricture, 3% for total urinary incontinence, 5% for fecal incontinence, and 1% for bowel injury requiring surgical repair.[1,14–16]

Comment: Both RCTs of radical prostatectomy were conducted before the advent of tests for prostate specific antigen and were too small to exclude a clinically important difference between groups. Radical prostatectomy may benefit selected groups of men with localized prostate cancer, particularly younger men with higher-grade tumors. However, the available data suggest that in most men the potential benefits in quality-adjusted life expectancy are at best small and sensitive to patients' preferences.[8] Studies have found no differences among groups treated with radical prostatectomy, radiation, or watchful waiting when evaluating general health-related quality of life.[17] Two ongoing trials are comparing radical prostatectomy versus watchful waiting.[18,19]

OPTION EXTERNAL-BEAM RADIATION

We found limited evidence from one small RCT that, compared with radical prostatectomy, external-beam radiation increases the risk of metastases in men with clinically localized prostate cancer. It has not been compared directly with watchful waiting.

Benefits: **Versus watchful waiting:** We found no RCTs. **Versus radical prostatectomy:** We found one RCT (*see* p. 418).[12]

Harms: The RCT made no mention of adverse effects of treatment.[12] A survey of men treated with external-beam radiation reported that 7% wore pads to control wetness, between 23% to 32% of men were impotent, and 10% reported problems with bowel dysfunction.[20] Treatment-related mortality is less than 0.5%.[1] External-beam radiation requires that men return for daily outpatient treatment for up to 6 weeks.

Comment: Up to 30% of men with clinically localized prostate cancer treated with radiotherapy still have positive biopsies 2 to 3 years after treatment.[21] Up to 60% have biochemical evidence of recurrence, which may reflect either distant or local recurrence.[22,23]

OPTION BRACHYTHERAPY

We found no direct evidence from RCTs that brachytherapy improves length or quality of life in men with clinically localized prostate cancer.

Benefits: We found no systematic review or RCTs.

Harms: Complication rates reported from case series include urinary retention (6%–7%), incontinence (1%–6%), cystitis/urethritis (4%–7%), proctitis, (1%–12%), and impotency (6%–50%).[24] Long-term outcomes from a representative national sampling of men have not been reported.

Comment: To be summarized in a future issue of *Clinical Evidence*.

OPTION CRYOSURGERY

We found no direct evidence from RCTs that cryosurgery improves length or quality of life in men with clinically localized prostate cancer.

Benefits: We found no systematic review or RCTs.

Harms: To be summarized in a future issue of *Clinical Evidence*.

Comment: None.

OPTION **ANDROGEN DEPRIVATION**

We found no direct evidence from RCTs that androgen deprivation improves length or quality of life in men with clinically localized prostate cancer.

Benefits: We found no systematic review or RCTs.

Harms: Adverse effects of androgen deprivation include osteoporosis, weight gain, hot flushes (10%–60%), loss of muscle mass, gynecomastia (5%–10%), impotence (10%–30%), and loss of libido (5%–30%).[25] These adverse effects are particularly important when considering treatment in men with long life expectancy or treatment duration, such as younger men with lower-grade cancers.

Comment: Treatment with androgen deprivation may help to relieve anxiety in men diagnosed with clinically localized prostate cancer by giving patients the sense that something is being done.

QUESTION **In men who have received primary treatment and remain asymptomatic, should androgen deprivation be offered when raised concentrations of prostate specific antigen are detected?**

The effects of initiating androgen suppression when concentrations of prostate specific antigen rise or persist after primary treatment have not yet been evaluated in RCTs.

Benefits: We found no systematic review or RCTs.

Harms: Potential harms include unnecessary or inappropriate treatment.

Comment: Clinicians often monitor blood concentrations of prostate specific antigen and offer androgen suppression when these rise. Consequently, more men with disease persistence are being considered for androgen suppression, and treatment is being initiated earlier in the natural history of the disease. RCTs are needed to evaluate the effectiveness of this approach and of intermittent treatment in which androgen suppression is initiated when concentrations of prostate specific antigen rise after primary treatment and is discontinued when the antigen concentrations return to nadir.

QUESTION **What are the effects of treatment in men with locally advanced prostate cancer?**

OPTION **ANDROGEN DEPRIVATION**

RCTs have found that, in men with locally advanced disease, androgen deprivation initiated at diagnosis reduces complications and may improve survival. Androgen deprivation improves survival in men with locally advanced disease treated with radiation.

Benefits: **Versus no initial treatment:** We found one systematic review, which identified no recent RCTs. Three RCTs performed between 1960 and 1975 compared androgen deprivation (diethylstilbestrol, orchiectomy, or estrogens) versus no initial treatment in approximately 4000 men with all stages of prostate cancer. They found no difference in overall survival. Reanalysis of updated data from these RCTs provided tentative evidence of a modest survival advantage with androgen deprivation.[26] **Immediate (initiated at diagnosis) versus deferred androgen deprivation:** We found one systematic review, which identified three RCTs ($n=2143$), two of which were conducted in the 1960s.[25] None had a uniform protocol for initiating deferred treatment, so deferred treatment in these trials reflects the varied practices of the treating clinicians. Meta-analysis found no significant survival difference at 5 years between immediate compared with deferred androgen deprivation (hazard ratio 0.914, 95% CI 0.81–1.03).[25] The more recent trial, which included 938 men with stage C (locally advanced) and D (asymptomatic metastatic) disease, reported a survival benefit from immediate treatment (62% of deaths were from prostate cancer compared with 71% in the deferred treatment arm, $p<0.001$). The survival benefit was limited to men with stage C disease.[27] Immediate androgen deprivation almost halved the risk of major complications, such as pathological fractures (AR 2.3% vs. 4.5% with deferred treatment), spinal cord compression (AR 1.9% vs. 4.9%), ureteric obstruction (AR 7% vs. 11.8%), and extraskeletal metastases (AR 7.9% vs. 11.8%). The report did not quote CIs nor make clear the time interval over which outcomes were recorded, though this appeared to be at least 10 years. Again, the lower incidence of complications was more apparent in men presenting with stage C disease. **Radiation plus androgen deprivation:** We found one systematic review, which identified four RCTs comparing early versus deferred androgen deprivation in men receiving external-beam radiation. Early androgen deprivation was initiated at the same time as radiation treatment for locally advanced or asymptomatic clinically evident metastatic prostate cancer and continued until the development of hormone refractory disease. The deferred group received radiation treatment alone, with androgen deprivation initiated only in those in whom the disease progressed.[25] Meta-analysis found a difference in overall 5-year survival in favor of early compared to deferred androgen deprivation (hazard ratio 0.63, 95% CI 0.48–0.83; percent surviving at 5 years 76.5% vs. 68.2%, ARR 8.3%; NNT at 5 years 12).[25]

Harms: Adverse events were not well reported in the RCTs. Earlier initiation of androgen deprivation means longer exposure to adverse effects, which include osteoporosis, weight gain, hot flushes (10%–60%), loss of muscle mass, gynecomastia (5%–10%), impotence (10%–30%), and loss of libido (5%–30%).[25] These adverse effects are particularly important when considering treatment of men with long life expectancy or younger men with lower-grade cancers.

Comment: The RCTs conducted in the 1960s[25] included men who were older and had more advanced cancers than those in the more recent RCT.[27] RCTs are needed to evaluate the effectiveness of neoadjuvant androgen deprivation to downstage the tumor before surgery when disease extends beyond the capsule.

REFERENCES

1. Middleton RG, Thompson IM, Austenfeld MS, et al. Prostate cancer clinical guidelines panel summary report on the management of clinically localized prostate cancer. *J Urol* 1995;154:2144–2148.
2. Landis SH, Murray T, Bolden S et al. Cancer Statistics. *CA Cancer J Clin* 1998;48:6–29.
3. Whitmore WF. Localized prostatic cancer: management and detection issues. *Lancet* 1994;343:1263–1267.
4. Adolfsson J, Steineck G, Hedund P. Deferred treatment of clinically localized low-grade prostate cancer: actual 10-year and projected 15-year follow-up of the Karolinska series. *Urology* 1997;50:722–726.
5. Johansson J-E, Holmberg L, Johansson S, et al. Fifteen-year survival in prostate cancer: prospective, population-based study in Sweden. *JAMA* 1997;277:467–471.
6. Brawley OW. Prostate carcinoma incidence and patient mortality. *Cancer* 1997;80:1857–1863.
7. Wingo PA, Ries LA, Rosenberg HM, et al. Cancer incidence and mortality, 1973–1995. *Cancer* 1998;82:1197–1207.
8. Fleming C, Wasson J, Albertsen PC, et al. A decision analysis of alternative treatment strategies for clinically localized prostate cancer. *JAMA* 1993;269:2650–2658.
9. Albertsen PC, Hanley JA, Gleason DF, Barry MJ. Competing risk analysis of men aged 55 to 74 years at diagnosis managed conservatively for clinically localized prostate cancer. *JAMA* 1998; 280:975–980.
10. Lu-Yao GL, Yao S. Population-based study of long-term survival in patients with clinically localised prostate cancer. *Lancet* 1997;349:906–910.
11. Iversen P, Madsen PO, Corle DK. Radical prostatectomy versus expectant treatment for early carcinoma of the prostate: 23 year follow-up of a prospective randomized study. *Scand J Urol Nephrol* 1995;172(suppl):65–72.
12. Paulsen DF, Lin GH, Hinshaw W, et al. The uro-oncology group: radical surgery versus radiotherapy for adenocarcinoma of the prostate. *J Urol* 1982;128:502–504.
13. Lu-Yao GL, McLerran D, Wasson JH, et al. An assessment of radical prostatectomy: time trends, geographic variation, and outcomes. *JAMA* 1993;269:2633–2636.
14. Anonymous. Screening for prostate cancer. *Ann Intern Med* 1997;126:480–484.
15. Fowler FJ, Barry MJ, Lu-Yao G, et al. Patient-reported complications and follow-up treatment after radical prostatectomy: the national Medicare experience 1988-1990 (updated June 1993). *Urology* 1993;42:622–629.
16. Bishoff JT, Motley G, Optenberg SA, et al. Incidence of fecal and urinary incontinence following radical perineal and retropubic prostatectomy in a national population. *J Urol* 1998;160: 454–458.
17. Litwin MS, Hays RD, Fink A, et al. Quality-of-life outcomes in men treated for localized prostate cancer. *JAMA* 1995;273:129–135.
18. Wilt TJ, Brawer MK. The prostate cancer intervention versus observation trial (PIVOT). *Oncology* 1997;11:1133–1143.
19. Norlen BJ. Swedish randomized trial of radical prostatectomy versus watchful waiting. *Can J Oncol* 1994;4(suppl 1):38–42.
20. Fowler FJ, Barry MJ, Lu-Yao G, Wasson JH, Bin L. Outcomes of external beam radiation therapy for prostate cancer: a study of Medicare beneficiaries in three surveillance, epidemiology, and end results areas. *J Clin Oncol* 1996;14:2258–2265.
21. Crook J, Perry G, Robertson S, Esche B. Routine prostate biopsies following radiotherapy for prostate care: results for 225 patients. *Urology* 1995;45:624–632.
22. Hanks GE, Lee WR, Schultheiss TE. Clinical and biochemical evidence of control of prostate cancer at 5 years after external beam radiation. *J Urol* 1995;154:456–459.
23. Health Care Financing Administration. Medicare Claims Data, Calendar Year 1995.
24. Blasko JC, Ragde H, Grimm PD. Transperineal ultrasound guided implantation of the prostate: morbidity and complications. *Scand J Urol Nephrol* 1991;137(suppl):113–118.
25. Technology Evaluation Center. *Relative effectiveness and cost-effectiveness of available methods of androgen suppression in the treatment of advanced prostate cancer*. Chicago, Illinois: Blue Cross Blue Shield Association, In press.
26. Byar DP, Corle DK. Hormone therapy for prostate cancer: results of the Veterans' Administration cooperative urologic research group studies. *National Cancer Institute Monograph* 1988;7:165–170.
27. The Medical Research Council Prostate Cancer Working Party Investigators Group. Immediate versus deferred treatment for advanced prostatic cancer: initial results of the Medical Research Council trial. *Br J Urol* 1997;79:235–246.

Timothy J Wilt, MD, MPH
Associate Professor of Medicine
Center for Chronic Diseases Outcomes Research
Minneapolis VA Hospital
Minneapolis
Minnesota
USA

Michael K Brawer, MD
Professor of Urology
Northwest Prostate Institute
Seattle
Washington
USA

Competing interests: None declared.

TABLE 1 Prostatic cancer staging systems. **(*See* text, p. 417.)**

The tumor, node, metastasis (TNM) classification system	
Tumor	
T0	Clinically unsuspected
T1	Clinically inapparent (not palpable or visible by imaging)
T2	Tumor confined within prostate
T3	Tumor outside capsule or extension into vesicle
T4	Tumor fixed to other tissue
Nodes	
N0	No evidence of involvement of regional nodes
N1	Involvement of regional node
Metastases	
M0	No evidence of distant metastases
M1	Evidence of distant metastases
The American urologic staging system	
Stage A	No palpable tumor
Stage B	Tumor confined to the prostate gland
Stage C	Extracapsular extension
Stage D	Metastatic prostate cancer
Stage D1	Pelvic lymph node metastases
Stage D2	Distant metastases

Metastatic prostate cancer

Matthew R Smith, MD, PhD, Philip Kantoff, MD, and James Talcott, MD

QUESTIONS

INTERVENTIONS

Key Messages

In men with metastatic cancer

- We found limited data from randomized controlled trials (RCTs) for survival advantage from androgen deprivation in men with metastatic prostate cancer. A systematic review of RCTs found no difference in effectiveness between different methods of androgen deprivation (orchiectomy, diethylstilbestrol, luteinizing hormone–releasing hormone [LHRH] agonists) but found that androgen deprivation improved symptoms and objective signs of disease in most men.
- Systematic reviews of RCTs provide no evidence of additional benefit from combined androgen blockade compared with androgen deprivation alone.
- RCTs found no evidence that deferring androgen deprivation until disease progression reduces survival compared with immediate treatment for men with metastatic disease. However, without surveillance, deferred androgen deprivation results in higher rates of complications. Immediate androgen deprivation may improve survival in men with advanced prostate cancer and no evidence of bone metastases.
- No trials have yet evaluated the long-term effects of intermittent androgen deprivation on mortality, morbidity, or quality of life.

In men with symptomatic androgen-independent prostate cancer

- RCTs found that chemotherapy has palliative benefit but does not prolong survival.
- External-beam radiation has not yet been compared with other palliative treatments. A systematic review of trials comparing different treatment schedules found pain relief in some men.

- We found limited evidence to suggest that radionuclides with selective bone localization decrease pain in some men.
- We found no adequate evidence to evaluate the effectiveness of bisphosphonates.

DEFINITION *See* nonmetastatic prostate cancer (p. 417). Androgen-independent metastatic disease is defined as disease progression following androgen deprivation.

INCIDENCE/ PREVALENCE *See* nonmetastatic prostate cancer (p. 417).

ETIOLOGY *See* nonmetastatic prostate cancer (p. 417).

PROGNOSIS Prostate cancer metastasizes predominantly to bone. Metastatic prostate cancer can result in pain, weakness, paralysis, and death.

AIMS To prevent premature death and disability, to control symptoms and maximize quality of life, and to minimize adverse effects of treatment.

OUTCOMES Survival; response in terms of symptoms and signs; quality of life; adverse effects of treatment.

METHODS *Clinical Evidence* search for systematic reviews to end of July 1998.

QUESTION What are the effects of treatment in men with metastatic prostate cancer?

OPTION ANDROGEN DEPRIVATION

We found limited evidence of a survival advantage from androgen deprivation in men with metastatic prostate cancer. A systematic review of RCTs found no difference in effectiveness between different methods of androgen deprivation (orchiectomy, diethylstilbestrol, LHRH agonists) but found that androgen deprivation improves symptoms and objective signs of disease in most men.

Benefits: **Versus no initial treatment:** We found no systematic review and no recent RCTs. Three RCTs performed between 1959 and 1975 compared androgen deprivation (diethylstilbestrol, orchiectomy, or estrogens) with no initial treatment in approximately 4000 men with all stages of prostate cancer. They found no difference in overall survival. Re-analysis of updated data from these RCTs found a modest survival advantage with androgen deprivation.[1] The report did not provide statistical details. **Different types of androgen deprivation:** We found one systematic review published in 1996, which identified 25 RCTs comparing different types of androgen deprivation in men with metastatic disease.[2] Interventions were orchiectomy, diethylstilbestrol, or an LHRH agonist. Disease-related symptoms (symptomatic response, range in different clinical trials 22%–90%) and measurable criteria, including radiographic findings and laboratory tests (objective response, range in different clinical trials 22%–90%), improved in most men. There were no significant differences in response rates, time to progression, or survival. For all forms of androgen deprivation, duration of response was 12 to 18 months, and overall survival was 24 to 36 months.

Harms: All forms of androgen deprivation are known to be associated with vasomotor flushing, loss of libido, gynecomastia, weight gain, osteoporosis, and loss of muscle mass; however, limited prospective data are available on the frequency for these adverse effects. **Diethylstilbestrol** is associated with an increased risk of cardiovascular events, gastric irritation, and allergic reactions, and for these reasons is not used routinely. **Orchiectomy** has cosmetic and potential psychological consequences. **LHRH agonists** may cause an initial clinical flare owing to transient increases in androgen levels.

Comment: The high cardiovascular event rate with high-dose diethylstilbestrol in the early RCTs[1] may have mitigated any survival benefit of androgen deprivation.

OPTION COMBINED ANDROGEN BLOCKADE

Evidence from systematic reviews of RCTs is conflicting. The largest review found no evidence of additional benefit from combined androgen blockade (androgen deprivation plus an antiandrogen) compared with androgen deprivation alone.

Benefits: We found two systematic reviews. The largest, published in 1995, identified 22 RCTs with 3283 deaths in 5710 men, most of whom had stage D2 disease. Individual patient data were obtained. Interventions were androgen deprivation (orchiectomy or LHRH agonist) with or without an antiandrogen.[3] There was no significant difference in 5-year survival (AR of dying within 5 years with androgen deprivation alone 77.2% compared with 73.8% with combined blockade, ARR 0.03, 95% CI 0–0.07, RR 0.96, 95% CI 0.93–1.00). Four of the 22 RCTs used cyproterone acetate, a steroidal antiandrogen with intrinsic androgenic activity and lower antiandrogenic activity than nonsteroidal antiandrogens. Exclusion of these four studies did not alter the results. The smaller systematic review, published in 1997, identified nine RCTs comparing androgen deprivation (orchiectomy or LHRH agonist) with or without nonsteroidal antiandrogens.[4] Combined androgen blockade improved overall survival (RR of death compared with androgen deprivation alone 0.78, 95% CI 0.67–0.90).

Harms: Combined androgen blockade with flutamide, a nonsteroidal antiandrogen, is associated with significantly higher rates of diarrhea (6.3% vs. 2.7%, $p=0.002$) and anemia (8.5% vs. 5.4%, $p=0.024$) than androgen deprivation alone.[5]

Comment An updated meta-analysis will be available shortly from the authors of the 1995 systematic review[3] (Clarke M, personal communication).

OPTION IMMEDIATE VERSUS DEFERRED ANDROGEN DEPRIVATION

In men with metastatic (stage D) disease, RCTs found no survival benefit from immediate treatment versus deferring androgen deprivation until disease progression. However, without surveillance, deferred androgen deprivation results in higher rates of complications. Immediate androgen deprivation may improve survival in men with locally advanced prostate cancer but no evidence of bone metastases (stage C).

Benefits: No systematic review. We found two RCTs in 2841 men with stage C and D prostate cancer, comparing immediate versus deferred androgen deprivation (orchiectomy or LHRH antagonist). Immediate androgen deprivation was initiated at diagnosis of prostate cancer; deferred androgen deprivation was initiated at the time of clinical disease progression. One RCT (already mentioned above) had no formal surveillance requirements or criteria for starting androgen deprivation in men assigned to deferred treatment.[6] It included 938 men with stage C (locally advanced) and D (asymptomatic metastatic) disease. It reported a survival benefit from immediate treatment (62% of deaths were from prostate cancer compared with 71% in the deferred treatment arm, $p<0.001$), which was limited to men with stage C disease.[6] Immediate androgen suppression almost halved the risk of major complications such as pathologic fractures (AR 2.3% vs. 4.5% with deferred treatment), spinal cord compression (AR 1.9% vs. 4.9%), ureteric obstruction (AR 7% vs. 11.8%), and extra-skeletal metastases (AR 7.9% vs. 11.8%). The report did not quote CIs nor make clear the time interval over which outcomes were recorded, although this seemed to be at least 10 years. Again, the lower incidence of complications was more apparent in men presenting with stage C disease. The other RCT had rigorous surveillance requirements and formal criteria for starting androgen deprivation in men assigned to deferred treatment. In men with evidence of distant metastases at study entry, there was no significant difference in overall survival. Of the men with distant metastases who died, 62% in the immediate treatment group died from prostate cancer compared with 71% assigned to delayed treatment ($p<0.001$). In men with no evidence of distant metastases, immediate androgen deprivation resulted in significantly better overall ($p=0.02$) and disease-specific survival compared with delayed treatment ($p<0.001$).[1]

Harms: We found no good data on adverse effects of androgen deprivation in men with metastatic prostate cancer, although these tend to be less of a concern than in men with nonmetastatic disease because of the shorter life expectancy.

Comment: The high rate of complications in men assigned to deferred treatment in the first RCT[1] suggests that deferred hormonal treatment in men with advanced prostate cancer is inappropriate without careful surveillance for signs and symptoms of disease progression. Approximately 10% of men assigned to deferred hormonal treatment were not treated until they developed a pathologic fracture or spinal cord compression.[1] The other RCT found no significant difference in rates of complication between immediate and deferred treatment.[1]

OPTION INTERMITTENT VERSUS CONTINUOUS ANDROGEN DEPRIVATION

The effects of intermittent androgen deprivation have not yet been evaluated adequately.

Benefits: We found no systematic review and no RCTs evaluating the long-term effect of intermittent androgen deprivation on mortality, morbidity, or quality of life.

Harms: Insufficient data.

Comment: None.

QUESTION **Are there any effective treatments for men with symptomatic androgen-independent metastatic disease?**

OPTION **CHEMOTHERAPY**

RCTs found that chemotherapy decreases pain and prolongs palliation in some men with symptomatic androgen-independent prostate cancer. We found no evidence that chemotherapy prolongs survival.

Benefits: We found no systematic review. We found three RCTs, all using crossover designs, only one of which has been published in full. This compared mitoxantrone plus prednisone versus prednisone alone in 161 men with symptomatic androgen-independent metastatic prostate cancer.[7] Men receiving chemotherapy were more likely to experience pain reduction (29% vs. 12%, $p=0.01$), enjoyed longer palliation (43 vs. 18 weeks, $p<0.0001$), and showed improvements in quality of life. There was no difference in overall survival. Two other RCTs are published only in abstract form. One compared mitoxantrone and prednisone versus prednisone alone in 242 men. Pain and analgesic use were reduced after chemotherapy.[8] The other compared suramin plus hydrocortisone versus hydrocortisone alone in 458 men.[9] Chemotherapy improved pain and duration of palliation.

Harms: The RCTs reported no treatment-related mortality. There were nine episodes of febrile neutropenia (World Health Organization grade 3 or 4) among 130 men treated with 796 courses of mitoxantrone. Five men experienced cardiac arrhythmias or decreased ejection fraction, including two who developed congestive heart failure.[7]

Comment: The crossover design of these RCTs precludes reliable conclusions about the effect of chemotherapy on survival, because men who died while in one arm of the study were not available for evaluation in the other.

OPTION **EXTERNAL-BEAM RADIATION**

One systematic review found no difference in effect between external beam radiation, strontium-89, or both treatments combined. One systematic review of RCTs comparing different radiation schedules found that external-beam radiation provides effective pain relief in some men. External-beam radiation has not been compared directly with other palliative treatments.

Benefits: **Versus other palliative treatments:** We found no RCTs. **Versus or as an adjunct to radionuclides:** We found one systematic review published in 1995, which identified two RCTs in men with prostate cancer and symptomatic bone metastases.[10] The first compared strontium-89 versus placebo in 126 men who had received external-beam radiation. It found no significant difference in median survival (27 vs. 34 weeks) or symptom relief (clinical response rate 80% vs. 60%). However, strontium-89 significantly reduced the number of new pain sites ($p<0.02$), the requirement for analgesia (17% stopped taking analgesics vs. 2% on placebo, $p<0.05$), and subsequent radiotherapy (median time to radiotherapy 35 weeks vs. 20 weeks on placebo, $p = 0.06$). The second RCT compared external-beam radiation versus strontium-89 in 305 men. Strontium-89 was associated with significantly fewer new sites of pain ($p < 0.05$), and for local radiotherapy reduced need for additional radiotherapy ($p < 0.04$). Effect on survival was not reported. **Different schedules and doses:** We found one systematic review published in 1997, which identified nine RCTs in 1486 men with symptomatic bone metastases from a variety of different malignancies. The trials compared different radiation treatment fractionation schedules and doses of external-beam radiation.[10] There were minimal differences in effectiveness between different fractionation schedules and doses. External-beam radiation produced more than 50% pain relief in 42% of men and complete pain relief in 27%.

Harms: External-beam radiation was associated with a 10% higher rate of gastrointestinal adverse effects.[10] However, thrombocytopenia occurred twice as often with strontium-89 (6.9% vs. 3.4% with external-beam radiation) and 3% of men receiving strontium-89 developed white blood cell toxicity.[10] There was no significant difference between treatment schedules and doses in rates of nausea, vomiting, or diarrhea.[10]

Comment: The systematic review provides no direct information on effectiveness of external-beam radiation in men with bone metastasis from prostate cancer, because all participants in the trials received some radiation treatment and not all metastases were due to prostate cancer.[11]

OPTION RADIONUCLIDE TREATMENT

We found limited evidence from one RCT that radionuclides with selective bone localization may reduce pain in men with symptomatic bone metastases. A systematic review of RCTs found no difference in palliation between radionuclides and external-beam radiation and no effect of radionuclides on survival.

Benefits: **Versus placebo:** We found no systematic review. We found one RCT comparing rhenium-186 with placebo in nine men with prostate cancer and symptomatic bone metastases.[12] Treatment with rhenium-186 resulted in significantly better pain control than placebo (no RR or CI reported). **Versus or as an adjunct to external-beam radiation:** *See* above.[10]

Harms: Strontium-89 results in thrombocytopenia (WHO grade 3 or 4) in 7% to 33% of patients, and leukopenia (WHO grade 3 or 4) in 3% to 12%.[11,13] Other radionuclides with selective bone localization have similar rates of hematologic toxicity.

Comment: None.

OPTION BISPHOSPHONATES

We found no adequate data to evaluate the effectiveness of bisphosphonates.

Benefits: A systematic review published in 1998 identified two RCTs in 156 men with prostate cancer and symptomatic bone metastases.[13] They found no significant reduction in bone pain with bisphosphonates.

Both RCTs were flawed. One did not use a pain scale. The other evaluated etidronate, a bisphosphonate that is pharmacologically unsuitable for treating bone metastases.

Harms: The systematic review identified a total of 18 RCTs of bisphosphonates in men with bone metastases from a variety of cancers.[13] No RCT reported major toxicity. Treatment with pamidronate was associated with increased frequency of anterior uveitis and episcleritis.

Comment: None.

REFERENCES

1. Byar DP, Corle DK. Hormone therapy for prostate cancer: results of the Veterans Administration cooperative urologic research group studies. *National Cancer Institute Monograph* 1988;7:165–170.
2. Robson M, Dawson N. How is androgen-dependent metastatic prostate cancer best treated? *Hematol Oncol Clin North Am* 1996;10:727–747.
3. Prostate Cancer Trialists' Collaborative Group. Maximum androgen blockade in advanced prostate cancer: an overview of 22 randomized trials with 3283 deaths in 5710 patients. *Lancet* 1995;346:265–269.
4. Caubet JF, Tosteson TD, Dong EW, et al. Maximum androgen blockade in advanced prostate cancer: a meta-analysis of published randomized controlled trials using nonsteroidal antiandrogens. *Urology* 1997;49:71–78.
5. Eisenberger MA, Blumenstein BA, Crawford ED, et al. Bilateral orchiectomy with or without flutamide for metastatic prostate cancer. *N Engl J Med* 1998;339:1036–1042.
6. Medical Research Council Prostate Cancer Working Party Investigators Group. Immediate versus deferred treatment for advanced prostatic cancer: initial results of the Medical Research Council trial. *Br J Urol* 1997;79:235–246.
7. Tannock IF, Osoba D, Stockler MR, et al. Chemotherapy with mitoxantrone plus prednisone or prednisone alone for symptomatic hormone-resistant prostate cancer: a Canadian randomized trial with palliative end points. *J Clin Oncol* 1996;14:1756–1764.
8. Kantoff PW, Conaway M, Winer E, et al. Randomized comparison of low-dose steroids in patients with hormone-refractory stage D carcinoma of the prostate: a phase III study (CALGB 9182) [abstract]. *Proc Am Soc Clin Oncol* 1996;15:2013.
9. Small EJ, Marshall E, Reyno L, et al. Superiority of suramin + hydrocortisone over placebo + hydrocortisone: results of a multicenter double-blind phase III study in patients with hormone refractory prostate cancer [abstract]. *Proc Am Soc Clin Oncol* 1998;17:1187.
10. McQuay HJ, Carroll D, Moore RA. Radiotherapy for painful bone metastases: a systematic review. *Clin Oncol (R Coll Radiol)* 1997;9:150–154.
11. Robinson RG, Preston DF, Schiefelbein M, et al. Strontium 89 therapy for the palliation of pain due to osseous metastases. *JAMA* 1995;274:420–424.
12. Maxon HR, Schroder LE, Hertzberg VS, et al. Rhenium-186(Sn)HEDP for treatment of painful osseous metastases: results of a double-blind crossover comparison with placebo. *J Nucl Med* 1991;32:1877–1881.
13. Bloomfield DJ. Should bisphosphonates be part of the standard therapy of patients with multiple myeloma or bone metastases from other cancers? An evidence-based review. *J Clin Oncol* 1998;16:1218–1225.

Matthew R Smith, MD, PhD
Instructor in Medicine
Massachusetts General Hospital
Boston
Massachusetts
USA

Philip Kantoff, MD
Director
Lank Center for Genitourinary Oncology
Dana Farber Cancer Institute
Boston
Massachusetts
USA

James Talcott, MD
Assistant Professor of Medicine
Harvard Medical School
Boston
Massachusetts
USA

Competing interests: None declared.

Epilepsy

Tony Marson, MB, ChB

QUESTIONS

INTERVENTIONS

Beneficial

Trade-off between benefits and harms

To be covered in future issues of *Clinical Evidence*

Treatment of infantile spasms
Treatment of drug-resistant generalized epilepsy
Temporal lobe surgery and vagus nerve stimulation for drug-resistant epilepsy

*Never evaluated in placebo-controlled trials

Key Messages

- Randomized controlled trials (RCTs) have found that treatment of single seizures reduces the risk of further seizures by approximately one half. However, we found no evidence that treatment alters long-term prognosis. Long-term anti-epileptic drug treatment is potentially harmful.
- The main anti-epileptic drugs (carbamazepine, lamotrigine, phenobarbital, phenytoin, primidone, valproate) have not been evaluated in placebo-controlled trials in people with newly diagnosed partial or generalized epilepsy. We found no good evidence on which to base a choice between drugs in terms of efficacy. RCTs have found that phenobarbital and primidone are less well tolerated than other drugs.
- One systematic review of RCTs has found that the addition of second-line drugs significantly reduces the seizure frequency in people with partial epilepsy who are not responding to usual treatment. Each additional drug increases the frequency of adverse effects, the need for withdrawal of additional treatment, or both. We found no good evidence from RCTs on which to base a choice between drugs.
- Anti-epileptic drug withdrawal for patients in remission is associated with a higher risk of seizure recurrence than continued treatment. Clinical predictors of relapse after drug withdrawal include age, seizure type, number of anti-epileptic drugs being taken, whether seizures have occurred since anti-epileptic drugs have been started, and the period of remission before drug withdrawal.

DEFINITION Epilepsy should be considered as a group of disorders rather than a single disease. Seizures can be partial (categorized as simple partial, complex partial, and secondary generalized tonic clonic seizures) or generalized (categorized as generalized tonic clonic, absence, myoclonic, tonic, and atonic seizures).[1]

INCIDENCE/ PREVALENCE Epilepsy is common, with an estimated prevalence in the developed world of 5 to 10/1000[2] and an annual incidence of 50/100,000. Approximately 3% of people will be given a diagnosis of epilepsy at some time in their lives.[3]

ETIOLOGY Epilepsy also can be classified according to etiology.[1] Idiopathic generalized epilepsies (such as juvenile myoclonic epilepsy or childhood-absence epilepsy) are largely genetic and have particular clinical and electroencephalographic characteristics. Symptomatic epilepsies result from a known cerebral abnormality—for example, temporal lobe epilepsy may result from a congenital defect, mesial temporal sclerosis, or a tumor. Cryptogenic epilepsies are those that cannot be classified as idiopathic or symptomatic and in which no causative factor has been identified.

PROGNOSIS For most people with epilepsy, the prognosis is good. Approximately 70% go into remission, defined as being seizure free for 5 years on or off treatment. This leaves 20% to 30% who will develop chronic epilepsy,[4] often requiring treatment with multiple anti-epileptic drugs. Approximately 60% of untreated people will suffer no further seizures in the 2 years after their first seizure.[5]

AIMS To reduce the risk of subsequent seizures, to improve the prognosis of the seizure disorder, and (in people in remission) to withdraw anti-epileptic drugs without causing seizure recurrence.

OUTCOMES For treatment after a single seizure: time to subsequent seizures; time to achieve remission; proportion achieving remission. For treatment of newly diagnosed epilepsy: retention on allocated treatment or time to withdrawal of allocated treatment; time to remission; time to first seizure after treatment. For treatment of drug-resistant epilepsy: percentage reduction in seizure frequency; proportion of responders. For drug withdrawal: time to seizure recurrence.

METHODS The Cochrane Epilepsy Group trials register was searched to the end of 1998. The register was established using a comprehensive MEDLINE search and hand searching of journals. Where possible, systematic reviews were sought. If none were found, the largest RCTs were reviewed.

QUESTION **Should single seizures be treated?**

RCTs have found that treatment with anti-epileptic drugs reduces the risk of further seizures by approximately half. However, we found no evidence that treatment alters long-term prognosis, and long-term anti-epileptic drug treatment is potentially harmful.

Benefits: A systematic review of prospective observational studies[5] concluded that, at 2 years from their first seizure, 40% (95% CI 37%–43%) of people will have had further seizures. No systematic review has examined the effects of treatment. We found three RCTs, the largest of which compared immediate versus no treatment in 419 patients (42% women, 28% aged ≤16 years, 65% aged 16–65 years, 6% aged ≥60 years).[6,7] Patients were randomized within 7 days of their first tonic clonic seizure and were followed for a minimum of 3 years. At 2 years, there were half as many second seizures in the treatment group compared with the control group (AR 25% vs. 51%, RR 0.36, 95% CI 0.24–0.53). However, there was no significant difference in the proportion of people achieving a 2-year remission (AR 60% vs. 68%, RR 0.82, 95% CI 0.64–1.03; RR adjusted for time of starting treatment 0.96, 95% CI 0.77–1.22).

Harms: The RCT did not report on adverse effects.[6,7] However, these are well known and include idiosyncratic reactions, teratogenesis, and cognitive effects.

Comment: The RCT was too small to exclude the possibility that treating a first seizure alters the long-term prognosis of epilepsy.[6,7]

QUESTION What are the effects of monotherapy in newly diagnosed partial epilepsy?

The main anti-epileptic drugs (carbamazepine, lamotrigine, phenobarbital, phenytoin, primidone, valproate) have not been evaluated in placebo-controlled trials in people with partial epilepsy. Trials comparing one drug with another have found that phenobarbital and primidone are less well tolerated than other drugs. With respect to efficacy, we found no evidence on which should be the drug of first choice in partial epilepsy.

Benefits: No systematic review. **Versus placebo:** We found no RCTs. **Versus each other:** We found more than 20 RCTs, although many were small and methodologically weak. The two largest RCTs are summarized here. The first randomized 622 patients (mean age 41 years, 87% men) to either carbamazepine, phenobarbital, phenytoin, or primidone.[8] At 36 months, patients allocated to primidone did significantly worse for the outcome "retention on allocated treatment" ($p < 0.001$). When the subgroup of patients with predominantly simple and/or complex partial seizures were considered, those allocated to phenobarbital and primidone did significantly worse for this outcome ($p < 0.02$). At 3 years, 39% of participants had remained seizure free, and no overall difference was found between groups. For patients with predominantly tonic clonic seizures, the proportion remaining seizure free was similar in all treatment groups (43%–48%), and no significant differences were found (no *p* values were quoted). For patients with predominantly complex partial seizures, those taking carbamazepine fared significantly better than those taking phenobarbital or primidone (proportions remaining seizure free 43%, 16%, 15%, $p < 0.03$). The second RCT randomized 480 patients (mean age 47 years, 93% men) to either valproate or carbamazepine.[9] At 12 months, no significant difference was found for the outcome "retention on allocated treatment," with 70% to 80%

of patients continuing to take allocated treatment (no *p* value quoted). Patients with predominantly complex partial seizures taking carbamazepine did significantly better for the outcome "time to first seizure" ($p < 0.02$). However, the proportion of patients remaining seizure free at 12 months did not differ (no *p* value quoted).

Harms: In the first RCT, people taking phenytoin were significantly more likely to suffer cosmetic adverse effects, including gum hypertrophy, acne, hirsutism, and rash (phenytoin 22%, carbamazepine 14%, phenobarbital 11%, primidone 10%; $p < 0.01$).[8] In the second RCT, rashes occurred in 11% of patients taking carbamazepine and 1% taking valproate ($p < 0.001$). Patients taking valproate were significantly more likely to gain weight (32% vs. 43%, $p = 0.02$), in particular to have weight gain of 5.5 kg or more (8% vs. 20%, $p < 0.001$), and to suffer hair loss or change in hair texture (6% vs. 12%, $p = 0.02$) and tremor (22% vs. 45%, $p < 0.001$).[9]

Comment: Placebo-controlled trials of these drugs now would be considered unethical. Patients recruited into the two largest comparative trials were predominantly male veterans and were therefore more likely to have epilepsy as a consequence of brain trauma, which may result in a more resistant partial epilepsy.

QUESTION **What are the effects of monotherapy in newly diagnosed generalized epilepsy?**

The main anti-epileptic drugs (carbamazepine, lamotrigine, phenobarbital, phenytoin, valproate) have not been evaluated in placebo-controlled trials in people with generalized epilepsy. Trials comparing one drug with another have failed to find consistent differences between drugs.

Benefits: No systematic review. **Versus placebo:** We found no RCTs. **Versus each other:** We found four RCTs of monotherapy, two in adults,[10,11] and two in children,[12 13] comparing carbamazepine versus valproate. One, in 200 adults, found that, at 3 years, retention on allocated treatment was more likely with valproate than carbamazepine (RR 0.34, 95% CI 0.1–0.72).[11] Another trial, in 160 children aged 5 to 16 years, found no difference in retention on allocated treatment (no measure of significance quoted).[13] Both trials found that approxiamtely 80% of patients achieved remission at 3 years, with no significant difference between groups.[11,13] The other two studies did not present results separately for partial and generalized epilepsy. However, on regression analysis they found no interaction between epilepsy type and drug for either retention on allocated treatment or time to first seizure.

Harms: The overall prevalence of adverse events was similar on the two drugs.[11,13] However, rashes occurred more often in patients on carbamazepine than on sodium valproate (11.2% vs. 1.7%, $p < 0.05$,[11] 6.3% vs. 3.4%, NS[13]), and more patients on sodium valproate reported weight gain (12.1% vs. 1.1%, $p < 0.05$,[11] 10.2% vs. 3.9% NS[13]), usually after at least 3-months' treatment. Other adverse events with carbamazepine were dizziness (6.7% vs. 2.9%, NS,[11] 6.3% vs. 0.8%, $p < 0.05$[13]), headaches (6.1% vs. 3.4%[13]), ataxia (2.2% vs. 0%[11]), somnolence (19.7% vs. 9.3%, $p < 0.05$[13]), fatigue (10.2% vs. 5.1%, NS[13]), diplopia (3.9% vs. 0%, NS[13]), and insomnia (3.9% vs. 0%, NS[13]). Other drug-related adverse events with sodium valproate were tremor (5.2% vs. 1.7%, NS[11]), alopecia (2.9% vs. 0.6%, NS,[11] 4.2% vs. 1.6%, NS[13]), and appetite increase (2.3% vs. 0%, NS,[11] 9.3% vs. 0%, $p<0.01$[13]). Treatment was withdrawn because of adverse events in 9.3 % of patients on valproate compared with 17.7% on carbamazepine[11] (18 vs. 15 patients).[13]

Comment: Placebo-controlled trials of these drugs now would be considered unethical. All four comparative trials recruited patients with partial and generalized epilepsy, but of the generalized epilepsy syndromes, only generalized tonic clonic seizures were measured, and not absence or myoclonus. The RCTs were too small to exclude potentially important differences in efficacy. In addition, results may have been confounded by errors in classification of patients' epilepsy.

QUESTION **Does the addition of second-line drugs benefit people with drug-resistant partial epilepsy?**

A systematic review of RCTs has found that the addition of second-line drugs significantly reduces the seizure frequency in people with partial epilepsy who are not responding to usual treatment. Each additional drug increases the frequency of adverse effects, the need for withdrawal of additional treatment, or both. We found no good evidence from RCTs on which to base a choice between these drugs.

Benefits: A systematic review identified 29 placebo-controlled RCTs in 4091 people with drug-resistant partial epilepsy.[14] It found that the addition of gabapentin, lamotrigine, tiagabine, topiramate, or vigabatrin to usual treatment significantly reduced the seizure frequency compared with placebo (Table 1).

Harms: Adverse effects were more frequent with additional treatment compared with placebo (Table 1). Lamotrigine is associated with a rash, which may be avoided by slower titration of the drug. Vigabatrin is not licensed in the USA because of concern over visual field defects.

Comment: Few RCTs have compared these drugs directly with each other.

QUESTION **Which patients are at risk of relapse on withdrawal of drug treatment?**

Observational studies have found that nearly one third of patients will relapse within 2 years if anti-epileptic drugs are withdrawn. Clinical predictors of relapse after drug withdrawal include age, seizure type, number of anti-epileptic drugs being taken, whether seizures have occurred since anti-epileptic drugs were started, and the period of remission before drug withdrawal.

Benefits: A systematic review of observational studies found that, at 2 years, 29% (95% CI 24%–34%) of patients in remission from all types of epilepsy would relapse if anti-epileptic drugs were withdrawn.[15] We found no systematic review of RCTs. The largest single RCT compared continued anti-epileptic treatment versus slow anti-epileptic drug withdrawal in 1013 people who had been seizure free for at least 2 years.[16,17] At 2 years, 78% of patients who continued treatment remained seizure free, compared to 59% in the withdrawal group. RRs with 95% CIs for the main factors predicting recurrence of seizures are given in Table 2.

Harms: Sixteen patients died during the trial, 10 in the continued treatment group, and six in the withdrawal group.[16,17] Only two deaths were attributed to epilepsy, and both of these occurred in patients randomized to continued treatment.

Comment: There were no significant differences in psychosocial outcomes between groups. Patients with a seizure recurrence were less likely to be in paid employment at 2 years.[16,17]

REFERENCES

1. Commission on classification and terminology of the international league against epilepsy. Proposal for revised classification of epilepsies and epileptic syndromes. *Epilepsia* 1989;30:389–399.
2. Hauser WA, Annegers JF, Kurland LT. Incidence of epilepsy and unprovoked seizures in Rochester, Minnesota 1935-84. *Epilepsia* 1993;34:453–468.
3. Hauser WA, Kurland LT. The epidemiology of epilepsy in Rochester, Minnesota, 1935 through 1967. *Epilepsia* 1975;16:1–66.
4. Cockerell OC, Johnson AL, Sander JW, Hart YM, Shorvon SD. Remission of epilepsy: results from the national general practice study of epilepsy. *Lancet* 1995;346:140–144.
5. Berg AT, Shinnar S. The risk of seizure recurrence following a first unprovoked seizure: a quantitative review. *Neurology* 1991;41:965–972.
6. First Seizure Trial Group (FIRST Group). Randomized clinical trial on the efficacy of antiepileptic drugs in reducing the risk of relapse after a first unprovoked tonic clonic seizure. *Neurology* 1993;43:478–483.
7. Musicco M, Beghi E, Solari A, Viani F, for the FIRST group. Treatment of first tonic clonic seizure does not improve the prognosis of epilepsy. *Neurology* 1997;49:991–998.
8. Mattson RH, Cramer JA, Collins JF, et al. Comparison of carbamazepine, phenobarbital, phenytoin, and primidone in partial and secondarily generalized tonic-clonic seizures. *N Engl J Med* 1985;313:145–151.
9. Mattson R, Cramer J, Collins J. A comparison of valproate with carbamazepine for the treatment of complex partial seizures and secondarily generalized tonic clonic seizures in adults: Department of Veterans Affairs epilepsy cooperative study No. 264 group. *N Engl J Med* 1992;327:765–771.
10. Heller AJ, Chesterman P, Elwes R, Crawford P, Chadwick D, Johnson AL, Reynolds EH. Phenobarbitone, phenytoin, or sodium valproate for newly diagnosed epilepsy: a randomized comparative monotherapy trial. *J Neurol Neurosurg Psychiatry* 1995;8:44–50.
11. Richens A, Davidson DL, Cartlidge NE, Easter DJ. A multicentre comparative trial of sodium valproate and carbamazepine in adult onset epilepsy: adult EPITEG collaborative group. *J Neurol Neurosurg Psychiatry* 1994;57:682–687.
12. de Silva M, MacArdle B, McGowan M, et al. Randomised comparative monotherapy trial of phenobarbitone, phenytoin, carbamazepine, or sodium valproate for newly diagnosed childhood epilepsy. *Lancet* 1996;347:709–713.
13. Verity CM, Hosking G, Easter DJ. A multicentre comparative trial of sodium valproate and carbamazepine in paediatric epilepsy: the paediatric EPITEG collaborative group. *Dev Med Child Neurol* 1995;37:97–108.
14. Marson AG, Kadir ZA, Hutton JL, Chadwick DW. The new antiepileptic drugs: a systematic review of their efficacy and tolerability. *Epilepsia* 1997; 38:859–880. (Search date 1995; primary sources Medline 1966–Dec 1995, hand search of key journals, contacting pharmaceutical companies.)
15. Berg AT, Shinnar S. Relapse following discontinuation of antiepileptic drugs. *Neurology* 1994;44: 601–608.
16. Medical Research Council Antiepileptic Drug Withdrawal Study Group. Prognostic index for recurrence of seizures after remission of epilepsy. *BMJ* 1993;306:1374–1378.
17. Medical Research Council Antiepileptic Drug Withdrawal Study Group. Randomised study of antiepileptic drug withdrawal in patients in remission. *Lancet* 1991;337:1175–1180.

Tony Marson, MBChB
Lecturer in Neurology
University of Liverpool
Liverpool
UK

Competing interests: The author has been paid for speaking at a meeting by Johnson and Johnson, manufacturer of topiramate, and by Janssen Cilag, Sanofi, and Glaxo Wellcome for attending conferences.

TABLE 1 **Effects of additional drug treatment in people not responding to usual treatment: results of a systematic review of RCTs.[14]*** **(See text p. 435.)**

Drug	Daily dose (mg)	Proportion of patients responding (~50% reduction in seizure frequency) % (95% CI)	Rate of treatment withdrawal (OR 95% CI)	Significant adverse effects (OR 95% CI)	Comment
Gabapentin	Placebo 600 900 1200 1800	9.9 (7.2–13.5) 14.4 (12.0–17.3) 17.3 (14.6–20.3) 20.6 (17.1–24.6) 28.5 (21.5–36.7)	1.36 (0.75–2.49)	Dizziness 2.25 (1.28–3.98) Fatigue 2.25 (1.09–4.63) Somnolence 2.04 (1.21–3.44)	4 RCTs. Efficacy increased with increasing dose. No plateauing of therapeutic effect, so doses tested may not have been optimal.
Lamotrigine†	200–500	OR versus placebo 2.32 (1.47–3.68)	1.19 (0.79–1.79)	Ataxia 2.98 (1.86–4.77) Diplopia 3.39 (2.05–5.61) Dizziness 2.38 (1.63–3.48) Nausea 1.70 (1.08–2.68)	10 RCTs.
Tiagabine	Placebo 16 30–32 56	6.2 (3.9–9.7) 9.8 (4.5–20.1) 21.6 (17.7–26.0) 29.8 (19.4–42.8)	1.81 (1.21–2.70)	Dizziness 1.88 (1.18–2.99) Tremor 3.17 (1.15–8.75)	3 RCTs.
Topiramate	Placebo 200 400–1000	11.6 (8.0–16.6) 26.7 (15.8–41.3) 45.7 (41.3–50.1)	2.56 (1.64–4.00)	Dizziness 1.99 (1.20–3.28) Fatigue 2.52 (1.47–4.31) Somnolence 2.86 (1.71–4.79) Difficulty thinking 3.95 (1.86–8.39)	6 RCTs. There was a clear plateauing of therapeutic effect. Doses above 400 mg showed no significant advantage.
Vigabatrin	Placebo 1000 or 2000 3000 or 6000	13.8 (9.7–19.2) 22.8 (14.5–34.0) 45.9 (39.5–52.5)	2.58 (1.26–5.27)	No adverse effects were significantly more frequent with vigabatrin.	4 RCTs.

*Results were generated from regression models rather than from multiple subgroup analyses. †Lamotrigine has been evaluated in several cross-over trials and one parallel group trial. As a result, we were unable to investigate the effects of different lamotrigine doses in regression models.

TABLE 2 **Factors predicting recurrence of seizures at 2 years after withdrawal of anti-epileptic drugs: results of the largest RCT comparing drug withdrawal versus combined treatment.[16,17] (*See* text, p. 435.)**

Prognostic variable	RR (95% CI)
Age < 16 years	1.75 (2.36–1.30)
Tonic clonic seizures	1.76 (1.09–2.22)
Myoclonus	1.84 (1.12–3.02)
Treatment with more than one anti-epileptic drug	1.85 (1.38–2.40)
Seizures since anti-epileptic drugs were started	1.86 (1.18–2.05)
Years free from seizures (1/years)	12.3 (5.80–26.11)
Any electroencephalographic abnormality	1.32 (1.00–1.75)

Primary open-angle glaucoma

Colm O'Brien, MBBCh, BAO, FRCS, FRCOphth, MD, and Jeremy P Diamond, FRCOphth, FRCS, PhD

QUESTIONS

INTERVENTIONS

Likely to be beneficial

To be covered in future issues of *Clinical Evidence*

Treatment of ocular hypertension and normal tension glaucoma
Early detection of glaucoma (opportunistic case finding, population screening)

Key Messages

- Randomized controlled trials (RCTs) have found that topical medical treatments reduce raised intraocular pressure in people with primary open-angle glaucoma, but their protective effect on visual fields is uncertain.
- We found limited evidence suggesting that laser trabeculoplasty and surgical trabeculectomy provide greater protection of visual fields than medical treatment. Trabeculectomy is associated with morbidity, including cataract formation and loss of visual acuity, and medical treatment also may be associated with significant morbidity, including cataract formation and systemic side effects.

DEFINITION Glaucoma constitutes a group of diseases characterized by progressive optic neuropathy. It is generally bilateral though asymmetrical. The different forms of glaucoma share features of optic nerve cupping and pallor and peripheral visual field loss. The most common forms are primary open-angle glaucoma (when the level of intraocular pressure is greater than the upper limit of normal of 21 mm Hg) and low-tension or normal-pressure glaucoma (intraocular pressure < 22 mm Hg).

INCIDENCE/ PREVALENCE Glaucoma is found in 1% to 2% of white people aged over 40 years, rising to 5% at 70 years. Primary open-angle glaucoma accounts for two thirds, and normal-pressure glaucoma for up to a quarter of those affected.[1,2] In black populations, glaucoma is more prevalent, presents earlier with higher pressures, is more difficult to control, and results in more blindness.[1] Glaucoma is the third most prevalent cause of blindness in the world, affecting more than 5 million people.[3]

ETIOLOGY The major risk factor for developing primary open-angle glaucoma is raised intraocular pressure. Lesser risk factors include family history, myopia, and race.

PROGNOSIS People often fail to recognize peripheral field loss, and consequently 20% of people with glaucoma have advanced field loss at diagnosis.[4] As the disease progresses, patients have difficulty moving from a bright room to a darker room, and judging steps and curbs. Blindness results from gross loss of visual field or loss of central vision. The rate of progression is probably dictated by the level of intraocular pressure.[5] Once early field defects have appeared, and where the intraocular pressure is > 30 mm Hg, untreated people may lose the remainder of the visual field in 3 years or less.[5]

AIMS To prevent progression of visual field loss.

OUTCOMES Visual acuity, visual fields. Optic disc cupping and intraocular pressure are intermediate outcomes.

METHODS *Clinical Evidence* search. All systematic reviews and RCTs were evaluated.

QUESTION What are the effects of treatments for established glaucoma?

OPTION TOPICAL MEDICAL TREATMENT

RCTs have found that topical medical treatment reduces intraocular pressure compared with placebo, but the few trials with long-term follow-up have found no benefit in terms of protection against loss of visual field.

Benefits: We found one systematic review published in 1993, which identified 102 RCTs published between 1975 and 1991 in people with primary open-angle glaucoma.[6] Eighty-six trials compared one drug with another and were excluded from the review. The remaining 16 RCTs compared active treatment versus placebo. It was not possible to identify the types of participants or topical treatments from the published report. **Intraocular pressure:** Pooled analysis of the 16 trials showed a significant reduction in mean intraocular pressure of 4.9 mm Hg (95% CI –7.3 to –2.5 mm Hg). **Visual field loss:** Data on long-term visual field change were available in only three RCTs (302 participants), which when combined failed to show a significant protective effect of medical treatment (OR for any worsening of visual field loss 0.75, 95% CI 0.42–1.35). Our search revealed no substantial RCTs published since the systematic review.

Harms: Systemic adverse effects of topical treatments are uncommon but may be serious, including exacerbation of chronic obstructive airways disease after use of nonselective topical β-blockers.[7]

Comment: Two RCTs sponsored by the US National Institutes of Health are under way: the early manifest glaucoma study and the advanced glaucoma intervention study.

OPTION LASER TRABECULOPLASTY

Limited evidence from a single RCT suggests greater long-term benefits from laser trabeculoplasty plus medical treatment than from medical treatment alone.

Benefits: We found no systematic review. We found one RCT in 203 participants selected from 271 people with newly diagnosed primary open-angle glaucoma. This compared initial laser trabeculoplasty versus medical treatment alone.[8] After a mean follow-up of 7 years, those treated initially with laser surgery had a 1.2 mm Hg greater reduction in intraocular pressure ($p = 0.001$), a 0.6 dB greater improvement in visual field ($p < 0.001$), and significantly less deterioration in optic disc appearance ($p = 0.005$) compared with those those given medical treatment only.

Harms: Adverse effects of argon laser trabeculoplasty are mild and include a transient rise in intraocular pressure (> 5 mm Hg in 91 of 271 participants) and formation of peripheral anterior synechiae (in 93 of 271 participants).[8]

Comment: This was a multicenter trial with multiple observers.[8] The report does not make clear whether or not the observers were blind to the intervention.

OPTION SURGICAL TRABECULECTOMY

Limited evidence from two RCTs suggests that early surgical trabeculectomy may offer greater protection of visual fields than medical treatment. Surgical drainage is associated with a reduction in central vision.

Benefits: We found no systematic review, but we found two RCTs. One RCT compared trabeculectomy (followed by medical treatment where indicated) versus medical treatment (followed by trabeculectomy in which medical treatment failed) in 116 people with newly diagnosed primary open-angle glaucoma. The authors concluded that, after a mean follow-up of 4.6 years, there was no significant difference in visual acuity between the groups, but the medical treatment group had significantly greater loss of visual field.[9] The second RCT randomized 186 people with glaucoma to receive laser, medication, or early trabeculectomy surgery. After 5 years, major deterioration in visual fields was found in participants on medical and laser treatment, but not in those receiving surgery. There was no difference in visual acuity between the three groups.[10]

Harms: As with any type of eye surgery, complications can occur that may result in loss of vision. Surgical trabeculectomy is associated with a reduction in central vision. In one study, 83% of participants lost two lines of Snellen visual acuity.[11]

Comment: It was not possible to extract numerical data from either report.

REFERENCES

1. Sommer A, Tielsch JM, Katz J, et al. Relationship between intraocular pressure and primary open angle glaucoma among white and black Americans. *Arch Ophthalmol* 1991;109: 1090–1095.
2. Coffey M, Reidy A, Wormald R, Xian WX, Wright L, Courtney P. The prevalence of glaucoma in the west of Ireland. *Br J Ophthalmol* 1993;77: 17–21.
3. Infeld DA, O'Shea JG. Glaucoma: diagnosis and treatment. *Postgrad Med J* 1998;74:709–715.
4. Sheldrick JH, Ng C, Austin DJ, Rosenthal AR. An analysis of referral routes and diagnostic accuracy in cases of suspected glaucoma. *Ophthalmic Epidemiol* 1994;1:31–39.
5. Jay JL, Murdoch JR. The rate of visual field loss in untreated primary open angle glaucoma. *Br J Ophthalmol* 1993;77:176–178.
6. Rossetti L, Marchetti I, Orzalesi N, Scorpiglione N, Torri V, Liberati A. Randomised clinical trials on medical treatment of glaucoma: are they appropriate to guide clinical practice? *Arch Ophthalmol* 1993;111:96–103. Search date 1991; primary source Medline.
7. Diamond JP. Systemic adverse effects of topical ophthalmic agents: implications for older patients. *Drugs Ageing* 1997;11:352–360.
8. Glaucoma Laser Trial Group. The glaucoma laser trial (GLT) and glaucoma laser trial follow-up study: Results. *Am J Ophthalmol* 1995;120:718–731.
9. Jay JL, Allan D. The benefit of early trabeculectomy versus conventional management in primary open angle glaucoma relative to severity of disease. *Eye* 1989;3:528–535.
10. Migdal C, Gregory W, Hitchins R. Long-term functional outcome after early surgery compared with laser and medicine in open angle glaucoma. *Ophthalmology* 1994;101:1651–1657.
11. Costas VP, Smith M, Spaeth GL, Gandham S, Markovitz B. Loss of visual acuity after trabeculectomy. *Ophthalmology* 1993;100: 599–612.

Colm O'Brien, MBBCh, BAO, FRCS, FRCOphth, MD
Ophthalmologist
University College Dublin
Dublin
Republic of Ireland

Jeremy P Diamond, FRCOphth, FRCS, PhD
Consultant Ophthalmic Surgeon
United Bristol Healthcare NHS Trust
Bristol
UK

Competing interests: None declared.

Recurrent tonsillitis

Martin Burton, DM, FRCS

QUESTIONS

INTERVENTIONS

Unknown effectiveness	To be included in subsequent issues of *Clinical Evidence*
Tonsillectomy 444	Intermittent antibiotics
	Long-term antibiotics

Key Messages

- No randomized controlled trials (RCTs) have evaluated tonsillectomy in adults, and the evidence from RCTs in children is inconclusive.

DEFINITION Tonsillitis is infection of the parenchyma of the palatine tonsils. It is only one cause of "sore throat," which may be caused by infection of other pharyngeal tissues. Severe tonsillitis has been defined as seven episodes in the preceding year, five episodes per year in the preceding 2 years, or three per year in the preceding 3 years.[1]

INCIDENCE/ PREVALENCE Recurrent sore throat has an incidence in general practice in the UK of 100 per 1000 population per year.[2] Acute tonsillitis is more common in childhood.

ETIOLOGY Common bacterial pathogens include β-hemolytic and other streptococci. The part played by viruses is uncertain.

PROGNOSIS There are no good data on the natural history of tonsillitis and recurrent sore throat in children and adults. Participants in RCTs who were randomized to medical treatment (courses of antibiotics as required) have shown a tendency toward improvement over time.[1,3]

AIMS To abolish tonsillitis, to reduce the frequency and severity of throat infections, to improve general well being, behavior, and educational achievement, with minimal adverse effects.

OUTCOMES Number and severity of episodes of tonsillitis or sore throat; requirement for antibiotics and analgesics; time off work or school; behavior, school performance, general well-being; morbidity and mortality of surgery, and adverse effects of drugs.

METHODS MEDLINE and EMBASE were searched for RCTs and controlled clinical trials using the terms *tonsillitis*, *tonsillectomy*, and *tonsil** to 1997.

QUESTION **Is tonsillectomy effective in severe tonsillitis in children and adults?**

OPTION **TONSILLECTOMY VERSUS ANTIBIOTICS**

Limited evidence from one RCT suggests that tonsillectomy may benefit some children with severe tonsillitis. We found no good evidence on tonsillectomy in adults. Many important outcome measures have not been considered.

Benefits: We found two reviews have been performed.[4,5] **Children:** Both reviews identified the same two RCTs as being the only ones that met their quality inclusion criteria.[1,3] The smaller RCT involved 91 children who fulfilled stringent diagnostic criteria for "severe tonsillitis" (see Definition above).[1] The children were randomized to tonsillectomy alone ($n=27$), adenotonsillectomy ($n=16$), or intermittent courses of antibiotics as needed ($n=48$). Some children ($n=16$) were withdrawn from the nonsurgical group by their parents and had surgery, and children who developed infections after surgery received antibiotics as necessary for each episode of infection. Secondary outcome measures such as time off school were also considered. The authors concluded that children undergoing tonsillectomy experienced significantly fewer throat infections than those on antibiotics, amounting to an average of three fewer throat infections in the first

2 years, but by the third year the difference was no longer significant. The larger RCT, in 246 "less severely affected children" is published only in abstract form.[3] Some patients in this study also underwent adenoidectomy. The limited data available suggest little difference between surgical and medical treatment. The second review[5] concluded that it was not possible to determine the effectiveness of tonsillectomy from these RCTs. In the smaller RCT,[1] there were significant baseline differences between groups before treatment, and the authors pooled the results of tonsillectomy and adenotonsillectomy, making it impossible to assess the effectiveness of tonsillectomy alone. **Adults:** The reviews found no RCTs that evaluated tonsillectomy in adults with recurrent tonsillitis or sore throats.

Harms: The risks of tonsillectomy include those associated with general anesthesia and those specific to the procedure. The overall complication rate in the smaller RCT[1] was 14% (all were "readily managed or self limiting") compared with 2.3% to 7.8% in the Scottish tonsillectomy audit.[6] Hemorrhage, either primary (in the immediate postoperative period) or secondary, occurred in 4% of patients studied in the larger RCT[3] and fewer than 1% of patients in the Scottish tonsillectomy audit.[6] The potentially harmful effects of nonsurgical treatment are principally those associated with antibiotic usage. In the smaller RCT[1] erythematous rashes occurred in 4% of children in the nonsurgical group while taking penicillin.

Comment: Tonsillectomy is one of the most frequently performed surgical procedures in the UK, particularly in children, and accounts for approximately 20% of all operations performed by otolaryngologists.[6] No RCT has considered general well-being, development, or behavior despite suggestions that these factors are influenced by tonsillectomy.[6] Adenoidectomy is now only performed with tonsillectomy when there is a specific indication to remove the adenoids as well as the tonsils.

REFERENCES

1. Paradise JL, Bluestone CD, Bachman RZ, et al. Efficacy of tonsillectomy for recurrent throat infection in severely affected children. *N Engl J Med* 1984;310:674–683.
2. Shvartzman P. Careful prescribing is beneficial. *BMJ* 1994;309:1101–1102.
3. Paradise JL, Bluestone CD , Rogers KD, et al. Comparative efficacy of tonsillectomy for recurrent throat infection in more versus less severely affected children [abstract]. *Pediatric Res* 1992; 31:126A.
4. Marshall T. A review of tonsillectomy for recurrent throat infection. *Br J Gen Pract* 1998;48: 1331–1335. (Date of search 1997, primary sources Cochrane Library, MEDLINE.)
5. Burton MJ, Towler B, Glasziou P. Tonsillectomy versus non-surgical treatment for chronic/recurrent acute tonsillitis. Submitted for publication to The Cochrane Library. (Date of search 1997, primary sources MEDLINE, EMBASE)
6. Blair RL, McKerrow WS, Carter NW, Fenton A. The Scottish tonsillectomy audit. *J Laryngol Otol* 1996;110(suppl 20):1–25.

Martin Burton, DM, FRCS
Consultant Otolaryngologist
Radcliffe Infirmary NHS Trust
Oxford
UK

Competing interests: None declared.

Otitis media with effusion

Ian Williamson, MBChB

QUESTIONS

INTERVENTIONS

Key Messages

- Strategies for preventing otitis media with effusion have not yet been adequately evaluated.
- We found no clear answers from the available evidence regarding the effectiveness of pharmacologic treatments. Antibiotics have a short-term benefit, but there are harms associated with treatment.
- We found insufficient evidence regarding sustained benefits from mechanical and surgical treatment.

DEFINITION Otitis media with effusion (OME), or "glue ear," is characterized by either serous or mucoid, but not mucopurulent, fluid in the middle ear. Children usually present with hearing loss and speech problems, and in contrast to those with acute otitis media (p. 485), do not suffer from acutely distressing otalgia, fever, or malaise. The hearing loss is usually mild, identified when parents express concerns about their child's behavior, school performance, or language development.

INCIDENCE/ PREVALENCE At any one time approximately 5% of children aged 2 to 4 years will have bilateral hearing loss persisting for at least 3 months associated with OME. The incidence declines considerably at age 6.[1] Approximately 80% of children have been affected at some time by 10 years of age. OME is the most common reason for referral for surgery in children in the UK. Middle ear effusions also occur infrequently in adults after upper respiratory tract infection or air travel.

ETIOLOGY The etiology is uncertain, but upper respiratory tract infection and the size of the upper respiratory airways are contributory factors. Established risk factors include age at first onset, day care center attendance, number of siblings, socioeconomic group, frequent upper respiratory tract infection, bottle feeding, and household smoking. Most have been reported as approximately doubling the risk of developing OME.[2]

PROGNOSIS In one in 20 preschool children, OME—as identified by tympanometric screening—persists for a year.[3,4] A large study of behavior and cognitive outcomes in children with middle ear disease, produced an adjusted OR of reported hearing difficulty at age 5 years was 1.44 (95% CI 1.18–1.76, $n=12,534$). Similar data were obtained for language development, with sequelae remaining even at 10 years of age.[5]

AIMS To improve hearing and well-being; to avoid poor behavioral, speech, and educational development; and to prevent recurrent otalgia and otitis media.

OUTCOMES Resolution of effusion (both speed and completeness) assessed by otoscopy, tympanometry, or global clinical assessment; hearing impairment, assessed by audiometry or tympanometry (although the positive predictive value of these tests has been reported as low as 49%)[6]; developmental and behavioral tests; language and speech development; adverse effects of treatment. Hearing losses as small as 15 dB may have potentially disabling consequences in children, so changes of this magnitude are probably clinically significant. Methods for assessing patient-centered outcomes such as disability and quality of life in children with OME need further development and evaluation.

METHODS We searched the Cochrane Library, MEDLINE, and EMBASE from 1966 to May 1998 as part of a standard *Clinical Evidence* search for systematic reviews and randomized controlled trials (RCTs). We included all systematic reviews identified.

QUESTION What are the effects of preventive interventions?

OPTION AVOIDANCE OF MODIFIABLE RISK FACTORS

Interventions to modify risk factors for OME, such as passive smoking and bottle feeding, have not been evaluated in RCTs.

Benefits: We found no systematic review or RCTs of interventions aimed at modifying risk factors for OME.

Harms: None documented.

Comment: There is good epidemiologic evidence that passive smoking[7] and bottle feeding[8] increase the risk of otitis media with effusion, but that most additional risk is attributable to a child's socioeconomic group and the number of other children to whom he or she is exposed.[8] Feasible interventions for preventing otitis media, such as strategies to reduce household smoking and encourage breast feeding, deserve attention.

QUESTION What are the effects of treatments?

OPTION ANTIMICROBIAL DRUGS

Systematic reviews of RCTs have found that OME resolves faster on antimicrobial drugs than placebo, but found no evidence of improved resolution from 6 weeks to 11 months.

Benefits: We found three systematic reviews,[6,9,10] the most recent of which, published in 1994, identified 10 effectively blinded RCTs in 1041 children with OME.[6] Antimicrobial drugs (amoxicillin with or without clavulanate, cefaclor, erythromycin, sulfisoxazole, sulfamethoxazole, or trimethoprim) were compared to placebo or no treatment. Treatment duration varied from 2 to 5 weeks, and follow up assessment was from 10 to 60 days. **Short-term outcomes:** At 1 month, resolution of effusion (assessed by pneumatic otoscopy, tympanometry, and audiometry) was significantly more likely with antimicrobial treatment (pooled ARR for nonresolution compared with placebo or no treatment 0.14, 95% CI 0.04–0.24, NNT 7).[9] **Longer-term outcomes:** A systematic review of eight RCTs found no significant difference in presence of effusions at between 6 weeks and 11 months after treatment (pooled ARR for presence of effusion compared with placebo 0.06, 95% CI –0.03–+0.014).[9]

Harms: Adverse effects were frequent. Diarrhea was reported in 20% to 30% and rashes in 3% to 5% of children taking amoxicillin, while for amoxycillin clavulanate, diarrhea was reported in 9%, nausea and vomiting in 4%, and skin rashes and urticaria in 3%.[6,11] For antibiotics overall, nausea and vomiting, diarrhoea, or both were reported in 2% to 32% of children, cutaneous reactions in $<5\%$, plus a variety of rare organ system effects and fatalities.[11] Adherence to longer courses of antibiotics is poor. Prescribing antibiotics for minor illness encourages reattendance[12] and antibiotic resistance.[13] The systematic reviews did not report rates of adverse events in children on placebo or no treatment.[6,9,10]

Comment: Although antibiotics such as amoxicillin, ampicillin, cotrimoxazole, and cefaclor, which are active against the major middle ear pathogens, were more effective than those that are not (e.g., erythromycin), these differences were not significant.[9]

OPTION **CORTICOSTEROIDS**

Systematic reviews of RCTs provide no evidence of benefit from oral steroids in children with OME. Topical steroids have not been adequately evaluated yet.

Benefits: We found two systematic reviews published in 1991 and 1994.[6,14] **Oral steroids versus placebo:** The reviews identified three placebo-controlled RCTs of oral steroids in 108 children with OME.[6,14] Presence of effusion was assessed clinically by pneumatic otoscopy, tympanometry, and audiometry after 7 to 14 days of treatment. There was no significant difference in mean improvement at 2 weeks after treatment (AR of clearance compared with placebo 0.18, 95% CI –0.03–+0.39). There were no available summary data beyond 6 weeks. **Added to antibiotic:** The systematic reviews identified four RCTs in 292 children comparing oral steroids versus antibiotic alone. Time to measurement of results varied from 1 week to 2 months. There was no significant difference in clearance rates with combined treatment versus antibiotic alone (ARR for nonclearance versus antibiotic alone 0.25, 95% CI –0.01–+0.5). **Topical steroids:** We found one RCT that compared intranasal beclomethasone with placebo as an adjunct to prophylactic antibiotics in 61 children with chronic middle ear infection.[15] It found significant improvement in middle ear pressure at 12 weeks ($p < 0.05$) and reduction in number of effusions at 4 and 8 weeks ($p \leq 0.05$) in those treated with intranasal steroids and antibiotics, compared with either antibiotics alone or with placebo spray.

Harms: Short courses of steroids can cause behavioral changes, increased appetite, and weight gain. Idiosyncratic reactions have been reported such as avascular necrosis of the femoral head and fatal varicella infections.

Comment: The quality of the evidence is suboptimal because of small numbers and diverse clinical populations.

OPTION **ANTIHISTAMINES AND DECONGESTANTS**

One systematic review of RCTs found no benefit from antihistamines and decongestants in children with OME.

Benefits: We found one systematic review, published in 1994, which identified four RCTs comparing oral antihistamines/decongestants versus placebo in 1202 infants and older children.[6] Treatment duration was 4 weeks. A Bayesian meta-analysis found that the antihistamine/decongestant combination had no significant effect on resolution of the effusion compared with placebo, as assessed by history, otoscopy, and tympanometry (WMD in clinical and tympanometric resolution –0.009, 95% CI –0.036–+0.054).

Harms: Adverse effects of antihistamines include hyperactivity, insomnia, drowsiness, behavioral change, blood pressure variability, and seizures. Courses of 3 weeks or more of decongestant nose drops can lead to iatrogenic rhinitis.

Comment: The RCTs included clinically heterogeneous groups (e.g., infants and older children) and selected individuals from ambulatory care or waiting lists. There were too few children with allergies for adequate subgroup analysis.

OPTION MUCOLYTICS

One systematic review of RCTs has found that 1- to 3-month courses of mucolytics provide modest benefits in resolution of effusions.

Benefits: We found one systematic review, which identified six RCTs comparing *S*-carboxymethylcysteine, its lysine salt, or both versus placebo or no treatment in 430 children.[16] Treatment lasted for 15 to 90 days. More children experienced complete resolution with mucolytics (OR 2.25, 95% CI 0.97–5.22). Three small RCTs comparing another mucolytic, bromhexine, versus placebo in 155 children and 195 ears found conflicting results.

Harms: The review gave no information on adverse effects.[16] Reported adverse effects of *S*-carboxymethylcysteine include gastric irritation, nausea, and rashes.

Comment: The RCTs were heterogeneous in their clinical outcomes and treatment durations. Adherence is important when prescribing long courses of treatment.

OPTION AUTOINFLATION

One systematic review of RCTs has found benefit from autoinflation using a nasal balloon, although some children may be unable to master the technique. The value of other methods of autoinflation have not yet been adequately evaluated.

Benefits: We found one unpublished systematic review, which identified six RCTs comparing autoinflation versus no treatment (Reidpath DD, personal communication; Suonpaa J, et al., 1995).[17–21] Improvement was variously defined as being effusion free, improved tympanogram, or improvement in hearing. The RCTs assessed different treatment effects and differed widely in their results. However, three trials evaluated nasal balloons in 386 children and found a homogeneous effect size. Children in the treatment group were three times more likely to improve within 1 week to 3 months than controls, using tympanometric and audiometric criteria (OR compared with treatment 1.85, 95% CI 1.22–2.8).

Harms: No serious adverse effects have been reported.

Comment: The eustachian tubes can be inflated by several methods, including getting the child to blow up a balloon through a plastic tube inserted into the nostril. Twelve percent of children in one of the

RCTs (age 3–10 years) were unable to use the balloon. The beneficial effects were noted when adherence was 70% or greater. The evidence is suboptimal because a variety of methods was used, the outcome assessments were not blinded, and follow-up was short. The value of other methods of autoinflation (e.g., forcible exhalation through the nostrils, with closed mouth, into an anesthetic mask with a flowmeter attachment) have not yet been adequately evaluated.

OPTION SURGERY

One systematic review of heterogenous RCTs has found that surgery (insertion of tympanostomy tubes, adenoidectomy, or both) many result in short-term hearing gain. Tympanostomy tubes and adenoidectomy, separately or combined, are equally effective. We found no evidence of benefit from tonsillectomy.

Benefits: We found one systematic review, which identified 19 RCTs of surgery in children with otitis media with effusion. Nine reported the data per child ($n=1508$) and 10 per ear ($n=1452$). None were placebo controlled, although some used patients as their own controls.[22] Outcomes were mean change in audiometry, tympanometry, and clinical and otoscopic evidence of OME. The review concluded that the evidence for the effectiveness of surgical interventions was still confused. **Tympanostomy tubes:** The review reported a mean 12 dB improvement in hearing after insertion of tympanostomy tubes (confidence intervals not available). However, the authors concluded that this was difficult to interpret clinically. **Tympanostomy tubes plus adenoidectomy:** The review found that adenoidectomy gave little additional benefit over tympanostomy tubes alone in terms of mean hearing gain, which varied from 1.1 to 2.6 dB. A subsequent RCT in 228 children compared adenotonsillectomy versus adenoidectomy or neither procedure.[23] All children had a grommet inserted into one ear. Outcomes were mean audiometric change and tympanometric and otoscopic clearance assessed over 6 months to 10 years after treatment. The trial found benefit in combining adenoidectomy with tympanostomy tubes. The median duration of glue ear assessed tympanometrically was reduced from 7.8 years without surgery to 4.9 years with gromments, to 4 years with adenoidectomy, and 2.8 years with adenoidectomy and tympanostomy tubes combined.

Harms: Otorrhoea occurred postoperatively in 13% of children after grommet insertion (AR 0.13, 95% CI 0.05–0.21) and persisted in 5% at 1 year.[24] The true incidence of persistent perforation beyond 1 year is not known. In a prospective cohort study, tympanosclerosis occurred in 51% of ears after surgery (AR 0.51, 95% CI 0.43–0.58) compared with 3% in chronic untreated otitis media.[25] Evidence of moderate sclerosis was noted on otoscopy at 5 years in those affected.[20] However, the effects of such scarring are unlikely to be clinically apparent, because no differences in hearing thresholds were noted in the first 5 years, and differences of only 2.3 dB were noted between sclerotic and nonsclerotic ears at 5 to 7 years after treatment. **Adenoidectomy:** Deaths have been reported in 1 in 16,700 to 25,000 children when combined with tonsillectomy (no figures available for adenoidectomy alone), and postoperative hemorrhage in 0.49%.[26]

Comment: Approximately half of children who have tympanostomy tubes inserted will undergo reinsertion within 5 years.[27] Resolution after surgery takes longer in younger children and in those whose parents smoke, irrespective of treatment.[23]

REFERENCES

1. Williamson IG, Dunleavey J, Bain J, Robinson D. The natural history of otitis media with effusion: a three year study of the incidence and prevalence of abnormal tympanograms in four SW Hampshire infant and first schools. *J Laryngol Otol* 1994: 108:930–934.
2. Haggard M, Hughes E. *Objectives, values and methods of screening children's hearing – a review of the literature*. London: HMSO, 1991.
3. Zielhuis GA, Rach GH, Broek PV. Screening for otitis media with effusion in pre-school children. *Lancet* 1989;1:311–314.
4. Fiellau-Nikolajsen M. Tympanometry in three year old children: prevalence and spontaneous course of MEE. *Ann Otol Rhinol Laryngol* 1980;89(suppl 68): 223–237.
5. Bennett KE, Haggard MP. Behaviour and cognitive outcomes from middle ear disease. *Arch Dis Child* 1999;80:28–35.
6. Stool SE, Berg SO, Berman S, et al. Otitis media with effusion in young children: clinical practice guideline number 12. AHCPR Publication 94-0622. Rockville, Maryland: Agency for Health Care Policy and Research, Public Health Service, United States Department of Health and Human Services, July, 1994. (Search date 1992; primary sources on line data base of National Library of Medicine; and 10 specialized bibliographic databases.)
7. Strachan DP, Cook DG. Health effects of parenteral smoking. 4. Passive smoking, middle ear disease and adenotonsillectomy in children. *Thorax* 1998;53:50–56. (Search date 1997; primary sources MEDLINE, EMBASE.)
8. Paradise JL, Rockette HE, Colborn DK, et al. Otitis media in 2253 Pittsburgh area infants: prevalence and risk factors during the first two years of life. *Pediatrics* 1997;99:318–333.
9. Williams RL, Chalmers TC, Strange KC, Chalmers FT, Bowlin SJ. Use of antibiotics in preventing recurrent acute otitis media and in treating otitis media with effusion: a meta-analytic attempt to resolve the brouhaha. *JAMA* 1993;270: 1344–1351. (Search date 1966 to 1993; primary source MEDLINE.)
10. Rosenfield RM, Port JC. Meta-analysis of antibiotics for the treatment of otitis media with effusion. *Otolaryngol Head Neck Surg* 1992;106; 378–386. (Search date 1980 to 1990; primary source English language MEDLINE.)
11. Computerised clinical information system. Denver, Colorado; Micromedex Inc, June 1993.
12. Little P, Gould C, Williamson I, Warner G. Gantley M, Kinmonth AL. Reattendance and complications in a randomised trial of prescribing strategies for sore throat: the medicalising effect of prescribing antibiotics. *BMJ* 1997;315: 350–352.
13. Wise, et al. Antimicrobial resistance is a major threat to public health [Editorial]. *BMJ* 1998;317: 609–610.
14. Rosenfield RM, Mandel EM, Bluestone CD. Systemic steroids for otitis media with effusion in children. *Arch Otolaryngol Head Neck Surg* 1991;117:984–989. (Search date 1990; primary sources not provided.)
15. Tracy JM, Demain JG, Hoffman KM, Goetz DW. Intranasal beclomethasone as an adjunct to treatment of chronic middle ear effusion. *Ann Allergy Asthma Immunol* 80;February 1998.
16. Pignataro O, Pignataro LD, Gallus G, Calori G, Cordaro CI. Otitis media with effusion and S-carboxymethylcysteine and/or its lysine salt: a critical overview. *Int J Pediatr Otorhinolaryngol* 1996; 35:231–241. (Search date 1993; primary sources MEDLINE, EMBASE, Biosis.)
17. Chan KH, Bluestone CD. Lack of efficacy of middle-ear inflation: treatment of otitis media with effusion in children. *Otolaryngol Head Neck Surg* 1989;100:317–323.
18. Blanshard JD, Maw AR, Bawden R. Conservative treatment of otitis media with effusion by autoinflation of the middle ear. *Clin Otolaryngol* 1993; 18:188–192.
19. Stangerup SE, Sederberg Olsen J, Balle V. Autoinflation as a treatment of secretory otitis media. A randomised control study. *Arch Otolaryngol Head Neck Surg* 1992;118: 149–152.
20. Fraser JG, Mehta M, Fraser PA. The medical treatment of secretory otitis media. A clinical trial of three commonly used regimes. *J Laryngol Otol* 1977;91:757–765.
21. Brooker DS, McNeice A. Autoinflation in the treatment of glue ear in children. *Clin Otolaryngol* 1992;17:289–290.
22. Freemantle N, Long A, Mason J, et al. The treatment of persistent glue ear in children. *Effective Health Care Bulletin* 1992;4. University of Leeds ISSN:0965–0. (Search date 1992; primary sources BIDS, MEDLINE, EMBASE.)
23. Maw R, Bawden R. Spontaneous resolution of severe chronic glue ear in children and the effect of adenoidectomy, tonsillectomy, and insertion of ventilation tubes. *BMJ* 1993;306:1756–1760.
24. Mclelland CA. Incidence of complications from tympanostomy tubes. *Arch Otolaryngol* 1980;106: 97–99.
25. Maw AR. Tympanic membrane atrophy, scarring, atelectasis and attic retraction in chronic untreated otitis media with effusion and following ventilation tube insertion. *Int J Pediatr Otorhinolaryngol* 1994;30:189–204.
26. Yardley MP. Tonsillectomy, adenoidectomy and adenotonsillectomy; are they safe day case procedures? *J Laryngol Otol* 1992;106:299–300.
27. Maw AR. Development of tympanosclerosis in children with otitis media with effusion and ventilation tubes. *J Laryngol Otol* 1991;105: 614–617.

Ian Williamson, MBChB
Senior Lecturer in Primary Medical Care
Southampton University
UK

Competing interests: None declared.

Ear pain and barotrauma

Simon Janvrin, MS, FRCS

QUESTIONS

INTERVENTIONS

Key Messages

- We found limited evidence to suggest that oral decongestants may be effective in reducing ear pain and trauma during air travel.

DEFINITION The effects of air travel on the middle ear can include tympanic membrane pain, vertigo, hearing loss, and perforation.

INCIDENCE/ PREVALENCE The prevalence of symptoms depends on the altitude, type of aircraft and characteristics of the passengers. One point-prevalence study found that 20% of adult and 40% of child passengers had a negative pressure in the middle ear after flight, and that 10% of adults and 22% of children had otoscopic evidence of damage to the tympanic membrane.[1] There are no data on the incidence of perforation, which seems to be extremely rare in commercial passengers.

ETIOLOGY During aircraft descent, the pressure in the middle ear drops relative to that in the ear canal. A narrow, inflamed, or poorly functioning eustachian tube impedes the necessary influx of air. As the pressure difference between the middle and outer ear increases, the tympanic membrane is pulled inward.

PROGNOSIS In most people, symptoms resolve spontaneously. Experience in military aviation shows that most ear drum perforations will heal spontaneously.

AIMS To prevent ear pain and trauma during air travel

OUTCOMES Incidence and severity of pain and hearing loss; incidence of perforation of tympanic membrane

METHODS *Clinical Evidence* search, July 1998. All randomized controlled trials (RCTs) were reviewed.

QUESTION What are the effects of preventive interventions?

OPTION ORAL DECONGESTANTS

We found limited evidence from two RCTs suggesting that oral pseudoephedrine can reduce the incidence of pain and hearing loss during flight in passengers prone to symptoms.

Benefits: We found no systematic review. We found two RCTs comparing oral pseudoephedrine (120 mg given 30 minutes before flight) versus placebo in a total of 350 adult passengers.[2,3] All participants had a history of ear pain during air travel. Those with acute or chronic ear problems were excluded. A total of 272 passengers completed the post-flight questionnaires. The incidence of symptoms in the combined treatment groups was 33% versus 64% in those receiving placebo (RR 0.51, 95% CI 0.31–0.84).

Harms: "Dry mouth or drowsiness" was reported by 7% to 15% of participants taking pseudoephedrine versus 2% on placebo.[2,3]

Comment: None.

OPTION **TOPICAL NASAL DECONGESTANTS**

Topical decongestants have not been evaluated adequately in this setting.

Benefits: We found one RCT comparing oxymetazoline nasal spray versus placebo nasal spray in 83 participants during air travel.[2] There was no significant difference in reported ear pain between the two groups.

Harms: Nasal irritation was reported by 14% of the oxymetazoline group. The rate in the placebo group was not reported.

Comment: The RCT was too small to rule out an effect of topical decongestants.

REFERENCES

1. Stangerup S-E, Tjernstrom O, Klokker M, Harcourt J, Stokholm J. Point prevalence of barotitis in children and adults after flight, and effect of autoinflation. *Aviat Space Environ Med* 1998; 69:45–49.
2. Jones JS, Sheffield W, White LJ, Bloom MA. A double-blind comparison between oral pseudoephedrine and topical oxymetazoline in the prevention of barotrauma during air travel. *Am J Emerg Med* 1998;16:262–264.
3. Csortan E, Jones J, Haan M, Brown M. Efficacy of pseudoephedrine for the prevention of barotrauma during air travel. *Ann Emerg Med* 1994;23: 1324–1327.

Simon Janvrin, MS, FRCS
Former Senior Medical Officer
Civil Aviation Authority
West Sussex
UK

Competing interests: None declared

Impacted wisdom teeth

Stephen F Worrall, MBBS

QUESTIONS

INTERVENTIONS

Likely to be ineffective or harmful

Key Messages

- We found limited evidence suggesting that the harms of removing asymptomatic impacted wisdom teeth outweigh the benefits.

DEFINITION Wisdom teeth are third molars that develop in almost all adults by approximately 20 years of age. In some people, the teeth become partially or completely impacted below the gumline because of lack of space, obstruction, or abnormal position. Impacted wisdom teeth may be diagnosed because of pain and swelling or incidentally by routine dental radiography.

INCIDENCE/ PREVALENCE Third-molar impaction is common. Over 72% of Swedish people aged 20 to 30 have at least one impacted lower third molar.[1] The surgical removal of impacted third molars (symptomatic and asymptomatic) is the most common procedure performed by oral and maxillofacial surgeons. It is performed on approximately 4 in 1000 people per year in England and Wales, making it one of the top 10 in patient and day case procedures.[2–4] Up to 90% of people on oral and maxillofacial surgery hospital waiting lists are awaiting removal of wisdom teeth.[3]

ETIOLOGY Impacted wisdom teeth are partly a by-product of improved oral hygiene and changes in diet. Less gum disease and dental caries, and less wear and tear on teeth because of more refined diet, have increased the likelihood of retaining teeth into adult life, leaving less room for wisdom teeth.

PROGNOSIS Impacted wisdom teeth can cause pain, swelling, and infection, as well as destroying adjacent teeth and bone. The removal of diseased and symptomatic wisdom teeth alleviates pain and suffering and improves oral health and function. There are no good data on what happens without treatment in people with asymptomatic impacted wisdom teeth.

AIMS To prevent harms and maximize benefits of wisdom teeth removal.

OUTCOMES Pain; rates of infection; oral health and function.

METHODS MEDLINE search (1966 to 1998).

QUESTION **Should asymptomatic impacted wisdom teeth be removed prophylactically?**

The prophylactic removal of asymptomatic impacted wisdom teeth has not been evaluated in randomized controlled trials (RCTs). Nonrandomized studies provide no evidence of benefit. Removal of lower wisdom teeth causes permanent numbness of the lower lip or tongue in approximately 1 in 200 people.

Benefits: We found one systematic review of English language studies, published in 1997, which identified at least 69 primary studies concerning the surgical removal of third molars.[5] There were no RCTs. The authors concluded that there was no good evidence of benefit from the removal of pathology-free impacted third molars. Two formal decision analyses also concluded that nonintervention was the optimal treatment for disease-free, asymptomatic third molars.[6,7]

Harms: Pain and swelling are almost universal after removal of impacted wisdom teeth.[8,9] The removal of the lower wisdom teeth carries the risk of damage to the inferior alveolar nerve (injured in 1.3%–7.8% of cases,[10,11] permanently injured in 0.5%–1%[12]), and to the lingual nerve (permanently injured in 0.3%–0.8% of cases[13]). The risks appear to be greater with greater depth of impaction. The risks are the same whether the wisdom tooth is symptomatic or asymptomatic.

Comment: All studies identified in the review were of poor quality. It is likely to take an RCT with 10 years follow-up to provide a definitive answer to the question. Anecdotal accounts and evidence from developing countries suggest that the answer would be negative.[5] Surgical morbidity following third-molar removal increases as patients become older. When there are reasons to remove them, it is prudent to do so in early adulthood.[14] Surgical morbidity is operator and technique sensitive.[15] Permanent sensory lingual nerve disturbance rates of 0% over a 20-year follow-up period have been reported recently.[15,16]

REFERENCES

1. Hugoson A, Kugelberg CF. The prevalence of third molars in a Swedish population. An epidemiological study. *Community Dental Health* 1988;5:121–138.
2. Mercier P, Precious D. Risks and benefits of removal of impacted third molars. *Int J Oral Maxillofac Surg* 1992;21:17–27.
3. Shepherd JP, Brickley M. Surgical removal of third molars. *BMJ* 1994;309:620–621.
4. Worrall SF, Riden K, Haskell R, Corrigan AM. UK National Third Molar project: the initial report. *Br J Oral Maxillofac Surg* 1998;36:14–18.
5. Song F, Landes DP, Glenny AM, Sheldon TA. Prophylactic removal of impacted third molars: an assessment of published reviews. *Br Dent J* 1997;182:339–346.
6. Tulloch JF, Antczak AA, Wilkes JW. The application of decision analysis to evaluate the need for extraction of asymptomatic third molars. *J Oral Maxillofac Surg* 1987;45:855–865.
7. Brickley M, Kay E, Shepherd JP, Armstrong RA. Decision analysis for lower third molar surgery. *Medical Decision Making* 1995;15:143–151.
8. Bramley P. Sense about wisdoms? *J R Soc Med* 1981;74:867–869.
9. Capuzzi P, Montebugnoli L, Vaccaro MA. Extraction of impacted third molars. *Oral Surg Oral Med Oral Pathol* 1994;77:341–343.
10. Schultze-Mosgau S, Reich RH. Assessment of inferior alveolar and lingual nerve disturbances after dentoalveolar surgery, and recovery of sensitivity. *Int J Oral Maxillofac Surg* 1993;22:214–217.
11. Rood JP. Permanent damage to inferior alveolar nerves during the removal of impacted mandibular third molars: comparison of two methods of bone removal. *Br Dent J* 1992;172:108–110.
12. Blackburn CW, Bramley PA. Lingual nerve damage associated with removal of lower third molars. *Br Dent J* 1989;167:103–107.
13. Robinson PP, Smith KG. Lingual nerve damage during lower third molar removal: a comparison of two surgical methods. *Br Dent J* 1996;180:456–461.
14. Bruce RA, Frederickson GC, Small GS. Age of patients and morbidity associated with mandibular thrid molar surgery. *J Am Dent Assoc* 1980;101:240.
15. Sisk AL, Hammer WB, Shelton DW, Joy ED Jr. Complications following removal of impacted third molars: the role of the experience of the surgeon. *J Oral Maxillofac Surg* 1986;44:855–859.
16. Moss CE, Wake MJC. Lingual access for third-molar surgery: a 20-year retrospective audit. *Br J Oral Maxillofac Surg* 1999;39:255–258.

Stephen F Worrall, MBBS
Consultant and senior lecturer in oral and maxillofacial surgery
North Staffordshire Hospital
Stoke-on-Trent
UK

Competing interests: None declared.

Depression

John Geddes, MD, MRCPsych

QUESTIONS

INTERVENTIONS

Beneficial

Tricyclic and heterocyclic antidepressants 461
Selective serotonin-reuptake inhibitors and related drugs 461
Monoamine oxidase inhibitors .461
Cognitive therapy (in mild to moderate depression) 464
Interpersonal therapy (in mild to moderate depression) 464
Continuation drug treatment (reduces risk of relapse) ...465

Likely to be beneficial

Saint Johnswort (in mild to moderate depression) 463
Problem-solving therapy (in mild to moderate depression) ...464

See Glossary, p. 466

Combining drug and psychological treatment (in severe depression) 464
Maintenance drug treatment (may prevent recurrence) ...465

Unknown effectiveness

Exercise 464
Bibliotherapy 465
Nondirective counselling 464
Psychological treatments in severe depression 464
Clinician collaboration and patient education 463

To be covered in future issues of *Clinical Evidence*

Electroconvulsive therapy
Behavior therapy
Treatment for bipolar affective disorder

Key Messages

- Randomized controlled trials (RCTs) have found that several treatments are effective in the treatment of mild to moderate depression. These include prescription antidepressant drugs, cognitive therapy, and interpersonal therapy. Less robust RCTs have found that problem-solving therapy and Saint Johnswort are also effective. Specific psychological treatments such as cognitive and interpersonal therapy have been shown to be as effective as drugs, and there is no clinically significant difference between antidepressant drugs, although they vary in adverse effects and costs.
- We found limited evidence that other treatments—including exercise, bibliotherapy, and nondirective counseling—may be effective, but further research is needed.
- We found no reliable evidence that one type of treatment (drug or nondrug) is superior to another. Limited evidence suggests that combining drug and psychological treatments may be effective in severe but not in mild to moderate depression.

- Of the interventions examined in this issue, prescription antidepressant drugs are the only treatment for which there is good evidence of effectiveness in severe and psychotic depressive disorders. We found no RCTs comparing drug and nondrug treatments in severe depressive disorder.
- RCTs have found that 1) continuing antidepressant drug treatment for 4 to 6 months after recovery reduces the risk of relapse, and 2) maintenance therapy in recurrent depressive disorder reduces the risk of recurrence.
- We found no evidence of a difference between treatments in terms of long-term benefits.

DEFINITION Depressive disorders lead to impaired functioning and are characterized by persistent low mood, loss of interest and enjoyment, and reduced energy.

PREVALENCE Depressive disorders are common, with a prevalence of major depression between 5% and 10% in primary care patients.[1] Two to three times as many patients have depressive symptoms but do not meet the full criteria for major depression. Women are twice as often affected as men. Depressive disorders are the fourth most important cause of disability worldwide and are expected to become the second most important cause by 2020.[2,3]

ETIOLOGY The causes are uncertain but are probably both genetic and environmental, including childhood events and current psychosocial adversity.

PROGNOSIS Approximately half of people suffering a first episode of major depressive disorder experience further symptoms in the next 10 years.[4] Different levels of severity[5,6] indicate different prognosis and treatment:

- mild to moderate depression, characterized by depressive symptoms and some functional impairment. Many patients recover in the short term, but approximately half experience recurrent symptoms.[6]
- severe depression, characterized by additional agitation or psychomotor retardation with marked somatic symptoms. In this review, treatments are considered to have been evaluated in severe depression if the RCTs included inpatients.
- psychotic depression, characterized by hallucinations, delusions, or both.

AIMS To improve mood, social and occupational functioning, and quality of life; to reduce morbidity and mortality; to prevent recurrence of depressive disorder; and to minimize adverse effects of treatment.

OUTCOMES Depressive symptoms rated by patient and clinician, social functioning, occupational functioning, quality of life, admission to hospital, rates of self-harm, relapse of depressive symptoms, rates of adverse events. Trials often use continuous scales to measure depressive symptoms (e.g., the Hamilton depressive rating scale, the Beck depression inventory). Changes in continuous measures can be dealt with in two ways. They can be dichotomized in an arbitrary, but clinically helpful, manner (e.g., taking a reduction in depressive symptoms of >50% as an end point), which allows results to be expressed as relative risks and numbers needed to treat. Alternatively, they can be treated as continuous variables, as is done for meta-analysis. In this case, the pooled estimate of effect (the effect size) expresses the degree of overlap between the range of scores in the control and experimental groups. The effect size can be used to estimate the proportion of people in the control group who had a poorer outcome than the average person in the experimental group.

METHODS A validated search for systematic reviews and RCTs was conducted between May and September 1998 from the Cochrane Database of Systematic Reviews and the Database of Abstract of Reviews of Effectiveness, *Best Evidence* and *Evidence-Based Mental Health*, MEDLINE (SilverPlatter), Psychlit, and EMBASE. Studies were included using epidemiologic criteria and relevance to the clinical question.

QUESTION **What are the effects of treatments?**

OPTION **PRESCRIPTION ANTIDEPRESSANT DRUGS**

Systematic reviews of RCTs have found that antidepressant drugs are effective in the acute treatment of all grades of depressive disorders. They also have found no clinically significant difference in effectiveness between different kinds of antidepressant drugs. However, the drugs did differ in their adverse event profiles. On average, people seem to tolerate selective serotonin-reuptake inhibitors (SSRIs) slightly better than older drugs, although this difference is too small to consider it grounds for a policy of always choosing an SSRI as first-line treatment. We found no strong evidence that fluoxetine is associated with increased risk of suicide. Abrupt withdrawal of SSRIs is associated with symptoms, including dizziness and rhinitis in some patients, and this is more likely, and probably more severe, with drugs with a short half-life, such as paroxetine.

Benefits: **Versus placebo**: We found two systematic reviews. The first, published in 1996, pooled data from 49 RCTs in people with depressive disorder.[7] Five trials included only inpatients (probably more severely ill), 40 included only outpatients, and two included both types of patient. Each RCT compared two antidepressant drugs and included a placebo control group. Meta-analysis found a mean effect size of 0.50 for antidepressant drug versus placebo, which means that 69% of those taking placebo did worse than the average person taking antidepressants. Drugs were more effective in those with depressive disorders diagnosed according to standard criteria (mainly Diagnostic and Statistical Manual, 3rd revision [DSM-III]).[7] The second systematic review, updated in 1998, identified 15 RCTs (1871 participants) comparing antidepressant versus placebo in patients with dysthymia (chronic mild depressive disorders).[8] Response to treatment was approximately twice as likely in the antidepressant group (RR versus placebo 1.9, 95% CI 1.6–2.3; NNT 4, 95% CI 3–5). **Tricyclic antidepressants versus SSRIs:** Two systematic reviews published in 1993 and 1997 compared SSRIs versus the tricyclic antidepressants (TCAs) in people with all grades of depression.[9,10] These found no clinically significant difference in effectiveness, but SSRIs seemed to be slightly more acceptable to patients than TCAs as measured by the total number of dropouts from clinical trials. We found no reliable evidence that TCAs are more effective than SSRIs in more severely depressed patients. **Monoamine oxidase inhibitors versus**

TCAs: A systematic review published in 1995 identified 55 RCTs comparing monoamine oxidase inhibitors (MAOIs) versus TCAs in several subgroups of depressed patients. It found that MAOIs were less effective in patients with severe depressive disorders but may be more effective in atypical depressive disorders (depressive disorders with reversed biological features, for example, increased sleep, increased appetite, mood reactivity, and rejection sensitivity).[11]

Harms: **Common adverse events:** A systematic review of RCTs published in 1998 compared TCAs versus SSRIs in people with all severities of depression. The findings are summarized in Table 1.[12] There also may be differences between SSRIs. A large cohort study of people receiving four different SSRIs (fluvoxamine [*n*=10,983], fluoxetine [*n*=12,692], sertraline [*n*=12,734], and paroxetine [*n*=13,741]) in British primary care found that reports of common adverse events (nausea/vomiting, malaise/lassitude, dizziness, and headache/migraine) varied between SSRIs (fluvoxamine 78 per 1000 patient-months; fluoxetine 23 per 1000 patient-months; RR versus fluvoxamine 0.29, 95% CI 0.27–0.32; paroxetine 28 per 1000 patient-months, RR 0.35, 95% CI 0.33–0.37; sertraline 21 per 1000 patient-months, RR 0.26, 95% CI 0.25–0.28) (calculated from data in the article).[13] Only 52% of patients responded to the questionnaire, although this response rate was similar for all four drugs. A study of spontaneous reports to the UK Committee on Safety of Medicines found no difference in safety profiles between the same four SSRIs.[14] **Suicide:** A systematic review published in 1991 pooled data from 17 double-blind RCTs in people with depressive disorder comparing fluoxetine (*n*=1765) versus a TCA (*n*=731) or placebo (*n*=569). There was no significant difference in the rate of suicidal acts between the groups (fluoxetine 0.3%, placebo 0.2%, TCAs 0.4%), while development of suicidal ideation was less in the fluoxetine group (1.2% fluoxetine vs. 2.6% placebo, $p=0.042$, and vs. 3.6% TCAs, $p=0.001$).[15] A historical cohort study followed 172,598 people who had at least one prescription for one of 10 antidepressants during the study period in general practice in the UK. The risk of suicide was higher in patients who received fluoxetine (19 per 10,000 person-years, 95% CI 9–34) (calculated from data in the article) than those receiving dothiepin (RR of suicide versus dothiepin 2.1, 95% CI 1.1–4.1).[16] In a nested case-controlled subanalysis in patients with no history of suicidal behavior or prior antidepressant prescription, the risk remains the same although the confidence interval broadened to make the result indeterminate (RR 2.1, 95% CI 0.6–7.9). Although the apparent association may be due to residual confounding, there remains uncertainty about the possible association between fluoxetine and suicide. However, any absolute increase in risk is unlikely to be large. **Withdrawal effects:** We found one RCT comparing abrupt discontinuation of fluoxetine (*n*=96) versus continued treatment (*n*=299) in people who had been taking the drug for 12 weeks. Abrupt discontinuation was associated with increased dizziness (7% vs. 1%), dysmenorrhea (3% vs. 0%), rhinitis (10% vs. 3%), and somnolence (4% vs. 0%). There was, however, a high dropout rate in this study because of return of symptoms of depression (39%), so these may be underestimates of the true rate of withdrawal symptoms.[17] The rate of spontaneous reports of suspected withdrawal reactions per million defined daily doses to the World Health Organization Collaborating Centre for International Drug Monitoring between 1987 and 1995 was higher for paroxetine than for sertraline and fluoxetine.[18]

The most common withdrawal effects were dizziness, nausea, paraesthesia, headache, and vertigo.

Comment: It is probably best to tailor the treatment to the patient's needs by considering the specific adverse-effect profiles of each drug. Note that dothiepin is not available in the US. Note also that there are other antidepressants (e.g., monotricyclic NE and 5HT reuptake inhibitors, DA active agents, 5HT antagonists and reuptake inhibitors, NE and 5HT antagonists) for which few, if any, RCT data exist.

OPTION CLINICIAN COLLABORATION AND PATIENT EDUCATION

We found limited evidence that the effectiveness of drug treatment may be improved by collaborative working between primary care clinicians and psychiatrists, and by intensive patient education.

Benefits: We found no systematic review. An RCT in 217 patients with mild to moderate depressive disorders in primary care in the USA found that, compared with standard treatment, outcomes were improved by collaborative working between primary care physician and psychiatrist, and by intensive patient education. Clinical outcomes were improved only in the subgroup of patients meeting DSM-III criteria for major depressive disorder ($n = 91$): a clinical response (> 50% reduction on symptom checklist) occurred in 44% of control patients compared with 74% of intervention patients (NNT 4; 95% CI 3–10).[19]

Harms: None reported.

Comment: More research is required on the benefits of enhancing routine treatment of depressive disorder.

OPTION SAINT JOHNSWORT (*Hypericum perforatum*)

One systematic review of RCTs has found that Saint Johnswort (*Hypericum perforatum*) is more effective than placebo in mild-to-moderate depressive disorders and is as effective as prescription antidepressant drugs. However, these findings have yet to be confirmed in fully representative groups of patients and with standardized preparations.

Benefits: We found one systematic review, updated in 1998, that identified 27 RCTs in 2291 people with mild to moderate depression.[20] Seventeen trials (1168 patients) were placebo controlled. Ten trials (1123 patients) compared *Hypericum* (eight studies using single preparations, two using combinations of *Hypericum* and *Valeriana*) versus other antidepressant or sedative drugs. *Hypericum* preparations were significantly superior to placebo in terms of clinical improvement (RR 2.47, 95% CI 1.69–3.61) but did not differ significantly from standard antidepressants (single preparations RR 1.01, 95% CI 0.87–1.16; combinations RR 1.52, 95% CI 0.78–2.94).

Harms: Adverse effects are poorly described in trials but seemed mainly to consist of mild photosensitivity. They were reported by 26% of patients on *Hypericum* single preparations versus 45% on standard antidepressants (RR 0.57, 95% CI 0.47–0.69), and 15% on combinations of *Hypericum* and *Valeriana* versus 27% on amitriptyline or desipramine (RR 0.49, 95% CI 0.23–1.04).[21]

Comment: This evidence must be interpreted cautiously because 1) it is unclear how closely the participants in these trials match patients in clinical practice, and 2) the preparations and doses of *Hypericum* and types and doses of standard antidepressants varied. More studies are required on clearly defined clinically representative patients with standardized preparations.

OPTION SPECIFIC PSYCHOLOGICAL TREATMENTS

A systematic review of RCTs has found that cognitive therapy is effective—and may be more effective than drug treatment—in people with mild to moderate depression. Less strong evidence from RCTs suggests that interpersonal psychotherapy, problem-solving therapy, and nondirective counseling may be as effective as drug treatment in mild to moderate depression. We found very limited evidence on the relative efficacy of drug and nondrug treatment in severe depression.

Benefits: The evidence is summarized in Table 2.[21–26]

Harms: *See* Table 2.

Comment: Large RCTs are needed in representative patients in a range of clinical settings, including primary care. Note that, because of varying exclusion criteria, the ability to generalize the studies shown in Table 2 is questionable. Other factors to be considered when psychological treatments are compared with drug treatment include 1) whether therapeutic doses of drugs are achieved (as documented by serum concentrations), 2) whether changes in medication are allowed (reflecting standard clinical practice), and 3) whether studies reflect the natural history of major depressive disorder.

OPTION SPECIFIC PSYCHOLOGICAL TREATMENTS PLUS DRUG TREATMENT

We found limited evidence from RCTs that, in severe depression, the addition of drug treatment to interpersonal or cognitive therapy is more effective than either psychological therapy alone. No such effect was observed in mild to moderate depression.

Benefits: We found no systematic review. A meta-analysis of six RCTs (595 patients) found no advantage in combining drug and specific psychological treatments in mild to moderate depressive disorders. However, in more severe depressive disorders, the combination of drug and interpersonal therapy or cognitive therapy was more effective than interpersonal therapy or cognitive therapy alone.[27]

Harms: No adverse effects have been reported.

Comment: The results of this meta-analysis may be unreliable because it included only the studies undertaken at one center and was therefore not based on a thorough search for all available studies.[27] A Cochrane systematic review is currently under way (Churchill R, personal communication).

OPTION EXERCISE

RCTs have found that exercise, alone or in combination with other treatments, improves mild to moderate depression.

Benefits: We found one systematic review published in 1990 that examined exercise in depressive disorders. However, it was difficult to interpret because it included nonrandomized studies and did not clearly describe participants.[28] Since then, several RCTs have found that exercise (alone and as an adjunct) was beneficial in mild to moderate depressive disorders.

Harms: None reported.

Comment: Further systematic review of these studies is required.

OPTION BIBLIOTHERAPY

We found limited evidence from a systematic review of RCTs that bibliotherapy may reduce mild depressive symptoms.

Benefits: We found one systematic review published in 1997. This identified six small short-term RCTs of bibliotherapy in 273 participants recruited by advertisement through the media and probably very mildly ill.[29] The mean effect size of bibliotherapy was 0.82 (95% CI 0.50–1.15). This means that 79% of control patients had a worse outcome than the average member of the group receiving bibliotherapy.

Harms: None reported.

Comment: Further studies are needed in clinical samples of patients.

QUESTION What are the effects of continuation and maintenance treatment with antidepressant drugs?

RCTs have found that 1) continuing treatment with antidepressant drugs for 4 to 6 months after recovery reduces the risk of relapse, and 2) maintenance treatment in recurrent depressive disorder reduces the risk of recurrence.

Benefits: **Continuation treatment:** We found one systematic review published in 1991 that identified six small RCTs (312 participants). Continuation of antidepressant medication for 4 to 6 months after acute treatment reduced the relapse rate by nearly half (RR 0.6; 95% CI 0.4–0.7).[30] Several more recent RCTs confirm this reduction in risk of early relapse with continuing antidepressant treatment for 6 to 12 months after acute treatment. **Maintenance treatment:** We found no adequate systematic review. Several RCTs found that maintenance treatment reduced the relapse rate compared with placebo in recurrent depressive disorder. The most recent and largest of these compared sertraline versus placebo in 161 people who had had chronic depression for more than 2 years and had responded to both short-term (12-week) and continuation (4-month) treatment with sertraline. During 76-weeks' follow-up, the recurrence rate on sertraline was 6% and on placebo 23% (NNT 6, 95% CI 4–18), although the reliability of these results is limited by the high dropout rates from this study.[31]

Harms: Adverse effects appear to be similar to those reported in the shorter-term studies.

Comment: Further large-scale studies are needed of continuation and maintenance treatment in people with all severities of major depressive disorder.

QUESTION **Which treatments are most effective at improving long-term outcome?**

We found no evidence of a difference between treatments in terms of long-term benefits.

Benefits: We found one systematic review published in 1998 that identified eight small RCTs looking at long-term (at least 1-year) recovery or relapse rates after treatment was stopped. The trials compared cognitive therapy versus antidepressants in people with mainly mild to moderate depressive disorders.[24] No quantitative review was attempted. However, the number of people who recovered and subsequently relapsed seemed higher in those taking antidepressants.

Harms: As above.

Comment: The authors of the review did not present the data on the proportion of people who recovered and remained well in the long term. The largest RCT found that only one fifth of participants remained well over 18 months follow-up, and there were no significant differences between interpersonal psychotherapy, cognitive therapy, or drug treatment.[24] It is possible that different people respond to different treatments. Further large-scale comparative studies are required of the long-term effectiveness of treatments in people with all severities of depressive disorders.

GLOSSARY

Cognitive therapy is a brief (20 sessions over 12–16 weeks) structured treatment aimed at changing the dysfunctional beliefs and negative automatic thoughts that characterize depressive disorders.[32] It requires a high level of training in the therapist.

Interpersonal psychotherapy is a standardized form of brief psychotherapy (usually 12–16 weekly sessions) primarily intended for outpatients with unipolar nonpsychotic depressive disorders. It focuses on improving the patient's interpersonal functioning and identifying the problems associated with the onset of the depressive episode.[33]

Problem solving consists of several stages: 1) identifying the main problems for the patient, 2) generating solutions, 3) trying out the solutions. It is potentially briefer and simpler than cognitive therapy and may be feasible in primary care.[24]

Brief, nondirective counseling aims to help the patient to express feelings and clarify thoughts and difficulties. The therapist suggests alternative understandings and does not give direct advice but tries to encourage patients to solve their own problems.[21]

Bibliotherapy consists of advising the patient to read written material such as *Feeling Good: The New Mood Therapy* by David Burns (New York: New American Library; 1980).

Continuation treatment is the continuation of antidepressants after acute treatment to decrease the chances of early relapse.

Maintenance treatment is the long-term treatment of recurrent depressive disorder to decrease the chances of further episodes.

REFERENCES

1. Katon W, Schulberg H. Epidemiology of depression in pimary care. *Gen Hosp Psychiatry* 1992;14:237–247.
2. Murray CJ, Lopez AD. Regional patterns of disability-free life expectancy and disability-adjusted life expectancy: global burden of disease study. *Lancet* 1997;349:1347–1352.
3. Murray CJ, Lopez AD. Alternative projections of mortality and disability by cause 1990–2020: global burden of disease study. *Lancet* 1997;349:1498–1504.
4. Persons JB. Most patients with a first episode of major depressive disorder experienced multiple levels of depressive symptoms over time Commentary on: Judd LL, Akiskal HS, Maser JD, et al. A prospective 12 year study of subsyndromal and syndromal depressive symptoms in unipolar major depressive disorders. *Arch Gen Psychiatry* 1988;55:694–700. In: *Evidence Based Mental Health* 1999;2:23.
5. American Psychiatric Association. *Diagnostic and statistical manual of mental disorders,* 4th ed. Washington, DC: American Psychiatric Association, 1994.
6. World Health Organization. *The ICD-10 classification of mental and behavioural disorders.* Geneva: World Health Organization, 1992.
7. Joffe R, Sokolov S, Streiner D. Antidepressant treatment of depression: a meta-analysis. *Can J Psychiatry* 1996;41:613–616. (Search date not given; primary source Medline 1966–June 1995.)
8. Lima MS, Moncrieff J. A comparison of drugs versus placebo for the treatment of dysthymia: a systematic review. In: Oakley-Brown M, ed. Cochrane Database of Systematic Reviews. Oxford: Update Software, 1998. (Search date 1997; primary sources Biological Abstracts 1984–1997, Medline 1966–Jan 1997, Psychlit 1974–Jan 1997, Embase 1980–Jan 1997, Lilacs 1982–Jan 1997, Cochrane library; and personal communication, conference abstracts, unpublished trials from the pharmaceutical industry, book chapters on the treatment of depression.)
9. Song F, Freemantle N, Sheldon TA, et al. Selective serotonin reuptake inhibitors: meta-analysis of efficacy and acceptability. *BMJ* 1993;306:683–687. (Search date not given; primary sources Medline and Index Medicus, manual cross referencing, and discussion with experts.)
10. Hotopf M, Hardy R, Lewis G. Discontinuation rates of SSRIs and tricyclic antidepressants: a meta-analysis and investigation of heterogeneity. *Br J Psychiatry* 1997;170:120–127. (Search date not given but based on Cochrane Review dated 1997; primary sources RCTs in previous meta analyses, Medline 1966 onwards, Embase 1974 onwards, hand search key journals.)
11. Thase ME, Trivedi MH, Rush AJ. MAOIs in the contemporary treatment of depression. *Neuropsychopharmacology* 1995;12:185–219. (Search date not given; primary sources Medline and Psychological Abstracts 1959–July 1992.)
12. Trindade E, Menon D. Selective serotonin reuptake inhibitors differ from tricyclic antidepressants in adverse events [Abstract]. *Selective serotonin reuptake inhibitors (SSRIs) for major depression. Part I. Evaluation of the clinical literature.* Ottawa: Canadian Coordinating Office for Health Technology Assessment, 1997 August Report 3E. *Evidence-Based Mental Health* 1998;1:50. (Search date 1996; primary sources Medline, Embase, PsycINFO, International Pharmaceutical Abstracts, Pascal, Health Planning & Administration, Mental Health Abstracts, PharmacoEconomics & Outcomes News, and Current Contents databases; scanning bibliographies of retrieved articles; hand searching journals; and consulting researchers.)
13. Mackay FJ, Dunn NR, Wilton LV, et al. A comparison of fluvoxamine, fluoxetine, sertraline and paroxetine examined by observational cohort studies. *Pharmacoepidemiology and Drug Safety* 1997;6:235–246.
14. Price JS, Waller PC, Wood SM, Mackay AV. A comparison of the post marketing safety of four selective serotonin reuptake inhibitors including the investigation of symptoms occurring on withdrawal. *Br J Clin Pharmacol* 1996;42:757–763.
15. Beasley CM Jr, Dornseif BE, Bosomworth JC, et al. Fluoxetine and suicide: a meta-analysis of controlled trials of treatment for depression. *BMJ* 1991;303:685–692. (Search date not given; primary sources not given in detail but based on clinical report form data from trials, and data from the Drug Experience Network Database.)
16. Jick SS, Dean AD, Jick H. Antidepressants and suicide. *BMJ* 1995;310:215–218.
17. Zajecka J, Fawcett J, Amsterdam J, et al. Safety of abrupt discontinuation of fluoxetine: a randomised, placebo controlled study. *J Clin Psychopharmacol* 1998;18:193–197.
18. Stahl MM, Lindquist M, Pettersson M, et al. Withdrawal reactions with selective serotonin reuptake inhibitors as reported to the WHO system. *Eur J Clin Pharmacol* 1997;53:163–169.
19. Katon W, Von Korff M, Lin E, et al. Collaborative management to achieve treatment guidelines: impact on depression in primary care. *JAMA* 1995;273:1026–1031.
20. Linde K, Mulrow CD. St John's Wort for depression (Cochrane Review). In: The Cochrane Library, Issue 4, 1998. Oxford: Update Software. (Search date 1998; primary sources Medline 1983–1997, Embase 1989–1997, Psychlit 1987–1997, Psychindex 1987–1997), and specialized databases [Cochrane Complementary Medicine Field, Cochrane Depression & Neurosis CRG, Phytodok] and by checking bibliographies of pertinent articles; and by contacting manufacturers and researchers.)
21. Friedli K, King MB, Lloyd M, Horder J. Randomised controlled assessment of non-directive psychotherapy versus routine general practitioner care. *Lancet* 1997;350:1662–1665.
22. Gloaguen V, Cottraux J, Cucherat M, et al. A meta-analysis of the effects of cognitive therapy in depressed patients 1998. *J Affect Disord* 1998;49:59–72. (Search date not given; primary sources Medline 1966–1 December 1996; Embase till December 1996, references in books and papers, previous reviews and meta-analyses, abstracts from congress presentations and preprints sent by authors.)
23. Elkin I, Shea MT, Watkins JT, et al. National Institute of Mental Health treatment of depression collaborative research program: general effectiveness of treatments. *Arch Gen Psychiatry* 1989;46:971–982.
24. Mynors-Wallis LM, Gath DH, Lloyd-Thomas, AR, Tomlinson D. Randomised controlled trial comparing problem solving treatment with amitriptyline and placebo for major depression in primary care. *BMJ* 1995;310:441–445.
25. Scott AI, Freeman CP. Edinburgh primary care depression study: treatment outcome, patient satisfaction, and cost after 16 weeks. *BMJ* 1992;304:883–887.
26. Harvey I, Nelson SJ, Lyons RA, et al. A randomized controlled trial and economic evaluation of counselling in primary care. *Br J Gen Pract* 1998; 48:1043–1048.

27. Thase ME, Greenhouse JB, Frank E, et al. Treatment of major depression with psychotherapy or psychotherapy–pharmacotherapy combinations. *Arch Gen Psychiatry* 1997;54:1009–1015. (Pooled results of six research protocols conducted between 1982 and 1992 at the Mental Health Clinical Research Center, University of Pittsburgh School of Medicine.)
28. North TC, McCullagh P, Tran ZV. Effect of exercise on depression. *Exerc Sport Sci Rev* 1990;18:379-415. (Search date not given; primary sources dissertation abstracts online, ERIC, PsychInfo, Medline, books, abstracts from meetings up to 1 June 1989.)
29. Cuijpers P. Bibliotherapy in unipolar depression: a meta-analysis. *J Behav Ther Exp Psychiatry* 1997; 28:139–147. (Search date not given; primary sources PsychLit, PsychInfo, Medline dates not given.)
30. Loonen AJ, Peer PG, Zwanikken GJ. Continuation and maintenance therapy with antidepressive agents: meta-analysis of research *Pharm Weekbl Sci* 1991;13:167–175. (Search date not given; primary sources references of textbooks and review articles, Medline 1977–1988, Embase 1977–1988, review of reference lists of primary studies.)
31. Keller MB, Kocsis JH, Thase ME, et al. Maintenance phase efficacy of sertraline for chronic depression: a randomized controlled trial. *JAMA* 1998;280:1665–1672.
32. Haaga DAF, Beck AT. Cognitive therapy. In: Paykel ES, ed. *Handbook of affective disorders.* Edinburgh: Churchill Livingstone, 1992:511–523.
33. Klerman GL, Weissman H. Interpersonal psychotherapy. In: Paykel ES, ed. *Handbook of affective disorders.* Edinburgh: Churchill Livingstone, 1992:501–510.

John Geddes, MD, MRCPsych
Senior Clinical Research Fellow and Honorary Consultant Psychiatrist
University of Oxford
Oxford
UK

Competing interests: None declared.

TABLE 1 **Adverse events (% of patients) with selective serotonin-reuptake inhibitors (SSRIs) versus tricyclic antidepressants (TCAs).[12] (*See text p. 462.*)**

Adverse effects	SSRI event rates (%)	TCA event rates (%)
Dry mouth	21	55
Constipation	10	22
Dizziness	13	23
Nausea	22	12
Diarrhoea	13	5
Anxiety	13	7
Agitation	14	8
Insomnia	12	7
Nervousness	15	11
Headache	17	14

TABLE 2 Effects of specific psychological treatments for depressive disorders. **(See text, p. 404.)**

Intervention	Evidence	Benefits	Harms/disadvantages
Cognitive therapy	A systematic review identified 48 RCTs of psychological therapies ($n = 2765$ people, mainly outpatients in secondary care therefore probably with mild to moderate depression; patients with psychotic or bipolar symptoms were excluded). 20 RCTs compared cognitive therapy with waiting list or placebo, and 17 compared it with drug treatment.[22]	79% of patients in the placebo control group were more symptomatic than the average patient treated with cognitive therapy (effect size 0.82, 95% CI 0.81–0.83).[22] 65% of patients treated with cognitive therapy were less symptomatic than the average patient treated with antidepressant drugs (effect size –0.38, 95% CI –0.39 to –0.37).[22]	No harms reported. Requires extensive training. Limited availability. RCTs in primary care suggest limited acceptability to some patients.
Interpersonal psychotherapy	No systematic reviews. One large RCT, including patients with mild to moderate depressive disorders, compared interpersonal psychotherapy versus drug treatment, cognitive therapy, or placebo plus clinical management, of 16-weeks' duration.[23]	Recovery rates were: placebo-clinical management (21%); interpersonal psychotherapy (43%, NNT 5, 95% CI 3–19), imipramine (42%, NNT 5, 95% CI 3–22).[23]	No harms reported. Requires extensive training. Limited availability.
Problem-solving therapy	No systematic reviews. Several small RCTs comparing problem solving versus drug treatment in primary care patients with mild depressive disorders.[24]	Problem solving was as effective as drug treatment.	No harms reported. Requires some training. Limited availability.
Nondirective counseling	No systematic review (protocol registered with the Cochrane database). Small RCTs comparing 1) counseling plus treatment as usual versus treatment as usual, and 2) counseling versus cognitive therapy or drug treatment in patients in primary care with mild to moderate depressive disorders.[21,25,26]	No consistent advantage to adding counseling to treatment as usual. Acceptable to patients.	No harms reported. Requires some training. Limited availability.

Schizophrenia

Stephen M Lawrie, MD

QUESTIONS

INTERVENTIONS

Key Messages

- Systematic reviews of randomized controlled trials (RCTs) have found that:
  - Chlorpromazine improves clinical outcomes but that adverse effects make it unacceptable for approximately half of patients in the short term and most patients in the long term.
  - Risperidone is at least as effective as standard antipsychotic drugs and has fewer adverse effects.
  - Clozapine is more effective than standard antipsychotic drugs but is associated with potentially fatal blood dyscrasias.
- Systematic reviews of RCTs have found that relapse rates are reduced significantly by continuing antipsychotic medication for at least 6 months after an acute episode and by family interventions. Social skills training may reduce relapse rates, but the evidence for this is poor.
- No intervention has been shown to reduce negative symptoms of reduced emotion, motivation, and self-care consistently. Evidence on the effects of newer drugs will be available soon.
- So far, only clozapine has been shown to benefit patients who are resistant to standard treatment.
- There is a need for larger trials over longer time periods with harder end points, including standardized, validated symptom scales. We also need to examine the desirability of different outcomes to patients and caregivers.

DEFINITION Schizophrenia is characterized by the "positive symptoms" (auditory hallucinations, delusions, and thought disorder) and the "negative symptoms" (reduced emotion, motivation, and self-care).[1]

INCIDENCE/ PREVALENCE Onset of symptoms typically occurs in early adult life (average age 25 years) and is more usual in younger men than women. Prevalence in the UK is 2 to 4 per 1000, and 1 in 100 people will develop schizophrenia in their lifetime.[2] These rates are similar in the US.

ETIOLOGY Risk factors include a family history (although no major genes have yet been identified), obstetric complications, developmental difficulties, central nervous system infections in childhood, cannabis use, and acute life events. The precise contributions of these factors and ways in which they may interact have yet to be determined.

PROGNOSIS Even with treatment, approximately three quarters of patients suffer recurrent relapse and continued disability,[3] although outcomes were worse in the pretreatment era.[4] Outcome may be worse in people with a strong family history or an insidious onset with delayed initial treatment and in those who continue to misuse drugs. Drug treatment is generally successful in treating positive symptoms, but up to 30% of people fail to derive much benefit, and negative symptoms are notoriously difficult to treat.[5] Approximately half of patients do not adhere to treatment in the short term. The figure is even higher in the longer term. The lifetime risk of suicide in patients with schizophrenia is 10% to 13%.[6]

AIMS To relieve symptoms, and to improve quality of life.

OUTCOMES Severity of positive and negative symptoms; global clinical improvement; global clinical impression (composite measure of symptoms and everyday functioning); rate of relapse; adverse effects of treatment.

METHODS *Clinical Evidence* search July 1998. Schizophrenia research currently comprises mainly small short-term trials using many different outcome measures.

QUESTION **What are the effects of drug treatment?**

OPTION **CHLORPROMAZINE**

One systematic review of RCTs has found that chlorpromazine is an effective antipsychotic drug. However, adverse effects make it unacceptable for approximately half of patients in the short term and most patients in the long term.

Benefits: We found one systematic review, updated in 1997, of 42 RCTs comparing chlorpromazine (mean dose of 511 mg/d, range 25–2000 mg/d) versus placebo.[7,8] Chlorpromazine was more effective than placebo in terms of psychiatrist-rated global improvement (OR 2.86, 95% CI 2.08–3.85; NNT 7, 95% CI 5–10) and global severity (OR 1.30, 95% CI 1.25–1.43; NNT 5, 95% CI 4–8).

Harms: Adverse effects make chlorpormazine unacceptable for approximately half of patients in the short and medium term and to most patients in the long term. Adverse central nervous system effects include sedation (OR 3.0, 95% CI 2.2–4.0; NNH 6, 95% CI 4–8) as well as the extrapyramidal effects of acute dystonias (OR 2.8, 95% CI 1.4–6.0) and parkinsonism (OR 2.6, 95% CI 1.8–3.7).[7,8] Other adverse effects include weight gain (OR 5.0, 95% CI 2–10; NNH 3, 95% CI 2–5), skin photosensitivity (OR 6, 95% CI 3–11), dizziness caused by hypotension (OR 2.4, 95% CI 1.7–3.5), jaundice (OR 17, 95% CI 9–90), dry mouth (OR 4, 95% CI 1.7–11), and blood dyscrasias (OR 2.6, 95% CI 0.7–9.9). No long-term information is available on the risk of tardive dyskinesia or the rare but potentially fatal neuroleptic malignant syndrome.

Comment: The review did not make specific reference to positive or negative symptoms as this information was rarely available from the trials. The ORs and NNTs were based on 6-months' data. Despite the frequent adverse effects, treated patients were more likely to stay in the studies than those receiving placebo in both the short and the medium term. Sensitivity analyses of the effects of the patients' age or sex, drug dosage, and time trends will be available in subsequent updates of the review.

OPTION RISPERIDONE

One systematic review of RCTs has found that risperidone is at least as effective as standard antipsychotic drugs and has fewer adverse effects.

Benefits: We found one systematic review updated in 1998 of 12 RCTs (2696 patients).[9,10] Risperidone (mean daily dose 6.1 mg, range 1–20 mg) was more effective than standard antipsychotic drugs (usually haloperidol) in achieving "clinical improvement" (variably defined but usually a 20% reduction in general symptoms) in the short term (< 12 weeks) (OR 1.32, 95% CI 1.07–1.59; NNT 17). No such benefit was observed for the outcome of global clinical impression.[8,9]

Harms: Compared with patients on typical antipsychotic drugs, fewer patients on risperidone developed extrapyramidal adverse effects (OR 0.43, 95% CI 0.34–0.55; NNT 4.5), required antiparkinsonian medication (NNT 5), or dropped out of treatment (OR 0.73, 95% CI 0.59–0.90; NNT 20), but more gained weight (OR 1.51, 95% CI 1.14–2.00; NNH 10).[9,10]

Comment: Risperidone is one of the new antipsychotic drugs. The reported benefits over standard drugs are marginal and subject to publication bias,[9] and need to be balanced against the greater expense of the drug.[10]

OPTION CLOZAPINE

One systematic review of RCTs has found that clozapine is more effective than standard antipsychotic drugs. However, it is associated with potentially fatal blood dyscrasias.

Benefits: We found one systematic review of clozapine updated in 1998 (31 RCTs in 2560 patients). This reported greater clinical improvement (OR 2.5, 95% CI 2.0–5.0; NNT 6, 95% CI 5–7) in both the short and the long term than did standard antipsychotics such as chlorpromazine and haloperidol.[11,12]

Harms: Compared with other commonly used neuroleptics,[11] clozapine was more likely to cause hypersalivation (OR 5.2, 95% CI 3.6–7.5; NNH 4), temperature increases (OR 3.4, 95% CI 2.0–5.6; NNH 10), and sedation (OR 1.8, 95% CI 1.3–2.4; NNH 10) but less likely to cause dry mouth (OR 0.3, 95% CI 0.2–0.4; NNT 6) and extrapyramidal adverse effects (OR 0.4, 95% CI 0.2–0.8; NNT 6). **Blood dyscrasias:** Leucopenia was reported in 3% of a large observational case series of 99,502 patients over a 5-year period, but the risk of agranulocytosis can be minimized by monitoring white cell (neutrophil) counts (0.38%, 95% CI 0.35–0.42).[13] Dyscrasias were much more common in younger patients (OR 14, 95% CI 2–98; NNH 2 vs. NNH 52 in adults). The drug seems to be more acceptable to many patients than standard antipsychotic drugs, despite the requirement for regular blood tests, as fewer dropped out from treatment than with drugs like chlorpromazine (OR 0.6, 95% CI 0.4–0.9; NNT 3).[11]

Comment: The risk of neutropenia has caused the drug company to provide a blood monitoring service, resulting in a high price for a drug that has been used for 30 years.

QUESTION Which interventions reduce relapse rates?

OPTION MEDICATION

One systematic review of follow-up studies has found that continuing antipsychotic medication for at least 6 months after an acute episode significantly reduces relapse rates and that some benefit of continuing treatment is apparent for up to 2 years. The choice of drug or preparation does not affect relapse rates greatly. Good evidence that individual drugs reduce relapse rates is available only for chlorpromazine and clozapine.

Benefits: **Continuing antipsychotic drugs:** We found one systematic review, published in 1995, of 66 studies (including 29 controlled trials) in 4365 patients taking antipsychotic drugs (mean dose 630 mg chlorpromazine equivalents per day, range 228–1736 mg) with a mean follow-up of 6.3 months.[14] This reported relapse rates of 16.2% in 1224 patients maintained on treatment compared with 51.5% in 3141 withdrawn from treatment (ARR 0.35, NNT 3). Over time, the relapse rate in patients maintained on antipsychotic treatment approached that in patients withdrawn from treatment but was still lower in treated patients at 2 years (ARR 0.22, NNT 5). **Choice of drug:** In the review,[14] the choice of drug or preparation did not seem to affect relapse rates.[14,15] A systematic review, updated in 1997, of six RCTs comparing oral versus depot fluphenazine supports this finding.[16] However, it lacked power to find a difference if one existed. A systematic review updated in 1997 of placebo-controlled RCTs of chlorpromazine[7,8] found that relapse rates over 6 to 24 months were significantly lower on chlorpromazine (OR 0.3, 95% CI 0.16–0.56; NNT 3, 95% CI 2.5–4). A systematic review, updated in 1997, identified 30 RCTs comparing clozapine versus standard antipsychotic drugs. It found that relapse rates up to 12 weeks were significantly lower with clozapine (OR 0.6, 95% CI 0.4–0.8; NNT 21).[11,12]

Harms: Mild transient cholinergic rebound (nausea, malaise, diaphoresis, vomiting, and insomnia) and dyskinesia were reported in an unspecified number of patients after sudden drug cessation but were usually acceptable with gradual dose reduction.[15] Annual incidence of tardive dyskinesia was 5%.[14,15]

Comment: In the systematic review of continued versus withdrawal of treatment, the 29 controlled trials had a longer mean follow-up of 9.7 months.[14] However, meta-analysis gave similar results to those obtained when all 66 studies were included (ARR 0.37, NNT 3). The review was weakened because all study results were used rather than weighted comparisons, no length of time was given since the last acute episode, and no distinction was made between patients experiencing a first episode and those with chronic illness.[14,15]

OPTION FAMILY INTERVENTION

One systematic review of RCTs has found that family intervention significantly reduces relapse rates.

Benefits: We found one systematic review, updated in 1996, of 12 RCTs comparing family interventions (mainly education about the illness and training in problem solving over at least five weekly sessions) versus usual care.[17,18] Three of the trials were in people experiencing their first episode. Family interventions significantly reduced relapse rates at 12, 18, and 24 months. At 1 year, the odds of relapse were reduced by 0.42 (95% CI 0.26–0.67), such that seven families would have to be treated to avoid one additional relapse (and likely hospitalization) in the family member with schizophrenia (NNT 6.5, 95% CI 4.3–14.0).[17,18]

Harms: No harms were reported, although illness education of patients possibly could have adverse consequences on morale and outlook.

Comment: The mechanism for the effects of family intervention remains unclear. It is thought to work by reducing "expressed emotion" (hostility and criticism) in patients' relatives, but may also act through improved compliance with medication. The time-consuming nature of this intervention, which must normally take place at nights or weekends, can limit its availability despite its apparent cost effectiveness; recent research, however, suggests that the work can be done as effectively in groups of families. It cannot be applied to people with little contact with home-based caregivers.

OPTION **SOCIAL SKILLS TRAINING**

Limited evidence from RCTs suggests that social skills training may reduce relapse rates.

Benefits: We found one nonsystematic meta-analysis, published in 1990, of 27 RCTs comparing social skills training versus usual care.[19] The trials were mainly in male inpatients (not all of whom had schizophrenia) using a number of techniques generally including instruction and rehearsal in social interaction. Four studies provided quantitative information, of which three defined relapse as rehospitalization. Social skills training significantly reduced relapse rates (weighted mean effect size 0.47 standard deviation units, meaning that the average treated patient would be 69% less likely to relapse than the average untreated patient; NNTs not calculable). However, sensitivity analysis indicated that only five null results (from unpublished studies) would render the difference nonsignificant. A meta-analysis published in 1991 of 73 RCTs in people with a variety of psychiatric disorders found similar results but suggested that motivation was an important predictor of benefit from treatment.[20]

Harms: None reported.

Comment: Many of the studies simultaneously compared the effects of other interventions (medication, education), so the effects of individual interventions are difficult to assess.[19] Overall, it remains uncertain whether people at different stages of illness and function require different approaches. Selected patients may benefit even from interventions of short duration.

QUESTION **Which interventions are effective in people resistant to standard treatment?**

So far, only clozapine has been shown, in a systematic review, to benefit patients who are resistant to standard treatment.

Benefits: **Clozapine:** We found one systematic review, updated in 1998, of studies comparing clozapine versus standard antipsychotic drugs.[11,12] A subanalysis of data from 349 people who were resistant to treatment found that clozapine achieved clinical improvement in 31% compared with 11% on standard antipsychotic drugs (OR for improvement compared with standard antipsychotic drugs 7.1, 95% CI 4.0–12.5; NNT 5). There was no difference in relapse rates.[11,12]
Other interventions: We found no good evidence of their effects in people resistant to standard treatment.

Harms: As above.

Comment: None.

REFERENCES

1. Andreasen NC. Symptoms, signs and diagnosis of schizophrenia. *Lancet* 1995;346:477–481.
2. Cannon M, Jones P. Schizophrenia. *J Neurol Neurosurg Psychiatry* 1996;61:604–613.
3. Johnstone EC, et al. Disabilities and circumstances of schizophrenia: a follow-up study. Police contact. *Br J Psychiatry* 1991; 159(suppl 13):37–39;44–46.
4. Hegarty JD, Baldessarini RJ, Tohen M, Waternaux C, Oepen G. One hundred years of schizophrenia: a meta-analysis of the outcome literature. *Am J Psychiatry* 1994;151:1409–1416.
5. Davis JM. Recent developments in the drug treatment of schizophrenia. *Am J Psychiatry* 1976; 133:208–214.
6. Caldwell CB, Gottesman II. Schizophrenia—a high-risk factor for suicide: clues to risk reduction. *Suicide Life Threat Behav* 1992;22: 479–493.
7. Thornley B, Adams CE, Awad G. Chlorpromazine versus placebo for those with schizophrenia. The Cochrane Library, Issue 4, 1998. Oxford: Update Software. Last substantially amended 1 December 1997. Search date October 1997; primary sources Biological Abstracts 1982 to date, EMBASE 1980 to date, MEDLINE 1966 to date, Psychlit 1974 to date, SciSearch, Cochrane Library, reference lists, pharmaceutical companies.
8. Barnes TRE. Commentary on reference 6. *Evidence-Based Mental Health* 1998;1:83.
9. Kennedy E, Song F, Hunter R, Gilbody S. Risperidone versus 'conventional' antipsychotic medication for schizophrenia. The Cochrane Library, Issue 4, 1998. Oxford: Update Software. Last substantially amended 28 November 1997. Search date 1997; primary sources Biological Abstracts 1980 to date, EMBASE 1980 to date, MEDLINE 1966 to date, Psychlit 1974 to date, SciSearch, Cochrane Library Issue 1 February 1998, reference lists, pharmaceutical companies.
10. Soares KVS. Commentary on reference 8. *Evidence-Based Mental Health* 1998;1:15.
11. Essali MA, Rezk E, Wahlbeck K, et al. Clozapine versus 'typical' neuroleptic medication for schizophrenia. The Cochrane Library, Issue 4, 1998. Oxford: Update Software. Last substantially amended 21 August 1998. Search date July 1998; primary sources BiologicaL Abstracts January 1982 to December 1997, Cochrane Schizophrenia Group's register October 1997, Cochrane Library, Issue 2, 1998, EMBASE January 1980 to December 1997, Lilacs January 1982 to September 1995; MEDLINE January 1966 to July 1998; Psyclit January 1974 to December 1997; Scisearch — Science Citation Index references of all identified studies. The first author of each study published since 1980, manufacturer of clozapine.
12. McGrath J. Commentary on reference 10. *Evidence-Based Mental Health* 1998;1:17.
13. Honigfeld G, Arellano F, Sethi J, Bianchini A, Schein J. Reducing clozapine-related morbidity and mortality: five years experience of the Clozaril national registry. *J Clin Psychiatry* 1998;59(suppl 3):3–7.
14. Gilbert PL, Harris MJ, McAdams LA, Jeste DV. Neuroleptic withdrawal in schizophrenic patients: a review of the literature. *Arch Gen Psychiatry* 1995;52:173–188. Search date not given; Primary source MEDLINE.
15. Jeste DV, Gilbert PL, McAdams LA, Harris MJ. Considering neuroleptic maintenance and taper on a continuum: need for an individual rather than dogmatic approach. *Arch Gen Psychiatry* 1995;52:209–212.
16. Adams CE, Eisenbruch M. Depot fluphenazine versus oral fluphenazine for those with schizophrenia. The Cochrane Library, Issue 4, 1998. Oxford: Update Software. Last substantive amendment 27 August 1997. Search date May 1995; primary sources Biological Abstracts January 1982 to May 1995, Cochrane Library, Cochrane Schizophrenia Group's register, EMBASE January 1980 to May 1995, MEDLINE January 1966 to May 1995, Psyclit January 1974 to May 1995, Science Citation Index, references and companies producing depot products were asked for published and unpublished, positive and negative trials.
17. Mari JJ, Streiner D. Family intervention for schizophrenia. The Cochrane Library, Issue 4, 1998. Oxford: Update Software. Last substantially amended 23 February 1996. Search date June 1995; primary sources MEDLINE 1966 to June 1995, EMBASE January 1981 to June 1995, Cochrane Schizophrenia Group's Register of Trials, and reference lists of review articles.
18. McGrath J. Commentary on reference 4. *Evidence-Based Medicine* 1996;1:121.
19. Benton MK, Schroeder HE. Social skills training with schizophrenics: a meta-analytic evaluation. *J Consult Clin Psychol* 1990;58:741–747. Search date: no details given.
20. Corrigan PW. Social skills training in adult psychiatric populations: a meta-analysis. *J Behav Ther Exp Psychiatry* 1991;22:203–210. Search date August 1988; primary sources Psychological Abstracts 1970 to August 1988.

Stephen M Lawrie, MD
Senior Clinical Research Fellow
University of Edinburgh
Edinburgh
UK

Competing interests: The author has been paid for speaking at symposia by Janssen, the manufacturer of risperidone.

Psychiatric services

Max Marshall, MB, ChB, MD, MRCPsych

QUESTIONS

INTERVENTIONS

Key Messages

- One systematic review has found that diversion to assertive community treatment can reduce the proportion of people requiring inpatient care as well as the duration of inpatient care. It is unclear whether it is safe to divert high-risk patients.
- Randomized controlled trials (RCTs) have found that admission of low-risk patients to a day hospital reduced the proportion of people requiring inpatient care as well as the duration of inpatient care.
- One systematic review has found that assertive community treatment can reduce the proportion of people with chronic psychiatric disorder requiring inpatient care as well as the duration of inpatient care. However, costs may be increased when the intervention is not restricted to patients who previously were high users of inpatient care.
- One systematic review has found that case management for people with chronic psychiatric disorder can increase the proportion admitted to hospital as well as the duration of inpatient care.

DEFINITIONS Modern psychiatric services face increasing pressure to limit the use of inpatient hospitalization for the treatment of the severely mentally ill.[1,2] In order to reduce admission rates, services have been reconfigured into two types: interventions designed to divert patients about to be admitted to hospital and interventions designed to prevent future admissions in high-user patients not requiring immediate admission. Although some interventions are now well defined (e.g., assertive community treatment and acute day hospital care), others are not (e.g., case management and home-based care), so some authors use the terms "assertive community treatment," "case management," and "home-based care" interchangeably. To avoid confusion, this review classifies interventions according to three criteria: 1) whether it consists of "diversion" from hospital or "prevention" of future admissions, 2) the nature of the intervention, and 3) the type of patient to whom it is applied (acute or chronically ill). Although the interventions described below are distinct, they are not grouped according to an internationally accepted classification.

Interventions designed to divert patients about to be admitted to hospital

Assertive community treatment—Patients are diverted to the care of a community-based, multidisciplinary team, including psychiatrists, nurses, and social workers. The team carries small case loads and frequently sees patients in the patients' own homes, with 24-hour coverage. Such teams care for the full range of acutely ill patients, including those who are suicidal or potentially violent.

Acute day hospital treatment—Patients are admitted to a highly staffed, acute day hospital, from which they may return home at night. Care is provided for the full range of acutely ill patients, but those who are suicidal or potentially violent usually are excluded.

Interventions designed to reduce admissions in patients at high risk of future admission (with chronic disorders, usually schizophrenia, or those who are acutely ill but do not require immediate admission who are at high risk of relapse)

Assertive community treatment—As above.

Case management—Patients with chronic psychiatric disorders are assigned a case manager who takes personal responsibility for assessing their needs, maintaining contact, and ensuring that they receive appropriate care. Case management may be of low or high intensity but is more individualistic than the team-based assertive community treatment.

Home-based care—Acutely ill patients requiring urgent psychiatric assessment are seen and treated at home by a multidisciplinary team, rather than in the emergency room or outpatient clinic. Follow-up is provided at home by the appropriate team member and may vary depending on the patient's needs.

AIMS To reduce admissions to hospital and duration of admissions; to improve clinical and social outcome; to reduce the costs of care; and to minimize harm to patients, caregivers, and members of the public.

OUTCOMES Frequency and duration of stay in hospital; clinical and social functioning; direct costs to health services; total costs, including nonhospital accommodation and welfare costs; rate of death and other serious adverse events; burden on caregivers.

METHODS We conducted validated searches[3] for systematic reviews and RCTs between May and August 1998 from the Cochrane Library, *Best Evidence, Evidence Based Mental Health*, MEDLINE, Psychlit, and EMBASE. Where systematic reviews were not available, RCTs were selected according to relevance, size, and recent date.

QUESTION **How effective are alternatives to regular hospital admission for patients with acute psychiatric disorders who are about to be admitted?**

OPTION **ASSERTIVE COMMUNITY TREATMENT**

One systematic review of RCTs has found that diversion to assertive community treatment reduces admissions to hospital and duration of hospital stay. The effects on cost and on caregiver burden are uncertain but tend to favor assertive community treatment. The effect on frequency of serious adverse events is uncertain.

Benefits: We found one systematic review, updated in 1998, that identified five RCTs in 719 severely ill patients about to be admitted to hospital.[4] Although it specifically studied "crisis intervention" rather than assertive community treatment, it seems admissible here because four of the five trials examined assertive community treatment,[5–8] and the fifth (a small early trial) examined an intervention similar to assertive community treatment.[9] All five trials found a reduction in admissions, although 44.8% of patients diverted from hospital were admitted within 12 months (no CIs given). Four of the five studies reported significant reductions in the duration of hospital stay (by 65%,[5] 76%,[6] 83%,[7] and 84%,[8] but no CIs were available and data could not be combined because of skew). No data were available from the fifth trial at the time of writing. Four trials reported data on costs of care (three reporting health care costs and three total costs); no CIs were available, and the data could not be combined. For costs to health services, one trial showed a small increase of 3% relative to standard care,[6] and two showed decreases of 20%[8] (no significance test applied) and 65% (significant).[7] For total costs, three trials showed decreases relative to standard care of 8% (nonsignificant),[6] 39% (significant),[5] and 45% (significant).[7] Data on caregiver burden and patient satisfaction generally favored the intervention, but data were insufficient for definitive conclusions to be drawn on clinical and social outcome.

Harms: The systematic review[4] reported lower rates of death from all causes (RR 0.75, 95% CI 0.3–1.88) and suicide (RR 0.74, 95% CI 0.24–2.32) with intervention compared with control, but CIs were too wide to permit conclusions. One trial reported a homicide by a patient in the intervention group.[7] Serious self-harm was more common among patients in the intervention group, but again CIs were too wide to permit conclusions.

Comment: There are concerns about the safety of assertive community treatment programs that divert high-risk patients.[10] It is unlikely that questions about harm will be resolved until there is a large scale trial or cohort study with frequency of serious adverse events as the main outcome.[10]

OPTION **DAY HOSPITAL CARE**

RCTs have found that diverting low-risk patients to day hospital care reduces admissions and duration of hospital stay. Effects on cost and on caregiver burden are uncertain but tend to favor day hospital care. There seems to be little effect on clinical and social outcome. Data on serious adverse events are limited.

Benefits: We found no systematic review. Three recent RCTs (one in the USA, two in the UK) examined diversion of 486 patients about to be admitted to day hospital care.[11–13] Two trials reported on the proportion of patients who could be diverted (28%,[11] 8%,[12] no CIs) and two reported on the impact on use of inpatient care (reduced by 12%[11] and 66%,[13] no significance tests or CIs available). Two reported health service costs, one finding a nonsignificant reduction of 20.9%[11] and the other a significant reduction of 36%.[13] Clinical and social outcome were similar for intervention and control groups in all three trials.

Harms: The trials did not provide data on serious adverse events. One trial reported four deaths but did not indicate how many of these were in the intervention group.[12] One trial (using a rating scale for measuring burden) found that diversion to day hospital significantly reduced burden on caregivers,[13] whereas another (using the same scale) reported no difference.[12]

Comment: In two of the trials, day hospital treatment was augmented with other interventions. One trial included outreach from a community psychiatric nurse,[13] whereas another included emergency accommodation in a nonhospital setting.[11] Therefore, the data reported cannot be taken as evidence for the effectiveness of pure "stand alone" day hospitals.

QUESTION **How effective are interventions designed to reduce admissions in patients who are at high risk of future admissions to hospital but who do not require immediate admission?**

OPTION **ASSERTIVE COMMUNITY TREATMENT**

One systematic review of RCTs has found that assertive community treatment reduces admissions and duration of hospital stay. Cost outcomes are uncertain but tend to favor assertive community treatment, so long as the intervention is restricted to previous high users of inpatient care. There is at worst no difference in clinical and social outcome, and some indices tend to favor assertive community treatment. Effects on frequency of serious adverse effects are uncertain and on caregiver burden are unknown.

Benefits: We found one systematic review, updated in 1998 (14 RCTs, 2647 people), that examined assertive community treatment for people aged 18 to 65 years with severe mental disorder.[3] Those receiving assertive community treatment were less likely to be admitted to hospital than those receiving standard care (RR 0.75, 95% CI 0.64–0.87), spent less time in hospital (weighted average from eight trials showed a 42% reduction; no CIs available), and were less likely to become homeless (RR 0.22, 95% CI 0.09–0.56). Reports on health service costs varied widely, from reductions of up to 55%[14] (including the cost of the care team) to increases of 325%.[15] No data were available on total costs of care. Meta-analysis found no differences in clinical outcomes.[3] A second systematic review published in 1998 included trials of case management as well as assertive community treatment but did not use meta-analysis.[16] It concluded (qualitatively) that psychiatric symptoms may have improved with assertive community treatment.[16]

Harms: Only five of the 14 trials reported mortality data.[3] Deaths from all causes were slightly worse for patients receiving assertive community treatment (5/264 vs. 8/427 controls, RR 1.13, 95% CI 0.38–3.3), but CIs were too wide to permit definitive conclusions. Data on caregiver burden were unavailable.

Comment: The large increase in health service costs was recorded in a trial that admitted all patients with severe mental disorder, irrespective of previous levels of service use.[15] Other trials restricted entry to patients who were either high users of care or homeless (a factor known to be associated with high rates of hospitalization).

OPTION CASE MANAGEMENT

One systematic review has found that case management increases admissions and duration of hospital stay. Data on costs and on serious adverse effects are unclear. There is no difference in clinical or social outcome. The effect on caregiver burden is unknown.

Benefits: We found one systematic review, updated in 1997 (11 RCTs), in 1751 people with severe mental disorder aged 18–65 years.[17] Those receiving case management were more likely to be admitted to hospital than those receiving standard care (RR 1.59, 95% CI 1.31–1.93) and spent more time in hospital (weighted average from trials showed a 53.6% increase in days in hospital, no CIs available). However, there was heterogeneity between trials, with four out of six trials, including the two largest, showing substantial increases[18–21] and two trials showing substantial decreases in rates and duration of admission.[14,22] Cost data were skewed and could not be combined. Three of the four trials reporting costs to health services recorded increases for the case management group (7.6%,[23] 5%,[20] and 152%[19]), none of which were significant. One trial reported a nonsignificant decrease of 38%.[14] Data on total costs of care were sparse, but two trials showed nonsignificant reductions in favor of case management (8%,[22] 28%[20]). There were no differences in clinical or social outcome between case management and standard care.

Harms: Six trials reported mortality data. There was a slight increase in all-cause mortality in the case management group, but CIs were too wide to permit conclusions (RR 1.25, 95% CI 0.69–2.3). There were no data on caregiver burden.

Comment: None.

OPTION HOME-BASED CARE

Two RCTs have found that home-based care for patients requiring acute psychiatric assessment reduces admissions and duration of hospital stay. Health service costs are probably reduced. There is no difference in clinical or social outcome. There is inconclusive evidence of a reduction in serious adverse events. There is no evidence of an increase in burden of care on relatives.

Benefits: We found no systematic review dealing exclusively with this intervention. We found two recent RCTs in 432 patients.[24,25] Both found a reduction in admissions (RR 0.57, 95% CI 0.34–0.97[24]; RR 0.47, 95% CI 0.21–1.05[25]). Use of inpatient care also was reduced by 51% (significant but no CIs available)[24] and 87% (not significant).[25] Both studies reported nonsignificant reductions in health service costs of 16%[24] and 54%.[25] There were no differences in clinical or social outcome.

Harms: Rates of death (from suicide and natural causes) were lower in the intervention groups in both trials (all deaths: RR 0.54, 95% CI 0.0–5.8,[25] RR 0.52, 95% CI 0.14–1.98[24]; suicide: RR 0.36 95% CI 0.0–8.6[25]; RR 0.4, 95% CI 0.0–3.9[24]) but CIs were too wide to permit conclusions. One trial (using a rating scale) found no increase in burden of care on relatives.[24]

Comment: Providing home-based care involves radical changes in working practices for all disciplines. It is not clear at present how far such changes can be implemented and sustained outside specialist centers.

REFERENCES

1. Strathdee G, Thornicroft G. The principles of setting up mental health services in the community. In: Bhugra D, Leff J, eds. *Principles of social psychiatry.* London: Blackwell Science, 1993.
2. Ellison D, Rieker P, Marx J. Organisational adaptation to community mental health. In: Roman P, ed. *Sociological perspectives on community mental health.* Philadelphia: Davis Co, 1974.
3. Marshall M, Lockwood A. Assertive community treatment for people with severe mental disorders (Cochrane Review). In: The Cochrane Library, Issue 2, 1998. Oxford: Update Software. Updated quarterly. Search date May 1997; primary sources CINAHL 1982 to May 1997, EMBASE 1980 to May 1997, The Cochrane Schizophrenia Group's Register, MEDLINE 1966 to May 1997, Psychlit 1974 to May 1997 and reference lists, and cited reference searching.
4. Joy CB, Adams CE, Rice K. Crisis intervention for people with severe mental illnesses (Cochrane Review). In: The Cochrane Library, Issue 1, 1999. Oxford: Update Software. Search date August 1998; primary sources Biological Abstracts 1985 to February 1998, CINAHL 1982 to February 1998, Cochrane Library, The Cochrane Schizophrenia Group's Register, EMBASE 1980 to February 1998, MEDLINE, 1966 to February 1998, Psychlit 1974 to February 1998, Sociofile 1974 to February 1998 and reference lists, cited reference searching, personal contact and hand searching of key journals.
5. Fenton FR, Tessier L, Struening EL. A comparative trial of home and hospital psychiatric care: one year follow-up. *Arch Gen Psychiatry* 1979;36:1073–1079.
6. Stein LI, Test MA, Marx AJ. Alternative to the hospital: a controlled study. *Am J Psychiatry* 1975; 132:517–522.
7. Muijen M, Marks I, Connolly J, Audini B. Home based care and standard hospital care for patients with severe mental illness: a randomised controlled trial. *BMJ* 1992;304:749–754.
8. Hoult J, Reynolds I, Charbonneau-Powis M, Weekes P, Briggs J. Psychiatric hospital versus community treatment: the results of a randomized trial. *Aust NZ J Psychiatry* 1983;101: 160–167.
9. Pasamanick B, Scarpitti FR, Lefton M, Dinitz S, Wernert JJ, McPheeters H. Home vs hospital care for schizophrenics. *JAMA* 1964;187: 177–181.
10. Kuhlman TL. Unavoidable tragedies in Madison, Wisconsin: a third view. *Hosp Community Psychiatry* 1992;43:72–73.
11. Sledge WH, Tebes J, Rakfeldt J, Davidson L, Lyons L, Druss B. Day hospital/crisis respite care versus inpatient care, part I: clinical outcomes. *Am J Psychiatry* 1996;153:1065–1073.
12. Creed F, Black D, Anthony P, Osborn M, Thomas P, Tomenson B. Randomised controlled trial of day patient versus inpatient psychiatric treatment. *BMJ* 1990;300:1033–1037.
13. Creed F, Mbaya P, Lancashire S, Tomenson B, Williams B, Holme S. Cost effectiveness of day

and inpatient psychiatric treatment: results of a randomised controlled trial. *BMJ* 1997;314: 1381–1385.
14. Quinlivan R, Hough R, Crowell A, Beach C, Hofstetter R, Kenworthy K. Service utilization and costs of care for severely mentally ill clients in an intensive case management program. *Psychiatr Serv* 1995;46:365–371.
15. Chandler D, Meisel J, McGowen M, Mintz J, Madison K. Client outcomes in two-model capitated integrated service agencies. *Psychiatr Serv* 1996;47:175–180.
16. Mueser KT, Bond GR, Drake RE, Resnick SG. Models of community care for severe mental illness: a review of research on case management. *Schizophr Bull* 1998;24:37–74. Search date 1997; no detail given about primary sources except "Relevant articles, presentations, reports to government granting agencies, and unpublished papers were identified through literature reviews, searches of computer data bases, attendance at conferences, our own knowledge of the literature, and contacts with other researchers in the field."
17. Marshall M, Gray A, Lockwood A, Green R. Case management for people with severe mental disorders (Cochrane Review). In: The Cochrane Library, Issue 2, 1998. Oxford: Update Software. Updated quarterly. Search date 1997; primary sources: The Cochrane Schizophrenia Group's Register 1997, EMBASE January 1980 to May 1995, MEDLINE January 1966 to May 1995, PsycLIT January 1974 to May 1995 and CINAHL, and searching of reference lists and hand searching of key journals.
18. Curtis JL, Millman EJ, Struening E, D'Ercole A. Effect of case management on rehospitalisation and utilisation of ambulatory care services. *Hosp Community Psychiatry* 1992;43:895–899.
19. Ford R, Ryan P, Beadsmoore A, Craig T, Muijen M. Intensive case management for people with serious mental illness—site 2: clinical and social outcome. *J Ment Health* 1997;6:181–190.
20. Muijen M, Cooney M, Strathdee G, Bell R, Hudson A. Community Psychiatric Nurse Teams: Intensive support versus generic care. *Br J Psychiatry* 1994;165:211–217.
21. Tyrer P, Morgan J, Van Horn E, et al. A randomised controlled study of close monitoring of vulnerable psychiatric patients. *Lancet* 1995;345: 756–759.
22. Marshall M, Lockwood A, Gath D. Social services case-management for long-term mental disorders: a randomised controlled trial. *Lancet* 1995;345:409–412.
23. Jerrell JM. Toward managed care for persons with severe mental illness: implications from a cost-effectiveness study. *Health Affairs* 1995;14: 197–207.
24. Burns T, Beadsmoore A, Bhat AV, Oliver A, Mathers C. A controlled trial of home-based acute psychiatric services. I: Clinical and social outcome. *Br J Psychiatry* 1993;163:49–54.
25. Merson S, Tyrer P, Oynett S, et al. Early intervention in psychiatric emergencies: a controlled clinical trial. *Lancet* 1992;339:1311–1314.

Max Marshall, MB, ChB, MD, MRCPsych
Senior Lecturer in Psychiatry
University of Manchester
Preston
UK

Competing interests: None declared.

Acute otitis media

Paddy O'Neill, MB, BS, MRCPG, DCCH, DRCOG, DPD

QUESTIONS

INTERVENTIONS

Key Messages

In children with acute otitis media

- We found limited evidence from one randomized controlled trial (RCT) that NSAIDs are more effective than placebo in relieving pain.
- Evidence on the effectiveness of antibiotics is conflicting. We found no clear evidence favoring a particular antibiotic.
- One systematic review of RCTs has found greater immediate benefit but no difference in long-term outcome with short (≤5 days) rather than longer courses of antibiotics.

In children with recurrent otitis media

- One systematic review of RCTs has found that long-term antibiotic prophylaxis has a modest effect in preventing recurrences of acute otitis media. The questions of which antibiotic to use, for how long, and how many episodes of acute otitis media justify treatment have not yet been evaluated adequately.

DEFINITION Otitis media is inflammation and effusion in the middle ear. Subcategories include acute otitis media (AOM), otitis media with effusion (OME; also known as "glue ear"; *see* p. 446), recurrent AOM, and chronic suppurative otitis media. AOM presents with systemic and local signs and has a rapid onset. The persistence of an effusion beyond 3 months without signs of infection defines otitis media with effusion, whereas chronic suppurative otitis media is characterized by continuing inflammation in the middle ear giving rise to otorrhea and a perforated tympanic membrane.

INCIDENCE/ PREVALENCE AOM is a common condition with a high morbidity and low mortality. In the UK approximately 30% of children less than 3 years of age visit their general practitioner with AOM each year, and 97% receive antimicrobial treatment. Roughly one in 10 children will have an episode of AOM by 3 months of age. It is the most common reason for outpatient antimicrobial treatment in the USA.[1]

ETIOLOGY The most common bacterial causes for AOM are *Streptococcus pneumoniae*, *Haemophilus influenzae*, and *Moraxella catarrhalis*. The incidence of penicillin resistant *S. pneumoniae* has risen, but rates differ between countries. The most important risk factors for getting AOM are young age and attendance at day care centers, such as nursery schools. Others include white race, male sex, history of enlarged adenoids, tonsillitis, and asthma. Other factors that may make the condition more likely include multiple previous episodes, bottle feeding, a history of ear infections in parents or siblings, use of a soother or pacifier, and parental smoking.[2]

PROGNOSIS In approximately 80% of children the condition resolves without antibiotic treatment in approximately 3 days. Complications are rare but include hearing loss, mastoiditis, meningitis, and recurrent attacks.[1]

AIMS To reduce the severity and duration of pain and other symptoms, to prevent complications, and to minimize adverse effects of treatment.

OUTCOMES Pain control, which can be assessed by proxy measures in infants (e.g., parental observation of distress/crying and analgesic use); incidence of complications (e.g., deafness [usually divided into short- and long-term hearing loss], recurrent attacks of otitis media, mastoiditis, and meningitis); resolution of otoscopic abnormalities; incidence of adverse effects of treatment.

METHODS *Clinical Evidence* search, July 1998. Priority was given to relevant systematic reviews. When more than one was found, both were included for comparison. Where these were unavailable, RCTs (preferably double blind) were used.

QUESTION What are the effects of treatments?

OPTION ANALGESIA

We found limited evidence from one RCT suggesting that nonsteroidal anti-inflammatory drugs (NSAIDs) are more effective than placebo in relieving

pain. The RCT found no significant difference between acetominophen and placebo, but the dosing regimen may not have been optimal and the trial may have been too small.

Benefits: We found no systematic review. We found one double-blind multicenter RCT comparing thrice daily treatment with ibuprofen, acetominophen, or placebo for 48 hours in 219 children aged 1 to 6 years with otoscopically proven AOM.[3] All children received antibiotic treatment with cefaclor. The proportions of children still experiencing pain by the second day were 7% on NSAIDs, 10% on acetominophen, and 25% on placebo. Compared with placebo, ibuprofen was significantly more effective ($p<0.01$) but acetominophen was not (p value not quoted).There was no significant difference between placebo and active treatments for other outcomes (appearance of the tympanic membrane, rectal temperature, and parental assessment).

Harms: All treatments were equally well tolerated.

Comment: The trial may have been too small to detect a significant difference between acetominophen and placebo. The lack of significant difference also may be explained by the use of a three times daily regimen, because acetominophen usually is given four times daily. The evidence from this trial may be limited further because the assessment of the child's pain relief was based on parental observation, using a scale of 0 or 1.

OPTION ANTIBIOTICS

Evidence from systematic reviews of RCTs is conflicting. The more recent and inclusive review suggests that antibiotics reduce the proportion of children still in pain at 2 to 7 days and the risk of developing contralateral AOM, but have no immediate beneficial effect in terms of reduced pain within 24 hours and no long-term effect in terms of rates of subsequent attacks or deafness at 1 month. Rates of adverse effects are almost doubled in children on antibiotics compared with placebo. There is no clear evidence favoring a particular antibiotic.

Benefits: **Versus placebo or no treatment:** We found two systematic reviews. The first identified four RCTs comparing antibiotics versus placebo or no treatment in 535 children aged 4 months to 18 years with AOM.[4] Co-intervention with analgesics and other symptomatic relief was allowed in most trials. At 7 to 14 days after treatment, the spontaneous rate of primary control—without antibiotics or tympanocentesis—was 81% (95% CI 69%–94%). Compared with placebo or no drug, antimicrobial therapy increased primary control by 13.7% (95% CI 8.2%–19.2%). This means that seven children would need to be treated with antibiotics for one additional child to achieve complete resolution of signs and symptoms or that six of every seven children with AOM either do not need or will not respond to antibiotic treatment (NNT 7, no CI was given). The second systematic review identified six RCTs comparing early use of antibiotics versus placebo in children aged 7 months to 15 years with AOM.[5] Most trials did not state the time interval between onset of symptoms and starting treatment: the two that did stated 1 to 24 and approximately 30 hours. Data from the three trials that reported pain outcomes 24 hours after presentation ($n=633$) suggested that antibiotic treatment had no effect (proportion of children pain free 61% on antibiotics vs. 60% on placebo). Data from all six trials showed that, 2 to 7 days after presentation (when only 14% of children on placebo still had pain) the proportion of children still in pain was significantly lower on antibiotics (RRR compared with placebo 41%, 95% CI 15%–60%, ARR 5.6%) as was the rate of contralateral AOM (RRR compared with placebo 43%, 95% CI 9%–64%). There was no significant difference in the rate of subsequent attacks of AOM (ARR 0.1%, 95%CI −4% to +4%) or deafness at 1 month (ARR 2.3%, 95% CI −6% to 11%). This means that 20 children would need to be treated with antibiotics early to prevent one additional child from experiencing pain at 2 to 7 days after presentation (NNT 20, 95% CI 13–46).[6] **Versus each other:** We found one systematic review, which identified 33 RCTs of antibiotics in children aged 4 months to 18 years with AOM ($n=5400$).[4] Compared to placebo or no treatment, the rate of treatment success (absence of all presenting signs and symptoms of AOM at approximately 7–14 days after treatment was started) was significantly higher with penicillin (ARI 15.7%, 95% CI 4.7%–26.7%), ampicillin/amoxicillin (ARI 12.9%, 95% CI 6.8%–19%), and for any antibiotic (ARI 13.7%, 95% CI 8.2%–19.2%). No significant differences were found between antimicrobial agents in rate of treatment success at 7 to 14 days or of middle ear effusion at 30 days.

Harms: The first review gave no information on adverse events.[4] In the second review, antibiotics were associated with a near doubling of the risk of vomiting, diarrhea, or rashes (OR 1.97, 95% CI 1.19–3.25).[5]

Comment: The first review[4] excluded two placebo-controlled trials that were included in the second[5] on the basis that they included myringotomy as part of treatment. This may have biased results in favor of antibiotic treatment and may explain the lower NNT quoted in the first review.

OPTION SHORT VERSUS LONGER COURSES OF ANTIBIOTICS

A systematic review of RCTs has found increased risk of relapse or reinfection approximately 10 days but no difference in long-term outcome with short courses (≤5 days) rather than longer courses of antibiotics.

Benefits: We found one systematic review, which identified 32 RCTs of antibiotic treatment in children aged 4 weeks to 18 years with AOM.[7] Treatment failure, relapse, or reinfection at an early evaluation (8–19 days) were significantly more likely with shorter courses of antibiotics (≤5 days) than with longer courses (8–10 days); summary OR compared to longer courses 1.52 (95% CI 1.17–1.98). However, by 20 to 30 days, there were no significant differences between treatment groups (OR 1.22, 95% CI 0.98–1.54, ARR 2.3%, 95% CI −0.2% to 4.9%).

Harms: A RCT of amoxicillin plus clavulanate potassium in 868 children aged between 2 months and 12 years reported protocol defined diarrhea in 26.7% of children on three times daily treatment for 10 days, compared with 9.6% in children on twice daily treatment for 10 days ($p<0.0001$), and 8.7% in children on twice daily treatment for 5 days ($p<0.0001$).[8] No p value was quoted for the comparison between 10- and 5-day twice-daily treatments. The trial made no mention of other adverse effects such as rash.

Comment: The 5-day treatment group did not receive a placebo from days 6 to 10, which may have biased the results.

QUESTION What are the effects of preventive interventions?

OPTION LONG-TERM ANTIBIOTIC PROPHYLAXIS

One systematic review of RCTs has found that long-term antibiotic prophylaxis has a modest effect in preventing recurrences of AOM. The questions of which antibiotic to use, for how long, and how many episodes of AOM justify treatment have not yet been evaluated adequately.

Benefits: **Versus placebo:** We found one systematic review, which identified 33 RCTs comparing antibiotics versus placebo to prevent recurrent otitis media and otitis media with effusion.[9] Nine of the trials ($n=945$) looked only at recurrent otitis media. It was not clear from the review which of the studies referred only to children; four either included the word "children" in the title or appeared in pediatric journals. Most studies defined recurrent otitis media as at least three episodes of AOM in 6 months. The most commonly used antibiotics were amoxicillin, cotrimoxazole, and sulfisoxazole given for 3 months to 2 years. All nine studies showed a lower rate of recurrence on antibiotic treatment, although in seven the difference was not significant. Pooled results showed an AR of 0.08 recurrences per patient per month on active treatment compared to 0.19 on placebo (ARR 0.11 episodes per month, 95% CI 0.03 to 0.19 episodes per month). This is a small effect favoring antibiotics, meaning that nine children with recurrent otitis media would need to be treated for 1 month to prevent one additional acute episode (NNT 9, no CI quoted). **Choice and duration of antibiotic:** The same systematic review found no significant difference in rate of recurrence between antibiotics. Greater treatment effect was seen with treatment lasting less than 6 months, but the CIs overlapped (AR of recurrence with courses <6 months 0.21, 95% CI –0.07 to 0.49; AR with courses >6 months 0.04, 95% CI –0.01 to +0.09).[9]

Harms: No evidence was presented on the harmful effects of prophylactic treatment.

Comment: None.

REFERENCES

1. Froom J, Culpepper L, Jacobs M, et al. Antimicrobials for acute otitis media? A review from the International Primary Care Network. *BMJ* 1997;315:98–102.
2. Uhari M, Mantysaari K, Niemela M. A meta-analytic review of the risk factors for acute otitis media. *Clin Infect Dis* 1996;22:1079–1083.
3. Bertin L, Pons G, d'Athis P, et al. A randomized double blind multicentre controlled trial of ibuprofen versus acetaminophen and placebo for symptoms of acute otitis media in children. *Fundam Clin Pharmacol* 1996;10:387–392.
4. Rosenfeld RM, Vertrees JE, Carr J, et al. Clinical efficacy of antimicrobial drugs for acute otitis media: meta-analysis of 5400 children from thirty-three randomised trials. *J Pediatr* 1994;124: 355–367. (Search date 1966 to June 1992; primary sources MEDLINE, Current Contents.)
5. Del Mar C, Glasziou P, Hayem M. Are antibiotics indicated as initial treatment for children with acute otitis media? A meta-analysis. *BMJ* 1997;314:1526–1529. (Search date 1966 to August 1994; primary sources MEDLINE, Current Contents.)
6. Johansen HK, Gøtzsche PC. Antibiotics as initial treatment for children with acute otitis media. *BMJ* 1997;315:879 [letter].
7. Kozyrskyj AL, Hildes Ripstein E, Longstaffe SEA, et al. Treatment of acute otitis media with a shortened course of antibiotics: a meta-analysis. *JAMA* 1998;279:1736–1742. (Primary sources MEDLINE 1966 to 1997, EMBASE 1974 to 1997, Current Contents, Science Citation Index.)
8. Hoberman A, Paradise JL, Burch DJ, et al.

Equivalent efficacy and reduced occurrence of diarrhoea from a new formulation of amoxicillin/clavulanate potassium (Augmentin) for treatment of acute otitis media in children. *Pediatr Infect Dis J* 1997;16:463–470.
9. Williams RL, Chalmers TC, Stange KC, Chalmers FT, Bowlin SJ. Use of antibiotics in preventing recurrent acute otitis media and in treating otitis media with effusion: a meta-analytic attempt to resolve the brouhaha. *JAMA* 1993;270: 1344–1351. [Published erratum appears in *JAMA* 1994;271:430.] (Search date 1966 to April 1993; primary sources MEDLINE, Current Contents.)

Paddy O'Neill, MB, BS, MRCPG, DCCH, DRCOG, DPD
General Practitioner
Norton Medical Centre
Stockton on Tees
UK

Competing interests: None declared.

Croup

David Evans, BMBCh, MA, MRCP

QUESTIONS

INTERVENTIONS

Key Messages

- Treatment of croup in primary care has not yet been evaluated adequately in randomized controlled trials (RCTs).
- RCTs in pediatric emergency departments found that systemic steroids, nebulized steroids, and nebulized epinephrine (adrenaline) all improve symptoms. Systemic and nebulized steroids also have been found to reduce the risk of admission to hospital.
- In children admitted to hospital, RCTs have found that systemic steroids, nebulized steroids, and nebulized epinephrine all improve symptoms. Systemic and nebulized steroids also have been found to reduce hospital stay.
- Limited data from RCTs provide no evidence of a difference between systemic and nebulized steroids.
- None of the RCTs we reviewed described a single death in over 1000 cases of childhood croup related either to croup itself or any associated treatment.

DEFINITION Croup is an acute clinical syndrome characterized by a harsh, barking cough, inspiratory stridor, and hoarse voice, caused by laryngeal or tracheal obstruction. Mild fever and rhinorrhea also may be present. The most important differential diagnoses are acute epiglottitis, inhalation of a foreign body, and bacterial tracheitis.

INCIDENCE/ PREVALENCE Every year croup occurs in approximately 30 per 1000 children under 6 years of age.[1,2]

ETIOLOGY Croup is believed to be mainly viral in origin, but atopy plays a part in some cases. The most common virus isolated is parainfluenza types 1, 2, or 3. Others include influenza, adenovirus, respiratory syncitial, and rhinovirus.

PROGNOSIS Fewer than 2% of children with croup are admitted to the hospital.[1] Of those admitted only 0.5% to 1.5% require intubation and mortality rates are low; two of 208 children who required artificial airways over a 10-year period died.[3] Symptoms of upper airway obstruction can be extremely distressing to the child and the family.

AIMS To reduce suffering and distress, need for hospital admission, duration of hospital stay, rates of intubation and mortality without undue adverse effects.

OUTCOMES Severity of symptoms and signs of upper airway obstruction, rates of hospital admission, visits to a medical practitioner or return to the emergency department, intubation rates, mortality, and adverse effects of treatment. A commonly used definition of a clinically significant improvement was approximately 2 points of the validated Westley score (maximum score 17),[4] within a predefined timescale. Intubation and death are rare in children with croup, thus, large numbers of children would be needed to exclude a difference in rates between interventions.

METHODS MEDLINE, EMBASE, and the Cochrane Library were searched to August 1998 for systematic reviews and RCTs evaluating interventions in croup, laryngotracheitis, and laryngotracheobronchitis. Data were extracted from trials that used randomization (not quasirandomization) and intention to treat analysis. Common exclusion criteria were previous upper airway abnormalities, previous prolonged intubation, severe croup (cyanosis with impaired consciousness), and recent treatment with steroids. The conclusions presented below should not be applied to children with these clinical features. Most children in the studies were cared for in institutions with excellent staffing and monitoring facilities. RCTs performed in hospital settings studied children with more severe croup than those based in assessment units.

QUESTION **What are the effects of treatment in primary care settings?**

We found no RCTs evaluating interventions in acute childhood croup within a primary care setting.

QUESTION What are the effects of treatment in primary pediatric assessment units?

OPTION SYSTEMIC STEROIDS

Three RCTs found that a single dose of oral or intramuscular steroids significantly improved symptoms within 5 hours, reduced the likelihood of admission to hospital by 75%, and reduced the need for further treatment after discharge by 70%.

Benefits: We found no systematic review. We found three RCTs in 230 children seen at primary pediatric assessment units in Canada, the USA, and Australia. One compared a single intramuscular dose of 0.6 mg/kg dexamethasone given shortly after arrival in the assessment unit versus placebo.[5] The others compared 0.15 mg/kg oral dexamethasone[6] and 0.6 mg/kg intramuscular dexamethasone[7] versus placebo in children ready for discharge from the assessment unit. **Symptom improvement:** The use of 0.6 mg/kg intramuscular dexamethasone significantly increased improvement in the croup score within 5 hours.[5] **Admission to hospital:** Intramuscular dexamethasone given shortly after arrival in the assessment unit reduced admissions to hospital (RR of admission compared with placebo 0.25, 95% CI 0.13–0.49, NNT to prevent one additional admission 2, 95% CI 1–3)[5] **Return to medical care:** For the week after discharge, all three RCTs reported lower rates of return to any medical practitioner or institution in children given steroids (RR for return compared to placebo 0.32, 95% CI 0.11–0.88, NNT to prevent one additional child return 12, 95% CI 6–60).[5–7]

Harms: None reported.

Comment: The children were observed for up to 5 hours in a pediatric assessment unit before a decision was made to discharge them. Some children were treated with nebulized epinephrine.[7] Treatment in an assessment unit that involves a potentially prolonged period of monitoring may have resource implications.

OPTION NEBULIZED STEROIDS

RCTs have found that nebulized steroids reduced by more than half the risk of a poor response within 2 to 5 hours and reduced by half the risk of hospital admission compared with placebo, with no evidence of a significant difference in the need for further treatment after discharge.

Benefits: We found no systematic review. **Symptom improvement:** We found four RCTs (250 children) evaluating treatment in assessment units. These compared a single dose of inhaled steroids (budesonide 2 mg[8,9] or 4 mg[5] and dexamethasone 10 mg [<8 kg bodyweight], 15 mg [8–12 kg] or 20 mg [>12 kg][10]) versus placebo. Treatments were given after humidified oxygen. Combined data from the three trials that dichotomized outcomes into either good or poor response showed a significantly reduced risk of a poor response within 2 to 5 hours after treatment (RR compared with placebo 0.44, 95% CI 0.29–0.67).[8–10] **Admission to hospital:** Rate of hospitalization was reduced by 50% (RR for hospitalization compared with placebo 0.51, 95% CI 0.36–0.72,

NNT to prevent one additional admission 4, 95% CI 3–8).[5,8–10] **Return to medical care:** There was no evidence of a significant difference in rates of further admission (RR 0.74, 95% CI 0.26–2.08[5,8–10]) or consultations with other health practitioners (RR 0.86, 95% CI 0.34–2.19[9]) in the week after discharge from the emergency department.

Harms: The use of nebulized steroids appears to be well tolerated. In one of these four trials, two neutropenic children suffered bacterial tracheitis after treatment with nebulized dexamethasone.[10]

Comment: The optimal regimen of nebulized steroids has not yet been established; furthermore, nebulized steroids are not approved for use in the US. All children were observed for up to 5 hours in the assessment unit, all received humidified air or oxygen, and in one study both groups also received oral dexamethasone 0.6 mg/kg.[9]

OPTION SYSTEMIC VERSUS NEBULIZED STEROIDS

RCTs have found that systemic dexamethasone and nebulized budesonide were equally effective in reducing symptoms. In one trial, oral dexamethasone resulted in a smaller proportion of children requiring admission than nebulized budesonide.

Benefits: We found no systematic review. We found two RCTs comparing oral dexamethasone 0.6 mg/kg versus nebulized budesonide 2 mg[11] and intramuscular dexamethasone 0.6 mg/kg versus nebulized budesonide 4 mg[5] in 230 children with acute croup attending an assessment unit. These found no significant difference between nebulized budesonide and systemic dexamethasone in the rates of symptom resolution or reattendance after discharge, although fewer children on oral dexamethasone were admitted (RR of admission compared with nebulized steroids 0.53, 95% CI 0.34–0.81).[5]

Harms: None reported.

Comment: Nebulized steroids are not approved for use in the US.

OPTION NEBULIZED EPINEPHRINE (ADRENALINE)

One small RCT has found that nebulized epinephrine given in the assessment unit to children suffering from croup significantly improves symptoms within 30 minutes compared with placebo. Symptoms returned to preintervention severity in one third of children within 2 hours.

Benefits: We found no systematic review. We found one RCT comparing nebulized racemic epinephrine (0.5 mg/kg diluted to 2 mL with 0.9% sodium chloride) versus saline placebo in 54 children with stridor at rest seen in an assessment unit.[12] This found a significant improvement in croup scores 30 minutes after treatment with epinephrine (mean scores 2.0 vs. 3.6 on placebo, $p < 0.01$).[12] There was no significant reduction in the duration of stay in the assessment unit.

Harms: Of the children who had improved by 30 minutes, a higher proportion relapsed (croup scores returned to the pretreatment value) 2 hours after treatment with epinephrine than with placebo (35% vs.

25%), although this difference was not significant (RR of relapse at two hours compared with placebo 1.41, 95% CI 0.36–5.51). This raises the question of whether children given nebulized epinephrine and then discharged home may come to harm when symptoms recur. However, no children discharged in the RCT reattended for further treatment.[12] Children were observed for a minimum of 5 hours (ranging up to 24 hours). During this time, 40% of treated children and 48% of controls were given another dose of epinephrine. Also, 52% of treated children and 58% of controls received oral betamethasone 6 mg before final discharge. These differences were not significant.

Comment: Two recent nonrandomized cohort studies have examined the outcome in children treated with nebulized epinephrine and dexamethasone 0.6 mg/kg in an assessment unit. Of the 55% to 66% who responded satisfactorily, all were discharged after 3 to 4 hours of observation and none reattended for further medical care within 24 to 48 hours.[13,14]

QUESTION What are the effects of treatment in hospital?

OPTION INHALATION OF HUMIDIFIED AIR/OXYGEN

The effectiveness of inhaling humidified air/oxygen has not been evaluated adequately.

Benefits: We found no systematic review. We found one RCT in 16 children.[15] This compared up to 12 hours' care in a humidified atmosphere (relative humidity 87%–95%) versus normal care. It found no significant difference in recovery rates.

Harms: None reported.

Comment: The study was not blinded; selection, performance, and detection biases remain a possibility.

OPTION SYSTEMIC STEROIDS

RCTs have found that children admitted with croup are more likely to show a clinically significant symptomatic improvement by 12 hours and have a shorter duration of hospital stay if given systemic corticosteroids. Limited evidence suggests that a single dose of oral dexamethasone 0.3 mg/kg is as effective as 0.6 mg/kg in children admitted with croup.

Benefits: We combined data from seven RCTs (830 children) reported within a systematic review published in 1989[16] with data from three subsequent RCTs comparing systemic steroids versus placebo in 180 children admitted to hospital with croup.[17–19] The most common regimen was intramuscular or oral dexamethasone 0.3 to 0.6 mg/kg as a single dose on admission or repeated over 24 to 48 hours. **Symptom improvement:** The trials that evaluated symptomatic improvement at 12 hours found significantly fewer children not responding to steroids than to placebo (RR of inadequate response compared with placebo 0.43; 95% CI 0.33–0.57; NNT to avoid one additional child with an inadequate response 4, 95% CI 3–6).[16–18] **Hospital stay:** Three RCTs evaluated duration of hospital stay. Two found a significant reduction in hospital stay on dexamethasone 0.6 mg/kg compared with placebo (median stay 20 vs. 13 hours[18] and mean stay 91 vs. 49 hours[19]). The other found no significant difference.[17] **Intubation rates:** Seven RCTs in the systematic review and one subsequent RCT gave data on intubation rates.[16,18] Combining these data, we found no significant difference (RR of intubation compared with placebo 0.48, 95% CI 0.09–2.55). However, intubation is rare in children with croup. Larger numbers of children would be needed to exclude a significant difference between interventions. **Different systemic steroid regimens:** We found no systematic review. We found one RCT comparing different single doses of oral dexamethasone (0.6 vs. 0.3 mg/kg and 0.3 vs. 0.15 mg/kg) in 120 children admitted with croup.[19] There were no significant differences in rate of improvement in croup score, duration of hospital stay, or intubation rates. However, children on 0.15 mg/kg were more likely to be given nebulized adrenaline than those on 0.3 mg/kg (RR 2.32, 95% CI 1.02–5.28).We found no studies comparing other systemic regimens.

Harms: Systemic steroids seem to be well tolerated. Only two RCTs in 100 children reported rates of secondary bacterial infection.[17,20] The cases reported were five pneumonia, one otitis media, and one sinusitis. Five cases were in the treated groups and two in the control groups (RR for infection compared with placebo 2.14; 95% CI 0.49–9.30).

Comment: A significant reduction in the time to symptom resolution may not mean a shorter hospital stay. This is because the duration of hospital stay is influenced by hospital policies and referral patterns, availability of treatment in the community, parental access to transportation and communications, and the tendency of hospitals to discharge patients at a certain time each day.[21]

OPTION NEBULIZED STEROIDS

RCTs have found that children admitted with croup improved more rapidly and left hospital sooner if given nebulized corticosteroids. We found insufficient evidence on the effect of nebulized steroids on intubation rates.

Benefits: We found no systematic review. We found three RCTs.[18,22,23] These compared nebulized steroids versus placebo in 170 children admitted with croup. **Symptom improvement:** One trial evaluated budesonide 1 mg, two doses 30 minutes apart.[22] The risk of an inadequate response by 2 hours was reduced significantly (RR compared with placebo 0.40, 95% CI 0.19–0.83; NNT to prevent one additional inadequate response 2, 95% CI 1–8). **Hospital stay:** Another trial compared nebulized budesonide 2 mg initially, followed by 1 mg every 12 hours, versus placebo and found a significant reduction in hospital stay (mean stay 55 vs. 36 hours).[23] The third RCT compared budesonide (2 mg single dose) versus placebo and reported a significant reduction in the number of children staying in hospital for more than 24 hours (RR 0.37, 95% CI 0.16–0.88; NNT 3, 95% CI 2–14).[18] **Intubation rates:** Using data from the three trials, there was no demonstrable effect on intubation rates (RR of intubation on steroid compared with placebo 0.18, 95% CI 0.01–3.67).[18,22,23]

Harms: The use of nebulized steroids seems to be well tolerated. Only one trial reported adverse effects: one episode of nausea and one episode of distress caused by firm application of the face mask for 10 minutes.[23]

Comment: The optimal regimen of nebulized steroids has not yet been established.

OPTION SYSTEMIC VERSUS NEBULIZED STEROIDS

One small RCT found that oral dexamethasone and nebulized budesonide were equally effective in reducing symptoms, duration of stay, and return to medical care.

Benefits: We found no systematic review. We found one RCT comparing oral dexamethasone 0.6 mg/kg versus nebulized budesonide 2 mg in 50 children admitted with croup.[18] There were no significant differences in rate of symptom resolution, duration of hospital stay, or reattendance after discharge.

Harms: None reported.

Comment: None.

OPTION NEBULIZED EPINEPHRINE (ADRENALINE)

Small RCTs have found some benefit of nebulized epinephrine, with no increased risk of cardiovascular events.

Benefits: We found no systematic review. **Versus placebo:** We found three RCTs comparing nebulized epinephrine versus placebo in 53 children admitted to hospital with croup. Two trials failed to show improvement with epinephrine treatment but were too small to exclude a clinically significant difference.[24,25] Another small RCT compared aerosolized racemic epinephrine versus 0.9% sodium chloride placebo, both delivered by intermittent positive-pressure breathing.[4] Children given epinephrine experienced greater reductions in croup score. The reduction was greatest within 30 minutes of treatment and was not apparent at 2 hours. **Nebulizer versus intermittent positive-pressure breathing:** We found one RCT in 14 children comparing nebulized epinephrine delivered by intermittent positive-pressure breathing versus nebulized epinephrine alone.[26] It found no significant difference in resolution of symptoms. **L-epinephrine versus racemic epinephrine:** We found one RCT comparing racemic epinephrine versus L-epinephrine in 31 children.[27] This found no significant difference in croup scores.

Harm: There was no significant difference in the risk of cardiovascular adverse effects with L-epinephrine or racemic epinephrine. Three children receiving racemic epinephrine were intubated but this risk was not significant (RR of intubation compared with L-epinephrine 6.59, 95% CI 0.37–117.8).[27] Patients given nebulized epinephrine need medical observation because of the possibility that symptoms will return to their pretreatment severity (*see* p. 494).

Comment: Racemic epinephrine comprises equal amounts of D and L isomers and was historically chosen in favor of the more readily available L form in the belief that it caused fewer cardiovascular adverse effects.

OPTION NEBULIZED EPINEPHRINE VERSUS STEROIDS

We found no good evidence with which to compare the effectiveness of nebulized epinephrine and steroids.

Benefits: We found no systematic review. We found one RCT comparing nebulised epinephrine 4 mg versus nebulized budesonide 2 mg in 66 children admitted to hospital with croup.[28] This found no significant difference in croup scores or duration of hospital stay. We found no RCTs comparing nebulized epinephrine versus oral steroids.

Harms: None reported.

Comment: Nebulized epinephrine and steroids may have an additive effect through different modes of action, although whether this leads to improved outcomes is not proved.

REFERENCES

1. Denny FW, Murphy TF, Clyde WA Jr, Collier AM, Henderson FW. Croup: an 11-year study in a pediatric practice. *Pediatrics* 1983;71:871–876.
2. Phelan PD, Landau LI, Olinsily A. *Respiratory illness in children,* 2nd ed. Oxford: Blackwell Science, 1982:32–33.
3. McEniery J, Gillis J, Kilham H, Benjamin B. Review of intubation in severe laryngotracheobronchitis. *Pediatrics* 1991;87:847–853.
4. Westley CR, Cotton EK, Brooks JG. Nebulized racemic epinephrine by IPPB for the treatment of croup: a double-blind study. *Am J Dis Child* 1978;132:484–487.
5. Johnson DW, Jacobson S, Edney PC, Hadfield P, Mundy ME, Schuh S. A comparison of nebulized budesonide, intramuscular dexamethasone, and placebo for moderately severe croup. *N Engl J Med* 1998;339:498–503.
6. Geelhoed GC, Turner J, Macdonald WB. Efficacy of a small single dose of oral dexamethasone for outpatient croup: a double blind placebo controlled clinical trial. *BMJ* 1996;313:140–142.
7. Cruz MN, Stewart G, Rosenberg N. Use of dexamethasone in the outpatient management of acute laryngotracheitis. *Pediatrics* 1995;96:220–223.
8. Klassen TP, Feldman ME, Watters LK, Sutcliffe T, Rowe PC. Nebulized budesonide for children with mild-to-moderate croup. *N Engl J Med* 1994; 331:285–289.
9. Klassen TP, Watters LK, Feldman ME, Sutcliffe T, Rowe PC. The efficacy of nebulized budesonide in dexamethasone-treated outpatients with croup. *Pediatrics* 1996;97: 463–466.
10. Johnson DW, Schuh S, Koren G, Jaffe DM. Outpatient treatment of croup with nebulized dexamethasone. *Arch Pediatr Adolesc Med* 1996; 150:349–355.
11. Klassen TP, Craig WR, Moher D, et al. Nebulized budesonide and oral dexamethasone for the treatment of croup: a randomized controlled trial. *JAMA* 1998;279:1629–1632.
12. Kristjansson S, Berg-Kelly K, Winso E. Inhalation of racemic adrenaline in the treatment of mild and moderately severe croup: clinical symptom score and oxygen saturation measurements for evaluation of treatment effects. *Acta Paediatr* 1994;83:1156–1160.
13. Ledwith CA, Shea LM, Mauro RD. Safety and efficacy of nebulized racemic epinephrine in conjunction with oral dexamethasone and mist in the outpatient treatment of croup. *Ann Emerg Med* 1995;25:331–337.
14. Kunkel NC, Baker MD. Use of racemic epinephrine, dexamethasone, and mist in the outpatient management of croup. *Pediatr Emerg Care* 1996; 12:156–159.
15. Bourchier D, Dawson KP, Fergusson DM. Humidification in viral croup: a controlled trial. *Aust Paediatr J* 1984;20:289–291.
16. Kairys SW, Olmstead EM, O'Connor GT. Steroid treatment of laryngotracheitis: a meta-analysis of the evidence from randomized trials. *Pediatrics* 1989;83:683–693. (Search date 1998; primary sources MEDLINE, EMBASE, and Cochrane Library.)
17. Super DM, Cartelli NA, Brooks LJ, Lembo RM, Kumar ML. A prospective randomized double-blind study to evaluate the effect of dexamethasone in acute laryngotracheitis. *J Pediatr* 1989;115:323–329.
18. Geelhoed GC, Macdonald WB. Oral and inhaled steroids in croup: a randomized, placebo-controlled trial. *Pediatr Pulmonol* 1995;20:355–361.
19. Geelhoed GC, Macdonald WB. Oral dexamethasone in the treatment of croup: 0.15 mg/kg versus 0.3 mg/kg versus 0.6 mg/kg. *Pediatr Pulmonol* 1995;20:362–368.
20. Kuusela AL, Vesikari T. A randomized double-blind, placebo-controlled trial of dexamethasone and racemic epinephrine in the treatment of croup. *Acta Paediatr Scand* 1988;77:99–104.
21. Kemper KJ. Medically inappropriate hospital use in a pediatric population. *N Engl J Med*

1988;318:1033–1037.
22. Husby S, Agertoft L, Mortensen S, Pedersen S. Treatment of croup with nebulised steroid (budesonide): a double blind, placebo controlled study. *Arch Dis Child* 1993;68:352–355.
23. Godden CW, Campbell MJ, Hussey M, Cogswell JJ. Double blind placebo controlled trial of nebulised budesonide for croup. *Arch Dis Child* 1997;76:155–158.
24. Gardner HG, Powell KR, Roden VJ, Cherry JD. The evaluation of racemic epinephrine in the treatment of infectious croup. *Pediatrics* 1973;52: 52–55.
25. Taussig LM, Castro O, Beaudry PH, Fox WW, Bureau M. Treatment of laryngotracheobronchitis (croup). *Am J Dis Child* 1975;129:790–793.
26. Fogel JM, Berg IJ, Gerber MA, Sherter CB. Racemic epinephrine in the treatment of croup: nebulization alone versus nebulization with intermittent positive pressure breathing. *J Pediatr* 1982;101:1028–1031.
27. Waisman Y, Klein BL, Boenning DA, et al. Prospective randomized double-blind study comparing L-epinephrine and racemic epinephrine aerosols in the treatment of laryngotracheitis (croup). *Pediatrics* 1992;89:302–306.
28. Fitzgerald D, Mellis C, Johnson M, Allen H, Cooper P, Van Asperen P. Nebulized budesonide is as effective as nebulized adrenaline in moderately severe croup. *Pediatrics* 1996;97:722–725.

David Evans, BMBCh, MA, MRCP
Lecturer in Paediatrics and Child Health
University of Leeds
UK

Competing interests: None declared.

TABLE 1 **Effects of treatment in acute childhood croup: results of placebo-controlled RCTs**

Intervention (versus placebo)	Outcome				
	Symptoms	**Hospital stay**	**Intubation***	**Hospital admission**	**Return to medical care after discharge**
Humidified air/oxygen	NE	NE	NE	NE	NE
Systemic steroids					
(i) In assessment units	Improved[5]	NE	NE	Reduced RR 0.25 (0.13–0.49) NNT 2 (1–3)[5]	Reduced RR 0.32 (0.11–0.88) NNT 12 (6–60)[5–7]
(ii) In hospital	Improved RR 0.43 (0.33–0.57) NNT 4 (3–6)[16–18]	Reduced[18,19]; no difference[17]	No difference RR 0.48 (0.09–2.55)[16,18]	NE	NE
Nebulized steroids					
(i) In assessment units	Improved RR 0.44 (0.29–0.67) NNT 3 (2–6)[8–10]	NE	NE	Reduced RR 0.51 (0.36–0.72) NNT 4 (3–8)[5,8–10]	NE
(ii) In hospital	Improved RR of inadequate response 0.40 (0.19 to 0.83) NNT 2 (1–8)[22]	Reduced[23]	No difference RR 0.18 (0.01–3.67)[18,22,23]	NE	NE
Nebulized epinephrine					
(i) In assessment units	Improved, but possible increased risk of relapse at 2 h[12]	NE	NE	NE	NE
(ii) In hospital	Improved[4] No difference[24,25]	NE	NE	NE	NE

NE = no or inadequate evidence. *Intubation is rare in children with croup, so large numbers would be needed to exclude a difference in intubation rates between interventions. Relative risk (RR) and numbers needed to treat (NNT) given for dichotomous outcomes; 95% CI given in parentheses.

Childhood asthma

Duncan Keeley, MB, MRCP

QUESTIONS

INTERVENTIONS

ACUTE ASTHMA
Beneficial
Oxygen .503
Ipratropium bromide added to β_2-agonists .503
Spacer devices for delivery of β_2-agonists (as effective as nebulizers) .504
Systemic corticosteroids .504

Unlikely to be beneficial
Intravenous theophylline .504

PROPHYLAXIS IN CHILDREN WITH ASTHMA
Beneficial
Inhaled corticosteroids .505
Oral theophylline .505
Inhaled sodium cromoglycate .505

ACUTE WHEEZING IN INFANCY
Unknown effectiveness
β_2-agonists .506

Unlikely to be beneficial
Systemic corticosteroids .507
Anticholinergic agents .507

PROPHYLAXIS IN WHEEZING INFANTS
Unknown effectiveness
Inhaled corticosteroids .508

Unlikely to be beneficial
Oral theophylline .508
Sodium cromoglycate .508

To be covered in future issues of *Clinical Evidence*
Long acting β_2-agonists for prophylactic treatment of childhood asthma

Key Messages

- Experience suggests that oxygen should be given for acute severe asthma.
- Evidence from a systematic review suggests that adding ipratropium bromide to β_2-agonists in acute severe asthma leads to marginal improvement.
- Evidence from a systematic review suggests that nebulizer and metered-dose inhaler/spacers for delivering β_2-agonists are equally effective in acute severe asthma.
- Evidence from systematic reviews suggests that systemic corticosteroids in acute asthma reduce the likelihood of hospital admission and of early relapse.
- Long-term follow-up randomized controlled trials (RCTs) in children with asthma show that prophylactic inhaled steroids, oral theophylline, and inhaled sodium cromoglycate improve symptoms and lung function, with inhaled steroids being more effective than theophylline or sodium cromoglycate.

- Long-term follow-up studies have failed to find evidence of growth retardation in groups of asthmatic children treated with inhaled steroids, although short-term studies have detected reduction in growth velocity in some children.
- Evidence for the effectiveness of treatments used for wheezing in infancy is weak or conflicting, possibly caused in part by diagnostic difficulties.

DEFINITION Childhood asthma is characterized by chronic or recurrent cough and/or wheeze, supported by demonstration of reversible airways obstruction in those old enough to perform peak flow measurements or spirometry. Making a diagnosis of asthma in children involves excluding other causes of recurrent respiratory symptoms. Wheezing in infancy may be due to a wide variety of causes, including acute viral infection (bronchiolitis), episodic viral associated wheeze, or asthma, and these are not easy to distinguish clinically.

INCIDENCE/ PREVALENCE Epidemiologic data suggest that the prevalence of wheeze, shortness of breath, and diagnosed asthma are rising in children over and above a recognized tendency for asthma to be diagnosed more readily. One questionnaire study from Aberdeen, Scotland, surveyed 2510 children (8–13 years old) in 1964 and 3403 children in 1989. Over the 25 years, prevalence of wheeze rose from 10.4% to 19.8%, episodes of shortness of breath from 5.4% to 10.0%, and diagnosis of asthma from 4.1% to 10.2%.[1] In one prospective cohort study of 826 newborns followed up at 3 and 6 years of age, 34% of the overall sample had had at least one wheezing illness before age 3, 14% wheezed before age 3 and were still wheezing at age 6, and 15% reported a wheezing illness in the past year at age 6 but had not wheezed before age 3.[2]

ETIOLOGY The etiology of asthma is multifactorial, although it is more common in children with a personal or family history of atopy. Precipitating factors are known to include infection, house dust mite, allergens from pet animals, exposure to tobacco smoke or cold air, and anxiety.

PROGNOSIS A study of wheezing in the first year of life found that 14% of children with one attack and 23% of children with four or more attacks (recalled at age 5 years) had had at least one wheezing illness in the past year at age 10.[3]

AIMS To reduce or abolish symptoms of cough and wheeze, to attain best possible lung function, to reduce the risk of severe attacks, to minimize sleep disturbance and absence from school, to minimize adverse effects of treatment, and to allow normal growth.

OUTCOMES Wheeze; cough; nights disturbed by asthma; days lost from school or normal activities; emergency department visits; hospital admission; duration of stay in hospital; lung function tests (peak expiratory flow rate [PEFR] and forced expiratory volume in one second [FEV_1]); blood oxygen saturation in acute attacks.

METHODS *Clinical Evidence* search May and September 1998. All relevant systematic reviews and RCTs that were identified were reviewed.

QUESTION How effective are treatments for acute severe asthma?

OPTION OXYGEN

Observational data and clinical experience support the need for oxygen in acute severe asthma.

Benefits: We found no systematic review or RCTs. One double-blind prospective cohort study of 280 children found that decreased oxygen saturation on entry to an emergency department was correlated with increased hospital admission or later readmission, as well as the administration of intravenous aminophylline and steroids. The likelihood ratio for admission/readmission was: 35 (95% CI 11–150) for arterial oxygen saturation (SaO_2) ≤91% compared with ~96%; and 4.2 (95% CI 2.2–8.8) for SaO_2 of 92% to 95% compared with ~96%.[4]

Harms: We found no evidence of harm.

Comment: An RCT of oxygen in acute asthma would be considered unethical. Although the evidence from the cohort study shows only that low oxygen saturation is correlated with more severe outcomes and does not directly address whether oxygen should be given therapeutically, it does suggest, along with clinical experience, that oxygen should continue to be given promptly to children with acute severe asthma.[4] Oxygen is useful during acute attacks, especially when nebulized β-agonists are given to prevent transient desaturation.[5]

OPTION IPRATROPIUM BROMIDE ADDED TO β_2-AGONISTS

The effectiveness of β_2-agonists is unquestioned. Adding anticholinergic agents improves lung function and may reduce admission rates.

Benefits: We found one systematic review of 10 RCTs (participants aged 18 months to 17 years) comparing combined inhaled anticholinergics and β_2-agonists versus β_2-agonists alone.[6] It found improvement in one lung function test (FEV_1) for children with milder asthma on combination treatment at 1 hour (WMD 16%, 99% CI 2%–30%) and 2 hours (WMD 17%, 99% CI 4–15) but not in other tests. With multiple-dose protocols for severe exacerbations (five RCTs), combination treatment was found to reduce the rate of hospital admission by 9% (NNT 11; OR 0.6, 99% CI 0.3 to 1.1), although no differences were found in oxygen saturation. A recent, large RCT (90 patients aged 6–18 years) found greater lung function improvement (at 30 and 120 minutes: increase in PEFR 22.7% vs. 15.4%; increase in FEV_1 19.5% vs. 14.3%, $p < 0.0001$ for all results) but no reduction in admission rate with combination treatment.[7]

Harms: No difference in the rate of adverse effects was noted in either study.

Comment: None.

OPTION NEBULIZER VERSUS SPACER WITH METERED DOSE INHALER

A systematic review of RCTs has found that the use of a metered-dose inhaler with spacer is as effective as nebulization for delivering β_2-agonists in acute asthma.

Benefits: We found one systematic review of 12 RCTs comparing nebulizers versus metered-dose inhaler with spacer for the administration of β_2-agonists in children with acute asthma. Six RCTs studied children over 2 years, excluding life threatening cases, and three included children under 5 years.[8] The review analyzed data on adults and children separately. It found no significant difference in hospital admission rates (OR 0.71, 95% CI 0.23–2.23), but one large RCT showed that time spent in the emergency department was lower in children treated with spacers (WMD –0.62 hours, 95% CI –0.84 to –0.40 hours).[9] Rate of increase in pulse rate was higher with nebulizers (WMD 10% from baseline, 95% CI 5.87%–14.13% from baseline). Two RCTs in children reported blood gas results showing less deterioration with spacer than with nebulizer. No outcomes were worse with spacer.

Harms: There were no reports of serious adverse effects with either mode of delivery.[8]

Comment: These findings suggest that the use of metered-dose inhalers plus spacers could be substituted for wet nebulization in the treatment of most children with acute asthma in emergency departments and hospital wards.

OPTION SYSTEMIC CORTICOSTEROIDS

Two systematic reviews have found that systemic corticosteroids reduce the likelihood of hospital admission and relapse in the first week after discharge from emergency departments.

Benefits: We found two systematic reviews. Both identified the same two RCTs comparing early use of systemic corticosteroids versus placebo for asthma exacerbations in children.[10,11] The first review found a reduced risk of admission (range of OR 0.06–0.42). The second found fewer relapses in children receiving steroids. Subgroup analysis was not performed.[11]

Harms: We found few adverse effects reported for short courses of systemic corticosteroids. Several case reports and case series have found an increased risk of severe varicella infection, whereas one case control study (167 cases, 134 controls) comparing otherwise immunocompetent children with complicated and uncomplicated varicella infection did not find significant risk attributable to corticosteroid exposure (OR 1.6, 95% CI 0.2–16.9).[12]

Comment: Any risk attached to the use of short courses of oral corticosteroids is extremely small. Failure to use oral corticosteroids in acute severe asthma is a recognized risk factor for asthma death.

OPTION **INTRAVENOUS THEOPHYLLINE**

We found no evidence of significant benefit from the addition of intravenous theophylline to treatment regimens.

Benefits: We found one systematic review of six small RCTs (total of 164 participants aged 1.5–18 years) that found no significant benefit in patients treated with theophylline in addition to other routine treatment.[13]

Harms: Theophylline has well-known, serious adverse effects (cardiac arrhythmia, convulsion) if therapeutic blood concentrations are exceeded.

Comment: The authors comment that the available studies were too small to exclude a clinically important effect of intravenous theophylline.

QUESTION **What are the effects of prophylactic treatments in childhood asthma?**

OPTION **INHALED CORTICOSTEROIDS, ORAL THEOPHYLLINE, AND INHALED SODIUM CROMOGLYCATE**

Prophylactic inhaled steroids, oral theophylline, and inhaled sodium cromoglycate all have been found to improve symptoms and lung function in children with asthma when compared with placebo. Inhaled steroids are more effective than theophylline or sodium cromoglycate.

Benefits: **Inhaled corticosteroids versus placebo:** We found one systematic review of 24 RCTs (1087 children, 10 of 24 trials in preschool children, duration 4–88 weeks) comparing regular inhaled steroids versus placebo.[14] It found an overall weighted relative improvement of 50% in symptom scores (95% CI 49%–51%), with a 37% (95% CI 36%–38%) reduction in β_2-agonist use, a 68% (95% CI 66%–70%) reduction in use of oral steroids, and a weighted mean overall improvement in PEFR of 11% predicted (95% CI 9.5%–12.5%). Three of the 24 RCTs showed no benefit with inhaled steroids. **Inhaled corticosteroids versus theophylline:** We found no systematic review. One double-blind, placebo-controlled RCT of 195 children aged 6 to 16 years, followed up for 12 months, compared oral theophylline versus inhaled beclomethasone (360 μg/d).[15] Beclomethasone gave comparable symptom control with less use of bronchodilators and oral steroids. Theophylline caused more adverse effects. **Inhaled corticosteroids versus sodium cromoglycate:** We found no systematic review. Several small comparative RCTs have found sodium cromoglycate to be less effective than inhaled steroids in improving symptoms and lung function.

Harms: **Inhaled corticosteroids:** One systematic review found no significant adverse effects, including no documented effects on growth (monitored in eight studies) or adrenal function (monitored in 12 studies).[16] Biochemical evidence of suppression of the hypothalamic-pituitary axis may be detectable at higher doses of inhaled steroids, but this has not been associated with any clinical effects. There is little or no biochemical evidence of alteration in bone metabolism with inhaled steroids, and studies of bone mineral density on asthmatic children treated with long-term inhaled corticosteroids have not shown any adverse effect.[16] Two studies screened a total of 198 young patients taking long-term inhaled steroids by slit lamp.[17,18] The only case of posterior subcapsular cataract was in a child who had received several prolonged courses of oral steroids. **Theophylline:** Continuous oral theophylline is associated with a higher frequency of headache, gastric irritation, and tremor.[15] One systematic review, which included 12 studies (340 children) of the behavioral and cognitive effects of theophylline, failed to find evidence of significant adverse effects.[19] **Sodium cromoglycate:** Sodium cromoglycate may cause cough, throat irritation, and bronchoconstriction, but no long-term adverse effects have been reported.

Comment: None.

QUESTION **Do inhaled corticosteroids affect growth in children with asthma?**

Long-term follow-up studies have found no evidence of growth retardation in asthmatic children treated with inhaled steroids. Some shorter-term clinical studies have detected reduced rates of growth velocity.

Evidence: We found one systematic review, published in 1994, which identified 21 studies that reported height for age in asthmatic children treated with steroids. No evidence of growth impairment was found in the 12 studies (331 patients) involving inhaled beclomethasone.[20] No detailed account of search methods or study selection was given. In one RCT of beclomethasone (360 µg/d) versus oral theophylline for 1 year in 195 children aged 6 to 16 years, there was a significant difference in rate of growth, more notable in boys, favoring the theophylline group (mean rate of growth in prepubescent boys 4.3 cm/year vs. 6.2 cm/year).[15] This effect was not sufficient to be noticed by the children or their parents, and no child was withdrawn from the study on this account. One controlled, prospective parallel group study compared 216 children treated with 400 to 600 µg budesonide daily versus 62 children treated with theophylline or sodium cromoglycate, with 3 to 5 years' of follow up. No evidence of growth impairment with budesonide was found.[21]

Comment: Many uncontrolled, medium- to long-term cohort studies have followed children treated with budesonide or beclomethasone. None has found growth impairment attributable to inhaled steroids. There may be individual variations in susceptibility, and height should still be monitored.

QUESTION **How should acute wheezing in infancy be treated?**

Evidence is conflicting, perhaps because of the difficulty in distinguishing asthmatic from nonasthmatic wheezing in infancy.

OPTION **β_2-AGONISTS BY NEBULIZER OR METERED-DOSE INHALER/SPACER**

The results of RCTs are inconsistent, although likelihood of response seems to increase with age. Transient hypoxia may be caused by nebulized

bronchodilators, particularly with air driven nebulizers, and seems less likely when using metered-dose inhaler/spacer.

Benefits: We found no systematic review. There have been many hospital-based RCTs of nebulized β_2-agonists versus normal saline in infants and young children with acute wheezing. Some, but not all, have found short-term improvements in clinical respiratory distress scores with β_2-agonists.[22] We found no systematic review and no large RCTs with clinical outcomes to determine the best mode of administration.

Harms: Some infants show a transient decrease in oxygen saturation after nebulization, especially with air driven nebulizers.[22] Nebulized β_2-agonists are known to cause tachycardia, tremor, and hypokalaemia, but serious adverse effects, if they occur at all, are rare.

Comment: Small RCTs with physiologic rather than clinical end points have found giving β_2-agonists by metered-dose inhaler with spacer to wheezy infants to be effective,[23] with less likelihood than nebulization to show transient adverse effects on lung function.[24]

OPTION INHALED ANTICHOLINERGIC DRUGS

We found no clear evidence of benefit from the use of these agents in the emergency room or hospital settings.

Benefits: We found one systematic review of six RCTs of anticholinergic drugs for wheeze in children under 2 years of age.[25] Of these, one emergency room study found that adding ipratropium bromide to β_2-agonists resulted in fewer children receiving further treatment 45 minutes after initial treatment, but a second similar study found no additional benefit. One study in 31 hospitalized children comparing ipratropium bromide versus placebo found no difference in the duration of hospitalization. Adding ipratropium bromide to β_2-agonist had no effect on duration of hospitalization compared with β_2-agonist treatment alone.

Harms: No evidence of harm specific to the use of anticholinergic agents was found in these studies.

Comment: The studies were too small to exclude a clinically important effect of ipratropium bromide. In one home-based, 2-month crossover study, regular nebulized ipratropium bromide was preferred to nebulized water by parents, but there was no reduction in the frequency of reported symptoms during treatment.

OPTION SYSTEMIC CORTICOSTEROIDS

We found no evidence that oral or parenteral steroids improve outcomes in acute wheezing in infancy.

Benefits: We found no systematic review. Five large RCTs did not find benefit for oral or intravenous steroids in acute bronchiolitis in infancy. An outpatient study compared oral prednisolone versus placebo in 38 acutely wheezing children aged 3 to 17 months, 30 of whom had been previously admitted with wheeze. It found no significant differences in outcome between the two groups in the 56 episodes studied.[26]

Harms: No important adverse effects were identified in these studies.

Comment: Although the clinical presentation of asthma and bronchiolitis may be similar, bronchiolitis does not appear to respond to standard asthma therapy.

QUESTION What are the effects of prophylactic treatments in wheezing infants?

Inhaled steroids may be beneficial in recurrent or persistent infant wheezing, the likelihood of benefit increasing with age. We found little evidence for the effectiveness of theophylline or sodium cromoglycate.

Benefits: We found no systematic review. Results of placebo-controlled trials on inhaled steroids in recurrent or persistent infant wheezing are inconsistent. Some have shown improvements in symptom scores and reduced administration of additional treatments. Other studies have failed to show any beneficial effect. There is a greater tendency for positive findings in studies of older children and in studies involving administration by metered-dose inhaler and spacer rather than nebulizer. There are no RCTs of continuous oral theophylline in infants, and the small numbers of trials with inhaled sodium cromoglycate are mainly negative.

Harms: We found no good evidence on the long-term safety of treatment with continuous inhaled steroids in infancy. Known effects include oral candidiasis and thinning of facial skin with the use of nebulizers and face masks.

Comment: Administration of inhaled treatments to infants is difficult and dependent on dosage and inhaler device. Randomized trials of treatment for infant wheezing employ a variety of drugs, dosages, and devices, but also may be conducted on study populations with differing proportions of subjects who have asthma rather than other types of infant wheeze. These factors may explain the inconsistent results of clinical trials in this area.

REFERENCES

1. Ninan TK, Russell G. Respiratory symptoms and atopy in Aberdeen schoolchildren: evidence from two surveys 25 years apart. *BMJ* 1992;304: 873–875.
2. Martinez FD, Wright AL, Taussig L, Holberg CJ, Halonen M, Morgan WJ, and the Group Health Medical Associates. Asthma and wheezing in the first six years of life. *N Engl J Med* 1995;332: 133–138.
3. Park ES, Golding J, Carswell F, Stewart-Brown S. Pre-school wheezing and prognosis at age 10. *Arch Dis Child* 1986;61:642–646.
4. Geelhoed GC, Landau LI, Le Souef PN. Evaluation of SaO_2 as a predictor of outcome in 280 children presenting with acute asthma. *Ann Emerg Med* 1994;23:1236–1241.
5. Douglas JG, Rafferty P, Fergusson RJ, et al. Nebulised salbutamol without oxygen in severe acute asthma: how effective and how safe? *Thorax* 1985;40:180–183.
6. Plotnick LH, Ducharme FM. Efficacy and safety of combined inhaled anticholinergics and beta 2 agonists in the initial management of acute paediatric asthma (Cochrane Review). In: The Cochrane Library, Issue 1 1999 Oxford: Update Software. Last updated February 1997. Search dates 1997; primary sources MEDLINE 1966-1997, EMBASE 1980-1997, Cinahl 1982-1997. Hand search of bibliographies of references, pharmaceutical companies contacted for details of unpublished trials and personal contact.
7. Qureshi F, Zaritsky A, Lakkis H. Efficacy of nebulised ipratropium in severely asthmatic children. *Ann Emerg Med* 1997;29:205–211.
8. Cates CJ. Comparison of holding chambers and nebulisers for beta-agonists in acute asthma. (Cochrane Review). In: The Cochrane Library, Issue 1 1999. Oxford: Update Software. Last

updated February 1998. Search dates Feb 1998; primary sources MEDLINE, Cochrane Airways Review Group Registery trials 1966 to February 1998.

9. Chou KJ, Cunningham SJ, Crain EF. Metered-dose inhalers with spacers vs nebulizers for pediatric asthma. *Arch Pediatr Adolesc Med* 1995;149: 201–205.
10. Rowe BH, Keller JL, Oxman AD. Effectiveness of steroid therapy in acute exacerbations of asthma: a meta-analysis. *Am J Emerg Med* 1992;10: 301–310. Search date February 1991; primary sources MEDLINE 1966-Feb 1991, Science Citation Search 1980-1990, and content experts, review articles, textbooks.
11. Rowe BH, Spooner CH, Ducharme FM, Bretzlaff JA, Bota GW. The effectiveness of corticosteroids in the treatment of acute exacerbations of asthma: a meta-analysis of their effect on relapse following acute assessment (Cochrane Review). In: The Cochrane Library, Issue1 1999. Oxford: Update Software. Last updated May 1997. Search dates May 1997; primary sources Cochrane Airways Group Register 1966-May 1997.
12. Patel H, Macarthur C, Johnson D. Recent corticosteroids use and the risk of complicated varicella in otherwise immunocompetent children. *Arch Pediatr Adolesc Med* 1996;150:409–414.
13. Goodman DC, Littenberg B, O'Connor GT, Brooks JG. Theophylline in acute childhood asthma: a meta-analysis of its efficacy. *Pediatr Pulmonol* 1996;21:211–218. Search date May 1994; primary sources MEDLINE 1966 to May 1994.
14. Calpin C, Macarthur C, Stephens D, Feldman W, Parkin P. Effectiveness of prophylactic inhaled steroids in childhood asthma: a systematic review of the literature. *J Allergy Clin Immunol* 1997;100:452–457. Search date December 1996; primary source MEDLINE, English language only.
15. Tinkelman DG, Reed C, Nelson H, Offord P. Aerosol beclomethasone diproprionate compared with theophylline as primary treatment of chronic, mild to moderately severe asthma in children. *Pediatrics* 1993;92:64–77.
16. Agertoft L, Pedersen S. Bone density in children during long term treatment with budesonide. *Eur Respir J* 1993;6:261S.
17. Simons FE, Persaud MP, Gillespie CA, Cheang M, Shuckett EP. Absence of posterior subcapsular cataracts in young patients treated with inhaled glucocorticoids. *Lancet* 1993;342:1306–1307.
18. Abuekteish F, Kirkpatrick JN, Russell G. Posterior subcapsular cataract and inhaled corticosteroid therapy. *Thorax* 1995;50:674–676.
19. Stein MA, Krasowski M, Leventhal BL, Phillips W, Bender BG. Behavioural and cognitive effects of methylxanthines: a meta-analysis of theophylline and caffeine. *Arch Pediatr Adolesc Med* 1996:50: 284–288.
20. Allen DB, Mullen M, Mullen B. A meta-analysis of the effect of oral and inhaled corticosteroids on growth. *J Allergy Clin Immunol* 1994;93: 967–976. Search date January 1993; primary sources literature search of leading medical journals 1956–1993.
21. Agertoft L, Pedersen S. Effects of long-term treatment with an inhaled corticosteroid on growth and pulmonary function in asthmatic children. *Respir Med* 1994;88:373–381.
22. Alario AJ, Lewander W, Dennehy P, Seifer R, Mansell A. The efficacy of nebulised metaproterenol in wheezing infants and young children. *Am J Dis Child* 1992;146:412–418.
23. Kraemer R, Frey U, Sommer CW, Russi E. Short term effect of albuterol, delivered via a new auxiliary device, in wheezy infants. *Am Rev Respir Dis* 1991;144:347–351.
24. Yuksel B, Greenough A. Comparison of the effects on lung function of different methods of bronchodilator administration. *Respir Med* 1994;88:229–333.
25. Everard M, Kurian M. Anticholinergic drugs for wheeze in children under the age of two years (Cochrane Review). In: The Cochrane Library, Issue 1, 1999. Oxford: Update Software. Last updated 28 May 1998. Search dates 1998; primary sources Cochrane Airways Group Register 1966 to May 1998, hand search of respiratory care and paediatric journals.
26. Webb M, Henry R, Milner AD. Oral corticosteroids for wheezing attacks under 18 months. *Arch Dis Child* 1986;61:15–19.

Duncan Keeley, MB, MRCP
General Practitioner
Thame
Oxfordshire
UK

Competing interests: The author has received occasional consultancy fees or assistance with organization of or travel to meetings from companies, including Allen and Hanburys, Astra, MSD, Zeneca, 3M, and Boots.

Constipation

Greg Rubin, MBChB, FRCGP

QUESTIONS

INTERVENTIONS

Key Messages

- One randomized controlled trial (RCT) found that dietary advice regarding increased fiber intake had little effect.
- We found no placebo-controlled trials of osmotic or stimulant laxatives. Small comparative RCTs suggest that both are effective.
- Three RCTs found no significant effect of biofeedback above that of laxative treatment.

DEFINITIONS Constipation is characterized by infrequent bowel evacuations, hard, small feces, or difficult or painful defecation. The frequency of bowel evacuation varies from person to person.[1] Encopresis is defined as involuntary bowel movements in inappropriate places at least once a month for 3 months or more, in children aged 4 years and older.[2]

INCIDENCE/ PREVALENCE Constipation with or without encopresis is common in children. It accounts for 3% of consultations to a pediatric outpatient clinic and 25% of pediatric gastroenterology consultations in the USA.[3] Encopresis has been reported in 1.5% of children at school entry.

ETIOLOGY Constipation is usually idiopathic (90%–95%) with peak incidence between 2 to 4 years of age. Psychosocial factors are often implicated, although most children with constipation are developmentally normal.[3] Chronic constipation can lead to progressive fecal retention, distension of the rectum, and loss of sensory and motor function. Organic causes for constipation are uncommon but should be considered, including Hirschsprung's disease (1/5000 births; male : females 4 :1 ; constipation invariably present from birth[3]), cystic fibrosis, anorectal physiologic abnormalities, anal fissures, constipating drugs, dehydrating metabolic conditions, and other forms of malabsorption.[3]

PROGNOSIS Childhood constipation can be difficult to treat, often requiring prolonged support, explanation, and medical treatment. In one long-term follow-up study of children presenting under the age of 5 years, 50% recovered within 1 year and 65% to 70% within 2 years, the remainder requiring laxatives for daily bowel movements or continuing to soil for years.[3] It is not known what proportion continue to have problems into adult life, although adults presenting with megarectum or megacolon often have a history of bowel problems from childhood.

AIMS To remove fecal impaction and to restore a bowel habit in which stools are soft and passed without discomfort.

OUTCOMES Number of defecations per week; number of episodes of soiling per month; no laxatives.

METHODS Search conducted by *Clinical Evidence* in June 1998 using the following key terms: constipation, diet therapy, diagnosis, therapy, psychology, stimulant laxatives, dietary fiber, lactulose. The search was limited to infants and children. No systematic reviews were identified. Trials were selected for inclusion if they focused on the management of constipation or encopresis or both, if they were relevant to primary health care, and if they included children without an organic cause for constipation.

QUESTION **What are the effects of dietary and medical treatments?**

OPTION **INCREASING DIETARY FIBER**

We found no direct evidence of benefit from increasing dietary fiber intake on colonic transit time or cure of constipation in children.

Benefits: We found no good trials of the effect of increasing dietary fiber on constipation in childhood. We found one RCT of the effect of laxatives plus advice about dietary fiber on chronic constipation and colonic transit time in 73 children with the same mean fiber intake as healthy controls but increased colonic transit time.[4] The study found that although advice significantly increased fiber intake, it did not significantly reduce colonic transit time or increase the cure of constipation at 6 months.

Harms: Adults who increase dietary fiber intake have reported abdominal pain and distension.

Comment: None.

OPTION OSMOTIC LAXATIVES

We found limited evidence that osmotic laxatives significantly increase stool frequency and, in infants, result in normal stools.

Benefits: We found no placebo-controlled trials of osmotic laxatives in children. We found two small RCTs comparing the effects of lactitol versus lactulose on stool frequency and consistency in 51[5] and 39[6] children with constipation. They found a significant increase in stool frequency at four weeks[5] and normal consistency of stool at two weeks[6] for both preparations. One RCT of 220 non–breast fed, constipated infants (aged 0–6 months) compared 2% versus 4% lactulose admixed to an artificial milk preparation.[7] It found parental observation of easy stools of normal or thin consistency at 14 days in over 90% of infants in both groups ($p < 0.05$).

Harms: One study found that children treated with lactulose experienced significantly more abdominal pain and flatus than those treated with lactitol.[5]

Comment: The benefits shown in these studies are before and after effects, and none were available in full English translation.[5,6]

OPTION STIMULANT LAXATIVES

Stimulant laxatives frequently form part of "standard treatment" in comparative studies. We found no placebo-controlled trials of their effect in children.

Benefits: We found no systematic review or placebo-controlled trial. All existing studies were comparative and used multiple interventions, small sample sizes, or both. One quasirandomized study compared senna versus mineral oil concentrate in 37 children aged 3 to 12 years with chronic constipation.[8] It found that mineral oil significantly reduced fecal soiling and decreased stool frequency at 1, 3, and 6 months, obviated the need for medication at 6 months (55% vs. 22%) and reduced relapses (66% vs. 89%).

Harms: None identified.

Comment: The study used last hospital number digit to randomize patients.[8]

OPTION **BIOFEEDBACK TRAINING**

RCTs have found no added benefit from biofeedback training in childhood constipation.

Benefits: We found no systematic review. Three RCTs compared conventional treatment with or without biofeedback in 192,[9] 129,[10] and 41[11] children with constipation. Although two studies found short-term benefit in defecation dynamics,[9,11] none found significant improvement in soiling, stool frequency, or laxative use at 1 year or more.

Harms: None identified.

Comment: None.

REFERENCES

1. Nelson R, Wagget J, Lennard-Jones JE, Barnes PRH. Constipation and megacolon in children and adults. In: Misiewicz JJ, Pounder RE, Venables CW. *Diseases of the gut and pancreas*, 2nd ed. Oxford, Blackwell Science, 1994.
2. American Psychiatric Association. *Diagnostic and statistical manual of mental disorders*, 4th ed. Washington, DC: American Psychiatric Association, 1994.
3. Loening-Baucke V. Chronic constipation in children. *Gastroenterology* 1993;105:1557–1563.
4. Mooren GCAH, Van der Plas RN, Bossuyt PMM, Taminiau JAJM, Buller HA. The connection between dietary fibre intake and chronic constipation in children. *Ned Tijdschr Geneeskd* 1996; 140:2036–2039.
5. Pitzalis G, Mariani P, Chiarini-Testa MB, et al. Lactitol in chronic idiopathic constipation of childhood. *Pediatr Med Chir* 1995;17:223–226.
6. Martino AM, Pesce F, Rosati U. The effects of lactitol in the treatment of intestinal stasis in childhood. *Minerva Pediatr* 1992;44:319–323.
7. Hejl M, Kamper J, Ebbesen F, Hansted C. Infantile constipation and allomin-lactulose. Treatment of infantile constipation in infants fed with breast milk substitutes: a controlled clinical trial of 2% and 4% allomin-lactulose. *Ugeskr Laeger* 1990;152:1819–1822.
8. Sondheimer JM, Gervaise EP. Lubricant versus laxative in the treatment of chronic functional constipation of children: a comparative study. *J Pediatr Gastroenterol Nutr* 1982;1:223–226.
9. Van der Plas RN, Benninga MA, Büller HA, et al. Biofeedback training in treatment of childhood constipation: a randomised controlled study. *Lancet* 1996;348:776–780.
10. Loening-Baucke V. Biofeedback treatment for chronic constipation and encopresis in childhood: long term outcome. *Pediatrics* 1995;96: 105–110.
11. Loening-Baucke V. Modulation of abnormal defecation dynamics by biofeedback treatment in chronically constipated children with encopresis. *J Pediatr* 1990;116:214–222.

Greg Rubin, MBChB, FRCGP
Senior Lecturer in Primary Care
University of Teesside
Middlesbrough
UK

Competing interests: None declared.

Enuresis

Sara Bosson, MBChB, BSc, MMedSci, and Natalie A Lyth, MBChB, MRCIP

QUESTIONS

INTERVENTIONS

Key Messages

- One systematic review has found desmopressin to be effective at short-term symptom relief.
- One systematic review has found alarms to be effective at long-term treatment of enuresis, with drugs (especially desmopressin) and behavioral treatments providing some additional benefit.

DEFINITION Primary nocturnal enuresis is the involuntary discharge of urine at night in the absence of organic disease at an age when a child reasonably could be expected to be dry—by consensus, at a developmental age of 5 years. Organic diseases are excluded by history, examination, and urinalysis. Secondary nocturnal enuresis is the return to nighttime wetting after nighttime bladder control has been achieved. Most nocturnal enuresis is primary.

ETIOLOGY Nocturnal enuresis is caused by several factors. A positive family history is often found, and linkage studies have identified possible enuresis loci on chromosomes 8q, 12q, 13q, and 22q11.[1–4] Other factors include small functional bladder capacity, nocturnal polyuria, and arousal dysfunction.

PROGNOSIS Nocturnal enuresis has widely differing outcomes, from spontaneous cure to apparent resistance to all current forms of treatment. Approximately 1% of adults remain enuretic. Without treatment approximately 15% of children become dry each year.[5]

AIMS To stay dry on particular occasions (such as when visiting friends), to reduce the number of wet nights, to lessen the impact of the enuresis on the child's lifestyle, to initiate successful continence, and to avoid relapse, with minimal adverse effects.

OUTCOMES Rate of initial success (14 consecutive dry nights); average number of wet nights per week; number of relapses after initial success; average number of wet nights after treatment has ceased.

METHODS We used validated searches to search Cochrane Library, MEDLINE, EMBASE, and Psychlit. One large, high-quality systematic review of 62 RCTs was identified as the best evidence currently available.

QUESTION **What are the effects of treatments for short-term relief of symptoms?**

OPTION **DESMOPRESSIN AND IMIPRAMINE**

A systematic review has found that desmopressin and imipramine are both effective in rapid symptom relief and that desmopressin has fewer adverse effects.

Benefits: We found one high-quality systematic review, which included a meta-analysis of good-quality placebo-controlled RCTs.[6] Short-term treatment (up to 6 weeks) was four times more effective than placebo (RR of initial success with desmopressin 4.6, 95% CI 1.4–15.0; with imipramine 4.2, 95% CI 1.2–15) (*see* Table 1).

Harms: **Desmopressin:** In this systematic review,[6] seven of 17 trials considering adverse effects found the following effects in a small number of children: anorexia, headache, rash, sight disturbance, upset stomach, bad taste, epistaxis, and nasal discomfort. Rarely, water intoxication has been reported in patients who have not restricted fluids or have had fluid imbalance. **Imipramine:** In the same systematic review,[6] nine of 11 trials reported adverse effects with imipramine: anorexia, anxiety reaction, burning sensation, constipation, depression, diarrhea, dizziness, drowsiness, dry mouth, headache, irritability, lethargy, sleep disturbance, upset stomach, and vomiting. Imipramine has been reported as fatal in overdose.[6]

Comment: This high-quality review included only studies reporting evaluations of interventions used to remedy either primary or secondary nonorganic nocturnal enuresis (shown by medical examination or explicitly mentioned in the trials' inclusion/exclusion criteria) and included a systematic measurement of baseline wetting and outcomes.[6]

QUESTION **What are the effects of available treatments for long-term management?**

OPTION **ALARMS, DRY BED TRAINING, AND DRUG TREATMENTS**

One systematic review found alarms to be most successful for initial success and to have lower relapse rates and the fewest adverse effects. Medication acts faster and is the treatment of choice when alarms are unacceptable. Desmopressin has a superior safety profile than imipramine.

Benefits: We found one systematic review of 62 RCTs of interventions in people with primary or secondary nonorganic enuresis.[6] Table 1 summarizes results of studies in children that compared behavioral, pharmacologic, and complementary treatments versus placebo, alarm, or no treatment controls.

Harms: **Medication:** *See* p. 515. **Alarms:** Four trials reported the following adverse effects to be most common: alarm failure, failure to wake the person, false alarms, fright, and disturbance to others.

Comment: None.

QUESTION **What is the best age to start treatment?**

We found no evidence indicating the youngest age at which treatment becomes effective. Children younger than 7 years are unlikely to possess the required level of commitment.

Benefits: We found no evidence.

Harms: We found no evidence.

Comment: In practice, reassurance is often all that is needed below the age of 7 years. If nocturnal enuresis becomes a problem, desmopressin and imipramine are licensed for use from the age of 6 years. Behavioral treatments, such as alarms, require motivation and commitment on the part of the child (usually present from the age of 7 years) and parent.

REFERENCES

1. Eiberg, H. Nocturnal enuresis is linked to a specific gene. *Scand J Urol Nephrol Suppl* 1995;173: 15–17.
2. Arnell H, Hjalmas K, Jagervall M, et al. The genetics of primary nocturnal enuresis: inheritance and suggestion of a second major gene on chromosome 12q. *J Med Genet* 1997;34:360–365.
3. Eiberg H, Berendt I, Mohr J. Assignment of dominant inherited nocturnal enuresis (ENUR 1) to chromosome 13q. *Nat Genet* 1995;10: 354–356.
4. Eiberg H. Total genome scan analysis in a single

extended family for primary nocturnal enuresis: evidence for a new locus (ENUR 3) for primary nocturnal enuresis on chromosome 22q11. *Eur Urol* 1998;33:34–36.
5. Forsythe WI, Redmond A. Enuresis and spontaneous cure rate: study of 1129 enuretics. *Arch Dis Child* 1974;49:259–263.
6. Lister-Sharp D, O'Meara S, Bradley M, Sheldon TA. A systematic review of the effectiveness of interventions for managing childhood nocturnal enuresis. University of York: NHS Centre for Reviews and Dissemination, August 1997. CRD Report 11. (Search date 1996; primary sources Cochrane Library, MEDLINE, EMBASE, Psychlit.)

Sara Bosson, MBChB, BSc, MMedSci
Staff grade community paediatrician
Mancunian Community Health NHS Trust
Manchester
UK

Natalie A Lyth, MBChB, MRCIP
Staff grade community paediatrician
The Friarage Hospital
Northallerton
UK

Competing interests: None declared.

TABLE 1 Effective treatments for enuresis: advantages and disadvantages[6]

	Initial success (14 consecutive dry nights)	Long-term success after treatment has finished	Evidence	Advantages	Disadvantages
Desmopressin	Four times more likely than with placebo (RR 4.6, 95% CI 1.4–15.0)	No better than placebo	Meta-analysis of three RCTs	Effective within days; safe; few adverse effects with appropriate pretreatment advice	Case reports of water intoxication; expensive
Imipramine (for 6 weeks)	Four times more likely than with placebo (RR 4.2, 95% CI 1.2–15.0)	No better than placebo (RR 1.1)	Meta-analysis of four RCTs	Effective within days; cheap	Risk of lethal overdose; frequent significant adverse effects
Alarm	Thirteen times more likely than with no treatment (RR 13.3, 95% CI 5.6–31.5)	31–61% still dry at 3 months; nine times less likely to relapse than with desmopressin	Meta-analysis of four RCTs	Safe	Takes longer to become dry; needs good cooperation from child and family
Alarm and medication	75% compared with 46% with alarm alone	Not studied	One RCT, $n=71$ (not included in systematic review)	More rapid effect than alarm alone	Same adverse effects as medication; cost of medication and alarm
Dry bed training without alarm	No better than no treatment (RR 2.5, 95% CI 0.55–11.41)	No better than no treatment (RR 0.4, 95% CI 0.14–1.13)	One good-quality RCT, $n=45$	Safe	Requires high degree of motivation
Dry bed training with alarm	Ten times more likely than with no treatment (RR 10, 95% CI 2.69–37.24)	No better than alarm alone (RR 1.0, 95% CI 0.7–1.5)	One RCT, $n=45$	Safe	Requires an even greater input from the family than either treatment alone

Urinary tract infection

James Larcombe, MB, ChB

QUESTIONS

INTERVENTIONS

Key Messages

- Treating symptomatic acute urinary tract infection (UTI) in children with an antibiotic is accepted clinical practice and trials would be considered unethical.
- We found little evidence on the effects of delaying treatment while awaiting microscopy or culture results, but retrospective observational studies suggest delayed treatment may be associated with increased rates of renal scarring.
- One systematic review of randomized controlled trials (RCTs) has found that antibiotic treatment for 7 days or longer is more effective than shorter courses.
- We found no convincing evidence of benefit from routine diagnostic imaging of all children with a first UTI, but subgroups at increased risk of future morbidity may benefit from investigation. Because such children cannot currently be identified clinically, investigating all young children with UTI may be warranted.
- Two small RCTs found that prophylactic antibiotics prevented recurrent UTI in children, particularly during the period of prophylaxis. The long-term benefits of prophylaxis have not been evaluated adequately, even for children with vesicoureteral reflux. The optimum duration of treatment is unknown.
- One systematic review and a subsequent multicenter RCT found no difference between surgery for vesicoureteral reflux and medical management in preventing recurrence or complications from UTI.

DEFINITION UTI is defined by the presence of a pure growth of more than 10^5 colony-forming units of bacteria per milliliter. Lower counts of bacteria may be clinically important, especially in boys and in specimens obtained by urinary catheter. Any growth of typical urinary pathogens is considered clinically important if obtained by suprapubic aspiration. In practice, three age ranges are usually considered on the basis of differential risk and different approaches to management: under 1 year of age; young children (1 to 4, 5, or 7 years of age, depending on the source); and older children (up to 12–16 years of age). Recurrent UTI is defined as a single further infection by a new organism. Relapsing UTI is defined as a further infection with the same organism.

INCIDENCE/ PREVALENCE Boys are more susceptible before the age of 3 months; thereafter, the incidence is substantially higher in girls. Estimates of the true incidence of UTI depend on rates of diagnosis and investigation. At least 8% of girls and 2% of boys will have a UTI in childhood.[1]

ETIOLOGY The normal urinary tract is sterile. Contamination by bowel flora may result in urinary infection if a virulent organism is involved, if the child is immunosuppressed, or both. In neonates, infection may originate from other sources. *Escherichia coli* accounts for approximately three quarters of all pathogens. Proteus is more common in boys (~30% of infections). Obstructive anomalies are found in 0% to 4% and vesicoureteral reflux in 8% to 40% of children being investigated for their first UTI.[2] Although vesicoureteral reflux is a major risk factor for adverse outcome, it is likely that other as yet unidentified triggers also need to be present.

PROGNOSIS After first infection, approximately 50% of girls have a further infection in the first year and 75% have one within 2 years; we found no figures for boys. Renal scarring is detected in 5% to 15% of children within 1 to 2 years of their first UTI, although 32% to 70% of these scars are noted at the time of initial assessment.[2] The incidence of new renal scars rises with each episode of infection.[3] Renal scarring is associated with future complications: poor renal growth, recurrent adult pyelonephritis, impaired glomerular function, early hypertension, and end-stage renal failure.[4–6] A combination of recurrent urinary infection, severe vesicoureteral reflux, and the presence of renal scarring at first presentation is associated with the worst prognosis.

AIMS To relieve acute symptoms; to eliminate infection; and to prevent recurrence, renal damage, and long-term complications.

OUTCOMES Acute: clinical symptoms (dysuria, frequency, fever); urine culture; incidence of new renal scars. Chronic: incidence of recurrent infection; prevalence of renal scarring; renal size and growth; renal function; prevalence of hypertension and renal failure.

METHODS Systematic reviews were extracted from validated searches of MEDLINE, EMBASE, and the Cochrane database in July 1999. RCTs and controlled cohort studies also were identified. We gave priority to studies on the basis of their methodology, relevance, and applicability.

QUESTION **What are the effects of different antibiotic regimens in acute UTI in children?**

We found little evidence on the effects of delaying treatment while awaiting microscopy or culture results, but retrospective studies suggest delayed treatment may be associated with increased rates of renal scarring. Placebo-controlled trials of antibiotics for symptomatic acute UTI in children would be considered unethical. One systematic review found that antibiotic treatment for 7 days or longer was more effective than short courses.

Benefits: **Immediate empiric versus delayed treatment:** We found no RCTs comparing immediate empiric treatment versus treatment delayed while awaiting microscopy or culture results. Five retrospective observational studies found increased rates of scarring in children in whom diagnosis was delayed from 4 days in acute UTI to 7 years when a child presented with chronic nonspecific symptoms.[2] **Long versus short courses:** We found one systematic review of 14 RCTs comparing short course (range single dose to 4 days) versus conventional treatment (range 7–10 days).[7] Short courses were less effective than courses of 7 days or longer. No RCTs were found comparing 5-day courses of antibiotics with other regimens.

Harms: The studies did not report comparative harms from long courses compared with short courses of antibiotics nor from immediate treatment compared with delayed treatment. Potential harms include the risk of unnecessary or inappropriate antibiotic prescription. Furthermore, empiric antibiotic treatment of a child with suspected UTI who ultimately proves not to have a UTI (i.e., negative urine culture) may interfere with further diagnostic tests for the true diagnosis.

Comment: We found no good evidence from which to predict which children are at high risk of complications after an acute UTI.[8] A recent RCT has shown the safety and efficacy of oral cefixime in young children with febrile UTI.[9] This finding, which contrasts with the long-held belief in the necessity for IV treatment, will be discussed further in future issues.

QUESTION **Which children benefit from diagnostic imaging?**

We found no convincing evidence of benefit from routine diagnostic imaging of all children with a first UTI. However, subgroups of children at increased risk of future morbidity may benefit from investigation. Because such children cannot be identified clinically, investigation of all young children with UTI may be warranted.

Benefits: We found no RCTs. One systematic review of 63 descriptive studies found no direct evidence to support the effectiveness of routine diagnostic imaging in children with UTI.[2] The quality of studies was generally poor and none included clinically important long-term outcome measures.

Harms: The studies reported no evidence on harms. Potential harms include those relating to radiation, invasive procedures, and allergic reactions to contrast media.

Comment: Although the studies showed no benefits overall, subgroups of children at high risk of future morbidity, including those with vesicoureteral reflux, may benefit from early investigation. These children cannot be identified clinically.[10] One prospective study found that the highest rates of renal scarring after an episode of pyelonephritis occurred between the ages of 1 and 5 years.[11] Older children with more severe presentations may need careful investigation.

QUESTION What are the effects of preventive interventions?

OPTION PROPHYLACTIC ANTIBIOTICS

Two small RCTs found that prophylactic antibiotics may prevent recurrent UTIs in children, particularly during the period of prophylaxis. The long term benefits of prophylaxis have not been evaluated adequately, even for children with vesicoureteral reflux.[12] The optimum duration of treatment is unknown.

Benefits: **Versus no prophylaxis:** We found no systematic review. One RCT of 45 children with either first or subsequent acute UTI compared 10 months treatment with prophylactic antibiotics versus no treatment.[13] During the 10-month prophylaxis period, recurrent UTIs were reported in none of the children in the intervention group compared with 11 in the control group. Twelve months after stopping prophylactic antibiotics, eight children (32%) in the intervention group compared with 13 (64%) in the control group had had a UTI. A further double-blind crossover trial of 18 girls aged 3 to 13 years found two episodes of infection in 1 year in the treatment groups compared with 35 in the control groups ($p < 0.01$).[14] **Duration of treatment:** We found no RCTs evaluating the optimum length of prophylaxis (although two studies of prolonged acute treatment were identified).

Harms: Potential harms include those of using antibiotics. In one study, although gut flora were affected by treatment, *E. coli* cultured from rectal swabs from 70% of children remained sensitive to the prophylactic antibiotic (co-trimoxazole).[15]

Comment: It is not possible to clinically identify children who are at high risk of subsequent UTIs and long-term damage.[8] Therefore, until the results are known, routine prophylaxis may be warranted, but current practice in the US precludes the use of continuous antibiotic prophylaxis in those without vesicoureteral reflux. The decision to stop prophylaxis may be based on trial periods without treatment or, for children with vesicoureteric reflux, two negative cystograms.[8]

OPTION SURGICAL CORRECTION FOR ANOMALIES OBSTRUCTING MICTURITION

We found no good studies evaluating surgical correction.

Benefits: We found no systematic review or RCTs. One small observational study suggested that children with minor anomalies do not develop renal scarring and therefore may not benefit from surgery.[16] Eight of 20 children with moderate degrees of vesicoureteral reflux had renal scars compared with none of the eight children with minor anomalies.

Harms: Potential harms include the usual risks of surgery.

Comment: In the presence of major anomalies, the prevention of UTIs is not the prime motive of surgical intervention. Minor anomalies may not be associated with significant morbidity, and surgical correction has not been evaluated in such children.

OPTION SURGICAL CORRECTION FOR VESICOURETERAL REFLUX

One systematic review and a subsequent multicenter RCT found no difference between surgery for vesicoureteral reflux and medical management in preventing recurrence or complications from UTIs.

Benefits: We found one systematic review of studies published before 1989 that included four RCTs (total 830 children) comparing surgical correction of moderate/severe (grades III–V) vesicoureteral obstruction versus medical management (continuous prophylactic antibiotics).[17] Surgery abolished reflux, but there were no significant differences in rates of subsequent UTIs, renal function, incidence of new renal scars, hypertension, or end-stage renal failure between groups over a period of 6 months to 5 years. A subsequent RCT in 132 children found that the incidence of pyelonephritis was lower in children receiving surgical treatment, but there was also no difference in overall clinical outcome.[18] In another arm of this study, six of 20 renal scars were thought to be associated with postoperative obstruction, which may have negated an otherwise beneficial effect of surgery over medical management.[19] **Long-term outcome:** We found no studies comparing long-term outcomes (>5 years).

Harms: The review did not mention surgical complications, and none of the individual studies was designed to compare harms.[17] As noted above, postoperative obstruction may negate the benefits of surgery.[19]

Comment: Better results were obtained by centers handling the greatest number of cases.[20] Surgery usually is considered only in children with more severe vesicoureteral reflux (grade III–V), who are less likely to experience spontaneous resolution.[21]

REFERENCES

1. Stark H. Urinary tract infections in girls: the cost-effectiveness of currently recommended investigative routines. *Pediatr Nephrol* 1997;11:174–177.
2. Dick PT, Feldman W. Routine diagnostic imaging for childhood urinary tract infections: a systematic overview. *J Pediatr* 1996;128:15–22. Search date 1994; primary source MEDLINE 1966 to October 1994; hand searching of article bibliographies and current contents.
3. Jodal U. The natural history of bacteriuria in childhood. *Infect Dis Clin North Am* 1987;1:713–729.
4. Berg UB. Long-term follow-up of renal morphology and function in children with recurrent pyelonephritis. *J Urol* 1992;148:1715–1720.
5. Martinell J, Claesson I, Lidin-Janson G, Jodal U. Urinary infection, reflux and renal scarring in females continuously followed for 13–38 years. *Pediatr Nephrol* 1995;9:131–136.
6. Jacobson S, Eklof O, Erikksson CG, Lins LE, Tidgren B, Weinberg J. Development of hypertension and uraemia after pyelonephritis in childhood: 27 year follow-up. *BMJ* 1989;299:703–706.
7. Moffatt M, Embree J, Grimm P, Law B. Short-course antibiotic therapy for urinary tract infections in children: a methodological review of the literature. *Am J Dis Child* 1988;142:57–61. No search date or primary sources given.
8. Greenfield SP, Ng M, Wan J. Experience with vesicoureteral reflux in children: clinical characteristics. *J Urol* 1997;158:574–577.
9. Hoberman A, Wald ER, Hickey RW, et al. Oral versus initial intravenous therapy for urinary tract infections in young febrile children. *Pediatrics* 1999;104:79–86.
10. Smellie JM, Normand ICS, Katz G. Children with urinary infection: a comparison of those with and those without vesicoureteric reflux. *Kidney Int* 1981;20:717–722.
11. Benador D, Benador N, Slosman D, Mermillod B, Girardin E. Are younger children at highest risk of renal sequelae after pyelonephritis? *Lancet* 1997;349:17–19.
12. Garin EH, Campos A, Homsy Y. Primary vesico-

ureteral reflux: a review of current concepts. *Pediatr Nephrol* 1998;12:249–256.
13. Smellie JM, Katz G, Gruneberg RN. Controlled trial of prophylactic treatment in childhood urinary tract infection. *Lancet* 1978;ii:175–178.
14. Lohr JA, Nunley DH, Howards SS, Ford RF. Prevention of recurrent urinary tract infections in girls. *Pediatrics* 1977;59:562–565.
15. Smellie JM, Gruneberg RN, Leakey A, Atkin WS. Long-term low-dose co-trimoxazole in prophylaxis of childhood urinary tract infection: clinical aspects/bacteriological aspects. *BMJ* 1976;ii: 203–206.
16. Pylkkanen J, Vilska J, Koskimies O. The value of level diagnosis of childhood urinary tract infection in predicting renal injury. *Acta Paediatr Scand* 1981;70:879–883.
17. Shanon A, Feldman W. Methodologic limitations in the literature on vesicoureteral reflux: a critical review. *J Pediatr* 1990;117:171–178. Search date 1988; primary source Medline 1972 to November 1988.
18. Weiss R, Duckett J, Spitzer A. Results of a randomized clinical trial of medical versus surgical management of infants and children with grades III and IV primary vesico-ureteral reflux (United States): the international reflux study in children. *J Urol* 1992;148:1667–1673.
19. Smellie JM, Tamminen-Mobius T, Olbing H, et al. Five-year study of medical or surgical treatment in children with severe reflux: radiological renal findings: the international reflux study in children. *Pediatr Nephrol* 1992;6:223–230.
20. Smellie JM. Commentary: management of children with severe vesicoureteral reflux. *J Urol* 1992;148:1676–1678.
21. Sciagra R, Materassi M, Rossi V, et al. Alternative approaches to the prognostic stratification of mild to moderate primary vesicoureteral reflux in children. *J Urol (Paris)* 1996;155:2052–2056.

James Larcombe, MB, ChB
General Practitioner
Sedgefield
UK

Competing interests: None declared.

The number needed to treat: adjusting for baseline risk

Adapted with permission from Chatellier et al[1]

BACKGROUND

The number needed to treat (NNT) to avoid a single additional adverse outcome is a meaningful way of expressing the benefit of an active treatment over a control. It can be used both to summarize the results of a therapeutic trial or series of trials and to help medical decision making about an individual patient.

If the absolute risk of adverse outcomes in a therapeutic trial is ARC in the control group and ART in the treatment group, then the absolute risk reduction (ARR) is defined as (ARC – ART). The NNT is defined as the inverse of the ARR:

$$\text{NNT} = 1/(\text{ARC} - \text{ART})$$

Because the Relative Risk Reduction (RRR) is defined as (ARC – ART)/ARC, it follows that NNT, RRR, and ARC are related by their definitions in the following way:

$$\text{NNT} \times \text{RRR} \times \text{ARC} = 1$$

This relationship can be used to estimate the likely benefits of a treatment in populations with different levels of baseline risk (i.e., different levels of ARC). This allows extrapolation of the results of a trial or meta-analysis to people with different baseline risks. Ideally, there should be experimental evidence of the RRR in each population. However, in many trials, subgroup analyses show that the RRR is approximately constant in groups of patients with different characteristics. Cook and Sackett[2] therefore proposed that decisions about individual patients could be made by using the NNT calculated from the RRR measured in trials and the baseline risk in the absence of treatment estimated for the individual patient.

The method may not apply to periods of time different from that studied in the original trials.

USING THE NOMOGRAM

The nomogram shown on the next page allows the NNT to be found directly without any calculation. A straight line should be drawn from the point corresponding to the estimated absolute risk for the patient on the left-hand scale to the point corresponding to the relative risk reduction stated in a trial or meta-analysis on the center scale. The intercept of this line with the right-hand scale gives the NNT. By taking the upper and lower limits of the confidence interval of the RRR, the upper and lower limits of the NNT can be estimated.

REFERENCES

1. Chatellier G, Zapletal E, Lemaitre D, Menard J, Degoulet P. The number needed to treat: a clinically useful nomogram in its proper context. *BMJ* 1996;312:426–429.
2. Cook RJ, Sackett DL. The number needed to treat: a clinically useful measure of treatment effect. *BMJ* 1995;310:452–454.

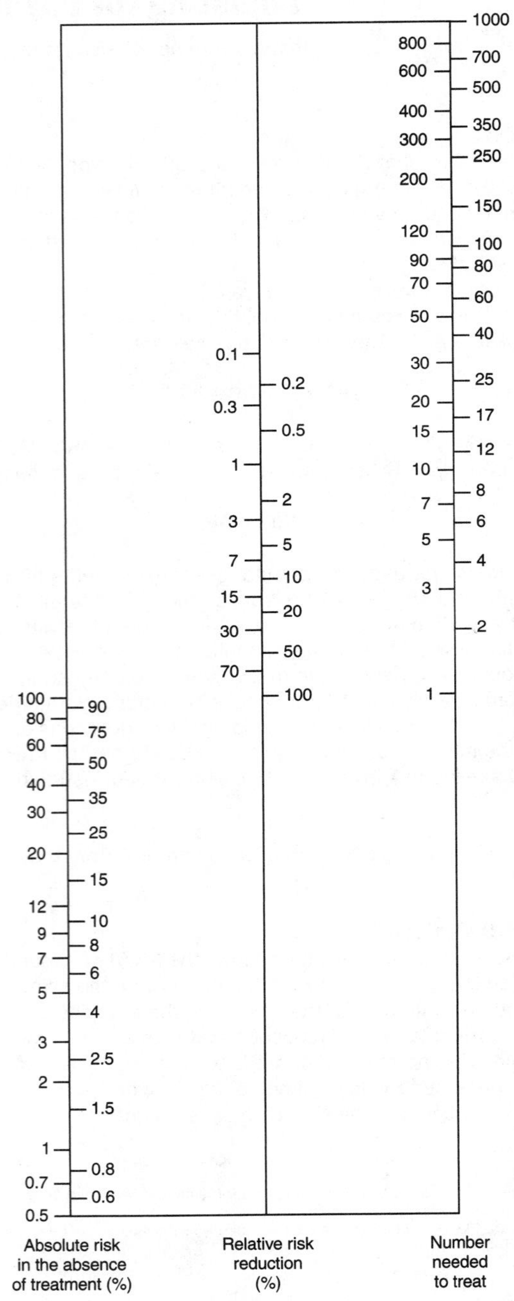

FIGURE **Nomogram for calculating the number needed to treat. Published with permission[1]**

Subject index

Note

When looking up a class of drug, the reader is advised to also look up specific examples of that class of drug where additional entries may be found. The reverse situation also applies.

INDEX

Subject index